MW00994342

ALL · IN · ONE

CISA®
Certified Information Systems Auditor
EXAM GUIDE

ABOUT THE AUTHOR

Peter H. Gregory, CISM, CISA, CRISC, CISSP, CIPM, CCISO, CCSK, PCI-QSA, is a 30-year career technologist and an executive director at Optiv Security, the largest security systems integrator (SSI) in the Americas. He has been developing and managing information security management programs since 2002 and has been leading the development and testing of secure IT environments since 1990. Also, Gregory spent many years as a software engineer and architect, systems engineer, network engineer, and security engineer. Throughout his career, he has written many articles, white papers, user manuals, processes, and procedures, and has conducted numerous lectures, training classes, seminars, and university courses.

Peter is the author of more than 40 books about information security and technology, including *Solaris Security* (Prentice Hall, 1999), *CISSP Guide to Security Essentials* (Cengage Learning, 2014), *CISM Certified Information Security Manager All-In-One Exam Guide* (McGraw-Hill Education, 2018), and *CISA Certified Information Systems Auditor All-In-One Exam Guide* (McGraw-Hill Education, 2016). He has spoken at numerous industry conferences, including RSA, Interop, ISACA CACS, (ISC)² Congress, SecureWorld Expo, West Coast Security Forum, OptivCon, Victoria (BC) Privacy and Security Conference, IP3, Society for Information Management, Interface, Tech Junction, SOURCE, the Washington Technology Industry Association, and InfraGard.

Peter is an advisory board member at the University of Washington's certificate program in information security and risk management and the lead instructor (emeritus) and advisory board member for the University of Washington certificate program in cybersecurity. He is an advisory board member and instructor at the University of South Florida's Cybersecurity for Executives program, a former board member of the Washington State chapter of InfraGard, and a founding member of the Pacific CISO Forum. He is a 2008 graduate of the FBI Citizens' Academy and a member of the FBI Citizens' Academy Alumni Association.

Peter resides with his family in Washington State and can be contacted at www .peterhgregory.com.

About the Technical Editor

Bobby E. Rogers is an information security engineer working as a contractor for Department of Defense agencies, helping to secure, certify, and accredit their information systems. His duties include information system security engineering, risk management, and certification and accreditation efforts. He retired after 21 years in the U.S. Air Force, serving as a network security engineer and instructor, and has secured networks all over the world. Bobby has a master's degree in information assurance (IA) and is pursuing a doctoral degree in cybersecurity from Capitol Technology University in Maryland. His many certifications include CISSP-ISSEP, CRISC, CEH, and MCSE: Security, as well as the CompTIA A+, CompTIA Network+, and CompTIA Security+ certifications. He is the author of *CRISC Certified in Risk and Information Systems Control All-In-One Exam Guide* (McGraw-Hill Education, 2016) and *CompTIA Mobility+ All-In-One Exam Guide* (McGraw-Hill Education, 2014). Bobby is also the technical editor for numerous books, including the eighth edition of *CISSP All-in-One Exam Guide* (McGraw-Hill Education, 2018).

ALL·IN·ONE

CISA®
Certified Information Systems Auditor
EXAM GUIDE
Fourth Edition

Peter H. Gregory

New York   Chicago   San Francisco
Athens   London   Madrid   Mexico City
Milan   New Delhi   Singapore   Sydney   Toronto

Library of Congress Control Number: 2019913240

McGraw-Hill Education books are available at special quantity discounts to use as premiums and sales promotions, or for use in corporate training programs. To contact a representative, please visit the Contact Us pages at www.mhprofessional.com.

CISA® Certified Information Systems Auditor All-in-One Exam Guide, Fourth Edition

5 6 7 8 9   LCR   25 24 23

ISBN   978-1-260-45880-0
MHID   1-260-45880-6

Sponsoring Editor Amy Stonebraker Gray	**Technical Editor** Bobby E. Rogers	**Production Supervisor** Pamela Pelton
Editorial Supervisor Janet Walden	**Copy Editor** Lisa Theobald	**Composition** Cenveo Publisher Services
Project Manager Radhika Jolly, Cenveo® Publisher Services	**Proofreader** Rick Camp	**Illustration** Cenveo Publisher Services
Acquisitions Coordinator Emily Walters	**Indexer** Karin Arrigoni	**Art Director, Cover** Jeff Weeks

To Rebekah

CONTENTS AT A GLANCE

CONTENTS

Figure Credits

Figure 4-6 courtesy of Digital Aardvark, Inc.

Figure 4-7 courtesy of AXELOS Limited. Copyright © AXELOS Limited 2016. PRINCE2® is a registered trade mark of AXELOS Limited. Used under permission of AXELOS Limited. All rights reserved.

Figure 4-10 courtesy of Don Wells.

Figure 4-11 courtesy of Oxford University Press, Inc. From Alexander et al., *The Oregon Experiment*, 1975, p. 44. Used by Permission of Oxford University Press, Inc.

Figure 5-2 courtesy of Fir0002/Flagstaffotos with permission granted under the terms of the GNU Free Documentation License, Version 1.2, http://commons.wikimedia.org/wiki/Commons:GNU_Free_Documentation_License,_version_1.2.

Figure 5-3 courtesy of Sassospicco with permission granted under the terms of the Creative Commons Attribution Share-Alike 2.5 License, http://creativecommons.org/licenses/by-sa/2.5/.

Figure 5-4, courtesy of Robert Jacek Tomczak, has been released into the public domain by its author at the Polish Wikipedia project.

Figure 5-5 courtesy of Robert Kloosterhuis with permission granted under the terms of the Creative Commons Attribution Share-Alike 2.5 License, http://creativecommons.org/licenses/by-sa/2.5/.

Figure 5-15 courtesy of Rebecca Steele.

Figure 5-16 courtesy of Harout S. Hhedeshian with permission granted under the terms of the Creative Commons Attribution 3.0 Unported License, http://creativecommons.org/licenscs/by/3.0/.

Figure 5-17 courtesy of Stephanie Tsacas with permission granted under the terms of the Creative Commons Attribution Share-Alike 2.5 License, http://creativecommons.org/licenses/by-sa/2.5/.

(Continued)

Figure 5-18 courtesy of Fdominec with permission granted under the terms of the GNU Free Documentation License, Version 1.2, http://commons.wikimedia.org/wiki/Commons:GNU_Free_Documentation_License,_version_1.2.

Figure 6-3 courtesy Ingersoll Rand Security Technologies.

Figure 6-10 courtesy of Rstubbs2 - Own work, CC BY-SA 4.0, https://commons.wikimedia.org/w/index.php?curid=44105524.

ACKNOWLEDGMENTS

I am especially grateful to Wendy Rinaldi for managing the revision process and helping to have this book published on a tight timeline.

Heartfelt thanks to Amy Stonebraker Gray for her project oversight and Claire Yee (and later, Emily Walters) for proficiently managing the submissions phase of this project, facilitating rapid turnaround, and equipping me with the information I needed to produce the manuscript.

I want to thank Bobby Rogers, who took on the task of tech reviewing the manuscript. Bobby carefully and thoughtfully read the entire draft manuscript and made many useful suggestions that have improved the book's quality.

Many thanks to contributors Tanya Scott, who wrote Chapter 1 and Appendix B of the first edition of this book and revised it for the second edition of this book; Chris Tarnstrom, who wrote the original Appendix A; and Justin Hendrickson, a CISA and consultant who practices in Seattle, for updates of Appendix A and B for the third edition. Also, thanks to security and privacy expert John Clark (CISA, CISSP, Security+, CIPP/E, CIPT, CIPM, FIP, PMP), for his revisions of Appendix B. These important texts help readers better understand the CISA certification process and help IS auditors to be more effective in their work. Tanya, Chris, Justin, and John's professional auditing experience and insight add considerable value to this book, long after readers become CISA-certified. My vision for this book includes value for aspiring as well as practicing IS auditors; these contributions allow the book to fulfill this vision.

Many thanks to Lisa Theobald for her excellent copyediting and further improving readability; Lisa caught several errors and made numerous suggestions for this edition. Much appreciation to Cenveo Publisher Services for the page layout. Like Olympic athletes, they make hard work look easy.

Special thanks to Radhika Jolly and Janet Walden for overseeing the production of the book and wringing out errors.

Many thanks to my literary agent, Carole Jelen, for diligent assistance during this and many other projects. Sincere thanks to Rebecca Steele, my business manager, publicist, and research assistant for her long-term vision, for keeping me on track, and for photos that she obtained for earlier editions of the book that are still in use.

Despite having written more than 40 books, I have difficulty putting into words my gratitude for my wife, Rebekah, for tolerating my frequent absences (in the home office) while I revised and added content for this fourth edition. This project could not have been completed without her unfailing support. She deserves the credit.

INTRODUCTION

The dizzying pace of information systems innovation has made vast expanses of information available to organizations and the public. Often, design flaws and technical vulnerabilities bring unintended consequences, often in the form of information theft and disclosure. The result: a patchwork of laws, regulations, and standards such as Sarbanes-Oxley, GLBA, HIPAA, PCI-DSS, NYDFS, PIPEDA, GDPR, CCPA, and scores of U.S. state laws requiring public disclosure of security breaches involving private information. Through these, organizations are either required or incentivized to perform their own internal audits or undergo external audits that measure compliance in order to avoid penalties, sanctions, and embarrassing news headlines.

These developments continue to drive demand for IT security professionals and IS auditors. These highly sought professionals play a crucial role in the development of better compliance programs and reduced risk.

The Certified Information Systems Auditor (CISA) certification, established in 1978, is indisputably the leading certification for IS auditing. Demand for the CISA certification has grown so much that the once-per-year certification exam was changed to twice per year in 2005, then three times each year, and is now offered on a continuous basis. In 2005, the CISA certification was awarded accreditation by the American National Standards Institute (ANSI) under international standard ISO/IEC 17024. CISA is also one of the few certifications formally approved by the U.S. Department of Defense in its Information Assurance Technical category (DoD 8570.01-M). In 2009 and 2017, *SC Magazine* named CISA the best professional certification program. In 2016, there were more than 129,000 professionals holding the certification.

IS auditing is not a "bubble" or a flash in the pan. Instead, IS auditing is a permanent fixture in organizations that have to contend with new technologies; new systems; new threats; and new data security and privacy laws, regulations, and standards. The CISA certification is the gold standard certification for professionals who work in this domain.

Purpose of This Book

Let's get the obvious out of the way: This is a comprehensive study guide for the security or audit professional who needs a serious reference for individual or group-led study for the Certified Information Systems Auditor (CISA) certification. The majority of the content in this book contains the technical information that CISA candidates are required to know.

This book is also a reference for aspiring and practicing IS auditors. The content that is required to pass the CISA exam is the same content that practicing auditors need to be familiar with in their day-to-day work. This book is an ideal CISA exam study guide as well as a desk reference for those who have already earned their CISA certification.

This book is also invaluable for security and business professionals who are required to undergo external audits from audit firms and examinations from regulators. Readers will gain considerable insight into the practices and methods used by auditors; this helps not only in internal audit operations but also in understanding external auditors and how they work. This knowledge and insight will lead to better audit outcomes.

This book is an excellent guide for someone exploring the IS audit profession. The study chapters explain all the relevant technologies and audit procedures, and the appendices explain process frameworks and the practical side of professional audits. The glossary contains a rich collection of terms used by IT security and IS auditors. These are useful for those readers who may wonder what the IS audit profession is all about.

How This Book Is Organized

This book is logically divided into four major sections:

- **Introduction**   This Introduction to the book plus Chapter 1 provide an overview of the CISA certification and the IS audit profession.

- **CISA study material**   Chapters 2 through 6 contain everything an aspiring CISA candidate is required to know for the CISA exam. This same material is a handy desk reference for aspiring and practicing IS auditors.

- **IS auditor reference**   Appendix A walks the reader through the entire process of a professional IS audit, from audit planning to delivery of the final report. Appendix B discusses control frameworks; this will help an IS auditor who needs to understand how control frameworks function, or who is providing guidance to an organization that needs to implement a control framework.

- **Practice exams**   Appendix C explains the CISA practice exams and TotalTester Online test engine that accompany this book.

Notes on the Fourth Edition

ISACA has historically recalibrated the contents of its certifications every five years. In late 2018, ISACA announced that it would update the CISA job practice (the basis for the exam and the requirements to earn the certification), effective in the June 2019 examination. In order to keep this book up to date, I contacted Wendy Rinaldi at McGraw-Hill so that we might develop a plan for the fourth edition of this book as quickly as possible. This book is the result of that effort.

The new CISA job practice information was made available in late December 2018. We began work at that time to update the third edition manuscript. The result is this book, which has been updated to reflect all of the changes in the CISA job practice, as well as changes in audit practices, information security, and information technology since the second edition was published.

Changes to the CISA Job Practice

Table 1 illustrates the previous and current CISA job practices and their relation to chapters in this book.

2016 CISA Job Practice		2019 CISA Job Practice		All-in-One Coverage
1. The Process of Auditing Information Systems	21%	1. Information Systems Auditing Process	21%	Chapter 3: The Audit Process
2. Governance and Management of IT	16%	2. Governance and Management of IT	17%	Chapter 2: IT Governance and Management
3. Information Systems Acquisition, Development, and Implementation	18%	3. Information Systems Acquisition, Development, and Implementation	12%	Chapter 4: IT Life Cycle Management
4. Information Systems Operation, Maintenance, and Service Management	20%	4. Information Systems Operations and Business Resilience	23%	Chapter 5: IT Service Management and Continuity
5. Protection of Information Assets	25%	5. Protection of Information Assets	27%	Chapter 6: Information Asset Protection

Table 1   Previous and Current CISA Job Practices

For the 2019 CISA job practice, ISACA reformatted the way that the practice areas are described. Previously, each job practice had a set of Knowledge Statements and Task Statements. In the 2019 edition, each job practice consists of two major categories, and each category has four to eleven subtopic areas. This is followed by 39 Supporting Tasks for CISA overall that are not specifically associated with the five domains.

As is typical for each new job practice and revision of this *CISA All-In-One Exam Guide*, I perform a gap analysis to understand what subject matter has been added to the new job practice and what has been eliminated. While the change in structure made this a bit more tedious, in general here are the noteworthy changes in content:

- Audit Project Management is a new topic.

- Audit Data Analytics is a new topic.

- Privacy Principles is a new topic.

- Business continuity planning and disaster recovery planning moved from domain 2 (Governance and Management of IT) to domain 4 (Information Systems Operations and Business Resilience) but are otherwise unchanged.

- Enterprise Architecture moved from domain 3 to domain 2.

- IoT is a new topic.

In addition to the changes to the CISA practice, there are several topics that are altogether new or expanded from the third edition. These changes include

- Segmentation and microsegmentation

- Virtualization, containerization, and virtual keyboards

- 5G
- A greater emphasis on systems acquisition with the systems development life cycle, which reflects the migration away from custom software development toward the acquisition of shrink-wrap software and Software-as-a-Service for core business applications
- The impact of digital transformation
- Zero Trust principles of enterprise architecture
- The NIST Cybersecurity Framework (CSF)
- New laws and regulations such as GDPR and CCPA
- Agile methodology for managing changes to infrastructure and business processes
- Several new development methodologies
- Cloud responsibility models
- Passwords, and whether they should periodically expire
- The threat of ransomware and destructware
- Changes in the meaning of remote access and VPNs
- Addition of numerous new technologies such as BLE and WPA3
- Removal of long-deprecated technology such as X.25
- Addition of 64 new items and cross-references to the glossary (and a few deprecated items removed)

By the time we completed this book, there were even more new developments, technologies, techniques, and breaches that provided additional insight and the promise of still more improvements. Like the surface of Saturn's moon, Io, our profession is ever changing. The technology boneyard is filled with vendors, products, protocols, techniques, and methodologies that once held great promise, later replaced with better things. This underscores the need for IS auditors (and IT, security, and risk professionals) to stay current by reading up on current events, new technologies, and techniques.

## CHAPTER 1

Becoming a CISA

This chapter discusses the following topics:

- What it means to be a CISA-certified professional
- Getting to know ISACA, its code of ethics, and its standards
- Undergoing the certification process
- Applying for the exam
- Maintaining your certification
- Getting the most from your CISA journey

Congratulations on choosing to become a Certified Information Systems Auditor (CISA). Whether you have worked for several years in the field of information systems auditing or have just recently been introduced to the world of controls, assurance, and security, don't underestimate the hard work and dedication required to obtain and maintain CISA certification. Although ambition and motivation are essential, the rewards of being CISA certified can far exceed the effort.

You probably never imagined you would find yourself working in the world of auditing or looking to obtain a professional auditing certification. Perhaps the increase in legislative or regulatory requirements for information system security led to your introduction to this field. Or possibly you noticed that CISA-related career options are increasing exponentially and you have decided to get ahead of the curve. You aren't alone: since the inception of CISA certification in 1978, more than 129,000 professionals worldwide reached the same conclusion and have earned this well-respected certification. In 2009 and again in 2017, *SC Magazine* named CISA certification the winner of the *Best Professional Certification Program*, and in 2014 it was a finalist for the same award. The 2016 Global Knowledge *IT Skills and Salary Report*, as well as a recent *IT Skills and Certifications Pay Index* (ITSCPI) from Foote Partners, show the CISA certification among the highest-paying IT certifications. Welcome to the journey and the amazing opportunities that await you.

I have put together this information to help you understand the commitment needed, prepare for the exam, and maintain your certification. Not only is it my wish that you prepare for and pass the exam with flying colors, but I also provide you with the information and resources to maintain your certification and to represent yourself and the professional world of information system (IS) auditing proudly with your new credentials.

ISACA (formerly known as the Information Systems Audit and Control Association) is a recognized leader in the areas of control, assurance, and IT governance. Formed in 1967, this nonprofit organization represents more than 140,000 professionals in more than 180 countries. ISACA administers several exam certifications, including the CISA, the Certified Information Security Manager (CISM), the Certified in Risk and Information Systems Control (CRISC), and the Certified in the Governance of Enterprise IT (CGEIT) certifications. The certification program itself has been accredited by the American National Standards Institute (ANSI) under International Organization for Standardization and International Electrotechnical Commission standard ISO/IEC 17024:2012, which means that ISACA's procedures for accreditation meet international requirements for quality, continuous improvement, and accountability.

If you're new to ISACA, I recommend that you tour the organization's web site (www .isaca.org) and become familiar with the guides and resources available. In addition, if you're near one of the 200-plus local ISACA chapters in more than 80 countries worldwide, consider taking part in the activities and even reaching out to the chapter board for information on local meetings, training days, conferences, or study sessions. You may be able to meet other IS auditors who can give you additional insight into the CISA certification and the audit profession.

Established in 1978, the CISA certification primarily focuses on audit, controls, assurance, and security. It certifies the individual's knowledge of testing and documenting IS controls and his or her ability to conduct formal IS audits. Organizations seek out qualified personnel for assistance with developing and maintaining strong control environments. A CISA-certified individual is a great candidate for this.

Through the phenomenon of digital transformation, organizations in every industry sector around the world are becoming increasingly reliant on information systems for daily business operations. Further, the upward trend in IT outsourcing in the form of Software-as-a-Service (SaaS), Platform-as-a-Service (PaaS), and Infrastructure-as-a-Service (IaaS) offerings means organizations are put in a position of having to trust those service providers that the SaaS, PaaS, and IaaS platforms are secure. This reliance compels organizations to rely heavily on IS auditors to provide assurances that IT environments have the necessary security, integrity, and resilience that today's organizations require.

Benefits of CISA Certification

Obtaining the CISA certification offers several significant benefits:

- **Expands knowledge and skills, builds confidence** Developing knowledge and skills in the areas of audit, controls, assurance, and security can prepare you for advancement or expand your scope of responsibilities. The personal and professional achievement can boost confidence that encourages you to move forward and seek new career opportunities.

- **Increases marketability and career options** Because of various legal and regulatory requirements, such as the Health Insurance Portability and Accountability Act (HIPAA), the Payment Card Industry Data Security Standard (PCI-DSS), Sarbanes-Oxley (SOX), the Gramm-Leach-Bliley Act (GLBA), the Food and Drug Administration (FDA), the Federal Energy Regulatory Commission/North American Electric Reliability Corporation (FERC/NERC), the European General Data Protection Regulation (GDPR), and the California Consumer Privacy Act (CCPA), along with the growing need for information systems and automation, controls, assurance, and audit experience, demand is growing for individuals with experience in developing, documenting, and testing controls. In addition, obtaining your CISA certification demonstrates to current and potential employers your willingness and commitment to improve your knowledge and skills in information systems auditing. Having a CISA can provide a competitive advantage and open up many doors of opportunity in various industries and countries.

- **Helps you meet other certification requirements** The Payment Card Industry Qualified Security Assessor (PCI-QSA) certification requires that all certificate holders have a current security audit certification, either CISA or ISO 27001 Lead Auditor.

- **Helps you meet employment requirements** Many government agencies and organizations, such as the United States Department of Defense (DoD), require CISA certifications for positions involving IS audit activities. DoD Directive 8140.01 (formerly DoD Directive 8570.01-M) mandates that those personnel performing information assurance activities within the agency are certified with a commercial accreditation approved by the DoD. The DoD has approved the ANSI-accredited CISA certificate program because it meets ISO/IEC 17024:2012 requirements. All Information Assurance Technical (IAT) Level III personnel are mandated to obtain CISA certification, as are those who are contracted to perform similar activities.

- **Builds customer confidence and international credibility** Prospective customers needing control or audit work will have faith that the quality of the audits and controls documented or tested are in line with internationally recognized standards.

Regardless of your current position, demonstrating knowledge and experience in the areas of IT controls, audit, assurance, and security can expand your career options. The certification does not limit you to auditing; it can provide additional value and insight to those in or seeking the following positions:

- Executives such as chief executive officers (CEOs), chief financial officers (CFOs), and chief information officers (CIOs)
- Chief audit executives, audit partners, and audit directors
- Security and IT operations executives (chief technology officers [CTOs], chief information security officers [CISOs], chief information risk officers [CIROs], chief security officers [CSOs]), directors, managers, and staff
- Compliance executives and management
- Security and audit consultants
- Audit committee members

The CISA Certification Process

To become a CISA, you are required to pay the exam fee, pass the exam, prove that you have the required experience and education, and agree to uphold ethics and standards. To keep your CISA certification, you are required to take at least 20 continuing education hours each year (120 hours in three years) and pay annual maintenance fees. This is depicted in Figure 1-1.

The following list outlines the major requirements for becoming certified:

- **Experience**   A CISA candidate must be able to submit verifiable evidence of at least five years' experience, with a minimum of two years' professional work experience in IS auditing, control, assurance, or security. Experience can be in any of the job content areas, but it must be verified. For those with less than five years' experience, substitution and waiver options for up to three years' experience are available.

- **Ethics**   Candidates must commit to adhere to ISACA's Code of Professional Ethics, which guides the personal and professional conduct of those certified.

- **Standards**   Those certified agree to abide by IS auditing standards and minimum guidelines for performing IS audits.

- **Exam**   Candidates must receive a passing score on the CISA exam. A passing score is valid for up to five years, after which the score is void. This means that a CISA candidate who passes the exam has a *maximum* of five years to apply for CISA certification; candidates who pass the exam but fail to act after five years will have to take the exam again if they want to become CISA certified.

- **Application**   After successfully passing the exam, meeting the experience requirements, and having read through ISACA's Code of Professional Ethics and Information Systems Auditing Standards, a candidate is ready to apply for certification. An application must be received within five years of passing the exam.

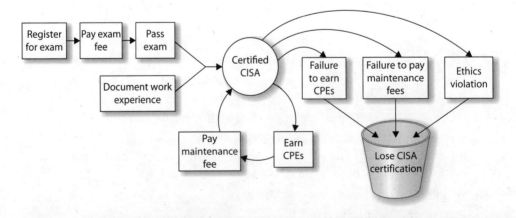

Figure 1-1   The CISA certification life cycle

- **Education**   Those certified must adhere to the CISA Continuing Education Policy, which requires a minimum of 20 continuing professional education (CPE) hours each year, with a total requirement of 120 CPEs over the course of the certification period (three years).

Experience Requirements

To qualify for CISA certification, you must have completed the equivalent of five years' total work experience. These five years can take many forms, with several substitutions available. Additional details on the minimum certification requirements, substitution options, and various examples are discussed next.

 NOTE   Although it is not recommended, a CISA candidate can take the exam before completing any work experience directly related to IS auditing. As long as the candidate passes the exam and the work experience requirements are fulfilled within five years of the exam date, and within ten years from application for certification, the candidate is eligible for certification.

Direct Work Experience

You are required to have a minimum of two years' work experience in the field of IS audit, controls, or security. This is equivalent to 4,000 actual work hours, which must be related to one or more of the five following CISA job practice areas:

- **Information Systems Auditing Process**   Planning and conducting information systems audits in accordance with IS standards and best practices, communicating results, and advising on risk management and control practices.

- **Governance and Management of IT**   Ensuring that adequate organizational structures and processes are in place to align and support the organization's strategies and objectives.

- **Information Systems Acquisition, Development, and Implementation** Ensuring that appropriate processes and controls are in place for the acquisition, development, testing, and implementation of information systems in order to provide reasonable assurance that the organization's strategies and objectives will be met.

- **Information Systems Operations and Business Resilience**   Ensuring that systems and infrastructure have appropriate operations, maintenance, and service management processes and controls in place to support meeting the organization's strategies and objectives.

- **Protection of Information Assets**   Ensuring that the organization's security policies, standards, procedures, and controls protect the confidentiality, integrity, and availability of information assets.

All work experience must be completed within the ten-year period before completing the certification application or within five years from the date of initially passing the

CISA exam. You will need to complete a separate Verification of Work Experience form for each segment of experience.

There is only one exception to this minimum two-year direct work experience requirement: if you are a full-time instructor. This option is discussed in the next section.

Substitution of Experience

Up to a maximum of three years' direct work experience can be substituted with the following to meet the five-year experience requirement:

- One year of information systems or one year of non-IS auditing experience can be substituted for up to one year of direct work experience.

- Completion of a two- or four-year degree (60 to 120 completed university semester credit hours), regardless of when completed, can be substituted for one or two years of direct work experience, respectively. Transcripts or a letter confirming degree status must be sent from the university attended to obtain the experience waiver.

- If you have completed a bachelor's or master's degree from a university that enforces an ISACA-sponsored curriculum, it can be substituted for one or two years of direct work experience, respectively (for information on ISACA-sponsored Model Curricula and participating universities, see www.isaca.org/modeluniversities). Transcripts or a letter confirming degree status must be sent from the university to obtain an experience waiver. This option cannot be used if you have already substituted or waived three years of direct work experience.

- Association of Chartered Certified Accountants (ACCA) members and Chartered Institute of Management Accountants (CIMA) members with full certification can apply for a two-year educational waiver.

- Those applying with a master's degree in information systems or information technology (IT) from an accredited university can apply for a one-year experience waiver.

As noted, there is only one exception to the experience requirements. Should you have experience as a full-time university instructor in a related field (that is, information security, computer science, or accounting), each two years of your experience can be substituted for one year of required direct work experience, without limitation.

Here is an example CISA candidate whose experience and education are considered for CISA certification:

> Jane Doe graduated in 2004 with a bachelor's degree in accounting. She spent five years working for an accounting firm conducting non-IS audits, and in January 2009, she began conducting IS audits full time. In January 2011, she took some time off work for personal reasons and rejoined the workforce in December 2017, working for a public company in its internal audit department documenting and testing financial controls. Jane passed the CISA exam in June 2018 and applied for CISA certification in January 2019. Does Jane have all of the experience required? What evidence will she need to submit?

- **Two-year substitution**   Jane obtained a bachelor's degree in accounting, which equates to two years' experience substitution.

- **Two years' direct experience**   She can count her two full years of IS audit experience (in 2009 and 2010).

- **One-year substitution**   She cannot take into account one year of non-IS audit experience completed between January 2008 to January 2009, as it was not completed within ten years of application.

- **One-year substitution**   Jane would want to utilize her new internal audit financial controls experience for experience substitution rather than her earlier non-IS audit experience.

Jane would need to send the following with her application to prove experience requirements are met:

- Verification of Work Experience forms filled out and signed by her supervisors (or any superior) at the accounting firm, verifying both the IS and non-IS audit work conducted.

- Transcripts or letter confirming degree status sent from the university.

 NOTE   I recommend you also read the CISA certification qualifications on the ISACA web site. From time to time, ISACA changes the qualification rules, and I want you to have the most up-to-date information available.

IS vs. IT

You're probably noticing the use of the terms "IS" and "IT" in this chapter. Indeed, you'll find these terms throughout the entire book. IS means *information systems*, an inclusive term that can mean a single computer, its operating system, an application running on the system, a network device, a virtual machine, or a collection of systems that work together to fulfill some purpose. In the world of auditing information systems, a person who examines information systems is an IS auditor.

Notice also that the letters "IS" in CISA stand for *information systems*, not *information security*, as is sometimes believed. A CISA is expected to know how to audit all aspects of an information system, not just security controls used to protect systems and information.

IT means *information technology* and refers to the technology found in computers, software, storage systems, and applications. In most organizations, the group of people who manage information technology is known as the IT department. Some organizations, however, ascribe the term IS department.

Often, IS and IT are used interchangeably, and generally, such usage is not considered inappropriate or incorrect.

ISACA Code of Professional Ethics

Becoming a CISA means that you agree to adhere to the ISACA Code of Professional Ethics, a formal document outlining those things you will do to ensure the utmost integrity and that best support and represent the organization and certification.

The ISACA Code of Professional Ethics requires ISACA members and certification holders to do the following (from www.isaca.org/Certification/Code-of-Professional-Ethics/Pages/default.aspx):

1. Support the implementation of, and encourage compliance with, appropriate standards and procedures for the effective governance and management of enterprise information systems and technology, including: audit, control, security and risk management.

2. Perform their duties with objectivity, due diligence and professional care, in accordance with professional standards.

3. Serve in the interest of stakeholders in a lawful manner, while maintaining high standards of conduct and character, and not discrediting their profession or the Association.

4. Maintain the privacy and confidentiality of information obtained in the course of their activities unless disclosure is required by legal authority. Such information shall not be used for personal benefit or released to inappropriate parties.

5. Maintain competency in their respective fields and agree to undertake only those activities they can reasonably expect to complete with the necessary skills, knowledge and competence.

6. Inform appropriate parties of the results of work performed including the disclosure of all significant facts known to them that, if not disclosed, may distort the reporting of the results.

7. Support the professional education of stakeholders in enhancing their understanding of the governance and management of enterprise information systems and technology, including: audit, control, security and risk management.

Failure to follow the code of ethics can result in an investigation of the person's actions; potential disciplinary measures range from a written warning to the loss of certification and/or membership.

You'll find the full text and terms of enforcement of the ISACA Code of Ethics at www.isaca.org/ethics.

ISACA IS Standards

An auditor can gather information from several credible resources to conduct an audit with integrity and confidence. ISACA has developed its own set of standards of mandatory requirements for IS auditing and reporting, known as the ITAF: Information Technology Assurance Framework.

ITAF offers multiple levels of IS audit and assurance guidance: standards, guidelines, and tools and techniques. Standards are higher level *mandatory* requirements that inform IS audit and assurance professionals of minimal performance expectations. Guidelines provide additional guidance in applying the standards, while tools and techniques provide examples of procedures that audit and assurance professionals may follow.

As a CISA, you are required to abide by and promote the IS standards where applicable, encouraging compliance and supporting their implementation. As you prepare for certification and beyond, you will need to read through and become familiar with these standards. These standards were created to define the minimum level of acceptable performance needed to meet the professional requirements as defined by ISACA and to help set expectations. They have been established, vetted, and approved by ISACA.

For more about ITAF, visit www.isaca.org/itaf.

General standards represent guiding principles by which the profession conducts IT audit and assurance activities. General standards include

- Audit charter
- Organizational independence
- Professional independence
- Reasonable expectation
- Due professional care
- Proficiency
- Assertions
- Criteria

Performance standards focus on the IT audit or assurance professional's conduct of assurance activities—such as the design, evidence, findings, and conclusions. These standards include

- Engagement planning
- Risk assessment in planning
- Performance and supervision
- Materiality
- Evidence
- Using the work of other experts
- Irregularity and illegal acts

Reporting standards cover the report produced by the IT audit or assurance professional, such as

- Reporting
- Follow-up activities

NOTE I recommend that you check the ISACA web site periodically for updates to these standards. As an ISACA member, you will automatically be notified when changes have been submitted and the documents are open for review (www.isaca.org/standards).

The Certification Exam

The certification exam is offered almost continuously throughout the year in periods known as *testing windows* that are generally several months in length. The ISACA web site will have information about current testing windows and sometimes about future testing windows. When you begin planning for your CISA examination, you'll want to consult the ISACA web site to see what scheduling options are available in your testing window. Other terms and conditions change from time to time, from one testing window to the next.

In 2019, the schedule of exam fees in U.S. dollars was

- CISA application fee: $50
- Regular registration: $575 member/$760 nonmember

The exam is administered by an ISACA-approved testing vendor, PSI Services, at numerous locations. For additional details on the locations nearest you, go to www.isaca.org/examlocations.

Once registration is complete, you will immediately receive an e-mail acknowledging your registration, and within four weeks of processing you will receive a hard copy of the letter and a registration receipt in the mail. Two to three weeks prior to the test date you will receive an exam admission ticket via e-mail and regular mail. You will need the admission ticket to enter the test site—be sure to keep it unmarked and in a safe place until test time.

Each registrant has four hours to take the multiple-choice-question exam. There are 150 questions on the computerized exam representing the five job practice areas. Each question has four answer choices; test-takers can select only one best answer by clicking it. You will be scored for each job practice area and then provided one final score. Before you close out the computerized exam, you will be notified of your tentative pass/fail status. All exam scores are scaled. Scores range from 200 to 800; however, a final score of 450 is required to pass.

Exam questions are derived from a job practice analysis study conducted by ISACA. The areas selected represent those tasks performed in a CISA's day-to-day activities and represent the background knowledge required to perform IS audit, control, assurance, and security tasks. More detailed descriptions of the task and knowledge statements can be found at www.isaca.org/cisajobpractice.

The CISA exam is quite broad in its scope. The exam covers five job practice areas, as shown in Table 1-1.

Independent committees have been developed to determine the best questions, review exam results, and statistically analyze the results for continuous improvement. Should you come across a horrifically difficult or strange question, do not panic. This question

Domain	CISA Job Practice Area	Percentage of Exam
1	Information Systems Auditing Process	21
2	Governance and Management of IT	17
3	Information Systems Acquisition, Development, and Implementation	12
4	Information Systems Operations and Business Resilience	23
5	Protection of Information Assets	27

Table 1-1   CISA Exam Practice Areas

may have been written for another purpose. A few questions on the exam are included for research and analysis purposes and will not be counted against your score.

Exam Preparation

The CISA certification requires a great deal of knowledge and experience from the CISA candidate. You need to map out a long-term study strategy to pass the exam. The following sections offer some tips and are intended to help guide you to, through, and beyond exam day.

Before the Exam

Consider the following list of tips on tasks and resources for exam preparation. They are listed in sequential order.

- **Read the ISACA Exam Candidate Information Guide**   For information on the certification exam and requirements for the current year, see www.isaca.org/ Certification/Pages/Candidates-Guide-for-Exams.aspx. Be sure to download the correct (usually the most recent) version of the guide.

- **Register**   Register to solidify your commitment to moving forward with this professional achievement.

- **Become familiar with the CISA job practice areas**   The job practice areas serve as the basis for the exam and requirements. Beginning with the June 2019 exam, the job practice areas have changed. Ensure that your study materials align with the current list at www.isaca.org/cisajobpractice.

- **Self-assess**   Run through the questions in the two practice exams, provided as additional resources with this book; see Appendix C for more information. You may also go to the ISACA web site for a free 50-question CISA self-assessment.

- **Iterative study**   Depending on how much work experience in IS auditing you have already, I suggest you plan your study program to take at least two months but as long as six months. During this time, periodically take practice exams and note your areas of strength and weakness. Once you have identified your weak areas, focus on those areas weekly by rereading the related sections in this book and retaking practice exams, and note your progress.

- **Avoid cramming** We've all seen the books on the shelves with titles that involve last-minute cramming. Just one look on the Internet reveals a variety of web sites that cater to teaching individuals how to cram for exams most effectively. There are also research sites claiming that exam cramming can lead to susceptibility to colds and flu, sleep disruptions, overeating, and digestive problems. One thing is certain: many people find that good, steady study habits result in less stress and greater clarity and focus during the exam. Because of the complexity of this exam, I highly recommend the long-term, steady-study option. Study the job practice areas thoroughly. There are many study options. If time permits, investigate the many resources available to you.

- **Find a study group** Many ISACA chapters have formed specific study groups or offer less expensive exam review courses. Contact your local chapter to see if these options are available to you. In addition, be sure to keep your eye on the ISACA web site.

- **Admission ticket** Approximately two to three weeks before the exam, you will receive your admission ticket. Do not write on or lose this ticket. Put it in a safe place, and take note of what time you will need to arrive at the site. Note this on your calendar.

- **Logistics check** Check the Candidate Information Guide and your admission ticket for the exact time you are required to report to the test site. Check the site a few days before the exam—become familiar with the location and tricks to getting there. If you are taking public transportation, be sure that you are looking at the schedule for the day of the exam. If you are driving, know the route and know where to park your vehicle.

- **Pack** Place your admissions ticket and a photo ID in a safe place, ready to go. Your ID must be a current, government-issued photo ID that matches the name on the admission ticket and must not be handwritten. Examples of acceptable forms of ID are passports, driver's licenses, state IDs, green cards, and national IDs. Make sure you leave food, drinks, laptops, cell phones, and other electronic devices behind, as they are not permitted at the test site. For information on what can and cannot be brought to the exam site, see www.isaca.org/cisabelongings.

- **Notification decision** Decide whether you want your exam results e-mailed to you. You will have the opportunity to consent to e-mail notification of the exam results. If you are fully paid (zero balance on exam fee) and have consented to the e-mail notification, you should receive a single e-mail a few weeks from the date of the exam with your exam results.

- **Sleep** Get a sound night's sleep before the exam. Research suggests that you should avoid caffeine at least four hours before bedtime, keep a notepad and pen next to the bed to capture late-night thoughts that might keep you awake, eliminate as much noise and light as possible, and keep your room a good temperature for sleeping. In the morning, arise early so as not to rush and subject yourself to additional stress.

Day of the Exam

Consider the following list of tips that can help you on exam day:

- **Arrive early**   Check the Candidate Information Guide and your admission ticket for the exact time you are required to report to the test site. The ticket and the Candidate Information Guide explain that you must be at the test site *no later* than approximately 30 minutes *before* testing time. If you are late, you may miss your opportunity to take the exam on that day, and you'll have to reschedule your exam.

- **Observe test center rules**   There may be rules about taking breaks. This will be discussed by the examiner along with exam instructions. If at any time during the exam you need something and are unsure as to the rules, be sure to ask first. For information on conduct during the exam, see www.isaca.org/cisabelongings.

- **Answering exam questions**   Read questions carefully, but do not try to overanalyze. Remember to select the *best* solution. There may be several reasonable answers, but one is *better* than the others.

After the Exam

Although you'll be shown your preliminary pass/fail results when you have completed and closed your exam, you will receive your official exam results by e-mail or regular mail within a few weeks from the date of the exam. Each job practice area score will be noted in addition to the overall final score. Should you receive a passing score, you will also receive the application for certification.

Those unsuccessful in passing will also be notified. These individuals will want to take a close look at the job practice area scores to determine areas for further study. They may retake the exam as many times as needed on future exam dates, as long as they have registered and paid the applicable fees. Regardless of pass or fail, exam results will not be disclosed via telephone, fax, or e-mail (with the exception of the consented one-time e-mail notification).

 CAUTION   You are not yet permitted to use the CISA moniker after passing the exam. You must first apply for CISA certification, which is described in the next section.

Applying for CISA Certification

To apply for certification, you must be able to submit evidence of a passing score and related work experience. Keep in mind that once you receive a passing score, you have five years to use this score on a CISA application. After this time, you will need to take the exam again. In addition, all work experience submitted must have been within ten years of your new certification application.

To complete the application process, you need to submit the following information:

- **CISA application**   Note the exam ID number located in your exam results letter; list the information systems audit, control, security experience, and/or any experience substitutions; and identify which ISACA job practice area(s) the experience pertains to.
- **Verification of Work Experience form(s)**   These must be filled out and signed by your immediate supervisor or a person of higher rank in the organization to verify work experience noted on the application. You must fill out a complete set of Work Experience forms for each separate employer.
- **Transcript or letter**   If you are using an educational experience waiver, you must submit an original transcript or a letter from the college or university confirming degree status.

As with the exam, after you've successfully mailed the application, you must wait approximately eight weeks for processing. If your application is approved, you will receive a package in the mail containing your letter of certification, a certificate, and a copy of the Continuing Education Policy. You can then proudly display your certificate and use the designation ("CISA") on your CV, résumé, e-mail profile, or business cards.

Retaining Your CISA Certification

There is more to becoming a CISA than merely passing an exam, submitting an application, and receiving a paper certificate. Being a CISA is an ongoing lifestyle. Those with the CISA certification not only agree to abide by the Code of Professional Ethics and adhere to the IS standards, but they must also meet ongoing education requirements and pay certification maintenance fees. Let's take a closer look at the education requirements and explain the fees involved in retaining certification.

Continuing Education

The goal of continuing professional education (CPE) requirements is to ensure that individuals maintain CISA-related knowledge so that they can better manage, assess, and design controls around IS. To maintain CISA certification, individuals must obtain 120 CPE hours within three years, with a minimum requirement of 20 hours per year. Each CPE hour is to account for 50 minutes of active participation in educational activities.

What Counts as a Valid CPE Credit?

In order for training and activities to be utilized for CPEs, they must involve technical or managerial training that is directly applicable to IS assessments, audit, controls, or security. The following list of activities has been approved by the CISA certification committee and can count toward your CPE requirements:

- ISACA professional education activities and meetings.
- If you are an ISACA member, you can take *ISACA Journal* CPE Quizzes online or participate in monthly webcasts. For each webcast, CPEs are rewarded after you pass a quiz.

- Non-ISACA professional education activities and meetings.
- Self-study courses.
- Vendor sales or marketing presentations (ten-hour annual limit).
- Teaching, lecturing, or presenting on subjects related to job practice areas.
- Publication of articles and books related to the profession.
- CISA exam question development and review.
- Passing related professional examinations.
- Participation in ISACA boards or committees (20-hour annual limit per ISACA certification).
- Contributions to the IS audit and control profession (ten-hour annual limit).
- Mentoring (ten-hour annual limit).

For more information on what is accepted as a valid CPE credit, see the continuing professional education policy (www.isaca.org/cisacpepolicy).

Tracking and Submitting CPEs

Not only are you required to submit a CPE tracking form for the annual renewal process, but you also should keep detailed records for each activity. Records associated with each activity should include the following:

- Name of attendee
- Name of sponsoring organization
- Activity title
- Activity description
- Activity date
- Number of CPE hours awarded

It is in your best interest to track all CPE information in a single document or worksheet. ISACA has developed a Verification of Attendance form for your use at www.isaca.org/cisacpepolicy. To make it easy on yourself, consider keeping all related records such as receipts, brochures, and certificates in the same place. Retain documentation throughout the three-year certification period and for one additional year afterward. This is especially important, because you may someday be audited. If this happens, you would be required to submit all paperwork. So why not be prepared?

For new CISAs, the annual and three-year certification period begins January 1 of the year following certification. You are not required to report CPE hours for the first partial year after your certification; however, the hours earned from the time of certification to December 31 can be utilized in the first certification reporting period the following year. Therefore, should you get certified in January, you will have until the following January to accumulate CPEs and will not have to report them until you report the totals for the following year, which will be in October or November. This is known as the *renewal period*. During this time, you will receive an e-mail directing you to the web site to enter CPEs earned over the course of the year. Alternatively, the renewal will be mailed to you, and you can record CPEs on the hard-copy invoice and send them with your maintenance fee payment. CPEs and maintenance fees must be received by January 15 to retain certification.

Notification of compliance from the certification department is sent after all of the information has been received and processed. Should ISACA have any questions about the information you have submitted, they will contact you directly.

Sample CPE Submission

Table 1-2 contains an example of a CPE submission.

CPE Maintenance Fees

To remain CISA certified, you must pay CPE maintenance fees each year. These fees are (as of 2019) $45 for members and $85 for nonmembers each year. These fees are in

Name: John Jacob
Certification Number: 67895787
Certification Period: 1/1/2019 to 12/31/2019

Activity Title/Sponsor	Activity Description	Date	CPE Hours	Support Docs Included?
ISACA presentation/lunch	PCI compliance	2/12/2019	1 CPE	Yes (receipt)
ISACA presentation/lunch	Security in SDLC	3/12/2019	1 CPE	Yes (receipt)
Regional Conference, RIMS	Compliance, risk	1/15–17/2019	6 CPEs	Yes (CPE receipt)
Brightfly webinar	Governance, risk, and compliance	2/16/2019	3 CPEs	Yes (confirmation e-mail)
ISACA board meeting	Chapter board meeting	4/9/2019	2 CPEs	Yes (meeting minutes)
Presented at IIA meeting	IT audit presentation	6/21/2019	1 CPE	Yes (meeting notice)
Published an article in XYZ	Journal article on SOX ITGC	4/12/2019	4 CPEs	Yes (article)
Vendor presentation	Learned about GRC tool capability	5/12/2019	2 CPEs	Yes
Employer-offered training	Change management course	3/26/2019	7 CPEs	Yes (certificate of course completion)

Table 1-2   Sample CPE Submission

addition to ISACA membership and local chapter dues (which are not required to maintain your CISA certification).

Revocation of Certification

A CISA-certified individual may have his or her certification revoked for the following reasons:

- Failure to complete the minimum number of CPEs during the required period.
- Failure to document and provide evidence of CPEs in an audit.
- Failure to submit payment for maintenance fees.
- Failure to comply with the Code of Professional Ethics; this can result in investigation and ultimately lead to revocation of certification.

If you have received a revocation notice, you will need to contact the ISACA Certification Department at certification@isaca.org for more information.

CISA Exam Preparation Pointers

Following are a few general pointers for exam prep:

- Register for the exam early to ensure that you can take the exam at a location and date of your choosing.
- When studying for the exam, take as many practice exams as possible.
- Memorization will not work—for this exam, it is critical that you understand the concepts.
- If you have time while studying for the exam, begin gathering relevant Work Experience Verification forms from past employers and original transcripts from your college or university (if using the education experience waiver).
- Do not arrive late to the exam site. Latecomers are immediately disqualified and they forfeit exam fees.
- Begin keeping track of CPEs as soon as you obtain certification.
- Mark your calendar for CPE renewal time, which begins in October/November each year and ends January 15. Don't wait for the e-mail; set your own reminder.
- Become familiar with the Code of Professional Ethics and IS standards.
- Become involved in your local ISACA chapter for networking and educational opportunities.

Summary

Becoming and being a CISA is a lifestyle, not just a one-time event. It takes motivation, skill, good judgment, and proficiency to be a strong leader in the world of information systems auditing. The CISA was designed to help you navigate the IS auditing world with greater ease and confidence.

In the following chapters, each CISA job practice area is discussed in detail, and additional reference material is presented. Not only is this information useful for studying prior to the exam, but it is also meant to serve as a resource throughout your career as an audit professional.

IT Governance and Management

This chapter covers CISA Domain 2, "Governance and Management of IT," and discusses the following topics:

- IT governance structure
- Human resources management
- IT policies, standards, processes, and procedures
- Management practices
- IT resource investment, use, and allocation practices
- IT contracting and contract management strategies and practices
- Risk management practices
- Monitoring and assurance

The topics in this chapter represent 17 percent of the CISA examination.

IT governance should be the wellspring from which all other IT activities flow.

Properly implemented, *governance* is a process whereby senior management exerts strategic control over business functions through policies, objectives, delegation of authority, and monitoring. Governance is management's control over all other IT processes to ensure that IT processes continue to meet the organization's business objectives effectively.

Business alignment is a critical characteristic of IT governance. IT's primary mission should be the support of the overall business mission, goals, and objectives. The alignment of IT to the business must be intentional and deliberate for IT and the organization to succeed.

Organizations usually establish governance through an IT steering committee that is responsible for setting long-term IT strategy and by making changes to ensure that IT processes continue to support IT strategy and the organization's needs. This is accomplished through the development and enforcement of IT policies, requirements, and standards.

IT governance typically focuses on several key processes, such as personnel management, sourcing, change management, financial management, quality management, security management, and performance optimization. Another key component is the establishment of an effective organization structure and clear statements of roles and responsibilities. An effective governance program will use a balanced scorecard (BSC) or other means to monitor these and other key processes, and through a process of continuous improvement, IT processes will be changed to remain effective and to support ongoing business needs.

IT Governance Practices for Executives and Boards of Directors

Governance starts at the top.

Whether the organization has a board of directors, council members, commissioners, or some other top-level governing body, governance begins with the establishment of top-level objectives and policies that are translated into more actions, policies, processes, procedures, and other activities downward through each level in the organization.

This section describes governance practices recommended for IT organizations, including a strategy-developing committee, measurement via the BSC, and security management.

 NOTE Governance is not merely an IT practice. Rather, governance is practiced in the business apart from IT to facilitate management's control over all aspects of business operations, including IT.

IT Governance

The purpose of IT governance is to align the IT organization with the needs of the business. The term *IT governance* refers to a collection of top-down activities intended to control the IT organization from a strategic perspective to ensure that the IT organization supports the business. The artifacts and activities that flow out of healthy IT governance include the following:

- **Policy**   At its minimum, IT policy should directly reflect the mission, objectives, and goals of the overall organization.

- **Priorities**   Priorities in the IT organization should flow directly from the organization's mission, objectives, and goals. Whatever is most important to the organization as a whole should be important to IT as well.

- **Standards**   The technologies, protocols, and practices used by IT should reflect the organization's needs. On their own, standards help to drive a consistent approach to solving business challenges; the choice of standards should facilitate solutions that meet the organization's needs in a cost-effective and secure manner.

- **Resource management**   The budget, personnel, equipment, and other resources are planned, selected, managed, and measured to ensure that the IT organization has the ability to meet its objectives.

- **Vendor management**   The suppliers and service providers that IT selects should reflect IT and business priorities, standards, and practices.

- **Program and project management**   IT programs and projects should be organized and performed in a consistent manner that reflects IT and business priorities and supports the business.

While IT governance contains the elements just described, strategic planning is also a key component of governance. Strategy development is discussed in the next section.

IT Governance Frameworks

Every organization may have a unique mission, objectives, goals, business models, tolerance for risk, and so on, but organizations need not invent governance frameworks from scratch to manage their IT and business objectives. Several good frameworks can be adapted to meet organizations' needs, including the following:

- **COBIT**   This IT management framework was developed by the IT Governance Institute and ISACA. COBIT's five domains are Evaluate, Direct, and Monitor; Align, Plan, and Organize; Build, Acquire, and Implement; Deliver, Service, and Support; and Monitor, Evaluate, and Assess.

- **ISO/IEC 27001**   This is the well-known international standard for top-down information security management. In the context of IT security governance, most important here are the requirements (sometimes referred to as the *clauses*) in ISO/IEC 27001, not the security controls that appear in its appendix. This is a good opportunity to point out that governance frameworks and control frameworks are not the same thing.

- **ITIL**   Formerly an acronym for *IT Infrastructure Library*, ITIL is a framework of processes for IT service delivery. ITIL was originally sponsored by the UK Office of Government Commerce to improve its IT management processes, but it is now owned by AXELOS. The international standard, ISO/IEC 20000, is adapted from ITIL.

- **ISO/IEC 38500**   This international standard on corporate governance of information technology is suitable for small and large organizations in the public or private sector.

- **COSO**   This framework was developed by the Committee of Sponsoring Organizations of the Treadway Commission to combat internal fraud. COSO is a framework of internal controls, mainly targeting financial accounting systems and implicitly underlying relevant IT controls.

These and other frameworks are discussed in greater detail in Appendix B.

Digital Transformation

The phenomenon known as *digital transformation* represents the trend of increasing reliance of businesses on information technology. DX, as it is sometimes known, surpasses the mere *support* of business processes with information technology, but also includes business processes entirely based on information technology. The United States is leading this revolution, with the UK and Europe not far behind. This trend underscores the need for IS auditors, and even the digital transformation of IS audit itself.

IT Strategy Committee

In organizations where IT provides significant business value, the board of directors should have an IT strategy committee. This group will advise the board of directors on strategies to enable better IT support of the organization's overall strategy and objectives.

The IT strategy committee can meet with the organization's top IT executives to impart the board's wishes directly to them. This works best as a two-way conversation, where IT executives can inform the strategy committee of their status on major initiatives, as well as on challenges and risks. This ongoing dialogue can take place as often as needed, usually once or twice per year.

Readers should note that this suggestion of the IT strategy committee communicating with IT management is not an attempt to circumvent communications through intermediate layers of management. Those individuals should be included in this conversation as well.

The Balanced Scorecard

The *balanced scorecard* (BSC) is a management tool that is used to measure the performance and effectiveness of an organization. The BSC is used to determine how well an organization can fulfill its mission and strategic objectives, and how well it is aligned with overall organizational objectives.

In the BSC, management defines key performance indicators in each of four perspectives:

- **Financial** Key financial items measured include the cost of strategic initiatives, support costs of key applications, and capital investment.
- **Customer** Key measurements include the satisfaction rate with various customer-facing aspects of the organization.
- **Internal processes** Measurements of key activities include the number of projects and the effectiveness of key internal workings of the organization.
- **Innovation and learning** Human-oriented measurements include turnover, illness, internal promotions, and training.

Each organization's BSC will represent a unique set of measurements that reflects the organization's type of business, business model, and style of management.

The BSC methodology of greatest interest to readers of this book is the standard IT balanced scorecard, discussed in the next section.

The Standard IT Balanced Scorecard

The BSC should be used to measure overall organizational effectiveness and progress. A similar scorecard, the standard IT balanced scorecard (IT-BSC), can be used specifically to measure IT organization performance and results.

Like the BSC, the standard IT-BSC has four perspectives:

- **Business contribution**   Key indicators here are the perception of IT department effectiveness and value as seen from other (non-IT) corporate executives.

- **User**   Key measurements include end-user satisfaction rate with IT systems and the IT support organization. Satisfaction rates of external users should be included if the IT department builds or supports externally facing applications or systems.

- **Operational excellence**   Key measurements include the number of support cases, amount of unscheduled downtime, and defects reported.

- **Innovation**   This includes the rate at which the IT organization utilizes newer technologies to increase IT value and the amount of training made available to IT staff.

The IT-BSC should flow directly out of the organization's overall BSC. This will ensure that IT will align itself with corporate objectives. Although the perspectives between the overall BSC and the IT-BSC vary, the approach for each is similar, and the results for the IT-BSC can "roll up" to the organization's overall BSC.

Information Security Governance

Security governance is the collection of management activities that establishes key roles and responsibilities, identifies and treats risks to key assets, and measures key security processes. Depending upon the structure of the organization and its business purpose, information security governance may be included in IT governance, or security governance may stand on its own (but if so, it should still be linked to IT governance so that these two activities are kept in sync). Security governance helps to align information security with business goals and objectives.

The main roles and responsibilities for security should be as follows:

- **Board of directors**   The board is responsible for establishing the tone for risk appetite and risk management in the organization. To the extent that the board of directors establishes business and IT security, so, too, should the board consider risk and security in that strategy.

- **Steering committee**   The security steering committee should establish the operational strategy for security and risk management in the organization. This includes setting strategic and tactical roles and responsibilities in more detail than was done by the board of directors. The security strategy should be in harmony with the strategy for IT and the business overall. The steering committee should also ratify security policy and other strategic policies and processes developed by the chief information security officer.

- **Chief information security officer (CISO)**   The CISO should be responsible for developing security policy; conducting risk assessments; developing processes for risk management, vulnerability management, incident management, identity and access management, security awareness and training, third-party risk management, and compliance management; and informing the steering committee and board of directors of incidents and new or changed risks. In some organizations, this is known as the chief information risk officer (CIRO).

 NOTE   Some organizations may employ a chief security officer (CSO) who is responsible for logical security as described in the CISO role, as well as physical security, including workplace and personnel safety, physical access control, and investigations.

- **Chief information officer (CIO)**   The CIO is responsible for overall management of the IT organization, including IT strategy, development, operations, and service desk. In some organizations the CISO or another top-ranking security individual reports to the CIO, while in other organizations they are peers.

- **Management**   Every manager in the organization should be at least partially responsible for the conduct of his or her employees. This approach helps to establish a chain of accountability from the top of the organization all the way down to individual employees.

- **All employees**   Every employee in the organization should be required to comply with the organization's security policy, as well as with security requirements and processes. All senior and executive management personnel should demonstrably comply with these policies as an example for others.

Security governance is not only for the identification and enforcement of applicable laws, regulations, and other legal requirements, but also for the fulfillment of goals and objectives, as well as management, monitoring, and enforcement of policies and processes.

Security governance should also make it clear that compliance with policies is a condition of employment; employees who fail to comply with policy are subject to discipline or termination of employment.

Whom Should the CISO Report To?

The "whom should the CISO report to" debate rages on. Some argue that the CISO should report to the CIO, while others insist they be peers. While there is no right answer for all organizations, it is often suggested that the CISO organization be bifurcated as follows: governance, policy, investigations, and risk should remain with the CISO as a peer of the CIO, while security operations activities may reside within a security operations function that reports to the CIO. This way, the CISO—for activities such as policy development and risk management—remains independent of IT.

Reasons for Security Governance

Organizations are dependent on their information systems. This has progressed to the point where organizations—including those whose products or services are not information-related—are completely dependent on the integrity and availability of their information systems to continue operations; this is the trend of digital transformation (DX). Security governance, then, is needed to ensure that the probability and impact of security-related incidents are minimized and do not threaten critical systems and their support of the ongoing viability of the organization.

Security Governance Activities and Results

Within an effective security governance program, the organization's management will see to it that information systems necessary to support business operations will be adequately protected. Following are some of the activities that will take place:

- **Risk management** Management will ensure that risk assessments will be performed to identify risks in information systems. Follow-up actions—primarily, risk treatment—will be carried out that will reduce the risk of system failure and compromise to acceptable levels that align with the organization's risk appetite or risk tolerance.

- **Process improvement** Management will ensure that key changes will be made to business processes that will result in security improvements.

- **Incident response** Management will implement incident response procedures that will help to avoid incidents, reduce the impact and probability of incidents, and improve response to incidents so that their impact on the organization is minimized.

- **Improved compliance** Management will be sure to identify all applicable laws, regulations, and standards and carry out activities to confirm that the organization is able to attain and maintain compliance.

- **Business continuity and disaster recovery planning** Management will define objectives and allocate resources for the development of business continuity and disaster recovery plans.

- **Third-party risk management**   With increased reliance on external service providers, management will direct the assessment and management of third-party service providers that process and store critical information and perform critical functions for the organization.

- **Effectiveness measurement**   Management will establish processes to measure key security events such as incidents, policy changes and violations, audits, and training.

- **Resource management**   The allocation of manpower, budget, and other resources to meet security objectives will be monitored by management.

- **Improved IT governance**   An effective security governance program will result in better strategic decisions in the IT organization that keep risks at an acceptably low level.

These and other governance activities are carried out through scripted interactions among key business and IT executives at regular intervals. Meetings will include a discussion of effectiveness measurements, recent incidents, recent audits, and risk assessments. Other discussions may include such things as changes to the business, recent business results, and any anticipated business events such as mergers or acquisitions.

There are two key results of an effective security governance program:

- **Increased trust**   Customers, suppliers, and partners trust the organization to a greater degree when they see that security is managed effectively.

- **Improved reputation**   The business community, including customers, investors, and regulators, will hold the organization in higher regard.

IT Strategic Planning

In a methodical and organized way, a good strategic planning process answers the question of *what to do*, often in a way that takes longer to answer than it does to ask. Although IT organizations require personnel who perform the day-to-day work of supporting systems and applications, some IT personnel need to spend at least part of their time developing plans for what the IT organization will be doing two, three, or more years in the future.

Strategic planning needs to be part of a formal, iterative planning process, not an ad hoc, chaotic activity. Specific roles and responsibilities for planning need to be established, and those individuals must carry out planning roles as they would any other responsibility. A part of the struggle with the process of planning stems from the fact that strategic planning is partly a creative endeavor that includes analysis of reliable information about future technologies and practices, as well as long-term strategic plans for the organization itself. In a nutshell, the key question is this: *In five years, when the organization will be performing specific activities in a particular manner, how will IT systems enable and support those activities?*

But it's more than just understanding how IT will support future business activities. Innovations in IT may help to shape *what* activities will take place, or at least *how* they will take place. On a more down-to-earth level, IT strategic planning is about the ability to provide the capability and capacity for IT services that will match the levels of and the types of business activities that the organization expects to achieve at certain points in the future. In other words, if organization strategic planning predicts specific transaction volumes (as well as new types of transactions) at specific points in the future, the job of IT strategic planning will be to ensure that cost-effective IT systems of sufficient processing capacity will be up and running to support those features and workloads. As digital transformation sweeps across industries, increasingly IT does not merely *support* a business process; IT *is* a business process.

Discussion of new business activities, as well as the projected volume of current activities at certain times in the future, is most often discussed by a steering committee.

The IT Steering Committee

A *steering committee* is a body of senior managers or executives that meets from time to time to discuss high-level and long-term issues in the organization. An *IT steering committee* will typically discuss the future states of the organization and how the IT organization will meet the organization's needs. A steering committee will typically consist of senior-level IT managers as well as business unit leaders, and key internal customers or constituents. This provider-customer dialogue will help to ensure that IT, as the organization's technology service arm, will fully understand the future vision of the business (in business terms) and be able to support future business activities in terms of capacity, cost-effectiveness, and the ability to support new activities that do not yet exist.

NOTE   The IT steering committee also assesses the results of recent initiatives and major projects to gain a high-level understanding of past performance in order to shape future activities. The committee also needs to consider industry trends and practices, risks as defined by internal risk assessments, and current IT capabilities.

The role of the IT steering committee is depicted in Figure 2-1.

Figure 2-1
The IT steering committee synthesizes a future strategy using several inputs.

A steering committee's mission, objectives, roles, and responsibilities should be formally defined in a written charter. Steering committee meetings should be documented and minutes published.

The steering committee needs to meet regularly to consider strategic issues and make decisions that translate into actions, tasks, and projects in IT and elsewhere.

Not all organizations have an IT steering committee. The role is sometimes filled by key senior staff members, with or without an official charter. And in some organizations, the role is not filled at all; as a result, the IT organization is directionless and not aligned to the business.

Policies, Processes, Procedures, and Standards

Policies, processes, procedures, and standards define IT organizational behavior and uses of technology. They are part of the written record that defines how the IT organization performs the services that support the organization.

Policy documents should be developed and ratified by IT management. Policies state only *what* must be done (or not done) in an IT organization. They should not state *how* something must be done (or not done). That way, a policy document will be durable—meaning it may last many years with only minor edits from time to time.

IT policies typically cover many topics, including the following:

- **Roles and responsibilities**   These will range from general to specific, usually by describing each major role and responsibility in the IT department and then specifying which position is responsible for it. IT policies will also make general statements about responsibilities that all IT employees will share.

- **Development and acquisition practices**   IT policy should define the processes used to acquire, develop, and implement software for the organization. Typically, IT policy will require a formal development methodology that includes a few specific ingredients, such as quality review and the inclusion of security requirements and testing.

- **Operational practices**   IT policy defines the high-level processes that constitute IT's operations. This will include service desk, backups, system monitoring, metrics, and other day-to-day IT activities.

- **IT processes, documents, and records**   IT policy will define other important IT processes, including incident management, project management, vulnerability management, and support operations. IT policy should also define how and where documents such as procedures and records will be managed and stored.

IT policy, like any other organization policy, is generally focused on what should be done and on what parties are responsible for different activities. However, policy generally steers clear of describing how these activities should be performed. That, instead, is the role of procedures and standards, discussed later in this section.

The relationship between policies, processes, procedures, and standards is shown in Figure 2-2.

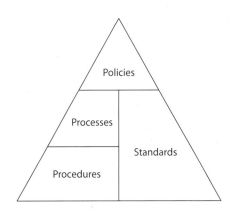

Figure 2-2
Policy pyramid showing the relationships between policies and the underlying processes, procedures, and standards

Information Security Policy

The *information security policy* defines how an organization will protect its important assets and respond to threats and incidents. Like IT policy, information security policy defines several fundamental principles and activities:

- **Roles and responsibilities**   Security policy should define specific roles and responsibilities, including the roles of specific positions in the organization as well as the responsibilities of all staff members.

- **Risk management**   Security policy should define how the organization identifies, manages, and treats risks. An organization should perform periodic risk assessments and risk analysis, which will lead to decisions about risk treatment for specific risks that are identified, and which align with established risk tolerance levels.

- **Security processes**   Security policy should define important security processes, such as vulnerability management and incident management, and incorporate security into other business processes, such as software development and acquisition, vendor selection and management, and employee screening and hiring.

- **Acceptable use**   Security policy should define the types of activities and behaviors that are acceptable and those that are not.

The best practice for information security policy is the definition of a top-down, management-driven information security program that performs periodic risk assessments to identify and focus on the most important risks in the organization. Roles and responsibilities define who is responsible for carrying out these activities. Executive management should have visibility and decision-making power, particularly in the areas of policy review and risk treatment.

It is generally accepted that security policy and security management should be separate from IT policy and IT management. This permits the security organization function to operate outside of IT, thereby permitting security to be objective and independent of IT. This puts security in a better position to be able to assess IT systems and processes objectively without fear of direct reprisal.

Privacy Policy

One of the most important policies an organization will develop that is related to information security is a privacy policy. A *privacy policy* describes how the organization will treat information that is considered private because it is related to a private citizen. A privacy policy defines two broad activities in this regard:

- **Protecting private information**   An organization that is required to collect, store, or transmit private information is duty-bound to protect this information so that it is not disclosed to unauthorized parties. This part of a privacy policy will describe what information is obtained and how it is protected.

- **Handling private information**   Aside from the actual protection of private information, some organizations may, in the course of their business activities, transmit some or all of this information to other parts of the organization or to other organizations. A privacy policy is typically forthright about this internal handling and the transmittals to other parties. Further, a privacy policy describes how the information is used by the organization and by other organizations to which it is transmitted. The privacy policy typically describes how a private citizen may confirm whether his or her private information is stored by the organization, whether it is accurate, and how the citizen can arrange for its removal if he or she wishes.

 NOTE   Many countries have privacy laws that require an organization to have a privacy policy and to enact safeguards to protect private information.

Data Classification Policy

A *data classification policy* defines degrees of sensitivity for various types of information used in the organization. A typical data classification policy will define two or more (but rarely more than five) data classification levels, such as the following:

- Top Secret
- Secret
- Sensitive
- Public

Along with defining levels of classification, a data classification policy will define policies and procedures for handling information in various settings at these levels. For instance, a data classification policy will state the conditions at each level in which sensitive information may be e-mailed, faxed, stored, transmitted, or shipped. Note that some methods for handling may be forbidden—such as e-mailing a top-secret document over the Internet.

EXAM TIP   While the CISO is responsible for establishing the organization's data classification policy, it is usually the responsibility of a document owner to classify and mark a document correctly. It is then the responsibility of any party who uses a document to handle it according to its classification level. All personnel who work with the document are responsible for handling it according to the classification policy.

System Classification Policy

A data classification policy may specify levels of security for systems storing classified information. A *system classification policy* will establish levels of system security that correspond to levels of data classification. Such a policy will help the organization to be more deliberate in its system hardening standards so that the most sensitive information will be stored only on systems with the highest levels of hardening (often, those higher levels of hardening are more costly and time consuming to manage; otherwise, an organization might just make all of its systems as secure).

Site Classification Policy

A *site classification policy* defines levels of security for an organization's work sites. This policy sets levels of physical security that corresponds to one or more factors:

- Criticality of staff that works at the site
- Criticality or value of business processes performed at the site
- Value of assets located at the site
- Sensitivity or value of data stored or processed at the site
- Siting risks associated with a site (human-made or natural hazards)

Based on the classification of a site, an organization may have additional security controls, such as video surveillance, guards, fences, visitor controls, and so on. Just as it does not make sense to protect all data at a single level, it also is sensible to have the appropriate level of physical security at each site according to the information, equipment, or activity that takes place there.

Access Control Policy

An *access control policy* defines the need for specific processes and procedures related to the granting, review, and revocation of access to systems and work areas. This policy will state which roles are permitted to manage access controls, what levels of approval are required for access requests, how often access reviews will take place, and what access control records will be kept.

Often, there will be linkage between a data classification policy and an access control policy, since access controls protecting the most sensitive information may be stricter than access controls protecting less-sensitive information.

Mobile Device Policy

A *mobile device policy* defines the use of mobile devices and personally owned devices in the context of business operations and access to business information and information systems. This policy will state the types of devices that may be permitted, the rules and conditions of their use, and the responsibilities of device owners and users. A mobile device policy often addresses the business rules related to the use of BYOD (bring your own device), wherein employees may want to use personally owned devices such as smartphones and home computers to access and manage business information.

Social Media Policy

A *social media policy* defines employees' use of social media. Generally, this encompasses online behavior and employees' online representations of their personal and professional conduct. A social media policy may include the following components:

- **Personal social media**   Policy may limit the posting of content that could put the employee or the organization in a bad light.
- **Professional social media**   Policy may address or restrict how employees describe their positions and activities in the workplace.
- **Disclosure of company information**   Policy may restrict the types of information that employees are permitted to disclose to the public.

Although organizations generally don't try to restrict employees' use of social media, organizations use social media policy to reaffirm their ownership of official information about the organization.

Other Policies

Organizations may have additional technology-related policies, including the following:

- **Equipment control and use**   Policy may address the appropriate use of IT and other equipment, perhaps including equipment assigned to employee use in the field.
- **Data destruction**   Policy defines acceptable and required methods for the disposal of information when it's no longer needed.
- **Moonlighting**   Policy addresses matters regarding outside employment, such as employees who have a second job or who perform volunteer work.
- **Intellectual property**   Policy addresses matters related to the ownership of intellectual property that is created, accessed, or used.

Processes and Procedures

Process and procedure documents, sometimes called *SOPs* (standard operating procedures), describe in step-by-step detail how IT processes and tasks are performed. Formal procedure documents ensure that tasks are performed consistently and correctly, even when performed by different IT staff members.

In addition to the actual steps in support of a process or task, a procedure document needs to contain several pieces of metadata:

- **Document (or process) ownership**   The document should contain the name of the person or department responsible for its review, revision, and publication.

- **Document revision information**   The procedure document should contain the name of the person who wrote the document and the person who made the most recent changes to the document. The document should also include the name or location where the official copy of the document can be found.

- **Review and approval**   The document should include the name of the manager who last reviewed the procedure document, as well as the name of the manager (or higher) who approved the document.

- **Dependencies**   The document should specify which other procedures are related to each procedure. This includes other procedures that are dependent upon a procedure, and any other procedures that each procedure depends on. For example, a document that describes the database backup process will depend on database management and maintenance documents; documents on media handling will depend on this document.

IT process and procedure documents are not meant to be a replacement for vendor task documentation. For instance, an IT department does not necessarily need to create a document that describes the steps for operating a data storage device when the device vendor's instructions are available and sufficient. Also, IT procedure documents need not be remedial and include every specific keystroke and mouse click: they can usually assume that the reader has experience in the subject area and needs to know how things are done in *this* organization only. For example, a procedure document that includes a step that involves the modification of a configuration file does not need to include instructions on how to operate a text editor.

 TIP   An IT department should maintain a catalog of its procedure documents to facilitate convenient document management. This will permit IT management to better understand which documents are in its catalog, when each was last reviewed and updated, and which will be impacted by specific IT or business changes.

Standards

IT standards are official, management-approved statements that define the technologies, protocols, suppliers, and methods that are used by an IT organization. Standards help to drive consistency into the IT organization, which will make the organization more cost-efficient and cost-effective.

An IT organization will have different types of standards, including these:

- **Technology/product standards** These standards specify what software and hardware technologies or products are used by the IT organization. Examples include operating systems, database management systems, application servers, storage systems, backup media, and so on.

- **Protocol standards** These standards specify the protocols that are used by the organization. For instance, an IT organization may opt to use Transmission Control Protocol/Information Protocol (TCP/IP) v6 for its internal networks, Cisco gateway routing protocols (GRP), Transport Layer Security (TLS) for secure transmission of data, Secure Shell (SSH) for device management, and so forth.

- **Supplier standards** These define which suppliers and vendors are used for various types of supplies and services. Using established suppliers can help the IT organization through specially negotiated discounts and other arrangements.

- **Methodology standards** These refer to practices used in various processes, including software development, system administration, network engineering, and end-user support.

- **Configuration standards** These standards refer to specific detailed configurations that are to be applied to servers, database management systems, end-user workstations, network devices, and so on. This enables users, developers, and technical administrative personnel to be more comfortable with IT systems, because the systems will be consistent with one another. This helps reduce unscheduled downtime and improves quality.

- **Architecture standards** These standards refer to the technology architecture at the database, system, or network level. An organization may develop reference architectures for use in various standard settings. For instance, a large retail organization may develop specific network diagrams to be used in every retail location, down to the colors of wires to use and how equipment is situated on racks or shelves.

 TIP Standards enable the IT organization to be simpler, leaner, and more efficient. IT organizations with effective standards will have fewer types of hardware and software to support, which reduces the number of technologies that must be managed by the organization. An organization that standardizes on one operating system, one database management system, and one server platform need only build expertise in those technologies. This enables the IT organization to manage and support the environment more effectively than if many different technologies were in use.

Enterprise Architecture

Enterprise architecture (EA) is both a business function and a technical model. In terms of a business function, the establishment of an EA consists of activities that ensure that important business needs are met by IT systems overall. EA may also involve the construction of a model that is used to map business functions into the IT environment and IT systems in increasing levels of detail so that IT professionals can more easily understand the organization's technology architecture at any level.

The Zachman Framework

The Zachman enterprise architecture framework, established in the late 1980s, continues to be the dominant EA standard today. Zachman likens IT EA to the construction and maintenance of an office building: at a high (abstract, not number of floors) level, the office building performs functions such as containing office space. As we look into increasing levels of detail in the building, we encounter various trades (steel, concrete, drywall, electrical, plumbing, telephone, fire control, elevators, and so on), each with its own specifications, standards, regulations, construction and maintenance methods, and so on.

In the Zachman framework, IT systems and environments are described at a high, functional level, and then in increasing detail, encompassing systems, databases, applications, networks, and so on. The Zachman framework is illustrated in Table 2-1.

While the Zachman framework enables an organization to peer into cross-sections of an IT environment that supports business processes, the model does not convey the relationships between IT systems. *Data flow diagrams*, discussed in the next section, are instead used to depict information flows.

The U.S. government takes EA quite seriously. All U.S. government agencies are required to develop EA and use it in their strategic planning activities. Often the DoD Architecture Framework (DoDAF) is used for this purpose.

	Data	Functional (Application)	Network (Technology)	People (Organization)	Time	Strategy
Scope	List of data sets important in the business	List of business processes	List of business locations	List of organizations	List of events	List of business goals and strategy
Enterprise Model	Conceptual data/object model	Business process model	Business logistics	Workflow	Master schedule	Business plan
Systems Model	Logical data model	System architecture	Detailed system architecture	Human interface architecture	Processing structure	Business rule model
Technology Model	Physical data/class model	Technology design	Technology architecture	Presentation architecture	Control structure	Rule design
Detailed Representation	Data definition	Program	Network architecture	Security architecture	Time definition	Rule speculation
Function Enterprise	Usable data	Working function	Usable network	Functioning organization	Implemented schedule	Working strategy

Table 2-1 Zachman Framework Shows IT Systems in Increasing Levels of Detail

Data Flow Diagrams

Data flow diagrams (DFDs) are frequently used to illustrate the flow of information between IT applications. Like the Zachman model, a DFD can begin as a high-level diagram, where the labels of information flows are expressed in business terms. Written specifications about each flow can accompany the DFD; these specifications would describe the flow in increasing levels of detail, all the way to field lengths and communication protocol settings.

Similar to Zachman, DFDs enable nontechnical business executives to understand the various IT applications and the relationships between them. A typical DFD is shown in Figure 2-3.

Data Storage Diagrams

A counterpart to data flow diagrams are *depictions* (visual, or tabular) or *data storage diagrams*. These depict data at rest across the enterprise. The purpose of data storage diagrams (or data storage catalogs) is to document the intended and expected instances of stored information in the organization.

Data storage diagrams document the *structured data* that resides in an organization. The term "structured data" refers to the fact that data in this instance resides in formal management systems (often, database management systems, or DBMSs) that have a structured design, usually known as a *schema*. Contrast structured data to *unstructured data*, which is the data that resides in network file shares and end-user workstations in a

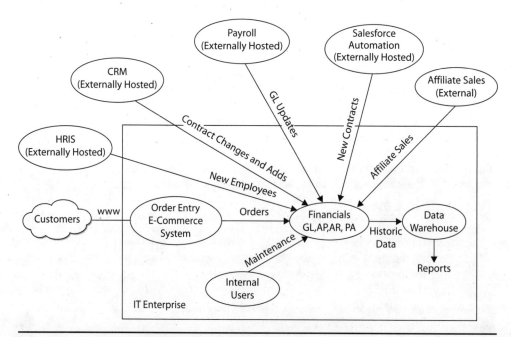

Figure 2-3   A typical DFD shows the relationship between IT applications.

mostly or entirely ad hoc fashion. Unstructured data often exists as a result of the ability for business applications to produce extracts and reports, which users create, download, and store on their local workstations or on network file shares.

Zero Trust

Zero trust is an architecture model wherein one or more portions of an environment are considered untrusted. The first such model is the greater Internet itself: networks and workstations external to an organization (on the Internet) are not controlled by the organization and, hence, are untrusted. This model applies not only to the technology in place, but also to the intent of the people using that technology (consider hackers and cybercriminal organizations).

The zero trust model is increasingly being used by organizations in various contexts. Consider, for instance, an organization with a traditional data center and office networks with end-user computing. An organization may adopt a zero trust model with respect to the relationship between the information systems and applications in its data center, and its workstations. The design of its data centers, information systems, and applications assume that the entire set of end-user systems are untrusted (which is rarely the *actual* case, but stay with me here). This thought process gives rise to a different way of thinking about security controls protecting the data center with its applications: if one assumes that an organization's end-user computing environment is like the Internet itself (completely untrusted), then this naturally gives rise to a more rigorous protection of the data center environment by protecting it from *all* endpoints, including those managed by the organization.

This is an entirely valid approach. In many organizations, end users are permitted to change the configuration of their workstations, and they are sometimes permitted to use their own workstations. Further, consider the threat and effect of malware, which often strikes end-user workstations, and the additional threat therein. Given these conditions, it is often prudent to apply protective controls to a data center as though all end-user workstations were uncontrolled and untrusted (because, often, that is exactly the case).

Zero trust principles apply in other instances as well. The result is generally the same: communications between one environment (or system) and another must be verified in various ways to ensure that no unplanned or hostile activities can interfere with computing and business operations.

Applicable Laws, Regulations, and Standards

Organizations need to identify all of the laws, regulations, and standards that are applicable to their operations. As IT has become more critical for organizations in many industry sectors, many nations and local governments have enacted new laws and regulations concerning the processing and protection of information.

The board of directors, strategy committee, or chief legal counsel should appoint an executive to be responsible for identifying all potentially applicable laws and regulations. This appointee should then consult with inside or outside legal counsel to determine their scope and applicability.

Once applicable laws and regulations have been identified, the organization needs to determine how they affect the following:

- **Enterprise architecture**   Laws and regulations may require that organizations use specific IT components or configurations that affect the organization's EA.
- **Controls**   Laws and regulations may require that additional controls be enacted or existing controls be changed.
- **Business processes**   Laws and regulations may require that the organization perform certain tasks that may affect processes.
- **Personnel**   Laws and regulations may require that certain personnel possess specific qualifications, certifications, or licenses.

Many factors will determine whether specific laws are applicable to an organization, including these:

- Type of data that is stored, processed, or transmitted by the organization's systems
- Industry sector
- Location and management of stored, processed, or transmitted data
- Location of the owner(s) and steward(s) of stored, processed, or transmitted data

Organizations may also be required to comply with specific standards. For example, organizations that process, store, or transmit credit card numbers may be required to comply with the Payment Card Industry Data Security Standard (PCI-DSS), even though there may be no laws requiring organizations to do so.

Risk Management

Organizations need to understand the internal activities, practices, and systems, as well as external threats, that are introducing risk into their operations. The span of activities that seek, identify, and manage these risks is known as *risk management*. Like many other processes, risk management is a life cycle activity that has no beginning and no end. It's a continuous and phased set of activities that includes the examination of processes, records, systems, and external phenomena in order to identify risks. This is continued by an analysis that examines a range of solutions for reducing or eliminating risks, followed by formal decision-making that brings about a resolution to risks.

Risk management needs to support the overall business objectives. This support will include the adoption of a *risk appetite* that reflects the organization's overall approach to risk. For instance, if the organization is a conservative financial institution, the organization's risk management program will probably adopt a position of being risk averse. Similarly, a high-tech startup organization that, by its very nature, is comfortable with overall business risk will probably be less averse to risks identified in its risk management program.

Regardless of its overall risk appetite, when an organization identifies risks, the organization can take one of four possible actions:

- **Accept** The organization accepts the risk as is.
- **Mitigate (or reduce)** The organization acts to reduce the level of risk.
- **Transfer (or share)** The organization shares the risk with another entity, often an insurance company.
- **Avoid** The organization discontinues the activity associated with the risk.

These choices are known as *risk treatments*. Often, a particular risk will be treated with a blended solution that consists of two or more of the actions just listed.

This section dives into the details of risk management, risk analysis, and risk treatment.

The Risk Management Program

An organization that operates a risk management program should establish principles that will enable the program to succeed. These may include the following:

- **Objectives** The risk management program must have a specific purpose; otherwise, it will be difficult to determine whether the program is successful. Example objectives include reducing the number of industrial accidents, reducing the cost of insurance premiums, and reducing the number or severity of security incidents. If objectives are measurable and specific, then the individuals who are responsible for the risk management program can focus on its objectives to achieve the best possible outcome.

- **Scope** Management must determine the scope of the risk management program. This is a delicate undertaking because of the many interdependencies found in IT systems and business processes. However, in an organization with several distinct operations or business units (BUs), a risk management program could be isolated to one or more operational arms or BUs. In such a case, where there are dependencies on other services in the organization, those dependencies can be treated like external service providers (or customers).

- **Authority** The risk management program is being started at the request of one or more executives in the organization. It is important to know who these individuals are and their levels of commitment to the program.

- **Roles and responsibilities** This defines specific job titles, together with their respective roles and responsibilities, in the risk management program. In a risk management program involving several individuals, it should be clear which individuals or job titles are responsible for which activities in the program.

- **Resources** The risk management program, like other activities in the business, requires resources to operate. This will include a budget for salaries as well as for workstations, software licenses, and possibly travel.

- **Policies, processes, procedures, and records** The various risk management activities, such as asset identification, risk analysis, and risk treatment, along with some general activities such as recordkeeping, should be included in business records.

 NOTE An organization's risk management program should be documented in a *charter*. A charter is a formal document that defines and describes a business program and becomes a part of the organization's record.

The risk management life cycle is depicted in Figure 2-4.

The Risk Management Process

Risk management is a life cycle set of activities used to identify, analyze, and treat risks. These activities are methodical and, as mentioned in the previous section, should be documented so that they will be performed consistently and in support of the program's charter and objectives.

The risk management process is a part of a larger risk framework, such as ISACA's Risk IT Framework, whose components are the following:

- **Risk Governance** This includes integration with the organization's enterprise risk management (ERM) process, the establishment and maintenance of a common risk view, and the ability to ensure that business decisions include the consideration of risk.

- **Risk Evaluation** This includes asset identification, risk analysis, and the maintenance of a risk profile.

- **Risk Response** This includes the management and articulation of risks and the response to events.

 EXAM TIP CISA candidates are not required to memorize the Risk IT Framework, but familiarity with its principles is important.

Figure 2-4
The risk management life cycle

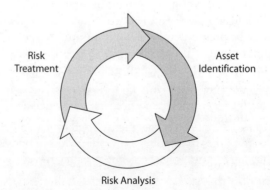

Risk Treatment

Asset Identification

Risk Analysis

Asset Identification

The risk management program's main objective (whether formally stated or not) is the protection of the organization's assets. These assets may be tangible or intangible, physical, logical, or virtual. Some examples of assets include the following:

- **Buildings and property**   These assets include structures and other improvements.
- **Equipment**   This can include machinery, vehicles, and office equipment such as copiers and fax machines.
- **IT equipment**   This includes computers, printers, scanners, tape libraries (the devices that create backup tapes, not the tapes themselves), storage systems, network devices, and phone systems.
- **Supplies and materials**   These can include office supplies as well as materials that are used in manufacturing.
- **Records**   These include business records, such as contracts, video surveillance tapes, visitor logs, and much more.
- **Information**   This includes data in software applications, documents, e-mail messages, and files of every kind on workstations and servers.
- **Intellectual property**   This includes an organization's trade secrets, designs, architectures, software source code, processes, and procedures.
- **Personnel**   In a real sense, an organization's personnel *are* the organization. Without its staff, the organization cannot perform or sustain its processes.
- **Reputation**   One of the intangible characteristics of an organization, reputation is the individual and collective opinion about an organization in the eyes of its customers, competitors, shareholders, and the community.
- **Brand equity**   Similar to reputation, this is the perceived or actual market value of an individual brand of product or service that is produced by the organization.

Grouping Assets   For risk management purposes, an electronic inventory of assets will be useful in the risk management life cycle. It is not always necessary to list each individual asset: often, it is acceptable to instead list *classes* or *groups* of assets as a single asset entity for risk management purposes. For instance, a single entry for laptop computers may be preferred over listing every laptop computer; this is because the risks for all laptop computers are roughly the same (ignoring behavior differences among individual employees or employees in specific departments). This eliminates the need to list them individually.

Similarly, groups of IT servers, network devices, and other equipment can be named instead of all of the individual servers and devices, again because the risks for each of them will usually be similar. One reason to create multiple entries for servers, however, might be their physical location or their purpose: servers in one location may have different risks than servers in another location, and servers containing high-value information will have different risks than servers that do not contain high-value information.

Sources of Asset Data An organization that is undergoing its initial risk management cycle may need to build its asset database from scratch. Management will need to determine where this initial asset data will come from, such as the following:

- **Financial system asset inventory** An organization that keeps all of its assets on the books will have a wealth of asset inventory information. It may not be entirely useful, however: asset lists often do not include the location or purpose of the asset and whether it is still in use. Correlating a financial asset inventory to assets in actual use may consume more effort than the other methods for creating the initial asset. However, for organizations that have a relatively small number of highly valued assets (for instance, a rock crusher in a gold mine or a mainframe computer), knowing the precise financial value of an asset is highly useful because the actual depreciated value of the asset is used in the risk analysis phase of risk management. Knowing the depreciated value of other assets is also useful, as this will figure into the risk treatment choices that will be identified later.

TIP Financial records that indicate the value of an asset do not include the value of information stored on (or processed by) the asset or the revenue earned through operation of the asset (or the financial consequences through its loss).

- **Interviews** Discussions with key personnel for purposes of identifying assets are usually the best approach. However, to be effective, several people usually need to be interviewed to be sure to include all relevant assets.
- **IT systems portfolio** A well-managed IT organization will have formal documents and records for its major applications. Although this information may not encompass every single IT asset in the organization, it can provide information on the assets supporting individual applications or geographic locations.
- **Online data** An organization with numerous IT assets (systems, network devices, and so on) can sometimes utilize the capability of local online data to identify those assets. For instance, a systems or network management system often includes a list of managed assets, which can be a good starting point when creating the initial asset list.
- **Asset management system** Larger organizations may find it more cost effective to use an asset management application dedicated to this purpose, rather than rely on lists of assets from other sources.

TIP Organizations need to keep in mind that some information assets will physically reside in service provider environments (mainly, information assets).

Collecting and Organizing Asset Data   It is rarely possible to take (or create) a list of assets from a single source. Rather, more than one source of information is often needed to be sure that the risk management program has identified at least the important, in-scope assets that it needs to worry about.

NOTE   As a part of IT governance, management needs to determine which person or group is responsible for maintaining an asset inventory.

It is usually useful to organize or classify assets. This will help to get the assets under study into smaller chunks that can be analyzed more effectively. There is no single way to organize assets, but here are a few ideas:

- **Geography**   A widely dispersed organization may classify its assets according to their locations. This will aid risk managers during the risk analysis phase, since many risks are geographic-centric, particularly natural hazards. Mitigation of risks is often geography based: for instance, it's easier to put a fence around one data center than to put up fences around buildings in every location.

- **Business process**   Because some organizations rank the criticality of their individual business processes, it can be useful to group assets according to the business processes that they support. This helps in the risk analysis and risk treatment phases, because assets supporting individual processes can be associated with business criticality and treated appropriately.

- **Organizational unit**   In larger organizations, it may be easier to classify assets according to the organizational units they support.

- **Sensitivity**   Usually ascribed to information, sensitivity relates to the nature and content of that information. Sensitivity usually applies in two ways: to an individual, where the information is considered personal or private, and to an organization, where the information may be considered a trade secret. Sometimes sensitivity is somewhat subjective and arbitrary, but often it is defined in laws and regulations.

- **Regulation**   For organizations that are required to follow government or private regulation regarding the processing and protection of information, it will be useful to include data points that indicate whether specific assets are considered in scope for specific regulations. This is important because some regulations specify how assets should be protected, so it's useful to be aware of this during risk analysis and risk treatment.

There is no need to choose which of these three methods will be used to classify assets. Instead, an IT analyst should collect several points of metadata about each asset (including location, process supported, and organizational unit supported). This will enable the risk manager to sort and filter the list of assets in various ways better to understand which assets are in a given location or which ones support a particular process or part of the business.

 TIP Organizations should consider managing information about assets in a fixed-assets application.

Risk Analysis

Risk analysis is the activity in a risk management program where individual risks are identified. A risk consists of the intersection of threats, vulnerabilities, probabilities, and impact. In its simplest terms, risk is described in the following formula:

$$Risk = Probability \times Impact$$

This equation implies that risk is always used in quantitative terms, but risk is equally used in qualitative risk analysis. An alternative formula is sometimes used:

$$Risk = Probability \times Impact \times Asset\ Value$$

Other definitions of risk include the following:

- The combination of the probability of an event and its consequence (source: ISACA Cybersecurity Fundamentals Glossary)
- The probable frequency and probable magnitude of future loss (source: "An Introduction to Factor Analysis of Information Risk (FAIR)," Risk Management Insight, LLC)
- The potential that a given threat will exploit vulnerabilities of an asset or group of assets and thereby cause harm to the organization (source: ISO/IEC 27005)

These definitions convey essentially the same message: the amount of risk is directly proportional to the probability of occurrence and the impact that a risk would have if realized.

A risk analysis consists of identifying threats and their impact of realization against each asset. It usually also includes a vulnerability analysis, where assets are studied to determine whether they are vulnerable to identified threats. The sheer number of assets may make this task appear daunting; however, threat and vulnerability analyses can usually be performed against groups of assets. For instance, when identifying natural and human-made threats against assets, it often makes sense to perform a single threat analysis against all of the assets that reside in a given location. After all, the odds of a volcanic eruption are the same for any of the servers in the room—the threat need not be called out separately for each asset.

Threat Analysis   The usual first step in a risk analysis is to identify threats against an asset or group of assets. A *threat* is an event that, if realized, would bring harm to an asset and, hence, to the organization. Often called *threat modeling*, a typical approach is to list all of the threats that have some realistic opportunity of occurrence; those threats that are highly unlikely to occur can be left out. For instance, the listing of meteorites, tsunamis in landlocked regions, and wars in typically peaceful regions will just add clutter to a risk analysis.

A more reasonable approach in a threat analysis is to identify all of the threats that a reasonable person would believe could occur, even if the probability is low. For example, include flooding when a facility is located near a river, hurricanes for an organization located along the southern or eastern coast (and inland for some distance) of the United States, or a terrorist attack in practically every major city in the world. All of these would be considered reasonable in a threat analysis.

It is important to include the entire range of both natural and human-made threats. The full list could approach or even exceed 100 separate threats. The categories of possible threats include these:

- **Severe storms**   These may include tornadoes, hurricanes, windstorms, ice storms, and blizzards.

- **Earth movement**   This includes earthquakes, landslides, avalanches, volcanoes, and tsunamis.

- **Flooding**   This can include both natural and human-made situations.

- **Disease**   This includes sickness outbreaks and pandemics, as well as quarantines that result.

- **Fire**   This includes forest fires, range fires, and structure fires, all of which may be natural or human-caused.

- **Labor**   This includes work stoppages, sick-outs, protests, and strikes.

- **Violence**   This includes riots, looting, terrorism, and war.

- **Malware**   This includes all kinds of viruses, worms, Trojan horses, root kits, ransomware, destructware, and associated malicious software.

- **Hacking attacks**   These include automated attacks (think of an Internet worm that is on the loose) as well as targeted attacks by employees, former employees, or criminals.

- **Hardware failures**   These include any kind of failure of IT equipment or failures of related environmental equipment, such as heating, ventilation, and air conditioning (HVAC).

- **Software failures**   These can include any software problem that precipitates a disaster. Examples are the software bug that caused a significant power blackout in the U.S. Northeast in 2003 and the Nest home thermostat bug in 2016.

- **Utilities**   These includes electric power failures, water supply failures, and natural gas outages, as well as communications outages.

- **Transportation**   This may include airplane crashes, railroad derailments, ship collisions, and highway accidents.

- **Hazardous materials**   This includes chemical spills. The primary threat here is direct damage by hazardous substances, casualties, and forced evacuations.
- **Criminal**   This includes extortion, embezzlement, theft, vandalism, sabotage, and hacker intrusion. Note that company insiders can play a role in these activities.
- **Errors**   These include mistakes made by personnel that result in disaster situations.

Alongside each threat that is identified, the risk analyst assigns a probability or frequency of occurrence. This may be a numeric value, expressed as a probability of one occurrence within a calendar year. For example, if the risk of a flood is 1 in 100, it would be expressed as 0.01, or 1 percent. Probability can also be expressed as a ranking; for example, Low, Medium, and High; or it can be expressed on a numeric probability scale from 1 to 5 (where 5 can be either highest or lowest probability).

An approach for completing a threat analysis is to:

- **Perform a geographic threat analysis for each location**   This will provide an analysis on the probability of each type of threat against all assets in each location.
- **Perform a logical threat analysis for each type of asset**   This provides information on all of the logical (that is, not physical) threats that can occur to each asset type. For example, the risk of malware on all assets of one type is probably the same, regardless of the assets' locations.
- **Perform a threat analysis for each highly valued asset**   This will help to identify any unique threats that may have appeared in the geographic or logical threat analysis, but with different probabilities of occurrence.

Threat Forecasting Data Is Sparse

One of the biggest problems with information security–related risk management is the lack of reliable data on the probability of many types of threats. While the probability of some natural threats can sometimes be obtained from local disaster response agencies, the probabilities of most other threats are difficult to predict accurately.

The difficulty in predicting security events sits in stark contrast to volumes of available data related to automobile and airplane accidents, as well as human life expectancy. In these cases, insurance companies have been accumulating statistics on these events for decades, and the variables (for instance, tobacco and alcohol use) are well known. On the topic of cyber-related risk, there is a general lack of reliable data, and the factors that influence risk are not well known from a statistical perspective. It is for this reason that risk analysis still relies on educated guesses for the probabilities of most events. But given the recent surge in popularity for cyber insurance, the availability and quality of cyber-attack risk factors may soon be more accurately determined.

Vulnerability Identification   A *vulnerability* is a weakness or absence of a protective control that increases the probability of one or more threats occurring. A *vulnerability analysis* is an examination of an asset to discover weaknesses that could lead to a higher than normal rate of occurrence or potency of a threat.

Here are some examples of vulnerabilities:

- Missing or inoperative antivirus software
- Outdated and unsupported software in use
- Missing security patches
- Weak password settings
- Missing or incomplete audit logs
- Inadequate monitoring of event logs
- Weak or defective application session management
- Building entrances that permit tailgating
- Insufficient coverage of video surveillance

In a vulnerability analysis, the risk manager needs to examine the asset itself as well as all of the protective measures that are—or should be—in place to protect the asset from relevant threats.

Vulnerabilities are usually ranked by severity. Vulnerabilities are indicators that show the effectiveness (or ineffectiveness) of protective measures. For example, an antivirus program on a server that updates its virus signatures once per week might be ranked as a medium vulnerability, whereas the complete absence (or malfunction) of an antivirus program on the same server might be ranked as a high vulnerability. Severity is an indication of the likelihood that a given threat might be realized. This is different from *impact*, which is discussed later in this section.

TIP   A vulnerability, and its ranking, should not be influenced by the probability that a threat will be realized. Instead, a vulnerability ranking should depend on whether the threat will actually bring about harm to the asset. Also, the ranking of a vulnerability should not be influenced by the value of the asset or the impact of a realized threat. These factors are covered separately in risk management.

Probability Analysis   For any given threat and asset, the probability that the threat will actually be realized needs to be estimated. This is often easier said than done, as there is a lack of reliable data on security incidents. A risk manager will need to perform some research and develop a best guess based on any available data.

Impact Analysis   A threat, when actually realized, will have some effect on the organization. *Impact analysis* is the study of estimating the impact of specific threats on specific assets.

In impact analysis, it is necessary for the analyst to understand the relationship between an asset and the business processes and activities that the asset supports. The purpose of impact analysis is to identify the impact on business operations or business processes. This is because risk management is not an abstract identification of abstract risks, but instead a search for risks that have real impact on business operations.

In an impact analysis, the impact can be expressed as a rating such as H-M-L (High-Medium-Low) or as a numeric scale, and it can also be expressed in financial terms. But what is also vitally important in an impact analysis is the inclusion of a *statement of impact* for each threat. Example statements of impact include "inability to process customer support calls" and "inability for customers to view payment history." Statements such as "inability to authenticate users" may be technically accurate, but they do not identify the business impact.

 NOTE Because of the additional time required to quantify and develop statements of impact, impact analysis is usually performed only on the highest ranked threats on the most critical assets.

Qualitative Risk Analysis   A *qualitative risk analysis* is an in-depth examination of in-scope assets with a detailed study of threats (and their probability of occurrence), vulnerabilities (and their severity), and statements of impact. The threats, vulnerabilities, and impact are all expressed in qualitative terms such as High-Medium-Low or in quasi-numeric terms such as a 1–5 numeric scale.

The purpose of qualitative risk analysis is to identify the most critical risks in the organization based on these rankings.

Qualitative risk analysis does not get to the issue of "how much does a given threat cost my business if it is realized?"—neither does it mean to do this. The value in a qualitative risk analysis is the ability to identify the most critical risks quickly without the additional burden of identifying precise financial impacts.

The individual(s) performing risk analysis may want to include threat-vulnerability pairing as well as asset-threat pairing. These techniques may help a risk analyst better understand the probability or impact of specific threats.

 NOTE Organizations that do need to perform quantitative risk analysis often begin with qualitative risk analysis to determine the highest ranked risks that warrant the additional effort of quantitative analysis.

Quantitative Risk Analysis   *Quantitative risk analysis* is a risk analysis approach that uses numeric methods to measure risk. Quantitative risk analysis offers statements of risk in terms that can be easily compared with the known values of their respective assets. In other words, risks are expressed in the same units of measure as most organizations' primary unit of measure: financial.

Despite this, quantitative risk analysis must still be regarded as an effort to develop estimates, not exact figures. Partly this is because risk analysis is a measure of events that *may* occur, not a measure of events that *do* occur.

Standard quantitative risk analysis involves the development of several figures:

- **Asset value (AV)**   This is the value of the asset, which is usually (but not necessarily) the asset's replacement value.

- **Exposure factor (EF)**   This is the financial loss that results from the realization of a threat, expressed as a percentage of the asset's total value. Most threats do not completely eliminate the asset's value; instead, they reduce its value. For example, if a construction company's $500,000 earth mover is destroyed in a fire, the equipment will still have salvage value, even if that is only 10 percent of the asset's value. In this case, the EF would be 90 percent. Note that different threats will have different impacts on EF, because the realization of different threats will cause varying amounts of damage to assets.

- **Single loss expectancy (SLE)**   This value represents the financial loss when a threat is realized one time. SLE is defined as $AV \times EF$. Note that different threats have a varied impact on EF, so those threats will also have the same multiplicative effect on SLE.

- **Annualized rate of occurrence (ARO)**   This is an estimate of the number of times that a threat will occur per year. If the probability of the threat is 1 in 50, then ARO is expressed as 0.02. However, if the threat is estimated to occur four times per year, then ARO is 4.0. Like EF and SLE, ARO will vary by threat.

- **Annualized loss expectancy (ALE)**   This is the expected annualized loss of asset value due to threat realization. ALE is defined as $SLE \times ARO$.

ALE is based upon the verifiable values AV, EF, and SLE, but because ARO is only an estimate, ALE is only as good as ARO. Depending upon the value of the asset, the risk manager may need to take extra care to develop the best possible estimate for ARO, based upon whatever data is available. Sources for estimates include

- History of event losses in the organization

- History of similar losses in other organizations

- History of dissimilar losses

- Best estimates based on available data

TIP   When the analyst is performing a quantitative risk analysis for a given asset, the ALE for all threats can be added together. The sum of all ALEs is the annualized loss expectancy for the total array of threats. A particularly high sum of ALEs would mean that a given asset is confronted with a lot of significant threats that are more likely to occur. But in terms of risk treatment, ALEs are better off left as separate and associated with their respective threats.

Developing Mitigation Strategies An important part of risk analysis is the investigation of potential solutions for reducing or eliminating risk. This involves understanding specific threats and their impact (EF) and likelihood of occurrence (ARO). Once a given asset and threat combination has been *baselined* (that is, the existing asset, threats, and controls have been analyzed to understand the threats as they exist at a given point in time), the risk analyst can then apply various hypothetical means for reducing risk, documenting each one in terms of its impact on EF and ARO.

For example, suppose a risk analysis identifies the threat of attack on a public web server. Specific EF and ARO figures have been identified for a range of individual threats. Now the risk analyst applies a range of fixes (on paper), such as an application firewall, an intrusion prevention system (IPS), and a patch management tool. Each solution will have a specific and unique impact on EF and ARO (these are all estimates, of course, just like the estimates of EF and ARO on the initial conditions); some will have better EF and ARO figures than others. Each solution should also be rated in terms of cost (financial or H-M-L) and effort to implement (financial or H-M-L).

NOTE Developing mitigation strategies is the first step in risk treatment, where various solutions are put forward, each with its cost and impact on risk.

While security analysts may have the responsibility for documenting vulnerabilities, threats, and risks, it is senior management's responsibility (through the security steering committee) to formally approve the treatment of risk. Risk treatment is discussed later in this chapter.

Risk Analysis and Disaster Recovery Planning Disaster recovery planning (DRP) and business continuity planning (BCP) utilize risk analysis to identify risks that are related to application resilience and the impact of disasters. The risk analysis performed for DRP and BCP is the same risk analysis that is discussed in this chapter—the methods and approach are the same, although the overall objectives are somewhat different. Business continuity planning and disaster recovery planning are discussed in detail in Chapter 5.

High-Impact Events The risk manager is likely to identify one or more high-impact events during the risk analysis. These events, which may be significant enough to threaten the very viability of the organization, require risk treatment that warrants executive management visibility and belongs in the categories of business continuity planning and disaster recovery planning. These topics are discussed in detail in Chapter 5.

Risk Treatment

When risks to assets have been identified through qualitative or quantitative risk analysis, the next step in risk management is to decide what to do about the identified risks. During risk analysis, one or more potential solutions may have been examined, along with their cost to implement and their impact on risk. In risk treatment, a decision about whether to proceed with any of the proposed solutions (or others) is needed.

Risk treatment pits available resources against the need to reduce risk. In an enterprise environment, not all risks can be mitigated or eliminated, because there are not enough resources to treat them all. Instead, a strategy for choosing the best combination of solutions that will reduce risk by the greatest possible margin is needed. For this reason, risk treatment is often more effective when all the risks and solutions are considered together, instead of considering each one separately. Then they can be grouped, compared, and prioritized.

When risk treatment is performed at the enterprise level, risk analysts and technology architects can devise ways to bring about the greatest possible reduction in risk. This can be achieved through the implementation of solutions that will reduce many risks for many assets at once. For example, a firewall can reduce risks from many threats on many assets; this will be more effective than individual solutions for each asset.

So far, I have been talking about risk mitigation as if it were the only option available when handling risk. But there are actually four primary ways to treat risk: mitigation, transfer, avoidance, and acceptance. And there is always some leftover risk, called *residual risk*. These approaches are discussed here.

Risk Mitigation

Risk mitigation, or risk reduction, involves the implementation of some solution that will reduce an identified risk. For instance, the risk of advanced malware being introduced onto a server can be mitigated with advanced malware prevention software or a network-based IPS. Either of these solutions would constitute mitigation of this risk on a given asset.

An organization usually decides to implement some form of risk mitigation only after performing some cost analysis to determine whether the reduction of risk is worth the expenditure of risk mitigation.

Back to the term *solution*, as mentioned here. Readers should not automatically think of new devices, systems, or features such as firewalls, IPSs, antivirus software, data loss prevention systems, or other hardware or software products. Instead, a solution may be as simple as an update to a written policy, a configuration change, or the modification of a firewall rule, or it may be as complex as network segmentation that could take many months to implement.

Risk Transfer

Risk transfer, or risk sharing, means that some or all the risk is being transferred to some external entity, such as an insurance company or business partner. When an organization purchases an insurance policy to protect an asset against damage or loss, the insurance company is assuming part of the risk in exchange for payment of insurance premiums.

The details of a cyber-insurance policy need to be carefully examined to ensure that any specific risk is transferrable to the policy. Cyber-insurance policies typically have exclusions that limit or deny payment of benefits in certain situations.

TIP Organizations considering cyber-insurance policies should carefully read the terms and conditions of such policies to ensure the selection of an appropriate policy. Some policies assume and require that the organization have specific measures in place. Further, policies have exclusions that must be well understood. Some organizations are denied benefits from malware attacks that insurance companies claim are acts of war, a common exclusion.

Risk Avoidance

In risk avoidance, the organization abandons the potential risk activity altogether, effectively taking the asset out of service so that the threat is no longer present. In another scenario, the organization may decide that the risk of pursuing a given business activity is too great so that specific activity is completely avoided.

 NOTE Organizations do not often back away completely from an activity because of identified risks. Generally, this avenue is taken only when the risk of loss is great and the perceived probability of occurrence is high.

Risk Acceptance

Risk acceptance occurs when management is willing to accept an identified risk as is, with no effort taken to reduce it. Risk acceptance also takes place (sometimes implicitly) for residual risk, after other forms of risk treatment have been applied.

Residual Risk

Residual risk is the risk that is leftover from the original risk after some of the risk has been removed through mitigation or transfer. For instance, if a particular threat had a probability of 10 percent before risk treatment and 1 percent after risk treatment, the residual risk is that 1 percent leftover. This is best illustrated by the following formula:

$$Original\ Risk - Mitigated\ Risk - Transferred\ Risk = Residual\ Risk$$

It is unusual for risk treatment to eliminate risk altogether; rather, various controls are implemented that remove some of the risk. Often, management implicitly accepts the leftover risk; however, it's a good idea to make that acceptance of residual risk more formal by documenting the acceptance in a risk management log or decision log.

Compliance Risk: The Risk Management Trump Card

Organizations that perform risk management are generally aware of the laws, regulations, and standards they are required to follow. For instance, U.S.-based banks, brokerages, and insurance companies are required to comply with the Gramm-Leach-Bliley Act (GLBA), and organizations that store, process, or transmit credit card numbers are required to comply with PCI-DSS (Payment Card Industry Data Security Standard). The European General Data Protection Regulation (GDPR) has an especially long reach, applying to organizations throughout the world that store and process personally identifiable information about European citizens.

GDPR, GLBA, HIPAA, PCI-DSS, and other regulations often state in specific terms what controls are required in an organization's IT systems. This brings to light the matter of *compliance risk*. Sometimes, the risk associated with a specific control (or lack of a control) may be rated as a low risk, either because the probability of a risk event is low or because the impact of the event is low. However, if a given law, regulation, or standard requires that the control be enacted anyway, the organization must consider the compliance risk. The risk of noncompliance may result in fines or other sanctions against the organization, which may (or may not) have consequences greater than the actual risk.

The result of this is that organizations often implement specific security controls because they are required by laws, regulations, or standards—not because their risk analysis would otherwise compel them to do so.

IT Management Practices

The primary services in the IT organization typically are development, operations, and support. These primary activities require the support of a second layer of activities that together support the delivery of primary IT services to the organization. The second layer of IT management practices consists of the following:

- Personnel management
- Sourcing
- Third-party service delivery management
- Change management
- Financial management
- Quality management
- Portfolio management
- Controls management
- Security management
- Performance and capacity management

Some of these activities the IT organization undertakes itself, while some are usually performed by other parts of the organization. For instance, most of the personnel management functions are typically carried out by a human resources department. This is another essential reason for the existence of an organization-wide IT steering committee that is represented by members of other departments such as human resources. This enables the entire spectrum of IT management to be centrally controlled even when other departments perform some IT management functions.

Personnel Management

Personnel management encompasses many activities related to the status of employment, training, and the acceptance and management of policy. These personnel management activities ensure that the individuals who are hired into the organization are suitably vetted, trained, and equipped to perform their functions. It is important that they are provided with the organization's key policies so that their behavior and decisions will reflect the organization's needs.

Hiring

The purpose of the employee hiring process is to ensure that the organization hires persons who are qualified to perform their stated job duties and that their personal, professional, and educational histories are appropriate. The hiring process includes several activities necessary to ensure that candidates being considered are suitable.

Background Verification   Various studies suggest that 30 to 80 percent of employment candidates exaggerate their education and experience on their résumé, and some candidates commit outright fraud by providing false information about their education or prior positions. Because of this, employers need to perform their own background investigation on an employment candidate to obtain an independent assessment of the candidate's true background.

Employers should examine the following parts of a candidate's background prior to hiring:

- **Employment background**   The employer should check at least two years back, although five to seven years is needed for mid- or senior-level personnel.

- **Education background**   The employer should confirm that the candidate has earned the degrees or diplomas listed on his or her résumé. There are many "diploma mills," enterprises that will print a fake college diploma for a fee.

- **Military service background**   If the candidate served in any branch of the military, this must be verified to confirm whether the candidate served at all, whether he or she received relevant training and work experience, and whether the candidate's discharge was honorable or otherwise.

- **Professional licenses and certifications**   If a position requires that the candidate possess licenses or certifications, these need to be confirmed, including whether the candidate is in good standing with the organizations that manage those licenses and certifications.

- **Criminal background**   The employer needs to investigate whether the candidate has a criminal record. In countries with a national criminal registry, such as the National Crime Information Center (NCIC) in the United States, this is simpler than in countries that have no nationwide criminal records database. Some industrialized countries do not permit criminal background checks (believe it or not).

- **Credit background**   Where permitted by law, the employer may want to examine a candidate's credit and financial history. There are two principal reasons for this type of check: first, a good credit history indicates the candidate is responsible, while a poor credit history may be an indication of irresponsibility or poor choices (although in many cases a candidate's credit background is not entirely his or her own doing); second, a candidate with excessive debt and a poor credit history may be considered a risk for embezzlement, fraud, or theft.

- **Terrorist association**   Some employers want to know whether a candidate has documented ties with terrorist organizations. In the United States, an employer can request verification of whether a candidate is on one of several lists of individuals and organizations with whom U.S. citizens are prohibited from doing business. Lists are maintained by the Office of Foreign Assets Control (OFAC), by a department of the U.S. Treasury, and by the U.S. Bureau of Industry and Security.

- **References**   The employer may want to contact two or more personal and professional references—people who know the candidate and will vouch for his or her background, work history, and character.

 TIP   In many jurisdictions, employment candidates are required to sign a consent form that will allow the employer (or a third-party agent acting on behalf of the employer) to perform the background check.

Employers also frequently research a candidate's background through word-of-mouth inquiries, Internet searches, and social media. Much useful information can be obtained that can help an employer corroborate information provided by a candidate.

Background checks are a prudent business practice to identify and reduce risk. In many industries, they are a common practice or even required by law. And in addition to performing a background check at the time of hire, many organizations perform them annually for employees in high-risk or high-value positions.

Employee Policy Manuals   Sometimes known as an *employee handbook*, an employee policy manual is a formal statement of the terms of employment, facts about the organization, benefits, compensation, conduct, and other policies.

Employee handbooks are often the cornerstone of corporate policy. A thorough employee handbook usually covers a wide swath of territory, including the following topics:

- **Welcome**   This welcomes a new employee into the organization, often in an upbeat letter that makes the new employee glad to have joined the organization. This may also include a brief history of the organization.

- **Policies**   These are the most important policies in the organization, which include security, privacy, code of conduct (ethics), and acceptable use of resources. In the United States and other countries, the handbook may also include antiharassment and other workplace behavior policies.

- **Compensation**   This describes when and how employees are compensated.

- **Benefits**   This describes company benefit programs.

- **Work hours**   This discusses work hours and basic expectations for when employees are expected to report to work and how many hours per week they are expected to work.

- **Dress code**   This provides a description and guidelines for required attire in the workplace.

- **Performance review**   This describes the performance review policy and program that is used periodically to evaluate each employee's performance.

- **Promotions**   This describes the criteria used by the organization to consider promotions for employees.

- **Time off**   This describes compensated and uncompensated time off, including holidays, vacation, illness, disability, bereavement, sabbaticals, military duty, and leaves of absence.

- **Security**   This discusses basic expectations on the topics of physical security and information security, as well as expectations for how employees are expected to handle confidential and sensitive information.

- **Regulation**   If the organization is subject to regulation, this may be mentioned in the employee handbook so that employees will be aware of this and conduct themselves accordingly.

- **Safety**   This discusses workplace safety, which may cover evacuation procedures, emergency procedures, permitted and prohibited items and substances (for example, weapons, alcoholic beverages, other substances and items), procedures for working with hazardous substances, and procedures for operating equipment and machinery.

- **Conduct**   This covers basic expectations for workplace conduct, both with fellow employees and with customers, vendors, business partners, and other third parties.

- **Discipline**   Organizations that have a disciplinary process usually describe its highlights in the employee handbook.

 NOTE   Employees are often required to sign a statement that affirms their understanding of and compliance with the employee handbook. Many organizations require that employees sign a new copy of the statement on an annual basis, even if the employee handbook has not changed. This helps to affirm for employees the importance of policies contained in the employee handbook.

Initial Access Provisioning   New employees may need access to office locations, computers, networks, and/or applications to perform their required duties. This will necessitate the provisioning of access to one or more buildings and to computer or network user accounts, as required to perform their work-related tasks.

An access-provisioning process should be used to determine which access privileges a new employee should be given. A template of job titles and access privileges should be set up in advance so that management can easily determine which access privileges any new employee will receive. Even with such a plan, each new employee's manager should formally request that these privileges be set up for new employees.

Job Descriptions   A job description is a formal document that describes the roles, responsibilities, and experience required. Each position in an organization, from chief executive officer to office clerk, should have a formal job description.

Job descriptions should also state that employees are required to support company policies, including but not limited to security and privacy, code of conduct, and acceptable use policies. By listing these in a job description, an employer is stating that all employees are expected to comply with these and other policies.

 NOTE   Employers usually are required to include several boilerplate items or statements (such as equal opportunity clauses) in job descriptions to conform to local labor and workplace safety laws.

Employee Development

Once hired into the organization, employees will require training in the organization's policies and practices so that their contributions will be effective and further the organization's goals. Regular evaluations will help employees to focus their long-term efforts on personal and organization goals and objectives.

Training   To be effective, employees need to receive periodic training. This includes the following:

- **Skills training**   Employees should learn how to use tools and equipment properly. In some cases, employees are required to receive training and prove competency before they are permitted to use some tools and equipment. Sometimes this is required by law.

- **Practices and techniques**   Employees need to understand how the organization uses its tools and equipment for its specific use.

- **Policies**   Organizations often impart information about their policies in the context of training. This helps the organization make sure that employees comprehend the material.

Performance Evaluation   Many organizations utilize a performance evaluation process to examine each employee's performance against a set of expectations and objectives. A performance evaluation program also helps to shape employees' behavior over the long term and helps them to reflect on how their efforts contribute toward the organization's overall objectives. A performance evaluation is frequently used to determine whether (and by how much) an employee's compensation should be increased.

Career Path   In many cultures, employees believe that they can be successful if they understand how they can advance within the organization. A career path program can help employees understand what skills are required for other positions in the organization and how they can strive toward positions that they desire in the future.

Mandatory Vacations

Some organizations, particularly those that deal with high-risk or high-value activities, require mandatory vacations of one week or longer for some or all employees. This practice can accomplish three objectives:

- **Cross-training** An absence of one week or longer will force management to cross-train other employees so that the organization is less reliant upon specific individuals.

- **Audit** A minimum absence gives the organization an opportunity to audit the absent employee's work to make sure that the employee is not involved in any undesired behavior.

- **Reduced risk** Knowing that they will be away from their day-to-day activities for at least one or two contiguous weeks each year, employees are less apt to partake in prohibited activities that could be discovered by colleagues or auditors during their absence.

Termination

When an employee leaves an organization, several actions need to take place:

- *Physical access to all work areas must be immediately revoked.* Depending upon the sensitivity of work activities in the organization, the employee may also need to be escorted out of the work area and have his or her personal belongings gathered by others and delivered to the departed employee's residence.

- *Each of the employee's computer and network access accounts needs to be locked.* The purpose of this is to protect the integrity of business information by permitting only authorized employees to access it. Locking computer accounts also prevents other employees from accessing information using the former employee's credentials.

CAUTION The issue of whether a former employee's account should be removed or merely locked depends upon the nature of the application or system. In some cases, the record of actions taken by employees (such as an audit log) depends upon the existence of the employee's ID on the system; if a former employee's ID is removed, then those audit records may not properly reference who is associated with them.

If the organization chooses to lock rather than remove computer or network accounts for terminated employees, those accounts must be locked or restricted in a way that positively prohibits any further access. For instance, merely changing the passwords of terminated accounts to "locked" would be considered a highly *unsafe* practice in the event that anyone discovers the password. If changing the account's password is the only way to lock it, then a long and highly random password must be used and then forgotten so that even the account administrator cannot use it.

 NOTE In some jurisdictions, employers may be required to permit former employees to be able to access their compensation and tax records.

Transfers and Reassignments

In many organizations, employees will move between positions over time. These position changes are not always upward through a career path, but can be lateral moves from one type of work to another.

Unless an organization is very careful about its access management processes and procedures, employees who transfer and are promoted tend to accumulate access privileges. This happens because a transferring employee's old privileges are not revoked, even though those privileges are no longer needed. Over a period of years, an employee who is transferred or promoted can accumulate many excessive privileges that can indicate significant risk should the individual choose to perform functions in the applications to which he or she is no longer officially authorized to use. This phenomenon is sometimes known as *accumulation of privileges* or *privilege creep*.

Privilege creep happens frequently in company accounting departments. An individual, for example, can move from role to role in the accounting department, all the while accumulating privileges that eventually result in the ability for that employee to defraud his or her employer by requesting, approving, and disbursing payments to himself/herself or to accomplices. Similarly, this can occur in an IT department, when an employee transfers from the operations department to the software development department (which is a common career path). Unless the IT department deliberately removes the transferring employee's prior privileges, it will end up with an employee who is a developer with access to production systems—a red flag to auditors who examine roles and responsibilities.

Contractor Management

For years, HR organizations refused to have anything to do with workers who were not employees of the organization. From the perspective of access management, this usually resulted in substandard practices for managing temporary workers, bringing increased risk to organizations. Thankfully, the tide is turning, and HR organizations are beginning to embrace the management of temporary workers. In part, this is because modern HR information systems are easily able to distinguish employees from all types of temporary workers. Still, because of their often-itinerant nature, temporary workers must be properly and accurately tracked. In the realm of access controls in sensitive environments, this represents an important risk reduction factor.

Sourcing

Sourcing refers to the choices that organizations make when selecting the personnel who will perform functions and where those functions will be performed. Sourcing options include the following:

- **Insourced** The organization hires employees to perform work. These workers can be full time, part time, or temporary.
- **Outsourced** The organization utilizes contractors or consultants to perform work.
- **Hybrid** The organization can utilize a combination of insourced and outsourced workers.

Next, the options include where personnel will perform tasks:

- **On-site** Personnel work at the organization's work site(s).
- **Off-site, local** Personnel are not located on-site, but are near the organization's premises, usually in or near the same community.
- **Off-site, remote** Personnel are in the same country, but not near the organization's premises.
- **Offshore** Personnel are located in a different country.
- **Nearshore** Outsourced personnel are located in a nearby country.
- **Onshore** Outsourced personnel are located in the same country.

 NOTE Organizations are often able to work out different combinations of insourced or outsourced personnel and where they perform their work. For instance, an organization can open its own office in a foreign country and hire employees to work there; this would be an example of offshore insourcing. Similarly, an organization can use contractors to perform work on-site; this is on-site outsourcing.

Insourcing

Insourcing, which is the practice of hiring employees for long-term work, is discussed earlier in this chapter in the "Personnel Management" section.

Outsourcing

Outsourcing is the practice of using contractors or consultants to perform work for the organization. An organization will decide to outsource a task, activity, or project for a wide variety of reasons:

- **Project duration** An organization may require personnel only for a specific project, such as the development of or migration to a new application. Often, an organization will opt to use contractors or consultants when it cannot justify hiring permanent workers.

- **Skills**   An organization may require personnel with certain hard-to-find skills but may not need them on a full-time basis. Persons with certain skills may command a higher salary than the organization is willing to pay, and the organization may not have sufficient work to keep such a worker interested in permanent employment.

- **Variable demand**   Organizations may experience seasonal increases and decreases of demand for certain workers. Organizations often cannot justify hiring full-time employees for peak demand capacity, when at other times those workers will not have enough work to keep them busy and productive. Instead, organizations will usually staff for average demand and augment staff with contractors for peak demand.

- **High turnover**   Some positions, such as IT helpdesk and call center positions, are inherently high-turnover positions that are costly to replace and train. Instead, an organization may opt to outsource some or all of the personnel in these positions.

- **Focus on core activities**   An organization may concentrate on hiring for positions related to its core purpose and to outsource functions that are considered "overhead." For instance, an organization that produces computer hardware products may elect to outsource its IT computer support department so that it can focus on its product development and support.

- **Financial**   A decision to outsource may be based primarily on financial issues. Usually an organization seeking to reduce costs of software development and other activities will outsource and off-shore these activities to service organizations located in other countries.

- **Complete time coverage**   An organization that needs to have personnel available around the clock may choose to outsource part of that function to personnel at work centers in other time zones.

An organization that chooses to hire employees only in its core service areas can outsource many of its noncore functions, including these:

- **IT helpdesk and support**   This is often a high-turnover function, as well as variable in demand, making it a good candidate for outsourcing.

- **Software development**   An organization that lacks employees with development and programming skills can elect to have contractors or consultants perform this work.

- **Software maintenance**   An organization may choose to keep its developers and analysts focused on new software development projects and to leave maintenance of existing software to contractors.

- **Customer support**   An organization may choose to outsource its telephone and online support to personnel or organizations in countries with lower labor costs.

TIP   Although outsourcing decisions appear, on the surface, to be economically motivated, some of the other reasons stated here may be even more important in some organizations. For example, the flexibility afforded by outsourcing may help to make an organization more agile, which may improve quality or increase efficiency over longer periods.

Outsourcing Benefits   Organizations that are considering outsourcing need to weigh the benefits and the costs carefully to determine whether the effort to outsource will result in measurable improvement in processing, service delivery, or finances. In the 1990s, when many organizations rushed to outsource development and support functions to operations in other countries, they did so with unrealistic short-term gains in mind and without adequately considering all of the real costs of outsourcing. This is not to say that outsourcing is bad, however; many organizations made outsourcing decisions without fully understanding their implications.

Outsourcing can bring many benefits:

- **Available skills and experience**   Organizations that may have trouble attracting persons with specialized skills often turn to outsourcing firms with highly skilled personnel who can ply their trade in a variety of client organizations.

- **Economies of scale**   Often, specialized outsourcing firms can achieve better economies of scale through discipline and mature practices that organizations are unable to achieve.

- **Objectivity**   Some functions are better done by outsiders. Personnel in an organization may have trouble being objective about some activities, such as process improvement and requirements definition. Also, auditors frequently must be employed by an outside firm to achieve sufficient objectivity and independence.

- **Reduced costs**   When outsourcing involves offshore personnel, an organization may be able to lower its operating costs and improve its competitive market position, usually through currency exchange rates and differences in the standards of living in headquarters versus offshore countries.

When an organization is making an outsourcing decision, it needs to consider these advantages together with risks that are discussed in the next section.

Risks Associated with Outsourcing   Although outsourcing can bring many tangible and intangible benefits to an organization, it is not without certain risks and disadvantages. Naturally, when an organization employs outsiders to perform some of its functions, it relinquishes some control. The risks of outsourcing include these:

- **Higher than expected costs**   Reduced costs were the main driver for offshore outsourcing in the 1990s. However, many organizations failed to anticipate all the operational realities. For instance, when outsourcing to overseas operations, IT personnel back in U.S.-based organizations may have to make many more expensive overseas trips than expected. Also, changes in international currency exchange rates can transform this year's bargain into next year's high cost.

- **Poor quality**   The outsourced work product may be lower in quality than the product created when the function was performed in-house.

- **Poor performance**   The outsourced service may not perform as expected. The capacity of networks or IT systems used by the outsourcing firm may cause processing delays or longer than acceptable response times.

- **Loss of control**   An organization that is accustomed to being in control of its workers may undergo a loss of control of its outsourced workers. Making small adjustments to processes and procedures may be more time-consuming or may increase costs.

- **Employee integrity and background**   It may be decidedly more difficult to determine the integrity of employees in an outsourced situation, particularly when the outsourcing is taking place offshore. Some countries, even where outsourcing is popular, lack the support of nationwide criminal background checks and other means for making a solid determination on an employee's background.

- **Loss of competitive advantage**   If the services performed by the outsourcing firm are not flexible enough to meet the organization's needs, this can result in the organization losing some of its competitive advantage. For example, suppose an organization outsources its corporate messaging (e-mail and other messaging) to a service provider. Later, the organization wants to enhance its customer communication by integrating its service application with e-mail. The e-mail service provider may be unable or unwilling to provide the necessary integration, which will result in the organization losing a competitive advantage.

- **Errors and omissions**   The organization performing outsourcing services may make serious errors or may fail to perform essential tasks. For instance, an outsourcing service may suffer a data security breach that may result in the loss or disclosure of sensitive information. This can be a disastrous event when it occurs within an organization's four walls, but when it happens in an outsourced part of the business, the organization may find that the lack of control will make it difficult to take the proper steps to contain and remediate the incident. If an outsourcing firm has undergone a security breach or similar incident, it may put its own interests first and only secondarily watch out for the interests of its customers.

- **Vendor failure**   The failure of the organization to provide outsourcing services may result in increased costs and delays in service or product delivery.

- **Differing mission and goals**   An organization's employees are going to be loyal to its mission and objectives. However, the employees in an outsourced organization usually have little or no interest in the hiring organization's interests; instead, they will be loyal to the outsourcing provider's values, which may at times be in direct conflict. For example, an outsourcing organization may place emphasis on maximizing billable hours, while the hiring organization emphasizes efficiency. These two objectives conflict with each other.

- **Difficult recourse** If an organization is dissatisfied with the performance or quality of its outsourced operation, contract provisions may not sufficiently facilitate any remedy. If the outsourced operation is in a foreign country, applying remediation in the court system may also be futile.

- **Lowered employee morale** If an organization chooses to outsource work and lays off some full-time workers, employees who remain may be upset because some of their colleagues have lost their jobs as a result of the outsourcing. Further, remaining employees may fear that their own jobs may soon be outsourced or eliminated. They may also believe that their organization is more interested in saving money than in taking care of its employees. Personnel who have lost their jobs may vent their anger at the organization through a variety of harmful actions that can threaten assets or other workers.

- **Audit and compliance** An organization that outsources a part of its operation that is in-scope for applicable laws and regulations may find it more challenging to perform audits and achieve compliance. Audit costs may rise, as auditors need to visit the outsourced work centers. Requiring the outsourced organization to make changes to achieve compliance may be difficult or expensive.

- **Applicable laws** Laws, regulations, and standards in headquarters and offshore countries may impose requirements on the protection of information that can complicate business operations or enterprise architectures.

- **Cross-border data transfer** Governments around the world are paying attention to the flow of data, particularly the sensitive data of its citizens. Many countries have passed laws that attempt to exert control over data about their citizens when it is transferred out of their jurisdictions.

- **Time zone differences** Communications will suffer when an organization outsources some of its operations to offshore organizations that are several time zones distant. It will be more difficult to schedule telephone conferences if there is very little overlap between work hours in each time zone. It will take more time to communicate important issues and to make changes.

- **Language and cultural differences** When outsourcing crosses language and cultural barriers, it can result in less than optimal communication and results. The outsourcing customer will express its needs through its own language and culture, and the outsourcing provider will hear those needs through its own language and culture. Both sides may be thinking or saying, "They don't understand what we want" and "We don't understand what they want." This can result in unexpected differences in work produced by the outsourcing firm. Delays in project completion or delivery of goods and services can occur as a result.

- **Political conditions** When offshoring labor and when using foreign workers with work visas, changes in political conditions can result in restrictions of the use of foreign workers, wherever they are working. For example, restrictions on certain types of work visas for foreign workers have forced some organizations to change their strategies for attracting offshore talent.

CAUTION Some of the risks associated with outsourcing are intangible or may lie outside the bounds of legal remedies. For instance, language and time zone differences can introduce delays in communication, adding friction to the business relationship in a way that may not be easily measurable.

Mitigating Outsourcing Risk   The only means of exchange between an outsourcing provider and its customer organization are money and reputation. In other words, the only leverage that an organization has against its outsourcing provider is the withholding of payment and communicating the quality (or lack thereof) of the provider's services to other organizations. This is especially true if the outsourcing crosses national boundaries. Therefore, an organization that is considering outsourcing must carefully consider how it will enforce contract terms so that it receives the goods and services that it is expecting.

Many of the risks of outsourcing can be remedied through contract provisions. Some of the remedies are listed here:

- **Service level agreement (SLA)**   The contract should provide details on every avenue of work performance and communication, including escalations and problem management.

- **Quality**   Depending upon the product or service, this may translate into an error or defect rate, a customer satisfaction rate, or system performance.

- **Security policy and controls**   Whether the outsourcing firm is safeguarding the organization's intellectual property, keeping business secrets, or protecting information about its employees or customers, the contract should spell out the details of the security controls that it expects the outsourcing firm to maintain. The organization should also require periodic third-party audits and the results of those audits. The contract should contain a "right to audit" clause that allows the outsourcing organization to examine the work premises, records, and work papers on demand.

- **Business continuity**   The contract should require the outsourcing firm to have reasonable measures and safeguards in place to ensure resilience of operations and the ability to continue operations with minimum disruption in the event of a disaster.

- **Employee integrity**   The contract should define how the outsourcing firm will vet its employees' backgrounds so that it is not inadvertently hiring individuals with a criminal history and so employees' claimed education and work experience are proven genuine.

- **Ownership of intellectual property**   If the outsourcing firm is producing software or other designs, the contract must define ownership of those work products and whether the outsourcing firm may reuse any of those work products for other engagements.

- **Roles and responsibilities**   The contract should specify in detail the roles and responsibilities of each party so that each will know what is expected of them.

- **Schedule**   The contract must specify when and how many items of work products should be produced.

- **Regulation**   The contract should require both parties to conform to all applicable laws and regulations, including but not limited to intellectual property, data protection, and workplace safety.

- **Warranty**   The contract should specify terms of warranty for the workmanship and quality of all work products so that there can be no ambiguity regarding the quality of goods or services performed.

- **Dispute and resolution**   The contract should contain provisions that define the process for handling and resolving disputes.

- **Payment**   The contract should specify how and when the outsourcing provider will be paid. Compensation should be tied not only to the quantity but also to the quality of work performed. The contract should include incentive provisions for additional payment when specific schedule, quantity, or quality targets are exceeded. The contract should also contain financial penalties that are enacted when SLA, quality, security, audit, or schedule targets are missed.

The terms of an outsourcing contract should adequately reward the outsourcing firm for a job well done, which should include the prospect of earning additional contracts as well as referrals that will help it to earn outsourcing contracts from other customers.

Outsourcing Governance   You cannot outsource accountability. Outsourcing is a convenient way to transfer some operations to an external organization, thereby allowing the outsourcing organization to be more agile and to improve focus on core competencies. Although senior managers can transfer these activities to external organizations and even specify rewards for good performance and penalties for substandard performance, those senior managers are still ultimately accountable for the delivery of these services, whether they are outsourced or performed by internal staff.

In the context of outsourcing, the role of governance must be expanded to include the aggregation of activities that control the work performed by external organizations. Governance activities may include the following:

- **Contracts**   The overall business relationship between the organization and its service providers should be defined in detailed legal agreements. The terms of legal agreements should define the work to be done (in general), the expectations of all parties, service levels, quality, the terms of compensation, and remedies in case expectations fail to be met. Appropriate levels of management must approve the content in contracts.

- **Work orders**   Sometimes called *statements of work* (SOWs), work orders describe in greater detail the work that is to be performed. While contracts are seldom changed, work orders operate in short-term intervals and are specific to currently delivered goods or services. Like contracts themselves, work orders should include precise statements regarding work output, timeliness, quality, and remedies.

- **SLAs**   These documents specify service levels in terms of the quantity of work, quality, timeliness, and remedies for shortfalls in quality or quantity.

- **Change management**   A formal method is needed so that changes in delivery specifications can be formally controlled.

- **Security**   If the service provider has access to the organization's records or other intellectual property, the organization will require that specific security controls be in place. In higher risk situations, the organization will want to validate periodically that the service provider's security controls are effective.

- **Quality**   Minimum standards for quality should be expressed in detail so that both service provider and customer have a common understanding of the expected quality of work to be performed.

- **Metrics**   Often, the outsourcing organization will want to actively measure various aspects of the outsourced activity to gain short-term visibility into work output as well as the ability to understand long-term trends.

- **Audits**   The outsourcing organization may require that audits of the outsourced work be performed. These audits may be performed by a competent third party (such as a public accounting firm performing an SSAE 16, ISAE 3402, SOC 1, or SOC 2 audit), by an independent security consulting firm, or by the customer. Often, an outsourcing organization will negotiate a "right to audit" clause in the contract but will exercise this only if the organization encounters irregularities or issues related to the work performed.

Depending on the nature of specific outsourcing arrangements, the preceding activities may be combined or performed separately.

Benchmarking   *Benchmarking* measures a process to compare its performance and quality against the same process in other organizations. Its purpose is to discover opportunities for improvement that may result in lower costs, fewer resources, and higher quality.

In the context of outsourcing, benchmarking can be used to measure the performance of an outsourced process against the same process performed by other outsourcing firms, as well as to compare it with the same process performed internally by other organizations. The objective is the same: to learn whether a particular outsourcing solution is performing effectively and efficiently. Benchmarking is discussed in further detail in Chapter 4.

Third-Party Service Delivery Management

Service delivery management is the institution of controls and metrics to ensure that services are performed properly and with a minimum of incidents and defects. When activities are transferred to a service provider, service delivery management has some added dimensions and considerations.

When service delivery management is used to manage an external service provider, the service provider is usually required to maintain detailed measurements of its work output. The organization utilizing an external service provider also needs to maintain detailed records of work received, and it should perform its own defect management controls to ensure that the work performed by the service provider meets quality standards. Problems and incidents encountered by the organization should be documented and transmitted to the service provider to improve quality.

These activities should be included in the SLA or in the contract to ensure that the customer will be able to impose financial penalties or other types of leveraging onto the service provider to improve quality while maintaining minimum work output.

Service delivery standards related to IT service management are defined in the international standard ISO/IEC 20000:2011. Relevant controls from this standard can be used to impose a standard method for managing service delivery by the service provider.

Third-party risk management (TPRM) is a similar activity with regard to the management of service providers. TPRM is discussed in detail in Chapter 6.

SaaS, IaaS, and PaaS Considerations

Organizations such as SaaS (Software-as-a-Service), IaaS (Infrastructure-as-a-Service), and PaaS (Platform-as-a-Service) provide cloud-based application or computing resources to clients that cannot justify building their own.

SaaS is an arrangement in which an organization obtains a software application for use by its employees, where the software application is hosted by the software provider as opposed to the customer organization. IaaS is an arrangement in which an organization rents IT infrastructure from a service provider. PaaS is a service that enables organizations to deploy applications without having to deal with underlying infrastructure such as servers and database management systems.

The primary advantages of using SaaS, IaaS, and PaaS as opposed to self-hosting are as follows:

- **Capital savings** The SaaS/IaaS/PaaS provider makes its software, infrastructure, or platform resources available to its customers on its own servers, thereby eliminating a customers' need to purchase dedicated hardware and software.

- **Labor savings** The SaaS/IaaS/PaaS provider performs many administration functions, including typical administrative tasks such as applying software or operating system patches, managing performance and capacity, upgrading software, and troubleshooting.

CAUTION An organization that is considering a SaaS, an IaaS, or a PaaS provider for one of its environments will need to ensure that the provider has adequate controls in place to protect the organization's data. Specifically, an organization needs to understand the security responsibility model thoroughly to determine which controls are performed by the service provider and which need to be implemented by the organization. Further, the provider should have controls in place that will prevent one customer from being able to view the data associated with a different customer.

An organization can consider the SaaS/IaaS/PaaS provider to be similar to other service providers. Generally, methods used to determine the integrity and quality of the SaaS/IaaS/PaaS provider would be the same as those used with other service providers.

Business Process as a Service

As the cybersecurity skills shortage widens, service organizations are developing numerous business process-as-a-service offerings to help businesses continue critical security processes. Examples of new service offerings include Identity-as-a-Service, Vulnerability Management-as-a-Service, and Patch Management-as-a-Service. One of the first security-related "as-a-service" offerings was security event monitoring, which is still popular.

Change Management

Change management is a business process that is used to control changes made to an IT environment. A formal change management process consists of several steps that are carried out for each change:

1. Request
2. Review
3. Approve
4. Perform
5. Verify
6. Back out (when verification of a successful change fails)

Each step in change management includes recordkeeping. Change management is covered in detail in Chapter 4.

Financial Management

Sound financial management is critical in any organization. Because IT is a cost-intensive activity, it is imperative that the organization be well managed, with short-term and long-term budget planning, and that it track actual spending.

One area where senior management needs to make strategic financial decisions in IT is the manner in which it acquires software applications. At the steering committee level, IT organizations carefully need to weigh "make versus buy" with its primary applications. This typically falls into three alternatives:

- *Develop the application.* The organization develops the application using in-house or contracted software developers, designers, and analysts.
- *Purchase the application.* The organization licenses the application from a software vendor and installs it on servers that it leases or purchases.

- *Rent the application.* This generally refers to the cloud computing or SaaS model, whereby the cloud/application service provider hosts the application on its own premises (or on an Internet data center) and the organization using the software pays either a fixed fee or an on-demand fee. The purchasing organization will have no capital cost for servers and little or no development cost (except, possibly, for interfaces to other applications).

The choice that an organization makes is not just about the finances, but is also concerned with the degree of control that the organization requires.

IT financial management is about not only applications, but also the other services that an IT organization provides. Other functions such as service desk, PC build and support, e-mail, and network services can likewise be insourced or outsourced, each with financial and other implications.

 NOTE   Many larger organizations employ a "chargeback" feature for the delivery of IT services. In this method, an IT organization charges (usually through budget transfers but occasionally through real funds) for the services that it provides. The advantage to chargeback is that the customers of the IT organization are required to budget for IT services and are less likely to make frivolous requests of IT, since every activity has a cost associated with it. Chargeback may also force an IT organization to be more competitive, as chargeback may invite IT's customers to acquire services from outside organizations and not from the internal IT organization. Chargeback can thus be viewed as outsourcing to the internal IT organization.

Quality Management

Quality management refers to the methods by which business processes are controlled, monitored, and managed to bring about continuous improvement. The scope of a quality management system in an IT organization may cover any or all of the following activities:

- Software development
- Software acquisition
- Service desk
- IT operations
- Security

The components that are required to build and operate a quality management system are as follows:

- **Documented processes**   Each process that is part of a quality management system must be fully documented. This means that all of the tasks, notifications, records, and data flows must be fully described in formal process documents that are themselves controlled.

- **Key measurements**   Each process under quality management must have some key measurement points so that management will be able to understand the frequency and effort expended for the process. Measurement goes beyond simply tallying and must include methods for recognizing, classifying, and measuring incidents, events, problems, and defects.

- **Management review of key measurements**   Key measurements need to be regularly analyzed and included in status reports that provide meaningful information to various levels of management. This enables management to understand how key processes are performing and whether they are meeting management's expectations.

- **Audits**   Processes in a quality management system should be periodically measured by internal or external auditors to ensure that they are being operated properly. These auditors need to be sufficiently independent of the processes and of management itself so that they can objectively evaluate processes.

- **Process changes**   When key measurements suggest that changes to a process are needed, a business or process analyst will make changes to the design of a process. Examples of process changes include the addition of data fields in a change request process, the addition of security requirements to the software development process, or a new method for communicating passwords to the users of newly created user accounts.

 TIP   An organization should document and measure its quality management processes, just as it does with all of the processes under its observation and control. This will help to confirm whether the quality management system itself is effective.

ISO/IEC 9000

Established in the 1980s, ISO/IEC 9000 remains the world's standard for quality management systems. The ISO/IEC 9001, 9002, 9003, and 9004 standards have been superseded by the single ISO/IEC 9001:2015 Quality Management System standard.

Organizations that implement the ISO/IEC 9001:2015 standard can voluntarily undergo regular external audits by an accredited firm to earn an ISO/IEC 9001:2015 certification. More than one million ISO/IEC 9001 certificates have been issued to organizations around the world since 1978.

ISO/IEC 9000 began as a manufacturing product quality standard. While many manufacturing firms are certified to ISO/IEC 9000, the standard is growing in popularity among service providers and software development organizations.

ISO/IEC 20000

Many IT organizations have adopted the IT Infrastructure Library (ITIL) of IT service management processes as a standard framework for IT processes. Organizations that desire a certification can be evaluated by an accredited external audit firm to the ISO/IEC 20000 IT Service Management standard. ISO/IEC 20000 supersedes the earlier BS 15000 standard.

The ITIL framework consists of 26 processes in five volumes:

- Service Strategy
- Service Design
- Service Transition
- Service Operation
- Continual Service Improvement

ITIL's processes are interrelated and together constitute an effective framework for IT's primary function: delivering valuable services to enable key organization processes.

Portfolio Management

Portfolio management refers to the systematic management of IT projects, investments, and activities. The purpose of portfolio management is to measure the value derived from IT projects, investments, and activities and to make adjustments periodically to maximize that value for the organization.

The principles of IT portfolio management are similar to those of financial investment portfolio management. All of the activities in IT are treated like investments, with a careful look at the value they bring to the organization.

Mature organizations that practice IT portfolio management typically develop three portfolios:

- Project portfolio
- Infrastructure portfolio
- Application portfolio

The items in these portfolios are measured, examined, and scrutinized for their continuing contribution to, and alignment with, the organization's mission and main objectives. Management can make periodic adjustments to the level of resources associated with IT projects and activities to maximize value to the organization.

ISACA's Val IT (IT Value Delivery) framework is one such IT portfolio management framework and is now fully a part of COBIT. More information can be found at www .isaca.org/valit.

Controls Management

IT organizations employ controls to ensure specific outcomes within business processes, IT systems, and personnel. Better organizations adopt one of several standard frameworks of controls and then periodically assess risk and control performance, resulting in changes to controls as well as the addition or removal of controls.

Controls are generally enacted as a result of one or more of the following:

- **Policies**   Controls can be established to ensure compliance to policy and to measure a policy's effectiveness.

- **Regulations** Organizations often establish controls to ensure compliance to regulations.

- **Requirements** Legal or operational requirements, such as terms and conditions in contracts with customers or suppliers, compel an organization to enact controls to ensure compliance.

- **Risks** An internal or external risk assessment may compel an organization to enact controls to reduce risks to acceptable levels.

- **Incidents** A compelling incident or event may prompt an organization to enact controls to prevent similar incidents from recurring.

It is not enough for organizations to develop and implement controls. Organizations need to examine controls periodically to determine whether they are operating properly and ensuring their intended outcomes. The entire discipline of internal and external audit is brought to bear on the subject of control examination and effectiveness. The process and practice of audits is explored in detail in Chapter 3 and Appendix A.

Well-known control frameworks include the following:

- **COBIT** Developed by ISACA, COBIT is a general-purpose IT controls framework.

- **NIST 800-53** Developed by the U.S. Department of Commerce, NIST 800-53 is a comprehensive set of security controls that are required for U.S. government information systems. This framework has been adopted by many nongovernment organizations as well.

- **NIST Framework for Improving Critical Infrastructure Cybersecurity (CSF)** This framework organizes controls into five principle activities: Identify, Protect, Detect, Respond, and Recover. CSF also serves as a guide for organizations to determine their security maturity.

- **ISO/IEC 20000** This is the international standard with its roots in the ITIL, the framework of IT service management.

- **ISO/IEC 27002** This is the international standard framework of IT security controls, and it is widely adopted worldwide.

- **PCI-DSS (Payment Card Industry Data Security Standard)** This is the IT security controls framework required for systems and networks that store, process, or transmit credit card data.

- **HIPAA (Health Insurance Portability and Accountability Act) Security Rule** This is the framework of controls required for organizations that store, process, or transmit electronic patient health information (ePHI).

- **Center for Internet Security (CIS) Controls** Originally developed by the SANS Institute, CIS Controls is a proven framework of controls that is ideal for organizations that are not required to adopt NIST, ISO, HIPAA, or PCI.

As an integral part of information security and IT audit, controls are discussed throughout this book.

Security Management

Security management refers to several key activities that work together to identify risks and risk treatment for the organization's assets. In most organizations these activities include the following:

- **Security governance**   This is the practice of setting organization security policy and then taking steps to ensure that the policy is followed. Security governance also is involved with the management and continuous improvement of other key security activities discussed in this section.

- **Risk assessment**   This is the practice of identifying key assets in use by the organization and identifying vulnerabilities in, and threats against, each asset. This is followed by the development of risk treatment strategies that attempt to mitigate, transfer, avoid, or accept identified risks.

- **Incident management**   This practice is concerned with the planned response to security incidents when they occur in the organization. An *incident* is defined as a violation of security policy; such an incident may be minor (such as a user choosing an easily guessed password) or major (such as a hacking attack and theft of sensitive information). Some of the aspects of incident management include computer forensics (the preservation of evidence that could be used in later legal action) and the involvement of regulatory authorities and law enforcement.

- **Vulnerability management**   This is the practice of proactively identifying vulnerabilities in IT systems, as well as in business processes, that could be exploited to the detriment of the organization. Activities that take place in vulnerability management include security scanning, vulnerability assessment, code review, patch management, and reviewing threat intelligence and risk advisories issued by software vendors and security organizations.

- **Identity and access management**   These practices are used to control which persons and groups may have access to which organization applications, assets, systems, workplaces, and functions. Identity management is the activity of managing the identity and access history of each employee, contractor, temporary worker, supplier worker, and, optionally, customer. These records are then used as the basis for controlling which workplaces, applications, IT systems, and business functions each person is permitted to use.

- **Compliance management**   Security management should be responsible for knowing which laws, regulations, standards, requirements, and legal contracts the organization is required to comply with. Verification of compliance may involve internal or external audits and other activities to confirm that the organization is in compliance with all of these legal and other requirements.

- **Third-party risk management**   This is the practice of identifying and managing risks associated with third-party organizations that store, process, or transmit sensitive information on behalf of the organization. Activities include up-front due diligence and periodic assessment of critical control effectiveness and overall business risk.

- **Business continuity and disaster recovery planning**   These practices enable the organization to develop response plans in the event that a disaster should occur that would otherwise threaten the ongoing viability of the organization. Business continuity and disaster recovery planning is covered in detail later in this chapter.

Control frameworks for security management include the following:

- **ISO/IEC 27001 requirements**   The first half of the ISO/IEC 27001 standard contains a set of requirements that describe a scalable and flexible Information Security Management System (ISMS) that is based on a life cycle of risk assessment, controls examination, and controls development, with an overarching theme of executive oversight and control.

Performance and Capacity Management

Performance optimization is concerned with the continual improvement of IT processes and systems. This set of activities is concerned not only with financial efficiency, but also with the time and resources required to perform common IT functions. The primary objective of IT performance optimization is to ensure that the organization is getting the maximum benefit from IT services for the lowest possible expenditure of resources.

An organization that measures process performance is more apt to recognize opportunities for making improvements to business processes. Organizations that reach a level of process maturity that includes measurement and feedback will be able to adopt a culture of continuous improvement. Then management can track improvement opportunities and assign resources accordingly.

Performance optimization is considered a rather mature approach to the management of IT processes and systems. It requires mature processes with key controls and measurement points, and it is one of the natural results of effective quality management. An organization that is not already monitoring and managing its processes is probably not ready to undertake performance optimization. See the earlier section, "Quality Management," for more information on this perspective.

Performance optimization is a complicated undertaking, because IT systems and processes usually change frequently over time; it can be difficult to attribute specific changes in systems or processes to changes in performance metrics.

Maturity models such as Capability Maturity Model Integration (CMMI) can be used to determine the level of an organization's processes. CMMI focuses on whether an organization's processes have a level of maturity associated with measurement and continuous improvement.

The COBIT framework also contains facilities to identify and measure key performance indicators (KPIs), with the aim of enabling continuous improvement to processes and technology. The COBIT framework contains 37 key IT processes, along with the means for any individual organization to determine how much (and what kind of) control is appropriate for the organization, based on its business objectives and how IT supports them.

A typical organization will not have the same level of maturity across all of its departments and processes. Instead, some processes and departments will be more mature than others, often by a wide variance.

Benchmarking

An organization may decide to benchmark its key processes. *Benchmarking* is a process of performing a detailed comparison of a business process (or system, or almost any other aspect of an organization) with the same process in other organizations. This will help an organization better understand how similar organizations are solving similar business problems, which could lead the organization to enact process improvements on its own.

In the past, it was common for organizations to benchmark the overall cost of information technology or information security. Today, however, IT and security costs are more ambiguous, particularly considering the trend of outsourcing business and IT services to third parties. Hence, it has become more useful to benchmark process maturity or risk appetite as a way of comparing an organization to its peers.

Organization Structure and Responsibilities

Organizations require structure to distribute responsibility to groups of people with specific skills and knowledge. The structure of an organization is depicted in an organization chart (org chart). Figure 2-5 shows a typical IT organization chart.

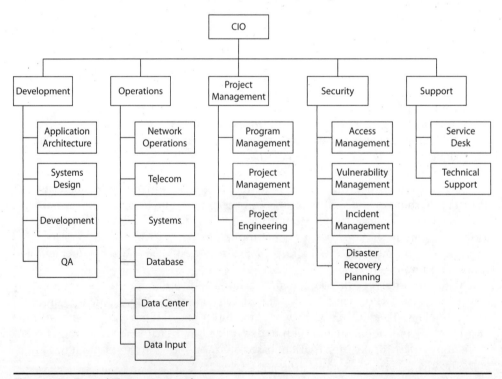

Figure 2-5 Typical IT organization chart

Organizing and maintaining an organization structure requires that many factors be considered. In most organizations, the org chart is a living structure that changes from time to time, based upon several conditions, including the following:

- **Short- and long-term objectives**   Organizations sometimes move departments from one executive to another so that departments that were once far from each other (in terms of the org chart structure) will be near each other. This provides new opportunities for developing synergies and partnerships that did not exist before the reorganization. These organizational changes are usually performed to help an organization meet new objectives that were less important before and that require new partnerships and teamwork.

- **Market conditions**   Changes in market positions can cause an organization to realign its internal structure to strengthen itself. For example, if a competitor lowers its prices based on a new sourcing strategy, an organization may need to respond by changing its organizational structure to put experienced executives in charge of specific activities.

- **Regulations**   New laws, regulations, or standards may induce an organization to change its organizational structure. For instance, an organization that becomes highly regulated may elect to move its security and compliance group away from IT and place it under the legal department, since compliance has much more to do with legal compliance than industry standards.

- **Attrition and available talent**   When someone leaves the organization or moves to another position within the organization, particularly in positions of leadership, a space opens in the org chart that often cannot be filled right away. Instead, senior management will temporarily change the structure of the organization by moving the leaderless department under the control of someone else. Often, the decisions of how to change the organization will depend upon the talent and experience of existing leaders, in addition to each leader's workload and other factors. For example, if the director of IT program management leaves the organization, the existing department could temporarily be placed under the IT operations department, in this case because the director of IT operations used to run IT program management. Senior management can see how that arrangement works out and later decide whether to replace the director of IT program management position or do something else.

TIP   Many organizations use formal succession planning as a way of preparing for unexpected changes in the organization, especially terminations and resignations. A succession plan helps the organization temporarily fill an absent position until a long-term replacement can be found.

This structure serves as a top-down and bottom-up conduit of communication. Figure 2-6 depicts the communication and control that an organization provides.

Figure 2-6
Communication
and control flow
upward and
downward in an
organization.

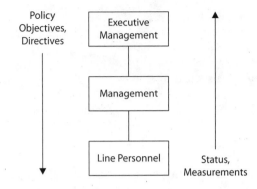

Roles and Responsibilities

The topic of roles and responsibilities is multidimensional: it encompasses positions and relationships on the organization chart, it defines specific job titles and duties, and it denotes generic expectations and responsibilities regarding the use and protection of assets.

Individual Roles and Responsibilities

Several roles and responsibilities fall upon all individuals throughout the organization:

- **Board of directors** The organization's governing body is legally responsible for overseeing the organization's activities, as well as the selection, support, and review of the chief executive. In private industry, directors are composed of the organization's senior executives as well as executives from other firms, including firms with a significant investment in the organization. In government, directors are often elected. Increasingly, directors are held to a higher standard of personal responsibility regarding the management and outcomes of the organizations they lead.

- **Executive management** The most senior managers and executives in an organization are responsible for developing the organization's mission, objectives, and goals, as well as policy. Executives are responsible for enacting security policy, which defines (among other things) the protection of assets.

- **Owner** An owner is an individual (usually but not necessarily a manager) who is the designated owner-steward of an asset. Depending upon the organization's security policy, an owner may be responsible for the maintenance and integrity of the asset, as well as for deciding who is permitted to access the asset. If the asset is information, the owner may be responsible for determining who can access and make changes to the information.

- **Manager** Managers are, in the general sense, responsible for understanding the organization's policies and procedures and making them available to their staff members. They should also, to some extent, be responsible for their staff members' behavior.

- **User**   Users are individuals (at any level of the organization) who use assets in the performance of their job duties. Each user is responsible for how he or she uses the asset, and each user does not permit others to access the asset in the user's name. Users are responsible for performing their duties lawfully and for conforming to organization policies.

These generic roles and responsibilities should apply across the org chart to include every person in the organization. Persons in these roles may be full-time or part-time employees, or they may be temporary workers such as contractors and consultants.

   TIP   The roles and responsibilities of executives, owners, managers, and users should be formally defined in an organization's security policy.

Job Titles and Job Descriptions

A *job title* is a label that is assigned to a *job description*. A job title denotes a position in the organization that has a given set of responsibilities and that requires a certain level and focus of education and prior experience. A job description is a list of those responsibilities and required education and experience.

   EXAM TIP   The CISA exam may present questions that address proper procedures for the audit of a specified job title. When considering your response, think about the job role assigned to the specific title rather than focusing on the title itself. Questions that address job titles are intended to examine your understanding of their related roles—an example being the Network Management role associated with the Network Engineer title.

An organization with a program of career advancement may have a set of career paths or career ladders that model how employees may advance. For each job title, a career path will show the possible avenues of advancement to other job titles and the experience required to reach those job titles.

Job titles in IT have matured and are quite consistent across organizations. This consistency helps organizations in several ways:

- **Recruiting**   When the organization needs to find someone to fill an open position, the use of standard job titles will help prospective candidates more easily find positions that match their criteria.
- **Compensation baselining**   Because of the chronic shortage of talented IT workers, organizations are forced to be more competitive when trying to attract new workers. To remain competitive, many organizations periodically undertake a regional compensation analysis to understand the levels of compensation paid to IT workers in other organizations. The use of standard job titles makes the task of comparing compensation far easier.

- **Career advancement**   When an organization uses job titles that are consistent in the industry, IT workers have a better understanding of the functions of positions within their own organizations and can more easily plan how they can advance.

The remainder of this section includes many IT job titles with a short description (not a full job description by any measure) of the function of that position.

Virtually all organizations also include titles that denote the level of experience, leadership, or span of control in an organization. These titles may include executive vice president, senior vice president, vice president, executive director, senior director, director, general manager, senior manager, manager, and supervisor. Larger organizations will use more of these and possibly additional titles such as regional manager, district manager, group manager, or area manager.

Executive Management   Executive managers are the chief leaders and policymakers in an organization. They set objectives and work directly with the organization's most senior management to help make decisions affecting the future strategy of the organization:

- **CIO (chief information officer)**   This is the title of the topmost leader in a larger IT organization.
- **CTO (chief technical officer)**   This position is usually responsible for an organization's overall technology strategy. Depending upon the purpose of the organization, this position may be separate from IT.
- **CRO (chief risk officer)**   This position is responsible for all aspects of risk, including information risk, business risk, compliance risk, and market risk. This role is separate from IT.
- **CSO (chief security officer)**   This position is responsible for all aspects of security, including information security, physical security, and possibly executive protection (protecting the safety of senior executives). This role is separate from IT.
- **CISO (chief information security officer)**   This position is responsible for all aspects of information-related security. This usually includes incident management, disaster recovery, vulnerability management, and compliance. This role is usually separate from IT.
- **CIRO (chief information risk officer)**   This position is responsible for all aspects of information-related risk management. The CIRO position symbolizes the risk management emphasis of information security.
- **CPO (chief privacy officer)**   This position is responsible for the protection and use of personal information. This position is present in organizations that collect and store sensitive information for large numbers of persons. This is sometimes known as a data privacy officer (DPO).
- **CCO (chief compliance officer)**   This position has broad responsibility for compliance, including information protection and privacy. Organizations under a heavy regulatory burden employ a CCO who is responsible for compliance across a broad spectrum of regulations and requirements.

Software Development   Positions in software development are involved in the design, development, and testing of software applications:

- **Systems architect**   This position is usually responsible for the overall information systems architecture in the organization. This may or may not include overall data architecture as well as interfaces to external organizations.

- **Systems analyst**   A systems analyst is involved with the design of applications, including changes in an application's original design. This position may develop technical requirements, program design, and software test plans. In cases where organizations license applications developed by other companies, systems analysts design interfaces to other applications.

- **Software engineer/developer**   This position develops application software. Depending upon the level of experience, persons in this position may also design programs or applications. In organizations that utilize purchased application software, developers often create custom interfaces, application customizations, and custom reports.

- **Software tester**   This position tests changes in programs made by software engineers/developers.

Data Management   Positions in data management are responsible for developing and implementing database designs and for maintaining databases:

- **Data manager**   This position is responsible for data architecture and data management in larger organizations.

- **Data scientist**   This position is responsible for employing scientific methods to gain knowledge from data.

- **Big data architect**   This position develops data models and data analytics for large, complex data sets.

- **Database architect**   This position develops logical and physical designs of data models for applications. With sufficient experience, this person may also design an organization's overall data architecture.

- **Database administrator (DBA)**   This position builds and maintains databases designed by the database architect and those databases that are included as a part of purchased applications. The DBA monitors databases, tunes them for performance and efficiency, and troubleshoots problems.

- **Database analyst**   This position performs tasks that are junior to the database administrator, carrying out routine data maintenance and monitoring tasks.

 EXAM TIP   The roles of data manager, data scientist, big data architect, database architect, database administrator, and database analyst are distinct from the data owner. The former are IT department roles for managing data technology, whereas the data owner role governs the business use of data in information systems.

Network Management Positions in network management are responsible for designing, building, monitoring, and maintaining voice and data communications networks, including connections to outside business partners and the Internet:

- **Network architect** This position designs data and voice networks and designs changes and upgrades to networks as needed to meet new organization objectives.
- **Network engineer** This position implements, configures, and maintains network devices such as routers, switches, firewalls, and gateways.
- **Network administrator** This position performs routine tasks in the network such as making configuration changes and monitoring event logs.
- **Telecom engineer** This position works with telecommunications technologies such as telecom services, data circuits, phone systems, conferencing systems, and voicemail systems.

Systems Management Positions in systems management are responsible for architecture, design, building, and maintenance of servers and operating systems. This may include desktop operating systems as well.

- **Systems architect** This position is responsible for the overall architecture of systems (usually servers), which includes both the internal architecture of a system and the relationship between systems. This position is usually also responsible for the design of services such as authentication, e-mail, and time synchronization.
- **Systems engineer** This position is responsible for designing, building, and maintaining servers and server operating systems.
- **Storage engineer** This position is responsible for designing, building, and maintaining storage subsystems.
- **Systems administrator** This position is responsible for performing maintenance and configuration operations on systems.

Operations Positions in operations are responsible for day-to-day operational tasks that may include networks, servers, databases, and applications:

- **Operations manager** This position is responsible for overall operations that are carried out by others. Responsibilities include establishing operations shift schedules.
- **Operations analyst** This position may be responsible for the development of operational procedures; examining the health of networks, systems, and databases; setting and monitoring the operations schedule; and maintaining operations records.
- **Controls analyst** This position is responsible for monitoring batch jobs, data entry work, and other tasks to make sure that they are operating correctly.

- **Systems operator**   This position is responsible for monitoring systems and networks, performing backup tasks, running batch jobs, printing reports, and other operational tasks.

- **Data entry**   This position is responsible for keying batches of data from hard copy or other sources.

- **Media manager**   This position is responsible for maintaining and tracking the use and whereabouts of backup tapes and other media.

Security Operations   Positions in security operations are responsible for designing, building, and monitoring security systems and security controls to ensure the confidentiality, integrity, and availability of information systems:

- **Security architect**   This position is responsible for the design of security controls and systems such as authentication, audit logging, intrusion detection systems, IPSs, and firewalls.

- **Security engineer**   This position is responsible for building and maintaining security services and systems that are designed by the security architect.

- **Security analyst**   This position is responsible for examining logs from firewalls, intrusion detection systems, and audit logs from systems and applications. This position may also be responsible for issuing security advisories to others in IT.

- **Access administrator**   This position is responsible for accepting approved requests for user access management changes and performing the necessary changes at the network, system, database, or application level. Often, this position is carried out by personnel in network and systems management functions; only in larger organizations is user account management performed in security or even in a separate user access department.

- **Security auditor**   This position is responsible for performing internal audits of IT controls to ensure that they are being operated properly.

CAUTION   The security auditor position needs to be carefully placed in the organization so that persons in this role can be objective and independent from the departments they audit. In U.S. public companies and other organizations, the internal audit function often reports directly to the audit committee of the board of directors.

Service Desk   Positions at the service desk are responsible for providing frontline support services to IT and IT's customers:

- **Service desk manager**   This position serves as a liaison between end users and the IT service desk department.

- **Helpdesk analyst**   This position is responsible for providing frontline user support services to personnel in the organization.

- **Technical support analyst**   This position is responsible for providing technical support services to other IT personnel and perhaps to IT customers.

Quality Assurance   Positions in quality assurance are responsible for developing IT processes and standards and for measuring IT systems and processes to confirm their accuracy:

- **QA manager**   This position is responsible for facilitating quality improvement activities throughout the IT organization.

- **QC manager**   This position is responsible for quality control through the testing of IT systems and applications to confirm whether they are free of defects.

Other Roles   Other roles in IT organizations include the following:

- **Vendor manager**   This position is responsible for maintaining business relationships with external vendors, measuring their performance, and handling business issues.

- **Project manager**   This position is responsible for creating project plans and managing IT projects.

Segregation of Duties

Information systems often process large volumes of information that is often highly valuable or sensitive. IT organizations should take measures to ensure that individuals do not possess sufficient privileges to carry out potentially harmful actions on their own. Checks and balances are needed so that high-value and high-sensitivity activities involve the coordination of two or more authorized individuals. The concept of *segregation of duties* (SOD), sometimes known as *separation of duties*, ensures that single individuals do not possess excess privileges that could result in unauthorized activities such as fraud or the manipulation, exposure, or compromise of sensitive data.

The concept of SOD has long been established in organization accounting departments, where, for instance, separate individuals or groups are responsible for the creation of vendors, the request for payments, and the remittance of payments. Since accounting personnel frequently handle checks, currency, and other payment instruments, the principles and practices of SOD controls in accounting departments are the norm.

IT departments are lagging behind somewhat, because the functions in IT are less often involved in direct monetary activities, except in some industries such as banking. But thanks to financial scandals in the 1980s and 1990s that involved the illicit manipulation of financial records and the emergence of new laws such as Sarbanes-Oxley, the need for full and formal IT-level SOD is now well recognized.

CAUTION   At its most basic form, the rule of segregation of duties specifies that no single individual should be permitted or be able to perform high-value, high-sensitivity, or high-risk actions. Instead, two or more parties must be required to perform these functions.

Segregation of Duties Controls

Preventive and detective controls should be implemented to manage SOD matters. In many organizations, both the preventive and detective controls will be manual, particularly when it comes to unwanted combinations of access between different applications. However, in some transaction-related situations, controls can be automated, although they may still require intervention by others.

Some examples of SOD controls include the following:

- **Transaction authorization**   Information systems can be programmed or configured to require two (or more) persons to approve certain transactions. Many of us see this in retail establishments, where a manager is required to approve a large transaction or a refund. In IT applications, transactions meeting certain criteria (for example, exceeding normally accepted limits or conditions) may require a manager's approval to be able to proceed.

- **Split custody of high-value assets**   Assets of high importance or value can be protected using various means of *split custody*. For example, a password to an encryption key that protects a highly valued asset can be split in two halves—one half assigned to two persons, and the other half assigned to two persons—so that no single individual knows the entire password. Banks do this for central vaults, where a vault combination is split into two or more pieces so that two or more people are required to open it.

- **Workflow**   Applications that are workflow-enabled can use a second (or third) level of approval before certain high-value or high-sensitivity activities can take place. For example, a workflow application that is used to provision user accounts can include extra management approval steps in requests for administrative privileges.

- **Periodic reviews**   IT or internal audit personnel can periodically review user access rights to identify whether any SOD issues exist. The access privileges for each worker can be compared against a SOD control matrix. Table 2-2 shows an example matrix.

When SOD issues are encountered during a review, management will need to decide how to mitigate the matter. The choices for mitigating an SOD issue include the following:

- **Reduce access privileges**   Management can reduce individual user privileges so that the conflict no longer exists.

- **Introduce a new control**   If management has determined that a person needs to retain privileges that are viewed as a conflict, then new preventive or detective controls need to be introduced that will prevent or detect unwanted activities. Examples of mitigating controls include increased logging to record the actions of personnel, improved exception reporting to identify possible issues, reconciliations of data sets, and external reviews of high-risk controls.

	Management	Systems Analyst	SW Developer	SW Test	DB Admin	Systems Admin	Network Admin	Security Admin	Systems Operator	Helpdesk
Management		OK	X	X	X	X	X	X	X	X
Systems Analyst	OK		OK	X	X	X	X	X	X	X
SW Developer	X	OK		X	X	X	X	X	X	X
SW Test	X	X	X		X	X	X	X	X	X
DB Admin	X	X	X	X		OK	X	X	X	X
Systems Admin	X	X	X	X	OK		OK	X	OK	OK
Network Admin	X	X	X	X	X	OK		X	X	X
Security Admin	X	X	X	X	X	X	X		X	X
Systems Operator	X	X	X	X	X	OK	X	X		OK
Helpdesk	X	X	X	X	X	OK	X	X	OK	

Table 2-2 Example Segregation of Duties Matrix Identifies Forbidden Combinations of Privileges

TIP An organization should periodically review its SOD matrix, particularly if new roles or high-value applications are added or changed.

Auditing IT Governance

IT governance is more about business processes than it is about technology. This will make audits of IT governance rely more on interviews and documentation reviews than on inspections of information systems. Effective or ineffective IT governance is discernible in interviews of IT personnel as well as of business customers and end users.

EXAM TIP Governance questions on the exam will consider ISACA's COBIT strategies as the standard but will be generic enough in nature to ensure that an understanding of other common IT governance methods will remain applicable to the test-taker. Focus here on the measures and instruments used to validate the governance model.

Problems in IT governance will manifest themselves through a variety of symptoms:

- **Discontentment among staff or end users** Burned-out or overworked IT staff, low IT morale, high turnover, and malaise among end users about IT-supported systems can indicate an IT department that lacks maturity and is falling behind on its methodology or is applying Band-Aid fixes to systems.

- **Poor system performance**   Excessive incidents of unscheduled downtime, a large backlog of support tasks, and long wait times indicate a lack of attention to the quality of applications.

- **Nonstandard hardware or software**   A mix of hardware or software technologies among applications or end-user systems may indicate a lack of technology standards or the failure to enforce standards that are already in place.

- **Project dysfunction**   An IT department suffering from late projects, aborted projects, and budget-busting projects indicates a lack of program and project management discipline.

- **Highly critical personnel**   A disproportionate overreliance on a few IT personnel indicates that responsibilities are not fairly apportioned over the entire IT staff. This may be a result of a lack of training, unqualified personnel, or high turnover.

Auditing Documentation and Records

The heart of an IT audit is the examination of documentation and records. They tell the story of IT control, planning, and day-to-day operations. When auditing IT governance, the IS (information systems) auditor will need to review many documents:

- **IT charter, strategy, and planning**   These documents will indicate management's commitment to IT strategic planning as a formally required activity. Other documents that should be requested include IT steering committee meeting agendas, minutes, and decision logs.

- **IT organization chart and job descriptions**   These documents give an indication of the organization's level of maturity regarding the classification of employees and their specific responsibilities. An org chart also depicts the hierarchy of management and control. Job description documents describe detailed responsibilities for each position in the IT organization. An IS auditor's interviews should include some inquiry into the actual skills and experience of IT personnel to determine whether they correspond to their respective job descriptions.

- **HR/IT employee performance review process**   The IS auditor should review the process and procedures used for employee performance reviews. In particular, the IS auditor should view actual performance goals and review documents to see how well individual employees' goals align with IT department objectives. Further, any performance problems identified in performance reviews can be compared with documents that describe the outcomes of key IT projects.

- **HR promotion policy**   It will be helpful for the IS auditor to determine whether the organization has a policy (written or not) of promoting from within. In other words, when positions become available, does the organization first look within its ranks for potential candidates, or are new hires typically outsiders? This will influence both employee morale and the overall effectiveness of the IT organization.

- **HR manuals**   Documents such as the employee handbook, corporate policies, and HR procedures related to hiring, performance evaluation, disciplinary action, and termination should exist and reflect both regular management reviews and practices that meet the organization's business needs.

- **Life cycle processes and procedures**   Processes such as the software development life cycle and change management should reflect the needs of IT governance. The IS auditor should request records from the SDLC (specifically, documents that describe specific changes to IT systems and supporting infrastructure) and change management process to see how changes mandated at the steering group level are carried out.

- **IT operations procedures**   IT operations process documents for activities such as service desk, monitoring, and computer and network operations should exist. The IS auditor should request records for these activities to determine whether these processes are active.

- **IT procurement process**   An IT organization needs to take a consistent and effective approach to the procurement process. The process should reflect management's attention to requirements development, bidding, vendor selection, and due diligence so that any supplier risks are identified and mitigated in the procurement phase and reflected in the service agreement contract. The goods and services provided by suppliers should be required to adhere to the organization's IT policies, processes, and standards; exceptions should be handled in an exception process. Records should exist that reflect ongoing attention to this process.

- **Quality management documents**   An IT organization that is committed to quality and improvement will have documents and records to support this objective.

- **Business continuity and disaster recovery documents**   These include documents such as the business impact assessment, critical assessment, and statements of impact, as well as evidence of periodic updates to recovery documentation and regular testing. Audits of business continuity and disaster recovery planning are covered in Chapter 5.

Another indication of a healthy governance system is evidence of regular review and update of all of these documents. Often this is found in each document's modification history, but it may also be present in a separate document management system.

Like any other facets of an audit, the IS auditor needs to conduct several interviews and walkthroughs to gain a level of confidence that these documents reflect the actual management and operations of an IT organization. These interviews should include staff from all levels of management, as well as key end users who can also attest to IT's organization and commitment to its governance program and the maturity of its processes.

NOTE The IS auditor should also review the processes related to the regular review and update of IT governance documents. Regular reviews attest to active management involvement in IT governance. The lack of recent reviews might suggest that management began a governance program but subsequently lost interest in it.

Auditing Contracts

The IS auditor who is examining IT governance needs to examine the service agreements between the organization and its key IT-related suppliers. Contracts should contain several items:

- **Service levels** Contracts should contain a section on acceptable service levels and the process followed when service interruptions occur. Service outages should include an escalation path so that management can obtain information from appropriate levels of the supplier's management team.

- **Quality levels** Contracts should contain specifications on the quality of goods or services delivered, as well as remedies when quality standards are not met.

- **Right to audit** Contracts should include a right-to-audit clause that permits the organization to examine the supplier's premises and records upon reasonable notice.

- **External audits** Contracts should include provisions that require the supplier to undergo appropriate and regular external audits. Audit reports should be available upon request, including remediation plans for any significant findings found in audits.

- **Conformance to security policies** Suppliers should be required to provide goods or services that can meet the organization's security policies. For instance, if the organization's security policy requires specific password-quality standards, then the goods or services from suppliers should be able to meet those standards.

- **Protection and use of sensitive information** Contracts should include detailed statements that describe how the organization's sensitive information will be protected and used. This is primarily relevant in an online, SaaS, or application service provider (ASP) model, where some of the organization's data will reside on systems or networks that are under the control of a supplier. The contract should include details that describe how the supplier tests its controls to ensure that they are still effective. Third-party audits of these controls may also be warranted, depending upon the sensitivity of the information in question.

- **Compliance with laws and regulations** Contracts should require that the supplier conform to all relevant laws and regulations, including those that the organization itself is required to comply with; in other words, compliance with laws and regulations should flow to and include suppliers. For example, if a health-care organization is required to comply with HIPAA, any suppliers that store or manage the organization's health-care–related information must be also required to be in compliance with HIPAA regulations.

- **Incident notification**   Contracts should contain specific language that describes how incidents are handled and how the organization is notified of incidents. This includes not only service changes and interruptions, but also security incidents. The supplier should be required to notify the organization within a specific period, and also required to provide periodic updates as needed.

- **Source code escrow**   If the supplier is a software organization that uses proprietary software as a means for providing services, the supplier should be required to deposit its software source code regularly into a software escrow. A software escrow firm is a third-party organization that will place software into a vault and release it to customer organizations in the event of the failure of the supplier's business.

- **Liabilities**   Contracts should clearly state which parties are liable for which actions and activities. They should further specify the remedies available should any party fail to perform adequately.

- **Termination terms**   Contracts should contain reasonable provisions that describe the actions to be taken if the business relationship is terminated.

 NOTE   Although the IS auditor may not be required to understand the nuances of legal contracts, the auditor should look for these sections in contracts with key suppliers. The IS auditor should also look for other contractual provisions in supplier contracts that are specific to any unique or highly critical needs that are provided by a supplier.

Auditing Outsourcing

When an auditor is auditing an organization's key processes and systems, those processes and systems that are outsourced require just as much (if not more) scrutiny than if they were performed by the organization's own staff using its own assets. However, it may be difficult to audit the services provided by a third-party supplier, for several reasons:

- **Distance**   The supplier may be located in a remote region, and travel to the supplier's location may be costly.

- **Lack of audit contract terms**   The organization may not have a clause in its contract with the supplier that requires cooperation with auditors. While it may be said that the organization should have negotiated a right-to-audit clause, this point may be moot at the time of the audit.

- **Lack of cooperation**   The supplier might not cooperate with the organization's auditors. Noncooperation takes many forms, including taking excessive time to return inquiries and providing incomplete or inadequate records. An audit report may include one or more findings (nonconformities) related to the lack of cooperation; this may provide sufficient leverage to force the supplier to improve its cooperation or for the organization to look for a new supplier.

In an ideal situation, a supplier undergoes regular third-party audits that are relevant to the services provided and the supplier makes those audit results available on request.

Chapter Review

IT governance is the top-down management and control of an IT organization. Governance is usually undertaken through a steering committee that consists of executives from throughout the organization. The steering committee is responsible for setting overall strategic direction and policy, ensuring that IT strategy is in alignment with the organization's strategy and objectives. The wishes of the steering committee are carried out through projects and tasks that steer the IT organization toward strategic objectives. The steering committee can monitor IT progress through a balanced scorecard.

The IT steering committee is responsible for IT strategic planning. The IT steering committee will develop and approve IT policies and appoint managers to develop and maintain processes, procedures, and standards, all of which should align with one another and with the organization's overall strategy.

Security governance is accomplished using the same means as IT governance: it begins with board-level involvement that sets the tone for risk appetite and is carried out through the chief information security officer (CISO) or chief information risk officer (CIRO), who develops security and privacy policies as well as strategic security programs, including incident management, vulnerability management, and identity and access management.

Enterprise architecture provides a meaningful way to depict complex IT environments in functional terms. The Zachman framework is most often used to represent IT architecture in various layers of detail. Similarly, data flow diagrams illustrate the relationship between IT applications.

Risk management is the practice of identifying key assets and the vulnerabilities they may possess and the threats that may harm them if permitted. This is accomplished through a risk assessment that identifies assets, threats, and vulnerabilities in detail, and is followed by specific risk treatment strategies used to mitigate, transfer, avoid, or accept risks. A risk assessment may be qualitative, where threats and risks are labeled on scales such as "high," "medium," and "low," or it may be quantitative, where risks are expressed in financial terms.

Key management practices will help ensure that the IT organization will operate effectively. These practices include *personnel management*, which encompasses the hiring, development, and evaluation of employees, as well as onboarding and offboarding processes, and development of the employee handbook and other policies. Another key practice area is *sourcing*, which is the management of determining where and by whom key business processes will be performed; the basic choices are insourced or outsourced and on-site or off-site. The third key practice area is *change management*, the formal process whereby changes are applied to IT environments in a way that reduces risk and ensures highest reliability. The next practice area is *financial management*, a key area, given that IT organizations are cost-intensive and require planning and analysis to guarantee the best use of financial resources. Another practice area is *quality management*, where processes are carefully measured and managed so that they may be continuously improved over time. Another practice is *portfolio management*, which is the systematic management of IT projects, investments, and activities. The next key practice is *controls management*, which is the life cycle of activities related to the creation, measurement, and improvement of controls. The next practice area is *security management*, which encompasses several activities, including risk assessments, incident management, vulnerability management, access and identity management, compliance management, business continuity planning, and performance and capacity management.

The IT organization should have a formal management and reporting structure, as well as established roles and responsibilities and written job descriptions. Roles and responsibilities should address the need for segregation of duties to ensure that high-value and high-risk tasks are carried out by two or more persons and recorded.

Quick Review

- IT executives and the board of directors are responsible for imposing an IT governance model encompassing IT strategy, information security, and formal enterprise architectural mandates.

- Strategic planning is accomplished by a steering committee, addressing the near-term and long-term requirements aligning business objectives and technology strategies.

- Policies, procedures, and standards enable validation of business practices against acceptable measures of regulatory compliance, performance, and standard operational guidelines.

- Risk management involves the identification of potential risks and the appropriate responses for each risk based on impact assessment using qualitative and/or quantitative measures for an enterprise-wide risk management strategy.

- Assigned IT management roles ensure that resource allocation, enterprise performance, and operational capabilities coordinate with business requirements by validating alignment with standards and procedures for change management and compliance with sourcing, financial, quality, and security controls.

- Formal organizational structure ensures alignment between operational roles and responsibilities within the enterprise, where a separation of duties ensures individual accountability and validation of policy alignment between coordinated team members.

- Regular audit of the IT governance process ensures alignment with regulatory and business mandates in the evolving enterprise by ensuring that all documentation, contracts, and sourcing policies are reviewed and updated to meet changes in the living enterprise.

Questions

1. IT governance is most concerned with

    A. Security policy

    B. IT policy

    C. IT strategy

    D. IT executive compensation

2. One of the advantages of outsourcing is

    A. It permits the organization to focus on core competencies.

    B. It results in reduced costs.

    C. It provides greater control over work performed by the outsourcing agency.

    D. It eliminates segregation of duties issues.

3. An external IS auditor has discovered a segregation of duties issue in a high-value process. What is the best action for the auditor to take?

    A. Implement a preventive control.

    B. Implement a detective control.

    C. Implement a compensating control.

    D. Document the matter in the audit report.

4. An organization has chosen to open a business office in another country where labor costs are lower and has hired workers to perform business functions there. This organization has

    A. Outsourced the function

    B. Outsourced the function offshore

    C. Insourced the function on-site

    D. Insourced the function at a remote location

5. What is the purpose of a criticality analysis?

    A. Determine feasible recovery targets.

    B. Determine which staff members are the most critical.

    C. Determine which business processes are the most critical.

    D. Determine maximum tolerable downtime.

6. An organization needs to better understand whether one of its key business processes is effective. What action should the organization consider?

    A. Audit the process.

    B. Benchmark the process.

    C. Outsource the process.

    D. Offshore the process.

7. Annualized loss expectancy (ALE) is defined as

   A. Single loss expectancy (SLE) × annualized rate of occurrence (ARO)

   B. Exposure factor (EF) × the annualized rate of occurrence (ARO)

   C. Single loss expectancy (SLE) × the exposure factor (EF)

   D. Asset value (AV) × the single loss expectancy (SLE)

8. A quantitative risk analysis is more difficult to perform because

   A. It is difficult to get accurate figures on the impact of a realized threat.

   B. It is difficult to get accurate figures on the probability of specific threats.

   C. It is difficult to get accurate figures on the value of assets.

   D. It is difficult to calculate the annualized loss expectancy of a specific threat.

9. A collection of servers that is designed to operate as a single logical server is known as what?

   A. Cluster

   B. Grid

   C. Cloud

   D. Replicant

10. What is the purpose of a balanced scorecard?

   A. Measures the efficiency of an IT organization

   B. Evaluates the performance of individual employees

   C. Benchmarks a process in the organization against peer organizations

   D. Measures organizational performance and effectiveness against strategic goals

11. An organization has discovered that some of its employees have criminal records. What is the best course of action for the organization to take?

   A. Terminate the employees with criminal records.

   B. Immediately perform background checks, including criminal history, on all existing employees.

   C. Immediately perform background checks, including criminal history, on all new employees.

   D. Immediately perform background checks on those employees with criminal records.

12. The options for risk treatment are

   A. Risk mitigation, risk reduction, and risk acceptance

   B. Risk mitigation, risk reduction, risk transfer, and risk acceptance

   C. Risk mitigation, risk avoidance, risk transfer, and risk acceptance

   D. Risk mitigation, risk avoidance, risk transfer, and risk conveyance

13. An IS auditor is examining the IT standards document for an organization that was last reviewed two years earlier. What is the best course of action for the IS auditor?

    A. Locate the IT policy document and see how frequently IT standards should be reviewed.

    B. Compare the standards with current practices and make a determination of adequacy.

    C. Report that IT standards are not being reviewed often enough.

    D. Report that IT standards are adequate.

14. The most important step in the process of outsourcing a business function is

    A. Developing a business case

    B. Measuring the cost savings

    C. Measuring the change in risk

    D. Performing due diligence on the external service provider

15. An organization has published a new security policy. What is the best course of action for the organization to undertake to ensure that all employees will support the policy?

    A. The company CEO should send an e-mail to all employees, instructing them to support the policy.

    B. The company should provide training on the new security policy.

    C. The company should publish the policy on an internal web site.

    D. The company should require all employees to sign a statement agreeing to support the policy.

Answers

1. **C.** IT governance is the mechanism through which IT strategy is established, controlled, and monitored through the balanced scorecard. Long-term and other strategic decisions are made in the context of IT governance.

2. **A.** Outsourcing is an opportunity for the organization to focus on its core competencies. When an organization outsources a business function, it no longer needs to be concerned about training employees in that function. Outsourcing does not always reduce costs, because cost reduction is not always the primary purpose for outsourcing in the first place.

3. **D.** The external auditor can only document the finding in the audit report. An external auditor is not in a position to implement controls.

4. **D.** An organization that opens a business office in another country and staffs the office with its own employees is insourcing, not outsourcing. Outsourcing is the

practice of using contract labor, which is clearly not the case in this example. In this case, the insourcing is taking place at a remote location.

5. **C.** A criticality analysis is used to determine which business processes are the most critical by ranking them in order of criticality.

6. **B.** An organization that needs to understand whether a key process is effective should consider benchmarking the process. This will help the organization better understand whether its approach is similar to that of other organizations.

7. **A.** Annualized loss expectancy (ALE) is the annual expected loss to an asset. It is calculated by multiplying the single loss expectancy (SLE—the financial loss experienced when the loss is realized one time) by the annualized rate of occurrence (ARO—the number of times that the organization expects the loss to occur).

8. **B.** The most difficult part of a quantitative risk analysis is determining the probability that a threat will actually be realized. It is relatively easy to determine the value of an asset and the impact of a threat event.

9. **A.** A server cluster is a collection of two or more servers that is designed to appear as a single server.

10. **D.** The balanced scorecard is a tool that is used to quantify the performance of an organization against strategic objectives. The focuses of a balanced scorecard are financial, customer, internal processes, and innovation/learning.

11. **B.** An organization that has discovered that some employees have criminal records should have background checks performed on all existing employees, and it should also begin instituting background checks (which should include criminal history) for all new employees. It is not necessarily required to terminate these employees; the specific criminal offenses may not warrant termination.

12. **C.** The options for risk treatment are the actions that management will take when a risk has been identified. The options are risk mitigation (where the risk is reduced), risk avoidance (where the activity is discontinued), risk transfer (where the risk is transferred to an insurance company), and risk acceptance (where management agrees to accept the risk as is).

13. **C.** IT standards that have not been reviewed for two years are out of date. If the IS auditor finds an IT policy that says that IT standards can be reviewed every two years, then there is a problem with IT policy as well; two years is far too long between reviews of IT standards.

14. **A.** Development of a business case is the most important step when considering the outsourcing of a business function. The other items (measuring cost savings and changes in risk, and performing due diligence on service providers) are parts of development of a business case.

15. **D.** All employees should be required to sign a statement agreeing to support the policy. The other actions are important but less effective.

The Audit Process

This chapter covers CISA Domain 1, "Information Systems Auditing Process," and discusses the following topics:

- Audit management
- ISACA auditing standards and guidelines
- Audit and risk analysis
- Internal controls
- Performing an audit
- Control self-assessments
- Audit recommendations

The topics in this chapter represent 21 percent of the CISA examination.

The IS audit process is the procedural and ethical structure used by auditors to assess and evaluate the effectiveness of the IT organization and how well it supports the organization's overall goals and objectives. The audit process is backed up by the Information Technology Assurance Framework (ITAF) and the ISACA code of ethics. The ITAF is used to ensure that auditors will take a consistent approach from one audit to the next throughout the entire industry. This will help to advance the entire audit profession and facilitate its gradual improvement over time.

Audit Management

An organization's audit function should be managed so that an audit charter, strategy, and program can be established; audits can be performed; recommendations can be enacted; and auditor independence can be assured throughout. The audit function should align with the organization's mission and goals, and it should work well alongside IT governance and operations.

The Audit Charter

As with any formal, managed function in the organization, the audit function should be defined and described in a charter document. The charter should clearly define roles and responsibilities that are consistent with ISACA audit standards and guidelines, including but not limited to ethics, integrity, and independence. The audit function should have sufficient authority so that its recommendations will be respected and implemented, but not so much power that the audit tail will wag the IS dog. An audit charter would also include statements about scope, both in terms of business units and business lines, and also about applicable regulations. For instance, an audit charter in a U.S. public company would include financially relevant systems for Sarbanes-Oxley compliance but may exclude PCI-DSS.

The Audit Program

The *audit program* describes the audit strategy and audit plans that include scope, objectives, resources, and procedures used to evaluate a set of controls and deliver an audit opinion. You could say that an audit program is the plan for conducting audits over a given period.

The term *program* in this case is intended to evoke a similar "big picture" point of view as the term *program manager* does. A program manager is responsible for the performance of several related projects in an organization. Similarly, an audit program is a plan for conducting several audits, types of audits, or audits of varying scope in an organization.

Strategic Audit Planning

The purpose of audit planning is to determine the audit activities that need to take place in the future, including an estimate of the resources (tools, budget, and staff) required to support those activities. Audit planning is really just project planning for projects that are audits or are related to audits.

Factors that Affect an Audit

As with security planning, audit planning must take into account several factors:

- **Organization's strategic goals and objectives**   The organization's overall goals and objectives should flow down to individual departments and their support of these goals and objectives. These goals and objectives will translate into business processes, technology to support business processes, controls for both the business processes and technologies, and audits of those controls. This is depicted in Figure 3-1.

- **New organization initiatives**   Closely related to goals and objectives are new initiatives that organizations often undertake, including new products, new services, or new ways of delivering existing products and services.

- **Mergers and acquisitions**   Recent mergers and acquisitions can throw a wrench into any audit program when organizations have been grafted together; business integration objectives, no matter how simple or extensive, are also affected. A merged organization is a moving target; planning must be done carefully to factor in business conditions during the actual audit.

Figure 3-1
The organization's goals and objectives translate down into audit activities.

Goals and Objectives

Business Processses

Information Technology

Controls

Audits

- **Market conditions**   Changes in the product or service market may have an impact on auditing. For instance, in a product or services market where security is becoming more important, market competitors could decide to undergo audits voluntarily to show that their products or services are safer or better than those from competing organizations. Other market players may need to follow suit for competitive parity. Changes in the supply or demand of supply-chain goods or services can also affect audits.

- **Changes in technology**   Enhancements in the technologies that support business processes may affect business or technical controls, which in turn may affect audit procedures for those controls. An organization that moves its applications or services from on-premises locales to the cloud is a good example of this.

- **Changes in regulatory requirements**   Changes in technologies, markets, or security-related events can result in new or changed regulations. Maintaining compliance may require changes to the audit program. In the 20-year period preceding the publication of this book, many new information security–related regulations have been passed or updated, including the Gramm-Leach-Bliley Act (GLBA), the Sarbanes-Oxley Act (SOX), the Health Insurance Portability and Accountability Act (HIPAA), the European General Data Protection Regulation (GDPR, and its predecessor, the European Privacy Directive), as well as national and state laws related to information security and privacy.

All of the changes listed here usually translate into new business processes or changes in existing business processes. Often, changes to information systems and changes to the controls supporting systems and processes are also involved.

Changes in Audit Activities

External factors may affect auditing in the following ways:

- **New internal audits** Business and regulatory changes sometimes compel organizations to audit more systems or processes. For instance, SOX requires that U.S. publicly traded companies perform internal audits of IT systems that support financial business processes.

- **New external audits** New regulations or competitive pressures could introduce new external audits. For example, virtually all banks, as well as many merchants and service providers, are required to undergo external Payment Card Industry Data Security Standard (PCI-DSS) audits.

- **Market competition** In certain industries, such as financial services, service providers are voluntarily undertaking new audits such as SOC 1 (SSAE 18 in the United States and ISAE 3402 elsewhere), SOC 2, TrustArc (formerly TRUSTe), HITECH (in the healthcare industry), and ISO/IEC 27001 certification, partly to support marketing claims that their security is superior to that of their competitors.

- **Increase in audit scope** The scope of existing internal or external audits could increase to include more systems, processes, or business units.

- **Impacts on business processes** This could take the form of additional steps in processes or procedures, or additions/changes in recordkeeping or record retention.

- **Changes in audit standards** Also undergoing continuous improvement, general and specific audit rules occasionally change, which may alter sampling methodologies as well as audit procedures. For example, the PCI-DSS 3.0 update requires penetration tests to include network segmentation validation, which can result in significant increases in costs and the time required for penetration testing.

Resource Planning

At least once per year, management needs to consider all of the internal and external factors that affect auditing to determine the resources required to support these activities. Primarily, resources will consist of the budget for external audits and staff for internal audits. External audits also require staff resources to meet with external auditors and provide evidence.

Additional external audits usually require additional staff hours to meet with external auditors; discuss scope; coordinate meetings with process owners and managers; discuss audits with process owners and managers; discuss audit findings with auditors, process owners, and management; and organize remediation work.

Internal and external audits usually require information systems to track audit activities and store evidence. Taking on additional audit activities may require additional capacity on these systems or new systems altogether.

Additional internal audits require all of these factors, plus time for performing the internal audits themselves. All of these details are discussed in this chapter and throughout this book.

Audit and Technology

ISACA auditing standards require that the auditor retain technical competence. With the continuation of technology and business process innovation, auditors need to continue learning about new technologies, how they support business processes, and how they are controlled. As with many professions, IS auditors are required to undergo hours of continuing education to stay current with changes in technology.

Here are some of the ways that an IS auditor can update his or her knowledge and skills:

- **ISACA training and conferences** As the developer of the CISA certification, ISACA offers many valuable training and conference events, including
  - Computer Audit, Control, and Security (CACS) Conference
  - Governance, Risk, and Control (GRC) Conference
  - Cybersecurity Nexus (CSX) Conference
  - ISACA Training Week
- **University courses** These can include both for-credit and noncredit classes on new technologies. Some universities offer certificate programs on many new technologies; this can give an auditor a real boost of knowledge, skills, and confidence.
- **Vo-tech (vocational-technical) training** Many organizations offer training in information technologies, including MIS Training Institute, SANS Institute, Computer Security Institute, and ISACA.
- **Training webinars** These events are usually focused on a single topic and last from one to three hours. ISACA and many other organizations offer training webinars, which are especially convenient because they require no travel, and many are offered at no cost.
- **ISACA chapter training** Many ISACA chapters offer training events so that local members can acquire new knowledge and skills close to where they live.
- **Other security association training** Many other security-related trade associations offer training, including ISSA (International Systems Security Association), SANS Institute, and IIA (The Institute of Internal Auditors). Training sessions are offered online, in classrooms, and at conferences.
- **Security conferences** Several security-related conferences include lectures and training. These conferences include those hosted by RSA, SANS, ISSA, Gartner, and SecureWorld Expo. Many local ISACA and ISSA chapters organize local conferences that include training.

 EXAM TIP ISACA requires CISA certification holders to undergo at least 120 hours of training every three years (and a minimum of 20 hours per year) to maintain their certification. Chapter 1 provides more information on this requirement.

Audit Laws and Regulations

Laws and regulations are some of the primary reasons why organizations perform internal and external audits. Regulations on industries generally translate into additional effort on the part of target companies to track and verify their compliance. Tracking and verification are undertaken via internal auditing, and new regulations sometimes also require external audits. Moreover, while other factors such as competitive pressures can compel an organization to begin or increase auditing activities, this section discusses laws and regulations that require auditing.

Digital Transformation Brings New Regulation

Automating business processes with information systems is still a relatively new phenomenon. Modern businesses have been around for the past two or three centuries, but information systems have been playing a *significant* role in business process automation for only about the past 20 years. Before that time, most information systems supported business processes, but only in an ancillary way. Automation of entire business processes is still relatively young, and so many organizations have messed up in such colossal ways that legislators and regulators have responded with additional laws and regulations to make organizations more accountable for the security and integrity of their information systems.

Almost every industry sector is subject to laws and regulations that affect organizations' use of information and information systems. These laws are concerned primarily with one or more of the following characteristics and uses of information and information systems:

- **Security**   Some information in information systems is valuable and/or sensitive, such as financial and medical records. Many laws and regulations require such information to be protected so that it cannot be accessed by unauthorized parties, and they require that information systems be free of defects, vulnerabilities, malware, and other threats.

- **Integrity**   Some regulations are focused on the integrity of information to ensure that it is correct and that the systems it resides on are free of vulnerabilities and defects that could make or allow improper changes.

- **Privacy**   Many information systems store information that is considered private. This includes financial records, medical records, and other information about people.

Computer Security and Privacy Regulations

This section contains several computer security and privacy laws in the United States, Canada, Europe, and elsewhere. The laws here fall into one or more of the following categories:

- **Computer trespass**   Some of these laws bring the concept of trespass forward into the realm of computers and networks, making it illegal to access a computer or network without explicit authorization.

- **Protection of sensitive information**   Many laws require that sensitive information be protected, and some include required public disclosures in the event of a breach of security.

- **Collection and use of information**   Several privacy laws define the boundaries regarding the collection and acceptable use of information, particularly private information.

- **Offshore data flow**   Some security and privacy laws place restrictions or conditions on the flow of sensitive data (usually about citizens) out of a country.

- **Law enforcement investigative powers**   Some laws clarify and expand the search and investigative powers of law enforcement.

The consequences of the failure to comply with these laws vary. Some laws have penalties written in as a part of the law; however, the absence of an explicit penalty doesn't mean there aren't any! Some of the results of failing to comply include

- **Loss of reputation**   Failure to comply with some laws can make front-page news, with a resulting reduction in reputation and loss of business. For example, if an organization suffers a security breach and is forced to notify customers, word may spread quickly and be picked up by news media outlets, which will further spread the bad news.

- **Loss of competitive advantage**   An organization that has a reputation for sloppy security may begin to see its business diminish and move to its competitors. A record of noncompliance may also result in difficulty winning new business contracts.

- **Government sanctions**   Breaking many federal laws may result in sanctions from local, regional, or national governments, including losing the right to conduct business.

- **Lawsuits**   Civil lawsuits from competitors, customers, suppliers, and government agencies may be the result of breaking some laws. Plaintiffs may file lawsuits against an organization even if there were other consequences. Large-scale violations sometimes lead to costly class-action lawsuits.

- **Fines**   Monetary consequences are frequently the result of breaking laws.

- **Prosecution**   Many laws have criminalized behavior such as computer trespassing, stealing information, or filing falsified reports to government agencies. Executives and board members are sometimes found to be personally liable in the event of security violations. Breaking some laws may result in imprisonment.

Knowledge of these consequences provides an incentive for organizations to develop management strategies to comply with the laws that apply to their business activities. These strategies often result in the development of controls that define required activities and events, plus analysis and internal audit to determine whether the controls are effectively keeping the organization in compliance with those laws. Although organizations often initially resist undertaking these additional activities, they usually accept them as a requirement for doing business and seek ways of making them more cost-efficient in the long term.

Determining Applicability of Regulations   An organization should take a systematic approach to determine the applicability of regulations as well as the steps required to attain compliance with applicable regulations and remain in a compliant state.

Determination of applicability often requires the assistance of legal counsel who is an expert on government regulations, as well as experts in the organization who are familiar with the organization's practices.

Next, the language in the applicable law or regulation needs to be analyzed and a list of compliant and noncompliant practices identified. These are then compared with the organization's practices to determine which practices are compliant and which are not. Those practices that are not compliant need to be corrected; one or more accountable individuals should be appointed to determine what is required to achieve and maintain compliance.

Another approach is to outline the required (or forbidden) practices specified in the law or regulation and then "map" the organization's relevant existing activities into the outline. Where gaps are found, the organization must develop or change processes or procedures to bring the organization into compliance.

PCI-DSS: A Highly Effective Non-law

The Payment Card Industry Data Security Standard (PCI-DSS) is a data security standard that was developed by a consortium of the major credit card brands: VISA, MasterCard, American Express, Discover, and JCB. The major brands have the contractual right to levy fines and impose sanctions, such as the loss of the right to issue credit cards, process payments, or accept credit card payments. PCI-DSS has gotten much attention, and by many accounts it has been more effective than many state and national laws.

Regulations Are Not Always Clear

Sometimes, the effort to determine what's needed to achieve compliance is substantial. For instance, when the Sarbanes-Oxley Act was signed into law, virtually no one knew precisely what companies had to do to achieve compliance. Guidance from the Public Company Accounting Oversight Board was not published for almost a year. It took another two years before audit firms and U.S. public companies were familiar and comfortable with the basic approach to achieve compliance with the act.

Similarly, organizations are still struggling to determine what actions they are required to take to be compliant with the European General Data Protection Regulation (GDPR) as well as the California Consumer Privacy Act (CCPA). Primarily, this is because laws state *what* must be done, but not *how* it must be done.

U.S. Regulations Selected security and privacy laws and standards applicable in the United States include

- Privacy Act of 1974
- Access Device Fraud, 1984
- Computer Fraud and Abuse Act of 1984
- Electronic Communications Privacy Act (ECPA) of 1986
- Computer Matching and Privacy Protection Act of 1988
- Communications Assistance for Law Enforcement Act (CALEA) of 1994
- Economic and Protection of Proprietary Information Act of 1996
- National Infrastructure Protection Act of 1996
- Health Insurance Portability and Accountability Act (HIPAA) of 1996
- Economic Espionage Act (EEA), 1996
- No Electronic Theft (NET) Act, 1997
- Digital Millennium Copyright Act (DMCA), 1998
- Children's Online Privacy Protection Act (COPPA) of 1998
- Identity Theft and Assumption Deterrence Act of 1998
- Gramm-Leach-Bliley Act (GLBA) of 1999
- Cyberspace Electronic Security Act of 1999
- Federal Energy Regulatory Commission (FERC) with its legally binding standards
- Uniting and Strengthening America by Providing Appropriate Tools Required to Intercept and Obstruct Terrorism (USA PATRIOT) Act of 2001 (expired in 2015, succeeded by the USA Freedom Act)
- Sarbanes-Oxley Act of 2002
- Cyber Security Enhancement Act (CSEA) of 2002
- Federal Information Security Management Act (FISMA) of 2002
- Controlling the Assault of Non-Solicited Pornography and Marketing (CAN-SPAM) Act of 2003
- California privacy law SB 1386 of 2003 (the first such U.S. state privacy regulation; those in most other states are excluded from this list)
- Identity Theft and Assumption Deterrence Act of 2003
- Basel II, 2004, an international accord
- Payment Card Industry Data Security Standard (PCI-DSS), 2004; updated 2016
- North American Electric Reliability Corporation (NERC), 1968/2006, with its legally binding standards
- Massachusetts security breach law, 2007

- Red Flags Rule, 2008
- Health Information Technology for Economic and Clinical Health Act (HITECH) of 2009
- USA Freedom Act, 2015
- Cybersecurity Information Sharing Act (CISA) of 2015

Canadian Regulations   Selected security and privacy laws and standards in Canada include

- Interception of Communications (Section 184 of the Canada Criminal Code)
- Unauthorized Use of Computer (Section 342.1 of the Canada Criminal Code)
- Privacy Act, 1983
- Personal Information Protection and Electronic Documents Act (PIPEDA), 2000
- Digital Privacy Act, 2015
- Protecting Canadians from Online Crime Act

European Regulations   Selected security and privacy laws and standards from Europe include

- Convention for the Protection of Individuals with Regard to Automatic Processing of Personal Data, 1981, Council of Europe
- Computer Misuse Act (CMA), 1990, U.K.
- Directive on the Protection of Personal Data (95/46/EC), 2003, European Union
- Data Protection Act (DPA) 1998, U.K.
- Regulation of Investigatory Powers Act 2000, U.K.
- Anti-Terrorism, Crime, and Security Act 2001, U.K.
- Privacy and Electronic Communications Regulations 2003, U.K.
- Fraud Act 2006, U.K.
- Police and Justice Act 2006, U.K.
- General Data Protection Regulation (GDPR), 2016

Other Regulations   Selected security and privacy laws and standards from the rest of the world include

- Cybercrime Act, 2001, Australia
- Information Technology Act, 2000, India
- Cybersecurity Law, 2017, China

ISACA Auditing Standards

ISACA has published its Information Technology Assurance Framework in the *ITAF: A Professional Practices Framework for IS Audit/Assurance* (currently in its third edition and available free of charge at www.isaca.org/ITAF). ITAF consists of the ISACA Code of Professional Ethics, IS audit and assurance standards, IS audit and assurance guidelines, and IS audit and assurance tools and techniques. This section discusses the Code of Professional Ethics, standards, and guidelines. The relationship between these is illustrated in Figure 3-2.

 EXAM TIP   ISACA does not require CISA candidates to memorize ITAF, but they should understand its importance and purpose.

ISACA Code of Professional Ethics

Like many professional associations, ISACA has published a Code of Professional Ethics. The purpose of the code is to define principles of professional behavior that are based on the support of standards, compliance with laws and standards, and the identification and defense of the truth.

Audit and IT professionals who earn the CISA certification are required to sign a statement that declares their support of the ISACA Code of Professional Ethics. If someone who holds the CISA certification is found to violate the code, he or she may be disciplined and may possibly lose his or her certification. The full text of the ISACA Code of Professional Ethics can be viewed at www.isaca.org/ethics.

 EXAM TIP   The CISA candidate is not expected to memorize the ISACA Code of Professional Ethics, but is required to understand and be familiar with it.

ISACA Audit and Assurance Standards

The ISACA audit and assurance standards framework, known as the Information Technology Assurance Framework (ITAF), defines minimum standards of performance

Figure 3-2
Relationship between ISACA audit standards, audit guidelines, and Code of Professional Ethics

Audit Guidelines
(optional)

Audit Standards
(mandatory)

Code of Ethics
(mandatory)

related to security, audits, and the actions that result from audits. This section lists the standards and paraphrases each.

The full text of these standards is available at www.isaca.org/standards.

 EXAM TIP ISACA does not require CISA candidates to memorize frameworks or audit standards, but they should understand its importance and purpose.

1001, Audit Charter

Audit activities in an organization should be formally defined in an audit charter. This should include statements of scope, responsibility, and authority for conducting audits. Senior management should support the audit charter through direct signature or by linking the audit charter to corporate policy.

1002, Organizational Independence

The IS auditor's placement in the command-and-control structure of the organization should ensure that the IS auditor can act independently.

1003, Professional Independence

Behavior of the IS auditor should be independent of the auditee. The IS auditor should take care to avoid even the appearance of impropriety.

1004, Reasonable Expectation

IS auditors and assurance professionals shall have a reasonable expectation that an audit engagement can be completed according to ISACA and other audit standards, that the audit scope enables completion of the audit, and that management understands its obligations and responsibilities.

1005, Due Professional Care

IS auditors and assurance professionals shall exercise due professional care, including but not limited to conformance with applicable audit standards.

1006, Proficiency

IS auditors and assurance professionals shall possess adequate skills and knowledge on the performance of IS audits and of the subject matter being audited, and shall continue in their proficiency through regular continuing professional education and training.

1007, Assertions

IS auditors and assurance professionals shall review audit assertions to determine whether they are capable of being audited, and whether the assertions are valid and reasonable.

1008, Criteria

IS auditors and assurance professionals shall select objective, measurable, and reasonable audit criteria.

1201, Engagement Planning

IS auditors shall perform audit planning work to ensure that the scope and breadth of an audit is sufficient to meet the organization's needs, that it is in compliance with applicable laws, and that it is risk-based.

1202, Risk Assessment in Planning

The IS auditor should use a risk-based approach when making decisions about which controls and activities should be audited and the level of effort expended in each audit. These decisions should be documented in detail to avoid any appearance of partiality.

A risk-based approach looks not only at security risks, but at overall business risk. This will probably include operational risk and may include aspects of financial risk.

1203, Performance and Supervision

IS auditors shall conduct an audit according to the plan and on schedule; shall supervise audit staff; shall accept and perform audit tasks only within their competency; and shall collect appropriate evidence, document the audit process, and document findings.

1204, Materiality

The IS auditor should consider materiality when prioritizing audit activities and allocating audit resources. During audit planning, the auditor should consider whether ineffective controls or an absence of controls could result in a significant deficiency or material weakness.

In addition to auditing individual controls, the auditor should consider the effectiveness of groups of controls and determine if a failure across a group of controls would constitute a significant deficiency or material weakness. For example, if an organization has several controls regarding the management and control of third-party service organizations, failures in many of those controls could represent a significant deficiency or material weakness overall.

1205, Evidence

The IS auditor should gather sufficient evidence to develop reasonable conclusions about the effectiveness of controls and procedures. The IS auditor should evaluate the sufficiency and integrity of audit evidence, and this evaluation should be included in the audit report.

Audit evidence includes the procedures performed by the auditor during the audit, the results of those procedures, source documents and records, and corroborating information. Audit evidence also includes the audit report.

1206, Using the Work of Other Experts

An IS auditor should consider using the work of other auditors when and where appropriate. Whether an auditor can use the work of other auditors depends on several factors, including:

- The relevance of the other auditors' work
- The qualifications and independence of the other auditors
- Whether the other auditors' work is adequate (this will require an evaluation of at least some of the other auditors' work)
- Whether the IS auditor should develop additional test procedures to supplement the work of another auditor(s)

If an IS auditor uses another auditor's work, his report should document which portion of the audit work was performed by the other auditor, as well as an evaluation of that work.

1207, Irregularity and Illegal Acts

IS auditors should have a healthy but balanced skepticism regarding irregularities and illegal acts: The auditor should recognize that irregularities and/or illegal acts could be ongoing in one or more of the processes that he is auditing. He should recognize that management may or may not be aware of any irregularities or illegal acts.

The IS auditor should obtain written attestations from management that state management's responsibilities for the proper operation of controls. Management should disclose to the auditor any knowledge of irregularities or illegal acts.

If the IS auditor encounters material irregularities or illegal acts, he should document every conversation and retain all evidence of correspondence. The IS auditor should report any matter of material irregularities or illegal acts to management. If material findings or irregularities prevent the auditor from continuing the audit, the auditor should carefully weigh his options and consider withdrawing from the audit. The IS auditor should determine if he is required to report material findings to regulators or other outside authorities. If the auditor is unable to report material findings to management, he should consider withdrawing from the audit engagement.

1401, Reporting

The IS auditor should develop an audit report that documents the process followed, inquiries, observations, evidence, findings, conclusions, and recommendations from the audit. The audit report should follow an established format that includes a statement of scope, period of coverage, recipient organization, controls or standards that were audited, and any limitations or qualifications. The report should contain sufficient evidence to support the findings of the audit.

1402, Follow-up Activities

After the completion of an audit, the IS auditor should follow up at a later time to determine if management has taken steps to make any recommended changes or apply remedies to any audit findings.

ISACA Audit and Assurance Guidelines

ISACA audit and assurance guidelines contain information that helps the auditor understand how to apply ISACA audit standards. These guidelines are a series of articles that clarify the meaning of the audit standards. They cite specific ISACA IS audit standards and COBIT controls and provide specific guidance on various audit activities. Last updated in 2014, ISACA audit guidelines also provide insight into why each guideline was developed and published.

The full text of these guidelines is available at www.isaca.org/guidelines.

2001, Audit Charter

This guideline provides information on the following IS audit standards topics:

- Mandate
- Contents of the audit charter

2002, Organizational Independence

This guideline provides information on the following IS audit standards topics:

- Position in the enterprise
- Reporting level
- Non-audit services
- Assessing independence
- Audit charter and audit plan

2003, Professional Independence

This guideline provides information on the following IS audit standards topics:

- Conceptual framework
- Threats and safeguards
- Managing threats
- Non-audit services or roles
- Non-audit services or roles that do not impair independence
- Non-audit services or roles that do impair independence
- Relevance of independence when providing non-audit services or roles
- Governance of the admissibility of non-audit services or roles
- Reporting

2004, Reasonable Expectation

This guideline provides information on the following IS audit standards topics:

- Standards and regulations
- Scope

- Scope limitations
- Information
- Acceptance of a change in engagement terms

2005, Due Professional Care

This guideline provides information on the following IS audit standards topics:

- Professional skepticism and competency
- Application
- Life cycle of the engagement
- Communication
- Managing information

2006, Proficiency

This guideline provides information on the following IS audit standards topics:

- Professional competence
- Evaluation
- Reaching the desired level of competence

2007, Assertions

This guideline provides information on the following IS audit standards topics:

- Assertions
- Subject matter and criteria
- Assertions developed by third parties
- Conclusion and report

2008, Criteria

This guideline provides information on the following IS audit standards topics:

- Selection and use of criteria
- Suitability
- Acceptability
- Source
- Change in criteria during the audit engagement

2201, Engagement Planning

This guideline provides information on the following IS audit standards topics:

- IS audit plan
- Objectives

- Scope and business knowledge
- Risk-based approach
- Documenting the audit engagement project plan
- Changes during the course of the audit

2202, Risk Assessment in Planning

This guideline provides information on the following IS audit standards topics:

- Risk assessment of the IS audit plan
- Risk assessment methodology
- Risk assessment of individual audit engagements
- Audit risk
- Inherent risk
- Control risk
- Detection risk

2203, Performance and Supervision

This guideline provides information on the following IS audit standards topics:

- Performing the work
- Roles and responsibilities, knowledge and skills
- Supervision
- Evidence
- Documenting
- Findings and conclusions

2204, Materiality

This guideline provides information on the following IS audit standards topics:

- IS v. financial audit engagements
- Assessing materiality of the subject matter
- Materiality and controls
- Materiality and reportable issues

2205, Evidence

This guideline provides information on the following IS audit standards topics:

- Types of evidence
- Obtaining evidence

- Evaluating evidence
- Preparing audit documentation

2206, Using the Work of Other Experts
This guideline provides information on the following IS audit standards topics:

- Considering the use of work of other experts
- Assessing the adequacy of other experts
- Planning and reviewing the work of other experts
- Evaluating the work of other experts who are not part of the audit engagement team
- Additional test procedures
- Audit opinion or conclusion

2207, Irregularity and Illegal Acts
This guideline provides information on the following IS audit standards topics:

- Irregularities and illegal acts
- Responsibilities of management
- Responsibilities of the professionals
- Irregularities and illegal acts during engagement planning
- Designing and reviewing engagement procedures
- Responding to irregularities and illegal acts
- Internal reporting
- External reporting

2208, Audit Sampling
This guideline provides information on the following IS audit standards topics:

- Sampling
- Design of the sample
- Selection of the sample
- Evaluation of sample results
- Documentation

2401, Reporting
This guideline provides information on the following IS audit standards topics:

- Types of engagements
- Required contents of the audit engagement report

- Subsequent events
- Additional communication

2402, Follow-up Activities

This guideline provides information on the following IS audit standards topics:

- Follow-up process
- Management's proposed actions
- Assuming the risk of not taking corrective action
- Follow-up procedures
- Timing and scheduling of follow-up activities
- Nature and extent of follow-up activities
- Deferring follow-up activities
- Form of follow-up responses
- Follow-up by professionals on external audit recommendations
- Reporting of follow-up activities

Relationship Between Standards and Guidelines

The ISACA audit standards and guidelines have been written to assist IS auditors with audit- and risk-related activities. They are related to each other in this way:

- *Standards* are statements that all IS auditors are expected to follow, and they can be considered a rule of law for auditors.
- *Guidelines* are statements that help IS auditors better understand how ISACA standards can be implemented.

The ISACA Code of Professional Ethics encompasses the standards and guidelines through the requirement of proper professional behavior.

Risk Analysis

In the context of an audit, a *risk analysis* is the activity used to determine the areas that warrant additional examination and analysis.

In the absence of a risk analysis, an IS auditor is likely to follow his or her "gut instinct" and apply additional scrutiny in areas where he or she *feels* risks are higher. Alternatively, an IS auditor may give all areas of an audit equal weighting, putting equal resources into low-risk areas and high-risk areas. Either way, the result is that an IS auditor's focus is not necessarily on the areas where risks really are higher. This results in a disservice to the audit client.

Better audits are risk-driven. That is, some method of risk analysis is performed to determine which controls, activities, processes, or locations warrant additional attention, and to determine the areas that are deemed to be lower risk, requiring less attention. The factors that contribute to a risk determination include

- Value or criticality of a process, system, or business unit
- Focus of regulatory burden
- History of security events
- Results of prior audits

 NOTE Although the performance of a risk analysis is not as empirical as, say, the observation of a system to determine whether it has specific configuration settings, basing risk on a risk analysis is likely to be more consistent than basing it on gut instinct. The ISACA Risk IT Framework, discussed a bit later, gives details on performing risk analysis.

Auditors' Risk Analysis and the Corporate Risk Management Program

A risk analysis that is carried out by IS auditors is distinct and separate from risk analysis that is performed as part of the corporate risk management program, which carries out risk analysis using different personnel and for somewhat differing reasons. A comparison of IS auditor and IS management risk analysis is shown in Table 3-1.

 NOTE In Table 3-1, I am not attempting to show a *polarity* of focus and results, but instead a *tendency* for focus based on the differing missions and objectives of IS audit and IS management.

Activity	IS Audit Focus Tendency	IS Management Focus Tendency
Perspective	Objective	Subjective
Focus of risk assessment	All areas of potential risk	Existing controls
Identify a high risk in an existing control	Additional audit scrutiny on the control during the audit	Continue operating control
Identify a high risk; no existing control	Additional audit scrutiny on the activity as though control exists; recommend creation of control	Create and operate control*

* Many organizations do not look for risks outside of their control frameworks; this can result in risks that are overlooked altogether.

Table 3-1 Comparison of IS Audit and IS Management Risk Analysis

Figure 3-3
The ISACA Risk
IT Framework
high-level
components

The ISACA Risk IT Framework

Auditors' risk analysis and corporate risk management can both be performed using the ISACA Risk IT Framework. This framework, which is depicted in Figure 3-3, approaches risk from the enterprise perspective, encompassing all types of business risk, including IT risk.

NOTE   Although the Risk IT Framework exists as a stand-alone standard, it is fully incorporated into the COBIT controls framework.

The Risk IT Framework consists of three primary activities:

- **Risk governance**   Ensure that IT risk is integrated into the organization's enterprise risk management (ERM) program.
- **Risk evaluation**   Provide a framework of processes for performing risk assessments against business assets and explained in business terms.
- **Risk response**   Provide a framework of processes for responding to identified risks through reporting and risk treatment.

Like other business frameworks, the Risk IT Framework contains detailed top-down explanations of business processes and includes references to COBIT, ISACA audit standards, and Val IT—another ISACA framework concerned with achieving business value from IT investments.

The Risk IT Framework is available from ISACA at www.isaca.org/riskit.

EXAM TIP   ISACA does not require CISA candidates to memorize the Risk IT Framework, but candidates should understand its importance and purpose.

Evaluating Business Processes

The first phase of a risk analysis is an evaluation of business processes to determine the purpose, importance, and effectiveness of business activities. Even though parts of a risk analysis may focus on technology, remember that technology exists to support business processes, not the other way around.

When a risk analysis starts with a focus on business processes, it is appropriate that the auditor consider the entire process and not just the technology that supports it. When an auditor examines business processes, it is essential that he or she obtain all available business process documentation, including the following:

- **Charter or mission statement**   Often, an organization will develop and publish a high-level document that describes the process in its most basic terms. This usually includes the reason that the process exists and how it contributes to the organization's overall goals and objectives.

- **Process architecture**   A complex process may have several procedures, flows of information (in electronic form or otherwise), internal and external parties that perform functions, assets that support the process, resources required, and the locations and nature of records. In a strictly IT-centric perspective, this would be a data flow diagram or an entity-relationship diagram, but starting with either of those would be too narrow a focus. Instead, it is necessary to look at the *entire* process, with the broadest view of its functions and connections with other processes and parties.

- **Procedures**   Looking closer at the process will reveal individual procedures—documents that describe the individual steps taken to perform activities that are part of the overall process. Procedure documents usually describe who (if not by name, then by title or department) performs what functions with what tools or systems. Procedures will cite business records that may be faxes, reports, databases, phone records, application transactions, and so on.

- **Records**   Business records contain the events that take place within a business process. Records will take many forms, including faxes, computer reports, electronic worksheets, database transactions, receipts, canceled checks, and e-mail messages.

- **Information system support**   When processes are supported by information systems, it is necessary that the auditor examine all available documents that describe information systems that support business processes. Examples of documentation are architecture diagrams, requirements documents (which were used to build, acquire, or configure the system), computer-run procedures, network diagrams, database schemas, and so on.

In addition to reviewing documentation, the auditor must interview personnel involved with each process so that they can describe their understanding of the process, its procedures, and other relevant details. The auditor can then compare descriptions from individuals with details in process and procedure documents. This will help the auditor understand the degree to which processes and procedures are performed consistently and in harmony with documentation.

Once the IS auditor has obtained business documents and interviewed personnel, he or she can begin to identify and understand any risk areas that may exist in the process.

NOTE The risk analysis method described here is no different from the risk analysis that takes place during the business impact assessment phase in a disaster recovery project, covered in Chapter 5.

Identifying Business Risks

The process of identifying business risks is partly analytical and partly based on the auditor's experience and judgment. An auditor will usually consider both within the single activity of risk identification.

An auditor will usually perform a *threat analysis* to identify and catalog risks. A threat analysis is an activity whereby the auditor considers a large body of possible threats and selects those that have some reasonable possibility of occurrence, however small. In a threat analysis, the auditor will consider each threat and document a number of facts about each, including

- **Probability of occurrence** This may be expressed in qualitative (high, medium, low) or quantitative (percentage or number of times per year) terms. The probability should be as realistic as possible, recognizing the fact that actuarial data on business risk is difficult to obtain and more difficult to interpret. Here, an experienced auditor's judgment is required to establish a reasonable probability.

- **Impact** This is a short description, from a few words to a couple of sentences, of the results if the threat is actually realized.

- **Loss** This is usually a quantified and estimated loss should the threat actually occur. This figure might be a loss of revenue per day (or week or month) or the replacement cost for an asset, for example.

- **Possible mitigating controls** This is a list of one or more countermeasures that can reduce the probability or the impact of the threat, or both.

- **Potential for transfer** This is an analysis of the potential for transferring risk to another party, such as an insurance company.

- **Countermeasure cost and effort** The cost and effort to implement each countermeasure should be identified, either with a high-medium-low qualitative figure or a quantitative estimate.

- **Updated probability of occurrence** With each mitigating control, a new probability of occurrence should be cited. A different probability, one for each mitigating control, should be specified.

- **Updated impact** With each mitigating control, a new impact of occurrence should be described. For specific threats and countermeasures, the impact may be the same, but for some threats, it may be different. For example, for a threat of fire, a mitigating control may be an inert gas fire suppression system. The new impact (probably just downtime and cleanup) will be much different from the initial impact (probably water damage from a sprinkler system).

The auditor will put all of this information into a chart (or electronic spreadsheet) to permit further analysis and the establishment of conclusions—primarily, which threats are most likely to occur and which ones have the greatest potential impact on the organization.

Because it is not the usual role of auditors to suggest solutions to risks, auditors sometimes forego the analysis of countermeasures. A more likely outcome is the identification of high-risk controls that warrant additional audit scrutiny.

 TIP　The establishment of a list of threats, along with their probability of occurrence and impact, depends heavily on the experience of the IS auditor and the resources available to him or her.

Risk Mitigation

The actual mitigation of risks addressed in the risk assessment is the implementation of one or more of the countermeasures identified in the risk assessment. In simple terms, mitigation could be as easy as a small adjustment in a process or procedure, or it could be a significant project to introduce new controls in the form of system upgrades, new components, or new procedures.

When the IS auditor is conducting a risk analysis prior to an audit, risk mitigation may take the form of additional audit scrutiny on certain activities during the audit. Such subsequent analysis will give the IS auditor additional insight about the effectiveness of high-risk controls: a control that the auditor identified as high risk could end up performing well, while other, lower risk activities could actually be the cause of control failures. Determining which of the two represents higher risk to the organization requires further analysis.

Additional audit scrutiny could take several forms, including one or more of the following:

- More time spent in inquiry and observation
- More personnel interviews
- Higher sampling rates
- Additional tests
- Re-performance of some control activities to confirm accuracy or completeness
- Corroboration interviews
- Peer reviews of audit work

Countermeasures Assessment

Depending upon the severity of an identified risk, mitigation could also take the form of additional (or improved) controls, even prior to (or despite the results of) the audit itself. The new or changed control may be major or minor, and the time and effort required to implement it could range from almost trivial to a significant project.

The cost and effort required to implement a new control (or whatever the counter-measure is that is designed to reduce the probability or impact of a threat) should be determined before it is implemented. It probably does not make sense to spend $10,000 to protect an asset worth $100—unless, of course, there was considerable revenue or organizational reputation also associated with that $100 asset.

NOTE   The effort required to implement a control countermeasure should be commensurate with the level of risk reduction expected from the countermeasure. A quantified risk analysis may be needed if the cost and effort seem high, especially when compared to the value of the asset being protected.

Monitoring

After countermeasures are implemented, the IS auditor will need to reassess the controls through additional testing. If the control includes any self-monitoring or measuring, the IS auditor should examine those records to determine whether there is any visible effect of the countermeasures.

The auditor may need to repeat audit activities to determine the effectiveness of coun-termeasures. For example, additional samples selected after the countermeasure is imple-mented can be examined and the rate of exceptions compared to periods before the countermeasure's implementation.

Controls

Controls are the policies, procedures, mechanisms, systems, and other measures designed to reduce risk and assure desired outcomes. An organization develops controls to ensure that its business objectives will be met, risks will be reduced, and errors will be prevented or corrected.

Controls are used in two primary ways in an organization: they are created to ensure the occurrence of desired events and to help prevent unwanted events.

Control Classification

Several types, classes, and categories of controls are discussed in this section. Figure 3-4 depicts this control classification.

Types of Controls

The three types of controls are physical, technical, and administrative:

- **Physical**   These types of controls exist in the tangible, physical world. Examples of physical controls are video surveillance, bollards, and fences.
- **Technical**   Sometimes called *logical* controls, these controls are implemented in the form of information systems and are usually intangible. Examples of technical controls include encryption, computer access controls, and audit logs.

Figure 3-4
Control classification shows types, classes, and categories of controls.

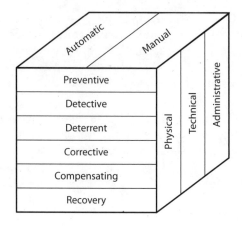

- **Administrative**   Also referred to as *managerial* controls, these are the policies and procedures that require or forbid certain activities. An example of an administrative control is a policy that forbids personal use of information systems for business purposes.

EXAM TIP   ISACA does not expressly use the terms "type," "class," or "category" to describe and distinguish the variety of controls and their basic characteristics. These terms are used in this book to highlight the multidimensional nature of controls and how they can be understood and classified. Like other constructs, these are models that better enable us to envision how controls operate and are used.

Classes of Controls

There are six classes of controls:

- **Preventive**   This type of control is used to prevent the occurrence of an unwanted event. Examples of preventive controls are computer login screens (which *prevent* unauthorized persons from accessing information), keycard systems (which *prevent* unauthorized persons from entering a building or workspace), and encryption (which *prevents* persons lacking an encryption key from reading encrypted data transmitted over an open network or stored in a public file share).

- **Detective**   This type of control is used to record both wanted and unwanted events. A detective control cannot enforce an activity (whether it is desired or undesired), but can only record whether, and how, the event occurred. Examples of detective controls include video surveillance and audit logs.

- **Deterrent**   This type of control exists to convince potential perpetrators not to perform some unwanted activity. Examples of deterrent controls include security guards, guard dogs, warning signs, and visible video surveillance cameras and monitors.

NOTE   Auditors and security professionals usually prefer preventive controls over detective controls, because preventive controls actually block unwanted events. Likewise, auditors prefer detective controls to deterrent controls, because detective controls record events while deterrent controls do not. However, there are often circumstances where cost, resource, or technical limitations force an organization to accept a detective control when it would prefer a preventive one. For example, there is no practical way to build a control that would prevent criminals from entering a bank, but a detective control (security cameras) would record what they did after they arrived.

- **Corrective**   This type of control is activated (manually or automatically) after some unwanted event has occurred. An example of a corrective control is an act of improving a process when it was found to be defective.
- **Compensating**   This type of control is enacted because some other direct control cannot be used. For example, a video surveillance system can be a compensating control when it is implemented to compensate for the lack of a stronger detective control, such as a keycard access system. A compensating control addresses the risk related to the original control. Note that the PCI-DSS requires the use of compensating controls when a control cannot be implemented for business, technical, or economic reasons.
- **Recovery**   This type of control is used to restore the state of a system or asset to its pre-incident state. An example of a recovery control is the use of a tool to remove a virus from a computer.

Auditors need to understand one key difference between preventive and deterrent controls: a deterrent control requires knowledge of the control by the potential violator, and it works only if they know it exists; a preventive control works regardless of whether or not the potential violator is aware of it.

NOTE   Many controls can be included in more than one class. For example, a video surveillance camera can be considered both a detective control (because it is part of a system that records events) and a deterrent control (because its visibility is designed to discourage persons from committing unwanted acts). Also, an audit log can be considered both a detective and a compensating control—detective because it records events and compensating because it may compensate for the lack of a stronger preventive control, such as a user IDs and password access control. In addition, the organization of controls described in this section is not according to any published standard.

Categories of Controls

There are two categories of controls:

- **Automatic**   This type of control performs its function with little or no human judgment or decision making. Examples of automatic controls include a login page on an application that cannot be circumvented and a security door that automatically locks after someone walks through the doorway.

- **Manual**   This type of control requires a human to operate it. A manual control may be subject to a higher rate of errors than an automatic control. An example of a manual control is a monthly review of computer user activity.

 NOTE   IS auditors and security professionals often prefer automatic controls to manual ones, because automatic controls are typically less prone to error. However, there are often circumstances in which an organization must settle for a manual control because of cost or some other factor, such as the requirement for human decision and intervention, perhaps during an emergency situation or disaster, for example.

Internal Control Objectives

Internal control objectives are statements of desired states or outcomes from business operations. Example control objectives include

- Protection of IT assets
- Accuracy of transactions
- Confidentiality and privacy
- Availability of IT systems
- Controlled changes to IT systems
- Compliance with corporate policies

Control objectives are the foundation for controls. For each control objective, one or more controls will exist to ensure the realization of the control objective. For example, the "Availability of IT Systems" control objective will be met with several controls, including

- IT systems will be continuously monitored, and any interruptions in availability will result in alerts sent to appropriate personnel.
- IT systems will have resource-measuring capabilities.
- IT management will review capacity reports monthly and adjust resources accordingly.
- IT systems will have anti-malware controls that are monitored by appropriate staff.

Together, these four (or more) controls contribute to the overall control objective on IT system availability. Similarly, the other control objectives will have one or more controls that will ensure their realization.

TIP   Control objectives should be established prior to the controls themselves.

IS Control Objectives

IS control objectives resemble ordinary control objectives but exist in the context of information systems. Examples of IS control objectives include

- Protection of information from unauthorized personnel
- Protection of information from unauthorized modification
- Integrity of operating systems
- Controlled and managed changes to information systems
- Controlled and managed development of application software

An organization will probably have several additional IS control objectives on other essential topics such as malware, availability, and resource management.

Like ordinary control objectives, IS control objectives will be supported by one or more controls.

EXAM TIP   CISA candidates are not required to memorize COBIT or other frameworks, but familiarity with them will help the CISA candidate understand how they contribute to effective IT governance and control.

The COBIT Controls Framework

To ensure that IT is aligned with business objectives, the COBIT controls framework of five principles and 37 processes is an industry-wide standard. The five principles are

- Meeting Stakeholder Needs
- Covering the Enterprise End-to-End
- Applying a Single, Integrated Framework
- Enabling a Holistic Approach
- Separating Governance from Management

COBIT contains more than 1100 control activities to support these principles.

Established in 1996 by ISACA and the IT Governance Institute, COBIT is the result of industry-wide consensus by managers, auditors, and IT users. Today, COBIT is accepted as a best-practices IT process and control framework.

Starting with Version 5, COBIT has absorbed ISACA's Risk IT Framework and Val IT Framework.

General Computing Controls

An IS organization supporting many applications and services will generally have some controls that are specific to each individual application. However, IS will also have a set of controls, usually called *general computing controls* (GCCs), that applies across *all* of its applications and services.

An organization's GCCs are general in nature and are often implemented in different ways on different information systems, based upon their individual capabilities and limitations, as well as applicability. Examples of GCCs include

- Applications require unique user IDs and strong passwords.
- Passwords are encrypted while stored and transmitted and are not displayed.
- Highly sensitive information, such as bank account numbers, is encrypted when stored and transmitted.
- All administrative actions are logged, and logs are protected from tampering.

Readers who are familiar with information systems technology will realize that these GCCs will be implemented differently across different types of information systems. Specific capabilities and limitations, for example, will result in somewhat different capabilities for password complexity and data encryption. Unless an organization is using really old information systems, the preceding four GCCs can probably be implemented everywhere in an IS environment. *How* they are implemented is the subject of the next section.

IS Controls

GCCs are implemented across a variety of information technologies. Each GCC is mapped to a specific IS control on each system type, where it is implemented. In other words, IS controls describe the implementation details for GCCs.

For example, a GCC for password management can be implemented through several IS controls—one for each type of technology platform in use in the organization: one for a central authentication service, one for Linux servers, one for network devices, and one for each application that performs its own access management. Those specific IS controls would describe implementation details that reflect the capabilities and limitations of each respective platform.

Performing an Audit

An audit is a systematic and repeatable process whereby a competent and independent professional evaluates one or more controls, interviews personnel, obtains and analyzes evidence, and develops a written opinion on the effectiveness of the control(s).

An IS audit, then, is an audit of information systems and the processes that support them. An IS auditor interviews personnel, gathers and analyzes evidence, and delivers a written opinion on the effectiveness of controls implemented in information systems.

An auditor cannot just begin an audit. Rather, audits need to be planned events. Formal planning is required that includes the following:

- **Purpose** The IS auditor and the auditee must establish a *reason* why an audit is to be performed. The purpose for a particular audit could be to determine the level of compliance to a particular law, regulation, standard, or contract. Another reason could be to determine whether specific control deficiencies identified in past audits have been remediated. Still another reason is to determine the level of compliance to a new law or standard that the organization may be subject to in the future.

- **Scope** The auditor and the auditee must also establish the *scope* of the audit. Often, the audit's purpose will make the scope evident, but not always. Scope may be multidimensional: it could be a given period (records spanning a start date and end date may comprise the body of evidence), geography (systems in a particular region or locale), technology (systems using a specific operating system, database, application, or other aspect), business process (systems that support specific processes such as accounting, order entry, or customer support), or segment of the organization.

- **Risk analysis** To know which areas require the greatest amount of attention, the IS auditor needs to be familiar with the levels of *risk* associated with the domain being audited. Two different perspectives of risk may be needed: First, the IS auditor needs to know the relative levels of risk among the different aspects of the domain being audited so that audit resources can be allocated accordingly. For example, if the audit is on an enterprise resource planning (ERP) system and the auditor knows that the accounts receivable function has been problematic in the past, the IS auditor will probably want to devote somewhat more resources and time on the accounts receivable function than on others. Second, the IS auditor needs to know about the absolute level of risk across the entire domain being audited. For example, if this is an audit to determine compliance to new legislation, the overall risk could be very high if the consequences of noncompliance are high. Both aspects of risk enable the IS auditor to plan accordingly.

- **Audit procedures** The purpose and scope of the audit may help to define the procedures that will be required to perform the audit. Requirements for a compliance audit, for example, may involve specific rules on sample sizes and sampling techniques, or they may call for auditors with specific qualifications to perform the audit. A compliance audit may also specify criteria for determining whether a particular finding constitutes a deficiency or not. There may also be rules for materiality.

- **Resources** The IS auditor must determine what resources are needed and available for the audit. In an external audit, the auditee (which is a client organization) may have a maximum budget figure available. For an external or internal audit, the IS auditor needs to determine the number of staff hours that will be required in the audit and the various skills required. Other resources that may be needed include specialized tools to gather or analyze information obtained from information systems—for example, an analysis program to process the roles and permissions in a database management system to identify high-risk areas. To a great degree, the purpose and scope of the audit will determine the resources that are required to complete it.

- **Schedule**   The IS auditor needs to develop an audit schedule that will allow enough time for interviews, data collection and analysis, and report generation. However, the schedule could also come in the form of a constraint, meaning the audit must be complete by a certain date. If the IS auditor is given a deadline, he or she will need to see how the audit activities can be made to fit within that period. If the date is too aggressive, the IS auditor will need to discuss the matter with the auditee to make required adjustments in scope, resources, or schedule.

Appendix A is devoted to a pragmatic approach to conducting professional audits.

Audit Objectives

Audit objectives are the specific goals for an audit. Generally, the objective of an audit is to determine whether controls exist and are effective in some specific aspect of business operations in an organization. Generally, an audit is performed as required by regulations, compliance, or legal obligations. It may also be performed as the result of a serious incident or event.

Depending on the subject and nature of the audit, the auditor may personally examine the controls and related evidence, or the auditor may instead focus on the business content that is processed by the controls. In other words, if the focus of an audit is an organization's accounting system, the auditor may focus on financial transactions in the system to see how they affect financial bookkeeping. Or the auditor could focus on the IS processes that support the operation of the financial accounting system. Formal audit objectives should make such a distinction so that the auditor has a sound understanding of the objectives. This tells the auditor what to examine during the audit. Of course, knowing the type of audit to be undertaken helps too; this is covered in the next section.

Types of Audits

The scope, purpose, and objectives of an audit will determine the type of audit that will be performed. IS auditors need to understand each type of audit, including the procedures that are used for each:

- **Operational audit**   This type of audit is an examination of the existence and effectiveness of IS controls, security controls, or business controls. The focus of an operational audit is usually the operation of one or more controls; it could concentrate on the IS management of a business process or on the business process itself. The scope of an operational audit is shaped to meet audit objectives. Do note that, *in this context*, an *operational audit* is the audit of a business process supporting the information system, *not* the business process supported *by* the information system. The latter would not be an IS audit but an audit of a business process.

- **Financial audit**   This type of audit is an examination of the organization's accounting system, including accounting department processes and procedures. The typical objective of a financial audit is to determine whether business controls are sufficient to ensure the integrity of financial statements.

- **Integrated audit**   This type of audit combines an operational audit and a financial audit in order for the auditor to gain a complete understanding of the entire environment's integrity. Such an audit will closely examine accounting department processes, procedures, and records, as well as the IS applications that support the accounting department. Virtually every organization uses a computerized accounting system for management of its financial records; the computerized accounting system and all of the supporting infrastructure (database management system, operating system, networks, workstations, and so on) will be examined to determine whether the IS department has the entire environment under adequate control.

- **IS audit**   This type of audit is a detailed examination of most or all of an IS department's operations. An IS audit looks at IT governance to determine whether IS is aligned with overall organization goals and objectives. The audit also looks closely at all of the major IS processes, including service delivery, change and configuration management, security management, systems development life cycle, business relationship and supplier management, and incident and problem management. This audit will determine whether each control objective and control is effective and operating properly.

- **Administrative audit**   This type of audit is an examination of operational efficiency within some segment of the organization.

- **Compliance audit**   This type of audit is performed to determine the level and degree of compliance to a law, regulation, standard, or internal control. If a particular law or standard requires an external audit, the compliance audit may have to be performed by approved or licensed external auditors; for example, a U.S. public company financial audit must be performed by a public accounting firm, and a PCI audit must be performed by a licensed QSA (qualified security assessor). If, however, the law or standard does not explicitly require audits, the organization may still want to perform one-time or regular audits to determine the level of compliance to the law or standard. This type of audit may be performed by internal or external auditors and typically is performed to help management better understand the level of compliance risk.

- **Forensic audit**   This type of audit is usually performed by an IS auditor or a forensic specialist in support of an anticipated or active legal proceeding. To withstand cross-examination and to avoid having evidence being ruled inadmissible, a forensic audit requires that strict procedures be followed, including the preservation of evidence and a chain of custody of evidence.

- **Fraud audit**   This audit is designed to reveal fraud and other business irregularities.

- **Service provider audit** Because many organizations outsource critical activities to third parties, often these third-party service organizations will undergo one or more external audits to increase customer confidence in the integrity of the third-party organization's services. In the United States, a Statement on Standards for Attestation Engagements No. 18, *Reporting on Controls at a Service Organization* (SSAE 18) can be performed on a service provider's operations and the audit report transmitted to customers of the service provider. SSAE 18 superseded SSAE 16 in 2016, which superseded the Statement of Accounting Standards No. 70 (SAS 70) audit in 2011. The SSAE 18 standard was developed by the American Institute of Certified Public Accountants (AICPA) for the purpose of auditing third-party service organizations that perform financial services on behalf of their corporate customers.

Internal and External Audits

The terms "internal audit" and "external audit" refer to the relationship between auditor and auditee, and not to the types of audits discussed in this section.

- **Internal audit** This audit is performed by personnel employed by the auditee organization. Internal auditors typically still have a degree of independence through their locations on the org chart.
- **External audit** This audit is performed by auditors who are not employees of the auditee. Typically, external auditors are employees of an audit firm.

There is, of course, some gray area here: in a large organization such as a holding company, auditors who are employees of the holding company may be considered as external auditors to the auditee.

Also, some organizations outsource the internal audit function, which means that the persons performing internal audit are not employees of the organization, but instead are consultants or contractors. This can be a source of confusion, based on appearances. What matters here is the specific audit function and how it is carried out, and not so much whether the persons performing it are employees or not.

TIP SSAE 18 is closely aligned with the global standard International Auditing and Assurance Standards Board (IAASB) *International Standard on Assurance Engagements 3402, Assurance Reports on Controls at a Service Organization* (ISAE 3402).

- **Pre-audit** While not technically an audit, a pre-audit is an examination of business processes, IS systems, and business records in anticipation of an upcoming external audit. Usually, an organization will undergo a pre-audit to get a better idea of its compliance to a law, regulation, or standard prior to an actual compliance audit. An organization can use the results of a pre-audit to implement corrective measures, thereby improving the outcome of the real audit.

Compliance vs. Substantive Testing

It is important for IS auditors to understand the distinction between compliance testing and substantive testing. These two types of testing are defined here:

- **Compliance testing**   This type of testing is used to determine whether control procedures have been properly designed and implemented and are operating properly. For example, an IS auditor may examine business processes, such as the systems development life cycle, change management, or configuration management, to determine whether information systems environments are properly managed.

- **Substantive testing**   This type of testing is used to determine the accuracy and integrity of transactions that flow through processes and information systems. For instance, an IS auditor may create test transactions and trace them through the environment, examining them at each stage until their completion.

IS audits sometimes involve both compliance testing and substantive testing. The audit objectives that are established will determine whether compliance testing, substantive testing, or both will be required.

Audit Methodology and Project Management

Like any business endeavor that involves the development of a plan, identification of resources, and the establishment of scope, procedures, and records, audits are projects that need to be managed as such. The reasons for employing formal project planning for audits include

- Development and management of a schedule and timelines
- Identification of resources
- Management of turnaround time for documentation and evidence requests
- Management of the time required for analysis and reporting writing
- Management of the time required for audit client report review, response, and acceptance

Project management principles and methodologies should be used throughout an audit, including periodic status meetings and status reports, tracking of schedule and activities, and retention of records.

Auditors do not always make good project managers. This may be the best reason to employ the services of project managers during larger audits.

Audit Methodology

An *audit methodology* is the set of audit procedures that is used to accomplish a set of audit objectives. An organization that regularly performs audits should develop formal methodologies so that those audits are performed consistently, even when carried out by different personnel.

The phases of a typical audit methodology are described in the remainder of this section.

Audit Subject Determine the business process, information system, or other domain to be audited. For instance, an IS auditor might be auditing an IT change control process, an IT service desk ticketing system, or the activities performed by a software development department.

Audit Objective Identify the purpose of the audit. For example, the audit may be required by a law, regulation, standard, or business contract. Or the audit may be needed to determine compliance with internal control objectives to measure control effectiveness.

Type of Audit Identify the type of audit that is to be performed. This may be an operational audit, financial audit, integrated audit, administrative audit, compliance audit, forensic audit, fraud audit, or a security provider audit.

Audit Scope The business process, department, or application that is the subject of the audit should be identified. Usually, a span of time needs to be identified as well so that activities or transactions during that period can be examined.

 NOTE The *subject* of an audit is a broad definition, whereas the *scope* further defines exactly which processes, locations, and systems will be audited.

Pre-Audit Planning Here, the auditor needs to obtain information about the audit that will enable him or her to establish the audit plan. Information needed includes

- Location or locations that need to be visited
- A list of the applications to be examined
- The personnel to be interviewed
- The technologies supporting each application
- Policies, standards, and diagrams that describe the environment and its requirements
- Information about business processes supported by the application

This and other information will enable the IS auditor to determine the resources and skills required to examine and evaluate processes and information systems. The IS auditor will be able to establish an audit schedule and will have a good idea of the types of evidence that are needed. The IS auditor may be able to make advance requests for certain other types of evidence even before the on-site phase of the audit begins.

For an audit with a risk-based approach, the auditor has a couple of options:

- Precede the audit itself with a risk assessment to determine which processes or controls warrant additional audit scrutiny.
- Gather information about the organization and historic events to discover risks that warrant additional audit scrutiny.

Audit Statement of Work   For an external audit, the IS auditor may need to develop a statement of work or an engagement letter that describes the audit purpose, scope, duration, and costs. The auditor may require a written approval from the client before audit work can officially begin.

Audit Procedures Development   Using information obtained regarding audit objectives and scope, the IS auditor can now develop procedures for this audit. For each objective and control to be tested, the IS auditor can specify

- A list of people to interview
- Inquiries to make during each interview
- Documentation (policies, procedures, and other documents) to request during each interview
- Audit tools to use
- Sampling rates and methodologies
- How and where evidence will be archived
- How evidence will be evaluated
- How findings will be reported

Communication Plan   The IS auditor will develop a communication plan to keep the IS auditor's management, as well as the auditee's management, informed throughout the audit project. The communication plan may contain one or more of the following:

- A list of evidence requested, usually in the form of a PBC (provided by client) list, which is typically a worksheet that lists specific documents or records and the names of personnel who can provide them (or who provided them in a prior audit).
- Regular written status reports that include activities performed since the last status report, upcoming activities, and any significant findings that may require immediate attention.
- Regular status meetings in which audit progress, issues, and other matters may be discussed in person or via conference call.
- Contact information for both IS auditor and auditee so that both parties can contact each other quickly if needed.

Report Preparation   The IS auditor needs to develop a plan that describes how the audit report will be prepared. This will include the format and the content of the report, as well as the manner in which findings will be established and documented.

The IS auditor will need to ensure that the audit report complies with all applicable audit standards, including ISACA IS audit standards.

If the audit report requires internal review, the IS auditor will need to identify the parties who will perform the review and make sure that they will be available at the time when the IS auditor expects to complete the final draft of the audit report.

Wrap-up   The IS auditor needs to perform a number of tasks at the conclusion of the audit, including the following:

- Deliver the report to the auditee.
- Schedule a closing meeting so that the results of the audit can be discussed with the auditee and so that the IS auditor can collect feedback.
- For external audits, send an invoice to the auditee.
- Collect and archive all work papers. Enter their existence in a document management system so that they can be retrieved later, if needed, and to ensure their destruction when they have reached the end of their retention life.
- Update PBC documents if the IS auditor anticipates that the audit will be performed again in the future.
- Collect feedback from the auditee and convey to audit staff as needed.

Post-Audit Follow-up   After a given period (which could range from days to months), the IS auditor should contact the auditee to determine what progress the auditee has made on the remediation of any audit findings. There are several good reasons for doing this:

- It establishes a tone of concern for the auditee organization (and an interest in its success) and demonstrates that the auditor is taking the audit process seriously.
- It helps to establish a dialogue whereby the auditor can help auditee management work through any needed process or technology changes as a result of the audit.
- It helps the auditor better understand management's commitment to the audit process and to continuous improvement.
- For an external auditor, it improves goodwill and the prospect for repeat business.

 NOTE   An audit methodology is a process. Like any process, it should be defined in an end-to-end document that is reviewed from time to time.

Audit Evidence

Evidence is the information collected by the auditor during the course of the audit project. The contents and reliability of the evidence obtained are used by the IS auditor to reach conclusions on the effectiveness of controls and control objectives. The IS auditor needs to understand how to evaluate various types of evidence and how (and if) it can be used to support audit findings.

The auditor will collect many kinds of evidence during an audit, including

- Observations
- Written notes

- Correspondence
- Independent confirmations from other auditors
- Internal process and procedure documentation
- Business records

When the IS auditor examines evidence, he or she must consider several characteristics about the evidence that will contribute to its weight and reliability. These characteristics include the following:

- **Independence of the evidence provider**   The IS auditor needs to determine the independence of the party providing evidence. The auditor will place more weight on evidence provided by an independent party than on evidence provided by the auditee. For instance, phone and banking records obtained directly from phone and banking organizations will be given more credence than an organization's own records (unless original statements are also provided). Some auditees may be able and inclined to "doctor" audit evidence, giving the appearance of process effectiveness.

- **Qualifications of the evidence provider**   The IS auditor needs to consider the qualifications of the person providing evidence. This is particularly true when evidence is in the form of highly technical information, such as source code, system configuration settings, or database extracts. The quality of the evidence will rest partly upon the evidence provider's ability to explain the source of the evidence, how it was produced, and how it is used. Similarly, the qualifications of the auditor come into play, as he or she will need to be able to understand the nature of the evidence thoroughly and be familiar enough with the technology to be able to determine its veracity. Some auditees like to "snowball" auditors by providing evidence that is irrelevant or incomplete, potentially to avoid disclosing details about controls that are ineffective.

- **Objectivity**   Objective evidence may be considerably more reliable than subjective evidence. An audit log, for instance, is quite objective, whereas an auditee's description or opinion of the audit log is less objective.

- **Timing**   The IS auditor needs to understand the availability of evidence in the systems being audited. Certain log files, extract files, debug files, and temporary files that may be of value during the examination of the system may be available only for short periods before they are recycled or removed. Often, intermediate files are not backed up or retained for long periods. For instance, Dynamic Host Configuration Protocol (DHCP) lease logs may be available only for a few hours or days. When tracing transactions through a system during substantive testing, an IS auditor will need to understand early on what files or intermediate data should be retrieved to be able to analyze the data later after those intermediate files have been cycled out.

NOTE The IS auditor needs to gain a thorough understanding of the sufficiency of evidence gathered using ISACA audit standards 1203, Performance and Supervision, and 1205, Evidence.

Gathering Evidence

The IS auditor must understand and be experienced in the methods and techniques used to gather evidence during an audit. The methods and techniques used most often in audits include the following:

- **Organization chart review**   The IS auditor should request a current org chart, as well as the job descriptions of key personnel. This will help the auditor to understand management, control, and reporting structures within the organization.

- **Review of department and project charters**   These documents describe the roles and responsibilities of the IS organization overall, as well as for specific departments within IS. The charters for any recent significant projects should be requested as well to understand newer objectives that could represent adjustments in organizational behavior. If the audit is going to focus on applications used by other departments, the auditor should request those departments' charters and descriptions, which will help the auditor better understand those departments' functions, roles, and responsibilities. In the absence of a formal charter, the auditor will need to interview a number of personnel to gain a consistent view of a department's or project's purpose, roles and responsibilities, and authority.

- **Review of third-party contracts and service level agreements (SLAs)**   Even if they are not a focus of the audit, certain third-party contracts and SLAs may provide additional insight into the workings and culture of the IS organization and specific systems and business processes.

- **Review of IS policies and procedures**   The auditor should obtain and review IS policies as well as process and procedure documents that are related to the audit. This will help the auditor better understand the tone and direction set by management and will provide information about how well organized the IS organization really is.

- **Review of risk register (also known as a risk ledger)**   The auditor should obtain the organization's risk register, which will provide insight into the kinds of risks identified by the organization.

- **Review of incident log**   The auditor should obtain the organization's security incident log. This will help the auditor understand the types of security incidents that have occurred, including those involving in-scope processes and systems.

- **Review of IS standards**   The auditor should obtain any IS standards documents to learn about current policy for vendors, products, methods, languages, and protocols in use. The auditor should review process and documentation standards as well to see how consistently the organization follows them; this will provide valuable insight into the discipline in the organization.

NOTE The IS auditor should pay attention to what IS charters, policies, and procedure documents do say, as well as what they don't say. He or she should perform corroborative interviews to determine whether these documents really define the organization's behavior or if they're just window dressing. This will help the auditor understand the maturity of the organization, a valuable insight that will be helpful when writing the audit report.

- **Review of IS system documentation**   If the subject of the audit (directly or indirectly) is an IS application, the auditor should obtain much of the project documentation that chronicles the development or acquisition of the system. This may include the following:
  - Feasibility study
  - Functional, technical, and security requirements
  - Requests for proposals (RFPs)/requests for information (RFIs)
  - Responses from vendors (at least the one chosen)
  - Evaluation of vendor responses
  - System design documentation, including data flow diagrams, entity-relationship diagrams, database schema, and so on
  - Test plans and results
  - Implementation guides and results
  - User manuals
  - Operations manuals
  - Business continuity plans
  - Changes made since initial release
  - Incidents and events
  - Reports of system stability, capacity, and availability
- **Personnel interviews (walkthroughs)**   The IS auditor should conduct walkthrough interviews with key personnel who can describe the function, design, use, and operation of the system. Rather than assume that all acquired documentation is absolutely complete and accurate, the auditor should ask open-ended questions to gain additional insight into *how well* the system really operates and how accurately the documentation describes the system in use and its operation. The auditor should develop questions in advance to keep the interview on track and to make sure that all topics are covered. The auditor should carefully select key questions and ask them of more than one individual to compare answers, which will provide more insight.

NOTE Some organizations may coach their personnel so that they do not provide any more than the minimum amount of information. An experienced auditor should recognize this and may need to get creative (without compromising ethics standards!) to get to key facts and circumstances. The IS auditor must always be polite, friendly, and request cooperation of each interviewee. He or she must always be truthful and never threaten any interviewee.

- **Re-performance** An auditor will create transactions to be executed by the process being audited, when practical, to confirm that the process produces expected results. Sometimes, however, re-performance is not feasible, in which case the auditor will have to observe planned/normal transactions critically to confirm the expected results.

- **Passive observation** When an IS auditor is embedded in an organization, people will "let their guard down" after they are accustomed to his or her presence. The auditor may be able to observe people being themselves and possibly will hear or see clues that will provide clear insights into the culture and tone of the organization.

Observing Personnel

It is rarely sufficient for an auditor to obtain and understand process documentation and be able to make judgments about the effectiveness of the process. Usually, the auditor will need to collect evidence in the form of observations to see how consistently a system's process documentation is actually followed. Following are some of the techniques used in observing personnel:

- **Real tasks** The auditor should request to see some IS functions actually being carried out. For example, if an auditor is examining user access management processes, he or she should request to observe the persons who manage user accounts to see how they perform their tasks. The auditor should compare the steps taken against procedure documentation and observe the configuration settings that the interviewee has made to determine whether they are being done according to procedure documents.

- **Skills and experience** The auditor should ask each interviewee about his or her career background to determine the interviewee's level of experience and career maturity. This will help the auditor to understand whether key responsibilities are in the hands of personnel who can really handle them.

- **Security awareness** The IS auditor should observe personnel to determine whether they are following security policies and procedures. The auditor can casually ask interviewees what they know about security procedures to determine whether the security awareness program is effective. This should implicitly be a part of every audit, even if not explicitly included in scope. Major deviations from policy or common sense could constitute deficiencies.

- **Segregation of duties**   The IS auditor should observe personnel to determine whether adequate segregation of duties (SOD) is in place. Lapses could include a user account administrator creating or changing a user account without official approval, or a systems engineer making a quick change on a system without going through the change management process or bypassing technical controls.

An experienced IS auditor will have a well-developed "sixth sense," an intuition about people that can be used to understand the people who execute procedures.

Sampling

Sampling refers to the technique that is used when it is not feasible to test an entire *population* of transactions. The objective of sampling is to select a portion of a population so that the characteristics observed will reflect the characteristics of the entire population.

There are several sampling methods including

- **Statistical sampling**   The IS auditor uses a technique of random or semi-random selection that will statistically reflect the entire population. The auditor will need to determine the size of the sample (usually expressed as a percentage of the entire population) so that the results obtained through testing will statistically reflect the entire population, where each event in the population has an equal chance of being selected.

- **Judgmental sampling (aka nonstatistical sampling)**   The IS auditor judgmentally and subjectively selects samples based on established criteria such as risk or materiality. For instance, when reviewing a list of user accounts to examine, the auditor can purposely select those users whose accounts represent higher risk than the accounts of others in the population.

- **Attribute sampling**   This technique is used to study the characteristics of a given population to answer the question, "How many?" The auditor selects a statistical sample and then examines the information. A specific attribute is chosen, and the samples are examined to see how many items have the characteristic and how many do not. For example, an auditor may test a list of terminated user accounts to see how many were terminated within 24 hours and how many were not. This is used to determine statistically the rate at which terminations are performed within 24 hours among the entire population.

- **Variable sampling**   This technique is used to determine statistically the characteristic of a given population to answer the question, "How much?" For example, an auditor who wants to know the total value of an inventory can select a sample and then statistically determine the total value in the entire population based on the total value of the sample.

- **Stop-or-go sampling**   This technique is used to permit sampling to stop at the earliest possible time. The IS auditor will use this technique when he or she believes that there is a low risk and a low rate of exceptions in the overall population.

- **Discovery sampling**   This technique is used when an IS auditor is trying to find at least one exception in a population. When the auditor is examining a population in which even a single exception would represent a high-risk situation (such as embezzlement or fraud), the auditor will recommend a more intensive investigation to determine whether additional exceptions exist.

- **Stratified sampling**   Here, the event population is divided into classes, or strata, based on the value of one of the attributes. Then samples are selected from each class, and results are developed from each class or combined into a single result. An example of where this could be used is a selection of purchase orders (POs), where the IS auditor wants to make sure that some of the extremely high-value and low-value POs will be selected to determine whether there is any statistical difference in the results in different classes.

When performing sampling, the IS auditor needs to understand several terms related to aspects of statistical sampling techniques:

- **Confidence coefficient**   Sometimes known as the reliability factor or confidence level, this is expressed as a percentage, as the probability that the sample selected actually represents the entire population. A confidence coefficient of 95 percent is considered high.

- **Sampling risk**   This is equal to 1 minus the confidence coefficient percentage. For example, if a given sample has a 93 percent confidence coefficient, the risk level is 7 percent (100 percent – 93 percent = 7 percent).

- **Precision**   This represents how closely the sample represents the entire population. A low precision figure means high accuracy, and a high precision figure means low accuracy. A smaller sample makes the precision higher, and the risk of exceptions in the entire population is higher.

- **Expected error rate**   This is an estimate that expresses the percentage of errors that may exist in the entire population. When the expected error rate is higher, the sample needs to be higher (because a population with a high rate of errors requires greater scrutiny). If the expected error rate is low, the sample can be smaller.

- **Sample mean**   This is the sum of all samples divided by the number of samples. This equals the average value of the sample.

- **Sample standard deviation**   This is a computation of the variance of sample values from the sample mean. This is a measurement of the "spread" of values in the sample.

- **Population standard deviation**   Within the entire evidence population, this is a computation of the variance of values from the mean. All other factors being equal, a larger population standard deviation means the auditor should select a larger set of samples.

- **Tolerable error rate**   This is the highest number of errors that can exist without a result being materially misstated.

NOTE   Part of the body of evidence in an audit is a description of how a sample was selected and why the particular sampling technique was used.

Reliance on the Work of Other Auditors

Audit departments and external auditors, like other IT service organizations, are challenged to find qualified audit professionals who understand all aspects of organizational technologies in use. Increased specialization in IT is resulting in auditors with increased technical knowledge in certain areas, and fewer auditors with all of the knowledge required to perform an audit. Third-party service providers usually do not permit customers to audit them; they instead rely on external auditors to perform audits and then make those audit reports available to customers. These and other factors are putting increasing pressure on organizations to outsource some auditing tasks (or entire audits) to third-party organizations and to rely upon audit reports from other sources.

When considering reliance upon other auditors, one must examine many potential issues, including

- Laws, regulations, standards, or contracts that may place restrictions on the use of third-party auditors
- Impact on risk
- Costs and the overhead required to manage external auditors
- Impact on audit schedule and reporting
- Impact on general and professional liability
- Audit standards and methodologies used by the third-party auditor
- Competence and experience of the third-party auditor
- Independence and objectivity of internal versus external auditors
- Methods for communication of audit issues and results
- Access by third-party auditor to internal records and systems
- Protection and privacy of information made available to external auditors
- Background checks, nondisclosure, and other agreements for third-party audit personnel
- Audit management controls used to manage external audit activities
- Compliance and/or compatibility with audit standards, regulations, and stipulations

Reliance on Third-Party Audit Reports

Another common setting for the reliance on third-party auditors occurs when an organization chooses to rely upon audit reports for an external service provider rather than audit the external service provider directly. A typical example is a case where an organization hires a payroll services provider that has its own SSAE 18 audit that was performed by qualified audit firms. The organization's own auditors will likely choose to rely on the payroll service provider's SSAE 18 audit rather than audit the payroll service provider directly.

From the service provider's point of view, the cost to commission an SSAE 18 audit and make the audit report available to its clients is less than the cost for even a small percentage of its customers to perform their own audits of the service provider's business.

 NOTE IS auditors should be familiar with ISACA audit guideline 2206, Using the Work of Other Experts, and standard 1203, Performance and Supervision, to manage the work performed by external auditors properly. Specific laws, regulations, or standards may also apply.

Audit Data Analytics

Data analytics techniques enable IS auditors to select and analyze potentially large data sets and use these techniques to determine control effectiveness. In the context of IS audits, data analytics represents a variety of computational techniques used to analyze larger volumes of audit data to assist IS auditors in determining control effectiveness. These techniques are described in this section.

The term *data analytics* may invoke visions of big data and data lakes used to obtain and analyze audit data, and this may be the situation at times. However, often there are far simpler situations where computational assistance in processing data is used. For example, programmatically cross-referencing badge access records with system logon data can help auditors detect potentially fraudulent user logins.

Audit data analytics can be performed using computer-assisted audit tools such as generalized audit software and continuous auditing. These topics are discussed next.

Computer-Assisted Audit and Automated Work Papers

When auditing complex information systems, IS auditors often need to obtain sample data from systems with a variety of operating systems, database management systems, record layouts, and processing methods. Auditors are turning to computer-assisted audit techniques (CAATs) to help them examine and evaluate data across these complex environments.

CAATs come in a variety of forms:

- **Direct extracts from database management systems** For off-the-shelf systems such as Oracle Financials and PeopleSoft Financials, auditors can obtain extracts from databases supporting these and other packaged applications and perform independent analysis on the data. Analytics software can then be run against extracted data to identify any transaction exceptions as well as fraud.

- **Test transactions** For standard financial and business management applications, auditors can prepare test transactions that will produce known, expected results. Such tests can determine the integrity of transaction processing by comparing test results with expected results.

- **Debugging and scanning software** Tools that reveal the details of transactions and data flow can help auditors better understand how transactions are processed by a system, to opine on their integrity and accuracy. Scanning software can be used to identify specific data in database management systems as well as unstructured data stores. Security scanning software can be used to identify known vulnerabilities in target systems. Code scanning software can examine application source code that will help reveal vulnerabilities and poor coding practices such as embedding login credentials in source code.

- **Test scripts** Tools that perform a variety of functions can be provided by an auditor and run on target systems. Such tools can reveal configuration details in operating systems, database management systems, and applications. A broad array of automated controls can be examined with test scripts.

When using CAATs, auditors need to document the evidence they obtain from systems and be able to link it to business transactions. Often, auditors will have to obtain several other items, including

- Application source code
- Online reports that correlate captured data to transactions and results
- Database schemas
- Data flow diagrams and flow charts
- Sample reports
- Operations procedures

Auditors should be able to stitch all these pieces back together to show a complete picture of the details behind business transactions.

Protecting Automated Work Papers

CAATs help IS auditors by making sampling easier and by capturing data that has varying degrees of persistence in an organization's application environment. That captured data will often be considered part of the body of work papers. Like the systems that are targets of audits, audit data needs to be protected to ensure its integrity. Controls such as the following need to be enacted to protect automated work papers:

- **Access control**   Only authorized persons (ideally, only the auditor) should have read access to automated work papers.
- **Protection from tampering and damage**   Automated work papers must be protected so that no person is able to change them, remove them, or threaten their integrity.
- **Backup**   Automated work papers should be included in data backups.
- **Encryption**   Automated work papers should be encrypted if they contain sensitive information. Effective key management procedures and controls must be in place.

Generalized Audit Software

IS auditors can use generalized audit software (GAS) to read and access data directly from database platforms and flat files. They can independently and directly acquire sample data from databases, which they can then analyze on a separate system. GAS has the ability to select samples, select data, and perform analysis on data. This can help the auditor better understand key data sets in a system to assist him or her in determining the integrity and accuracy of a system and the business transactions it supports.

Continuous Auditing

CAATs can also be used as part of a continuous audit approach, where samples are obtained automatically over long periods instead of just during audit engagements. This represents a paradigm shift from the traditional model of periodic sampling and reporting. To be truly effective, continuous auditing should include the following:

- Frequent notifications to auditors and control owners on audit results
- Triggers to notify auditors and control owners of control failures and other exceptions

There are several types of continuous auditing:

- **Audit hooks**   These components in software applications are used to provide additional transaction monitoring and to create alerts when certain events occur, such as a potential fraudulent transaction.
- **Integrated test facility (ITF)**   In a software application, additional "dummy" test records will be present that will be processed alongside actual business transactions. These additional records are usually created by auditors and are introduced during normal production transaction processing.
- **Continuous and intermittent simulation (CIS)**   This technique involves a connection to a live production environment; when new transactions are introduced, the transaction is simulated in a transaction simulator as well

as being executed in the live environment. The results of the simulation are compared to the actual transaction. In CIS, it is not necessary to simulate every transaction; instead, a sampling technique is used to simulate selected transactions.

- **Systems control audit review file and embedded audit modules (SCARF/ EAM)** This involves the development and embedding of specialized audit software directly into production applications. This audit software can perform various functions, including selecting transactions to audit, additional logging, and additional checks.

Additional guidance on the use of CAATs and continuous auditing is located in ISACA auditing guideline 2205, Evidence.

 NOTE IS auditors need to ensure that the effort required to set up the CAAT environment doesn't exceed the effort required by other methods for sampling and analysis.

Reporting Audit Results

The work product of an audit project is the *audit report*, a written report that describes the entire audit project, including audit objectives, scope, controls evaluated, opinions on the effectiveness and integrity of those controls, and recommendations for improvement.

Although an IS auditor or audit firm will generally use a standard format for an audit report, some laws and standards require that particular types of audit reports contain specific information or be presented in a particular format. Still, some variance is expected in the structure and appearance of audit reports created by different audit organizations.

The auditor is typically asked to present findings in a closing meeting, where he or she can explain the audit and its results and be available to answer questions about the audit. The auditor may include an electronic presentation to guide discussion of the audit.

Structure and Contents

Although there are often different methods for presenting audit findings, as well as regulations and standards that require specific content, an audit report will generally include several elements:

- **Cover letter** The cover letter briefly describes the audit, its scope and purpose, and the auditor's findings. Often, this letter is used alone as evidence to other organizations that the audit took place.
- **Introduction** The introduction describes the contents of the audit report.
- **Summary** The executive summary briefly describes the audit, its purpose and scope, and the auditor's findings and recommendations.
- **Description of the audit** The report includes a high-level description of the audit, its purpose, and its objectives.

- **Listing of systems and processes examined** The report should contain a list of systems, applications, and business processes that were examined.

- **Listing of interviewees** The report should contain a complete list of interviewees, when they were interviewed, and topics discussed.

- **Listing of evidence obtained** A detailed list of all evidence obtained, from whom, and when it was obtained is included. Electronic evidence should be described, including the time it was acquired, the system it was obtained from, and the method used to obtain it. The names of any staff members who assisted should be included.

- **Explanation of sampling techniques** Each time the auditor performed any sampling, the techniques used should be described.

- **Description of findings and recommendations** Detailed explanations describe the effectiveness of each control, based on evidence and the auditor's judgment. Exceptions are described in detail to demonstrate that they actually occurred. Information in this section may be organized according to criticality, technology in use, or business function, or it may be organized by several of these. Some audit reports do not include recommended remediation to avoid the appearance of influencing the organization in a consultative manner.

The IS auditor creating the report must ensure that it is balanced, reasonable, and fair. The report should not just be a list of everything that was bad; it should also include a list of controls that were found to be operating effectively.

The IS auditor also needs to take care when describing recommendations, realizing that any organization is capable of a finite amount of change in a given period. If the audit report contains many findings, the auditor needs to realize that the organization may not be able to remediate all of the issues before the next audit cycle. Instead, the organization will need to understand which findings should be remediated first—the audit report should provide this guidance through severity ratings on individual findings or groups of findings.

 NOTE It is typically *not* the auditor's role to describe *how* an audit finding should be remediated. Deciding the method(s) used to apply remediation is the role of auditee management.

Evaluating Control Effectiveness

When developing an audit report, the auditor needs to communicate the effectiveness of controls to the auditee. Often, this reporting is needed at several layers; for instance, the auditor may provide more detailed findings and recommendations to control owners, while the report for senior management may contain only the significant findings.

> ## Audit Reports Should Not Contain Surprises
>
> In a collaborative relationship between auditor and auditee, there should be a level of candor and trust, so that the auditee understands throughout the audit where things stand. At the end of the audit, when the auditor is presenting the audit results to management, those in management should already know with reasonably good (but not necessarily absolute) accuracy what the audit report will contain.
>
> This is not to say that auditee management will be *happy* with the audit results. Certainly, if there are deficiencies in the report, management, in its spirit of continuous improvement and quality, should not be satisfied with a less-than-perfect audit result. The point here is that auditors should not necessarily conceal their findings until the report is delivered.

One method that auditors frequently use is the development of a matrix of all audit findings, where each audit finding is scored on a criticality scale. This helps the auditor to illustrate the audit findings that are the most important and those that are less important, in the auditor's opinion. The auditor can also report on cases where an ineffective control is mitigated (fully or partially) by one or more compensating controls. For example, a system may not have the ability to enforce password complexity (for example, requiring upper- and lowercase letters, plus numbers and special characters), but this can be compensated through the use of longer than usual passwords and perhaps even more frequent expiration times.

 NOTE   The IS auditor should review ISACA auditing standard 1401, Reporting, and guideline 2401, Reporting, when developing the audit report to ensure that the report is complete and accurate.

Other Audit Topics

This section includes important discussions on topics related to IS audits.

Detecting Fraud and Irregularities

Fraud is defined as an intentional deception made for personal gain or to damage another party. In the context of corporate information systems and IS auditing, fraud is an act whereby a person discovers and exploits a weakness in a process or system for personal gain or personal satisfaction. An *irregularity* is an event that represents actions contrary to accepted practices or policy.

Management is responsible for implementing controls designed to prevent, deter, and detect fraud. However, no system or process is without weaknesses—worse yet, if two or more employees agree to a conspiracy to defraud the organization, it is possible for the conspirators to, at least temporarily, steal from the organization.

While detecting fraud and irregularities is certainly not the IS auditor's primary responsibility, an IS auditor surely has many opportunities to discover exploitable weaknesses in processes and systems that could be used to defraud the organization. Occasionally, the IS auditor will discover evidence of fraud while examining transaction samples during substantive testing.

When the auditor detects signs of fraud or irregularities, he or she should carefully evaluate these findings and then communicate them to the appropriate authorities. Precisely whom he or she contacts will depend on the nature and structure of the organization and whether there is regulatory oversight of the organization and/or the auditor. The auditor needs to be extremely careful when reporting findings within the organization because the person the auditor reports findings to could be the perpetrator—or could be associated with the perpetrator. This logic may prompt the auditor to report findings directly to the audit committee, thereby bypassing all potential perpetrators in the organization (usually, members of the audit committee are not employees in the organization, have no role in the organization's operations, and hence are probably not among the culprits).

If the organization has no audit committee or similar overseeing body, the auditor may be compelled to report irregularities to industry regulators or law enforcement.

When the auditor is representing an external audit organization, often the auditor will discuss the weakness, irregularity, or actual fraud with selected members of the audit organization to confirm his or her observations and agree on a plan for notifying the auditee or outside authorities.

Communication of the weakness or actual fraud or irregularity typically begins with a phone call or face-to-face conversation, which is followed up by a formal written letter. This will satisfy the need to inform the auditee quickly (via the phone call) and formally (via the written letter).

Audit Risk and Materiality

What if material errors in business processes remain undetected by the IS auditor? There are a number of ways in which this can occur, including the following:

- **Control risk**   This is the risk that a material error exists that will not be prevented or detected by the organization's control framework. For example, a manual control that is designed to detect unauthorized changes in an information system may fail if the person who reviews logs overlooks significant errors, irregularities, or fraud.

- **Detection risk**   This is the risk that an IS auditor will overlook errors or exceptions during an audit. Detection risk should be a part of the IS auditor's risk assessment that is carried out at the beginning of an audit; this would help the auditor focus on controls that require additional scrutiny (meaning higher sampling rates) and thereby improve the chances of detecting errors.

- **Inherent risk**   This is the risk that there are material weaknesses in existing business processes and that there are no compensating controls to aid in their detection or prevention. Inherent risks exist independent of the audit.

- **Sampling risk**   This is the risk that the sampling technique used will not detect transactions that are not in compliance with controls.
- **Overall audit risk**   This is the summation of all of the residual risks discussed in this section.

Materiality   In financial audits, *materiality* is established as a dollar amount threshold that is calculated in one of several possible ways, including a percentage of pretax income, a percentage of gross profit, a percentage of total assets, a percentage of total revenue, a percentage of equity, or blended methods using two or more of these.

When an auditor is examining transactions and controls during an audit, a finding can be classified as a material weakness if the dollar amount of the exceptions exceeds the materiality threshold. There is, however, some latitude (more in some cases and less in others) in the auditor's judgment as to whether a finding is material.

In an IS audit, the controls being examined usually do not have dollar figures associated with them, and deficiencies are not measured against materiality thresholds in the same way. Instead, materiality in an IS audit occurs when a control deficiency (or combination of related control deficiencies) makes it possible for serious errors, omissions, irregularities, or illegal acts to occur as a result of the deficiency or deficiencies. Here more than in a financial audit, the judgment of the IS auditor is very important in determining whether a finding is material.

Auditing and Risk Assessment

When assessing the effectiveness of controls in an organization, the IS auditor should take the time to understand how the organization approaches risk assessment and risk treatment.

Risk Assessment   Organizations should periodically undertake risk assessments to identify areas of risk that warrant management attention. A risk assessment should identify, prioritize, and rank risks. The subject of risk assessment should be those business processes and supporting information systems and infrastructures that are central to the organization's mission.

After the auditor identifies risks, the risk assessment should include one or more potential remedies, each with an analysis of the cost and effort required to implement it and the estimated reduction, transfer, avoidance, or acceptance of risk. When these remedies and their impact (in terms of risk reduction) are then ranked, the result should be a list of the most effective initiatives for reducing risk in the organization.

There are two types of risk assessment: qualitative and quantitative. A qualitative risk assessment rates risks as high-medium-low, whereas a quantitative risk analysis rates risks in terms of actual probabilities and costs. A quantitative risk assessment is considerably more difficult and time-consuming to perform, since it can be difficult to ascertain reasonable probabilities of threats and their financial impact. However, when seriously considering measures to reduce risk on the highest risk areas in the assessment, the auditor will find that it sometimes makes sense to perform some quantitative risk assessment to verify which investments will make the most difference.

Risk Treatment   Once risks have been identified, *risk treatment* involves the decision made and subsequent actions taken to address them. There are four possible avenues for risk treatment:

- **Risk reduction**   Sometimes known as *risk mitigation*, this involves making changes to processes, procedures, systems, or controls to reduce either the probability or the impact of a threat. For example, if the risk assessment identifies a threat of a SQL injection attack on an application, the organization can reduce risk by implementing an application firewall that will block such attacks.

- **Risk transfer**   This typically involves the use of insurance, which can compensate the organization for the financial losses or damages that would occur if the threat were realized. For example, the organization can transfer the risk of a denial-of-service attack by purchasing a cyber-insurance policy that would compensate the organization if such an attack were to occur.

- **Risk avoidance**   Here, the organization will cease the activity associated with the risk. For instance, if the risk assessment identifies risks associated with the implementation of an e-commerce capability, the organization may choose to abandon this idea, thereby avoiding e-commerce–related risk.

- **Risk acceptance**   In this case, the organization believes that the risk is acceptable and that no measures need to be taken to reduce the risk.

Rarely does an organization make a decision that fits entirely within a single risk treatment category. Rather, risk treatment is usually a blended approach, where, for instance, measures are taken to reduce risk; however, even a combination of measures rarely eliminates all risk—there is usually some risk left over after some risk treatment is performed. This leftover risk is known as *residual risk*. And like the remaining dirt that can't be picked up with a broom and dustpan after a few successive attempts, the leftover risk is usually accepted.

Control Self-Assessment

Control self-assessment (CSA) is a methodology used by an organization to review key business objectives, risks related to achieving these objectives, and the key controls designed to manage those risks. The primary characteristic of a CSA is that the organization takes initiative to self-regulate rather than engage outsiders, who may be experts in auditing but not in the organization's mission, goals, and culture.

Examples of CSA include

- **Sarbanes-Oxley mandated internal audit**   U.S. public companies are required to implement an internal audit function that examines financial controls.

- **PCI Self-Assessment Questionnaire (SAQ)**   The Payment Card Industry requires all merchants and service providers to comply with the PCI-DSS; organizations whose transaction volumes are below set thresholds are allowed to self-assess with a Self-Assessment Questionnaire (SAQ).

- **Voluntary internal audit**   Better organizations that realize that cybersecurity controls are important to protect their ongoing business undertake voluntary internal audits, not because a law or regulation requires them to, but because they understand it's a good method for ensuring that their controls continue to be effective.

CSA Advantages and Disadvantages

Like almost any business activity, CSAs have a number of advantages and disadvantages that the IS auditor and others should be familiar with. This will help the organization make the most of this process and avoid some common problems.

The advantages of a CSA include

- Risks can be detected earlier, because subject matter experts are involved earlier.
- Internal controls can be improved in a timely manner.
- CSA leads to greater ownership of controls through involvement in their improvement.
- CSA leads to improved employee awareness of controls through involvement in their improvement.
- CSA may help improve relationships between departments and auditors.

The disadvantages of a CSA include

- CSA could be mistaken by employees or management as a substitute for an internal audit.
- CSA may be considered extra work and dismissed as unnecessary.
- Employees may attempt to cover up shoddy work and misdeeds.
- CSA may be considered an attempt by the auditor to shrug off responsibilities.
- Lack of employee involvement would translate to little or no process improvement.

The CSA Life Cycle

Like most continuous-improvement processes, the CSA process is an iterative life cycle. The phases in the CSA are

- **Identify and assess risks**   Operational risks are identified and analyzed.
- **Identify and assess controls**   Controls to manage risks are identified and assessed. If any controls are missing, new controls are designed and implemented.
- **Develop questionnaire or conduct workshop**   An interactive session is conducted, if possible, for discussion of risks and controls. If attending personnel are distributed across several locations, a conference call can be convened or a questionnaire may be developed and sent to them.

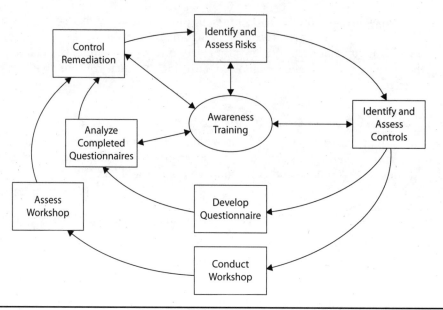

Figure 3-5   The control self-assessment life cycle

- **Analyze completed questionnaires or assess workshop**   If a workshop was held, the workshop results are assessed to see what good ideas for remediation emerged. If a questionnaire was distributed, the results are analyzed to see what good ideas for risk remediation were identified.

- **Control remediation**   Using the best ideas from the workshop or questionnaire, controls are designed or altered to better manage specific risks.

- **Awareness training**   This activity is carried out through every phase of the life cycle to keep personnel informed about the activities in the various phases.

The CSA life cycle is illustrated in Figure 3-5.

Self-Assessment Objectives

The primary objective of a CSA is to transfer some of the responsibility for oversight of control performance and monitoring to the control owners. The IS auditor's role is not diminished, because the IS audit still needs to test control effectiveness periodically, but control owners will play a more active role in the audit of their controls.

Another objective of CSA is the long-term reduction in exceptions. As control owners assume more responsibility for the performance of their controls, they will strive to avoid situations where IS auditors identify exceptions. The CSA gives control owners an opportunity and a process for cleaning house and improving audit results.

NOTE The IS auditor should be involved in CSAs to ensure that the CSA process is not hijacked by efficiency zealots who try to remove the controls from processes because they do not understand their significance.

Auditors and Self-Assessment

IS auditors should be involved in CSAs that various departments conduct. The role of an IS auditor should be that of an objective subject matter expert who can guide discussions in the appropriate direction so that controls will receive the right kind of development over time.

IS auditors should resist taking too large a role in CSAs, however. Responsibility for control development and maturation should lie within the department that owns the CSA. However, if a department is new at conducting a CSA, it may take some time before they are confident and competent enough to take full ownership and responsibility for the process.

Implementation of Audit Recommendations

The purpose of internal and external audits is to identify potential opportunities for making improvements in control objectives and control activities. The handoff point between the completion of the audit and the auditee's assumption of control is in the portion of the audit report that contains findings and recommendations. These are the imperatives that the auditor recommends the auditee perform to improve the control environment.

Implementation of audit recommendations is the responsibility of the auditee. However, there is some sense of shared responsibility with the auditor, as the auditor seeks to understand the auditee's business so that he or she can develop recommendations that can reasonably be undertaken and completed. In a productive auditor-auditee relationship, the auditor will develop recommendations using the fullest possible understanding of the auditee's business environment, capabilities, and limitations—in essence, saying, "Here are my recommendations to you for reducing risk and improving controls." And the auditee, having worked with the auditor to understand his or her methodology and conclusions, and having been understood by the auditor, will accept the recommendations and take full responsibility for them—in essence saying, "I accept your recommendations and will implement them." This is the spirit and intent of the auditor-auditee partnership.

In some auditor-auditee relationships, auditors do not include recommendations in their audit reports. Often this is because auditors are not permitted to play a role of influencing auditee business decisions. Put another way, auditors can tell an auditee organization *what* control exception to fix, but not *how* to fix the control exception.

Chapter Review

The audit function in an organization should be defined and described in a charter. The audit program and audit strategy should support the organization's mission and objectives and facilitate business development and growth.

Auditors need to establish and maintain technical competence so that they can effectively evaluate technical controls and identify technical control risks. They will need to attend periodic training in the technologies in use by the organization as well as in emerging technologies that the organization may use in the future.

The ISACA Code of Professional Ethics defines the standards of behavior and conduct for IS auditors. The ISACA auditing standards framework defines mandatory audit standards, guidelines that contain suggestions for implementing the standards. All persons who hold the CISA designation are required to uphold the ISACA Code of Professional Ethics; violations will result in investigations and possible disciplinary actions, including expulsion.

ISACA audit standards, guidelines, and procedures provide a framework that can be used to guide the development of an IT assurance program. The Information Technology Assurance Framework (ITAF) is a complete IT assurance and audit framework that borrows elements from COBIT and ISACA audit standards, guidelines, and procedures.

IS auditors may need to perform a risk analysis as an integral part of an audit project to identify risk areas that require additional audit resources. The result of the risk analysis will help the auditor to build a complete audit plan that includes the appropriate level of activities to be carried out during the audit.

The ISACA Risk IT Framework provides a set of processes for performing risk governance, risk evaluation, and risk response.

Internal controls are the policies, procedures, mechanisms, systems, and other means designed to reduce risk and facilitate the achievement of business objectives. Controls are classified in several different ways that describe how they are designed to control behaviors and outcomes.

Internal control objectives are statements of desired states and outcomes in the organization. They are supported by one or more controls that ensure the realization of control objectives. Controls should be measurable and are defined and enforced with processes, procedures, or automatic mechanisms within information systems. IS control objectives resemble internal control objectives but are focused on the desired states and outcomes within the context of information systems.

General computing controls (GCCs) are applied across an entire IS environment. An organization will likely have additional controls that are applied to individual applications or components in the environment.

An audit is the planned, methodical evaluation of controls and control objectives. A key activity in an audit is the identification and acquisition of evidence that supports the operation of controls and helps the auditor reach a conclusion about the effectiveness of a control.

IS auditors generally develop and follow an audit methodology, which is a process that ensures consistent, repeatable audits from start to finish. Often, the type and reason for an audit will determine the methodology to be used.

Evidence is the information collected by the auditor during the course of the audit. The reliability and relevance of evidence helps the auditor reach sound conclusions on the effectiveness of controls and control objectives.

Sampling is the technique used when it is not feasible to test an entire population of transactions. Sampling techniques need to be carefully considered so that they accurately represent the entire population.

Computer-assisted audit techniques (CAATs) are used to automate sampling and analysis of information in complex application environments. CAATs can help auditors analyze and correlate data in ways that would be too difficult to do manually. Continuous auditing consists of samples that are automatically gathered over long periods.

The audit report is the work product of the audit project. It contains a summary, a description of evidence gathered, and findings and conclusions.

In IS audits, materiality is the threshold where control deficiencies make it possible for serious errors, omissions, irregularities, or illegal acts to occur.

A control self-assessment (CSA) is an activity used by an organization to take ownership of controls and make improvements in the implementation of its controls through workshops and other activities.

Quick Review

- An audit program defines the audit strategy and the plans that include scope, objectives, resources, and procedures used to evaluate controls and processes.

- IS auditors need to stay current with technology through training courses, webinars, ISACA chapter training events, and industry conferences.

- Several laws, regulations, and standards require internal or external audits to ensure that organizations achieve and maintain compliance.

- The types of controls are physical, technical, and administrative.

- The classes of controls are preventive, detective, deterrent, corrective, compensating, and recovery.

- The categories of controls are automatic and manual.

- The types of audits are operational audits, financial audits, integrated audits, IS audits, administrative audits, compliance audits, forensic audits, and service provider audits. Pre-audits can be performed to help an organization prepare for an upcoming audit. Internal audits and external audits refer to the relationship of auditor to auditee.

- Compliance testing is used to determine whether control procedures are properly designed and are operating properly. Substantive testing is used to verify the accuracy and integrity of transactions as they flow through a system.

- Audit methodologies define an audit subject, audit objective, type of audit, audit scope, pre-audit planning, audit statement of work, audit procedures, communication plan, report preparation, wrap-up, and post-audit follow-up.

- The types of evidence that the auditor will collect during an audit include observations, written notes, correspondence, process and procedure documentation, and business records.

- During an audit, the auditor should obtain org charts, department charters, third-party contracts, policies and procedures, risk ledgers, incident logs, standards, and system documentation. He or she should conduct several interviews with pre-written questions and carefully observe personnel to understand their discipline as well as organizational culture and maturity.

- The types of sampling include statistical sampling, judgmental sampling, attribute sampling, variable sampling, stop-or-go sampling, discovery sampling, and stratified sampling. The IS auditor needs to understand the meaning of confidence coefficient, sampling risk, precision, expected error rate, sample mean, sample standard deviation, and tolerable error rate.

- An audit report usually includes a cover letter, introduction, summary, audit description, list of systems examined, interviewees, evidence, explanation of sampling techniques, findings, and, optionally, recommendations.

- The types of risks that are related to audits include control risk, detection risk, inherent risk, overall audit risk, and sampling risk.

- Computer-assisted audit techniques, generalized audit software, and continuous auditing present many challenges and opportunities that may result in more frequent and rapid reporting, which can help to reduce the time needed to mitigate control failures and exceptions.

- External auditors may be needed when the organization lacks specific expertise or resources to conduct an internal audit. However, some regulations and standards require external, independent audits.

Questions

1. An IS auditor is planning an audit project and needs to know which areas represent the highest risk. What is the best approach for identifying these risk areas?

   A. Perform the audit; control failures will identify the areas of highest risk.

   B. Perform the audit and then perform a risk assessment.

   C. Perform a risk assessment first, and then concentrate control tests in high-risk areas identified in the risk assessment.

   D. Increase sampling rates in high-risk areas.

2. An auditor has detected potential fraud while testing a control objective. What should the auditor do next?

   A. Notify the audit committee.

   B. Conduct a formal investigation.

    C. Report the fraud to law enforcement.

    D. Report the suspected fraud to management.

3. The possibility that a process or procedure will be unable to prevent or detect serious errors and wrongdoing is known as

    A. Detection risk

    B. Inherent risk

    C. Sampling risk

    D. Control risk

4. The categories of risk treatment are

    A. Risk reduction, risk transfer, risk avoidance, and risk acceptance

    B. Risk avoidance, risk transfer, and risk mitigation

    C. Risk avoidance, risk reduction, risk transfer, risk mitigation, and risk acceptance

    D. Risk avoidance, risk treatment, risk mitigation, and risk acceptance

5. An IS auditor needs to perform an audit of a financial system and needs to trace individual transactions through the system. What type of testing should the auditor perform?

    A. Discovery testing

    B. Statistical testing

    C. Compliance testing

    D. Substantive testing

6. An IS auditor is auditing the change management process for a financial application. The auditor has two primary pieces of evidence: change logs and a written analysis of the change logs performed by a business analyst. Which evidence is best and why?

    A. The change log is best because it is subjective.

    B. The written analysis is best because it interprets the change log.

    C. The change log is best because it is objective and unbiased.

    D. The written analysis is best because it is objective.

7. Under which circumstances should an auditor use subjective sampling?

    A. When the population size is low

    B. When the auditor believes that specific transactions represent higher risk than most others

    C. When the risk of exceptions is low

    D. When statistical sampling cannot be performed

8. An IS auditor has discovered a high-risk exception during control testing. What is the best course of action for the IS auditor to take?

   A. Immediately perform mitigation.

   B. Include the exception in the report and mark the test as a control failure.

   C. Immediately inform the auditee of the situation.

   D. Immediately inform the audit committee of the situation.

9. What is the appropriate role of an IS auditor in a control self-assessment?

   A. The IS auditor should participate as a subject matter expert.

   B. The IS auditor should act as facilitator.

   C. The IS auditor should not be involved.

   D. The IS auditor should design the control self-assessment.

10. Which of the following would *not* be useful evidence in an IS audit?

    A. Personnel handbook

    B. Organization mission statement and objectives

    C. Organization chart

    D. Organization history

11. An auditor has discovered that automated work papers were configured with read/write permissions for database administrators. What actions should the auditor take?

    A. Simply continue to rely on the automated work papers.

    B. Note an exception and continue to rely on these automated work papers.

    C. Recommend that permissions on automated work papers be changed so that no personnel have write access and so that this data may be relied upon in the future.

    D. Notify the board of directors or the audit committee.

12. During an audit, an auditor has discovered a process that is being performed consistently and effectively, but the process lacks procedure documentation. What action should the auditor take?

    A. Document the process.

    B. Find that the process is effective but recommend that it be documented.

    C. Write the procedure document for the auditee and include it in audit evidence.

    D. Find that the process is ineffective.

13. During audit planning, an auditor has discovered that a key business process in the auditee organization has been outsourced to an external service provider. Which option should the auditor consider?

    A. Audit the external service provider or rely on an SSAE 16 audit report if one is available.

    B. Audit the external service provider.

    C. Determine that the business process is not effective.

    D. Request that the external service provider submit its internal audit work papers.

14. Why should an auditor prefer bank statements over a department's own business records that list bank transactions?

    A. Bank statements can be provided in electronic format.

    B. Bank statements contain data not found in internal records.

    C. Bank statements are usually easier to obtain.

    D. Bank statements are independent and objective.

15. Which of the following statements is true about ISACA audit standards and guidelines?

    A. ISACA audit standards are mandatory, while ISACA audit guidelines are optional.

    B. ISACA audit standards are optional, while ISACA audit guidelines are mandatory.

    C. ISACA audit standards and guidelines are mandatory.

    D. ISACA audit standards and guidelines are optional.

Answers

1. **C.** The IS auditor should conduct a risk assessment first to determine which areas have highest risk, and then devote more testing resources to those high-risk areas.

2. **A.** When the IS auditor suspects fraud, he or she should conduct a careful evaluation of the matter and notify the audit committee. Because audit committee members are generally not involved in business operations, they will be sufficiently removed from the matter and they will have the authority to involve others as needed.

3. **D.** Control risk is the term that signifies the possibility that a control will fail to prevent or detect unwanted actions.

4. **A.** The four categories of risk treatment are risk reduction (sometimes called *risk mitigation,* where risks are reduced through a control or process change), risk transfer (where risks are transferred to an external party such as an insurance company), risk avoidance (where the risk-bearing activity is discontinued), and risk acceptance (where management chooses to accept the risk).

5. **D.** The auditor should perform substantive testing, which is a test of transaction integrity.

6. **C.** The change log is the best evidence because it is objective and not subject to human judgment.

7. **B.** Subjective sampling is used when the auditor wants to concentrate on samples known to represent higher risk.

8. **C.** The IS auditor should immediately inform the auditee when any high-risk situation is discovered.

9. **B.** The IS auditor should act as a facilitator of a control self-assessment, and management should make any decisions regarding changes to controls.

10. **D.** Of the choices given, the organization history would be the least useful. The others will provide insight into the organization's mission and goals and how it sets out to achieve them.

11. **C.** If an auditor has discovered that automated work papers could be updated by any personnel, the work papers should not be trusted to contain complete and accurate information. Once this is fixed by eliminating write access, the auditor can rely on this data going forward but should not rely on the information prior to that point in time.

12. **B.** The auditor should determine that the process is effective and recommend that it be documented. Some regulations, however, may require that such a process be judged ineffective specifically because it lacks documentation.

13. **A.** An auditor who has determined that a key business process has been outsourced needs to determine effectiveness of that process by auditing that process or by relying on a separate audit report of that process.

14. **D.** An auditor would prefer bank statements over internal records because bank statements are produced by a bank, which is independent and objective. A bank is unlikely to alter its records to improve the audit outcome of one of its customers.

15. **A.** ISACA audit standards are mandatory for all ISACA certification holders, including those with the CISA certification. ISACA audit guidelines are optional.

IT Life Cycle Management

This chapter covers CISA Domain 3, "Information Systems Acquisition, Development, and Implementation," and discusses the following topics:

- Program and project management
- The systems development life cycle (SDLC)
- Infrastructure development and implementation
- Maintaining information systems
- Business processes and business process reengineering
- Managing third-party risk
- Application controls
- Auditing the software development life cycle
- Auditing business and application controls
- Auditing third parties

The topics in this chapter represent 12 percent of the CISA examination.

Organizations employ business processes to organize the tasks related to the development and maintenance of application software and the supporting IT infrastructure. Business processes provide constraint and management control for high-value activities such as the acquisition, development, and maintenance of software and infrastructure, and these processes also provide the structure for projects and project management.

Organizations, for the most part, have undergone significant transformation in the past decade with regard to the nature of their business software applications. In the past, organizations developed or acquired software applications, heavily customized them with an internal staff of programmers, and operated them in on-premises data centers (once known as computer rooms). Contrast to today, where most organizations employ Software-as-a-Service (SaaS) business applications with integrations among them, and with few, if any, software developers on staff. The emphasis on the software development life cycle has now given way to the systems development (really, acquisition) life cycle.

Many organizations recognize that business processes themselves have the same intricacies as software, and that life cycle management is appropriate for, and similar to, the life cycle for software development. They also realize that business processes and application software are often tightly coupled and must often be managed as complex, multifaceted single entities.

IS auditors should pay particular attention to an organization's methodologies and practices for the acquisition, development, and management of software, infrastructure, and business processes. This is valuable information regarding the effectiveness of an organization's life cycle management and helps auditors determine how well the organization develops requirements and can transform them into applications and infrastructure that effectively support key business processes.

In addition to auditing the organization's development processes, auditors must audit software applications. Areas of particular interest include controls that govern input, processing, and output, as well as the application's ability to perform calculations correctly and maintain the integrity of data that is being accessed by many users simultaneously.

Benefits Realization

Benefits realization, sometimes called *business realization*, is the result of strategic planning, process development, and systems development, which all contribute toward a launch of business operations to reach a set of business objectives. This chapter focuses on process and systems acquisition and development, which are used to build the engine of business operations. Audits of these activities provide objective views of their effectiveness. Benefits realization is depicted in Figure 4-1.

Portfolio and Program Management

A *program* is an organization of many large, complex activities and can be thought of as *a set of projects that work to fulfill one or more key business objectives or goals*. A program is generally a multiyear effort that comprises many complex projects, each with its own project manager, project schedule, budget, and participants.

A program is usually run by a *program manager* who has oversight over all of the projects in the program. Figure 4-2 shows the relationship between a program manager and the projects that he or she manages.

Like a single project, a program has a defined scope, budget, resources, and a schedule. A program also helps to organize and coordinate the operation of its projects, identify dependencies between them, manage conflicts and issues, and manage common and shared resources used by project teams.

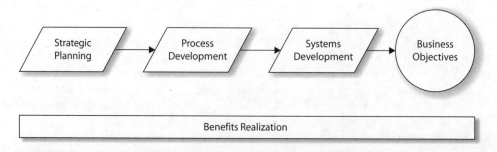

Figure 4-1   Benefits realization

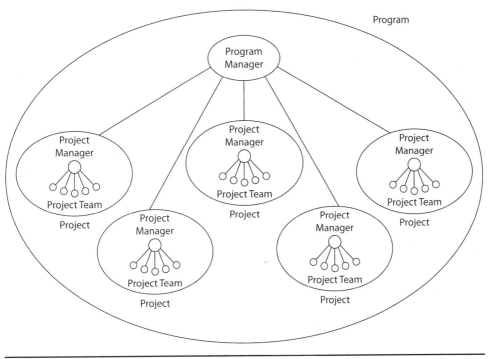

Figure 4-2 A program manager oversees several projects.

Starting a Program

When an organization sets objectives and goals that will be realized through a program, a number of activities usually take place:

- **Development of a program charter** A *charter* is a formal document that defines the objectives of a program, its main timelines, the sources of funding, the names of its principal leaders and managers, and the names of the business executive or executives who are sponsoring the program.

- **Identification of available resources** Senior management must identify the resources that will be used by the program. These will include funding, personnel, and business assets such as information systems and other equipment.

The charter and resources provide the direction and the means to begin a program that will move the business closer to realizing its objectives.

Titles vs. Roles

Many middle and senior managers are program managers, even if they don't have "program manager" in their title or job description. Any manager who is responsible for the execution of multiple concurrent projects, particularly if those projects are helping the organization get closer to common objectives, is a program manager.

Running a Program

After a program has been launched, the program manager needs to manage it actively to ensure that the program is on track and fulfilling its objectives. Some of the activities required may include

- **Monitoring project schedules**   Each of the projects running in the program will have its own schedule. The program manager will need to examine these schedules periodically to understand how each is progressing. This often requires the program manager to communicate frequently with program participants and project managers to get up-to-date statuses on project tasks.

- **Managing project budgets**   The program manager needs to monitor and manage spending by each of the projects in the program. The program manager may need to make spending adjustments periodically to keep the overall program budget under control.

- **Managing resources**   The program manager needs to understand how resources are being used across all the projects and to make changes as needed. Resources are scarce in most IT organizations, so this requires creativity; often, the program manager needs to *find* resources before those resources can be used to further program goals.

- **Identifying and managing conflicts**   Individual projects will often encounter resource conflicts—sometimes projects will vie for the same resources, or they may require resources in use outside of the program.

- **Creating program status reports for senior management**   As executive sponsors for the program, senior management needs to be kept informed of program status, in whatever level of detail required. Often, these status reports will describe issues and conflicts and how they are being resolved. Sometimes, however, status reports will describe unresolved conflicts that require senior management intervention in the form of resource prioritization to keep vital programs moving ahead.

These activities enable management to measure progress and to adjust resources and priorities to keep the program running smoothly.

Project Portfolio Management

The *project portfolio* is the organization's entire set of active projects at any given time. Unlike a program, where projects are related and support a common objective, a port-folio of projects is simply *all* the active projects, which may support many different and even unrelated objectives and be part of different programs.

An organization needs to maintain a collection of information about all its projects in a central location. Having this information will help a senior manager or executive quickly view high-level information about all the active projects in the organization. Often, this information will be stored electronically in a form that will enable an executive to sort and filter company projects in various ways. Some of the information that may be maintained in this portfolio of projects includes

- Executive sponsor
- Program manager
- Project manager
- Start and end dates
- Names of participants
- Objectives or goals that the project supports
- Budget
- Resources used
- Dependencies

NOTE Ease of access to project and program portfolios helps management better understand what activities are taking place and the resources that each is consuming.

Business Case Development

The prevalent point of view is that IT exists in support of business objectives. Given this assumption, every IT project should directly or indirectly result in tangible business benefits, regardless of how technical or abstract any particular IT project may be.

Before any IT project is permitted to begin, a *business case* for the project is developed. The purpose of a business case is to explain the benefits to the business that will be realized as a result of the project.

The development of a business case will normally follow a feasibility study. A *feasibility study* defines the business problem and describes potential solutions. It is possible, however, that none of the solutions will result in a benefit for the business. For example, each may be too costly or may incur excessive risk. However, the business case should go beyond the feasibility study in terms of business benefits and include actual figures for costs and benefits.

A typical business case is a written document that includes

- **Business problem** This is a description of the business problem in qualitative and quantitative terms.
- **Feasibility study results** The business case should include results of the feasibility study if one was performed.
- **High-level project plan** This should include a timeline and the number of persons required.

- **Budget**   This should include the cost to execute the project as well as costs associated with the solution.

- **Metrics**   The business case should include information on how business benefit will be measured, as well as expected before-and-after measurements. Estimates should be backed up by examples of the benefits of similar projects in the organization or in other organizations.

- **Risks**   The business case should include any risks that may occur, as well as how those risks can be mitigated. These risks may be market risks or financial risks.

 NOTE   Some organizations make the development of a business case the first phase in the actual project; however, this arrangement may be self-serving, as the project team may be taking the point of view of justifying the continuation of the project instead of focusing on whether the project will actually benefit the business. The development of a business case should be performed in an objective manner by persons who do not benefit from the result.

The start of a project is not the only time to assess the project's business case and decide whether to undertake the project. At key milestones throughout the project, the business case should be reevaluated. As a project unfolds, often situations develop that could not be anticipated earlier, and these situations sometimes result in added risks, costs, or other changes. For this reason, the business case should be reconsidered throughout the project so that senior management can determine whether the project should continue or not.

 NOTE   Decisions on whether to continue a project should be made not only by those people who benefit from the project, but also by other stakeholders who can be more objective. Otherwise, there is a risk that projects will be continued for their own sake instead of for the good of the business.

Measuring Business Benefits

In the mid-to-late 20th century, information technology was primarily used to automate tasks, and in that era it was fairly easy to measure the benefits derived from IT. Often, measuring the benefits was a matter of comparing the cost and time spent to perform tasks manually versus the cost and time spent to automate those tasks. Information technology's role today is *digital transformation* (sometimes abbreviated as *DX*), which provides benefits that are not so easily measured and are often not short-term in nature.

For example, an organization that invests in a new customer relationship management (CRM) application may do so to improve its customer service in measurable ways. Shortly after implementing a CRM system, productivity may actually decrease until individuals and teams learn how to operate and fully utilize the new system. But customer satisfaction may improve in future quarters. A year or more may be required to determine whether improvements in customer satisfaction is a blip or an actual upward trend attributable to the new CRM. The new system can also help the organization to improve its products and services; the benefits from these improvements may not be experienced for years after implementation of the new CRM.

Measuring business benefits requires that the organization select key performance indicators (KPIs) and measure them formally and accurately over the long term. When new projects and programs are considered, business benefits should be estimated and measurements should be taken before and after the project has completed to validate whether the project's predictions were valid. The nature of the project may require months or even years of measurements to validate project results.

NOTE   Major projects should include post-implementation reviews that take place long after the project's completion (as long as 24 months, or even longer) to determine whether trends in key metrics changed as predicted.

Business case development should include a description of the business benefits that are expected from the completed project, including how those benefits will be measured. These key metrics should be decided before the project begins. If key metrics are not being measured, those measurements should begin as soon as possible so that the organization will have enough "before-and-after" metrics to determine whether the project has benefited the organization or not.

NOTE   An organization that does not agree on key metrics is in danger of setting self-fulfilling metrics later on as a way of justifying the project, regardless of whether it actually benefits the organization.

In the spirit of continuous improvement, careful analysis of key metrics long after a project has been completed should lead the organization to consider additional improvements in its processes and technologies.

Finally, organizations that modernize business processes with automation often enjoy unexpected benefits, including insight gained through business analytics or business intelligence (BI), such as customer buying trends that could not have been known before.

Project Management

The preceding section on benefits realization is concerned with the high-level view across many projects. This section on project management takes a closer look at the management of individual projects.

A *project* is a coordinated and managed sequence of tasks that results in the realization of an objective or goal. The effort may be performed by a single individual or by many. A project's duration may be a few days or as long as two years or more.

Organizing Projects

Projects should be organized in a methodical way that supports the organization's objectives. Management should formally approve projects, which should be documented in a consistent manner.

In addition to being a collection of organized activities, a project has a social context and culture. A project consists of a project team that comprises the people who perform tasks for the project. The relationships among these people fall into four models:

- **Direct report**   A department manager serves as the project manager. Project team members report directly to the manager and are obliged to carry out the directives from the manager. In a slight variation, the department manager could be a project team member, and the project manager is someone who reports to the department manager.

- **Influencer**   The project manager has no direct management influence over project team members. The project manager must practice the art of influence and persuasion over the project team members to keep the project moving.

- **Pure project**   The project manager is given authority over the project team members, even though the team members do not report to the project manager.

- **Matrix**   The project manager and project team manager have authority over each project team member.

 NOTE   Although a project may have a formal plan and schedule, it's the people on the project team who help a project reach its objectives. Paying attention to the human side of projects is just as important as the project objectives themselves.

Initiating a Project

The formal project launch occurs when the project has been approved by the IT steering committee or a similar oversight body. Management will appoint a project manager as well as all project team members.

Management also needs to establish priorities for the team and for each team member. Because most or all project team members will probably have other work responsibilities, management must be very clear on where project activities fall on the work priority list.

In addition, management must express its support for the project schedule and important project milestones so that all project team members are aware of management's objectives for timely project completion. This will help to motivate project team members to start and complete tasks on time.

 NOTE   A project kickoff meeting is an effective way to convey these messages: management can gauge project team members' interest by studying their body language. A meeting is also an effective way to discuss issues and answer questions in real time.

Prior to the launch of a project, management should also discuss the upcoming project with individuals to learn their opinions regarding the makeup of the project team and its prospects for success.

Developing Project Objectives

The specific objectives of a project must be established and documented before the project begins. In fact, project objectives should be a part of the project's description when the project is being considered for approval by the IT steering committee. Project objectives should be specific, measurable, achievable, relevant, and time-bound (SMART). They should support and relate to business objectives and to the organization's key performance indicators.

Example project objectives are

- Reduce customer service call wait time by 70 percent.
- Reduce implementation time for new customers by five days.
- Reduce annual data storage system cost by 20 percent.

Additional objectives that are not a project's key objectives may also be developed; these objectives may clarify a project's purpose or the manner in which it will be performed.

Object Breakdown Structure

As a part of the project objectives, a project manager may develop an *object breakdown structure* (OBS), which represents the components of the project in graphical or tabular form. An OBS can help management and project team members better visualize the scope and objectives of the project. An example OBS appears in Figure 4-3.

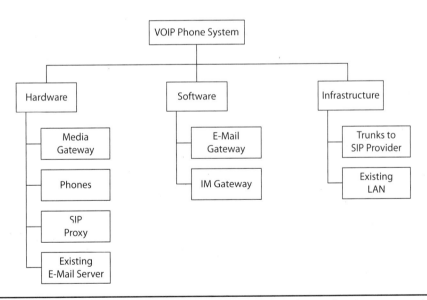

Figure 4-3   An object breakdown structure helps participants understand project scope and objectives.

An OBS is a visual or structural representation of the system, software, or application, in a hierarchical form, from high level to fine detail. An OBS· is not a schematic, architecture, or data flow diagram, although one or more of these may also need to be developed, either as a part of the design or as a tool to help project participants better understand the overall system.

Work Breakdown Structure

Another common method for depicting a project is the *work breakdown structure* (WBS). This is a logical representation of the high-level and detailed tasks that must be performed to complete the project. A WBS used for this purpose can also be used as the basis for the creation of the project schedule. An example WBS is shown in Figure 4-4.

The WBS created in this phase will be simpler than the full-fledged project plan, which will include the resources required to perform each task, task dependencies, and schedules.

In simpler projects, the WBS and the project plan are one and the same. Or, put another way, the WBS can be the *start* of the project plan, in terms of its containing all the tasks that need to be included in the project plan. With tools like WBS Planner, the WBS is the list of tasks in the left column, and the project plan is that same list when it also contains dependencies, dates, resources, and other details. Project planning is discussed in more detail later in this section.

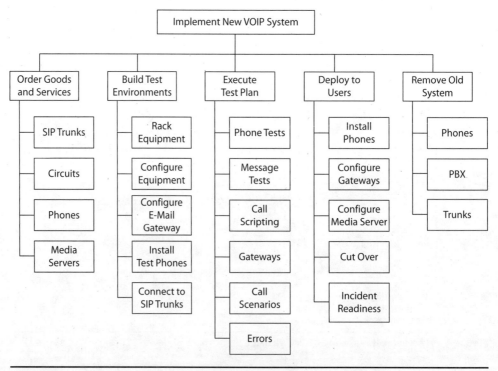

Figure 4-4   A work breakdown structure depicts a project's tasks.

Managing Projects

Projects should be managed by a project manager. The project manager is responsible for performing several activities:

- **Building and managing the project schedule**   The project manager may have developed the original project schedule, and he or she will be responsible for maintaining the schedule throughout the life of the project. As tasks are completed early, on time, or late, this will impact the rest of the project schedule, and the project manager will need to make adjustments to take into account these scheduling variations. In addition to changes in timing, other types of changes in the schedule will be required, including new tasks, new dependencies, and other unforeseen matters that could affect the schedule.

- **Recording task completion**   As tasks progress and are completed, the project manager must keep the project schedule up to date. The project schedule must accurately reflect the status of each task.

- **Running project meetings**   The project manager organizes regular meetings of project participants where project status and issues are discussed. The project manager facilitates project meetings to make sure that the meeting agenda is followed. The project manager is also responsible for sending meeting agendas, meeting minutes, and other updates to the project team.

- **Tracking project expenditures**   The project manager is responsible for tracking and reporting on project costs.

- **Communicating project status**   The project manager is responsible for communicating project status to project team members and also to management. A project status report will include details on task statuses and on whether the project is still on schedule and on budget, and a list of open and closed issues.

NOTE   The project manager needs to be a highly organized, methodical individual who is detail oriented and a good communicator and negotiator. While knowledge of the technologies in a project is useful, of utmost importance are the project manager's people skills, which enable the manager to work effectively with project team members and to be an effective facilitator and problem solver.

Project Roles and Responsibilities

Formal roles and responsibilities need to be established so that projects will be well organized and will have the greatest possible chance of success. Defined roles and responsibilities ensure that important tasks are known to all project participants. Typical roles and responsibilities include

- **Senior management**   Support the approval of the project, its funding, and resource allocation.

- **IT steering committee**   Commission the feasibility study, approve the project, assign IT and business resources to the project, and approve the project schedule. Periodically review project status and progress. Take corrective action when necessary—for example, when priorities conflict.

- **Project manager**   Develop the detailed project plan, identify and indicate dependencies, and estimate the time required to complete each task. Track progress at the task level. Call regular project meetings where project status and issues are discussed among project team members. Track spending and other resource allocation. Publish status reports to project team members and to senior management.

- **Project team members**   Participate in all project team meetings; complete tasks on time; identify issues and communicate them to the project manager; look for opportunities to optimize tasks, reduce necessary resources, and improve the project.

- **End-user management**   Assign staff to the project team and support the development of business requirements, test cases, test data, and system testing.

- **End users**   Develop business requirements, test cases, use cases, test data, and test systems, and report test results to the project manager. Participate in acceptance testing and provide accurate, timely results.

- **Project sponsor**   Define project objectives, provide budget and other resources, and work with the project manager and other management stakeholders to ensure that the project delivers the desired outcomes.

- **Systems development management**   Provide adequate hardware, software, tools, and resources to facilitate development. Assign competent, trained developers to the project, and support their participation in the project.

- **Systems developers**   Develop software and systems that conform to functional requirements, good coding practices, and organization IT standards. Perform unit, program, and system testing as required. Ensure that software and systems are free of software bugs, vulnerabilities, and security issues that could result in undesired activities such as a break-in or disclosure of sensitive information. Develop operational procedures.

- **Quality assurance**   Review the results and deliverables throughout the project to determine whether the project deliverables are in compliance with project requirements and any applicable regulatory requirements and other legal obligations.

- **Security manager**   Provide security requirements, privacy requirements, regulatory requirements, audit requirements, test plans, and test cases. Ensure that the system meets organizational controls and audit requirements. Perform security testing. Report test results to the project manager.

- **IT operations**   Provide operational requirements, review operational procedures, and participate in acceptance testing. Participate in system implementation, and operate the system after implementation. Report post-implementation problems to the project manager and developers.

- **IS auditor**   Subsequently audit the systems and processes built or changed in the project. Act in an advisory role and as a controls expert. The auditor should not otherwise act as a decision maker on the project team.

NOTE   In smaller organizations, one person may have two or more project roles. In large organizations (or large projects in any size organization), each role may be assigned to one person, a group, or even an entire team.

Project Planning

The term *project planning* refers to the activities related to the development and management of a project. The project manager is responsible for identifying all the activities required for the project, the sequence in which they must be performed, dependencies between tasks, the resources required, and the priorities of tasks and resources. The project manager will also be expected to determine how the project can make the most efficient use of resources and the shortest amount of time in which the entire project can be completed.

The RACI Matrix

Many organizations have adopted the RACI model for establishing responsibilities within projects as well as in other contexts. The four roles in the RACI model are presented here in hierarchical order (indicating why this model is sometimes called ARCI):

- **Accountable**   Usually a single individual who is accountable for the success of a project.

- **Responsible**   One or more individuals who are responsible for completing tasks in a project.

- **Consulted**   One or more individuals who may need to be consulted on various matters throughout a project. These are typically subject matter experts.

- **Informed**   One or more individuals who need to be informed.

Program managers and project managers often publish RACI charts so that all project participants know the responsibilities for each project team member.

Project planning encompasses many detailed activities:

- **Task identification**   One of the first steps in the development of a project plan is identifying all the tasks that must be performed to complete the project. This is often accomplished using a project management tool that can be used to build a detailed WBS. When completed, a WBS is a structural decomposition of the work necessary to complete the entire project, task by task, bit by bit.

- **Task estimation**   Once the project planner has identified all of the tasks required to complete the project, the next step is determining how much time and effort each task requires. There are a couple of different ways to measure this: actual effort and elapsed time. For example, it may take a painter one hour to paint a room, but there is also preparation and cleanup time to consider, and it may take four hours for the paint to dry (though while the paint is drying, the painter can be doing other tasks). Often, it is necessary to know how many hours or days of work are required for one or more persons to perform a task, but knowing elapsed time is critical also.

- **Task resources**   It is necessary to know what resources are required to perform a task. Resources include people (and not just any people—often a given task must be performed by specific people), equipment, consumable resources, outside professional services, materials, software licenses, and so on.

- **Task dependencies**   Often in a project there will be tasks that cannot be started until other tasks have been completed. Project managers must discern all of the dependencies between projects so that project teams don't run into unexpected obstacles.

- **Milestone tracking**   In larger projects, it is a good idea to identify milestones. Milestones are significant events in the project when major phases have been completed. Example milestones are completion of the design, completion of software development, completion of network wiring, and completion of software testing. Often management will want to schedule a project review meeting when these milestones have been completed; such reviews give management an opportunity to make go/no-go decisions on whether the project should be permitted to continue, or to see whether any lingering issues should first be addressed before the project is continued.

- **Task tracking**   When a project is in progress, the project manager must accurately track the status and progress of every task. He or she also must look toward the short-term and long-term futures, anticipate future resource needs, and make sure that tasks that have not started yet will be able to start without undue delays.

NOTE One of the most common pitfalls in project planning is the failure to identify task resources and dependencies properly. Sometimes a project planner will have "optimized" a project plan, only to find out that many tasks that could be done concurrently must be done consecutively. This happens, for instance, when several tasks that are slated to be done in parallel must all be performed by the same individual. For example, five tasks that take one day each were scheduled to all take place on the same day, but it turns out that the same person is required to perform all of those tasks; this results in those tasks being completed one day after another, requiring five days in all.

Estimating and Sizing Software Projects

Several tools and methods can be used to estimate the amount of effort required to complete tasks in a software project. Tools and methodologies can make the task of estimating work more accurate, because they rely on techniques that have been proven over the long run. Also, tools and methodologies can reduce the time required to perform the estimating work.

Using the OBS The OBS can be useful to depict the system and its components visually, particularly in complex projects where the tasks, costs, and other aspects of the project are not immediately evident. Object breakdown structures are described in more detail earlier in this chapter.

Using the WBS The WBS is a great way to get to the tasks in a complex project. A project manager or planner can decompose large efforts into smaller and smaller pieces, down to the task level.

Using Source Lines of Code Sizing for software projects has traditionally relied upon *source lines of code* (SLOC) estimates. Experienced systems analysts could make rough estimates on the numbers of lines of code required for a given software project. Then, using results from past projects, the analyst could make an accurate estimate for the time required to develop a program based on its length. A similar measuring unit is kilo lines of code (KLOC).

SLOC and KLOC offer the advantages of being quantitative and somewhat repeatable for a given computer language such as COBOL, FORTRAN, or BASIC. However, these methods are falling out of favor because many of the languages in use today are not textual in nature.

The most direct replacement for SLOC/KLOC are methods that estimate the effort required to program a form, page, window, report, cell, widget, file, or calculation. For example, the programming effort for a web application would be tied to the number of forms, pages, and windows in a web application and the number of fields and variables in each.

An analogy between the older and newer methods for estimating source code is to estimate the time required to develop engineering drawings for an automobile. Old methods would rely on the weight (number of pounds, akin to the number of lines of code) of the car. Newer methods rely on the number of individual features (engine size, number of doors, seats, lights, accessories, and so on).

Using Constructive Cost Model   The *Constructive Cost Model* (COCOMO) method for estimating software development projects was developed in the aerospace industry in the 1970s and represented an advancement in the ability to estimate the effort required to develop software. Three levels of COCOMO were developed: Basic COCOMO, Intermediate COCOMO, and Detailed COCOMO. Only Basic COCOMO is described here.

Basic COCOMO uses a minimal number of inputs:

- **KLOC**   The number of lines of code (in thousands)
- **Complexity rating**   The rating for the project, expressed as "organic" (a smaller project with experienced software engineers and less-than-rigid requirements), "semi-detached" (a larger project with a mix of rigid and semi-rigid requirements), or "embedded" (a large project with highly specific and restrictive requirements)

Equations in Basic COCOMO are

$$E = a(KLOC)^b$$

$$D = c(E)d$$

$$P = E/D$$

where the values a, b, c, and d are taken from Table 4-1, and

E = Effort required in man-months
D = Development time in months
P = Number of people required

Let's look at two examples. First, a software project has 32,000 lines of code and is classified as organic. Using the COCOMO estimating model, this effort will require 91.3 man-months, 13.9 months of elapsed time, and seven people.

In a second example, a software project requires 186,000 lines of code and is classified as embedded. Using the formulas here, this project will require 1,904 man-months, 28 months of elapsed time, and 68 people. This is a large project!

Table 4-1
COCOMO
Weighting
Factors

Project Type	a	b	c	d
Organic	2.4	1.05	2.5	0.38
Semi-detached	3.0	1.12	2.5	0.35
Embedded	3.6	1.20	2.5	0.32

Using Function Point Analysis   *Function point analysis* (FPA) is a time-proven estimation technique for larger software projects. Developed in the 1970s, it looks at the number of application functions and their complexity. FPA is not hindered by specific technologies or measuring techniques (such as lines of code), so it is more adaptable for today's graphical user interface (GUI)–based software.

In FPA, the analyst studies the detailed design specifications for an application program and counts the number of user inputs, user outputs, user queries, files, and external interfaces. The analyst then selects a complexity weighting factor for each of those five points. The number of inputs, outputs, queries, files, and interfaces are multiplied by their respective complexity weights, and those products are added together. The sum is called the number of unadjusted *function points* (FPs) for the program.

A *value adjustment factor* (VAF) is then determined for the application; this factor will raise or lower the function points based upon 14 criteria that address various aspects of application complexity. The total number of unadjusted function points is multiplied by the VAF to yield the total adjusted function points.

A sample FPA calculation table appears in Table 4-2.

The only disadvantage of FPA is that the value of an FP for a program does not directly specify the time required to develop it. However, an organization that has used FPA in the past will probably have a pretty good idea of the number of man-hours or man-months each FP requires.

Considering Other Costs   In addition to man-months, other costs will need to be considered in a software project, including

- **Development, modeling, and testing tools**   The project may require new tools for developers or additional licenses if there are more developers working on the project than the number of available licenses.

- **Workstations**   Developers, testers, or users may require additional (or more powerful) workstations.

Parameter	Count	Weighting			Results
		Simple	Average	Complex	
# of user inputs	_____	× 3	× 4	× 6	= _____
# of user outputs	_____	× 4	× 5	× 7	= _____
# of user queries	_____	× 3	× 4	× 6	= _____
# of files opened	_____	× 7	× 10	× 15	= _____
# of external interfaces	_____	× 5	× 7	× 10	= _____
			Total Unadjusted Function Points		= _____
			Multiplied by Value Adjustment Factor		× _____
			Total Adjusted Function Points		= _____

Table 4-2   Using FPA to Estimate Effort Required to Develop Complex Applications

- **Servers**   The project may require additional servers or upgrades to existing servers. Servers may be needed for production and for development and testing purposes.

- **Software licenses**   This includes licenses for operating systems, database management systems, application software, virtual network devices, and possibly more.

- **Network devices**   The project may require additional network devices (whether physical or virtual) such as switches, routers, or firewalls to tie everything together.

- **Storage**   The system may require more storage than was estimated.

- **Connectivity**   Higher capacity network connections might be required.

- **Training**   Developers or testers may need training on the use of their tools, and users may need training regarding the use of new software.

- **Equipment**   This could include office equipment such as copiers, and just about anything else.

- **Travel**   Staff, trainers, consultants, suppliers, and others may need to travel to various locations throughout the project.

Additional costs associated with a project may be specific to certain industries, regulations, or locales.

Scheduling Project Tasks

When the project manager or planner has established the complete breakdown of tasks and has determined resources, dependencies, and levels of effort for each, he or she can create the actual project schedule. Tools such as Trac, Microsoft Planner, Microsoft Project, and many others will automatically assign dates to tasks once their duration, dependencies, and resources are identified.

After the planner/manager has entered all of the tasks into a project planning tool, he or she will probably discover that the end date of the project (as calculated by the tool) is long after the date that senior management has defined as the end of the project.

This is where a good project planner/manager begins to earn his or her compensation.

This is a critical phase in the project, when the project manager begins to analyze the project plan and look for ways to shorten the overall duration. Methods for optimizing project duration and squeezing the project into management-supplied constraints include

- **Shorten task duration**   The project manager should consult with subject matter experts who provided time estimates for each task and see whether those estimates were high. A good project manager presses for details as he or she asks the expert to justify the time frames on the plan.

- **Reduce dependencies**   The project manager can consult with subject matter experts to find ways to reduce dependencies, which can enable more tasks to run in parallel (which is okay as long as there aren't multiple tasks stacking up on individual resources or teams).

- **Identify critical paths**   The project manager can perform critical path analysis (discussed in more detail later in this section). This will help to point out which parts of the project may need additional scrutiny.

Gantt Chart   A *Gantt chart* is a visual representation of a project in which individual tasks occupy rows on a worksheet and horizontal time bars depict the time required to complete each task relative to other tasks in the project. A Gantt chart can also show schedule dependencies and percent completion of each task. A sample Gantt chart is shown in Figure 4-5.

Program (or Project) Evaluation and Review Technique   A *program (or project) evaluation and review technique* (which is nearly always known just as PERT) chart provides a visual representation of project tasks, timelines, and dependencies. A PERT chart shows project tasks from left to right in time sequence, with connectors signifying dependencies. An example PERT chart is shown in Figure 4-6.

Critical Path Methodology (CPM)   A PERT chart helps to illustrate how a project is a "network" of related and sequenced tasks. In this network, it is possible to draw "paths" through ordered tasks from the beginning to the end of the project.

When a PERT chart includes notation regarding the elapsed time required for each task, you can follow each path through the network and add the elapsed time to get a total time for each path.

A project's *critical path* is that path through the PERT chart with the highest total elapsed time.

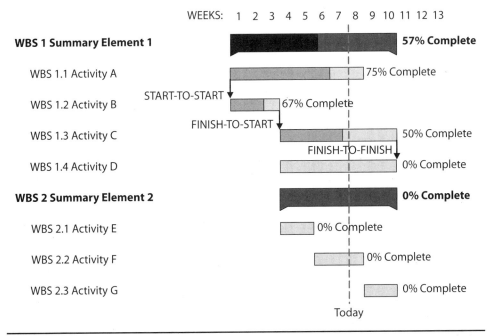

Figure 4-5   A Gantt chart illustrates task duration, schedule dependencies, and percent completion.

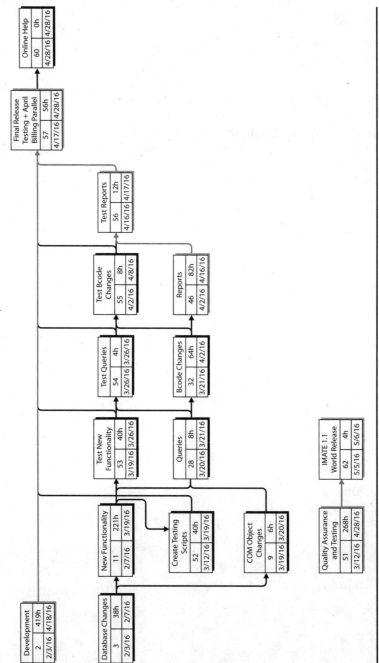

Figure 4-6 A PERT chart helps to visualize time sequence and dependencies in a project. (Image courtesy of Digital Aardvark, Inc.)

It is important to identify the critical path in a project, because this enables the project manager to understand which tasks are most likely to impact the project schedule and to determine when the project will finally conclude. When a project manager knows which tasks are on the critical path, he or she can perform analysis and attempt to improve the project plan through one of the following:

- **Start critical tasks earlier**   If a critical-path task on a project can be started earlier, this will directly affect the project's end date. To be able to start a task earlier, it may be necessary to change the way that earlier dependent tasks are performed. For example, a Unix system administrator can be brought into a project a week earlier to begin critical tasks such as building servers.

- **Reduce dependencies**   If earlier tasks in the project can be changed, it may be possible to remove one or more dependencies that will enable critical tasks to begin (and hence, end) earlier. For example, the "Install operating system" task depends on an earlier task, "Purchase server." If the organization has an available server in-house, the project does not need to wait to order, purchase, and receive a server. By using an in-house server, the "Install operating system" task can be started earlier.

- **Apply more resources to critical tasks**   Some labor-intensive tasks can be completed more quickly if more resources are available to assist with them. An experienced project manager will be able to identify the types of tasks that can be shortened by adding resources. As the saying goes, however, "Nine women cannot make a baby in one month." Experienced project managers are keenly aware of the concept behind this truth.

NOTE   It is impossible to rid a project of critical paths. It is possible, however, (and even essential) to perform one or more rounds of critical-path analysis to find opportunities to shorten the project schedule. This can also help to smooth out resource utilization so that people on a project team are used more constantly.

Squeeze to Fit

Left to their own accord, most projects would greatly overrun the period and budget intended by their sponsors and customers. An initial project plan for a simple software development project, for example, may span nine months—but management, being astute with the timing of software projects, wants it done in three.

Most project managers are capable of creating project plans whose schedules extend practically to infinity. However, management should (and does) apply pressure to shorten a project's schedule, often by a significant proportion.

What separates expert project managers from the rest is their ability to optimize a project plan by relentlessly seeking opportunities to compress the schedule by removing dependencies. They achieve this by becoming familiar with the details of every task and by asking tough questions of the experts on the team.

Peaks and valleys of resource utilization are costly and disruptive. They're more costly especially when external resources (for example, contractors and consultants) are used, since on-again, off-again resource utilization may incur extra fees. But they can also be costly for internal resources if personnel are being shuttled back and forth between projects. Starts and stops can mean that personnel incur startup time as they move back and forth between projects.

Timebox Management   For many projects, time is the primary constraint, and in such projects, the end date is non-negotiable. A *timebox* is a period in which a project (or a set of tasks within a project) must be completed.

Timeboxing can increase the chances that a large project can be completed within a certain time period by splitting it into several periods (each usually a few weeks long). Each timebox has its own budget, which is fixed. The deliverable for each timebox, however, can be adjusted somewhat, provided that the customer (or primary end user) agrees with any changes.

NOTE   Timeboxing overcomes problems of procrastination and projects whose timelines slip. One characteristic of software developers is a tendency to strive for perfection on a project. The result of this tendency is that developers will complete a task and then repeatedly "preen" the output, which takes considerable extra time with little tangible benefit.

A Project of Sprints

Many organizations are organizing their IT projects using agile methodology, which is not used just for software development anymore—in fact, many projects are broken down into one-to-four-week sprints. It's been recognized that sprints help a project team focus on intermediate goals and achieve them in short periods of time.

Project Records

Projects need to have written records of their proceedings, from project inception to shutdown. The purpose of these records is to help project managers and other project team members keep track of the details related to the project during its lifetime and beyond.

The types of records that most often need to be kept for a project include

- **Project plans**   This includes initial project plans as well as the records used to track task scheduling and completion.

- **Project changes**   Proposed and approved (as well as rejected) changes to the project schedule, deliverables, budget, and so on need to be recorded.

- **Legal documents**   Contracts, proposals, and statements of work (SOWs) that are a part of the project should be recorded. Internal and external SLAs fit in this category also.

- **Meeting agendas and minutes**   This includes issues, decisions, and other matters encountered and discussed from week to week.

- **Resource consumption**   Purchase orders, invoices, and receipts for equipment, supplies, and services should be recorded. This may also include time sheets and invoices for employees, contractors, consultants, and other service providers.

- **Task information**   Details associated with the performance and/or completion of project tasks should be recorded.

- **Draft and final deliverables**   Any work products that are produced as a part of the project need to be retained. If there are any approvals associated with final versions of deliverables, these need to be retained as well.

Good, Cheap, Fast: Pick Any Two

Experienced project managers are—consciously or unconsciously—aware of the Good-Cheap-Fast triad in project management. For any project, for the characteristics Good, Cheap, and Fast, management may choose which two characteristics are the most desirable. Whichever two they select, the third characteristic will take an inverse trend.

These are the principles:

- If a project is Good and Cheap, it will not be Fast.
- If a project is Good and Fast, it will not be Cheap.
- If a project is Cheap and Fast, it will not be Good.

While these statements are not absolute, they are reasonable principles to keep in mind when managing issues that affect budget, schedule, and the quality of the project's outcome.

Project Documentation

Virtually every IT project needs to include documentation that describes the system or application that is built or modified. Documentation helps a wide audience with many aspects of an application, including

- **Users**   End users of applications need to understand how the systems are supposed to be used. This includes the operation of all user interfaces, the business meaning of application controls, and how to solve typical problems and issues.

- **Support**   If end-user support is provided, these individuals need to know how to guide users through typical and not-so-typical problems and how to fix common problems.

- **IT operations**   System operators who monitor and operate systems and applications need to know what they are supposed to do. This can include application, database, operating system, or device monitoring; problem identification and resolution; backups; system recovery; and daily or weekly tasks.

- **Developers**   Detailed descriptions of the system will help current and future IT workers understand how the system works. Descriptions of the inner workings of individual programs, components, and tools; internal and external data flows; interfaces; and state diagrams will help developers and engineers understand a system so that they can more easily support problems and make future changes.

- **Auditors**   IT and business auditors who audit the systems, applications, or the business process(es) supported by the system need to know how the system works. This includes business controls such as access controls and the enforcement of business rules, as well as the manner in which business information is stored and processed.

- **Configuration management**   This includes information on the methods to be used to manage and record configuration changes in the system and in the supporting infrastructure and services.

- **Security**   This includes information on controls within and around the system that protect it, as well as event logging and incident response procedures.

- **Disaster recovery and business continuity planning**   If the system supports a business process that is in-scope for business continuity planning or disaster recovery planning, a complete set of documentation is required that describes system recovery and emergency operations.

- **Management**   Company management needs to understand how systems support critical business functions, as well as information about the internal and external resources required to build and support the system.

 NOTE   For software projects where existing systems are being updated, all of the existing documents associated with the system need to be reviewed and updated.

Project Change Management

When a project is launched, company management has agreed to sponsor and allocate resources to the project based upon the objectives of the project at its onset. As a project is launched and as it progresses week by week, the project manager and team will meet regularly to discuss the schedule and any issues that arise that were unanticipated at the start of the project.

   While managing the project schedule, a project manager could be tempted to adjust the end date on a task that is running late to adjust affected downstream tasks. However, doing so may affect the budget or the final project deliverable. Management might not appreciate the project manager making arbitrary changes to the project schedule without asking for permission. If management permits this degree of latitude from the project manager, it is likely that the schedule will continue to slip here and there, significantly affecting the final completion date as well as the budget and resource utilization. This type of change cannot be permitted to take place.

Issues that affect the overall project schedule, deliverables, resources, and budget need to be formally identified and submitted for approval through a formal change process. Management needs to establish parameters for changes to budget, schedule, deliverables, and resources. For example, any proposed project change that results in a change of budget or final delivery date would need to be approved by management. The procedure for making changes to the project should be done in two basic steps:

1. The project team, together with the project manager, should identify the specific issue, its impact on the project, and their proposed remedy. This information should be packaged into a formal request.

2. This change request should be presented to management, either in one of the regular project meetings or in a separate meeting that includes the project manager, any relevant project team members (experts in the specific matter to be discussed), and members of senior management—preferably those who are sponsoring the project. The proposed change and its impact on the project should be discussed, and management should make a decision on whether to approve the change.

It should be evident that not every small change needs to go through this process. A spending increase of $10 is hardly a reason to call a management review, but an increase of $50,000 done without any review may make management fuming mad. Management needs to set some parameters so that change reviews will take place only when changes exceed any set thresholds.

Smaller changes in schedule and budget can be made a part of a regular project status report that should be sent to management and project sponsors. Smaller issues of changes to budget, schedule, and resources can be highlighted so that management is aware of these less significant changes.

 NOTE Tracking changes in a project is as important as tracking the project's activities. Only by tracking project changes such as schedule, resource, and cost adjustments can the project manager and senior management understand the status of a project at any given time.

Project Closure

When the developed or updated application is completed, the system will be handed over to users (as applicable) and support staff. Before the project team disbands, some project closure activities need to take place:

- **Project debrief** Here, project team members conduct an honest assessment of the performance of the project. Every aspect of the project is considered: project management, management support, team member participation, user participation, tools and technologies, issues and how they were managed, and turnover. Lessons on what went well and what did not are included.

- **Project documentation archival**   All of the records associated with the project are archived for future reference. This includes project plans, correspondence, meeting agendas and minutes, budgets, drawings, specifications, requirements, documentation, and practically everything else.

- **Management review**   This is similar to the project debrief and may be the same activity or something different from the project debrief. Management provides the same kind of feedback on the performance of the project that project team members do themselves.

- **Training**   Users, operators, support, and analysts need to be trained on the new or changed system. In some cases, this should be handled prior to project closure, particularly if users will be using the system before that time.

- **Formal turnover to users, operations, and support**   When the project is completed, the project team formally relinquishes control of all the elements of the project. Responsibility for managing and operating the application is transferred to IT operations and support. Responsibility for using the application is transitioned to business owners and end users.

Project Management Methodologies

Planning, initiating, and managing a project is a complex undertaking, and many different types of projects are undertaken, even within an individual organization. Several project management methodologies are in use. These methodologies differ in approach, documentation, and management techniques.

Project Management Body of Knowledge (PMBOK)

The PMBOK guide is an international standard (IEEE Std 1490-2011 and ANSI/PMI 99-001-2008) that defines the essentials of project management. The PMBOK is process-based; processes are described as follows:

- Inputs (documentation, plans, designs, and so on)
- Tools and techniques (mechanisms applied to inputs)
- Outputs (documentation, products, or services)

In the PMBOK model, processes in most projects are arranged in five process groups and ten knowledge areas. The process groups for running a project are

1. Initiating
2. Planning
3. Executing
4. Controlling and Monitoring
5. Closing

The knowledge areas in a project are

1. Project Integration Management

2. Project Scope Management

3. Project Time Management

4. Project Cost Management

5. Project Quality Management

6. Project Human Resource Management

7. Project Communications Management

8. Project Risk Management

9. Project Procurement Management

10. Project Stakeholders Management

The process groups and knowledge areas form a matrix, wherein every process within project management falls into one knowledge area and one group.

NOTE The PMBOK is described in a publication called *A Guide to the Project Management Body of Knowledge,* published by the Project Management Institute (PMI).

Projects in Controlled Environments

The PRojects IN Controlled Environments (PRINCE2) is a project management framework that was developed by the U.K. Office of Government Commerce and is now managed by AXELOS. Like PMBOK, PRINCE2 is a process-driven framework. The elements of the framework are organized into seven top-level processes:

1. Starting Up a Project (SU)

2. Directing a Project (DP)

3. Initiating a Project (IP)

4. Controlling a Stage (CS)

5. Managing Product Delivery (MP)

6. Managing Stage Boundaries (SB)

7. Closing a Project (CP)

Each of these processes has its own structure and additional detail that describe steps and required activities. The PRINCE2 method that integrates principles, themes, and processes is depicted in Figure 4-7.

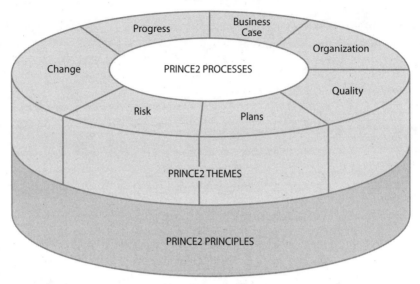

PROJECT ENVIRONMENT

Figure 4-7 The PRINCE2 method integrates principles, themes, and processes. (Image courtesy of AXELOS Limited)

NOTE PRINCE2 is the de facto project management framework in the United Kingdom and several other countries. PRINCE2 is available from https://www.axelos.com/best-practice-solutions/prince2/.

Scrum

Scrum is an iterative and incremental process most commonly used to manage an agile software development effort. Scrum defines several roles:

- **ScrumMaster** The project manager or team leader
- **Product owner** The customer or the customer's representative who speaks for the customer
- **Team** The project team members who do the actual project work
- **Users** The people who will be using the software once it has been developed or updated
- **Stakeholders** Other parties who contribute in some way to the project, such as customers, vendors, and suppliers
- **Managers** The individuals who provide resources to the project

These roles belong to two major groups: *stakeholders* and *employees*. The stakeholders are the ScrumMaster, product owner, and team members. The employees are everyone else on the team; though they are interested in the outcome of the project, their jobs are probably not on the line.

A typical Scrum team is just five to nine members. Larger projects are organized into a Scrum of Scrums that scales upward to include hundreds of programmers.

A typical Scrum project consists of a *sprint*, a focused effort to produce some portion of the total project deliverable. A sprint usually lasts from two to four weeks.

The project team meets every day in a meeting called the *daily standup* (or the *Daily Scrum*) that lasts no more than 15 minutes. It is called a *standup* because participants usually stand (it helps the meeting go faster). The ScrumMaster leads the meeting and asks three questions of each team member:

1. What have you done since yesterday?

2. What are you planning to do by tomorrow?

3. What obstacles are preventing you from completing your work?

Although employees are welcome to join the daily standup, only stakeholders are permitted to speak.

At the end of each sprint, a *sprint retrospective* is held, a meeting that is a reflection of the just-completed sprint. A retrospective is usually limited to four hours.

The documents that are created and maintained in a Scrum project are

- **Product backlog**   This list of required features describes deliverables for the entire project (not just the current sprint).
- **Sprint backlog**   This detailed document describes how the project team will implement requirements for the current sprint.
- **Burn down chart**   This document shows the number of remaining tasks for the current sprint or the count of items on the sprint backlog.

The Scrum process is illustrated in Figure 4-8.

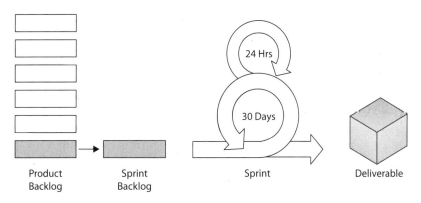

Product
Backlog

Sprint
Backlog

24 Hrs

30 Days

Sprint

Deliverable

Figure 4-8   The Scrum process consists of one or more sprints that produce project deliverables every two to four weeks.

NOTE Scrum is used by several large software product firms such as IBM and Microsoft.

Lean

You should think of *lean* more as an approach than as a process like waterfall or Scrum. Lean focuses on efficiency; it starts by identifying value and then achieves it through the mindset of continuous improvement and elimination of waste.

Lean was derived from the *lean manufacturing* methodology that originated in the Japanese manufacture of Toyota automobiles, which focused on the elimination of waste without sacrificing value.

The principles of lean are

- Eliminate waste.
- Amplify learning.
- Decide as late as possible.
- Deliver as fast as possible.
- Empower the team.
- Build integrity in.
- Optimize the whole.

Agile

Like lean, *agile* is more of an approach than a methodology or a process. The agile manifesto describes four principles:

- Individuals and interactions over processes and tools
- Working software over comprehensive documentation
- Customer collaboration over contract negotiation
- Responding to change over following a plan

Agile is mainly known as an iterative technique used to move a project toward success. Pundits would call agile a development process without a master plan, but with iterative plans instead. Like an artist rendering a painting, the artist adds basic shapes and hues, continually adding detail and touching up until the piece is finished.

Kanban

Also derived from the lean Toyota Production System manufacturing model, the root of Kanban is the visual Kanban board that shows the overall flow and progress of a project. Figure 4-9 shows an example Kanban board. Arguably, the greatest strength of Kanban is its visual display of planned tasks, work in progress, and completed tasks. While managing a project, a project manager will pull forward specific tasks as resources are available to complete them.

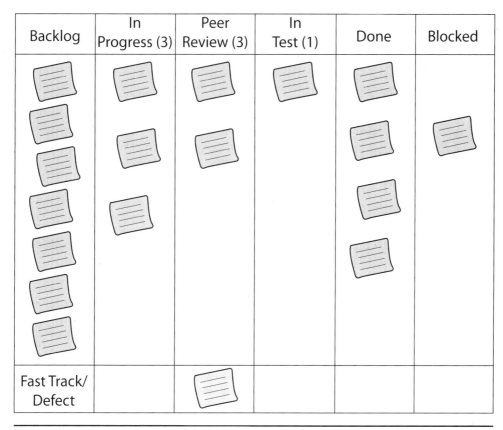

Figure 4-9   Example Kanban board (Image source: Dr. Ian Mitchell)

Scrumban

As the name suggests, *Scrumban* is a combination of Scrum and Kanban methodologies. Scrumban has the structure of Scrum with the flexibility of Kanban. Scrumban is suitable for Kanban-oriented teams that need more structure, or for Scrum teams that need more flexibility.

Extreme Programming

Extreme programming (XP) is an iterative development methodology used primarily in software development projects. Extreme programming has a set of values that are similar to Scrum:

- Simplicity
- Communication
- Feedback
- Respect
- Courage

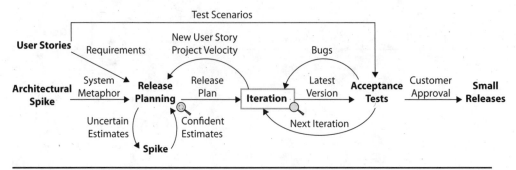

Figure 4-10 Extreme Programming process flow (Image courtesy of Don Wells)

Figure 4-10 depicts an XP workflow. More information on XP is available at www .extremeprogramming.org.

The Systems Development Life Cycle (SDLC)

Developing and maintaining information systems is a complex undertaking that requires a great deal of structure, organization, and discipline. Application software and other systems are used to automate or support key business processes. Organizations rely heavily on applications to be operating properly, on demand, and with sufficient capacity.

Designing, developing, and using information systems requires a diverse array of skills that are typically held by people located throughout an organization. These diverse skills are applied by persons with different levels and styles of education, and in the workplace, these different groups of people are sometimes suspicious of one another and believe that the others do not really understand "the way things ought to be." This is a part of the human dynamic that affects the performance of project teams and influences the outcome of larger development projects.

System development projects are expensive. Given the cost of developers, project managers, software tools, and computer hardware, even a "small" project can easily cost many tens of thousands of dollars, and large projects can cost several million.

Management wants the project to finish on time and on budget, and users want the software to operate as promised. Shareholders want the entire development process to be efficient and effective.

EXAM TIP The CISA exam may include multiple questions related to the SDLC or its business process equivalent, the Business Process Life Cycle (BPLC), covered later in this chapter. Familiarity with the phases of the SDLC is key to your success with these questions.

These factors are among those that demand that the software development process be highly organized and structured so that all activities are performed according to a plan. The SDLC is a framework for deciding what software should do, building it accordingly, performing testing to verify features, placing it in production, providing support, and maintaining it after initial implementation.

> ### The "S" in SDLC Now Stands for "Systems"
> IT and security professionals who have been in the business for more than ten years will sooner or later notice the switch in the well-known SDLC acronym. Originally, and for decades, SDLC referred to the "software development life cycle," for many organizations developed their own business applications and spent considerable effort maintaining and customizing those applications over many years.
>
> Two changes have occurred. First, fewer organizations develop their own business application software, and instead purchase off-the-shelf applications or (more often) subscribe to Software-as-a-Service (SaaS) services for their primary business applications. Second, the SDLC life cycle has been expanded to encompass projects such as the development of infrastructure. Hence, the "S" in SDLC has been changed to "systems" to represent a broader perspective than just that of software applications.

SDLC Phases

The *systems development life cycle* describes the end-to-end process for developing and maintaining software. A common structure for SDLC is a *waterfall*-style framework that consists of several distinct phases:

1. Feasibility study
2. Requirements definition
3. Design
4. Development
5. Testing
6. Implementation
7. Post-implementation

Organizations often employ a "gate process" approach to their SDLC by requiring that a formal review be held at the conclusion of each phase before the next phase is permitted to begin. The review is usually a formal meeting where project managers and other participants describe the status of the project; management, if satisfied that the current phase of the project has been completed successfully and that all requirements have been met, will permit the project to proceed to the next phase.

In addition to the waterfall SDLC model, iterative and spiral models are used in SDLC processes. The iterative and spiral models both operate in (visually) circular modes, as opposed to the linear waterfall model.

The *spiral* model consists of the development of requirements, design, and one or more prototypes, followed by additional requirements and design phases until the entire design is complete. Similarly, the development in the *iterative* model goes through one or more loops of planning, requirements, design, coding, and testing until development and implementation are considered complete.

The *DevOps* model is also often used for systems development processes. DevOps is an iterative development and operations model that is discussed later in this chapter.

SDLC in this section is described from the waterfall model's perspective. The activities discussed in this section in the waterfall model are quite similar to those in the iterative and spiral models.

Pre-SDLC: Software and Business Capabilities Imagined

The first phase of the SDLC is the *feasibility study*. But how does the feasibility study get started? It does not create itself; instead, the feasibility study is started as a result of some pre-SDLC event.

An instantiation of the SDLC is created when management has decided that some new software application is needed or some significant changes are needed in an existing application. By "instantiation" I mean that management has decided to initiate the process to develop or update a software application. Management makes such a decision as a response to an event, which could be any of the following:

- **Changes in market conditions**   For example, the entrance of a new competitor or the development of a new product or service feature by a competitor may spur management to respond by matching the competitor's capabilities. A competitor can also create a new market through innovation in products or services; this kind of a move sometimes needs to be answered by making a change to maintain parity with the competitor. Or *your* organization may be the one that creates a new market through some groundbreaking innovation in the way that it does business or in what it delivers to its customers.

- **Changes in costs or expenses**   Dramatic shifts in capital or expense costs may force an organization to make changes. For instance, higher fuel costs may prompt the organization to reduce field service calls, but doing so might require better remote diagnostic and self-healing capabilities. In the 1990s, the shift to software development outsourcing required transformations in development methodologies that prompted organizations to make or buy better defect-management applications. And dropping telecommunications costs and higher bandwidth meant that online service providers began to ratchet up their offerings, most of which required enhancements to existing online service applications, and sometimes brand-new ones.

- **Changes in regulation**   The rise in dependence on technology has resulted in some negative events, which in turn resulted in new legislation or changes in existing legislation. Examples of relatively recent and updated regulation include Sarbanes-Oxley; GLBA (Gramm Leach Bliley Act); HIPAA (Health Insurance

Portability and Accountability Act); FERC/NERC (regulations from the Federal Energy Regulatory Commission and the North American Electric Reliability Corporation); USA PATRIOT Act (Uniting and Strengthening America by Providing Appropriate Tools Required to Intercept and Obstruct Terrorism Act of 2001), which has been updated by the USA Freedom Act; European General Data Protection Regulation (GDPR), PCI DSS (Payment Card Industry Data Security Standard); and many others. Many of these regulations require organizations to implement additional safeguards, controls, and recordkeeping to information systems. Sometimes this results in an organization opting to discontinue use of an older information system in favor of making or buying a newer application that can more effectively comply with applicable laws.

- **Changes in risk**   New types of vulnerabilities are discovered with regularity, and new threats are developed in response to vulnerabilities as well as changes in economic conditions and organizational business models. In other words, hackers find new ways to try and attack systems for profit within the growing cyber-criminal enterprises of the world. Applications that were considered safe just a few years ago are now known to be too vulnerable to operate. Reducing risk sometimes means making changes to application logic, and sometimes it requires that an application be discontinued altogether.

- **Changes to business processes**   Many types of changes to business processes will require organizations to alter their business applications so that they continue to support those processes. For example, a change in the way that purchase orders are requested and approved may require changes to the financial accounting application.

- **Changes to legal agreements**   Changes in the legal agreements between organizations can compel an organization to make changes to its software applications. There are several possible reasons for this, including changes in risks or regulations imposed upon customer or partner organizations.

- **Changes in customer requirements**   Changes like those just discussed will often prompt customer organizations to ask for new features or for changes in existing features in the products and services they buy. Often this requires changes in processes and applications to meet these customers' needs.

It is important to understand that *innovation* is also a valid and frequent reason that an organization chooses to make changes to a software application. Generally, this means that an organization has developed new features or methods in a software application in an attempt to gain a competitive advantage.

 NOTE   Internal and external events prompt management to action by initiating changes in business processes, product designs, service models, and, frequently, the software applications that are used to support and manage them. What begins as an informal discussion turns to more formal actions and, finally, to the initiation of a project to make changes.

Feasibility Study

The *feasibility study* is the first formal phase in the SDLC. The feasibility study is an intellectual effort that seeks to determine whether a specific change or set of changes in business processes and underlying applications is practical to undertake.

Capital and money are the fuel and lubricant for an organization. Often the purpose of a feasibility study is not to answer the question, "Can a specific type of change be made to the business?" but rather, "Is a specific type of change to the business feasible from a cost and benefit perspective?" In other words, the feasibility study is an analysis of proposed changes to business processes and supporting applications, including the costs associated with making those changes and the benefits that are expected as a result of those changes. While there is often a qualitative aspect in the feasibility study, there is almost always a quantitative aspect that states, "These specific changes will cost XXX to build, YYY to maintain, and are anticipated to make a ZZZ impact on revenue."

Organizations don't always make changes to business processes to increase revenue or reduce costs. However, revenue and costs are nearly always the quantitative elements that receive attention. For example, if an organization is enacting changes to processes and systems to remain compliant with regulations, management is still going to be interested in the cost and revenue impact that the changes will bring about.

A feasibility study often will propose two or more approaches to a particular challenge. For instance, if a project has been initiated as a result of changes in market conditions, the purpose of the feasibility study may be to explore various ways to respond to those market conditions; for each way to respond, there may be two, three, or more ways to implement the change by using a variety of technologies or approaches. For example, when a ride-sharing service seeks ways of expanding its markets, it considers developing additional services such as the delivery of restaurant meals, flowers, and other goods.

The feasibility study should also include the following considerations:

- Time required to develop or acquire software (or to make changes) and whether the solution can be developed or acquired within that time frame
- A comparison between the cost of developing the application versus buying one
- Whether an existing system can meet the business need
- Whether the application supports strategic business objectives
- Whether a solution can be developed (or acquired) that is compatible with other IT systems
- The cost of building interfaces between the new system and other existing systems
- The impact of the proposed changes to the business regarding regulatory compliance
- Whether future requirements can be met by the system
- Whether an innovative change will result in an increase in market share

A feasibility study should seek to uncover every reasonable issue and risk that will be associated with the new system. The study should have the appearance and form of impartiality and should not reflect the biases and preferences of those who are taking part in the feasibility study or its outcome.

A feasibility study may also include or reference a formal business plan for the proposed new activity. A *business plan* is a formal document that describes the new business activity, its contribution and impact to the organization, resources required to operate the activity, benefits from operating the activity, and risks associated with the activity.

NOTE When the feasibility study has been completed, a formal management review should take place so that senior management fully understands the results and recommendations of the study and can determine whether the project should proceed or whether any changes to the plan should take place.

Requirements Definition

Requirements describe necessary characteristics of a new application or of changes being made to an existing application. They describe how the application should work as well as the technologies that it should support. The types of requirements used in software projects are

- Business functional requirements
- Technical requirements and standards
- Security and regulatory requirements
- Disaster recovery and business continuity requirements
- Privacy requirements

These types of requirements are described in detail in the remainder of this section.

Business Functional Requirements Nearly every software project will include *functional requirements*. These are statements that describe required characteristics that the software must have to support business needs. This includes both the way that the software accepts, processes, and produces information, and how users interact with the software in terms of technology, appearance, and user interface function.

Functional requirements should be a part of new software acquisitions as well as modifications or updates to software.

Example functional requirements resemble the following:

- Application supports payroll tax calculations for U.S. federal, states, counties, and cities
- Application supports payment by credit card, electronic check, and virtual currency
- Application encrypts credit card numbers, social insurance numbers, and driver's license numbers in storage and when transmitted

Notice that the preceding examples do not specify *how* the application is to accomplish these things. Business requirements are interested in *what* the application does; the application architect or designer will determine *how* the application will support those requirements.

In a few circumstances, new business requirements are not needed for a software modification. For example, if a software interface is being upgraded, an existing software program may need to be modified to work with the new interface. A change like this should be transparent to users, and the software should not differ in the way that it supports existing business requirements. So, in a way, it can be argued that business requirements apply even in this case: the program will still be required to adhere to existing business functional requirements.

 NOTE It is not unusual for a formal requirements document to span many hundreds of pages. This will be the case especially for larger and more complex applications such as customer relationship management (CRM), enterprise resource planning (ERP), manufacturing resource planning (MRP), or service management systems.

Technical Requirements and Standards To help the organization remain efficient, any new application or system should use the same basic technologies that are already in use (or that are planned on being used in the long term). The details related to maintaining the consistency that is required constitute the majority of technical requirements and standards.

An organization of any appreciable size should have formal technical standards in place. These standards are policy statements that cite the technologies, protocols, vendors, and services that make up the organization's core IT infrastructure. The purpose of standards is to increase technological consistency throughout the entire IT infrastructure, which helps to simplify the environment and reduce costs. Standards should include the following:

- Server hardware, virtualization platform, virtual machine, operating system, and operating system configuration
- Server tools and services
- Application programming interfaces (APIs)
- Database and storage management systems
- Network architecture, communications protocols, and services
- Authentication and authorization models and protocols
- Security architecture, hardening, configuration, and algorithms
- Software development methodologies, tools, languages, and processes
- User applications and tools
- Any other standards that describe methodologies, technologies, or practices

When an organization is considering the acquisition of a new system, the requirements for the new system should include the organization's IT and security standards. This will help the organization select a system that will have the lowest possible impact on capital and operational costs over the lifetime of the system.

Besides IT standards, many additional technical requirements will define the desired new system. These requirements will describe several characteristics of the system, including

- How the system will accept, process, and output data
- Specific data layouts for interfaces to other systems
- Support of specific modules or tools that will supplement or support application functions (for example, the type of tax table that will be used in an invoicing or payroll system)
- Language support
- Specific middleware support
- Client platform support

 NOTE The entire body of technical requirements should accomplish two sweeping objectives: ensure that the new system will blend harmoniously with the existing environment, and ensure that the new system will operate as required at the technical level.

Security and Regulatory Requirements Security and regulatory requirements must be developed to ensure that the new application will contain appropriate controls and characteristics that will protect sensitive information and comply with applicable regulations.

Security and regulation are sometimes strange bedfellows, and sometimes they are symbiotic. It is often better to split security and regulatory requirements into two separate sections. However, security and regulation are often mashed together, since the majority of recent applicable regulations seem to be security-related.

 NOTE I have kept these two topics in a single section because I suspect that most readers expect to find security and compliance together, but I recommend you separate them, because many security requirements are not associated with regulations, and because many regulations are not security-related. In the remainder of this subsection I will keep them separated.

Organizations should have an existing *security requirements document* that can be readily applied to any systems development or acquisition project. These requirements should describe the business and technical controls that address several security topics, including the following:

- **Authentication**   This broad category includes many specific requirements related to the manner in which application users authenticate onto the system. For systems that perform autonomous authentication, this will include all of the password quality requirements (minimum length, expiration, complexity, and so on), account lockout settings, password reset procedures, user account provisioning, and user ID standards. Authentication standards may also include requirements for machine and system accounts in support of automated functions in the application. For applications that use a network-based authentication service such as LDAP (Lightweight Directory Access Protocol), Kerberos, or a single-sign-on (SSO) solution, security requirements should describe how the application must interface with a network authentication service.

- **Authorization**   This category includes requirements related to the manner in which different users are granted access to different functions and data in the application. Authorization requirements may include the way in which roles are established, maintained, and audited. An organization may require that the application support a number of *roles*, which are templates that contain authorization details that can be applied to a user account.

- **Access control**   This category has to do with how the application is configured to permit access to users and/or roles. Unlike authorization, which is about assigning roles to users, access control is concerned with assigning access permissions to objects such as application functions and data. Depending upon the way in which an application is designed, permissions assignment may be user-centric, object-centric, or both.

- **Encryption**   Really another form of access control, encryption is used to hide data that, for whatever reason, may exist in "plain sight" in some contexts and yet must still be protected from those who do not have authorization to access it. Encryption standards fall into two broad categories: (1) data requiring encryption in certain settings and contexts, and with certain encryption algorithms and key lengths; and (2) key management to be handled in specific ways that permit the application to be operated similarly to other applications in the IT environment.

- **Data validation**   Applications should not blindly trust all input data to be properly formed and formatted. Instead, an application should perform validation checks against input data, whether a user types in input data on an application input form or the application receives the data via a batch feed from a trusted source. Data validation includes not only input data, but also the results of intermediate calculations and output data. Requirements should also specify what the application should do when it encounters data that fails a validation check.

- **Audit logging**   This is the characteristic whereby the application creates an electronic record of events. These events include changing application configuration settings, adding and deleting users, changing user roles and permissions, resetting user login credentials, changing access control settings, and, of course, the actions and transactions that the application is designed to handle. Requirements about audit logging will be concerned with the configuration that is used to control the types of events that are written to an audit log, as well as the controls used to protect the audit log from tampering (which, if permitted, could enable someone to "erase their tracks").

- **Security operational requirements**   Management of passwords, encryption keys, event logs, patching, and other activities is required to maintain an application's confidentiality, integrity, and availability.

- **Misuse and abuse requirements**   This category needs to include the full range of use (and misuse) cases through which a user may—deliberately or not—misuse or abuse the application. This includes malicious input and other methods that may cause the application to malfunction, resulting in an escalation of privilege, exposure of—or tampering with—sensitive data, and exhaustion of system resources. The list of requirements should not merely match the capabilities of any automated or manual testing tools used by the organization.

Disaster Recovery and Business Continuity Requirements   Applications that do—or may in the future—support critical business functions included in an organization's disaster recovery plans need to have certain characteristics. Depending upon specific recovery targets specified for the business process supported by the application, these requirements may include the ability for the application to run in the public cloud, on a server cluster, on a virtual machine, or in a load-balanced mode; to support data replication; to facilitate rapid recovery from backup tape or database redo logs; or to be installed on a cold recovery server without complicated, expensive, or time-consuming software licensing issues. Requirements could also dictate the ability for the application to be easily recovered from a server or virtual machine image on a storage area network (SAN), to operate correctly in a virtual server environment, and to operate correctly in a cloud environment such as AWS or Azure. An application might also be expected to work with a different brand or version of the database management system or to coexist with other applications, even though it may usually be configured to run on a server by itself.

Privacy Requirements   In the broadest sense, privacy is about two distinctly different issues. First, privacy has to do with the protection of personally sensitive information so that it cannot be accessed by unauthorized parties. This aspect of privacy neatly falls into the umbrella of security: security requirements can be developed that require access controls or encryption of personal information.

The other aspect of privacy is the prevention of proliferation and misuse of personally sensitive information. This has a lot less to do with security and more to do with how the organization treats and uses sensitive information and whether it permits this information to be passed on to other organizations for their own purposes. In this regard, privacy is about business functionality that is specifically related to how the application handles personal information.

For example, if an application includes canned reports about customers, and those reports are sent to third parties, those reports should be configurable so that they can contain (or omit) certain fields. For instance, customers' date of birth may be omitted from a report that is sent to a third-party organization to reduce the possibility of the third party using or abusing information to the detriment of individual customers. The rule in this case is this: "You can't abuse or misuse information you do not possess or cannot access." Indeed, regulations such as the European GDPR require that organizations collect sensitive data only as required to perform services, and that they retain the data for only as long as it is needed.

Increasingly, privacy is addressed by regulation, so an organization may choose to classify privacy requirements in a privacy section or in a regulations section.

Organizing and Reviewing Requirements   In a software project in which many individuals are contributing requirements, the project manager or another person should track each requirement back to a specific individual so that person can justify or explain those requirements if needed.

When all requirements have been collected and categorized, the project manager should check with each contributor to make sure that each requirement is actually a *requirement* and not merely a "nice-to-have" feature. Perhaps each requirement can be weighted or ranked in order of importance. This will help, especially in a request for proposals (RFP) situation, where analysts need to evaluate suppliers' conformance to individual requirements. This helps project personnel determine which vendors are best able to meet the requirements that matter most.

 TIP   The teams that develop requirements need to ensure that requirements are measurable. The reason for this is that the requirements developed in this phase of the project should flow directly into user acceptance testing plans (for functional requirements) and system testing plans (for technical requirements).

The RFP Process   The vast majority of mainstream business functions, such as accounting, customer relationship management, incident management, sales force management, and enterprise resource planning, can be handled exceedingly well using cloud-based Software-as-a-Service (SaaS) and common off-the-shelf (COTS) software. Advances in SaaS and COTS software have resulted in most IT organizations needing to develop only custom interfaces between SaaS or COTS applications and specialized programs that cannot be readily obtained. Thus, the SDLC process can be morphed somewhat to accommodate the fact that most big software projects are a matter of leasing or buying, not making. The result is the ever popular RFP activity used to communicate requirements and solicit proposals from vendors. Typical steps in the RFP process are

- **Research**   Personnel in the organization may need to learn more about available applications and solutions so that they can develop better requirements that will more closely align with business needs.

- **Requirements**   This trend makes the development of good requirements much more important, because the matching of different vendors' software products with business and technical requirements depends mostly on requirements. The software that is obtained is configurable only to a point, and it probably will not be able to perform other functions so easily. In an environment where a business analyst or project manager realizes that some requirements were omitted, if the organization wrote its own software, then it might be fairly easy to change the application. If, on the other hand, some important requirements were omitted and a product selection was made in the absence of those requirements, the organization may have to live without the functionality related to those requirements. It's kind of like specifying a four-passenger automobile because you forgot about that fifth family member; now that you've got the car, it's more difficult to make a change.

- **Vendor financial stability**   When an organization is considering purchasing or licensing software from a software vendor, the organization should examine the financial stability of the vendor. This is done as a way of determining whether the vendor is likely to be in business in the future. If the vendor's financial fundamentals are unhealthy, then purchasing software from this vendor is a risky proposition, since the vendor may not be in business in the future. This would probably require the organization to change its software in another expensive application migration that could have been avoided.

- **Product roadmap**   Although the software vendor may be healthy, it's also important to understand the vendor's long-term vision for its product. This includes not only business functionality but also the technical platforms that will be supported in the future. In this regard, it is also useful to know whether any of the vendors being considered can be deemed to be market leaders or market followers. If the organization shopping for software is likewise a market leader, it may make more sense to select a market-leading company that will be able to keep up with the organization's own vision and market leadership.

- **Experience**   It's important to understand how much experience a prospective vendor has. A suitable vendor should have many years of experience developing software for the solution that the organization is trying to solve. This will help to clarify whether the vendor has been in the business of developing this particular type of software for a long time or has only recently entered the market. Deep experience will give confidence that the vendor has experience helping its customers solve the types of business problems that its software is designed to solve, whereas a company with little experience will probably have more difficulty helping its customers solve even simpler business problems, not to mention unusual or complex problems. You do not want to be in the position of calling the software vendor to ask, "Hi, we have a new kind of problem that we need to solve," only to receive the answer, "Well, we won't be able to be of much help because we're new at this ourselves."

- **Vision**   Even for a software product as mundane as one for accounting, it is important to know each vendor's vision for how it aims to innovate and to approach business problems in the future. If a vendor's vision varies widely from your organization's vision, perhaps that particular vendor is not the best choice. Although difference in vision should rarely disqualify a vendor entirely, it should be just one more variable to consider in the long equation of vendor selection.

- **Multitenant data protection and data segregation**   For SaaS applications, it is important for those service providers to enact strict controls so that users in one customer organization are not able to access other customers' data, even in cases of software defects and intrusions.

- **References**   When an organization is considering leasing or purchasing software from an outside vendor, it is wise to discuss the vendor and its services with at least two or three reference customers. I suggest that a standard questionnaire be developed before any vendor contacts are made. A questionnaire will help the project manager or business analyst to collect the same information from each reference customer. This will help the organization more easily compare reference information that has been collected from several reference clients. Questions asked of reference clients fall into several areas:

  - **Satisfaction with implementation**   If the software vendor will be helping with software implementation, ask reference clients about the quality of this effort. Find out what kinds of specific issues came up and how the vendor managed them.

  - **Satisfaction with migration**   If the software vendor is going to be assisting with migrating business functionality to the new software application, ask each reference client about the quality of this effort. Whether it went well or not so well, get the names of specific personnel so that your organization can (if feasible) ask that certain vendor staff be there to support migration.

  - **Satisfaction with support**   Find out from each reference client whether they are satisfied with each vendor's support organization. See if the support organization provides timely, high-quality, and consistently good service.

  - **Satisfaction with long-term roadmap**   Ask the reference client if they are satisfied with each vendor's long-term product roadmap. Ask what strengths and weaknesses are in the roadmap.

  - **What went well**   Find out each vendor's strengths and try to determine if those strengths are associated with individual vendor employees or with the vendor overall. Ask if the reference client would choose the vendor again and why (or why not).

  - **What did not go so well**   Ask the reference client what parts of their software project did not go so well. Find out if the reference client believes their experience to be associated with one specific vendor employee or the entire company as a whole.

- **Other questions** Finally, ask each vendor's reference client if they have any other useful information that has not been discussed. Sometimes you'll find out about a completely different set of activities that were associated with the vendor's migration.

- **Evaluation** When you have received RFP responses from each vendor, you can begin to chart the responses in a multicolumn spreadsheet, with each vendor's responses in a separate column. You can even score each response with a Low-Medium-High rating, and use that to see how the vendors rank in terms of requirements and references. If you can reduce the field of potential vendors to the top two or three vendors, you may choose to evaluate their products in your IT environment for a time. This means installing the software in your organization to try out with some users. The evaluation should be highly scripted—not to "win" or "lose," but to verify systematically that the software performs as claimed and that the vendor's responses to your functional requirements are credible. If the software operates differently from their claims in the RFP responses, it's time either to ask hard questions or to disqualify the vendor for stretching the truth and move on.

- **Vendor support** Success with a given vendor's software product can rest on vendor support alone. Specifically, if there are problems and support is of insufficient quality, the project can stall or even fail. Support quality has a few dimensions to it, including timeliness, quality, and speed to escalation. If a vendor falls short in any of these areas, then that choice may have more risk.

- **Source code escrow** When an organization develops its own software, of course the software is already in the organization's custody. However, when a third-party vendor develops the software, the customer probably does not have a copy of it. Under ordinary business conditions, this is acceptable. However, should the vendor fail, the vendor will be unable to maintain the software and the organization would be stuck with a software package without source code or programmers to support it. Source code escrow is a viable solution to this problem, and it works like this: The software vendor sends an electronic copy of its source code to a third-party software escrow firm, which keeps control of the software. If, however, the software vendor goes out of business, the organization will be able to obtain a copy of the vendor's software for support purposes. This is a bad-case scenario, but it's better than the worst-case scenario, where the software vendor goes out of business and the organization has no source code at all.

- **Selection** After the organization has narrowed the search down to two or three vendors, it's time to do more critical thinking, discussing, and identifying of the primary strengths, weaknesses, and differentiators between the vendor finalists. The RFP team should make a recommendation to management on its choice, explaining why this particular vendor should be chosen over the others. The final decision on a software vendor should be made by management, with the RFP team being a consultative body. Remember that senior management will be making a business decision that partly considers the technology and partly considers the value proposition (the value derived from a given expenditure).

- **Contract negotiation** When the selection is made, the contract between the organization and the software vendor needs to be negotiated. There are plenty of ways that the software vendor can be held accountable in terms of delivering and supporting software that meets the business's needs. However, the organization purchasing the software will also likely have obligations of its own. I recommend that you *not* tell the other vendor finalists that they are out of the game too soon. If contract negotiations with the first-choice vendor do not proceed well, it may be smart to begin negotiations with one of the other finalists (management should decide which vendor). Contract negotiation should be left to the lawyers. However, lawyers on each side will often consult with IT experts or management to make sure that sections of contract language accurately describe systems, controls, security, and any other matters that lawyers may not have expertise in.

- **Closing the RFP** When the RFP process has concluded, the project team can begin preparations for testing and implementing the software. For obvious reasons, the design and development phases of the SDLC process are usually skipped altogether, unless the organization needs to build some custom interfaces or other programs that will enable the acquired software to work in the environment.

Request for Information A request for information (RFI) is similar to a request for proposal (RFP) in that organizations are soliciting information from one or more vendors or service providers. Compared to an RFP, an RFI is lightweight, as it requests information about vendors' products and services with no stated intent to purchase any services or products.

An RFI might precede a planned purchase, or it could precede an RFP. Mainly, the purpose of an RFI is to help individuals in an organization learn more about specific vendors or the products or services they sell.

Design

When all functional, technology, security, privacy, regulatory, and other requirements have been finalized, design of the application can begin. It is assumed that a high-level design was developed in the feasibility study, since an elementary design is necessary to estimate costs to compute the financial viability of the application—but, if not, the high-level design should be developed first.

The design effort should be a top-down process, starting with the major components of the application and then decomposing each module into increasingly detailed pieces.

It's difficult to say whether a data flow diagram (DFD), entity relationship diagram (ERD), or some other high-level depiction of the application should be developed first. This will depend partly upon the nature of the application and partly on the experience of the developers, analysts, and designers. Regardless, design should start at a high level and graduate to levels of increasing complexity, to the point where database designers and developers have sufficient detail to begin development.

Project team members who represent business owners/operators/customers should review the application design to confirm that the analysts' and designers' concept of the application agrees with that of the business owners. Reviews should be done at each level of design, not just at the top level. Business experts should be able to read and understand both a high-level design and a detailed design and to confirm whether the design is appropriate or not.

Design review by customers can be a step in the process where business customers and designers do not see eye-to-eye and where they might disagree on the design; any disagreements can be attributed either to differences in the understanding of technology or to practical versus abstract thinking. To end the design review prematurely could have costly consequences. The potential consequences of failing to come to an agreement on design are vividly depicted in the classic illustration shown in Figure 4-11.

Key activities in the software design phase include

- The use of a structured software design tool or methodology that records details of data flow and processing flow from high levels to detail levels
- Generalized and detailed database design at the logical and physical levels
- Storyboards showing user interaction with the application
- Details on reports that can be generated by the application

The application design effort should also include the development of test plans that will be used during the development and test phases of the project. Test plans need to be developed no later than the design phase, because developers will need to perform

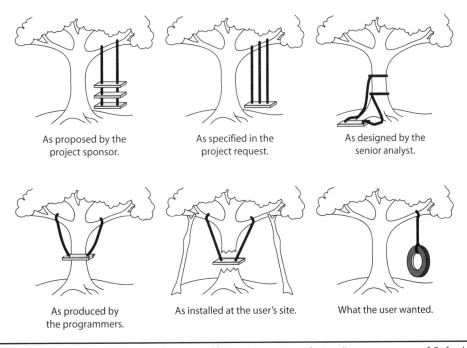

Figure 4-11 The potential consequences of failing to agree on design (Image courtesy of Oxford University Press, Inc.)

unit testing during development as a way of verifying that they have coded software modules properly (and they may need to consult test plan documents for confirmation that they are developing software correctly). If test plans are not developed until the test phase, developers will have to figure out tests on their own, or they might not perform enough testing, which will result in many more defects being discovered during the formal testing phase of the project.

When design reviews have concluded that the design is complete, a "design freeze" should be instituted, whereby no further changes to any level of design will be permitted. With a design freeze in effect, both designers and users are more inclined to really think through all of the details of the design and do a better job of confirming whether the design is correct.

An organization that does not institute a design freeze will find the design changing throughout the development phase, which will result in different parts of the application conforming to different "versions" of the ever-changing design. This will result in chaos during the development and testing phases and is sure to result in many more reported defects during user acceptance testing and after implementation. Management should strongly assert a design freeze, since changing the design during the development phase will drive up development costs when developers are forced to rework code that was written in conformance to earlier versions of the design.

NOTE   Organizations that have internal IT auditors on staff should include them in design reviews so that they can confirm whether the application design will result in an application whose integrity can be confirmed through auditing. Organizations that incur external audits may want to invite external auditors to review the design documents for this same purpose.

Development

The developers have been waiting all this time, and finally they can have their fun. Developers take the detailed design documents that were developed in the design phase and begin building the application. The activities in the development phase include

- **Coding the application**   Using tools selected for the project, developers will build the application code. Newer development tools may include design elements, code generators, debuggers, or testing tools that will make developers more productive.

- **Developing program- and system-level documents**   During development, developers document technical details such as program logic, data flows, and interfaces. This aids other developers later on when modifications to the application are needed.

- **Developing user procedures**   As they develop user interfaces, developers can write the procedure documents and help text that application users will read. In a more extensive, formal environment, developers may write the essential core of these documents, which will be completed by tech writers. But an even better idea may be this: end-user documentation is written by tech writers who derive procedures from requirements; then the software developers will use technical requirements and the completed end-user documentation to guide them on development of end-user software.

- **Working with users**   As they develop the parts of the application that interface with users, developers will need to work with them to ensure that the forms, screens, and reports that they build will meet users' needs.

Application Programming Languages   An organization that is considering an application development project has to make several strategic decisions regarding the technologies and techniques that will be used to perform the development and to operate the completed application.

Among those choices is the programming language(s) that will be used to write the application. Rarely does an organization have a wide-open choice of languages; rather, its choices will be constrained by several factors, including

- **Standards**   The organization's preferences for specific brands of computer hardware, operating systems, and databases will limit available languages to those that are available on its chosen application platform.

- **Available expertise**   Preferences will be further limited by available programming experience among staff or contracted developers. After the application has been developed and placed in use, the organization will need to make periodic changes; an experienced developer will be needed for that task as well.

- **Context and practicality**   For a given hardware and software environment, the nature of the application will make some of the available languages more desirable and others less so. For instance, an organization wants to write a professional-services invoicing application in a Unix environment where assembler, C, C++, C#, and Java are the available languages. Chances are good that assembler will be eliminated, because assembler is a poor choice for application development. Instead, C++, C#, or Java is likely to be chosen. Similarly, mobile applications on the Android platform are likely to be written in Java, and applications for iOS are likely to be written in Swift.

Another factor that will influence language selection is the availability of development and testing tools. With nearly as much scrutiny as for the application features themselves, the organization should carefully select an application development environment if it does not already have one (or if it has determined that its present capabilities are insufficient).

Requirements for a development environment must include functions that will permit developers to write software code that can meet functional requirements for the application itself. If, for example, functional requirements specify a high degree of accuracy in a way that requires a high volume of test cases, a development environment that can help to automate testing will enable developers to perform this rigorous testing more easily.

Development in a Software Acquisition Setting   In a software acquisition situation where an organization is purchasing or leasing software instead of developing it in-house, development activities may still be required. In a software acquisition project, software development is often needed to facilitate several needs:

- **Customizations**   Larger off-the-shelf applications make accommodations for customizations that must be developed. These customizations can take many forms, including application code modules, XML documents, and configurations.

- **Integration with other systems**   Applications rarely stand alone. Instead, they accept data from various sources and, in turn, provide data to other systems. Sometimes "bridge programs" or integration gateways need to be written that serve to move and transform data from one environment to another.

- **Authentication**   In an effort to improve security or make application adoption easier, organizations often desire that new applications use a system- or network-based authentication service. The primary advantage to this approach is that users do not need to remember yet another user ID and password. An application's authentication can often be tied to LDAP or Microsoft Active Directory, or it can be part of a federated identity environment.

- **Reports**   Complex applications may have a report writer module that is used to create custom reports. Depending upon the underlying technology, a developer may be needed to develop these reports. Even if a report authoring tool is intuitive and easy to use, a developer may still be needed to help users design reports.

 NOTE   An organization that is considering acquiring software should develop and enforce policies regarding the extent to which customizations will be permitted. Customizations can be costly when off-the-shelf software upgrades take place, because they may need to be rewritten to work with the upgraded software. The cost savings of using off-the-shelf software can be negated by the additional time required to manage and upgrade customizations.

Debugging   The first and most crucial part of software testing is performed by the developers themselves during development. *Debugging* is the process of testing software code to make sure that it operates properly and is free of defects. The testing that a developer performs is called *unit testing*; this means that the individual modules (units) that developers create are tested on their own. Wider scale testing is usually performed by others later on in the development cycle.

The objectives of debugging include the following:

- **Correct operations**   Software developers need to make sure that software modules are manipulating data and performing calculations correctly.

- **Proper input validation**   All input fields and input records should perform detailed checks on all input data to prevent errors and tampering. Manipulation of input data is one of the principal forms of application abuse and a significant cause of security incidents.

- **Proper output validation**   Modules must perform output validation to ensure that output data is within bounds. Output validation is one way to detect malfunctions that occur in an application module.

- **Proper resource usage**   Modules should be tested to make sure that they utilize resources such as memory correctly. Modules should properly request and relinquish resources so that malfunctions such as memory leaks do not occur.

NOTE   While it is tempting to gloss over debugging and unit testing, the effort usually pays big dividends by streamlining the integration effort and reducing the number of defects in system testing. Defects that could have been found during debugging usually take more resources to find during system testing, because a defect must first be isolated to a specific section of code before it can be diagnosed and corrected.

Source Code Management   In any size development effort, whether the development team is 1 developer or 250 developers, an organization should use a source code repository tool. Such a tool has several purposes:

- **Protection**   A source code management tool often includes access controls so that only authorized personnel are permitted to access application source code. This helps to protect the organization's intellectual property and to prevent other persons from learning the secrets of the application's inner workings or performing unauthorized changes to source code, either of which could lead to fraud or misuse of the application later on.

- **Control**   A source code management system utilizes "check out" and "check in" functions so that only one developer at a time may work on a specific part of the application. This helps to ensure the integrity of the application's source code.

- **Version control**   A source code management system tracks each version of the code as it is checked in by developers. The system tracks the changes made from version to version and can show the differences in code between versions, and it also permit the reversion to an older version if application problems arise later on.

- **Recordkeeping**   A source code management system maintains records related to check-outs, check-ins, and modifications to source code. This makes it possible for management to know what changes are being made to source code and who is making those changes.

Organizations that outsource some of their software development to third parties need to determine the business rules regarding those outsiders' access to source code.

Some portions of a software application may be considered intellectual property or may constitute trade secrets. Further, there may be sections that are security-related. In such cases, organizations should consider enacting and enforcing business rules that restrict outsourced developer access to these more sensitive portions of code.

 NOTE Source code management is not an activity that is limited to the period when the application is first developed; on the contrary, source code management is a vital activity that must continue throughout the life span of the application.

Testing

During the requirements, design, and even development phases of a software project, various project team members develop specific facts and behavioral characteristics about the application. Each of those characteristics must be verified before the application is approved for production use. This concept is depicted in a V-model in Figure 4-12. The V-model is sometimes used to depict the increasing levels of detail and complexity in the SDLC.

The stages of testing in a software development project are unit testing, system testing, functional testing, and user acceptance testing. Each stage is addressed in turn following a brief overview of test plans.

Test Plans Before testing can take place, it is first necessary to create test plans. Testing, at the overall project level and at the detail level, should be a methodical and repeatable process, not subject to the skills and experience of any individuals who are performing tests.

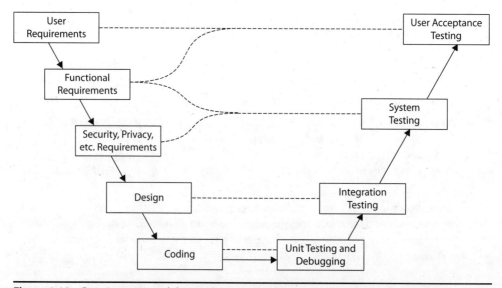

Figure 4-12 Requirements and design characteristics must all be verified through testing.

To a great extent, test plans are going to be derived directly from requirements that were developed prior to development taking place. There may, however, be other sources or types of testing that may not be explicitly stated in requirements, including

- Adequacy of business use cases
- Resistance against misuse and abuse cases
- The degree to which a program's operation and functions are self-evident to the user

Because of the volume and/or complexity of test cases, it may be necessary to create test plans. Test plans may be developed for several reasons, including

- Volume of tests need to be distributed to several individuals in some logical manner
- Testing performed by one or more outside parties or organizations
- Tests allocated based on the availability of individual testers or test teams
- Tests allocated based on the knowledge or skills of individual testers or test teams
- Tests allocated based on the tools required to perform testing (for example, workload testing or security defect testing)

Unit Testing   Unit testing is usually performed by developers during the coding phase of the software development project. When each developer is assigned the task of building a section of an application, the specifications that are given to the developer should include test plans or test cases that the developer will use to verify that the code works properly. This is true regardless of whether the part of the application that the developer is working on will be seen and used by end users or will be buried deep within the bowels of the application and never seen by anyone.

In a formal development environment, the unit test plans should be precise and list each test that the developer should undertake. The developer then performs each of the tests and records the results (usually the actual output) of the test. Those test results are then archived so that they can be referred to later if needed.

The archiving of unit testing records sometimes proves valuable when later phases of testing are taking place and some problem is found. Developers trying to isolate the cause of later testing problems can refer back to test plans and results at the unit testing phase to see whether the test plans and other unit testing activities were performed correctly, or whether they contained appropriate test cases. This evidence can save the project team a lot of time by eliminating the need to repeat unit testing.

Unit testing should be a part of the development of each module in the application. When a developer is assigned a programming task in a software development project, unit testing should be performed immediately after coding and debugging have taken place. In some organizations, developers work in pairs—the senior developer writes code, and the junior developer performs testing. This gives junior programmers an opportunity to learn more about advanced programming by observing the senior developer and by testing his or her code.

NOTE It can be easily argued that unit testing for a software module should not be performed by the developer who wrote the module. The developer may be under time pressure to complete development and testing and may overlook test cases or gloss over errors as irrelevant. Also, a developer can be too familiar with his or her code to be capable of objectively testing it. The methodology of "written by one and tested by another" has the advantage of objective testing, but it can be more difficult to carry out in smaller organizations where only a single developer may be writing all of the code.

System Testing As various parts of the application are developed and unit-tested, they will be installed into a test environment. When a sufficient number of modules or components has been completed, it will eventually become possible to begin end-to-end (or at least partial end-to-end) testing. In this way, it will be possible to test several components as a whole to verify whether they work together properly.

System testing includes *interface testing* to confirm that the application is communicating properly with other applications. This will include real-time interfaces as well as batch processing.

System testing also includes *migration testing*. When one application is replacing another, data from the old application is often imported into the new application to eliminate the need for both old and new applications to function at the same time. Migration testing ensures that data is being properly formatted and imported into the new application. This testing is often performed several times in advance of the real, live migration at cutover time.

As with unit testing, system testing should have pre-prepared test plans that were developed at the system design phase. And as with unit testing, system testing should probably not be performed by the developers who developed the modules under test or by the integrators who set them up in the test environment. Further, system testing results should be formally documented and archived in case they are needed later.

Functional Testing *Functional testing* is primarily concerned with the verification of functional requirements that were developed earlier in the application project.

Each functional requirement must be expressed in a way that makes it inherently verifiable. When each functional requirement is developed, one or more tests should also be developed, which are conducted during the functional testing phase of the project.

Functional tests should be formally recorded, including test input and test results. All of this should be archived in case it's needed if the application is suspected of malfunctioning. Often functional test results can verify whether the malfunction was present during the functional testing before the application went live.

User Acceptance Testing Before business users will formally approve and begin using a new (or updated) application, often a formal phase called *user acceptance testing* (UAT) is performed. UAT should consist of a formal, written body of specific tests that permits application users to determine whether the application will operate properly.

The detailed output of user acceptance testing should be archived, as it may be needed in the future.

UAT is often a stage in the acceptance of leased or purchased software, as well as in software that is developed by a third-party organization. User acceptance testing is the formal test that determines whether the customer organization will accept (and pay for, as the case may be) the application and begin formal use of it.

NOTE Acceptance criteria for UAT should be developed by end users and not by developers or designers; otherwise, internal or external customers are liable to end up with software that does not function as desired or expected.

Quality Assurance Testing *Quality assurance testing* (QAT) is a formal verification of system specifications and technologies. Users are usually not involved in QAT; instead, this testing is typically performed by IT or IS departments.

Like UAT, QAT should be a "gatekeeper" test in any situation where the organization is purchasing off-the-shelf software or the application software is being developed by an external organization. The results of QAT should also determine whether the organization will formally accept and pay for the application.

Implementation

Implementation is the phase of the project in which the completed application software is placed into the production environment and started.

Implementation must be started before UAT and QAT begin. UAT and QAT should be performed on the production environment that is anticipated to become the in-use production environment once approvals to use the application are obtained.

From the very day that construction of the implementation environment begins, that environment should be as controlled as a production environment. This means that all changes to the environment should go through a change management process. Also, administrative access to the production environment should be restricted to those personnel who will be supporting the environment after it goes live. The implementation timeline, in relation to other phases of the software development project, is depicted in Figure 4-13.

NOTE Because the production environment is the environment where UAT and QAT testing usually takes place, this environment must be pristine and free from the possibility of being accessed by developers and other personnel.

Implementation Planning Implementation is a complicated undertaking that requires advance planning. Some activities may have a long lead time associated with them, requiring some implementation activities to begin during development or earlier.

- *Prepare physical space for on-premises production systems.* For organizations implementing an application on physical servers, an existing data center may be used for an application's servers and other equipment. But if there isn't room, or if an existing data center's available space is insufficient, the organization may need to consider expanding an existing data center or consider a collocation center.

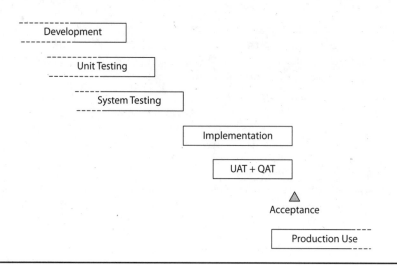

Figure 4-13 Implementation involves preparing the production environment prior to UAT and QAT.

- *Build production systems.* The actual servers that the application will use must be built and configured. If the organization does not have the necessary servers available, the hardware systems must be leased or purchased; depending upon the type of hardware, considerable lead time may be required. If the public cloud will be used, the organization needs to select a public cloud vendor (this should be done at design time, or earlier!) and implement server operating systems there. Once the hardware or virtualization platform is available, personnel will need to install and configure operating systems and possibly other subsystems such as database management systems or application management systems. Supporting infrastructure such as routers, switches, firewalls, and so forth must also be implemented at this time.

- *Prepare virtual machines for cloud-based production systems.* For an organization deploying its application in an Infrastructure-as-a-Service (IaaS; discussed later in the chapter), virtual machines need to be acquired and configured.

- *Install application software.* Once the systems are ready for the application software, it can be installed and configured.

- *Migrate the data.* For environments in which an existing application will be retired, data from the former environment usually needs to be transferred to the new environment. Often this procedure requires the development of one or more custom programs to extract, convert, and insert the data into the new environment. This procedure is usually performed more than once: it must be rehearsed at least one time to make sure that it works properly. Also, migrated data is often needed for functional testing, UAT, and training before the actual cutover.

NOTE As each phase of implementation is completed, the newly completed component should be locked down immediately and treated as though it is already in production. Usually this is the only way to ensure the integrity of the entire environment.

Training   The success of the entire software development project hinges on the knowledge and skills of several different people in the organization. The following are among those who may need training:

- **End users**   Personnel who will be using the application need to be trained so that they will know how to operate it properly.

- **Customers**   If outside customers will be using the new application, they will need an appropriate amount of information so that they will understand how to use it. In other cases, customers will not be using the application directly, but a new application can still influence how they interact with the organization. If customer service or sales personnel are using a new application for taking orders or for looking up customer data, they may be asking different questions or presenting different information to the customer.

- **Support staff**   Personnel who provide customer service to users and customers need to be trained in the workings of the application, as well as on administrative "back office" tools that they may use to assist users.

- **Trainers**   Organizations that employ a training organization will need to "train the trainers" so that, in turn, they will be able to train users and customers correctly.

The purpose of an application may require that others also receive training. This could include internal or external auditors, or regulators who have oversight over the organization.

Data Migration   In the context of the SDLC, the purpose of a data migration is to transfer data from an older, soon-to-be-retired system to a new system. Depending upon the nature of the old and new applications, the purpose of the data migration may be to make historical records that originated in the older system available in the newer system.

In some cases, an organization will continue to keep the older application running to facilitate access to historical data. In some circumstances, it may require fewer resources to keep the old application running than to migrate the historical data to the new application.

Data migration often requires the development of programs that extract data from the old application, perform required transformations, and then format the data and import it into the new application. This is frequently a complex task, as there may be differences so significant between the data models of the old and new applications that the meaning of stored data differs between them. In some cases, it will be necessary to create some parts of the database in the new application by extracting data from the old application and then performing calculations to create the data necessary in the new. Careful analysis is required in all cases to make sure that the *meaning* of data in each application is known so that the migration will be done properly. Following are some techniques and considerations that ensure a successful migration:

- **Record counts**   Programs or utilities should be used to count the number of records in counterpart tables in the old and new environments. This will confirm the completeness of the migration programs that move data from the old environment to the new one.

- **Batch totals**   Data records with numeric values can be added together in the old and new databases. This will help to confirm the integrity of key data elements in the old and new environments.

- **Checksums**   Programs that compute checksums can be run against old and new databases to ensure the accuracy of migrated data. Programmers do need to be aware of the methods used to store data, which could lead to differences in checksums. For instance, an address field in one application may pad the field with spaces, but in the other it may be padded with nulls. Also, the way that dates are stored can vary between applications. While using checksums can be valuable, programmers and analysts must be familiar with any differences in data representation between the old and new environments.

NOTE   Like other software projects, the migration programs themselves must be carefully designed and tested, and the results of tests must be analyzed to make sure that they are working properly. Often it is necessary to perform a test migration—well in advance of the scheduled cutover date—to give enough time to make sure that the migration programs have been properly written.

Cutover   When the production system has been constructed, applications loaded, data migrated, and all testing performed and verified, the project team has reached the cutover milestone. Often, management review and approval are required to verify that all necessary steps have been completed correctly.

Depending upon the nature of the application as well as external influences such as regulation or business requirements, an organization may transfer processing to the new environment in one of several ways:

- **Parallel cutover**   The organization may operate both the old and new applications in parallel for a time, making careful comparisons between old and new to ensure that the new application is working properly.

- **Geographic cutover**   In an application used throughout large geographic regions, such as a retail point-of-sale application, the organization may migrate individual locations to the new application instead of moving all locations at one time.

- **Module-by-module cutover**   The organization may migrate different parts of the application at different times. In a financial management application, for instance, the organization could move accounts receivable to the new environment, later move accounts payable, and still later move general ledger. During and between each of these phases, the organization must keep track of exactly which business information resides in which system.

- **All-at-once cutover**   An organization may elect to migrate the entire environment at one time.

The project team must analyze all available methods for a cutover and choose the method that will balance risk, efficiency, and cost-effectiveness.

Analysts may discover problems in data in the old environment that necessitate a cleanup be performed prior to the migration or as a part of the migration. Examples of the types of problems that can be found include duplicate records, incomplete records, or records that contain values that violate one or more business rules. Analysts who discover data inconsistencies such as these need to alert the project team to the matter and then help the project team decide how to remedy the situation.

Rollback Planning   Sometimes an organization will migrate an application from an old environment to a new one, and shortly afterward will discover a serious problem in the new environment that requires a return to the old environment. *Rollback planning* is a safety net that provides a last-resort path away from a situation where the organization cannot continue using the new environment.

A rollback is a serious undertaking and would be considered only when there is a problem in the new environment that is so serious that it cannot be easily remedied. However, rollback planning is recommended in environments where the availability and integrity of an application is critical to the organization, even if a rollback is never needed.

Post-Implementation

The software project is not completed when the application cutover has taken place. Several activities still must take place before the project is closed. This section describes these final tasks.

Post-Implementation Review   After the implementation of a new application, one or more formal reviews need to take place. The purpose of these reviews is to collect all known open issues and to identify and discuss the performance of the project. Because the organization is likely to undertake similar projects in the future, it is a valuable use of time to identify what parts of the project went well and what could have been done better. The implementation review should consider

- **System adequacy**   The project team should work with the users of the new system and collect issues and comments, which are then discussed in the implementation review. Any issues requiring further attention should be identified.

- **Security review**   The system's access controls and other security controls should be discussed and any issues or problems identified.

- **Privacy review**   The system's privacy features and controls need to be discussed and any problems identified.

- **Audit review**   The system's ability to be audited, as well as any early audit results, need to be discussed.

- **Issues**   All known problems regarding the new environment should be identified. This should include user feedback, operations feedback, and the accuracy and completeness of documentation and records. The project team needs to discuss each issue and assign it to one or more individuals who will address and remedy it.

- **Return on investment**   If the purpose for implementing the application was to establish or improve return on investment (ROI) or efficiency, then initial measurements need to be taken. The project team needs to recognize that several business cycles may be required before an accurate ROI can be determined.

More than one post-implementation review may be needed. To hold a single post-implementation review shortly after going live and then calling it good is probably inadequate for most organizations. Instead, a series of reviews may be needed, perhaps stretching over years.

 NOTE   IS auditors should be involved in every phase of the SDLC, including post-implementation reviews, to ensure that the application is functioning according to whatever control or regulatory requirements are attended to by auditors. Auditor feedback must be included in the body of issues and comments that is reviewed in the initial and subsequent reviews.

Software Maintenance   Immediately after implementation, the application enters the maintenance phase. From this point forward, all changes to the environment must be performed under formal processes, including incident management, problem management, defect management, vulnerability management, change management, and configuration management. All of these processes should have been developed and modified as necessary to accommodate the new application when cutover was completed.

Software Development Risks

Software development is not a risk-free endeavor. Even when management provides adequate resources for a software development project and supports a viable methodology, there are still many more paths to failure than to success.

Some of the specific risks that are associated with software development projects include

- **Application inadequacy**   The application may fail to support all business requirements. During the requirements and specifications phases of a software development project, some business requirements may have been overlooked, disregarded, misunderstood, or unappreciated. Whatever the reason, an application that falls short of meeting all business requirements may, as a result, be underutilized or even abandoned.

- **Security and privacy defects** The application may contain security or privacy defects that permit various forms of misuse and abuse, including denial of service, escalation of privilege, data disclosure, and data corruption.

- **Project risk** If the application development (or acquisition) project is not well run, the project may exceed spending budgets, time budgets, or both. This may result in significant delays and even abandonment of the project altogether if management has considered the project a failure.

- **Business inefficiency** The application may fail to meet business efficiency expectations. In other words, the application itself may be difficult to use, it may be exceedingly slow, or business procedures may require additional manual work to meet business needs. This can result in critical business tasks taking too long or requiring additional resources to complete.

- **Market changes** Between the time that a software development project is approved and when it is completed, sudden or unexpected changes in market conditions can spell disaster for the project. For instance, drastic supply or price shocks in a macro environment can have an adverse effect on costs that may make a new business activity no longer viable. Changes in the market can also result in reduced margins on products and services, which can turn the ROI of a project upside-down.

 NOTE Management is responsible for the business decisions that it makes; in ideal situations, management makes these decisions with sufficient information at hand. Usually, however, there are some unknowns.

Alternative Software Development Approaches and Techniques

For decades, the waterfall approach to software development was the de facto model used by most organizations. Breakthroughs and changes in technology in the 1970s and 1980s have led to new approaches in software development that can be every bit as effective as the waterfall model and, in many cases, more efficient and faster.

DevOps

DevOps is the growing movement that utilizes agile development methodology coupled with tighter integration of development teams, software QA, and IT operations. DevOps isn't complete without tools facilitating more effective (often automated) testing.

In DevOps, the lines between software development, QA, and IT operations are somewhat blurred. It is essential for organizations to ensure that access control models and capabilities continue to support regulatory and compliance requirements such as

- **Data segregation** Developers should never have access to production data.
- **Separation of duties** Critical processes such as change control still require administrative and technical controls so that no one person (such as a developer) can make unauthorized changes in production environments.

Figure 4-14
DevOps is the
integration of
development,
software QA
(testing), and
IT operations.

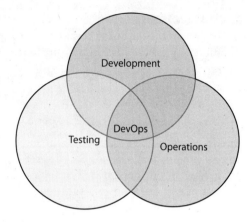

The relationship between development, software QA, and IT operations is depicted in Figure 4-14.

DevSecOps

DevSecOps is an offshoot of (some would say an improvement to) DevOps. DevSecOps represents the best of DevOps and includes security design and testing capabilities that are a part of the rapid development and automated testing process. Often, static and/or dynamic code-scanning capabilities are integrated into the software build environment so that security defects are identified as soon as possible. Further automated testing can be performed on production environments to reveal exploitable defects that can be remediated by developers in subsequent sprints.

Agile Development

Agile development is a software development model and is referred to as an alternate methodology that is appropriate for some organizations. The agile methodology utilizes the Scrum project methodology that is discussed in detail earlier in this chapter. In an agile development project, a larger development team is broken up into smaller teams of five to nine developers and a leader, and the project deliverables are broken up into smaller pieces that can each be attained in just a few weeks.

Prototyping

Application *prototyping* is a methodology whereby rapidly developed application prototypes are developed with user input and continuous involvement. In this method, users work closely with developers who build specific components in short periods and solicit frequent user feedback.

The primary advantage of prototyping is that the risks of the application turning out all wrong are reduced because users are constantly involved and can head off an incorrect approach before more time is wasted.

The main disadvantage of prototyping is that the system is developed based only on what the user sees and knows; other functional requirements that users may be unaware of may go unaddressed, resulting in a system with inadequate controls and resilience.

Rapid Application Development

Rapid application development (RAD) is a response to the slower and more structured application development methodologies (such as waterfall) that were developed in the 1970s. RAD is characterized by the following activities and features:

- Small development teams consisting of highly experienced developers and analysts
- The development of prototypes
- Development tools that integrate data design, data flow, user interface, and prototyping
- A central repository for software components with an emphasis on code reusability
- Design and prototype analysis sessions with end users
- Tight time frames

RAD can almost be thought of as a 1960s-era protest of the political and business establishment. In most cases, it takes the opposite approach to software development from the then-traditional and time-proven (but also inefficient and time-*consuming*) development models created in the decades before.

Data-Oriented System Development

Data-oriented system development (DOSD) is, as the name suggests, a data-centric software development methodology. In DOSD, data is the central focus, the "hub of the wheel" as it were, and the other development activities occur as a result of data analysis and design.

DOSD is utilized in some of the larger information processing environments that are interconnected by many organizations. For instance, airline reservations systems, merchant and payment processing systems, securities trading systems, medical records processing systems, and cloud-based Platform-as-a-Service (PaaS) vendors such as SalesForce.com and Concur all have well-defined data models and transaction interfaces. Organizations that want to participate in these larger systems will build their own applications that are focused on the published data interfaces on the systems they want to connect to.

DOSD can be applied to environments that utilize batches of transactions that are, for example, transmitted and processed in bulk, as well as transactions that are performed in real time, such as airline reservations or securities trading.

Object-Oriented System Development

Object-oriented (OO) system development is a world unto itself that contains an entire vocabulary to describe objects and many other software components. It is so different from traditional structured programming (such as FORTRAN, BASIC, and C) that it has its own languages and even databases if you want to implement one.

Entire books (and even series of books) have been written on OO development and technology. I will summarize the basic vocabulary and activities here.

The basic unit of OO technology is the *class*. A class describes the characteristics of an object, including its attributes, properties, fields, and the methods it can perform.

The instantiation of a class is called an *object*. You could think of a class as stored code and configuration, and when it's running, the part that is running is the object.

A *method* refers to the actions that an object can perform. If, for instance, an object is written to calculate the interest on a loan, the method is the software code in the object that performs the calculation. In other programming languages, subroutines and functions are basically the same thing as a method in OO.

Objects routinely employ another technique known as *encapsulation*. This is a common practice whereby any particular method may call other methods to perform its work. This is similar to a function calling another function. The point of encapsulation in OO is that the software developer does not need to know anything about the implementation details of a method, including whether it calls other methods.

At the beginning of this narrative I mentioned a class. OO frequently has a hierarchy of classes. A class can belong to a parent class, and in turn, a class can contain subclasses. But parent classes and subclasses are not just ways of arranging or storing classes. Instead, the relationship of classes is functional. The attributes of a parent class are passed down through *inheritance*.

Earlier I stated that when a class is instantiated, it becomes an object. Depending on the data that is passed on to the object, it may behave in different ways. This characteristic is known as *polymorphism*. For example, a class that computes shipping charges will behave in different ways, depending upon the source and destination addresses as well as on special circumstances such as customers. In this case, polymorphism is not just about the rate that is chosen for shipping, but possibly other objects will be called, such as objects to handle customs, taxes, or hazardous materials declarations.

OO programming and operational environments will have one or more *class libraries*. These take many forms, depending upon the operating system, languages, and subsystems that are in use. For instance, in the Java language, class libraries are stored in JAR (Java ARchive) files that are located on the system where programs can refer to them when needed.

Component-Based Development

Component-based development is an approach that reflects the software architecture of an application. Here, an application environment will be made up of several independent components, often located on different physical or virtual systems, which work together.

For example, a large application environment may consist of a group of centrally located servers that process primary transactions. These servers may contain interfaces, using standard interface technologies such as CORBA (Common Object Request Broker Architecture), RPC (Remote Procedure Call), or SOA (Service-Oriented Architecture), with which other parts of the overall application environment may communicate. For instance, auxiliary components such as batch input and output, data warehouses, static table updates (such as tax or shipping rates), and client programs may all be independent applications that communicate with the core system.

NOTE In a component-based environment, some components may be systems that are owned and operated by other organizations. This is especially true of modern distributed applications, PaaS environments, and web-based mashups, where applications may include components from external applications.

Web-Based Application Development

The creation of the HTML content-display standard and the HTTP communications protocol has revolutionized application development. The web browser is ubiquitous and has become the universal client platform that is not unlike an intelligent display terminal from earlier eras.

The Web, as it is popularized now, came along just in time: two-tier and three-tier client-server computing, the great new application development paradigm that was developed in the 1990s, was not living up to its promise, particularly in the areas of performance and upkeep of client software. Web software has dramatically simplified software development from the perspective of the user interface (UI); though the developer has a little less control over what and how data will be displayed on a user workstation, the trade-off in not having to maintain client-side software is viewed as acceptable.

From a development methodology perspective, web application development can be performed within virtually all of the development frameworks, including waterfall, DevOps, agile, RAD, DOSD, and OO (all discussed in this chapter). Primarily it's the target technology that differentiates web-based application development from its alternatives.

Important standards have been developed that facilitate communications between web-based applications, including JSON-RPC, SOAP (Simple Object Access Protocol), and Web Services Description Language (WSDL). JSON-RPC is an XML (eXtensible Markup Language)–based protocol coded in JavaScript Object Notation (JSON) used by a client system to request a method of a remote system.

SOAP is an XML-based application programming interface (API) specification that facilitates real-time communications between applications using the HTTP and HTTPS protocols. Functionally, SOAP operates similarly to RPC, wherein one application transmits a query to another application, and the other application responds with a query result. SOAP messages are based in the XML standard.

WSDL serves as a specification repository for the SOAP services available in a particular environment. This permits an application to discover what services are available on an application server.

Reverse Engineering

Reverse engineering is the process of analyzing a system to see how it functions, usually as a means for developing a similar system or for learning about how the system works. Reverse engineering usually requires tools that examine computer binary code and that build a programming language equivalent.

Reverse engineering can help to speed up a development project where an organization needs to build an application that is similar to another in its possession that exists in binary format only. Without reverse engineering, the organization would have to spend additional time in the software design and development phases of the project.

This practice is usually forbidden in software license agreements, because using it would reveal protected intellectual property that could economically damage the original software maker.

 NOTE Reverse engineering is a standard technique used in malware analysis to understand how the malware works.

System Development Tools

Application developers can create source code using tools ranging from simple text editors to advanced tools such as computer-aided software engineering and fourth-generation languages (4GLs). While there's little reason to discuss text editors such as vi, Notepad, or Emacs, advanced development tools are worth your attention and are discussed in this section.

Integrated Development Environment

Integrated development environments (IDEs) are a class of desktop software development tools that incorporates source code editing, source code version control, compilation, and debugging in a single tool. An IDE enables a developer to write, test, and debug code without having to switch between programs.

IDEs typically have multiple windows, or panes, that enable the software developer to view and edit code, run code and observe execution, and view the source code library. Other functions may be available as well.

Some IDEs have built-in security capabilities such as code analysis, as well as connectivity to external tools such as source code scanning tools that look for security defects.

Computer-Aided Software Engineering

Computer-aided software engineering (CASE) represents a broad variety of tools used to automate various aspects of application software development. CASE tools cover three basic realms of development:

- **Upper CASE** This includes activities ranging from requirements gathering to the development of data models, data flow diagrams, and interfaces.
- **Middle CASE** This involves the development of detailed designs, including screen layouts, report definitions, data design, and data flows.
- **Lower CASE** This involves the creation of program source code and data schemas.

These terms are loosely used to classify various CASE tools. Some CASE tools are strictly Upper CASE, while others include Middle CASE and/or Lower CASE, but many cover the entire range of functionality and can be used to capture specifications, create data structure and flow diagrams, define program functions, and generate source code.

CASE tools do not usually create source code that is ready for implementation and testing. Instead, they are used to create the majority (in the best cases) of code for a given program; then the developer(s) would add details and specific items that the CASE tool did not cover. CASE tools are not used to replace the work of a developer, but to help make the coding part of a development project take less time, to improve consistency, and to enhance program quality.

CASE tools often contain *code generators* that create the actual program source code.

 NOTE CASE tools do not eliminate the need for any of the essential phases of the SDLC. With or without CASE tools, it is still necessary for a project team to create requirements, specifications, and design. CASE does help to automate some of these activities, however.

Fourth-Generation Languages

Fourth-generation languages, or 4GLs, comprise a variety of tools that are used in the development of applications or that are parts of the applications themselves.

There is no universally accepted definition for 4GLs, unlike with first-, second-, and third-generation languages. 4GLs were developed independently by many different organizations and researchers, and they carry a diversity of concepts that contributes to the inability to describe all of them in a single definition. Common among nearly all of the 4GLs and tools is that they are event-driven rather than procedure-driven, and they are less detailed than procedural languages.

4GLs are most often used as adjuncts to applications rather than for their core functionality. For instance, 4GLs are useful for report generators, query generators, and other higher level functions. 4GLs are typically designed for use by nontechnical users who have few or no programming skills. 4GLs can also be used by developers as code generators.

Acquiring Cloud-Based Infrastructure and Applications

Organizations often choose to acquire a business application that is hosted in a cloud or SaaS environment, as opposed to hosting the application on their own systems. This section discusses issues that organizations should understand when considering this option.

The common options available for cloud-based application environments are

- **Software-as-a-Service** An application service provider is hosting its application software on its own infrastructure, often located in a data center and used by several customers. Users access the application in much the same way that they would if the application were hosted within the organization's own IT environment.

- **Infrastructure-as-a-Service**   A cloud service provider is providing an environment in which its customers build and operate virtual machines. While the client organization is relieved of the burden of purchasing network, system, and storage hardware, it still needs to create a network architecture, security architecture, systems architecture, and application architecture, and it must install and manage operating systems, virtual network devices such as switches and routers, and virtual security tools such as firewalls, intrusion prevention systems, and data loss prevention systems.

- **Platform-as-a-Service**   A cloud service provider is providing an application-based or data-based platform on which customers can develop and/or integrate their applications. PaaS services are typically organized around a business theme—for example, Salesforce.com for sales enablement or Concur.com for expense and travel management.

Regardless of the cloud model that is chosen, the organization needs to understand many details that are related to the manner in which the cloud provider provides its services to the organization. Some of these details are

- **Access control**   The cloud service provider must have an effective access control plan to ensure that only authorized personnel have access to infrastructure components and virtual machines. Often, the organization using cloud services will manage access control in upper layers (such as in operating systems, database management systems, and applications that it may install and maintain on cloud servers), while the cloud provider will manage access control in lower levels (such as in virtual machine hypervisors and via physical access).

- **Environment segregation**   The cloud service provider must effectively separate systems and data between customers so that no cloud customer is able to access systems and data of other customers.

- **Physical security**   The cloud services provider must provide adequate physical security so that only authorized personnel will have physical access to all cloud environment infrastructure and facilities.

- **Regulation**   The cloud service provider must provide controls that will meet all applicable regulatory needs for its customers.

- **Privacy**   The cloud service provider (and, indeed, the organization using cloud services) must implement safeguards to ensure appropriate protection and handling of personally identifiable information (PII) stored in cloud environments.

- **Legal jurisdiction**   The cloud service provider and its customers must have a firm understanding regarding the physical location of stored data, relative to the location of the owner(s) of that data. This will enable legal counsel to understand the applicability of security and privacy laws governing the use of stored data. This is particularly important in the context of data privacy and data sovereignty laws.

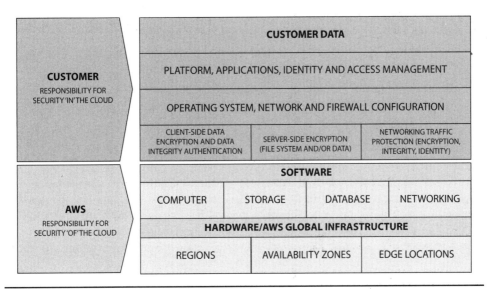

Figure 4-15 Typical cloud responsibility model (Image source: Amazon Web Services)

- **Availability**   The cloud services provider must deliver availability of services to customers at a level to meet customers' expectations. This applies not only to the steady availability of services, but also to on-demand availability.

- **Audit**   Many standards, regulations, and legal agreements require some level of auditing of systems, applications, and their supporting controls. The cloud environment must be verifiable in this regard.

Figure 4-15 shows a typical cloud responsibility model that illustrates which party is responsible for implementing and operating which aspects of security in a cloud environment.

NOTE   The Cloud Security Alliance (https://cloudsecurityalliance.org) is a high-quality resource for controls and guidance for cloud services providers as well as organizations using cloud-based services.

Infrastructure Development and Implementation

Infrastructure is used to connect applications to users and to other applications. Infrastructure is composed of the networks, servers, storage systems, and other facilities that support the use of applications.

While an organization may be able to acquire off-the-shelf or SaaS software for many of its core business activities, infrastructure is almost always custom-architected and integrated for the organization. Whereas software applications are like the tools in the hand of an astronaut, the infrastructure is like the astronaut's glove, which must be tailor-made to fit each astronaut's hand. Infrastructure needs to conform to the organization's geography, business model, security requirements, regulatory requirements, and culture.

Formal processes are required to design and develop infrastructure that is sure to meet the organization's needs. This section describes the detailed process of the infrastructure development life cycle that is needed to ensure that the infrastructure will adequately support the use of applications and other IT facilities and tools.

In the context of business applications and information systems, infrastructure is the collection of networks, network services, devices, facilities, and system software that facilitate access to, communications with, and protection of those business applications. For instance, a user who wants to access a business application uses a workstation that is connected to a local area network (LAN). To access the business application, the workstation communicates over networks formed with routers, switches, firewalls, and cabling. All of that "in-between" equipment and cabling constitutes infrastructure.

Infrastructure facilitates the communication and use of applications. Without infrastructure, applications cannot function or be accessed by users. Since infrastructure is so vital, its construction and maintenance requires the same level of formality and process as the business applications that it supports. In newer organizations, however, infrastructure serves only to connect workstations to the Internet and to facilitate a few business location services such as document scanning and printing.

 NOTE Cloud-based infrastructure in an IaaS environment is no less important than on-premises or co-lo infrastructure with respect to management processes described in this section.

Review of Existing Architecture

When an organization is considering an architecture change or an upgrade to some component or aspect of its infrastructure, it must first review what infrastructure already exists and how its components relate to one another. Changes or additions to infrastructure will be most effective when existing infrastructure is carefully analyzed. This permits the organization to make necessary additions and changes that will be most effective and at the lowest possible cost. Characteristics of existing architecture that need to be considered include

- Physical security, size, weight, and power requirements for on-premises environments
- Compatibility with virtualization platforms for cloud-based environments
- Compatibility with existing infrastructure and infrastructure that will be acquired in the future
- Operations and support
- Security architecture and operations

Requirements

The next step in any addition or upgrade of infrastructure is the development of requirements. As with the SDLC, it is essential to know precisely what is expected of the infrastructure in terms of specific features and capabilities. An analyst or project team should
develop specific requirements in a number of categories:

- **Business functional requirements**   These specify what the addition or change
  to the infrastructure is expected to do. For instance, networks or network services
  will be expected to support new or improved communications between users
  and applications, remote access, communications to service providers, or services
  between applications. Or segmentation may be planned to isolate a cardholder
  environment from the rest of the environment.

- **Technical requirements and standards**   These specify which technologies and
  standards must be followed for the new infrastructure. Additions or changes
  to infrastructure should support existing protocol and services standards such
  as TCP/IP, LDAP (used for authentication and authorization), product standards
  for devices such as routers and switches, and other standards that will permit
  the new infrastructure to work harmoniously with existing infrastructure with
  the smallest possible increases in support costs. Technical requirements for
  infrastructure should also include performance requirements such as availability,
  latency, and throughput so that the infrastructure will have the capacity to
  support all needed business functions.

- **Interoperability**   These requirements ensure that additions or upgrades will
  work in harmony with existing components and systems in an organization's
  environment.

- **Security and regulatory requirements**   These requirements specify how
  information is protected from unauthorized third parties. Examples include
  firewalls to limit access, intrusion detection systems to create alerts of possible
  tampering, and encryption to protect information from eavesdropping and
  interception.

- **Privacy requirements**   These requirements specify how information is
  protected and handled to limit the use of personal information to officially
  sanctioned purposes.

Design

Additions and changes to existing infrastructure (or even to brand-new infrastructure)
must be designed, and that design must be validated by subject matter experts. An infrastructure design may also include the use of specific protocols or services for authentication,
routing, encryption, device management, and administrative support. When an environment is being expanded or upgraded, generally the new components will need to work
with the same support and management methods that are used for existing infrastructure, except when the infrastructure change has to do with a change in these features.

The design should be detailed enough so that a network or systems engineer can determine the logical and physical components that are needed and can configure them to support business needs. If software or hardware vendors will be asked to make suggestions on the components required for the infrastructure, then the design must be detailed enough so that they can make appropriate recommendations that will meet business needs.

 NOTE With enough detail in business and technical requirements and sufficient discipline, any two qualified engineers should be able to take requirements and arrive at the same design result. Architecture and design is not so much about creativity as it is the development of a solution that will meet business needs.

Procurement

More often than not, additions or changes to infrastructure involve the procurement of infrastructure hardware and/or software.

Request for Proposals

Any significant expansion or upgrade to infrastructure may require the use of a *request for proposals* (RFP). This is a formal process whereby the organization gathers all business and technical requirements and forwards them to several qualified vendors, who produce formal written proposals that include detailed information on the equipment and services required to perform the upgrade. Some organizations require the RFP process to be used for any purchases that exceed a set amount.

When the project team receives RFP responses, the responses must be evaluated to determine which vendors are capable of meeting the organization's business and technical needs. The project team may also need to evaluate one or more of the vendors' solutions to "see for themselves" whether each vendor's proposed solution will successfully meet the organization's needs.

The *request for information* (RFI) process is similar to that of RFP, except that the primary request is not for business proposals, but instead for information that will help the organization select solutions.

Evaluation

If the project team will be evaluating potential solutions, the team will need to provide whatever facilities are required to house the equipment or software. The project team will also need to take whatever time is required to test the components to determine whether they can support business needs. This may require the team to provide other equipment to set up an end-to-end test.

Each of the business and technical requirements needs to be verified. This will require that one or more project team members work with the equipment being evaluated to see how that equipment works. A test checklist should be developed that has a one-to-one correspondence to each business and technical requirement. This will permit project team members to rate each feature from each vendor in an objective manner.

Testing

Before new infrastructure—or significant changes to existing infrastructure—can be made available for production users, the infrastructure should be formally and thoroughly tested. This helps to confirm that the infrastructure was built correctly and that it will be reliable and secure.

Each functional and technical requirement that was developed earlier needs to be systematically verified. This means that a detailed test plan needs to be developed that uses functional and technical requirements as a source. For instance, if a technical standard requires a specific routing protocol configuration setting, then a network engineer on the project team needs to verify whether network devices support that feature (a matter such as this should have been settled during requirements development).

Most organizations do not have a test network environment that completely mirrors their production network. This means that some of the testing needs to be creative, and some testing and verification can't be done until implementation time. The project team will need to discuss the hard-to-test characteristics of the new infrastructure and decide the best course of action that facilitates the greatest amount of testing and the lowest risk of project failure. In other words, the results of some testing won't be known until the new infrastructure goes live.

Tests that cannot be done until implementation will become part of the verification that implementation was performed correctly.

Proof of Concept

Because integration issues are often complex, organizations are turning to the *proof of concept* to evaluate a proposed new technology or system. In a proof of concept, the organization asks an infrastructure vendor, value-added reseller, or consultant to set up components in the organization's environment and perform some simple integrations with existing systems. This helps the organization to better understand the likely answer to the question, "Will this new technology work in *our* environment?" before committing to a particular solution.

The project team should carefully plan the proof of concept so that key features can be demonstrated. A proof of concept is usually performed over a relatively short period, and only a small proportion of integration will be performed. Also remember that the vendor is providing the proof-of-concept hardware and resources without compensation (but with the hope that its solution will be chosen); there is only so much that a vendor will be willing to do for free. Of course, the vendor or an integrator will be able to provide additional integrations for a fee. This is why it is important to identify the key, measurable objectives before the proof of concept is carried out.

Implementation

When evaluation and testing are complete and all obstacles and issues have been satisfied, the new infrastructure (or changes to existing infrastructure) can be implemented. This may involve the physical installation of cabling, devices, and other components, as well as the use of common carrier facilities such as communications circuits. In an implementation, the infrastructure is all assembled, tested, and placed into production use.

Maintenance

Infrastructure requires periodic maintenance, usually in the form of software and hardware upgrades and configuration changes to accommodate changes in the business and technical environments. These changes should be controlled through change management and configuration management processes that are described in detail earlier in this chapter and in the following section.

Maintaining Information Systems

The job is only half done when an application or system has been implemented. Like any system with moving parts (whether real or virtual), information systems and the environments that support them require frequent maintenance. There are dual aspects to system maintenance: business processes and changes to technology. This is embodied in the change management and configuration management processes discussed here.

Change Management

Change management is a formal process whereby every proposed and required change to an environment must be formally requested, reviewed, and approved before it is made. The purpose of change management—which is also known as *change control*—is to identify and reduce risks associated with changes to an IT environment. Change management also helps to reduce unscheduled downtime in an environment. The typical components in a change management process are

- **Change request**   The requestor describes, in structured detail, the desired change. The change request should include the business reason for the change, a procedure for making the change, who will make the change, and who will verify the change (this should be two different individuals or groups); a procedure for verifying that the change was made properly, when the change will be made, and a plan for backing out of the change if it is unsuccessful; and results from test implementations in a testing environment. The request should be distributed to all stakeholders to give them time to read and understand the change.

- **Change review**   A quorum of stakeholders (usually called the *change advisory board*, or CAB) meets to discuss the requested change. The person or group proposing the change should describe the change and why it is being made, and he or she should be able to answer questions from others about the change and its impact. If the stakeholders agree that the change may proceed, the change is approved.

- **Perform the change**   The person or team slated to perform the change does so at the agreed-upon date and time, using instructions that were agreed upon in the review phase of the change. Results from the change are recorded and archived.

- **Verify the change**   Any necessary tests are performed to verify that the change was executed properly and that it has produced the desired result. If the change takes too long, or if the change cannot be successfully verified, the organization "backs out" of the change according to the agreed-upon procedure.

- **Emergency changes**   When the performance of a change cannot wait until the next scheduled change review, organizations usually provide a process whereby developers or engineers are permitted to make an emergency change. Typically, some management approval is still required; personnel should never be permitted to make changes and then inform others after the fact. Emergency changes still need to be formally reviewed in a change review to ensure that all stakeholders understand what change was made to the environment. A long-term goal that should be realized from managing emergency changes is the reduction in the need to make emergency changes, but a change plan should provide enough information to enable the organization to anticipate situations and manage them proactively if they do occur.

NOTE   The change management process should be formalized and include a documented process, procedures, forms, and recordkeeping.

Unauthorized Changes

Organizations need to have tools and methods in place to detect unauthorized changes that are made to systems, and to respond to those changes. Two avenues of action need to take place: first is the behavioral aspect, whereby management discusses the unauthorized changes with the person(s) who made them; second, the impact of those unauthorized changes needs to be understood and appropriate actions taken as a result.

Controls should be in place to prevent unauthorized changes from occurring. Some of these controls include

- **Segregation of duties**   Critical activities such as application software changes should be apportioned among a group of individuals so that no single individual is able to make key changes. For instance, only developers should have access to source code and be able to make changes to a staging area. Next, only authorized personnel should be able to read changes from a staging area and place those changes into production. No single person should be able to do all of these things.

- **Application code review**   Before checking in any change to application code, an independent review should be performed to ensure that only approved changes are being made.

- **Least privilege access**   Only those personnel who have a need to access and make changes to a system should be able to do so. For example, developers should not be able to make changes to production systems.

- **File integrity monitoring**   Production systems should be equipped with file integrity monitoring (FIM) software that automatically detects and reports changes to files on a system. This will help to detect changes that may have been made without formal approval.

- **File activity monitoring**   Production systems should be equipped with file activity monitoring (FAM) software that automatically detects and reports activities on sensitive files. Generally, FAM tools are used to detect access to operating system files that are usually accessed infrequently. Such access can be an indicator of compromise or of unauthorized activity by trusted insiders.

Configuration Management

Configuration management (CM) is the combination of a business recordkeeping process and automated tool(s) where the configuration of components in an IT environment is independently recorded. This activity has many potential benefits:

- **Recovery**   When configuration information for IT systems is stored independent of the systems themselves, CM information can be used to recover a system or device in the event of a malfunction or failure.

- **Consistency**   Often, automated tools are used to manage systems and devices in an environment. A CM tool can help an organization drive consistency into the configuration of its systems and devices. This consistency will simplify administration, reduce mistakes, and result in less unscheduled downtime.

- **Troubleshooting**   When unexpected behavior and unplanned outages occur, information in a CM system can help with troubleshooting the problem.

Configuration management and change management processes together can help to reduce errors by requiring approval for changes and then by recording them when they are completed.

Controlling and Recording Configuration Changes

While CM is usually considered a means for recording changes made to a system, it can also be used to control those changes. Typically, this is achieved through the use of tools that control system configuration and through system access controls that prohibit changes that circumvent those tools.

Automated tools are almost always used for CM. These tools include a *configuration management database* (CMDB) that serves as a repository for every component in an environment and that contains information on every configuration change made to those components. The more sophisticated CM tools also permit their operator to revert a given component to a configuration that existed at any time in the past.

Configuration Management and Change Control

While controlling and recording changes in an environment is highly valuable for some organizations, CM is not a substitute for the change management process. Instead, CM is the means by which change management–approved changes are carried out and recorded on systems. Change management is the review and approval of changes, while configuration management is used to perform and record changes.

Business Processes

Organizations that are mature in their thinking and practices will treat their business processes almost like they do their software: both are carefully designed, constructed, operated, and measured, and any changes that are made for either one should be formally considered. Ongoing processes are measured, and continuous improvement and optimization are carried out over time.

Both software and processes should be considered as structured and procedural. The primary difference between the two is that software directs the processing of information in computers, while processes (usually) direct the activities of personnel.

Organizations that understand this type of approach to processes will control their processes like they control their software: through a life cycle.

The Business Process Life Cycle and Business Process Reengineering

Like software, business processes should not be constructed on a whim, but instead should be carefully planned, designed, and constructed, with the involvement of all concerned parties in the organization. These activities are a part of the *business process life cycle* (BPLC).

The most important component in the business process life cycle is *business process reengineering* (BPR), which is the set of activities related to the process of making changes to business processes.

A *process* is a set of procedures that achieves some business purpose or objective. These procedures should be formally documented and usually will require recordkeeping of the activities controlled by the process. The procedures will help ensure that the activities are carried out correctly and consistently. The records produced help to document the activities that occurred as the process was carried out over and over. Depending upon the nature of the process, the records serve as tangible evidence that each activity occurred at specific dates and times, by specific personnel, using specific resources. Records also record details about activities such as money spent, products or services processed or sold, and names of customers or others. Records are also used to create statistics about the process that help management understand how well the process is performing and how it is contributing to overall business goals.

There should be a process to control the creation of new processes as well as changes to existing processes. This process is remarkably similar to the SDLC (since software and processes are similar, this should be of little surprise) and consists of the following major steps:

1. **Feasibility study** This effort determines the viability of a new process or a change in an existing process. The amount of rigor needed here is proportional to the impact of the new or changed process.

2. **Requirements definition** This formal record details the process that must be included in the new or changed process. All stakeholders should contribute to the requirements definition process and review to ensure that everyone understands the details of the process.

3. **Design** When requirements are completed, the process can be designed. Depending upon the nature of the process, this may include descriptions of activities performed by various personnel; the business equipment, assets, or materials used; and the specific involvement of customers, partners, and suppliers.

4. **Development** The details of the process are developed, using all of the requirements and design as a guide. This will include detailed procedures, templates for recordkeeping, and whatever other details are required.

5. **Testing** When procedures have been developed, they are then tested to ensure their accuracy and suitability. Detailed test plans need to be developed that have a one-to-one correspondence to each of the requirements developed in that earlier phase.

6. **Implementation** When the process has been perfected through testing, it is ready to be implemented. This means using the process in actual business operations with real equipment, people, materials, and money.

7. **Monitoring** The process needs to be continually monitored (primarily through its recordkeeping) so that management can manage resource allocation in support of process operations and to determine whether the process is performing against stated goals.

8. **Post-implementation** After the process has been implemented, one or more formal reviews need to take place to review the development process itself as well as the new (or changed) process. Depending upon the size, impact, and scope of the process, several reviews may be required, possibly over several years, to measure the effectiveness of the process and its results.

The reality in business today is that information systems and applications are used to support most business processes. This means that software development and process development often occur side by side and must be coordinated so that software applications meet the needs of the business processes that they support.

As organizations began to understand that business processes can be designed, developed, and improved like software, the term *business process reengineering* as a beneficial activity came into being in 1990. BPR became popular almost overnight as U.S. companies struggled to stay competitive with foreign companies that were intruding into American market spaces.

Figure 4-16
The business
process
management life
cycle

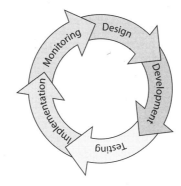

Business process management (BPM) is more often used to describe ongoing process improvement. A formal discipline of its own, BPM is a "Plan-Do-Check-Act" continuous improvement cycle described in the preceding paragraphs and illustrated in Figure 4-16.

Benchmarking a Process

Benchmarking describes the activity of continuous process improvement. The purpose of benchmarking is to compare key measurements in a business process to the same measurements performed by other organizations, particularly those that are considered to be top performers.

Typically, the steps in process benchmarking are

1. **Plan**   A critical process is selected and measurement techniques are identified. If the process has been through at least one improvement cycle, metrics may be available; otherwise, the team will need to determine how the process is measured in terms of throughput, cost, and quality.

2. **Research**   The team collects information about the target process over time. The team also identifies other organizations whose similar processes can be monitored and measured.

3. **Measure and observe**   The benchmarking team collects actual measurements on other organizations' processes. In "friendly" situations, the team will be able to visit the organizations and be permitted to collect measurements openly. In "unfriendly" situations, the team will need to make indirect measurements using whatever information is readily, legally, and ethically available. The team will also need to collect qualitative data about the processes that it is measuring in the other organizations so that it can understand how the other organizations' processes are performed.

4. **Analyze**   The team compares measurements of its own processes against those of the other organizations. Often the team will need to adjust measurements to account for known differences. Then the team will identify differences in metrics between its organization and those of the other organizations.

5. **Adapt** Here the team needs to understand the fundamental reasons why other organizations' measurements are better than its own. The team will need to understand not only the quantitative differences, but also the qualitative differences, between its organization's processes and the other organizations' processes to see how the other organizations achieve their metrics.

6. **Improve** Finally, the team recommends process improvements in its own organization. Management makes commitments to improve its process in specific ways to help its process to become more effective and efficient.

Benchmarking is relatively straightforward when other organizations are cooperative with regard to observation and measurement. But in a competitive situation, market rivals are unlikely to cooperate, and in some situations, cooperation may even be considered illegal.

Capability Maturity Models

Capability maturity models are another way to understand the effectiveness of an organization's business processes, particularly its software development processes. Three software development maturity models are discussed in this section.

Software Engineering Institute Capability Maturity Model

Developed at Carnegie Mellon University and now a part of ISACA, the Software Engineering Institute Capability Maturity Model (SEI CMM, often referred to as the CMM) is a conceptual model that helps an organization better understand the maturity of its own processes. This is a necessary step if an organization wants to improve its processes, particularly if the organization is not precisely sure how to begin this improvement.

The SEI CMM defines five levels of maturity:

- **Level 1 – Initial** This level has no process, no procedures, and no consistency. Success, when it is attained, is achieved through brute force and luck.

- **Level 2 – Repeatable** At this level of maturity, there is some consistency in the ways that individuals perform tasks from one time to the next, as well as some management planning and direction to ensure that tasks and projects are performed consistently.

- **Level 3 – Defined** The organization has developed a site-wide, documented software development process that is used for all development projects.

- **Level 4 – Managed** At this level, the documented software development process includes key measurement points used to measure effectiveness, efficiency, and defects. These measurements are performed and reported to management as a part of the life cycle.

- **Level 5 – Optimizing** At this highest level of maturity, the organization has instituted metrics-driven process improvement techniques to bring about continuous improvement in its SDLC.

Considerable effort is required for an organization to ascend from one level to the next. This model helps an organization better understand its current level of maturity and the process changes needed to improve its maturity over time.

How Mature Should We Be?

Confusion abounds on the topic of process maturity, and few organizations have the right perspective. Here's the myth: better-run organizations will aspire to improve their business processes until they are at the optimizing level—the top level in the CMM. Instead, consider this: in most organizations, a maturity level of around 3 is sufficient, for the long term. Organizations in some industries such as banking and aerospace should be closer to, or even a little beyond, level 4, managed. Few organizations should aspire to level 5, optimizing. The reason for this is that the cost of operations to rise from level 3 to level 4 is considerable, and for most organizations the amount of risk reduction does not warrant the expense.

The best way for organizations to approach process maturity is to determine the aspirational maturity level of each important business process—not merely a big average figure. In each organization, some processes need to be more mature, and others can acceptably be less mature. Organizations should ask two questions about each business process: how precise should this business process be run, and should we collect measurements on this process so that we can manage and improve it?

ISO/IEC 25010, Software Engineering

International standard ISO/IEC 25010 (previously ISO/IEC 9126) is used to evaluate the quality of software. This standard classifies software quality within a set of main characteristics:

- Functionality
- Reliability
- Usability
- Efficiency
- Maintainability
- Portability

Each of these characteristics has subcharacteristics that are further divided into attributes. Each attribute is objectively measured; these measurements contribute to measured software quality results.

ISO/IEC 33001, Information Technology—Process Assessment

International standard ISO/IEC 33001 (previously ISO/IEC 15504) is a maturity model for business processes. ISO/IEC 33001 is an introduction to the ISO/IEC 330XX family of process assessment standards and how they work together.

NIST Cybersecurity Framework

The U.S. NIST Cybersecurity Framework (CSF) is a controls and management framework, together with a scheme of framework implementation tiers. The tiers are

- Partial
- Risk Informed
- Repeatable
- Adaptive

The text of the CSF claims that these tiers are not maturity levels, but upon reading the tier descriptions, it is difficult to come to any other conclusion.

Executive Order (EO) 13636, *Improving Critical Infrastructure Cybersecurity*, (February 2013) reads, "directed NIST to work with stakeholders to develop a voluntary framework—based on existing standards, guidelines, and practices—for reducing cyber risks to critical infrastructure" (NIST, 2018). While required for implementation within the U.S. Federal Government, the CSF is voluntary guidance for private, commercial, and other organizations. It is heavily integrated into the latest version of the Risk Management Framework (RMF) (version 2, as of December 2018), and is essentially a catalog of cybersecurity activities. These activities are outcome-based and describe desired outcomes from performing these activities. As of the writing of this book, the current version of the CSF is 1.1, released in April 2018.

The CSF consists of 5 activities or *functions*, further broken down into 23 categories and 108 subcategories. Each of these is also matrixed with 5 Informative References—CIS, COBIT, ISA, ISO/IEC 27001, and NIST SP 800-53—although obviously the emphasis throughout is on the NIST control catalog. All of this together is referred to as the CSF *core*. The mapping to CIS, COBIT, ISA, ISO 27001, and NIST 800-53 alone makes the CSF a valuable reference tool.

The five CSF functions are Identify (ID), Protect (PR), Detect (DE), Respond (RS), and Recover (RC). Each of these functions dictates how a mature cybersecurity life cycle can be developed to protect an organization and its assets. These are essentially the functions and activities an organization performs on a daily basis to protect its assets and minimize or respond to risk.

A CSF tier is "the degree to which an organization's cybersecurity risk management practices exhibit the characteristics defined in the Framework" (NIST, 2018). The four tiers range from Partial (Tier 1) to Adaptive (Tier 4). The three areas that are measured for maturity in the CSF are the Risk Management Process (degree of rigor), the Integrated Risk Management Program (how well cybersecurity risk decisions are integrated into broader risk decisions), and the level of External Participation (the degree to which the organization shares and receives cybersecurity info from external parties).

For implementation in the private sector, the CSF can be customized into profiles. A *profile* is a particular customization of the CSF core for an organization or sector; it is based on the organization's or sector's unique requirements. NIST publishes profiles for a variety of industry sectors, such as the manufacturing and petroleum industries.

Managing Third Parties

The suppliers, vendors, service providers, and business partner organizations that assist the organization in the realization of its objectives are known as *third parties*. The standard of due care for the management of third parties requires that organizations carefully examine each third party during the selection process and thereafter. In response to the trend of outsourcing IT services to third-party organizations, the standard of due care has been steadily increasing. This is necessary to maintain risk parity, so that organizations have a reasonable amount of visibility into cyber-risk matters.

Risk Factors

The range and type of involvement of a third party in an organization's development and delivery of its products or services may vary widely. This means that the risks associated with individual third parties will also vary. Accordingly, the activities that an organization will need to undertake at the onset of each third-party relationship, and periodically thereafter, will also differ.

Examples of the factors that influence risk levels include the following:

- Does the third party assist in the design, development, or operations of important information systems?

- Does the third party have access to sensitive data?

- Is sensitive data transmitted to the third party for processing?

- Do members of the third-party organization have access to the organization's work centers?

- Are any of the activities performed by the third party in scope for laws, regulations, standards, or contracts with other parties?

The answers to these and other questions help organizations better understand various aspects of cybersecurity risk associated with each third-party organization.

Onboarding and Due Diligence

An organization typically embarks on a search of third-party service providers to find one or more candidate service providers. The organization will develop objectives and requirements and use these in an evaluation process to determine how successfully each candidate service provider will be able to assist the organization to fulfill its business objectives.

Often, organizations will conduct a formal RFP or RFI process, in which formal business and technical requirements are developed and sent to each candidate service provider. Those service providers will then respond to each requirement. The RFP process is described in more detail earlier in this chapter.

After vetting candidate service providers and making a final selection, the organization should determine the level and type of up-front and periodic (typically quarterly or

Table 4-3 Third-Party Risk Tiers	Classification	Access to Client Data	Access to Source Code	Access to Facilities
	High	Y	Y	Y
	Medium	N	N	Y
	Low	N	N	N

annual) due diligence that will take place. These activities should be described in legal agreements between the organization and the chosen third party.

Classification

Organizations with more than just a few third-party service providers should establish a *risk tiering scheme* to separate the third parties into similar risk groups. The purpose of this tiering is to serve as a part of a larger program of third-party risk management whereby the organization will determine various types of due diligence for third parties at each risk level. An example tiering scheme is depicted in Table 4-3. This is a simplistic example; organizations need to develop their own criteria to determine the number and type of risk levels and rules to select a risk tier for each third party.

Assessment

All third parties need to be periodically assessed, but not all assessments are the same. After risk tiering is used to determine the risk level for each third party, the activities to assess each third party are established. These activities correspond to risk levels; a simplistic example scheme of risk levels and assessments is shown in Table 4-4.

Remediation

Organizations should expect that the initial and ongoing processes of conducting due diligence on its third-party service providers are not going to proceed perfectly. Occasionally, an organization will discover that the third party is not performing all of the required or desired activities to its liking. At times, these deficiencies may put the organization in jeopardy with regulators.

For example, an organization may require its top-tier service providers to use two-factor authentication for all remote access; an organization may, through the use of questionnaires or a site visit, discover that the third party is not using two-factor

Table 4-4 Assessment Techniques for Each Level of Risk	Classification	High	Medium	Low
	Full Questionnaire	Y	Y	N
	Limited Questionnaire	N	N	Y
	On-site Visit	Y	N	N
	Penetration Test	Y	N	N

authentication for remote access. The organization may consider this a serious deficiency and must decide a course of action. Remediation can range from cessation of the relationship to acceptance of the risk. Neither of these is reasonable, but instead the organization generally will seek some middle ground whereby it will compel the third party to enact two-factor authentication for remote access within a reasonable period of time.

In situations where the third party is unable or unwilling to remediate a deficiency, the organization will need to consider its options carefully and find a path of action that brings together the right level of risk and continued business.

Risk Reporting

As personnel periodically assess third parties, a bigger picture can begin to form. Often, metrics or a risk dashboard are presented to senior management, so that management can understand where the risk "hot spots" are, as well as trends in third-party risk. This information helps management decide how to manage this important aspect of cybersecurity risk over time.

Application Controls

Software applications accept, process, store, and transmit information. Unless specifically programmed and configured, software applications lack the ability to properly distinguish valid and reasonable data from that which is not. Controls are necessary to ensure that information at each stage of processing retains its required integrity.

 EXAM TIP Exam questions may present a more complex situation than simple input, process, and output controls. Few business processes exist in a vacuum, so many process controls also need to have the full set of internal input, process, and output controls for each subprocess. Test-takers should watch for questions that address application controls that may deal with subprocess requirements, or in which the output of one process is presented as the input for the process under review (affecting which set of controls is appropriate to the question).

While there are marked differences in the architecture of software applications, the typical approach to controls is to apply these controls at the point of entry, processing, and exit. In other words, controls around input data, processing, and output data are needed.

Input Controls

Data that is presented to an application as input data must be validated for authorization, reasonableness, completeness, and integrity. Several controls must be implemented to ensure these points.

Input Authorization

All data that is input into a system must be authorized by management. The method of authorization can take many forms:

- **User access controls**   Only approved personnel, such as system operators, input clerks, business analysts, and customer service representatives, are permitted to log in and use applications. Each user must have unique login credentials.

- **Entity access controls**   Only authorized organizations are permitted to log in and access business applications. Entities in each such organization (including users, service accounts, and hosts) are required to have unique login credentials.

- **Workstation identification**   Only approved terminals and workstations are permitted to be used to input transactions. Identification can take many forms, including electronic serial number, network address, or digital certificate.

- **Approved transactions and batches**   Through manual signature, online approval, and other means, management and other approved personnel perform necessary checks and verifications before individual transactions and batches of transactions are permitted to be input and processed.

- **Source documents**   In some settings, data can be input only from existing source documents. This can include mailed invoices, checks, receipts, or forms filled in by customers. Source documents themselves should be controlled so that they cannot be altered, misplaced, or removed.

 NOTE   Well-designed applications include audit logs that record when specific data was input, how it was input, and who authorized its input. This permits an organization to research matters when a question arises regarding the source of specific input data after the fact.

Input Validation

The process of input validation is used to make sure that the types and values of information are appropriate and reasonable. The types of input validation include

- **Type checking**   Each input field should be programmed to accept only the type of data that is appropriate for the field. For instance, a numeric field should contain only numeric digits, and a name field should contain only alphabetic characters.

- **Range and value checking**   Input fields need to validate the range and value of characters. For instance, the day field in a date should only accept figures 1 through 31, and the month field 1 through 12. Even more intelligent checking is often warranted; for example, a date field often should be a date that is only in the past, or the future, or even a specific range of the past or future. Other examples include only valid ZIP or postal codes, only valid telephone numbers, and only valid IP addresses. In some cases, input data must match values in a table of data stored in the application; for instance, only valid city, state, or country codes; telephone area codes; or valid Universal Product Codes (UPCs).

- **Existence**   This simple check confirms that each input field actually contains data.

- **Consistency**   This check compares related data from different input fields. For instance, a ZIP code value in an input field can be validated by comparing it to the range of allowed ZIP codes for the city and state values.

- **Length**   Programs must validate the length of input data in an input field. Fields such as names and addresses are often limited to, say, 30 characters. This is especially important on interactive programs where intruders may attempt buffer overflow attacks in an attempt to cause the program to malfunction.

- **Check digits or hash totals**   Numeric values such as bank account numbers can be verified for integrity by recalculating their check digits or hash totals.

- **Spelling**   Input fields that are supposed to contain common words can be spell-checked.

- **Unwanted characters**   Input fields should filter out unwanted characters that could be a result of mistyping. However, unwanted characters can also be a sign of a software malfunction (on a system that is the source of input data) or of an attempted intrusion.

- **Batch controls**   Batches of data should include calculations and counts to ensure the integrity and completeness of a batch of data. Some available methods include transaction counts, control totals (the numeric sum of one or more numeric fields in all of the batch records), and hash totals (a computed "sum" of all of the input fields, regardless of their actual type).

Input validation is certainly necessary on user input forms in applications where users are filling in online forms. However, input validation is just as necessary on batch input and other automated functions; errors in other systems may occur that can cause input data to be entered into the wrong fields: failure to validate input data can result in inappropriate data being input and stored in a system, which can lead to other problems later.

Input Validation as Achilles Heel

In many, or dare I say most, organizations, insufficient input validation is the nexus for many critical system vulnerabilities and breaches (for example, SQL injection and buffer overflow conditions). With alarming regularity, we learn of critical vulnerabilities in commercial software products and systems such as buffer overflow and cross-site scripting. These vulnerabilities exist as a result of insufficient input validation.

Error Handling

As software programs perform all of the input validation checking described earlier, these programs must be programmed or configured to take specific actions when any of the input validations fail. There are many possible responses, depending upon the type of data being input as well as the method of input:

- **Batch rejection**   For input batches, if the transaction count, control totals, or hash totals of a batch do not agree with expected values, the entire batch should be rejected. Usually the application software will have no way to determine what exactly is wrong with the batch, so the only reasonable course of action is to reject the entire batch, which will require data control analysts to examine the batches to see what went wrong.

- **Transaction rejection**   For individual input transactions, whether automated or user input, the software application can reject the transaction.

- **Hold in suspense**   The entire batch will be held in suspense so that the error(s) in the batch can be corrected and the batch can be rerun.

- **Request re-input**   An interactive user program can request that the user re-input the entire form or just the specific field that appears to be incorrect.

When an application rejects input, in most cases the application will need to create a log entry, an error report, or another record of the rejected input so that data analysts will know that an error occurred and take steps to correct it. If the application does not create a record of the error, analysts are apt to believe that all data was input successfully, which could lead to problems later on when those invalid transactions cannot be found anywhere in the system. A lack of such records makes detailed troubleshooting far more difficult.

Processing Controls

It is necessary to ensure that data in a system retains its integrity. All new data that is created—for instance, as a result of calculations—must be checked for reasonableness to ensure that calculations are working properly and that bad information or program code is not creeping in through some other means. The controls used to ensure that data in the system retains its integrity are discussed in this section.

Editing

In many types of applications, data that is initially input into the system will be changed from time to time. For example, a subscriber's e-mail or mailing address may change, or a bank account number, passport number, or license plate number may change. Often these changes are performed either directly by customers or by a customer service representative during a telephone conversation. Sometimes these changes are made automatically as a result of trusted and validated data arriving from other sources.

Whenever values are changed, the new values must be validated before they are accepted and stored; otherwise, problems may ensue later on. The types of validation checks performed during editing are similar to those performed during initial input, described earlier in this section.

Calculations

When application programs are performing calculations, the results of those calculations need to be validated for accuracy and reasonableness to verify that the application is performing calculations properly. Several techniques are used to validate calculations:

- **Run-to-run totals**   This validates that specific stored or calculated data values retain their values throughout the steps in a transaction. This helps to ensure that no errors, tampering, or software malfunctions have occurred.

- **Limit checking**   Results of specific calculations can be checked for upper and lower limits. Calculation results that exceed predetermined limits can be rejected.

- **Batch totals**   When data is processed in batches, batch totals that are calculated at the beginning of the batch can be recalculated at the end of processing for the batch to ensure the integrity of the batch data.

- **Manual recalculation**   An analyst or clerk can recalculate certain transaction calculations manually, and those manual calculation results can be verified or keyed into the application.

- **Reconciliation**   When a set of records is processed that results in the creation of a second set of records—or the next stage of calculation results—totals from the old to new batches may need to be calculated to ensure that processing was done correctly and that no data corruption or calculation errors occurred.

- **Hash values**   The values in selected sets of numeric or text fields can be rehashed at various stages of calculations to verify that they have not been altered or tampered with.

Data File Controls

When processing is performed on data stored in data files, several types of controls are needed to ensure the security and integrity of those data files. Some of the controls available include

- **Data file and database security**   Access controls can be configured so that only authorized users or processes are permitted to access data files and databases.

- **Error handling**   Erroneous transactions that need to be corrected or re-input should be checked by personnel other than those who originally keyed them.

- **Internal and external labeling**   Labeling on removable storage media is vital to ensure that the correct volume (whether tape, disc, or other storage medium) has been loaded.

- **Data file version**   The version of a data file should be independently verified to ensure that the proper file is being processed. This would, for example, help to prevent processing yesterday's file twice.

- **Source files**   Data input at the beginning of a processing run should be retained for a minimum period in case a batch needs to be rerun many days or weeks later.

- **Transaction logs**   Log files containing transactions should be retained for a minimum period in support of later troubleshooting or the investigation of data errors weeks or months later.

Processing Errors

Errors that occur during processing must be recorded in a logfile or other output medium that will be examined by personnel. All errors need to be addressed, whether through rekeying of errant data, rerunning failed batch runs, correcting data transmission errors, or other means.

Processing errors that occur in interactive programs may display an error message to the user. Depending upon the type of program, the user may have an opportunity to correct or rekey information.

Output Controls

Applications accept input data, perform calculations, and produce output data. The results of final calculations and transformations need to be checked for reasonableness and validity. Several types of output controls are available, depending upon the type of activity and data.

Controlling Special Forms

Some calculation outputs are printed on special physical forms, such as checks, warrants, invoices, and certificates. These forms should be serialized and kept in a locked cabinet. In high-value situations, these forms should be kept in dual custody, where two individuals are required in order to access them.

A forms log should be maintained to account for the use of forms. This log should be examined frequently to ensure that forms are used only for their stated purpose and that all are accounted for.

Checks, warrants, bonds, and other negotiable instruments must be secured at all times to ensure that all are accounted for and properly handled. Just as with electronic data, physical forms must be inventoried and accounted for at each stage of processing and handling.

Signature devices and stamps, when used, must be secured at all times. They should be stored in locations separate from checks and certificates and should be under the control of separate individuals.

Report Distribution and Receipt

Application processing often results in the creation of reports that are sent to authorized personnel in paper or electronic form. Often these reports will contain sensitive information, which requires that the reports be safeguarded at all times in any form.

Reports that are printed and later delivered may need to be placed in tamper-proof or tamper-evident envelopes. Reports that remain in electronic form may need to be encrypted or password-protected. Reports that are transmitted over public networks need to be encrypted. If recipients send electronic reports to printers, special safeguards may be required so that sensitive data is not left on printers for others to view.

Reconciliation

Numeric and financial data on reports may need to be reconciled to input data, data from intermediate calculations, or control totals. This activity, when required, should be documented and logged.

Retention

Reports are sometimes the only human-readable data available during each business cycle. Whether reports deal with research, reference, or statutory requirements, it is often necessary to retain them for a minimum period of up to several years. Reports containing sensitive data will need to be physically safeguarded to prevent access by unauthorized personnel.

NOTE   Output controls are just as vital as input controls, because the outputs from one system do not necessarily become the inputs to another system that the organization has control over. Sometimes, one system's output will become another system's inputs where little or no input validation takes place.

Auditing the Systems Development Life Cycle

Audits of the processes used to create and maintain software will assist the organization in knowing how effective these processes are. This provides the organization with valuable information that can be used to make its processes more effective. If the IS auditor examines only an organization's applications and controls but not the processes used to create them, then the root cause of endemic problems in applications and processes may be unknowable.

EXAM TIP   The exam will expect you to have a general understanding of the details of each type of audit practice. Focus on the type of documentation and the mechanism for validation of each as you review this section. Watch for exam questions that begin with phrases such as "During the design phase…" or similar terminology to guide your response.

Auditing Program and Project Management

The IS auditor who is auditing an organization's program and project management is verifying whether the organization's projects are adequately controlled. Controls in project management ensure the integrity of the organization's projects so that the systems and processes that are built actually support the requirements that are supported and agreed to by management.

The activities that the IS auditor should review when auditing project management include

- Oversight by senior management and any steering committee(s)
- Risk management techniques used in the project
- Processes and methodologies used to build project plans
- Methods for dealing with issues
- Management of costs
- Status reporting to management
- Project change control
- Project recordkeeping, including decisions, approvals, resource utilization, and costs

Auditing the Feasibility Study

IS auditors should audit any feasibility studies that occur at the beginning of major projects. The activities that IS auditors should review include

- Budgets and cost justifications, and whether they can be independently verified
- Criticality of the project and/or the criticality of the business process supported by the project
- Alternatives that were considered, including the feasibility that existing systems could be used in support of the business need
- Reasonableness of the solution that was chosen and implemented

Auditing Requirements

An IS auditor should audit a project's requirements and the process that was used to develop them. The IS auditor needs to review several aspects of requirements:

- Identify all of the personnel who contributed requirements and determine whether this body of personnel actually represents all true stakeholders.
- Interview several of the requirements contributors to gain a better understanding of whether contributors' requirements were included and whether they were altered without their knowledge.
- Identify any ranking or alteration of requirements that may have occurred without the knowledge of those who contributed them.
- Perform some reasonableness checking of requirements to see if they support the project described in the feasibility stage.
- Determine whether the final body of requirements was approved by management.

Auditing Design

The IS auditor should audit the design and specifications that were developed during a project. During the audit, the IS auditor should consider whether

- The design actually reflects and supports requirements and the feasibility study.
- The design contains sufficient detail to enable application developers to produce software that will unambiguously meet the organization's requirements and business needs.
- The design was adequately reviewed and was approved by management.
- The design will reasonably result in a successful implementation that meets the users' needs.
- Testing and UAT (user acceptance testing) plans and criteria were developed by this phase in the project.

Auditing Software Acquisition

For software development projects where the organization acquires software from an outside vendor, an IS auditor should audit several aspects and activities in the acquisition stage of the project. The IS auditor should consider whether

- The organization performed a formal RFP or RFI process.
- All requirements were transferred to the RFP or RFI document.
- Suitable vendors were considered and their responses were properly analyzed against each of the requirements.
- The vendor that was selected could support a majority of the requirements.
- The organization did reference checking, evaluation, and/or pilot evaluation before purchase.
- The contract contains clauses that reasonably protect the organization in the event the software or the vendor fails to perform adequately.
- The contract was reviewed by the organization's legal department before being signed.

Auditing Development

For software development projects where the organization develops software on its own, the IS auditor should consider whether

- The developers were adequately trained and experienced in the languages and tools used in the project.
- The chosen design and development tools were adequate for the project.

- The chosen computer language and other related technologies were adequate for the project.

- The application contains adequate controls to ensure proper operation, recordkeeping, and support of business processes.

- Controls used to protect source code are adequate.

- The application was written in support of stated requirements.

- The application has adequate input, processing, and output controls.

- The application performs calculations correctly.

- The application produces adequate transaction and audit logs.

Auditing Testing

Software that is developed within the organization or acquired from an outside vendor needs to be tested to ensure that it meets the organization's requirements. When auditing software testing, the IS auditor should consider whether

- All test plans were developed during the requirements and design phases.

- Test plans reflect the entirety of requirements and design elements.

- All tests were performed and verified successfully.

- Actual test results are available for review as well as contact information for personnel who performed testing.

- Test results have been archived for later research if needed.

- Parallel tests were needed and, if so, were performed appropriately.

- UAT was performed, and the results of those tests are available.

Auditing Implementation

Implementation should be performed only after all testing has been successful and all issues identified during testing have been resolved. When auditing implementation, the IS auditor should consider whether

- Management approved the implementation.

- The system was implemented using established change control procedures.

- The system was administratively locked down before implementation, thereby preventing tampering by any developer or other persons who do not have authorization to access production systems.

- Data conversions were performed in a controlled manner, including controls to ensure correct conversion processing.

Auditing Post-Implementation

The IS auditor should audit all post-implementation activities, considering whether

- A post-implementation review took place and, if so, whether the review was documented and actions taken.
- The application supports the entire body of requirements established during the project.
- The application is being measured to verify whether it is meeting established performance and ROI targets.
- Excessive changes were made to the system after implementation, which could be an indicator of inadequate requirements or testing.
- Excessive unscheduled downtime or errors occurred, which could be an indicator of inadequate requirements or testing.
- Control balances indicate that the application is performing properly.

Auditing Change Management

Change management is the management process whereby all changes to an environment are controlled. The IS auditor should consider whether

- A change management policy and process exists and is followed in practice.
- Adequate records exist that indicate how much the change management process is followed.
- The number of emergency changes indicates inadequate requirements or testing.
- Proposed changes contain implementation procedures, back-out procedures, and test results.
- Minutes are kept of change management meetings.
- Emergency changes are adequately reviewed.

Auditing Configuration Management

Configuration management involves controlling, configuring, and recording configuration changes to information systems. When auditing configuration management, the IS auditor should consider whether

- Configuration management policies and controls exist and are followed.
- Configuration management tools are used to control and/or record changes made to systems.
- Changes are approved through the change management process.
- Configuration management tools are able to verify the integrity of systems and whether discrepancies are identified and resolved.

Auditing Business Controls

Business controls are points in time during business processes where key activities occur. The IS auditor needs to identify the key processes in an organization and understand the controls that are in place—or that should be in place—that govern the integrity of those processes.

Many business controls are supported by IT applications, but the auditor also needs to take a business process perspective and understand the control points from a strictly process viewpoint. This is necessary because, although controls may be automated by applications, personnel are still in control of and responsible for the correct operation of business processes. Further, processes, even when partly or entirely automated, must be monitored and managed by staff or management. And these processes must be documented—itself an important control.

 NOTE For the IS auditor to overlook business controls and focus only on IT applications would be a disservice to the organization, because the auditor could miss the obvious control points in key business processes. Remember that the IT system is not the process; instead, the IT system *supports* the process.

Auditing Application Controls

Application controls ensure that only valid data enters a system through input controls, that calculations yield only valid results, and that output data is valid. The IS auditor needs to examine system documentation to understand internal and external data flows and calculations. The IS auditor also needs to examine system records to ensure that all changes made to the system were authorized. Several aspects of application activity need to be examined; these are described in the remainder of this section.

Transaction Flow

The IS auditor should audit an application and follow transactions from end to end. The IS auditor should consider whether

- Any data flow diagrams or flowcharts exist that describe data flow in the transaction, and whether such diagrams or flowcharts correctly identify the flow of data
- Any data items in the transaction were altered in the data flow, and, if so, where alterations occurred and whether audit log entries recorded those changes, including who or what made them

Observations

During an audit of information systems, the IS auditor should make several observations, including whether

- Any segregations of duties (SODs) are established in terms of the entire transaction process flow

- Input data is validated, and how the validation is performed
- Input data is authorized, and how the authorization is documented
- Any balancing or reconciliation is performed to ensure data integrity
- Any errors occur, how they are detected, and how they are handled
- Reports and other outputs are generated, controlled, protected, examined, and acted upon

Data Integrity Testing

Data integrity testing is used to confirm whether an application properly accepts, processes, and stores information. Data integrity tests will determine whether there are any failures or errors in input, processing, or output controls in an application. The IS auditor should perform several tests on the application, in each case attempting to input data that is invalid or unreasonable to determine whether the application properly rejects such data. The auditor should also attempt to have the application perform calculations that should result in errors or exceptions—for example, a calculation result that should be rejected.

The IS auditor should test not only the stated input, calculation, and output rules for data integrity, but he or she should also assess the efficacy of the rules themselves. For example, an auditor should determine whether the absence of a rule forbidding the entry of negative hours in a time-reporting system constitutes a deficiency in the application's rules.

Testing Online Processing Systems

Online processing systems are characterized by their ability to process transactions for many users simultaneously. An online application must be able to compartmentalize each user's work so that the users do not interfere with one another, even if two or more users are attempting to read or update the same records. A typical database management system (DBMS) will be able to enforce record locking, and an application must have logic to deal with locked records gracefully and according to established business rules.

Business records and transactions in DBMSs are usually made up of rows in several different tables. *Referential integrity* is the characteristic that requires that the DBMS maintain the parent-child relationships between records in different tables and prohibit activities such as deleting parent records and transforming child records into orphans. Application logic must be designed to prevent these situations and other types of "collisions" and deadlocks that can occur when many users are performing different tasks in an application. The characteristic of *atomicity* states that a complex transaction, which could consist of simultaneous actions on many records in many different tables, is performed as a single unit of work: either it will all be completed properly or none of it will be completed. This helps to ensure the integrity of all data in the DBMS.

The IS auditor will need a complete understanding of the inner workings of an application, including the actions of different transactions on the underlying DBMS. Then the auditor will need to stage a number of different tests to see how the application handles situations that may challenge the integrity of business information. Some examples include

- Having two different users try to open the same transaction to update it
- Having one user try to remove the transaction while another user is trying to update it
- Having two different users open related records in a database, and then having one of the users attempt to remove records that the other user is viewing

These are simple examples, but they should serve to illustrate the need for the IS auditor to determine whether the application properly manages business records.

Auditing Applications

Applications must never be assumed to perform all of their input, processing, and output perfectly. This must be the mindset of the IS auditor: that every important function of applications must be verified to be operating correctly and completely.

Many techniques are available for auditing IT applications, including

- **Transaction tracing**   The IS auditor enters specific transactions and then carefully examines the application, data, and reports to see how the transaction is represented and processed in the application.
- **Test batches**   The IS auditor creates a batch of test transactions with expected outcomes and directs that they be processed by the system and their results compared against what is expected.
- **Software mapping**   The application software is traced during execution to determine whether there are any unused sections of code. Unused code could signify faulty program logic, obsolete code, or backdoors.
- **Baselining**   This process uses sets of input data (batch- or key-processed by the system) with known results. After system changes, the same sets of data are processed again to determine whether the expected results have changed.
- **Parallel testing**   Programs that simulate the application's function are used to process real data to determine whether results vary from the production system.

It is not suggested that an IS auditor employ all of these methods, but he or she should instead select those that will be most effective at verifying correct and complete processing at key points in an application.

Continuous Auditing

Continuous auditing permits the IS auditor to conduct audits of an online environment in a way that is less disruptive to business operations. Instead of more costly and invasive audits, IS auditors can test systems while they are running and with minimum or no involvement from IT staff. Continuous auditing techniques, also known as *computer-assisted audit techniques* (CAATs), are especially useful in applications such as an e-commerce operation with no paper audit trail. Several techniques are available to perform online auditing:

- **Audit hooks** Special audit modules are placed in key points in an application and are designed to trigger if a specific audit exception or special condition occurs. This can alert auditors to the situation, permitting them to decide whether additional action is required.

- **System Control Audit Review File and Embedded Audit Modules (SCARF/EAM)** Special audit software modules are embedded in the application; these modules perform continuous auditing and create an independent log of audit results.

- **Integrated test facility (ITF)** This permits test transactions to be processed in a live application environment. A separate test entity is required, however, so that test data does not alter financial or business results (because the test data does not present actual transactions).

- **Continuous and intermittent simulation (CIS)** The application contains an audit software module that examines online transactions. When a transaction meets audit criteria, the transaction is processed by the application and is also processed by a parallel simulation routine, and the results of the two are compared. These results are logged so that an auditor may examine them at a later time and decide whether any action is required based upon the results.

- **Snapshots** This technique involves the use of special audit modules embedded in an online application that samples specific transactions. The modules make copies of key parts of transactions, often by copying database records and storing them independently. This enables an auditor to trace specific transactions through an application to view the state of transactions as they flow through the application.

- **Online inquiry** An auditor has the ability to query the application and/or its database to retrieve detailed information on specific transactions or groups of transactions. The auditor typically must have an intimate knowledge of transaction and data structures to make use of this technique.

Auditing Third-Party Risk Management

Auditing third-party risk management involves careful examinations of policy and process documents as well as business records to determine whether all of the organization's third parties are represented in the organization's third-party risk management program. Several techniques and activities are available, including

- **Completeness of third-party population** When examining other activities in the business, auditors should determine third parties that are working with the organization and verify whether these third parties are a part of the organization's third-party risk process.

- **Risk criteria**   Auditors should examine stated risk criteria to determine whether they are measurable and complete, and whether they reflect risks present in the organization.

- **Legal agreements**   Auditors should examine legal agreements with third parties to see what security-related controls and obligations are required of each third party. The auditors should determine whether contract language adequately covers business risks and whether that language corresponds to any specific risks identified in the initial vetting of a third party.

- **Third-party classification**   Auditors should examine the classification of third parties and determine whether they were classified properly, according to the organization's risk tiering scheme (as covered earlier in the chapter in the section "Classification"). While the organization may have latitude for making exceptions (rating third parties higher risk or lower risk than usual), these exceptions should be documented and reasonable.

- **Examination of questionnaires**   Auditors should examine the various questionnaires that are sent to third parties to determine whether the contents and subject matter in the questionnaires cover risks adequately.

- **Questionnaire processing**   Auditors should examine questionnaires returned from third parties and look for responses that warrant attention or response. Auditors should follow the remediation process and see what actions were performed when third parties failed to answer questions or provided answers that warrant action. There should be a complete record of action from a returned questionnaire to remediation and issue closure.

Chapter Review

Organizations should have processes and procedures in place to manage the development, acquisition, and maintenance of software applications and supporting infrastructure. These processes ensure that all of the activities related to additions and changes to software applications are performed consistently and that all necessary considerations are included and documented.

Program management is the oversight of several projects and project teams. A program manager oversees project managers who manage individual projects in a program that contributes to an organization's objective. The program manager's oversight includes monitoring project schedules, budgets, resource allocation, conflicts, and the preparation of status reports for senior management. Another form of program management involves the management of a *project portfolio*, which is a collection of all of the active projects, regardless of whether they contribute to a single corporate objective or to many.

Management should approve any new project only after a valid business case has been developed, reviewed, and approved. A *business case* describes the business problem, the results of any feasibility studies, a project plan, a budget, and related risks. The project will be approved only if there is a reasonable expectation of business benefits; a business case should include one or more ways in which the outcome of the project can be measured so that management can determine whether the project resulted in actual business benefit.

Projects require formal planning that includes the development of a project schedule, creation of methods for estimating the time required for individual tasks, management of budgets and resources, methods for identification and resolution of issues and conflicts, management of project records, and creation of status reports for management. Changes to projects should be managed through a formal review and approval process. Project debriefs or reviews should take place when projects conclude so that the organization can identify lessons learned that will help improve future projects.

Software development and acquisition should be managed through a *systems development life cycle* (SDLC) or similar process. The SDLC is a rigorous set of activities that help ensure that new applications will meet the organization's business needs. The phases of the SDLC are feasibility study, requirements definition, design, development, testing, implementation, and post-implementation. These phases are all formally documented, reviewed, and measured.

The feasibility study and requirements definition phases help a project team develop a highly detailed set of specifications that developers can use to build the application. An organization that is purchasing off-the-shelf software can use requirements to make sure that the most appropriate software product will be selected.

The testing phase ensures that the application that was developed or acquired will actually perform as required. A test plan should be formally developed; this plan should be a direct derivation from formal requirements that were developed earlier in the project; essentially, every requirement must be measurable and confirmed during testing. Other critical activities in a software development project include data migration (where data is transferred from an older application to the new application), training (for users, operations, and technical support staff), and implementation of the new software application.

Some alternatives to the traditional SDLC process include agile development, prototyping, rapid application development (RAD), data-oriented system development (DOSD), object-oriented (OO) system development, component-based development, web-based development, and reverse engineering.

Software developers often use system development tools to aid in software development. These tools include integrated development environments (IDEs), computer-aided software engineering (CASE), and fourth-generation languages (4GLs) that can make developers more productive. Some organizations will integrate these environments with security testing tools such as dynamic application security testing (DAST) and static application security testing (SAST).

Acquiring cloud-based applications requires the same steps as software acquisition, although additional considerations need to be managed, including access control, environment segregation, and legal jurisdiction.

Change management and configuration management processes are used to manage changes to existing applications and infrastructure. Change management is a formal process whereby desired changes are planned, tested, and reviewed prior to implementation. Configuration management is a process (usually supported by automated tools) of recording configuration information in operating systems, software environments, and applications.

Like software applications and infrastructure, business processes should also be managed by a life cycle process that includes feasibility studies, requirements definition, business process engineering, testing, and implementation. Often, business processes are tightly coupled to software applications; frequently, changes to one will necessitate changes in the other.

Software applications should be equipped with controls that ensure the integrity of information and the integrity of processing and applications. These controls include input validation, processing validation, and output validation, all of which ensure that the data in the application is of the proper type and within required numeric ranges.

IS auditors who audit life cycle management activities need to obtain and examine documents that describe program and project management processes, charters, and records. They need to understand the processes that are used to develop and acquire software applications and supporting infrastructure, as well as the processes used to maintain them. IS auditors need to understand the processes that are in place and to examine records to help determine whether the processes are followed and effective.

Third parties should be assessed for risk and their compliance with the organization's requirements. Organizations with many third parties should establish a risk-tiering scheme and enact periodic assessment procedures commensurate with each level of risk. IS auditors need to audit an organization's third-party risk program to ensure that all third parties are included in the program, that third parties are correctly classified, and that issues are remediated. Metrics and specific issues on third-party risk should be reported to senior management.

Quick Review

- Benefits realization is the result of strategic planning, process development, and systems development, which all contribute toward a launch of business operations to reach a set of business objectives.

- Project management strategies guide program execution through the organization of resources and development of clear project objectives. Management of the project schedule, roles, change management, and subsequent completion or closure criteria determine the outcome of each project. Many project management methodologies exist to guide project expectations, requirements, and completion criteria.

- The systems development life cycle (SDLC) defines a subset of project management focusing on the requirements for the creation, implementation, and maintenance of application software. The SDLC relies on a sequence of events that may occur one time or cyclically as part of a formal continual improvement process. The SDLC phases include a feasibility study, definition of requirements, design, development, testing, implementation, and post-implementation phases.

- Application access is facilitated by the enterprise infrastructure, which is in turn developed, implemented, and maintained through a process similar to the SDLC.

Infrastructural development begins with a review of existing infrastructure elements, matching each to identified requirements to produce the initial design. After procurement to meet design requirements, the activities of testing, implementation, and post-implementation follow similarly to the SDLC.

- Post-implementation maintenance of information systems includes both change and configuration management strategies to ensure the enterprise remains aligned with business requirements and practices.

- The business process life cycle (BPLC) and business process reengineering (BPR) aid in coordinating business processes using a sequence of events similar to that of the SDLC focused on business process creation, implementation, and maintenance. Benchmarking facilitates continuous improvement within the BPLC, while capability maturity models can enable point-in-time assessment of business process and information system capability alignment.

- Application controls limit information system access at the point of entry (input controls), during consumption (process controls), and at the point of expression (output controls).

- Auditing each element of the enterprise's development life cycle validates alignment between business and regulatory controls against process and functional control strategies and standards. The auditor should be familiar with the project management strategy in place within an enterprise to ensure that both the elements and the process used to develop each are properly aligned with business process requirements.

- Auditing application controls validates the proper operation of input, process, and output controls by following transaction flow from initiation through conclusion and performing data integrity testing appropriate to the application design. Computer-aided audit techniques (CAATs) systems are particularly useful for the continuous audit of application controls.

Questions

1. What testing activities should developers perform during the development phase?
    A. Security testing
    B. Integration testing
    C. Unit testing
    D. Developers should not perform any testing

2. The purpose of function point analysis (FPA) is to
    A. Estimate the effort required to develop a software program.
    B. Identify risks in a software program.
    C. Estimate task dependencies in a project plan.
    D. Inventory inputs and outputs in a software program.

3. A project manager needs to identify the tasks that are responsible for project delays. What approach should the project manager use?

  A. Function point analysis

  B. Gantt analysis

  C. Project evaluation and review technique

  D. Critical path methodology

4. A software developer has informed the project manager that a portion of the application development is going to take five additional days to complete. The project manager should

  A. Inform the other project participants of the schedule change.

  B. Change the project schedule to reflect the new completion time.

  C. Create a project change request.

  D. Adjust the resource budget to account for the schedule change.

5. The phases and their order in the systems development life cycle are

  A. Requirements definition, feasibility study, design, development, testing, implementation, post-implementation

  B. Feasibility study, requirements definition, design, development, testing, implementation, post-implementation

  C. Feasibility study, requirements definition, design, development, testing, implementation

  D. Requirements definition, feasibility study, development, testing, implementation, post-implementation

6. What personnel should be involved in the requirements phase of a software development project?

  A. Systems administrators, network administrators, and software developers

  B. Developers, analysts, architects, and users

  C. Security, privacy, and legal analysts

  D. Representatives from each software vendor

7. The primary source for test plans in a software development project is

  A. Requirements

  B. Developers

  C. End users

  D. Vendors

8. The primary purpose of a change management process is to

   A. Record changes made to systems and infrastructure.

   B. Review and approve proposed changes to systems and infrastructure.

   C. Review and approve changes to a project schedule.

   D. Review and approve changes to application source code.

9. What is the purpose of a capability maturity model?

   A. To assess the experience of software developers

   B. To assess the experience of project managers

   C. To assess the integrity of application software

   D. To assess the maturity of business processes

10. The purpose of input validation checking is to

    A. Ensure that input values are within acceptable ranges.

    B. Ensure that input data contains the correct type of characters.

    C. Ensure that input data is free of hostile or harmful content.

    D. Ensure all of the above.

11. An organization is considering the acquisition of enterprise software that will be hosted by a cloud services provider. What additional requirements need to be considered for the cloud environment?

    A. Logging

    B. Access control

    C. Data segregation

    D. Performance

12. System operators have to make an emergency change in order to keep an application server running. To satisfy change management requirements, the systems operators should

    A. Document the steps taken.

    B. Fill out an emergency change request form.

    C. Seek approval from management before making the change.

    D. Do all of the above.

13. A global organization is planning the migration of a business process to a new application. What cutover methods can be considered?

    A. Parallel, geographic, module by module, or all at once

    B. Parallel, geographic, or module by module

    C. Parallel, module by module, or all at once

    D. Parallel, geographic, or all at once

14. The purpose of developing risk tiers in third-party management is to

    A. Determine whether to perform penetration tests.

    B. Satisfy regulatory requirements.

    C. Determine the appropriate level of due diligence.

    D. Determine data classification requirements.

15. The reason that functional requirements need to be measurable is

    A. Developers need to know how to test functional requirements

    B. Functional tests are derived directly from functional requirements

    C. To verify correct system operation

    D. To measure system performance

Answers

1. **C.** During the development phase, developers should perform only unit testing to verify that the individual sections of code they have written are performing properly.

2. **A.** Function point analysis (FPA) is used to estimate the effort required to develop a software program.

3. **D.** Critical path methodology helps a project manager determine which activities are on a project's "critical path."

4. **C.** When any significant change needs to occur in a project plan, a project change request should be created to document the reason for the change.

5. **B.** The phases of the systems development life cycle are feasibility study, requirements definition, design, development, testing, implementation, and post-implementation.

6. **B.** Requirements need to be developed by several parties, including developers, analysts, architects, and users.

7. **A.** The requirements that are developed for a project should be the primary source for detailed tests.

8. **B.** The main purpose of change management is to review and approve proposed changes to systems and infrastructure. This helps to reduce the risk of unintended events and unplanned downtime.

9. **D.** A capability maturity model helps an organization to assess the maturity of its business processes, which is an important first step to any large-scale process improvement efforts.

10. **D.** Input validation checking is used to ensure that input values are within established ranges, of the correct character types, and free of harmful content.

11. **C.** In addition to business, functional, security, and privacy requirements, an organization considering cloud-based services needs to understand how the cloud services provider segregates the organization's data from that of its other customers.

12. **D.** When making an emergency change, personnel should first seek management approval, document the details of the change, and initiate an emergency change management procedure.

13. **A.** The migration to a new application can be done in several ways: parallel (running old and new systems side by side); geographic (migrating users in each geographic region separately); module by module (migrating individual modules of the application); or migrate all users, locations, and modules at the same time.

14. **C.** Developing risk tiers in third-party management helps an organization determine the level of due diligence for third parties at each risk tier. Because the level of risk varies, some third parties warrant extensive due diligence, while a lighter touch is warranted for low-risk parties.

15. **B.** Functional requirements should be measurable, because test cases should be developed directly from functional requirements. The same can be said about security and privacy requirements—all must be measurable because all should be tested.

IT Service Management and Continuity

This chapter covers CISA Domain 4, "Information Systems Operations and Business Resilience," and discusses the following topics:

- Information systems operations
- Information systems hardware
- Information systems architecture and software
- Network infrastructure, technologies, models, and protocols
- Business continuity and disaster recovery planning
- Auditing infrastructure, operations, business continuity and disaster recovery planning

The topics in this chapter represent 23 percent of the CISA examination.

IT organizations are effective if their operations are effective. Management needs to be in control of information systems operations, which means that all aspects of operations need to be measured, those measurements and reports reviewed, and management-directed changes carried out to ensure continuous improvement.

IT organizations are service organizations—they exist to serve the organization and support its business processes. IT's service management operations need to be well designed, adequately measured, and reviewed by management.

In the age of *digital transformation* (DX), organizations are more dependent than ever before on information technology for execution of core business processes. This, in turn, changes the business resilience conversation and increases the emphasis on business continuity and disaster recovery planning, which has moved to this domain in the 2019 CISA job practice.

In addition to being familiar with IT business processes, IS auditors need to have a keen understanding of the workings of computer hardware, operating systems, and network communications technology. This knowledge will help the auditor better understand many aspects of service management and operations.

Information Systems Operations

IS operations encompass the day-to-day control of the information systems, applications, and infrastructure that support organizational objectives and processes. IS operations is composed of several sets of activities, which include management and control of operations:

- IT service management
- IT operations and exception handling
- End-user computing
- Software program library management
- Quality assurance
- Security management
- Media control
- Data management

These activities are discussed in detail in the remainder of this section, following a brief overview describing how IS operations need to be managed and controlled.

NOTE Don't get too hung up on the terms "IS operations" versus "IT operations"; often they are considered synonymous.

Management and Control of Operations

All of the activities that take place in an IT department should be managed and controlled. This means that all actions and activities performed by operations personnel should be a part of a control, procedure, process, or project that has been approved by management. Processes, procedures, and projects should have sufficient recordkeeping so that management can understand the statuses of these activities.

Management is ultimately responsible for all activities that take place in an IS operations department. The primary high-level management activities that govern IS operations are

- **Development of processes and procedures** Every repetitive activity performed by any operations personnel should be documented in the form of a *process* or *procedure*. This means that documents that describe each step of every process and procedure need to be developed, reviewed, approved by management, and made available to operations staff.

- **Development of standards** From the way that operations perform tasks to the brands and technologies used, *standards* drive consistency in everything that IS operations does.

- **Resource allocation**   Management is responsible for allocating resources that support IS operations, including manpower, technology, and budget. Resource allocation should align with the organization's mission, goals, and objectives.

- **Process management**   All IS operations processes should be measured and managed. This will ensure that processes are being performed properly, accurately, and within time and budget targets.

IT Service Management

IT service management (ITSM) is the set of activities that ensures the delivery of IT services is efficient and effective, through active management and the continuous improvement of processes.

ITSM consists of several distinct activities:

- Service desk
- Incident management
- Problem management
- Change management
- Configuration management
- Release management
- Service-level management
- Financial management
- Capacity management
- Service continuity management
- Availability management

Each of these activities is described in detail in this section.

ITSM is formally defined in the IT Infrastructure Library (ITIL) process framework, a well-recognized standard. The content of ITIL is managed by AXELOS. ITSM processes can be audited and registered to the ISO/IEC 20000:2011 standard, the international standard for ITSM.

Service Desk

Often known as the helpdesk or call center, the IT service desk function handles incidents and service requests on behalf of internal IT customers by acting as a single point of contact. The service desk performs end-to-end management of incidents and service requests (at least from the perspective of the customer) and also is responsible for communicating status reports to the customer for matters that take more time to resolve.

The service desk can also serve as a collection point for other ITSM processes, such as change management, configuration management, service-level management, availability management, and other ITSM functions.

Incident Management

ITIL defines an *incident* as "an unplanned interruption to an IT service or reduction in the quality of an IT service. Failure of a configuration item that has not yet affected service is also an incident—for example, failure of one disk from a mirror set."

Thus, an incident may be any of the following:

- Service outage
- Service slowdown
- Software bug

Regardless of the cause, incidents are a result of failures or errors in any component or layer in IT infrastructure.

In ITIL terminology, if the incident has been experienced before and its root cause is known, this is a *known error*. If the service desk is able to access the catalog of known errors, this may result in more rapid resolution of incidents, resulting in less downtime and inconvenience. The change management and configuration management processes are used to make modifications to the system in order to fix it temporarily or permanently.

If the root cause of the incident is not known, the incident may be escalated to a *problem*, which is discussed in the next section.

IT Infrastructure Library, Not Just for the United Kingdom

Although ITIL has its roots in the U.K., it has very much become an international standard. This is due in part to ITIL being adopted by the International Organization for Standardization (ISO)/International Electrotechnical Commission (IEC), in the ISO/IEC 20000 standard, and because IT management practices are becoming more standardized and mature.

Problem Management

When several incidents have occurred that appear to have the same or a similar root cause, a problem is occurring. ITIL defines a *problem* as "a cause of one or more incidents."

The overall objective of problem management is the reduction in the number and severity of incidents.

Problem management can also include some proactive measures, including system monitoring to measure system health and capacity management that will help management to forestall capacity-related incidents.

Examples of problems include

- A server that has exhausted available resources that result in similar, multiple errors (which, in ITSM terms, are known as *incidents*)
- A software bug in a service that is noticed by and affecting many users
- A chronically congested network that causes the communications between many IT components to fail

Similar to incidents, when the root cause of a problem has been identified, the change management and configuration management processes will be enacted to make temporary and permanent fixes.

Change Management

Change management is the set of processes that ensures all changes performed in an IT environment are controlled and performed consistently. ITIL defines change management as follows: "The goal of the change management process is to ensure that standardized methods and procedures are used for efficient and prompt handling of all changes, in order to minimize the impact of change-related incidents upon service quality, and consequently improve the day-to-day operations of the organization."

The main purpose of change management is to ensure that all proposed changes to an IT environment are vetted for suitability and risk, and to ensure that changes will not interfere with each other or with other planned or unplanned activities. To be effective, each stakeholder should review all changes so that every perspective of each change is properly reviewed.

A typical change management process is a formal "waterfall" process that includes the following steps:

1. **Proposal or request** The person or group performing the change announces the proposed change. Typically, a change proposal contains a description of the change, the change procedure, the IT components that are expected to be affected by the change, a verification procedure to ensure that the change was applied properly, a back-out procedure in the event the change cannot be applied (or failed verification), and the results of tests that were performed in a test environment. The proposal should be distributed to all stakeholders several days prior to its review.

2. **Review** This is typically a meeting or discussion about the proposed change, where the personnel who will be performing the change can discuss the change and answer stakeholders' questions. Since the change proposal was sent out earlier, each stakeholder should have had an opportunity to read about the proposed change in advance of the review. Stakeholders can discuss any aspect of the change during the review. The stakeholders may agree to approve the change, or they may request that it be deferred or that some aspect of the proposed change be altered.

3. **Approval** When a change has been formally approved in the review step, the person or group responsible for change management recordkeeping will record the approval, including the names of the individuals who consented to the change. If, however, a change has been deferred or denied, the person or group that proposed the change will need to make alterations to the proposed change so that it will be acceptable, or they can withdraw the change altogether.

4. **Implementation** The actual change is implemented per the procedure described in the change proposal. Here, the personnel identified as the change implementers perform the actual change to the IT system(s) identified in the approved change procedure.

5. **Verification** After the implementers have completed the change, they will perform the verification procedure to make sure that the change was implemented correctly and that it produces the desired result. Generally, the verification procedure will include one or more steps that include the gathering of evidence (and directions for confirming a correct versus an incorrect change) that shows the change is correct. This evidence will be filed with other records related to the change and may be useful in the future if there is any problem with the system where this change is suspected as a part of the root cause.

6. **Post-change review** Some or all changes in an IT organization will be reviewed after the change is implemented. In this activity, the personnel who made the change discuss the change with other stakeholders to learn more about the change and whether any updates or future changes may be needed.

These activities should be part of the duties of a *change control board*, a group of stakeholders from IT and every group that is affected by changes in IT applications and supporting infrastructure.

NOTE The change management process is similar to the system development life cycle (SDLC) in that it consists of life cycle activities that systematically enact changes to an IT environment.

Change Management Records Most or all of the activities related to a change should include updates to business records so that all of the facts related to each change are captured for future reference. In even the smallest IT organization, there are too many changes taking place over time to expect that anyone will be able to recall facts about each change later on. Records that are related to each change serve as a permanent record.

Emergency Changes Though most changes can be planned in advance using the change management process described here, there are times when IT systems need to be changed right away. Most change management processes include a process for emergency changes that details most of the steps in the nonemergency change management process, but they are performed in a different order. The steps for emergency changes are

- **Emergency approval** When an emergency situation arises, the staff members attending to the emergency should still seek management approval for the proposed change. This approval may be done by phone, in person, or in writing (typically, e-mail). If the approval was by phone or in person, e-mail or other follow-up communication is usually performed. Certain members of management should be designated in advance who can approve these emergency changes.

- **Implementation** Staff members perform the change.

- **Verification** Staff members verify that the change produced the expected result. This may involve other staff members from other departments or end users.

- **Review**   The emergency change is formally reviewed. This review may be performed alongside nonemergency changes with the change control board, the same group of individuals who discuss nonemergency changes.

Like nonemergency changes, emergency changes should be fully documented with records made available for future reference.

Linkage to Problem and Incident Management   Often, changes are made as a result of an incident or problem. Emergency and nonemergency changes should reference specific incidents or problems so that those incidents and problems may be properly closed once verification of their resolution has been completed.

Configuration Management

Configuration management (CM) is the process of recording the configuration of IT systems. Each configuration setting is known in ITSM parlance as a *configuration item* (CI). CIs usually include the following:

- **Hardware complement**   This includes the hardware specifications of each system (such as CPU speed, amount of memory, firmware version, adaptors, and peripherals).
- **Hardware configuration**   Settings at the hardware level may include boot settings, adaptor configuration, and firmware settings.
- **Operating system version and configuration**   This includes versions, patches, and many operating system configuration items that have an impact on system performance and functionality.
- **Software versions and configuration**   Software components such as database management systems, application servers, and integration interfaces often have many configuration settings of their own.

Organizations that have many IT systems may automate the CM function with tools that are used to record and change configuration settings automatically. These tools help to streamline IT operations and make it easier for IT systems to be more consistent with one another. The database of system configurations is called a *configuration management database* (CMDB).

Linkage to Problem and Incident Management   An intelligent problem and incident management system is able to access the CMDB to help IT personnel determine whether incidents and problems are related to specific configurations. This can be a valuable aid to those who are seeking to determine a problem's root cause.

Linkage to Change Management   Many configuration management tools are able to detect system configuration changes automatically. With some change and configuration management systems, it is possible to correlate changes detected by a configuration management system with changes approved in the change management process. Further, many changes that are approved by the change management process can be performed by configuration management tools, which can be used to push changes out to managed systems.

Release Management

Release management is the ITIL term used to describe the portion of the SDLC where changes in applications and other information systems are placed into production and made available to end users. Release management is used to control the changes that are made to software programs, applications, and environments.

The release process is used for several types of changes to a system, including the following:

- **Incidents and problem resolution**   Casually known as *bug fixes*, these types of changes are done in response to an incident or problem, where it has been determined that a change to application software is the appropriate remedy.

- **Enhancements**   New functions in an application are created and implemented. These enhancements may have been requested by customers, or they may be a part of the long-range vision on the part of the designers of the software program.

- **Subsystem patches and changes**   Changes in lower layers in an application environment may require a level of testing that is similar to what is used when changes are made to the application itself. Examples of changes are patches, service packs, and version upgrades to operating systems, database management systems, application servers, and middleware.

The release process is a sequential process—that is, each change that is proposed to an information system will be taken through each step in the release management process. In many applications, changes are usually assembled into a "package" for process efficiency purposes: it is more effective to discuss and manage groups of changes than it would be to manage individual changes.

The steps in a typical release process are preceded by typical SDLC process steps:

1. **Feasibility study**   This study seeks to determine the expected benefits of a program, project, or change to a system.

2. **Requirements definition**   Each software change is described in terms of a feature description and requirements. The *feature description* is a high-level description of a change to software that may explain the change in business terms. *Requirements* are the detailed statements that describe a change in enough detail for a developer to make changes and additions to application code that will provide the desired functionality. Often, end users will be involved in the development of requirements so that they may verify that the proposed software change is really what they desire.

3. **Design**   After requirements have been developed, a programmer/analyst or application designer will create a formal design. For an existing software application, this will usually involve changes to existing design documents and diagrams, but new applications will need to be created from scratch or copied from similar designs and modified. Regardless, the design will have a sufficient level of detail to permit a programmer or software engineer to complete development without having to discern the meaning of requirements or design.

4. **Development** When the requirements definition and design have been completed, reviewed, and approved, programmers, software engineers, or other IT engineers begin development. This involves actual coding in the chosen computer language with approved development tools, as well as the creation or update to ancillary components, such as a database design or application programming interface (API). Developers will often perform their own *unit testing*, where they test individual modules and sections of the application code to make sure that it works properly. In other cases, development will consist of planned configuration changes, patch application, or module upgrades made to an information system.

5. **Testing** When the developers have finished coding and unit testing (or other engineers have completed their initial work), a more formal and comprehensive test phase is performed. Here, analysts, dedicated software or systems testers, and perhaps end users, will test all of the new and changed functionality to confirm whether it is performing according to requirements. Depending on the nature of the changes, some amount of *regression testing* is also performed; this means that functions that were confirmed to be working properly in prior releases are tested again to make sure that they continue to work as expected. Testing is performed according to formal, written test plans designed to confirm that every requirement is fulfilled. Formal test scripts are used, and the results of all tests should be recorded and archived. The testing that users perform is usually called *user acceptance testing* (UAT). Often, automated test tools are used, which can make testing more accurate and efficient. After testing is completed, a formal review and approval are required before the process is allowed to continue.

6. **Implementation** When testing has been completed, the changes are implemented on production systems. Here, developers hand off the completed software or system changes to operations personnel, who install it according to instructions created by developers. This could also involve the use of tools to make changes to data and database design, operating systems, or network devices, to accommodate changes in the system. When changes are completed and tested, the release itself is carried out with these last two steps:

   a. **Release preparation** When UAT and regression testing have been completed, reviewed, and approved, a release management team will begin to prepare the new or changed system for release. Depending upon the complexity of the system and of the change itself, release preparation may involve not only software (or another component) installation but also the installation or change to database design, operating systems, network devices, and perhaps even customer data. Hence, the release may involve the development (or engineering) and testing of data conversion tools and other programs that are required so that the new or changed system will operate properly. As with testing and other phases, full records of testing and implementation of release preparation details need to be captured and archived.

b. **Release deployment**   When release preparation is completed (and perhaps reviewed and approved), the release is installed on the target system(s). Personnel deploying the release will follow the release procedure, which may involve the use of tools that will make changes to the target system at the operating system, database, or other level; any required data manipulation or migration; and the installation of the actual software. The release procedure will also include verification steps that will be used to confirm the correct installation of all components.

7. **Post-Implementation**   After system changes have been implemented, a post-implementation review takes place to examine matters of system adequacy, security, ROI, and any issues encountered during implementation.

Utilizing a Gate Process   Many organizations utilize a "gate process" approach in their release management process. This means that each step of the process undergoes formal review and approval before the next step is allowed to begin. For example, a formal design review will be performed and attended by end users, personnel who created requirements and feature description documents, developers, and management. If the design is approved, development may begin. But if there are questions or concerns raised in the design review, the design may need to be modified and reviewed again before development is allowed to begin.

Agile processes utilize gates as well, although the flow of agile processes is often parallel rather than sequential. The concept of formal reviews is the same, regardless of the SDLC process in use.

Service-Level Management
Service-level management is composed of the set of activities that confirms whether IS operations are providing adequate services to customers. This is achieved through continuous monitoring and periodic review of IT service delivery.

An IT department often plays two different roles in service-level management. As a provider of service to its own customers, the IT department will measure and manage the services that it provides directly. Also, many IT departments directly or indirectly manage services that are provided by external service providers. Thus, many IT departments are both service provider and customer, and often the two are interrelated. This is depicted in Figure 5-1.

Financial Management
Financial management for IT services consists of several activities, including

- Budgeting
- Capital investment
- Expense management
- Project accounting and project return on investment (ROI)

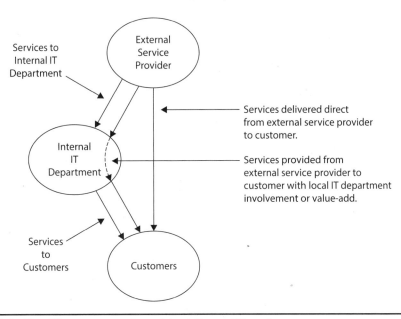

Figure 5-1 The different perspectives of the delivery of IT services

IT financial management is the portion of IT management that takes into account the financial value of IT services that support organizational objectives.

Capacity Management

Capacity management is a set of activities that confirms that sufficient capacity exists in IT systems and IT processes to meet service needs. Primarily, an IT system or process has sufficient capacity if its performance falls within an acceptable range, as specified in service level agreements (SLAs).

Capacity management is not just a concern for current needs; it must also consider future needs. This is attained through several activities, including

- **Periodic measurements**   Systems and processes need to be regularly measured so that trends in usage can be used to predict future capacity needs.

- **Considering planned changes**   Planned changes to processes and IT systems may have an impact on predicted workload.

- **Understanding long-term strategies**   Changes in the organization, including IT systems, business processes, and organizational objectives, may have an impact on workloads, requiring more (or less) capacity than would be extrapolated through simpler trend analysis.

- **Changes in technology**   Several factors may influence capacity plans, including the expectation that computing and network technologies will deliver better performance in the future and that trends in the usage of technology may influence how end users use technology.

Linkage to Financial Management   One of the work products of capacity management is a projection for the acquisition of additional computer or network hardware (whether physical devices or virtual in-the-cloud workloads) to meet future capacity needs. This information needs to be made a part of budgeting and spending management processes.

Linkage to Service Level Management   If there are insufficient resources to handle workloads, capacity issues may result in violations to SLAs. Systems and processes that are overburdened will take longer to respond. In some cases, systems may stop responding altogether.

Linkage to Incident and Problem Management   Systems with severe capacity issues may take excessive time to respond to user requests. In some cases, systems may malfunction or users may give up. Often, users will call the service desk, resulting in the logging of incidents and problems.

Service Continuity Management

Service continuity management is the set of activities that is concerned with the ability of the organization to continue providing services, primarily when a natural or manmade disaster has occurred. Service continuity management is ITIL parlance for the more common terms *business continuity planning* and *disaster recovery planning*.

Business continuity and disaster recovery are discussed later in this chapter.

Availability Management

The goal of availability management is to sustain IT service availability in support of organizational objectives and processes. The availability of IT systems is governed by

- **Effective change management**   When changes to systems and infrastructure are properly vetted through a change management process, changes are less likely to result in unanticipated downtime.

- **Effective system testing**   When changes to systems are made according to a set of formal requirements, review, and testing, the system is less likely to fail and become unavailable.

- **Resilient architecture**   When the overall architecture of an environment is designed from the beginning to be highly reliable, it will be more resilient and more tolerant of individual faults and component failures.

- **Serviceable components**   When the individual components of an environment can be effectively serviced by third-party service organizations, those components will be less likely to fail unexpectedly.

 NOTE   Organizations typically measure availability as a percentage of uptime of an application or service. Another common measure is the number of minutes of unscheduled downtime per month.

IT Operations and Exception Handling

Effective IT operations require that IT personnel understand and properly carry out operational tasks according to established processes and procedures. Personnel must also be trained to recognize exceptions and errors and to respond to them accordingly. The tasks that may be included in IT operations include

- Running jobs according to the job schedule
- Monitoring jobs and allocating resources to jobs based on priority
- Restarting failed jobs and processes
- Facilitating backup jobs by loading or changing backup media, or by ensuring readiness of target storage systems
- Monitoring systems, applications, and networks for availability and adequate performance
- Performing after-hours maintenance activities such as equipment cleaning and system restarts

IT organizations often employ a *production schedule*, which is a list of activities or tasks that are carried out periodically (daily, weekly, monthly, quarterly, and so on). Scheduled activities consist of system-borne activities such as backups as well as human-performed activities such as access reviews, reconciliations, and month-end close. Scheduled activities in systems may be automatically scheduled or manually invoked.

Larger organizations may have a network operations center (NOC) and perhaps also a security operations center (SOC), staffed by personnel who monitor activities in the organization's security devices, networks, systems, and applications. Often, some or all of these activities are outsourced to a managed security service provider (MSSP).

Exceptions and errors that occur within the context of IT operations are typically handled according to ITSM incident management and problem management processes, which were discussed in the preceding section.

Monitoring

Information systems, applications, and supporting infrastructure must be monitored to ensure that they continue to operate as required.

Monitoring tools and programs enable IT operations staff to detect when software or hardware components are not operating as planned. The IT operations staff must also make direct observations in order to detect some problems. The types of errors that should be detected and reported include

- System errors
- Program errors
- Communications errors
- Operator errors

Simply put, any event that represents unexpected or abnormal activity should be recorded so that management and customers may become aware of it. This requires that incident and problem management processes be developed. Incident and problem management are discussed in detail in the earlier section "IT Service Management."

 NOTE IT business processes also need to be monitored. Process monitoring is discussed in Chapters 2 and 3.

Security Monitoring

Many organizations perform several types of security monitoring as a part of their overall strategy to prevent and respond to security incidents. The types of monitoring that an organization may perform include

- Firewall exceptions
- Intrusion prevention system (IPS) alerts
- Data loss prevention (DLP) system alerts
- Cloud security access broker (CASB) alerts
- User access management system alerts
- Network anomaly alerts
- Web content filtering system alerts
- Endpoint management system alerts, including anti-malware
- Vendor security advisories
- Third-party security advisories
- Threat intelligence advisories
- Work center access system alerts
- Video surveillance system alerts

End-User Computing

A critical portion of an IT organization's function is the services it renders to organization personnel to facilitate their access and use of IT systems and applications. Operational models for supporting end-user computing include

- **Organization-provided hardware and software**   The organization provides all computing devices (typically, laptop or desktop computers and perhaps mobile computing devices such as tablets or smartphones) and software.
- **Personnel-provided hardware and software**   The organization provides network infrastructure and instructions on how end users may configure their computing devices to access the organization's IT applications and systems.

Some organizations provide a stipend to its personnel to pay for all or part of the costs of end-user computers.

- **Hybrid models**   Many organizations employ a hybrid of the organization and personnel models. Often, an organization provides laptop or desktop computers, and employees are permitted to access e-mail and some organization applications via personally owned devices such as home computers, tablets, and smartphones.

Usually the organization will employ enterprise management tools to facilitate efficient and consistent management of end-user computers. Typically, end-user computers are "locked down," which limits the amount of and types of configuration changes that end users may perform on their devices, including

- Operating system configuration
- Patch installation
- Software program installation
- Use of external data storage devices

Such restrictions may be viewed by end users as an inconvenience. However, these restrictions not only help to ensure greater security of end-user devices and the entire organization's IT environment, but they also promote greater consistency, which leads to reduced support costs.

Some organizations employ a *zero trust* model for end-user computing. This approach is sometimes used in conjunction with BYOD (bring your own device), where end users provide their own computing devices.

Software Program Library Management

The *software program library* is the facility that is used to store and manage access to an application's source and object code.

In most organizations, application source code is highly sensitive. It may be considered intellectual property, and it may contain information such as algorithms, encryption keys, and other sensitive information that should be accessed by as few persons as possible. In a very real sense, application source code should be considered information and be treated as such through the organization's security policy and data classification policy.

A software program library often exists as an information system with a user interface and several functions, including the following:

- **Access and authorization controls**   The program library should uniquely identify all individuals who attempt to access it and authenticate them with means that are commensurate with the sensitivity of the application. The program library should be able to manage different roles or levels of access so that each person is able to perform only the functions that they are authorized to perform. Also, the program library should be able to restrict access to different modules or applications stored within it; for example, source code that is more sensitive (such as the code related to access control or data encryption) should be accessible by fewer personnel than less sensitive source code.

- **Program check-out** This means that an authorized user is able to access some portion of application source code, presumably to make a modification or perform analysis. Check-out permits the user to make a copy of the source code module that might be stored elsewhere in the program library or on another computer. Often, check-out is permitted only upon management approval, or it may be integrated with a defect tracking system so that a developer is permitted to check out a piece of source code only if there is a defect in the program that has been assigned to the particular developer. When source code is checked out, the program library typically "locks" that section of source code so that another developer is not able to also check it out—thus preventing a "collision" where two developers are making changes to the same section of code at the same time.

- **Program check-in** This function enables an authorized user to return a section of application source code to the program library. A program library will usually permit only the person who checked out a section of code to check it back in. If the user who is checking in the code section made modifications to it, the program library will process those changes and may perform a number of additional functions, including version control and code scanning. If the section of code being checked in was locked, the program library will either automatically unlock it or ask the user whether it should remain locked if, for example, additional changes are to be made.

- **Version control** This function enables the program library to manage changes to the source code by tracking the changes that are made to it each time it is checked in. Each time a source code module is modified, an incremented "version number" is assigned. This enables the program library to recall any prior version of a source code module at any time in the future. This can be useful during program troubleshooting or investigations into a particular programmer's actions.

- **Code analysis** Some program library systems can perform different types of code analysis when source code is checked in. This may include a security scan that will examine the code for vulnerabilities or a scan that will determine whether the checked-in module complies with the organization's coding policies and standards.

These controls enable an organization to have a high degree of control over the integrity and, hence, quality and security of its software applications.

Quality Assurance

The purpose of quality assurance (QA) is to ensure that changes to software applications, operating system configuration, network device configuration, and other information systems components are performed properly. Primarily, this is carried out through independent verification of work.

QA can be carried out within most IT processes, including but not limited to

- Software development
- Change management
- Configuration management
- Service management
- Incident management
- Problem management
- Business process development

As a result of QA activities, improvements in accuracy and efficiency are sought and processes and systems are changed.

Security Management

Information security management is the collection of high-level activities that ensures that an organization's information security program is adequately identifying and addressing risks and operating properly overall. An information security management program usually consists of several activities:

- Development of security policy, processes, procedures, and standards
- Risk assessment and risk management
- Vulnerability management
- Incident management
- Security awareness training

In some organizations, security management also includes disaster recovery planning and business continuity planning.

Security management is discussed in detail in Chapters 2 and 6.

Media Control

Security standards and privacy laws have highlighted the need for formal processes to ensure the proper management of digital media, including its protection as well as destruction of data that is no longer needed. These processes are usually associated with data retention and data purging procedures so that data that is needed is adequately protected with physical and logical security controls, and data that is no longer needed is effectively discarded and erased. Procedures related to the disposal of media that is no longer needed now include steps to erase data on that media or make the data on that media irretrievable in another way.

Media that should be considered in scope for media management and destruction policies and procedures include

- Backup media
- Virtual tape libraries
- Optical media
- Hard drives and solid-state drives
- Flash memory in computers, network devices, disk drives, workstations, mobile devices, and portable USB storage devices
- Hard drives in printers, copiers, and scanners
- Hard copy

Policies and procedures for media sanitization need to be included in service provider contracts, as well as recordkeeping to track the destruction of media over time.

Media control is closely related to data management, discussed in the next subsection.

Data Management

Data management is the set of activities related to the acquisition, processing, storage, use, and disposal of data.

Arguably the most important activity in data management is planning. As with most human endeavors, data management activities have far better outcomes when planning precedes action. Mainly this is related to data architecture, which is the set of activities related to the design of databases and the flows of information between databases, systems, and organizations.

Data Life Cycle

The *data life cycle* is the set of activities that take place throughout the use of data in an organization. The phases of the data life cycle are

- **Planning**   Prior to the creation or acquisition of data, the organization needs to understand its structure, its sensitivity and value, its use, and its eventual destruction.
- **Design**   This is the actual process of creating the structure and protection of data. Typical activities at this stage include the creation of a database schema and configuration of physical and logical storage systems that will store databases.
- **Build/acquire**   In this phase, data is created or imported from another system.
- **Operations**   In this phase, data is processed, shared, and used.
- **Monitoring**   This includes examination of the data itself as well as activities related to the access and use of data to ensure that the data retains its quality and that it is protected from misuse and harm.

- **Archival** This is related to any long-term storage of data for legal or historical purposes.

- **Disposal** This is related to the discarding or erasure process that takes place at the end of the useful life of a set of data.

 NOTE DAMA International is a professional organization for people in the data management profession. Information is available at https://dama.org.

Data Quality Management

Data quality management encompasses several activities to ensure the confidentiality, integrity, and completeness of data. Activities in data quality management include

- **Application controls** Measures to ensure that applications enforce the integrity and completeness of data. This topic is covered in Chapter 4.

- **Systems development** Measures to ensure that applications that are developed or acquired enforce the integrity and completeness of data. This topic is covered in Chapter 4.

- **Systems integrity** Measures to ensure that information systems enforce the confidentiality and integrity of data. This topic is covered in Chapter 6.

Information Systems Hardware

Hardware is the elemental basis of information systems. It consists of circuit boards containing microprocessors and memory; other components connected through circuitry, such as hard disk drives or solid-state drives; and peripherals such as keyboards, printers, monitors, and network connections.

IS auditors need to understand at least the basic concepts of computer hardware architecture, maintenance, and monitoring so that they can properly assess an organization's use and care of information systems hardware. A lack of knowledge in this area could result in the auditor overlooking or failing to understand important aspects of an organization's operations.

The macro trend toward the use of cloud computing infrastructure versus on-premises computer hardware does not preclude the need to be familiar with the concepts of computing hardware. Although contact with computer hardware is absent when an organization is managing virtual workloads, organizations utilizing cloud-based infrastructure still need to be familiar with hardware concepts; this is applied through the configuration of virtual servers and the resources they use. Further, computer hardware is still used by end users in the form of desktop and laptop computers as well as tablet computers and smartphones.

Computer Usage

Computers are manufactured for a variety of purposes and contexts and are used for many different purposes. They can be classified by their capacity, throughput, size, use, or the operating system or software that they use.

Types of Computers

From a business perspective, computers are classified according to their size and portability. In this regard, the types of computers are

- **Supercomputer** These are the largest computers in terms of the number and/ or power of their central processing units (CPUs). Supercomputers are generally employed for scientific applications such as weather and climate forecasting, seismology, and other computer-intensive applications.

- **Mainframe** These business workhorse computers are designed to run large, complex applications that operate on enormous databases or support vast numbers of users. When computing began, mainframes were the *only* kind of computer; most of the other types were derived from the mainframe. Today, mainframes are still commonly used for larger financial transaction systems and other large-scale applications such as airline reservation systems.

- **Midrange** These computers are not as large and powerful as mainframe computers, but they are larger or more powerful than small servers. There are no hard distinctions between these sizes of computers, but only vague, rough guidelines.

- **Server** If mainframe computers are the largest business servers, the ordinary *server* is the smallest. In terms of its hardware complement and physical appearance, a server can be indistinguishable from a user's desktop computer.

- **Blade server** In this style of hardware design, servers are modules that plug in to a cabinet. Each module contains all of the internal components of a stand-alone computer. The cabinet itself will contain power supplies and network connectors.

- **Virtual server** This is a cloud-based server that exists in a hypervisor environment, whether in an on-premises private cloud or a public cloud.

- **Appliance** This type of computer typically comes with one or more tools or applications preinstalled. The term "appliance" is sometimes used to connote the fact that little or no maintenance is required on the system.

- **Desktop** This is a computer that is used by an individual worker. Its size makes it fairly easy to move from place to place, but it is not considered portable. The desktop computers of today are more powerful in many ways than the mainframe computers of a few decades ago. Desktop computers used to be called *microcomputers*, but the term is seldom used now.

- **Laptop/notebook** This computer is portable in every sense of the word. It is self-contained, equipped with a battery, and folds for storage and transport. Functionally, desktop and laptop computers are nearly identical: they may run the same operating system and programs.

- **Mobile**   These computers come in the form of smartphones and tablet devices.
- **Embedded**   These computers are built into products such as televisions, automobiles, medical devices, and many other industrial and consumer devices.

Uses for Computers

Aside from the sizes and types of computers discussed in the previous section, computers may also be used for several reasons, including

- **Application server**   This computer—usually a mainframe, midrange, or server—runs application-server software. An application server contains one or more application programs that run on behalf of users. Data used by an application server may be stored on a database server that contains a database management system.
- **Web server**   This is a server that runs a web server program to make web pages available to users. A web server will usually contain both the web server software and the content ("pages") that are requested by and sent to users' web browser programs. A web server can also be linked to an application server or database server to permit the display of business information, such as order forms, reports, and so on.
- **Database server**   Also a mainframe, midrange, or small server, a database server runs specialized database management software that controls the storage and processing of large amounts of data that resides in one or more databases.
- **Gateway**   A server that performs some manner of data transformation—for instance, converting messages from one format to another—between two applications.
- **File server**   This computer is used to provide a central location for the storage of commonly used files. File servers may be used by application servers or by a user community.
- **Print server**   In an environment that uses shared printers, a print server is typically used to receive print requests from users or applications and store them temporarily until they are ready to be printed.
- **Production server/test server**   The terms *production server* and *test server* denote whether a server supports actual business use (a production server) or is a separate server that can be used to test new programs or configurations (a test server). Most organizations will have at least one test server for every type of production server so that any new programs, configurations, patches, or settings can be tested on a test server, with little or no risk of disrupting actual business operations.
- **Thick client**   A thick client is a user's computer (of the desktop or laptop variety) that contains a fully functional operating system and one or more application programs. Purists will argue that a thick client is *only* a thick client if the system contains one or more software application client programs. This is a reasonable distinction between a thick client and a workstation, described later.

- **Thin client**   A thin client is a user's workstation that contains a minimal operating system and little or no data storage. Thin-client computers are often used in businesses where users run only application programs that can be executed on central servers and data is displayed on the thin client's screen. A thin client may be a desktop or laptop computer with thin-client software installed, or it may be a specialized computer with no local storage other than flash memory.

- **Workstation**   This is a user's laptop or desktop computer. For example, a PC running the Windows operating system and using Microsoft Office word processor and spreadsheet programs, a Firefox browser, and Skype messenger would be considered a workstation.

- **Virtual desktop**   This workstation operating system physically resides on a central server that is displayed by and used on a user's desktop computer.

- **Mobile device**   A user's smartphone or tablet device is considered a mobile device. Indeed, the lines between laptops and tablets are blurring as larger tablets, particularly with companion keyboards, function like laptops. And, laptop operating systems are appearing on larger tablet devices.

 NOTE   For the most part, computers are designed for general use in mind so that they may perform any of the functions listed here.

Computer Hardware Architecture

Computers made since the 1960s share common characteristics in their hardware architecture: They have one or more central processing units, a bus (or more than one), main memory, and secondary storage. They also have some means for communicating with other computers or with humans, usually through communications adaptors.

This section describes computer hardware in detail.

Mobile Devices, the New and Disruptive Endpoint

Much is said about endpoints being the weak link in IT infrastructure. But historically speaking, these proclamations are more about laptop computers, which, for the most part, can be well managed by enterprises.

Mobile devices are a different matter entirely. They are turning all of the rules about endpoint computing on their head. Principally,

- End users choose which models to purchase and own them outright.

- End users can install any application they choose.

- Mobile devices can be easily connected to corporate e-mail without any help (or consent) from the IT department.

- Few, if any, anti-malware or other anti-tampering tools are available.
- Mobile devices are easily lost and more easily broken into than laptop computers.
- Mobile device manufacturers have published application interfaces, thereby enabling the creation of malware that can steal data and alter operation of the device.

IS auditors need to understand how organizations are addressing the mobile device dilemma.

Central Processing Unit

The central processing unit, or CPU, is the main hardware component of a computer system. The CPU is the component that executes instructions in computer programs.

Each CPU has an *arithmetic logic unit* (ALU), a control unit, and a small amount of memory. The memory in a CPU is usually in the form of *registers*, which are memory locations where arithmetic values are stored.

The CPU in modern computers is wholly contained in a single large-scale integration integrated circuit (LSI IC), more commonly known as a microprocessor. A CPU is attached to a computer circuit board (often called a motherboard on a personal computer) by soldering or a plug-in socket. A CPU on a motherboard is shown in Figure 5-2.

Figure 5-2 A CPU that is plugged into a computer circuit board (Image courtesy of Fir0002/Flagstaffotos)

CPU Architectures   A number of architectures dominate the design of CPUs. Two primary architectures that are widely used commercially are

- **CISC (complex instruction set computer)**   This CPU design has a comprehensive instruction set, and many instructions can be performed in a single cycle. This design philosophy claims superior performance over RISC. Well-known CISC CPUs include Intel x86, VAX, PDP-11, Motorola 68000, and System/360.

- **RISC (reduced instruction set computer)**   This CPU design uses a smaller instruction set (meaning fewer instructions in its "vocabulary"), with the idea that a small instruction set will lead to a simpler microprocessor design and better computer performance. Well-known RISC CPUs include Alpha, MIPS, PowerPC, and SPARC. Few of these are produced today, but they are still found in some environments.

Another aspect of CPUs that is often discussed is the power requirements. Typically, the CPUs that are used for laptop computers and mobile devices are known as low-power CPUs, while other CPUs are used in desktop, server, and mainframe systems, where performance and speed are more important considerations than power consumption.

Computer CPU Architectures   Early computers had a single CPU. However, it became clear that many computing tasks could be performed more efficiently if computers had more than one CPU to perform them. Some of the ways that computers have implemented CPUs are

- **Single CPU**   In this design, the computer has a single CPU. This simplest design is still prevalent, particularly among small servers and personal computers.

- **Multiple CPUs**   A computer design can accommodate multiple CPUs, from as few as 2 to as many as 128 or more. There are two designs for multi-CPU computers: symmetric and asymmetric. In the symmetric design, all CPUs are equal in terms of how the overall computer's architecture uses them. In the asymmetric design, one CPU is the "master." Virtually all multi-CPU computers made today are symmetric.

- **Multicore CPUs**   A change in the design of CPUs themselves has led to multicore CPUs, in which two or more central processors occupy a single CPU chip. The benefit of multicore design is the ability for software code to be executed in parallel, leading to improved performance. Many newer servers and personal computers are equipped with multicore CPUs, and some are equipped with multiple multicore CPUs.

Bus

A *bus* is an internal component in a computer that provides the means for the computer's other components to communicate with one another. A computer's bus connects the CPU with its main and secondary storage as well as to external devices.

Most computers also utilize electrical connectors that permit the addition of small circuit boards that may contain additional memory, a communications device or adaptor (for example, a network adaptor or a modem), a storage controller (for example, a SCSI [Small Computer Systems Interface] or ATA [AT Attachment] disk controller), or an additional CPU.

Several industry standards for computer buses have been developed. Notable standards include

- **Universal Serial Bus (USB)**   This standard is used to connect external peripherals such as external storage devices, printers, and mobile devices. USB operates at data rates up to 40.0 Gbit/sec. USB is discussed in more detail later in this chapter.

- **Serial ATA (SATA)**   This standard is used mainly to connect mass storage devices such as hard disk drives, optical drives, and solid-state drives.

- **PCI Express (PCIe)**   This bus standard replaced older standards such as PCI and PCI-X and employs data rates from 250 Mbyte/sec to 128 Gbyte/sec.

- **Thunderbolt**   This hardware interface standard is a combination of PCI Express and DisplayPort (DP) in a single serial signal.

- **PC Card**   Formerly known as *PCMCIA*, the PC Card bus is prevalent in laptop computers and is commonly used for the addition of specialized communication devices.

- **ExpressCard**   Also developed by the PCMCIA, this bus standard replaces the PC Card standard.

It is not uncommon for a computer to have more than one bus. For instance, many PCs have an additional front-side bus (FSB), which connects the CPU to a memory controller hub, as well as a high-speed graphics bus, a memory bus, and the low pin count (LPC) bus that is used for low-speed peripherals such as parallel and serial ports, keyboard, and mouse.

Main Storage

A computer's *main storage* is used for short-term storage of information. Main storage is usually implemented with electronic components such as *random access memory* (RAM), which is relatively expensive but also relatively fast in terms of accessibility and transfer rate.

A computer uses its main storage for several purposes:

- **Operating system**   The computer's running operating system uses main storage to store information about running programs, open files, logged-in users, in-use devices, active processes, and so on.

- **Buffers**   Operating systems and programs will set aside a portion of memory as a "scratch pad" that can be used temporarily to store information retrieved from hard disks or information that is being sent to a printer or other device. Buffers are also used by network adaptors to store incoming and outgoing information temporarily.

Figure 5-3
Typical RAM
module for
a laptop,
workstation, or
server (Image
courtesy of
Sassospicco)

- **Storage of program code** Any program that the computer is currently executing will be stored in main storage so that the CPU can quickly access and read any portion of the program as needed. Note that the program in main storage is only a *working copy* of the program, used by the computer to reference instructions quickly in the program.

- **Storage of program variables** When a program is being run, it will store intermediate results of calculations and other temporary data. This information is stored in main storage, where the program can quickly reference portions of it as needed.

Main storage is typically *volatile*. This means that the information stored in main storage should be considered temporary. If electric power were suddenly removed from the computer, the contents of main storage would vanish and would not be easily recovered, if at all.

Different technologies are used in computers for main storage:

- **DRAM (dynamic RAM)** In the most common form of semiconductor memory, data is stored in capacitors that require periodic refreshing to keep them charged—hence the term *dynamic*.

- **SRAM (static RAM)** This form of semiconductor memory does not require periodic refresh cycles like DRAM.

A typical semiconductor memory module is shown in Figure 5-3.

Secondary Storage

Secondary storage is the permanent storage used by a computer system. Unlike primary storage (which is usually implemented in volatile RAM modules), secondary storage is persistent and can last many years.

This type of storage is usually implemented using hard disk drives or solid-state drives ranging in capacity from gigabytes to terabytes.

Secondary storage represents an economic and performance tradeoff from primary storage. It is usually far slower than primary storage, but the unit cost for storage is far less costly. At the time of this writing, the price paid for about 16GB of RAM could also purchase a 2TB hard disk drive, which makes RAM (primary) storage more than 1,000 times more expensive than hard disk (secondary) storage. A hard disk drive from a desktop computer is shown in Figure 5-4.

Figure 5-4
Typical computer hard disk drive (Image courtesy of Robert Jacek Tomczak)

A computer uses secondary storage for several purposes:

- **Program storage**   The programs that the computer executes are contained in secondary storage. When a computer begins to execute a program, it makes a working copy of the program in primary storage.

- **Data storage**   Information read into, created by, or used by computer programs is often stored in secondary storage. Secondary storage is usually used when information is needed for use at a later time.

- **Computer operating system**   The set of programs and device drivers that are used to control and manage the use of the computer is stored in secondary storage.

- **Temporary files**   Many computer programs need to store information for temporary use that may exceed the capacity of main memory. Secondary storage is often used for this purpose. For example, a user wants to print a data file onto a nearby laser printer; software on the computer will transform the stored data file into a format that is used by the laser printer to make a readable copy of the file; this "print file" is stored in secondary storage temporarily until the printer has completed printing the file for the user, and then the file is deleted.

- **Virtual memory**   This is a technique for creating a main memory space that is physically larger than the actual available main memory. Virtual memory (which should not be confused with virtualization) is discussed in detail later in this chapter in the section "Computer Operating Systems."

While secondary storage is usually implemented with hard disk drives, many newer systems use semiconductor flash memory in solid-state drives (SSDs). Flash is a nonvolatile semiconductor memory that can be rewritten and requires no electric power to preserve stored data.

Although secondary storage technology is persistent and highly reliable, hard disk drives and even SSDs are known to fail from time to time. For this reason, important data in secondary storage is often copied to other storage devices, either on the same computer or on a different computer, or it is copied onto computer backup tapes that are designed to store large amounts of data for long periods at low cost. This practice of data backup is discussed at length in the section "Information Systems Operations," earlier in this chapter.

Firmware

Firmware is special-purpose storage that is used to store the instructions needed to start a computer system. Typically, firmware consists of low-level computer instructions that are used to control the various hardware components in a computer system and to load and execute components of the operating system from secondary storage. This process of system initialization is known as an initial program load (IPL), or bootstrap (or just "boot").

Read-only memory (ROM) technology is often used to store a computer's firmware. Several available ROM technologies are in use, including

- **ROM**   The earliest forms of ROM are considered permanent and can never be modified. The permanency of ROM makes it secure, but it can be difficult to carry out field upgrades. For this reason ROM is not often used.

- **PROM (programmable read-only memory)**   This is also a permanent and unchangeable form of storage. A PROM chip can be programmed only once, and it must be replaced if the firmware needs to be updated.

- **EPROM (erasable programmable read-only memory)**   This type of memory can be written to with a special programming device and then erased and rewritten at a later time. EPROM chips are erased by shining ultraviolet (UV) light through a quartz window on the chip; the quartz window is usually covered with a foil label, although sometimes an EPROM chip does not have a window at all, which effectively makes it a PROM device.

- **EEPROM (electrically erasable programmable read-only memory)**   This is similar to EPROM, except that no UV light source is required to erase and reprogram the EEPROM chip; instead, signals from the computer in which the EEPROM chip is stored can be used to reprogram or update the EEPROM. Thus, EEPROM was one of the first types of firmware that could be updated by the computer on which it was installed.

- **Flash**   This memory is erasable, reprogrammable, and functionally similar to EEPROM, in that the contents of flash memory can be altered by the computer that it is installed in. Flash memory is the technology used in popular portable storage devices such as USB memory devices, Secure Digital (SD) cards, Compact Flash, and Memory Stick.

A well-known use for firmware is the ROM-based BIOS (basic input/output system) on Intel-based personal computers.

I/O and Networking

Regardless of their specific purpose, computers nearly always must have some means for accepting input data from some external source as well as for sending output data to some external destination. Whether this input and output are continuous or infrequent, computers usually have one or more methods for transferring data. These methods include

- **Input/output (I/O) devices**   Most computers have external connectors to permit the attachment of devices such as keyboards, mice, monitors, scanners, printers, and cameras. The electrical signal and connector-type standards include PS/2 (for keyboards and mice), USB, parallel, serial, and Thunderbolt. Some types of computers lack these external connectors; instead, special adaptor cards can be plugged into a computer's bus connector. Early computers required reprogramming and/or reconfiguration when external devices were connected, but newer computers are designed to recognize when an external device is connected or disconnected and will adjust automatically.

- **Networking**   A computer can be connected to a local or wide area data network. Then, one of a multitude of means for inbound and outbound data transfer can be configured that will use the networking capability. Some computers will have built-in connectors or adaptors, but others will require the addition of internal or external adaptors that plug into bus connectors such as PC Card, ExpressCard, PCI, or USB.

Multicomputer Architectures

Organizations that use several computers have a lot of available choices. Not so long ago, organizations that required several servers would purchase individual server computers. Now there are choices that can help to improve performance and reduce capital, including

- **Blade computers**   This architecture consists of a main chassis component that is equipped with a central power supply, cooling, network, and console connectors, with several slots that are fitted with individual CPU modules. The advantage of blade architecture is the lower-than-usual unit cost for each server module, since it consists of only a circuit board. The costs of power supply, cooling, and so on, are amortized among all of the blades. A typical blade system is shown in Figure 5-5.

- **Grid computing**   The term *grid computing* describes a large number of loosely coupled computers that are used to solve a common task. Computers in a grid may be in close proximity to each other or scattered over a wide geographic area. Grid computing is a viable alternative to supercomputers for solving computationally intensive problems.

- **Server clusters**   A *cluster* is a tightly coupled collection of computers that is used to solve a common task. In a cluster, one or more servers actively perform tasks, while zero or more computers may be in a "standby" state, ready to assume active duty should the need arise. Clusters usually give the appearance of a single computer to the perspective of outside systems. Clusters usually operate in one of two modes: *active-active* and *active-passive*. In active-active mode, all servers perform tasks; in active-passive mode, some servers are in a standby state, waiting to become active in an event called a *failover*, which usually occurs when one of the active servers has become incapacitated.

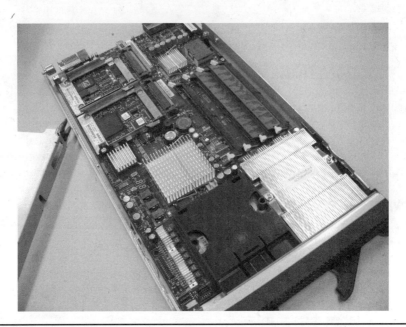

Figure 5-5   Blade computer architecture (Image courtesy of Robert Kloosterhuis)

These options give organizations the freedom to develop a computer architecture that will meet their needs in terms of performance, availability, flexibility, and cost.

Virtualization Architectures

Virtualization refers to the set of technologies that permits two or more running operating systems (of the same type or different types) to reside on a single physical computer. Virtualization technology enables organizations to use computing resources more efficiently.

Before I explain the benefits of virtualization, I should first state one of the principles of computer infrastructure management. It is a sound practice to use a server for one single purpose. Using a single server for multiple purposes can introduce a number of problems, including

- Tools or applications that reside on a single computer may interfere with one another.

- Tools or applications that reside on a single computer may interact with each other or compete for common resources.

- A tool or application on a server could, although rarely, cause the entire server to stop running; on a server with multiple tools or applications, this could cause the other tools and applications to stop functioning.

Prior to virtualization, the most stable configuration for running many applications and tools was to run each on a separate server. This would, however, result in a highly inefficient use of computers and of capital, as most computers with a single operating system spend much of their time in an idle state.

Virtualization permits IT departments to run many applications or tools on a single physical server, each within its own respective operating system, thereby making more efficient use of computers (not to mention electric power and data center space). Virtualization software emulates computer hardware so that an operating system running in a virtualized environment does not know that it is actually running on a virtual machine. Virtualization software, known as a *hypervisor*, includes resource allocation configuration settings so that each *guest* (a running operating system) will have a specific amount of memory, hard disk space, and other peripherals available for its use. Virtualization also facilitates the sharing of peripheral devices such as network connectors so that many guests can use an individual network connector, although each will have its own unique IP address.

Virtualization is the basis of cloud-based Infrastructure-as-a-Service (IaaS) services such as Amazon AWS, Google Cloud, and Microsoft Azure.

Virtualization software provides security by isolating each running operating system and preventing it from accessing or interfering with others. This is similar to the concept of *process isolation* within a running operating system, where a process is not permitted to access resources used by other processes.

A server with running virtual machines is depicted in Figure 5-6.

Many security issues need to be considered in a virtualization environment, including

- **Access control** Access to virtualization management and monitoring functions should be restricted to those personnel who require it.

- **Resource allocation** A virtualization environment needs to be carefully configured so that each virtual machine is given the resources it requires to function correctly and perform adequately.

- **Logging and monitoring** Virtual environments need to be carefully monitored so that any sign of security compromise will be quickly recognized and acted on.

- **Hardening** Virtual environments need to be configured so that only necessary services and features are enabled, and all unnecessary services and features are either disabled or removed.

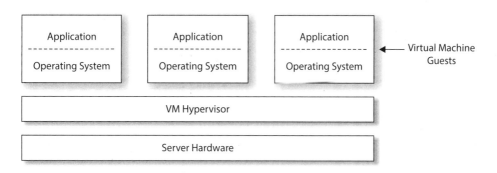

Figure 5-6 Virtualization

- **Vulnerability management**   Virtualization environments need to be monitored as closely as operating systems and other software so that the IT organization is aware of newly discovered security vulnerabilities and available patches.

Hardware Maintenance

In comparison to computer hardware systems that were manufactured through the 1980s, today's computer hardware requires little or no preventive or periodic maintenance. And with today's popular cloud-based computing, some organizations have little or no data center hardware to maintain at all.

Computer hardware maintenance is limited to periodic checks to ensure that the computer is free of dirt and moisture. From time to time, a systems engineer will need to open a computer system cabinet and inspect it for accumulation of dust and dirt, and he or she may need to remove this debris with a vacuum cleaner or filtered compressed air. Depending on the cleanliness of the surrounding environment, inspection and cleaning may be needed as often as every few months or as seldom as every few years.

Maintenance may also be carried out by third-party service organizations that specialize in computer maintenance.

When it is required, hardware maintenance is an activity that should be monitored. Qualified service organizations should be hired to perform maintenance at appropriate intervals. If periodic maintenance is required, management should establish a service availability plan that includes planned downtime when such operations take place.

Automated hardware monitoring tools can provide information that will help determine whether maintenance is needed. Automated monitoring is discussed in the next section.

Hardware Monitoring

Automated hardware monitoring tools can be used to keep a continuous watch on the health and utilization of server and network hardware. In an environment with many servers, this capability can be centralized so that the health of many servers and network devices can be monitored using a single monitoring program.

Hardware monitoring capabilities may vary among different makes of computer systems, but can include any or all of the following:

- **CPU**   Monitoring will indicate whether the system's CPU is operating properly and whether its temperature is within normal range.
- **Power supply**   Monitoring will show whether the power supply is operating properly, including input voltage, output voltage and current, cooling fans, and temperature.
- **Internal components**   Monitoring will specify whether other internal components such as storage devices, memory, chipsets, controllers, adaptors, and cooling fans are operating properly and within normal temperature ranges.
- **Resource utilization**   Monitoring will measure the amount of resources in use, including CPU, memory, disk storage, and network utilization.

- **Asset management**   Many monitoring systems can track the assets that are present in the environment, giving management an electronic asset inventory capability.

- **External environment**   Monitoring is usually considered incomplete unless the surrounding environment is also monitored. This usually includes temperature, humidity, the presence of water, and vibration in locales where earthquakes are common. Monitoring can also include video surveillance and access door alarms.

Centralized monitoring environments typically utilize the local area network for transmitting information from systems to a central console. Many monitoring consoles have the ability to send alert messages to the personnel who manage the systems being monitored. Often, reports can show monitoring statistics over time so that personnel can identify trends that could be indications of impending failure.

Public cloud IaaS vendors perform hardware monitoring on behalf of their customers.

 NOTE   Hardware monitoring is often included in network device and network traffic monitoring that is performed by personnel in a NOC.

Information Systems Architecture and Software

This section discusses computer operating systems, data communications, file systems, database management systems, media management systems, and utility software.

Computer Operating Systems

Computer operating systems (which are generally known as operating systems, or OSs) are large, general-purpose programs that are used to control computer hardware and facilitate the use of software applications. Operating systems perform the following functions:

- **Access to peripheral devices**   The operating system controls and manages access to all devices and adaptors that are connected to the computer. This includes storage devices, display devices, and communications adaptors.

- **Storage management**   The operating system provides for the orderly storage of information on storage hardware. For example, operating systems provide file system management for the storage of files and directories on SSDs or hard drives.

- **Process management**   Operating systems facilitate the existence of multiple processes, some of which will be computer applications and tools. Operating systems ensure that each process has private memory space and is protected from interference and eavesdropping by other processes.

- **Resource allocation** Operating systems facilitate the sharing of resources on a computer such as memory, communications, and display devices.

- **Communication** Operating systems facilitate communications with users via peripheral devices and also with other computers through networking. Operating systems typically have drivers and tools to facilitate network communications.

- **Security** Operating systems restrict access to protected resources through process, user, and device authentication.

Examples of popular operating systems include Linux, Solaris, macOS, Android, iOS, Chrome OS, and Microsoft Windows.

The traditional context of the relationship between operating systems and computer hardware is this: one copy of a computer operating system runs on a computer at any given time. Virtualization, however, has changed all of that. Virtualization is discussed earlier in this chapter.

Server Clustering

Using special software, a group of two or more computers can be configured to operate as a *cluster*. This means that the group of computers will appear as a single computer for the purpose of providing services. Within the cluster, one computer will be active and the other computer(s) will be in passive mode; if the active computer should experience a hardware or software failure and crash, the passive computer(s) will transition to active mode and continue to provide service. This is known as *active-passive* mode. The transition is called a *failover*.

Clusters can also operate in *active-active* mode, where all computers in the cluster provide service; in the event of the failure of one computer in the cluster, the remaining computer(s) will continue providing service.

Grid Computing

Grid computing is a technique used to distribute a problem or task to several computers at the same time, taking advantage of the processing power of each, to solve the problem or complete the task in less time. Grid computing is a form of distributed computing, but in grid computing, the computers are coupled more loosely and the number of computers participating in the solution of a problem can be dynamically expanded or contracted at will.

Cloud Computing

Cloud computing refers to dynamically scalable and usually virtualized computing resources that are provided as a service. Cloud computing services may be rented or leased so that an organization can have scalable application environments without the need for supporting hardware or a data center. Or cloud computing may include networking, computing, and even application services in a Software-as-a-Service (SaaS) or Platform-as-a-Service (PaaS) model. Cloud computing is discussed in more detail in Chapter 4.

Data Communications Software

The prevalence of network-centric computing has resulted in networking capabilities being included with virtually every computer and being built into virtually every computer operating system. Almost without exception, computer operating systems include the ability for the computer to connect with networks based on the TCP/IP suite of protocols, enabling the computer to communicate on a home network, enterprise business network, or the global Internet.

Data communications is discussed in greater detail later in this chapter in the section "Network Infrastructure."

File Systems

A *file system* is a logical structure that facilitates the storage of data on a digital storage medium such as a hard drive, SSD, CD/DVD-ROM, or flash memory device. The structure of the file system facilitates the creation, modification, expansion and contraction, and deletion of data files. A file system may also be used to enforce access controls to control which users or processes are permitted to access, alter, or create files in a file system.

It can also be said that a file system is a special-purpose database designed for the storage and management of files.

Modern file systems employ a storage hierarchy that consists of two main elements:

- **Directories** A *directory* is a structure that is used to store files. A file system may contain one or more directories, each of which may contain files and subdirectories. The topmost directory in a file system is usually called the "root" directory. A file system may exist as a hierarchy of information, in the same way that a building can contain several file rooms, each of which contains several file cabinets, which contain drawers that contain dividers, folders, and documents. Directories are sometimes called *folders* in some computing environments.

- **Files** A *file* is a sequence of zero or more characters that are stored as a logical whole. A file may be a document, spreadsheet, image, sound file, computer program, or data that is used by a program. A file can be small as zero characters in length (an empty file) or as large as many gigabytes (trillions of characters). A file occupies units of storage on storage media (which could be a hard disk, SSD, or flash memory device, for example) that may be called blocks or sectors; however, the file system hides these underlying details from the user so that the file may be known simply by its name, the directory in which it resides, and its contents.

Well-known file systems in use today include

- **FAT (File Allocation Table)** This file system has been used in MS-DOS and early versions of Microsoft Windows, and FAT is often used as the file system on portable media devices such as flash drives. Versions of FAT include FAT12, FAT16, and FAT32. FAT does not support security access controls, including specifying access permissions to files and directories. FAT also does not include any journaling features, making it more vulnerable to corruption if power is removed during write operations.

- **NTFS (NT File System)**   This is used in newer versions of Windows, including desktop and server editions. NTFS supports file- and directory-based access control and file system journaling (the process of recording changes made to a file system; this aids in file system recovery).

- **EXT3**   This journaled file system is used by the Linux operating system.

- **HFS (Hierarchical File System)**   This file system is used on computers running the Apple macOS operating system.

- **APFS (Apple File System)**   This file system is used on computers running the Apple macOS operating system.

- **Resilient File System (ReFS)**   This file system is used on Windows Server 2012 and later versions and is intended to become the replacement for NTFS.

- **ISO/IEC 9660**   This file system is used by CD-ROM and DVD-ROM media.

- **UDF (Universal Disk Format)**   This optical media file system is considered a replacement for ISO/IEC 9660. UDF is widely used on rewritable optical media.

Database Management Systems

A *database management system*, or DBMS, is a software program or collection of programs that facilitates the storage and retrieval of potentially large amounts of structured information. A DBMS contains methods for inserting, updating, and removing data; these functions can be used by computer programs and software applications. A DBMS also usually contains authentication and access control, thereby permitting control over which users may access what data.

DBMS Organization

Most DBMSs employ a data definition language (DDL) that is used to define the structure of the data contained in a database. The DDL defines the types of data stored in the database as well as relationships between different portions of that data.

DBMSs employ some sort of a data dictionary (DD) or directory system (DS) that is used to store information about the internal structure of databases stored in the DBMS.

To understand how they relate to each other, you can think of the DDL as the instructions for building a database's structure and data relationships; the DD or DS is where the database's structure and relationships are stored and used by the DBMS.

DBMSs also employ a data manipulation language (DML) that is used to insert, delete, and update data in a database. SQL is a popular DML that is used in the Oracle and SQL Server DBMSs.

DBMS Structure

There are three principal types of DBMSs in use today: relational, object, and hierarchical. Each is described in this section.

Relational Database Management Systems Relational database management systems (RDBMSs) represent the most popular model used for DBMSs. A relational database permits the design of a structured, logical representation of information.

Many relational databases are accessed and updated through the SQL (Structured Query Language) computer language. Standardized in ISO/IEC and ANSI standards, SQL is used in many popular relational DBMS products, including Oracle Database, Microsoft SQL Server, MySQL, and IBM DB2.

RDBMS Basic Concepts A relational database consists of one or more *tables*. A table can be thought of as a simple list of records, like lines in a data file. The records in a table are often called *rows*. The different data items that appear in each row are usually called *fields*.

A table often has a *primary key*. This is simply one of the table's fields whose values are unique in the table. For example, a table of healthcare patient names can include each patient's identification number, which can be made the primary key for the table.

One or more *indexes* can be built for a table. An index facilitates rapid searching for specific records in a table based upon the value of one of the fields other than the primary key. For instance, a table that contains a list of assets and their serial numbers can have an index of the table's serial numbers. This will permit a rapid search for a record containing a specific serial number; without the index, RDBMS software would have to examine every record in the table sequentially until the desired records are found.

One of the most powerful features of a relational database is the use of *foreign keys*. A foreign key is a field in a record in one table that can reference a primary key in another table. For example, a table that lists sales orders includes fields that are foreign keys, each of which references records in other tables. This is shown in Figure 5-7.

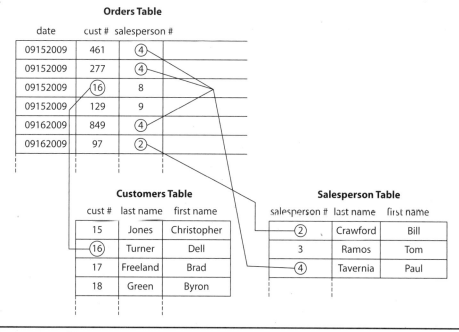

Figure 5-7   Fields in a sales order table point to records in other tables.

Relational databases enforce *referential integrity*. This means that the database will not permit a program (or user) to delete a row from a table if there are records in other tables whose foreign keys reference the row to be deleted. The database instead will return an error code that will signal to the requesting program that there are rows in other tables that would be "stranded" if the row was deleted. Using the example in Figure 5-7, a relational database will not permit a program to delete salesperson #2 or #4 since there are records in the sales order table that reference those rows.

The power of relational databases comes from their design and from SQL. Queries are used to find one or more records from a table using the SELECT statement. An example statement is

```
SELECT * FROM Orders WHERE Price > 100 ORDER BY Customer
```

One powerful feature in relational databases is a special query called a *join*, where records from two or more tables are searched in a single query. An example join query is

```
SELECT Salesperson.Name, count(*) AS Orders FROM Salesperson JOIN
Salesperson_Number ON Salesperson.Number = Orders.Salesperson GROUP BY
Salesperson.Name
```

This query will produce a list of salespersons and the number of orders they have sold.

Relational Database Security   Relational databases in commercial applications need to have some security features. Three primary security features are

- **Access controls**   Most relational databases have access controls at the table and field levels. This means that a database can permit or deny a user the ability to read data from or write data to a specific table or even a specific field. To enforce access controls, the database needs to authenticate users so that it knows the identity of each user making access requests. DBMSs employ a data control language (DCL) to control access to data in a database.

- **Encryption**   Sensitive data such as financial or medical records may need to be encrypted. Some relational databases provide field-level database encryption that permits a user or application to specify certain fields that should be encrypted. Encryption protects the data by making it difficult to read if an intruder is able to obtain the contents of the database by some illicit means.

- **Audit logging**   DBMSs provide audit logging features that permit an administrator or auditor to view some or all activities that take place in a database. Audit logging can show precisely the activities that take place, including details of database changes and the user who made those changes. The audit logs themselves can be protected so that they resist tampering, which can make it difficult for someone to make changes to data and erase their tracks.

Database administrators can also create *views*, which are virtual tables created via stored queries. Views can simplify viewing data by aggregating or filtering data. They can improve security by exposing only certain records or fields to users.

NoSQL   NoSQL DBMSs are nonrelational and designed to support large, sometimes disparate data sets across multiple systems. Several types of NoSQL databases are in use, including Column, Document, Key-Value, and Graph.

The motivation for the use of NoSQL databases is primarily applicability and usefulness: relational databases are not always the best choice for a DBMS in every application.

Object Database Management Systems   An *object database* (or object database management system, ODBMS) is a database where information is represented as objects that are used in object-oriented programming languages. Object-oriented databases are used for data that does not require static or predefined attributes, such as a fixed-length field or defined data structure. The data can even be of varying types. The data that is contained in an object-oriented database is unpredictable in nature.

Unlike the clean separation between programs and data in the relational database model, object databases make database objects appear as programming language objects. Both the data and the programming method are contained in an object. Object databases are really just the mechanisms used to store data that is inherently part of the basic object-oriented programming model. Thus, when a data object is accessed, the data object itself will contain functions (methods), negating the requirement for a query language such as SQL.

Object databases are not widely used commercially. They are limited to a few applications requiring high-performance processing on complex data.

Relational databases are starting to look a little more like object databases through the addition of object-oriented interfaces and functions; object-oriented databases are starting to look a little more like relational databases through query languages such as Object Query Language (OQL).

Hierarchical Database Management Systems   A *hierarchical database* is so named because its data model is a top-down hierarchy, with parent records and one or more child records in its design. The dominant hierarchical database management system product in use today is IBM's IMS (Information Management System) that runs on mainframes in nearly all of the larger organizations in the world.

A *network database* is similar to a hierarchical database, extended somewhat to permit lateral data relationships (like the addition of "cousins" to the parent and child records). Figure 5-8 illustrates hierarchical and network databases.

Media Management Systems

Information systems may employ automated tape management systems (TMSs) or disk management systems (DMSs) that track the tape and disk volumes that are needed for application processing.

Disk and tape management systems instruct system operators to mount specific media volumes when they are needed. These systems reduce operator error by requesting specific volumes and rejecting incorrect volumes that do not contain the required data.

TMSs and DMSs are most often found as a component of a computer backup system. Most commercial backup systems track which tape or disk volumes contain which

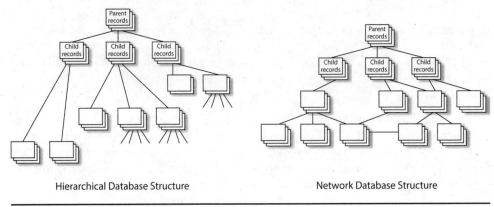

Hierarchical Database Structure   Network Database Structure

Figure 5-8   Hierarchical and network databases

backed-up files and databases. Coupled with automatic volume recognition (usually through barcode readers), backup systems maintain an extensive catalog of the entire collection of backup media and their contents. When data needs to be restored, the backup software (or the TMS or DMS) will specify which media volume should be mounted, verify that the correct media is available, and then restore the desired data as directed.

Significant reductions in the cost of storage, together with the trend toward cloud computing and cloud storage, have resulted in few new installations of TMSs and DMSs. Still, many organizations utilize these today, and IS auditors must be familiar with their function and operation.

Utility Software

Utility software comprises a broad class of programs that support the development or use of networks, information systems, operating systems, and applications. Utility software is most often used by IT specialists whose responsibilities include some aspect of system development, support, or operations. End users, on the other hand, most often use software applications instead of utilities.

Utility software can be classified into the following categories:

- **Software and data design**   This includes system, program, and data modeling tools that are used to design new applications or to model existing applications.

- **Software development**   These programs are used to facilitate the actual coding of an application (or another utility). Development tools can provide a wide variety of functions, including program language syntax checking, compilation, debugging, and testing.

- **Software testing**   Apart from unit testing that may be present in a development environment, dedicated software testing tools perform extensive testing of software functions. Automated testing tools can contain entire suites of test cases that are run against an application program, with the results stored for future reference.

- **Security testing**   Several different types of software tools are used to determine the security of software applications, operating systems, DBMSs, and networks. One type of security testing tool examines an application's source code, looking for potential security vulnerabilities. Another type runs the application program and inputs different forms of data to see if the application contains vulnerabilities in the way that it handles this data. Other security testing tools examine operating system and DBMS configuration settings. Still others send specially crafted network messages to a target system to see what types of vulnerabilities might exist that could be exploited by an intruder or a hacker.

- **Data management**   These utilities are used to manipulate, list, transform, query, compare, encrypt, decrypt, import, or export data. They may also test the integrity of data (for instance, examining an index in a relational database or the integrity of a file system) and possibly make repairs.

- **System health**   These utilities are used to assess the health of an operating system by examining configuration settings; verifying the versions of the kernel, drivers, and utilities; and making performance measurements and tuning changes. Some system utilities are used to assess the health of system components including CPU, main memory, secondary storage, and peripherals.

- **Network**   These utilities are used to examine the network to discover other systems connected to it, determine network configuration, and listen to network traffic.

Utilities and Security

Because some utilities are used to observe or make changes to access controls or security, organizations should limit the use of utilities to those personnel whose responsibilities require their use. All other personnel should not be permitted to use them.

Because many utilities are readily available, simply posting a policy will not prevent their use. Instead, strict access controls should be established so that unauthorized users who do obtain utilities would derive little or no use from them. These controls are typically implemented through one of two methods:

- **Remove local administrator privileges** from end users on their workstations so that they are unable to install software packages or change the configuration of their workstations' operating systems.

- **Employ software whitelisting software** that prohibits all but strictly permitted software programs from running on users' workstations.

Software Licensing

Most organizations purchase many software components in support of their software applications and IT environments overall. For example, organizations often purchase operating systems, software development tools, DBMSs, web servers, network management tools, office automation systems, and security tools. Organizations need to be aware of the licensing terms and conditions for each of the software products that they lease or purchase.

To be effective, an organization should centralize its records and expertise in software licensing to avoid licensing issues that could lead to unwanted and potentially costly and embarrassing legal actions. Some of the ways that an organization can organize and control its software usage include

- **Develop policy**   The organization should develop policies that define acceptable and unacceptable uses of software.

- **Centralize procurement**   This can help to funnel purchasing through a group or department that can help to manage and control software acquisition and use.

- **Implement software metering**   Automated tools that are installed on each computer (including user workstations) can alert IT of every software program that is installed and run in the organization. This can help to raise awareness of any new software programs that are being used as well as the numbers of copies of programs installed and in use.

- **Implement concurrent licensing**   The organization can use dynamic license management that controls the number of users who are able to use a program simultaneously. This can help reduce costs for expensive programs used infrequently by many employees.

- **Review software contracts**   The person or group with responsibility for managing software licensing should be aware of the terms and conditions of use.

Digital Rights Management

The Internet has provided a means for easily distributing content to large numbers of people. This ability, however, sometimes runs afoul of legal copyright protection afforded to the owners of copyrighted work. This encompasses software programs as well as documents and media.

Organizations also are faced with the problem of limiting the distribution of documents for privacy or intellectual property protection. For example, an organization may publish a technical whitepaper describing its services and desires that only its current customers be able to view the document.

Digital rights management (DRM) is a set of emerging technologies that permits the owner of digital information (such as documents) to control access to that information, even after it is no longer contained in the owner's environment. In some instances, these technologies are implemented in system hardware (such as electronic book readers), and in other cases they are implemented in software.

Whether implemented in hardware or software, the program or device displaying information will first examine the file to determine whether the information should be displayed or not. Some of the characteristics that the owner of a file may be able to set include

- **Expiration**   The owner of a file may be able to set an expiration date, after which time the file cannot be viewed or used.

- **Registration**   The owner of a file may be able to require anyone viewing the file to register him- or herself in a reliable way (such as through e-mail address verification).

- **Authentication**   The owner of a file may be able to require that persons viewing a file first authenticate themselves.

Network Infrastructure

Networks are used to transport data from one computer to another, either within an organization or between organizations. *Network infrastructure* is the collection of devices and cabling that facilitates network communications among an organization's systems as well as among the organization's systems and those belonging to other organizations. This section describes the following network infrastructure topics:

- Enterprise architecture
- Network architecture
- Network-based services
- Network models
- Network technologies
- Local area networks
- Wide area networks
- Wireless networks
- The TCP/IP suite of protocols
- The global Internet
- Network management
- Networked applications

Enterprise Architecture

There are two distinct facets related to the term *enterprise architecture*. The first is the overall set of infrastructure that facilitates access to applications and information: the networks, whether wired or wireless, local or wide area, together with resilience, access controls, and monitoring; the systems with their applications and tools; and the data and where it is stored, transmitted, and processed. The second facet is the ongoing activity carried out by one or more persons with titles such as *Enterprise Network Architect, Enterprise Data Architect, Enterprise Systems Engineer*, or *Enterprise Security Architect*, any and all of whom are concerned with "big picture" aspects of the organization and its mission, objectives, and goals, and whether the organization's infrastructure as a whole contributes to their fulfillment.

Enterprise architecture, done correctly, requires *standards*: consistent ways of doing things, and consistency in the components that are used and how those components are configured.

The goals of enterprise architecture include

- **Scalability** Enterprise architects should design the whole enterprise and its components so that systems, networks, and storage can be easily expanded where needed.
- **Agility** The overall design of the organization's infrastructure should be flexible enough to meet new goals and objectives.
- **Transparency** High-level and detailed diagrams should be readily available and up-to-date. There should be no secrets.
- **Security** The design of an organization's infrastructure should reflect the needs of the organization through means such as segmentation, the creation of security zones, monitoring, and the inclusion of security components including firewalls and intrusion prevention systems.
- **Consistency** The organization's infrastructure should reflect consistency through the use of common components and configurations. This makes troubleshooting and upkeep more effective when engineers are familiar with micro architectures, components, and configurations. For example, an organization with retail stores or branch offices should employ identical architectures in each of those locations; this makes support and troubleshooting easier because engineers don't first need to figure out how a local network is configured—they're all the same, or nearly so.
- **Repeatability** Consistency brings repeatability. In an organization with retail stores or branch offices, for instance, additions or changes are "cookie cutter" instead of time-consuming "one-off" efforts.
- **Efficiency** Repeatability and consistency yield efficiency. Upgrades, expansion, and configuration changes are consistent and repeatable. Troubleshooting takes less time.
- **Resilience** Enterprise architects need to understand where resilience is required, so that infrastructure will be continuously available even in the event of the failure of individual components, or in cases of maintenance.

The challenge facing many organizations is the temptation to cut corners and deviate from (or never implement) standard architectures. Short-term gains are almost sure to be smaller than long-term inefficiencies realized later. Vision and discipline are required to attain, and maintain, a consistent and effective enterprise architecture.

Network Architecture

The term *network architecture* has several meanings, all of which refer to the overall design of an organization's network communications. An organization's network architecture, like other aspects of its information technology, should support the organization's mission, goals, and objectives.

The facets of network architecture include

- **Physical network architecture**   This is concerned with the physical locations of network equipment and media. This includes, for instance, the design of a network cable plant (also known as *structured cabling*), as well as the locations and types of network devices. An organization's physical network architecture may be expressed in several layers. A high-level architecture may depict global physical locations or regions and their interconnectivity, while an in-building architecture will be highly specific regarding the types of cabling and locations of equipment.

- **Logical network architecture**   This is concerned with the depiction of network communications at a local, campus, regional, and global level. Here, the network architecture will include several related layers, including representations of network protocols, device addressing, traffic routing, security zones, and the utilization of carrier services.

- **Data flow architecture**   This is closely related to application and data architecture. Here, the flow of data is shown as connections among applications, systems, users, partners, and suppliers. Data flow can be depicted in nongeographic terms, although representations of data flow at local, campus, regional, and global levels are also needed, since geographic distance is often inversely proportional to capacity and throughput.

- **Network standards and services**   This is more involved with the services that are used on the network and less with the geographic and spatial characteristics of the network. Services and standards need to be established in several layers, including cable types, addressing standards, routing protocols, network management protocols, utility protocols (such as Domain Name System [DNS], Network Time Protocol [NTP], file sharing, printing, e-mail, remote access, and many more), and application data interchange protocols, such as SOA (Service-Oriented Architecture), SOAP (Simple Object Access Protocol), and XML (eXtensible Markup Language).

- **Security architecture**   This includes the creation of trust zones, segmentation, and security controls such as firewalls, intrusion prevention systems (IPSs), web content filtering, proxy servers, gateways, and security monitoring.

Types of Networks

Computer networks can be classified in a number of different ways. The primary method of classification is based on the size of a network. By *size*, we refer not necessarily to the number of nodes or stations on the network, but to its physical or geographic size. These types are (from smallest to largest)

- **Personal area network (PAN)**   Also known as a *piconet*, a PAN is generally used by a single individual. Its reach ranges from a few centimeters up to 3 meters and is used to connect peripherals and communication devices for use by an individual.

- **Local area network (LAN)**   The original type of network, a LAN connects computers and devices together in a small building or a residence. The typical maximum size of a LAN is 100 meters, which is the maximum cable length for popular network technologies such as Ethernet.

- **Campus area network (CAN)**   A CAN connotes the interconnection of LANs for an organization that has buildings in close proximity.

- **Metropolitan area network (MAN)**   The MAN network spans a city or regional area. Usually, this type of network consists of two or more in-building LANs in multiple locations that are connected by telecommunications circuits (such as Multiprotocol Label Switching [MPLS], T-1, Frame Relay, or dark fiber) or private network connections over the global Internet.

- **Wide area network (WAN)**   A WAN's size can range from regional to international. An organization with multiple locations across vast distances will connect its locations together with dedicated telecommunications connections or protected connections over the Internet. It is noted that an organization will also call a single point-to-point connection between two distant locations a "WAN connection."

The classifications discussed here are not rigid, nor do they impose restrictions on the use of any specific technology from one to the next. Instead, they are simply a set of terms that enable professionals to speak easily about the geographic extent of their networks with easily understood terms.

The relative scale of these network terms is depicted in Figure 5-9.

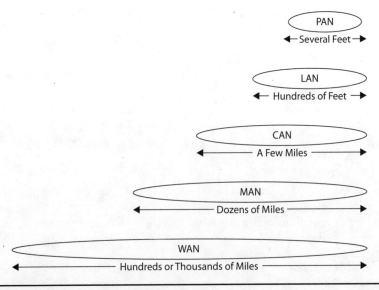

Figure 5-9   A comparison of network sizes

Network-Based Services

Network-based services are the protocols and utilities that facilitate system- and network-based resource utilization. In a literal sense, many of these services operate on servers; they are called network-based services because they facilitate or utilize various kinds of network communication.

Some of these services are

- **E-mail**   E-mail servers collect, store, and transmit e-mail messages from person to person. They accept incoming e-mail messages from other users on the Internet and likewise send e-mail messages over the Internet to e-mail servers that accept and store e-mail messages for distant recipients.

- **Print**   Print servers act as aggregation points for network-based printers in an organization. When users print a document, their workstation sends it to a specific printer queue on a print server. If other users are also sending documents to the same printer, the print server will store them temporarily until the printer is able to print them.

- **File storage**   File servers provide centralized storage of files for use among groups of users. Often, centralized file storage is configured so that files stored on remote servers logically appear to be stored locally on user workstations.

- **Directory**   These services provide centralized management of resource information. Examples include DNS, which provides translation between resource name and IP address, and Lightweight Directory Access Protocol (LDAP), which provides directory information for users and resources, and is often used as a central database of user IDs and passwords. An example of an LDAP-based directory service is Active Directory, which is the Microsoft implementation of and extensions to LDAP.

- **Remote access**   Network- and server-based services within an organization's network are protected from Internet access by firewalls and other means. This makes them available only to users whose workstations are physically connected to the enterprise network. Remote access permits authorized users to access network-based services remotely from anywhere on the Internet via an encrypted "tunnel" that logically connects the users to the enterprise network as though they were physically there. These *virtual private networks* (VPNs) are typically encrypted to prevent any eavesdropper from being able to view the contents of a user's network communication.

- **Terminal emulation**   In many organizations with mainframe computers, PCs have replaced "green screen" and other types of mainframe-centric terminals. Terminal emulation software on PCs enables them to function like those older mainframe terminals.

- **Virtual workstation**   Many organizations implement a virtual desktop infrastructure (VDI), wherein its workstations run operating systems that are actually stored on central servers. This simplifies the administration of those user operating systems since they are centrally stored.

- **Time synchronization** It is a well-known fact among systems engineers that the time clocks built in to most computers are not very accurate (some are, in fact, notoriously *inaccurate*). Distributed applications and network services have made accurate "timestamping" increasingly important. Time synchronization protocols enable an organization's time server system to ensure that all other servers' and workstations' time clocks are synchronized. And the time server itself will synchronize with one of several reliable Internet-based time servers, GPS-equipped time servers, or time servers that are attached to international standard atomic clocks.

- **Network connectivity and authentication** Many organizations have adopted one of several available methods that authenticate users and workstations before logically connecting them to the enterprise network. This helps to prevent nonorganization-owned or noncompliant workstations from being able to connect to an internal network, which is a potential security threat. Users or workstations that are unable to authenticate are connected to a "quarantine" network, where users can obtain information about the steps they need to take to get connected to enterprise resources. Network-based authentication can even quickly examine an organization workstation, checking it for proper security settings (anti-malware, firewall, security patches, security configuration, and so on), and allow it to connect logically only if the workstation is configured properly. Various protocols and technologies that are used to connect, verify, and authenticate devices to a network include Dynamic Host Configuration Protocol (DHCP), 802.1X, and network access control (NAC).

- **Web security** Most organizations have a vested interest in having some level of control over the choice of Internet web sites that their employees choose to visit. Web sites that serve no business purpose (for example, online gambling, porn, and online games) can be blocked so that employees cannot access them. Further, many Internet web sites (even legitimate ones) host malware that can be automatically downloaded to user workstations. Web security appliances can examine incoming content for malware, in much the same way that a workstation checks incoming files for viruses.

- **Cloud access control** Many organizations utilize a cloud access security broker (CASB) system to monitor and control access to cloud-based services, as a part of an overall data management and data protection program. A CASB can prevent users from uploading sensitive internal information to a nonsanctioned cloud storage service, for instance.

- **Anti-malware** Malware (viruses, worms, Trojan horses, and so on) remains a significant threat to organizations. Antivirus software on each workstation is still an important line of defense. Because of the complexity of anti-malware, many organizations have opted to implement advanced anti-malware solutions along with centralized management and control. Using a central anti-malware console, security engineers can quickly spot workstations under attack, as well as those whose anti-malware is not functioning, and they can force new anti-malware updates to some or all user workstations. They can even force user workstations to commence an immediate whole-disk scan for malware if an outbreak has started. Centralized anti-malware consoles can also receive virus infection alerts from workstations and keep centralized statistics on virus updates and outbreaks, giving security engineers a vital "big picture" status.

- **Network management**   Larger organizations with too many servers and network devices to administer manually often turn to network management systems. These systems serve as a collection point for all alerts and error messages from vital servers and network devices. They can also be used to configure network devices centrally, making wide-scale configuration changes possible by a small team of engineers working in a NOC. Network management systems also measure network performance, throughput, latency, and outages, giving network engineers vital information on the health of the enterprise network.

Network Models

Network models are the archetype of the actual designs of network protocols. While a model is often a simplistic depiction of a more complicated reality, the Open Systems Interconnection (OSI) and TCP/IP network models accurately illustrate what is actually happening in a network. It is fairly difficult to actually *see* the components of the network in action; the models help us to understand how they work.

These models were developed to build consensus among the various manufacturers of network components (from programs, to software drivers, to network devices and cabling) to improve interoperability between different types of computers. In essence, it was a move toward networks with "interchangeable parts" that would facilitate data communications on a global scale.

The two dominant network models that are used to illustrate networks are OSI and TCP/IP. Both are described in this section.

The OSI Network Model

The first widely accepted network model is the *Open Systems Interconnection* model. The OSI model was developed by the International Organization for Standardization (ISO) and the International Telecommunications Union (ITU). The working groups that developed the OSI model ignored the existence of the TCP/IP model, which was gaining in popularity around the world and has become the de facto world standard.

The OSI model consists of seven layers. Messages that are sent on an OSI network are encapsulated; a message that is constructed at layer 7 is placed inside of layer 6, which is then placed inside of layer 5, and so on. This is not figurative—this encapsulation literally takes place and can be viewed using tools that show the detailed contents of packets on a network. Encapsulation is illustrated in Figure 5-10.

The layers of the OSI model are, from bottom to top,

- Physical
- Data link
- Network

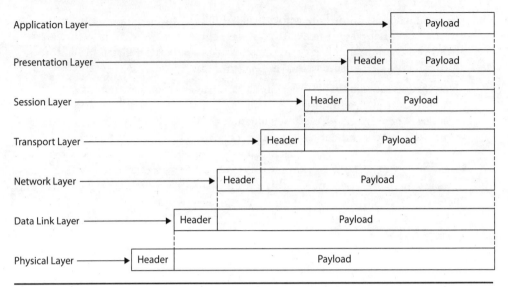

Figure 5-10   Encapsulation of packets in the OSI network model

- Transport
- Session
- Presentation
- Application

Because it is difficult for many people to memorize a list such as this, there are some memory aids to help remember the sequence of these layers, including the following:

- Please Do Not Throw Sausage Pizza Away
- Please Do Not Touch Steve's Pet Alligator
- All People Seem To Need Data Processing
- All People Standing Totally Naked Don't Perspire

The layers of the OSI model are explained in more detail in the remainder of this section.

OSI Layer 1: Physical   The *physical layer* in the OSI model is concerned with electrical and physical specifications for devices. This includes communications cabling, voltage levels, and connectors, as well as some of the basic specifications for devices that would connect to networks. At the physical layer, networks are little more than electric signals flowing in wires or radiofrequency airwaves.

At this layer, data exists merely as bits; there are no frames, packets, or messages here. The physical layer also addresses the modulation of digital information into voltage and current levels in the physical medium.

Examples of OSI physical layer standards include

- **Cabling**   10BASE-T, 100BASE-TX, 1000BASE-X, twinax, and fiber optics, which are standards for physical network cabling

- **Communications**   RS-232, RS-449, and V.35, which are standards for sending serial data between computers

- **Telecommunications**   T1, E1, SONET (Synchronous Optical Networking), DSL (Digital Subscriber Line), and DOCSIS (Data Over Cable Service Interface Specification), which are standards for common carrier communications networks for voice and data

- **Wireless communications**   Asynchronous Connection-Less (ACL) used by Bluetooth, 802.11a PHY (meaning the physical layer component of 802.11), and other wireless local area network (WLAN) airlink standards

- **Wireless telecommunications**   LTE (Long Term Evolution), WiMAX (Worldwide Interoperability for Microwave Access), CDMA (Code Division Multiple Access), W-CDMA, CDMA2000, TDMA (Time Division Multiple Access), and UMTS (Universal Mobile Telecommunications Service), which are airlink standards for wireless communications between cell phones and base stations (these standards also include some OSI layer 2 features)

OSI Layer 2: Data Link   The *data link layer* in the OSI model focuses on the method of transferring data from one station on a network to another station on the same local network. In the data link layer, information is arranged into *frames* and transported across the medium. Error correction is usually implemented as *collision detection*, as well as the confirmation that a frame has arrived intact at its destination, usually through the use of a checksum.

This layer is concerned only with communications on a LAN. At the data link layer, there are no routers (or routing protocols). Instead, the layer should be thought of as a collection of locally connected computers to a single physical medium. Data link layer standards and protocols are concerned only with getting a frame from one computer to another on that local network.

Examples of data link layer standards include

- **LAN protocols**   Ethernet, Token Ring, ATM (Asynchronous Transfer Mode), FDDI (Fiber Distributed Data Interface), and Fibre Channel are the protocols used to assemble a stream of data into frames for transport over a physical medium (the physical layer) from one station to another on a LAN. These protocols include error correction, primarily through collision detection, collision avoidance, synchronous timing, or tokens.

- **802.11 MAC/LLC**   This is the data link portion of the well-known Wi-Fi (wireless LAN) protocols.

- **Common carrier packet networks**   MPLS and Frame Relay are packet-oriented standards for network services provided by telecommunications carriers. Organizations that required point-to-point communications with various locations would often obtain an MPLS or Frame Relay connection from a local telecommunications provider. Frame Relay is being replaced by MPLS and is rapidly declining in use.

- **ARP (Address Resolution Protocol)** This protocol is used when one station needs to communicate with another and the initiating station does not know the receiving station's network link layer (hardware) address. ARP is prevalent in TCP/IP networks but is used in other network types as well.

- **Point-to-Point (PPP) and Serial Line Internet Protocol (SLIP)** These protocols are used to transport TCP/IP packets over point-to-point serial connections (usually RS-232). SLIP is now obsolete, and PPP is generally seen only in remote access connections that utilize dial-up services.

- **Tunneling** PPTP (Point-to-Point Tunneling Protocol), L2TP (Layer 2 Tunneling Protocol), and other tunneling protocols were developed as a way to extend TCP/IP (among others) from a centralized network to a branch network or a remote workstation, usually over a dial-up connection.

In the data link layer, stations on the network must have an address. Ethernet and Token Ring, for instance, use MAC (Media Access Control) addresses, which are considered hardware addresses. Most other multistation protocols also utilize some form of hardware addressing for each device on the network.

OSI Layer 3: Network The purpose of the OSI *network layer* is the delivery of messages from one station to another via one or more networks. The network layer can process messages of any length and will "fragment" messages so that they are able to fit into *packets* that the network is able to transport.

The network layer is concerned with the interconnection of networks and the packet *routing* between networks. Network devices called *routers* are used to connect networks. Routers are physically connected to two or more logical networks and are configured with (or have some ability to learn) the network settings for each network. Using this information, routers are able to make routing decisions that will enable them to forward packets to (or closer to) the correct network, moving them closer to their ultimate destination.

Examples of protocols at the network layer include

- **IP (Internet Protocol)** This network layer protocol is used in the TCP/IP suite of protocols. IP is concerned with the delivery of packets from one station to another, whether the stations are on the same network or on different networks. IP has the *IP address* scheme for assigning addresses to stations on a network; this is entirely separate from link layer (hardware) addressing such as Ethernet's MAC addressing. IP is the basis for the global Internet.

- **IPsec (Internet Protocol Security)** This protocol is used to authenticate, encapsulate, and encrypt IP traffic between networks. This protocol is often used for VPNs facilitating secure remote access.

- **ICMP (Internet Control Message Protocol)** This communications diagnostics protocol is also a part of the TCP/IP suite. One of its primary uses is the transmission of error messages from one station to another; these error messages are usually related to problems encountered when attempting to send packets from one station to another.

- **IGMP (Internet Group Management Protocol)**   This protocol is used to organize multicast group memberships between routers. IGMP is a part of the multicast protocol family.

- **Logical link control and adaptation protocol (L2CAP)**   This is the network layer used by Bluetooth.

- **AppleTalk**   This original suite of protocols was developed by Apple Computer for networking the Apple brand of computers. The suite of protocols includes the transmission of messages from one computer over interconnected networks, as well as routing protocols. AppleTalk has since been deprecated in favor of TCP/IP.

OSI Layer 4: Transport   The *transport layer* in the OSI model is primarily concerned with the *reliability* of data transfer between systems. The transport layer manages the following characteristics of data communications:

- **Connection orientation**   At the transport layer, communications between two stations can take place in the context of a *connection*. Here, two stations will initiate a unique, logical context (called a connection) under which they can exchange messages until a later time when the stations agree to end the connection. Stations can have two or more unique connections established concurrently; each is uniquely identified.

- **Guaranteed delivery**   Protocols at the transport layer can track individual packets to guarantee delivery. For example, the TCP uses something like a return receipt for each transported packet to confirm that each sent packet was successfully received by the destination.

- **Sequence of delivery**   The transport layer includes protocols that are able to track the sequence in which packets are delivered. Typically, each transported packet will have a serialized number that the receiving system will use to make sure that packets on the receiving system are delivered in proper order. When coupled with guaranteed delivery, a receiving system can request retransmission of any missing packets, ensuring that none are lost.

The protocols at the transport layer are doing the heavy lifting by ensuring the integrity and completeness of messages that flow from system to system. The ability for data communications to take place over the vast worldwide network that is the global Internet is made possible by the characteristics of protocols in the transport layer.

Examples of transport layer protocols include

- **TCP (Transmission Control Protocol)**   This is the "TCP" in the TCP/IP protocol suite. TCP is connection-oriented due to the formal establishment (three-way handshake) and maintenance (sequence numbers and acknowledgments) of a connection, using flags to indicate connection state. When a system sends a TCP packet to another system on a specific port, that port number helps the operating system direct the message to a specific program. For example, port 25 is used for inbound e-mail, ports 20 and 21 are used for FTP (File Transfer Protocol), and ports 80 and 443 are used for HTTP (Hypertext Transfer Protocol) and HTTPS (HTTP Secure), respectively. Hundreds of preassigned port numbers are the subject of Internet standards. TCP employs guaranteed delivery and guaranteed order of delivery.

- **UDP (User Datagram Protocol)**   This is the other principal protocol used by TCP/IP in the OSI transport layer. Unlike TCP, UDP is a lighter weight protocol that lacks connection orientation, order of delivery, and guaranteed delivery. UDP consequently has less computing and network overhead, which makes it ideal for some protocols that are less sensitive to occasional packet loss. Examples of protocols that use UDP are DNS (Domain Name System), TFTP (Trivial File Transfer Protocol), and VoIP (Voice over IP). Like TCP, UDP also employs port numbers so that incoming packets on a computer can be delivered to the right program or process. Sometimes UDP is called "unreliable data protocol," a memory aid that is a reference to the protocol's lack of guaranteed delivery.

The TCP/IP suite of protocols is described in more detail later in this chapter.

OSI Layer 5: Session   The *session layer* in the OSI model is used to control connections that are established between applications on the same, or different, systems. This involves connection establishment, termination, and recovery.

In the OSI model, connection control takes place in the session layer. This means that the concept of the establishment of a logical connection between systems is a session layer function. However, TCP—which is generally thought of as a transport layer protocol—handles this on its own.

Examples of session layer protocols include

- **Interprocess communications**   Sockets and named pipes are some of the ways that processes on a system (or on different systems) exchange information.
- **SIP (Session Initiation Protocol)**   SIP is used to set up and tear down VoIP and other communications connections.
- **RPC (Remote Procedure Call)**   This is another interprocess communication technology that permits an application to execute a subroutine or procedure on another computer.
- **NetBIOS (Network Basic Input/Output System)**   This permits applications to communicate with one another using the legacy NetBIOS API.

OSI Layer 6: Presentation   The *presentation layer* in the OSI model is used to translate or transform data from lower layers (session, transport, and so on) into formats that the application layer can work with. Examples of presentation layer functions include

- **Character set translation**   Programs or filters are sometimes needed to translate character sets between ASCII and EBCDIC (Extended Binary Coded Decimal Interchange Code), for instance.

- **Encryption/decryption**   Communications may be encrypted if data is to be transported across unsecure networks. Example protocols are SSL (Secure Sockets Layer), TLS (Transport Layer Security), and MIME (Multipurpose Internet Mail Extensions).

- **Codecs**   Protocols such as MPEG (Moving Picture Experts Group) use *codecs* to encode/decode or to compress/decompress audio and video data streams.

OSI Layer 7: Application   The *application layer* in the OSI model contains programs that communicate directly with the end user. This includes utilities that are packaged with operating systems, as well as tools and software applications.

Examples of application layer protocols include

- **Utility protocols**   DNS, SNMP (Simple Network Management Protocol), DHCP, and NTP

- **Messaging protocols**   SMTP (Simple Mail Transfer Protocol), NNTP (Network News Transfer Protocol), HTTP, VoIP, X.400, and X.500

- **Data transfer protocols**   NFS (Network File System) and FTP

- **Interactive protocols**   Telnet, IRC (Internet Relay Chat), SSH

End-user applications that communicate over networks do so via OSI layer 7.

OSI: A Model That Has Never Been Implemented—or Has It?

The OSI network model is a distinguished tool for teaching the concepts of network encapsulation and the functions taking place at each layer. However, the problem is that no actual, living network protocol environments have ever been built that contain all of the layers of the OSI model, and it is becoming increasingly apparent that none ever will. The world's dominant network standard, TCP/IP, is a layered protocol stack that consists of four layers, and it's not likely that TCP/IP's model will ever be increased to seven layers.

As the OSI model was being developed and socialized by ISO (and is now defined by ISO/IEC 7498-1), the rival TCP/IP model was quickly becoming the world's standard for data network communications. OSI has been relegated to a teaching tool, and the model itself is more of an interesting museum piece that represents an idea that never came to fruition.

There is a different and equally valid point of view regarding implementation of the OSI model: it can be said that all of the modern encapsulated network protocols—TCP/IP, IPX/SPX (Internetwork Packet Exchange/Sequenced Packet Exchange), AppleTalk, and Token Ring—are implementations, albeit incomplete, of the OSI model. This is a topic for technology philosophers and historians to take up.

The TCP/IP Network Model

The TCP/IP network model is one of the basic design characteristics of the TCP/IP suite of protocols. The network model consists of four "layers," where each layer is used to manage some aspect of the transmission, routing, or delivery of data over a network. In a layered model, each layer receives services from the next lowest layer and provides services to the next higher layer.

Like OSI, the TCP/IP network model utilizes *encapsulation*. This means that a message created by an application program is encapsulated within a transport layer message, which in turn is encapsulated within an Internet layer message, which is encapsulated in a link layer message, which is delivered to a network adaptor for delivery across a physical network medium. This encapsulation is depicted in Figure 5-11.

The layers of the TCP/IP model, from bottom to top, are

- Link
- Internet
- Transport
- Application

These layers are discussed in detail in this section.

One of the primary purposes of the layered model (in both the OSI and TCP/IP models) is to permit *abstraction*. This means that each layer need be concerned only with its own delivery characteristics, while permitting other layers to manage their own matters. For instance, order of delivery is managed by the transport layer; at the Internet and link layers, order of delivery is irrelevant. Also, the link layer is concerned with just getting a message from one station to another and with collisions and the basic integrity of the message as it is transported from one device to another; but the link layer has no concept of a logical connection or with order of delivery, which are addressed by higher layers.

TCP/IP Link Layer   The *link layer* is the lowest layer in the TCP/IP model. Its purpose is the delivery of messages (usually called *frames*) from one station to another on a local network. Being the lowest layer of the TCP/IP model, the link layer provides services to the transport layer.

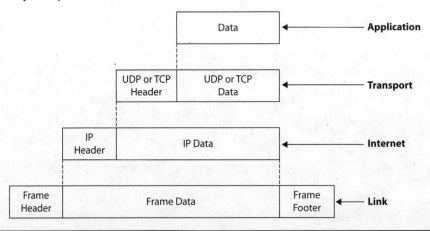

Figure 5-11   Encapsulation in the TCP/IP network model

The link layer is the physical layer of the network and is usually implemented in the form of hardware network adaptors. TCP/IP can be implemented on top of any viable physical medium that has the capacity to transmit frames from one station to another. Examples of physical media used for TCP/IP include those from standards such as Ethernet, ATM, USB, Wi-Fi, Bluetooth, GPRS (General Packet Radio Service), DSL, ISDN (Integrated Services Digital Network), and fiber optics.

The link layer is only concerned with the delivery of messages from one station to another on a local network. At this layer, there is no concept of neighboring networks or of routing; these are handled at higher layers in the model.

TCP/IP Internet Layer   The *Internet layer* of the TCP/IP model is the foundation layer of TCP/IP. The purpose of this layer is the delivery of messages (packets) from one station to another on the same network or on different networks. The Internet layer receives services from the link layer and provides services to the transport layer.

At this layer, the delivery of messages from one station to another is not guaranteed. Instead, the Internet layer makes only a best effort to deliver messages. The Internet layer also does not concern itself with the sequence of delivery of messages. Concerns such as these are addressed at the transport layer.

The primary protocol that has been implemented in the Internet layer is the Internet Protocol. IP is the building block for nearly all other protocols and message types in TCP/IP. One other protocol is common in the Internet layer: ICMP (Internet Control Message Protocol), a diagnostic protocol that is used to send error messages and other diagnostic messages over networks.

At the Internet layer, there are two types of devices: hosts and routers. *Hosts* are computers that could be functioning as servers or workstations. They communicate by creating messages that they send on the network. *Routers* are computers that forward packets from one network to another. In the early Internet, routers really *were* computers like others, with some additional configurations that they used to forward packets between networks.

The relationship between hosts and routers is depicted in Figure 5-12.

TCP/IP Transport Layer   The *transport layer* in the TCP/IP model consists of two main packet transport protocols, TCP and UDP, as well as a few other protocols that were developed after the initial design of TCP/IP. The transport layer receives services from the Internet layer and provides services to the application layer.

Several features are available at the transport layer for packet delivery, including

- **Reliable delivery**   This involves two characteristics: integrity of the packet contents and guaranteed delivery. TCP includes these two features that ensure confirmation that a packet sent from one station will be delivered to its destination and that the contents of the packet will not be altered along the way.

- **Connection orientation**   This involves the establishment of a persistent logical "connection" between two stations. This is particularly useful when a station is communicating on many simultaneous "conversations" from one or more source

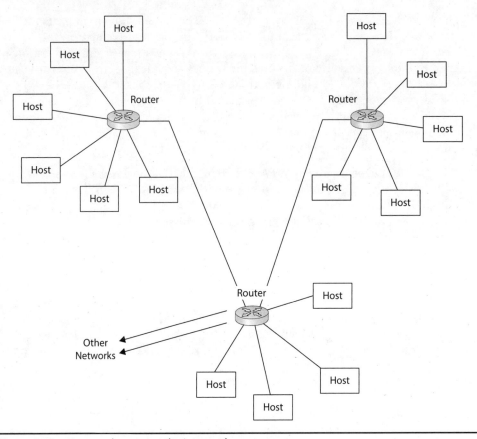

Figure 5-12 Hosts and routers at the Internet layer

stations. When a connection is established, the requesting system communicates on an arbitrary source port, to the destination system on standard ports (such as HTTP port 80, DNS port 53, and so on). The two stations will negotiate and agree on arbitrary high-numbered ports (channels) that will make each established connection unique.

- **Sequence of delivery** The sequence of delivery of packets can be guaranteed to match the order in which they were sent. This is implemented through the use of sequence numbers, which are used by the receiving system to deliver packets in the correct order to the receiving process.

- **Flow control** This means that the delivery of packets from one station to another will not overrun the destination station. For example, the transfer of a large file from a faster system to a slower system could overrun the slower system, unless the latter has a way to pause the transfer (flow control) periodically so that it can keep up with the inbound messages.

- **Port number**   A message on one station may be sent to a specific port number on a destination station. A port number essentially signifies the type of message that is being sent. A "listener" program can be set up on a destination system to listen on a preassigned port and then process messages received on that port number. The primary advantage of port numbers is that a destination system does not need to examine the contents of a message to discern its type; instead, the port number defines the purpose. There are many standard port numbers established, including 23 = Telnet, 25 = e-mail, 53 = Domain Name System, 80 = HTTP, and so on.

Note that not all transport layer protocols utilize all of these features. For instance, UDP utilizes flow control but none of the other features listed.

TCP/IP Application Layer   The *application layer* is the topmost layer of the TCP/IP model. This layer interfaces directly with applications and application services. The application layer receives services from the transport layer and may communicate directly with end users.

Application layer protocols include DNS, SNMP, DHCP, NTP, SMTP, NNTP, HTTP, HTTPS, NFS, FTP, and Telnet. There are many more.

The TCP/IP and OSI Models   The TCP/IP model was not designed to conform to the seven-layer OSI network model. However, the models are similar in their use of encapsulation and abstraction, and some layers between the two models are similar. Figure 5-13 shows the TCP/IP and OSI models side by side and how the layers in one model correspond to the other.

 EXAM TIP   Mapping TCP/IP and OSI models to each other has no practical purpose except to understand their similarities and differences. There is no unanimous agreement on the mapping of the models. It is easy to argue for some small differences in the way that they are conjoined.

Figure 5-13
The TCP/IP and
OSI network
models side
by side

OSI	TCP/IP
Application Presentation Session	Application
Transport	Transport
Network	Internet
Data Link Physical	Link

Network Technologies

Many network technologies have been developed over the past several decades. Some, such as Ethernet, DSL, and TCP/IP, are found practically everywhere, while other technologies, such as ISDN, Frame Relay, and AppleTalk, have had shorter lifespans.

The IS auditor needs to be familiar with network technologies, architectures, protocols, and media so that he or she may examine an organization's network architecture and operation. The following sections describe network technologies at a level of detail that should be sufficient for most auditing needs:

- **Local Area Networks**   This section discusses LAN topologies, cabling, and transport protocols (including Ethernet, ATM, Token Ring, USB, and FDDI).

- **Wide Area Networks**   This section discusses WANs, including transport protocols MPLS, SONET, T-Carrier, Frame Relay, and ISDN.

- **Wireless Networks**   This section discusses wireless network standards Wi-Fi, Bluetooth, Wireless USB, NFC, and IrDA.

- **TCP/IP Protocols and Devices**   This section discusses TCP/IP protocols in the link layer, Internet layer, transport layer, and application layer.

- **The Global Internet**   This section discusses global Internet addressing, DNS, routing, and applications.

- **Network Management**   This section discusses the business function, plus the tools and protocols used to manage networks.

- **Networked Applications**   This section discusses the techniques used to build network-based applications.

Local Area Networks

Local area networks exist within a relatively small area, such as a floor in a building, a lab, a storefront, an office, or a residence. Because of electrical signaling limitations, a LAN is usually several hundred feet in length or less.

Physical Network Topology   Wired LANs are transported over network cabling that runs throughout a building. Network cabling is set up in one of three physical topologies:

- **Star**   A separate cable is run from a central location to each computer. This is the way that most networks are wired today. The central location might be a wiring closet or a computer room, where all of the cables from each computer would converge at one location and be connected to network equipment such as a switch or hub.

- **Ring**   Cabling runs from one computer to the next. Early Token Ring and Ethernet networks were often wired this way. Where the network cable was attached to a computer, a "T" connector was used: one part connected to the computer itself, and the other two connectors were attached to the network cabling.

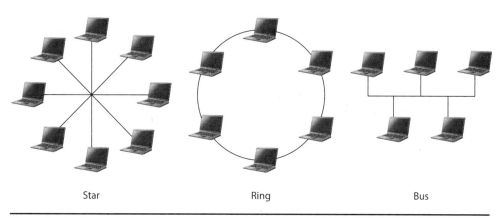

Figure 5-14   Network physical topologies: star, ring, and bus

- **Bus**   A central cable, with connectors along its length that facilitate "branch" cables connected to individual computers. Like the ring topology, this was used in early networks but is seldom used today.

These three topologies are depicted in Figure 5-14.

Note that the logical function and physical topology of a network may vary. For instance, a Token Ring network may resemble a physical star (with all stations connected to a central device), but it will function logically as a ring. An Ethernet network functions as a bus, but it may be wired as a star, bus, or ring, depending on the type of cabling used (and, as indicated earlier, star topology is prevalent). The point is that logical function and physical topology often differ from each other.

Cabling Types   Several types of cables have been used in LANs over the past several decades. This section will focus on the types in use today but will mention those that have been used in the past, which may still be in use in some organizations.

Twisted-Pair Cable   Twisted-pair cabling is a thin cable that contains four pairs of insulated copper conductors, all surrounded by a protective jacket. Several varieties of twisted-pair cabling are suitable for various physical environments and provide various network bandwidth capabilities.

Because network transmissions can be subject to interference, network cabling may include shielding that protects the conductors from interference. Some of these types are

- **Shielded twisted pair (U/FTP or STP)**   This type of cable includes a thin metal shield that protects each pair of conductors from electromagnetic interference (EMI), making it more resistant to interference.
- **Screened unshielded twisted pair (S/UTP)**   Also known as foiled twisted pair (FTP), this type of cable has a thin metal shield that protects the conductors from EMI.

- **Screened shielded twisted pair (S/STP or S/FTP)** This type of cable includes a thin layer of metal shielding surrounding each twisted pair of conductors, plus an outer shield that protects all of the conductors together. This is all covered by a protective jacket.

- **Unshielded twisted pair (UTP)** This type of cable has no shielding and consists only of the four pairs of twisted conductors and the outer protective jacket.

The abbreviations for twisted-pair cable have recently changed in compliance with international standard ISO/IEC 11801, "Information technology—Generic cabling for customer premises." The new standard takes the form X/YTP, where X denotes whether the entire cable has shielding, and Y indicates whether individual pairs in the cable are shielded. Table 5-1 shows the old and new names and their meanings. The old names are likely going to be in common use for many years, as office buildings and residences around the world are wired with twisted-pair cabling that is labeled with the old names; this wiring will likely last for decades in many locations.

Twisted-pair network cabling is also available with different capacity ratings to meet various bandwidth requirements. The common ratings include

- **Category 3** Known as "Cat-3," this is the oldest still-recognized twisted-pair cabling standard, capable of transporting 10Mbit Ethernet up to 100 meters (328 ft.). The 100BASE-T4 standard permitted up to 100Mbit Ethernet over Cat-3 cable by using all four pairs of conductors. Cat-3 cable is no longer installed but is still found in older networks.

- **Category 5** Cat-5 cabling grade has been in common use since the mid-1990s and is suitable for 10Mbit, 100Mbit, and 1000Mbit (1Gbit) Ethernet over distances up to 100 meters (328 ft.). Cat-5 cable is typically made from 24-gauge copper wire with three twists per inch. A newer grade, Category 5e, has better performance for Gigabit Ethernet networks.

- **Category 6** This is the cabling standard for Gigabit Ethernet networks. Cat-6 cabling greatly resembles Cat-5 cabling, but Cat-6 has more stringent specifications for crosstalk and noise. Cat-6 cable is typically made from 23-gauge copper. Cat-6 cabling is "backward compatible" with Cat-5 and 5e cabling, which means that Cat-6 cables can be used for 10Mbit and 100Mbit Ethernet networks as well as 1000Mbit (1Gbit).

Old Name	New Name	Cable Shielding	Pair Shielding
UTP	U/UTP	None	None
FTP	F/UTP	Foil	None
STP	U/FTP	None	Foil
S-FTP	SF/UTP	Foil, braiding	None
S-STP	S/FTP	Braiding	Foil

Table 5-1 Old and New Twisted-Pair Cabling Abbreviations and Meaning

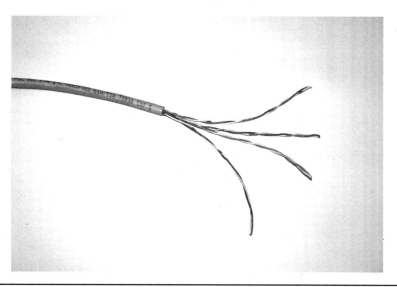

Figure 5-15   Category 5 twisted-pair cable (Image courtesy of Rebecca Steele)

- **Category 7**   This cable standard has been developed to permit 10Gbit Ethernet over 100 meters of cabling. Cat-7 cabling is almost always made from S/FTP cabling to provide maximum resistance to EMI. A newer grade, Category 7a, is designed to have telephone, cable TV, and 1GB networking in the same cable. This newer grade is still under development.

- **Category 8**   This is a new cable standard designed for high-speed networking over short distances, intended for use in data centers.

Twisted-pair cable ratings are usually printed on the outer jacket of the cable. Figure 5-15 shows a short length of Category 5 cable with the rating and other information stamped on it.

Fiber Optic Cable   Fiber optic cable is the transmission medium for fiber optic communications, which is the method of transmitting information using pulses of light instead of electric signals through metal cabling. The advantages of fiber optic cable are its much higher bandwidth, lower loss, and compact size. Because communications over fiber optic cable are based on light instead of electric current, they are immune from EMI.

In LANs, *multimode*-type fiber optic cable can carry signals up to 10 Gbit/sec up to 600 meters (and distances up to a few kilometers at lower bandwidths), sufficient for interconnecting buildings in a campus-type environment. For longer distances, *single-mode*–type fiber optic cable is used, usually by telecommunications carriers for interconnecting cities for voice and data communications.

Compared to twisted-pair and other network cable types, fiber optic cable is relatively fragile and must be treated with care. It can never be pinched, bent, or twisted—doing so will break the internal fibers. For this reason, fiber optic cabling is usually limited to

Figure 5-16
Fiber optic
cable with
its connector
removed to
reveal its interior
(Image courtesy
of Harout S.
Hedeshian)

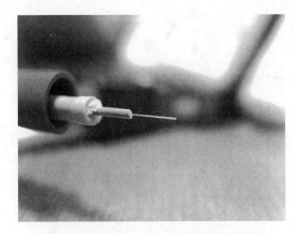

Figure 5-17
Connectors
link fiber optic
cable to network
equipment.
(Image courtesy
of Stephane
Tsacas)

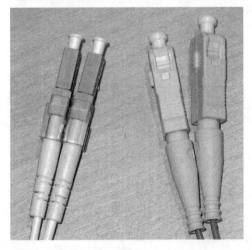

data centers requiring high bandwidths between systems, where network engineers will carefully route fiber optic cabling from device to device, using guides and channels that will prevent the cable from being damaged. But the advantage of fiber optic cabling is its high capacity and freedom from EMI.

Figures 5-16 and 5-17 show fiber optic cable and connectors.

Other Types of Network Cable Twisted-pair and fiber optic cable are the dominant LAN cable types. However, older types of cable have been used and are still found in many installations, including

- **Coaxial** Coaxial cable consists of a solid inner conductor that is surrounded by an insulating jacket, surrounded by a metallic shield. A plastic jacket protects the shield. Coaxial cables were used in early Ethernet networks with cable types such as 10BASE5 and 10BASE2. Twist-lock or threaded connectors were used to connect coaxial cable to computers or network devices. This is fundamentally the type of cable also used for "TV cable." A typical coaxial cable is shown in Figure 5-18.

Figure 5-18
Coaxial cable
(Image courtesy
of Fdominec)

- **Serial**   Point-to-point network connections can be established over USB or RS-232 serial cables. In the case of serial lines, in the 1980s, many organizations used central computers and user terminals that communicated over RS-232 serial cabling. At that time, these existing cable plants made the adoption of SLIP (Serial Line Internet Protocol) popular for connecting workstations and minicomputers to central computers using existing cabling. SLIP is all but obsolete now, displaced by USB.

Network Transport Protocols   Many protocols, or standards, have been developed to facilitate data communications over network cabling. Ethernet, ATM, Token Ring, USB, and FDDI protocols are described in detail in the following sections.

Ethernet   Ethernet is the dominant standard used in LANs. It uses a frame-based protocol, which means that data transmitted over an Ethernet-based network is placed into a "frame" that has places for source and destination addresses as well as contents.

   Shared Medium   Ethernet is a "broadcast" or "shared medium" type of protocol. This means that a frame that is sent from one station on a network to another station may be physically received by all stations that are connected to the network medium. When each station receives the frame, the station will examine the destination address of the frame to determine whether the frame is intended for that or another station. If the frame is destined for another station, the station will simply ignore the frame and do nothing. The destination station will accept the frame and deliver it to the operating system for processing.

   Collision Detection   Ethernet networks are *asynchronous*—a station that needs to transmit a frame may do so at any time. However, Ethernet also employs a "collision detection" mechanism whereby a station that wants to broadcast a frame will begin transmitting and also listen to the network to see if any other stations are transmitting at the same time. If another station is transmitting, the station that wants to transmit will "back off" and wait for a short interval and then try again (in a 10Mbit Ethernet, the station will wait for 9.6 microseconds). If a collision (two stations transmitting at the same time) does occur, both transmitting stations will stop, wait a short interval (the length of the interval is based on a randomly generated number), and then try again. The use of a random number as a part of the "back-off" algorithm ensures that each station has a statistically equal chance to transmit its frames on the network. This is essential for large networks with numerous stations.

Ethernet Addressing   On an Ethernet network, each station on the network has a unique address called a *Media Access Control* (MAC) address, expressed as a six-byte hexadecimal value. A typical address is displayed in a notation separated by colons or dashes, such as F0:E3:67:AB:98:02.

The Ethernet standard dictates that no two devices *in the entire world* will have the same MAC address; this is established through the issuance of ranges of MAC addresses that are allocated to each manufacturer of Ethernet devices. Typically, each manufacturer will be issued a range, which consists of the first three bytes of the MAC address; the manufacturer will then assign consecutive values for the last three bytes to each device that it produces.

For example, suppose a company is issued the value A0-66-01 (called its Organizationally Unique Identifier, or OUI). The devices that the company produces will have that value as the first three bytes of its MAC address and assign three additional bytes to each device that it produces, giving addresses such as A0-66-01-FF-01-01, A0-66-01-FF-01-02, A0-66-01-FF-01-03, and so on. This will guarantee that no two devices in the world will have the same address.

Ethernet Frame Format   An *Ethernet frame* consists of a header segment, a data segment, and a checksum. The header segment contains the destination MAC address, the source MAC address, and a two-byte Ethernet type field. The data segment ranges from 46 to 1,500 bytes in length—the maximum for any particular network is known as the *maximum transmission unit* (MTU). The checksum field is four bytes in length and is a CRC (cyclic redundancy check) checksum of the entire frame. An Ethernet frame is shown in Figure 5-19.

Network Devices   *Network devices* must not only facilitate the transmission of frames on Ethernet networks, but they must support all other network standards as well. These devices include

- **Network adaptor**   A network adaptor, commonly known as a *network interface card* (NIC), is a device that is directly connected to a computer's bus and contains one or more connectors to which an Ethernet network cable may be connected.

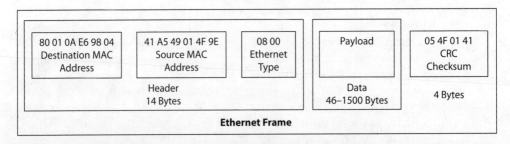

Figure 5-19   An Ethernet frame consists of a header, data, and checksum

Often, a computer's NIC is integrated with the computer's motherboard, but a NIC may also be a separate circuit card that is plugged into a bus connector.

- **Hub** Organizations came to realize that ring and bus topology networks were problematic with regard to cable failures. This gave rise to the star topology as a preferred network architecture, because a cable problem would affect only one station instead of many or all stations. A multiport repeater would be used to connect all of the devices to the network. Over time, this device became known as a *hub*. Like repeaters, Ethernet hubs propagate packets to all stations on the network.

- **Gateway** A *gateway* is a device that acts as a protocol converter or performs some other type of transformation of messages.

- **Repeater** A *repeater* is a device that receives and retransmits the signal on an Ethernet network. Repeaters are useful for situations in which cable lengths exceed 100 meters, or to interconnect two or more Ethernet networks. A disadvantage of repeaters is that they propagate collisions, errors, and other network anomalies onto all parts of the network. Repeaters as stand-alone devices are seldom used in Ethernet networks today; more modern devices have absorbed their functions.

- **Bridge** A *bridge* is a device used to interconnect Ethernet networks. For example, an organization may have an Ethernet network on each floor of a multistory building; a bridge can be used to interconnect each of the separate Ethernet segments. A bridge is similar to a repeater, except that a bridge does not propagate errors such as collisions, but instead propagates only well-formed packets. Bridges also, as stand-alone devices, are seldom seen in today's Ethernet networks.

- **Switch** An Ethernet *switch* is similar to a hub, but with one important difference: a switch will listen to traffic and learn the MAC address(es) associated with each port (connector) and will send packets only to destination ports. The result is potentially greater network throughput, because each station on the network will be receiving only the frames that are specifically addressed to it. When only one station is connected to each port on an Ethernet switch, theoretically, collisions will never occur. Switches are the dominant method for contemporary networks.

Devices such as routers, layer 3 switches, layer 4 switches, and layer 4-7 switches are discussed in the section "TCP/IP Protocols and Devices," later this chapter.

ATM ATM, or *Asynchronous Transfer Mode*, is a link-layer network protocol developed in the 1980s in response to the need to unify telecommunications and computer networks. ATM has been a dominant protocol in the core networks of telecommunications carriers, although IP is becoming more dominant.

Messages (called *cells*) on an ATM network are transmitted in synchronization with a network-based time clock. Stations on an Ethernet, on the other hand, transmit as needed, provided the network is quiet at the moment.

ATM cells are fixed at a length of 53 bytes (5-byte header and 48-byte payload). This small frame size improves performance by reducing jitter, which is a key characteristic of networks that are carrying streaming media such as broadcast television, VoIP, or video.

ATM is a connection-oriented link-layer protocol. This means that two devices on an ATM network that want to communicate with each other will establish a connection through a *virtual circuit*. A connection also establishes a Quality of Service (QoS) setting for the connection that defines the priority and sensitivity of the connection.

Cells that are transmitted from one station to another are transported through one or more ATM switches. The path that a cell takes is established at the time that the virtual circuit is established. An ATM switch is used even when two stations on the same LAN are communicating with each other.

Like Ethernet, ATM can be used to transport TCP/IP messages. TCP/IP packets that are larger than 48 bytes in length are transmitted over ATM in pieces and reassembled at the destination.

Token Ring　*Token Ring* is a LAN protocol that was developed by IBM in the 1980s. Historically, Token Ring was prevalent in organizations that had IBM mainframe or midrange computer systems. However, as TCP/IP and Ethernet grew in popularity, Token Ring declined and it is rarely found today.

Token Ring networks operate through the passage of a three-byte *token frame* from station to station on the network. If a station needs to send information to another station on the network, it must first receive the token; then it can place a frame on the network that includes the token and the message for the destination station. When the token frame reaches the destination station, the destination station will remove the message from the token frame and then pass an empty token (or a frame containing the token and a message for another station) to the next station on the network.

The principal Token Ring device is the *multistation access unit*, or MAU. A MAU is a device that contains several Token Ring cable connectors and connects network cables from the MAU to each station on the network. A typical MAU contains as many as eight connectors; if a Token Ring network is to contain more than eight stations, MAUs can be connected together using their ring in/ring out connectors. Figure 5-20 shows small and large Token Ring networks.

The design of Token Ring technology makes collisions impossible, since no station can transmit unless it possesses the token. A disadvantage of this design occurs if the station with the token encounters a malfunction that causes it not to propagate the token. This results in a momentary pause until the network goes into a recovery mode and regenerates a token.

Universal Serial Bus　*Universal Serial Bus* (USB) is not typically considered a network technology, but rather a workstation bus technology. This is primarily because USB is used to connect peripherals such as mice, keyboards, storage devices, printers, scanners, cameras, microphones, and network adaptors. However, the USB specification indeed contains full networking capabilities, which makes use of those small USB hubs possible.

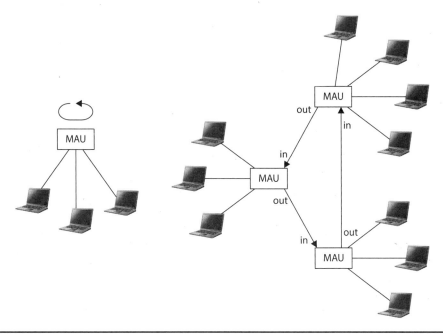

Figure 5-20   Token Ring network topologies

USB data rates are shown in Table 5-2.

Cable length for USB is restricted to 5 meters. The maximum number of devices on a USB network is 127.

One of the valuable characteristics of USB technology is the ability to "hot plug" devices. This means that USB devices can be connected and disconnected without the need to power down the workstation they are connected to. This is achieved primarily through the design specification for devices and device drivers that tolerate plugging and unplugging. This does not mean, however, that all types of USB devices may be plugged and unplugged at will. USB mass storage devices, for instance, should be logically "dismounted" to ensure the integrity of the file system on the device.

FDDI   *Fiber Distributed Data Interface* (FDDI) is a LAN technology whose range can extend up to 200 kilometers over optical fiber. FDDI is a "dual ring" technology that utilizes redundant network cabling and counter-rotating tokens, which together make

Table 5-2
USB Data Rates

USB Version	Data Rate
1.0	12 Mbit/sec
2.0	480 Mbit/sec
3.0	5.0 Gbit/sec
4.0	40 Gbit/sec

FDDI highly resilient. Each ring has a 100 Mbit/sec data rate, making the entire network capable of 200 Mbit/sec.

FDDI has been largely superseded by 100 Mbit/sec and 1 Gbit/sec Ethernet and is no longer common in commercial networks.

Wide Area Networks

Wide area networks (WANs) can extend for miles to thousands of miles between stations. The term WAN is generally used in two ways: to connote an organization's entire regional or global data network and as the label for the long-distance network connections used to join individual networks together. In the second usage, the terms "WAN link" and "WAN connection" are used.

Wide Area Transmission Modes   Before we discuss specific WAN protocols, it is important that you understand the basics of message transmission techniques used in WANs.

The basic problem of wide area communications is the need to route communications efficiently from many different endpoints to many destinations, without constructing dedicated connections between all possible communication sources and destinations. Instead, some scheme for sharing a common communication medium is needed. These methods are

- **Circuit-switched**   Here, a dedicated, end-to-end communications channel is established that lasts for the duration of a connection. The best-known example of circuit-switched technology is the old public-switched telephone network, where a telephone call from one telephone to another occupied a dedicated circuit that was assigned at the onset of the call and used until the call was finished.

- **Packet-switched**   Communications between endpoints takes place over a stream of packets, which are routed through switches until they reach their destination. Frame Relay and the TCP/IP Internet are good examples of packet-switched networks. And while landline telephone calls still have the appearance of being circuit-switched, telephone conversations are actually converted into packets for transmission through the core of a digital telecommunications network.

- **Message-switched**   Each message is switched to its destination when a communications path is available. An example of message switching is the transmission of individual e-mail messages between servers on the Internet.

- **Virtual circuit**   A logical communications channel is established between two endpoints on a packet-switched network. This communications channel may be known as a permanent virtual circuit (PVC) or a switched virtual circuit (SVC). Virtual circuits are used in ATM and Frame Relay networks. VPNs can also be thought of as virtual circuits.

Wide Area Network Protocols   This section describes several well-known protocols used in WANs.

MPLS *Multiprotocol Label Switching* (MPLS) is a variable-length, packet-switched network technology. In an MPLS network, each packet has one or more *labels* affixed to it that contain information that helps MPLS routers to make packet-forwarding decisions, without having to examine the contents of the packet itself (for an IP address, for instance).

MPLS can be used to carry many types of traffic, including Ethernet, ATM, SONET, and IP. It is often used to trunk voice and data networks over WAN connections between business locations in an enterprise network. One of the strengths of MPLS is its QoS (quality of service) properties, which facilitate the rapid transfer of packets using time-sensitive protocols such as VoIP and H.323.

MPLS employs two types of devices: label edge routers (LERs) and label switch routers (LSRs). Label edge routers are used at the boundaries of an MPLS network; LERs push a label onto incoming packets that enter the network. LSRs make packet-forwarding decisions based upon the value of the label. When a packet leaves the MPLS network, another LER pops the label off the packet and forwards it out of the MPLS network.

SONET *Synchronous Optical Networking* (SONET) is a class of telecommunications network transport technologies transmitted over fiber optic networks. It is a multiplexed network technology that can be used to transport voice and data communications at very high speeds over long distances.

SONET networks are almost exclusively built and operated by telecommunications network providers that sell voice and data connectivity services to businesses. Often, the endpoint equipment for SONET networks provides connectivity using a native technology such as MPLS, Ethernet, or T-1.

Telecommunications service providers often encapsulate older services, such as DS0, DS-1, T-1, and Frame Relay, over SONET networks.

The data rates available in SONET networks are shown in Table 5-3. Rates are expressed using the term *Optical Carrier Level*, abbreviated OC.

T-Carrier The term *T-Carrier* refers to a class of multiplexed telecommunications carrier network technologies developed to transport voice and data communications over long distances using copper cabling.

Table 5-3 SONET OC Levels	SONET OC Level	Data Rate
	OC-1	51,840 Kbit/sec
	OC-3	155,520 Kbit/sec
	OC-12	622,080 Kbit/sec
	OC-24	1,244,160 Kbit/sec
	OC-48	2,488,320 Kbit/sec
	OC-192	9,9539280 Kbit/sec
	OC-768	39,813,120 Kbit/sec
	OC-3072	159,252,240 Kbit/sec

Table 5-4	**T-Carrier Class**	**Data Rate**	**Number of DS-0 Channels**
T-Carrier Data	DS-0	64 Kbit/sec	1
Rates and	DS-1 (T-1)	1,544 Kbit/sec	24
Channels in	DS-2	6,312 Kbit/sec	96
North America	DS-3 (T-3)	44,736 Kbit/sec	672
	DS-4	274,176 Kbit/sec	4,032
	DS-5	400,352 Kbit/sec	5,760

The basic service in T-Carrier technology is known as DS-0, which is used to transport a single voice or data circuit. The data rate for a DS-0 is 64 Kbit/sec. Another basic T-Carrier service is the DS-1, also known as T-1. DS-1 contains 24 channels, each a DS-0. The total speed of a DS-1 is 1,544 Kbit/sec. There are additional services, all of which are shown, together with their respective data rates and channels, in Table 5-4. These services are unique to North America.

In Europe, T-Carrier circuits are known instead as E-1 and E-3, which multiplex 32 and 512 64 Kbit/sec circuits, respectively. The European E-Carrier standards are based on multiples of 32 circuits, whereas North American standards are based on multiples of 24 circuits. Otherwise, there isn't much practical difference between them. E-Carrier services are shown in Table 5-5.

T-Carrier and E-Carrier protocols are *synchronous*, which means that packets transported on a T-Carrier or E-Carrier network are transmitted according to the pulses of a centralized clock that is usually controlled by the telecommunications carrier. This is contrasted with Ethernet, which is *asynchronous*, meaning a station on an Ethernet may transmit a frame at any time of its choosing (provided the network is not busy at that exact moment).

Organizations that use a T-Carrier or E-Carrier service to carry data can utilize individual DS-0 channels (which are the same speed as a dial-up connection) or an entire T-1 (or E-1) circuit without multiplexing. This enables use of the entire 1,544 Kbit/sec (T-1) or 2,048 Kbit/sec (E-1) as a single resource.

Frame Relay   *Frame Relay* is a carrier-based, packet-switched network technology. It is most often used to connect remote data networks to a centralized network; for example, a retail store chain might use Frame Relay to connect each of its retail store LANs to the corporate LAN.

Table 5-5	**E-Carrier Class**	**Data Rate**
E-Carrier Services	E1	2,048 Kbit/sec
	E2	8 Mbit/sec
	E3	34 Mbit/sec
	E4	140 Mbit/sec

Frame Relay is often more economical than dedicated DS-0 or DS-1/T-1 circuits. By their nature, Frame Relay backbone networks are shared, in the sense that they transport packets for many customers.

Connections between locations using Frame Relay are made via a permanent virtual circuit (PVC), which is not unlike a VPN, except that the payload is not encrypted. For purposes of security and privacy, PVCs are generally considered private, like a T-1 circuit.

Frame Relay has all but superseded the older X.25 services. MPLS is rapidly overtaking Frame Relay.

ISDN   ISDN, or *Integrated Services Digital Network*, is best described as a digital version of the public-switched telephone network. In many regions of the United States, ISDN was the first "high-speed" Internet access available for residential and small business subscribers.

A subscriber with ISDN service will have a digital modem with one connection to a digital ISDN voice telephone and one connection (typically Ethernet) to a computer. The speed of the computer connection in this configuration is 64 Kbits/sec. Alternatively, the ISDN modem could be configured in a "bonded" state with no voice telephone and only a computer connection at 128 Kbits/sec. Both of these configurations use a BRI (basic rate interface) type of connection.

Higher speeds are also available, up to 1,544 Kbits/sec, and are known as a PRI (primary rate interface) type of connection.

ISDN utilizes a separate, but similar, environment where an ISDN modem "dials" a phone number, similar to dial-up Internet service.

Wide Area Network Devices   This section describes devices used to connect WAN components to each other and to an organization's internal network.

Modem   A modulator-demodulator unit, also known as a *modem*, is a device used to connect a telecommunications carrier network to a computer or a LAN. Early modems consisted of an analog telephone connector for connecting to the public telephone network and a serial port for connecting to a computer. Later versions connect to ISDN, cable, and DSL networks and include an Ethernet port for connecting to a single computer or a LAN.

Multiplexor   A *multiplexor* connects several separate signals and combines them into a single data stream. There are four basic types of multiplexing:

- **Time division**   Separate signals are combined into a pattern, where each individual signal occupies a separate dedicated timeslot.

- **Asynchronous time division multiplexing**   Separate signals are allocated into timeslots of varying sizes depending on need.

- **Frequency division multiplexing**   Separate signals are combined into a single stream, where each separate signal occupies a nonoverlapping frequency.

- **Statistical multiplexing**   Separate signals are inserted into available timeslots. This is different from time division multiplexing, where input signals are assigned to timeslots. In statistical multiplexing, input signals are dynamically assigned to available timeslots.

Channel Service Unit/Digital Service Unit   Also known as a CSU/DSU, this device is used to connect a telecommunications circuit (typically, a T-1 line) to a device such as a router. A CSU/DSU is essentially a modem for T-1 and similar telecomm technologies.

WAN Switch   *WAN switch* is a general term that encompasses several types of WAN switching devices, including ATM switches, Frame Relay switches, MPLS switches, and ISDN switches. See the respective sections on these technologies earlier in this chapter.

Router   A *router* is a device used to connect two or more logical local (occupying the same subnet) networks together. In the context of WANs, a router would be used to connect two or more WANs to each other.

See also the discussion of routers in the "TCP/IP Protocols and Devices" section, later in this chapter.

Wireless Networks

Several types of wireless technologies are available to organizations that want to implement data communications without constructing or maintaining a wiring plant. Furthermore, wireless networks permit devices to move from place to place, even outside of buildings, facilitating highly flexible and convenient means for high-speed communications.

The technologies discussed in this section are the type that an organization would set up on its own, without any services required from a telecommunications service provider.

Wi-Fi   *Wi-Fi* describes several similar standards developed around the IEEE 802.11i/a/b/n/ac/ad/af/ah/aj/aq/ax/ay/n standards. Wi-Fi, or WLAN, permits computers to communicate with each other wirelessly at high speeds over moderate distances from each other. The term "Wi-Fi" is a trademark of the Wi-Fi Alliance for certifying products as compatible with IEEE 802.11 standards. The generic term describing networks based on IEEE 802.11 standards is wireless LAN, or WLAN, although this term is not often used.

Wi-Fi Standards   The various Wi-Fi standards are outlined in Table 5-6.

Standard	Year Introduced	Maximum Data Rate	Indoor Range
802.11a	1999	54 Mbit/sec	35 m
802.11b	1999	11 Mbit/sec	38 m
802.11g	2003	54 Mbit/sec	38 m
802.11n	2009	150 Mbit/sec	70 m
802.11ad	2012	6.75 Gbit/sec	60 m
802.11ac	2013	780 Mbit/sec	35 m
802.11af	2014	568.9 Mbit/s	1 km
802.11ah	2017	347 Mbit/s	1 km
802.11ai	2017	This standard is concerned with faster connection setup time.	
802.11aj	2017	6.75 Gbit/sec	60 m

Table 5-6   Comparison of Wi-Fi Standards

Wi-Fi Security   Wi-Fi networks can be configured with several security features that protect the privacy as well as the availability of the Wi-Fi network. Available features include

- **Authentication**   Individual stations that want to connect with a Wi-Fi network can be required to provide an encryption key. Furthermore, the user may be required to provide a user ID and password. Without this information, a station is unable to connect to the Wi-Fi network and communicate with it. Wi-Fi access points can contain a list of user IDs and passwords, or they can be configured to utilize a network-based authentication service such as RADIUS, LDAP, or Active Directory. Use of the latter generally makes more sense for organizations that want to centralize user authentication information; this also makes access simpler for employees, who do not need to remember yet another user ID and password.

- **Access control**   A Wi-Fi network can be configured to permit only stations with known MAC addresses or specific digital certificates to connect to it. Any station without a permitted address or certificate will not be able to connect.

- **Encryption**   A Wi-Fi network can use encryption to protect traffic from interception through over-the-air eavesdropping. It can encrypt with the WEP (Wired Equivalent Privacy; now deprecated and should not be used), WPA (Wi-Fi Protected Access), WPA2, or WPA3 method. A Wi-Fi network can also be configured not to use encryption, in which case another station may be able to eavesdrop on any communications on the wireless network. When a Wi-Fi network uses encryption, only the airlink communications are encrypted; network traffic from the Wi-Fi access point to other networks will not be encrypted.

- **Network identifier**   A Wi-Fi access point is configured with a service set identifier (SSID) that identifies the network. For organizations that provide network access only for their own personnel, it is recommended that the SSID *not* be set to a value that makes the ownership or identity of the access point obvious. Using a company name, for instance, is not a good idea. Instead, a word—even a random set of characters—that does not relate to the organization's identity should be used. The reason for this is that the SSID will not itself identify the owner of the network, which could, in some circumstances, invite outsiders to attempt to access it. An exception to this is a "public hotspot" used to provide free network access, where the SSID will clearly identify the establishment providing access.

- **Broadcast**   A Wi-Fi access point can be configured to broadcast its SSID, making it easier for users to discover and connect to the network. However, broadcasting SSIDs also alerts outsiders to the presence of the network, which can compromise network security by encouraging someone to attempt to connect to it. However, turning off the SSID broadcast does not make the network absolutely secure: a determined intruder can obtain tools that will enable him or her to discover the presence of a Wi-Fi network that does not broadcast its SSID.

- **Signal strength** The transmit signal strength of a Wi-Fi access point can be configured so that radio signals from the access point do not significantly exceed the service area. Often, signal strength of access points will be set to maximum, which provides persons outside the physical premises with a strong signal. Instead, transmit signal strength should be turned down so that as small a signal as possible leaves the physical premises. This is a challenge in shared-space office buildings, however, and thus cannot be used as a Wi-Fi network's *only* security control.

CAUTION Because a Wi-Fi network utilizes radio signals, an untrusted outsider is able to intercept those signals, which could provide enough information for that outsider to penetrate the network. It is for this reason that all of the controls discussed in this section should be utilized to provide an effective defense-in-depth security protection.

WiMAX *WiMAX* (Worldwide Interoperability for Microwave Access) is a set of wireless telecommunications protocols that provides data throughput from 30 Mbit/sec to 1 Gbit/sec. WiMAX is an implementation of the IEEE 802.16 standard.

WiMAX networks were in service in the 2000s but have been largely discontinued in favor of LTE.

LTE *LTE* (Long Term Evolution) is a telecommunications standard for wireless voice and data communications for smartphones, mobile devices, and wireless broadband modems. LTE is a shared-medium technology that provides data rates up to 300 Mbit/sec.

Bluetooth *Bluetooth* is a short-range airlink standard for data communications between computer peripherals and low power consumption devices. Designed as a replacement for short-range cabling, Bluetooth also provides security via authentication and encryption.

Applications using Bluetooth include

- Mobile phone earsets
- In-car audio for smartphones
- Data transfer between smartphones and computers
- Music player headphones
- Computer mice, keyboards, and other low-power and low-speed peripherals
- Printers and scanners

Bluetooth is a lower-power standard, which supports the use of very small devices, such as mobile phone earsets. And yet, a new standard, Bluetooth Low Energy (BLE), uses far less power for devices such as security tokens. The Bluetooth standard includes one-time authentication of devices using a process called *pairing*. Communications over Bluetooth can also be encrypted so that any eavesdropping is made ineffective. Data rates range from 1 to 24 Mbit/sec.

WUSB   *Wireless USB* (WUSB) is a short-range, high-bandwidth wireless protocol used for personal area networks (PANs). Data rates range from 110 to 480 Mbit/sec. WUSB is typically used to connect computer peripherals that would otherwise be connected with cables.

WUSB can be thought of as a competitor to Bluetooth, and due to Bluetooth's success, WUSB is not widely used.

NFC   *Near-Field Communications* (NFC) is a standard of extremely short-distance radio frequencies that are commonly used for merchant payment applications. The typical maximum range for NFC is 10 centimeters (4 in.).

NFC supports two types of communications: active-active and active-passive. In active-active mode, the base station and the wireless node electronically transmit messages over the NFC airlink. In active-passive mode, the wireless node has no active power supply and instead behaves more like an RFID (radio frequency identification) card. Throughput rates range from 106 to 848 Kbit/sec.

Common applications of NFC include merchant payments using a mobile phone or credit card–sized card, and advanced building access control systems.

IrDA   IrDA (Infrared Data Association) is an organization that has developed technical standards for point-to-point data communications using infrared light. IrDA has been used for communications between devices such as laptop computers, PDAs, and printers.

IrDA is not considered a secure protocol: there is no authentication or encryption of IrDA-based communications.

Bluetooth and USB have largely replaced IrDA, and few IrDA-capable devices are now sold.

TCP/IP Protocols and Devices

TCP/IP, the technology that the Internet is built upon, contains numerous protocols. This section discusses many of the well-known protocols, layer by layer. First, link layer protocols are discussed, followed by Internet layer protocols, then transport layer protocols, and finally application layer protocols. This is followed by a discussion of network devices that are used to build TCP/IP networks.

Link Layer Protocols   The link layer (sometimes referred to as the network access layer) is the lowest logical layer in the TCP/IP protocol suite. Several protocols have been implemented as link layer protocols, including

- **ARP (Address Resolution Protocol)**   This protocol is used when a station on a network needs to find another station's MAC address when it knows its Internet layer (IP) address. Basically, a station sends a broadcast on a local network, asking, in effect, "What station on this network has IP address xx.xx.xx.xx?" If any station on the network does have this IP address, it responds to the sender. When the sending station receives the reply, the receiving station's MAC address is contained in the reply, and the sending station can now send messages to the destination station since it knows its MAC address. Another type of ARP message is known as a *gratuitous ARP* message that informs other stations on the network of the station's IP and MAC addresses, regardless of whether it was requested to do so or not. Gratuitous ARP messages can be used in network attacks and are often blocked by the switch.

- **RARP (Reverse Address Resolution Protocol)**   This protocol is used by a station that needs to know its own Internet layer (IP) address. A station sends a broadcast on a local network, asking, "This is my MAC address (xx.xx.xx.xx.xx.xx). What is my IP address supposed to be?" If a station configured to respond to RARP requests exists on the network, it will respond to the querying station with an assigned IP address. RARP has been largely superseded by BOOTP (Bootstrap Protocol) and later by DHCP.

- **OSPF (Open Shortest Path First)**   This routing protocol is implemented in the TCP/IP Internet layer. The purpose and function of routing protocols are discussed in detail later in this section.

- **L2TP (Layer 2 Tunneling Protocol)**   This tunneling protocol is implemented in the link layer. The purpose and function of tunneling protocols are discussed later in this section.

- **PPP (Point-to-Point Protocol)**   This packet-oriented protocol is used mainly over point-to-point physical connections such as RS-232 or HSSI (High-Speed Serial Interface) between computers.

- **Media Access Control (MAC)**   This is the underlying communications standard used by various media such as Ethernet, DSL, MPLS, and ISDN.

Internet Layer Protocols   Internet layer protocols are the fundamental building blocks of TCP/IP. The Internet layer is the lowest layer where a frame or packet is uniquely TCP/IP.

Protocols in the TCP/IP Internet layer include

- IP
- ICMP
- IGMP
- IPsec

IP   IP is the principal protocol used by TCP/IP at the Internet layer. The main transport layer protocols (discussed in the next section), TCP and UDP, are built on IP. The purpose of IP is to transport messages over internetworked networks. IP is the workhorse of the TCP/IP protocol suite: most communications used on the Internet are built on it.

Characteristics of IP include

- **IP addressing**   At the IP layer, nodes on networks have unique addresses. IP addressing is discussed in detail later in this section.

- **Best-effort delivery**   IP does not guarantee that a packet will reach its intended destination.

- **Connectionless** Each packet is individual and not related to any other packet.
- **Out-of-order packet delivery** No assurances for order of delivery are addressed by IP. Packets may arrive out of order at their destination.

Higher layer protocols such as TCP address reliability, connections, and sequence of delivery.

Multicast *Multicast* is a method for sending IP packets to multiple stations in a one-to-many fashion. This enables a sender to send a single packet to any number of receivers. Multicast uses the IP network range 224.0.0.0/24 for originating multicast traffic.

Network infrastructure such as switches and routers take care of the task of receiving individual multicast packets and relaying them to all receivers.

The list of receivers for any given multicast is maintained in multicast groups. Group membership can change in real time without involvement from the originator of the multicast traffic. The protocol used to manage group membership is the Internet Group Management Protocol (IGMP).

ICMP ICMP is used by systems for diagnostic purposes. Primarily, ICMP messages are automatically issued whenever there are problems with IP communications between two stations. For example, if one station attempts to send a message to another station, and a router on the network knows that there is no existing route to the destination station, the router will send an ICMP Type 3, Code 1 "No route to host" diagnostic packet back to the sending station to inform it that the destination station is not reachable.

ICMP message types are shown in Table 5-7.

The well-known "ping" command uses the ICMP 8 Echo Request packet type. If the target station is reachable, it will respond with ICMP 1 Echo Reply packets. The ping command is used to determine whether a particular system is reachable from another system over a TCP/IP network.

 NOTE The absence of a response to a ping message does not necessarily mean that the system does not exist or is not communicating. Some organizations block ICMP echo request messages at their network boundaries for security purposes.

IGMP IGMP provides a type of communications called *multicast*. Multicast is discussed earlier in this section.

IPsec The IPsec suite of protocols is used to secure IP-based communication. The security that IPsec provides is in the form of authentication and encryption.

IPsec authentication is used to confirm the identity of a station on a network. This is used to prevent a rogue system from easily masquerading as another, real system. Authentication is achieved through the establishment of a security association (SA) between two nodes, which permits the transmission of data from the originating node to the destination node. If the two nodes need to send messages in both directions,

Table 5-7	ICMP Message Type	Definition
ICMP Message Types	0	Echo reply
	1	(reserved)
	2	(reserved)
	3	Destination unreachable (contains 14 subcodes that describe the reason in detail)
	4	Source quench
	5	Redirect message (with 4 subcodes)
	6	Alternate host address
	7	(reserved)
	8	Echo request
	9	Router advertisement
	10	Router solicitation
	11	Time exceeded (with 2 reason subcodes)
	12	Parameter problem: bad IP header (with 3 reason subcodes)
	13	Timestamp
	14	Timestamp reply
	15	Information request
	16	Information reply
	17	Address mask request
	18	Address mask reply
	19–29	(reserved)
	30	Traceroute
	31–255	(seldom used or reserved for future use)

two SAs need to be established. The *Internet Key Exchange* (IKE) protocol is used to set up associations.

IPsec has two primary modes of operation:

- **Transport mode**   Only the payload of an incoming packet is authenticated or encrypted. The original IP header is left intact. The original headers are protected with hashes; if the headers are altered, the hashes will fail and an error will occur.

- **Tunnel mode**   Each entire incoming packet is encapsulated within an IPsec packet. The entire incoming packet can be encrypted, which protects the packet against eavesdropping. This mode is often used for protecting network traffic that traverses the Internet, thereby creating a VPN between two nodes, between two networks, or between a remote node and a network. IPsec tunnel mode is shown in Figure 5-21.

Figure 5-21 IPsec tunnel mode protects all traffic between two remote networks.

Internet Layer Node Addressing: IPv4 To specify the source and destination of messages, TCP/IP utilizes a numeric address scheme. In TCP/IP, a station's address is known as an "IP address." On a given network, no two stations will have the same IP address; this uniqueness permits any station to communicate directly with any other station.

The TCP/IP address scheme also includes a *subnet mask*, which permits a station to determine whether any particular IP address resides on the same subnetwork. Furthermore, an IP address plan usually includes a *default gateway*, a station on the network that is able to forward messages to stations on other subnets or networks.

IP Addresses and Subnets The notation of an IP address is four sets of integers, separated by periods. The value of each integer may range from 0 through 255; hence, each integer is an eight-bit value. A typical IP address is 141.204.13.240. The entire IP address is 32 bits in length.

Each station on a network is assigned a unique IP address. Uniqueness permits any station to send messages to any other station; the station needs to know only the IP address of a destination station.

A larger organization may have hundreds, thousands, or even tens of thousands of stations on many networks. Typically, a network is the interconnection of computers within a single building or even part of a building. Within a larger building or collection of buildings, the individual networks are called subnetworks, or subnets. Those subnets are joined together by network devices such as routers or switches; they function as gateways between networks.

Subnet Mask A *subnet mask* is a numeric value that determines which portion of an IP address is used to identify the network and which portion is used to identify a station on the network.

For example, an organization has the network 141.204.13. On this network the organization can have up to 256 stations, numbered 0 through 255. Example station IP addresses on the network are 141.204.13.5, 141.204.13.15, and 141.204.13.200.

A subnet mask actually works at the bit level. A "1" signifies that a bit in the same position in an IP address is the *network identifier*, while a "0" signifies that a bit in the same position is part of the station's address. In the previous example, where the first three numbers in the IP address signify the network, the subnet mask would be 255.255.255.0. This is illustrated in Figure 5-22.

Station IP Address	141.204.13.15	10001101.11001100.00001101.00001111
Subnet Mask	255.255.255.0	11111111.11111111.11111111.00000000
Network Portion	141.204.13.0	10001101.11001100.00001101.00000000
Station Portion	0.0.0.15	00000000.00000000.00000000.00001111

Network Address   Station Address

Figure 5-22 A subnet mask denotes which part of an IP address signifies a network and which part signifies a station on the network.

Default Gateway Networks are usually interconnected so that a station on one network is able to communicate with a station on any other connected network (subject to any security restrictions). When a station wants to send a packet to another station, the sending station will examine its own network ID (by comparing its IP address to the subnet mask) and compare that to the IP address of the destination. If the destination station is on the same network, the station may simply send the packet directly to the destination station.

If, however, the destination station is on a different network, the sending station cannot send the packet to it directly. Instead, the sending station will send the packet to a node called the *default gateway*—usually a router that has knowledge of neighboring and distant networks and is capable of forwarding packets toward their destination. Any network that is interconnected to other networks will have a *default gateway*, which is where all packets for "other" or "unknown" networks are sent. The default gateway will forward the packet closer to its ultimate destination. A default gateway can be thought of as "the way out of this network to all other networks."

For example, suppose a station at IP address 141.204.13.15 wants to send a packet to a station at IP address 141.204.21.110. The sending station's subnet mask is 255.255.255.0, which means it is on network 141.204.13. This is a different network from 141.204.21.110, so the sending station will send the packet instead to the default gateway at 141.204.13.1, a router that can forward the packet to 141.204.21.110.

When the packet reaches a router that is connected to the 141.204.21 network, that router can send the packet directly to the destination station, which is on the same network as the router.

Classful Networks The original plan for subnets and subnet masks allowed for the network/node address boundary to align with the decimals in IP addresses. This was expressed in several classes of networks, shown in Table 5-8.

The matter of the shortage of usable IP addresses in the global Internet is related to classful networks. This is discussed later in this chapter in the section "The Global Internet."

Table 5-8
Classes of
Networks

Class	Subnet Mask	Number of Stations Per Network
A	255.0.0.0	16,777,216
B	255.255.0.0	65,536
C	255.255.255.0	256

Table 5-8 Classes of Networks

Classless Networks   It became clear that the rigidity of Class A, Class B, and Class C networks as the only ways to create subnets was wasteful. For instance, the smallest subnet available was a Class C network with its 256 available addresses. If a given subnet had only one station on it, the other 255 addresses were wasted and unused. This situation gave rise to *classless networks*, where subnet masks could divide networks at any arbitrary boundary.

Classless networks don't have names like the classful networks' Class A, Class B, and Class C. Instead, they just have subnet masks that help to serve the purpose of preserving IP addresses and allocating them more efficiently. The method, classless interdomain routing (CIDR), is used to create subnets with any arbitrary subnet mask.

Table 5-9 shows some example subnet masks that can be used to allocate IP addresses to smaller networks.

A more rapid way of expressing an IP address with its accompanying subnet mask has been developed, where the number of bits in the subnet mask follows the IP address after a slash. For example, the IP address 141.204.13.15/26 means the subnet mask is the first 26 bits (in binary) of the IP address, or 255.255.255.192. This is easier than expressing the IP address and subnet mask separately.

Virtual Networks (VLANs)   In the preceding discussions of IP addresses and subnets, the classic design of TCP/IP LANs specifies that LANs are physically separate. Each LAN will have its own physical cabling and devices.

Virtual networks, known as VLANs, are logically separate networks that occupy the same physical network. VLANs are made possible through advanced configuration of network devices, including switches and routers.

Subnet Mask (Decimal)	Subnet Mask (Binary)	CIDR Notation	Number of Nodes
255.255.255.254	11111111.11111111.11111111.11111110	/31	2
255.255.255.252	11111111.11111111.11111111.11111100	/30	4
255.255.255.248	11111111.11111111.11111111.11111000	/29	8
255.255.255.240	11111111.11111111.11111111.11110000	/28	16
255.255.255.224	11111111.11111111.11111111.11100000	/27	32
255.255.255.192	11111111.11111111.11111111.11000000	/26	64
255.255.255.128	11111111.11111111.11111111.10000000	/25	128
255.255.255.0	11111111.11111111.11111111.00000000	/24	256

Table 5-9   Classless Network Subnet Masks

The primary advantage of VLAN technology is the cost savings realized through the use of fewer network cables and devices. Another advantage of VLAN technology is the ability to divide a single network into logically separate networks, thereby creating smaller broadcast domains and reducing the potential for information leakage.

The main disadvantage is that, while they are logically separate, VLANs occupy a single physical medium: traffic on one VLAN has the potential to disrupt traffic on other VLANs, since they must share the physical network. Even with QoS capabilities, a given physical network has finite bandwidth that all VLANs must share.

Special IP Addresses   Other IP addresses are used in IP that have not been discussed thus far. These other addresses and their functions are

- **Loopback**   The IP address 127.0.0.1 (or any other address in the entire 127 address block) is a special "loopback" address that is analogous to earlier technologies, where a physical loopback plug would be connected to a network connector to confirm communications within a system or device. The 127.0.0.1 loopback address serves the same function. If a system attempts to connect to a system at IP address 127.0.0.1, it is essentially communicating with itself. A system that is able to connect to itself through its loopback address is testing its IP drivers within the operating system; during network troubleshooting, it is common to issue a "ping 127.0.0.1" or similar command to verify whether the computer's IP software is functioning correctly.

- **Broadcast**   The highest numeric IP address in an IP subnet is its broadcast address. When a packet is sent to a network's broadcast address, all active stations on the network will logically receive and potentially act on the incoming message. For example, in the network 141.204.13/24, the broadcast address is 141.204.13.255. Any packet sent to that address would be sent to all stations. A ping command sent to a network's broadcast address will cause all stations to respond with an echo reply.

Internet Layer Node Addressing: IPv6   The IP version IPv4 had a number of shortcomings, namely in the total number of available IP addresses for use in the global Internet. The new version, IPv6, takes care of the problem of available addresses, as well as other matters.

The total number of IP addresses available in IPv4 is 2^{32}, or 4,294,967,296 addresses. Because IP was originally designed prior to the proliferation of network-enabled devices, over 4 billion available IP addresses seemed more than sufficient to meet world demand. The number of IP addresses available in IPv6 is 2^{128}, or about 3.4×10^{38} addresses.

Many new network-enabled devices support IPv6, which is enabling organizations to slowly migrate their networks. However, it is expected that IPv4 will be with us for many years. Network devices today support "dual stack" networks where IPv4 and IPv6 coexist on the same network medium.

The format of an IPv6 address is eight groups of four hexadecimal digits, separated by colons. For example,

```
2001:0db8:0000:0042:0000:07cc:1028:1948
```

Unlike IPv4 with its various schemes of subnetting, the standard size of an IPv6 subnet is 64 bits. Protocols for assigning addresses to individual nodes such as stateless address autoconfiguration generally work with /64 networks.

Transport Layer Protocols The two principal protocols in TCP/IP's transport layer are TCP and UDP. The majority of Internet communications are based on these. This section explores TCP and UDP in detail.

TCP and UDP support the two primary types of Internet-based communication: that which requires highly reliable and ordered message delivery, and that which has a high tolerance for lost messages, respectively. TCP and UDP are uniquely designed for these two scenarios.

TCP TCP is a highly reliable messaging protocol that is used in situations where high-integrity messaging is required. The main characteristics of TCP-based network traffic are

- **Unique connections** TCP utilizes a *connection* between two stations. TCP supports several concurrent connections between any two stations, potentially numbering in the tens of thousands.

- **Guaranteed message integrity** TCP performs checks on the sent and received segments to ensure that the segments arrived at their destination fully intact. If the checksum indicates that the segment was altered in transit, TCP will handle retransmission.

- **Guaranteed delivery** TCP guarantees message delivery. This means that if an application sends a message to another application over an established TCP connection and the function sending the message receives a "success" code from the operating system, then the message was successfully delivered to the destination system. This is contrasted with the message delivery used by UDP that is discussed later in this section.

- **Guaranteed delivery sequence** Segments sent using TCP include sequence numbers so that the destination system can assemble arriving segments into the correct order. This guarantees that an application receiving segments from a sending application over TCP can be confident that segments are arriving in the same order in which they were sent.

UDP UDP is a lightweight messaging protocol used in situations where speed and low overhead are more important than guaranteed delivery and delivery sequence.

Unlike the connection-oriented TCP, UDP is *connectionless*. This means that UDP does not need to set up a connection between sending and receiving systems before datagrams can be sent; instead, the sending system just sends its datagrams to the destination system. Like TCP, datagrams can be sent to a specific port number on a destination system.

UDP does nothing to assure order of delivery. Hence, it is entirely possible that datagrams may arrive at the destination system out of order. In practice, this is a rarity, but the point is that UDP does not make any effort to reassemble datagrams into their original order upon arrival.

One might ask, why use UDP with all these shortcomings? The answer is efficiency and throughput. Without the overhead of connections and acknowledgment for every packet, UDP is simpler and requires far less bandwidth than TCP.

Protocol Data Units (PDUs)

In the telecommunications and network industry, discrete terms are used to signify the messages that are created at various layers of encapsulated protocols such as TCP/IP. These terms include

Technology	PDU
Network cable	Bit
Ethernet	Frame
ATM	Cell
TCP	Segment
UDP	Datagram
IP	Packet

Frequently, the term *packet* is used to signify messages at every layer, although it is useful to know the specific terms used for each.

Furthermore, not only does UDP not guarantee the sequence of delivery, but it also does not even guarantee that the destination system will receive a datagram. In UDP, when an application sends a message to a target system, the "success" error code returned by the operating system means only that the datagram was sent. The sending system receives no confirmation that the datagram was received by the destination system.

Application Layer Protocols   Scores of protocols have been developed for the TCP/IP application layer. Several are discussed in this section; they are grouped by the type of service that they provide.

File Transfer Protocols

- **FTP (File Transfer Protocol)**   An early and still widely used protocol for batch transfer of files or entire directories from one system to another. FTP is supported by most modern operating systems, including Unix, OS X, and Windows. One drawback of FTP is that the login credentials (and all data) are transmitted unencrypted, which means that anyone eavesdropping on network communications can easily intercept them and reuse them for potentially malicious purposes.

- **FTPS (File Transfer Protocol Secure, or FTP-SSL)**   This is an extension to the FTP protocol where authentication and file transfer are encrypted using SSL or TLS.

- **SFTP (SSH File Transfer Protocol, also Secure File Transfer Protocol)**   This is an extension to the FTP protocol where authentication and file transfer are encrypted using SSH.

- **SCP (Secure Copy)**   This is a file transfer protocol that is similar to rcp (remote copy) but which is protected using SSH.

- **rcp (remote copy)**   This is an early Unix-based file transfer protocol that is used to copy files or directories from system to system. The main drawback with rcp is the lack of encryption of credentials for transferred data.

Messaging Protocols

- **SMTP (Simple Mail Transfer Protocol)**   This is the protocol used to transport virtually all e-mail over the Internet. SMTP is used to route e-mail messages from their source over the Internet to a destination e-mail server. It is an early protocol that lacks authentication and encryption. It is partly for this reason that people should consider their e-mail to be nonprivate.

- **SMTPS (Simple Mail Transfer Protocol Secure)**   This is a security-enhanced version of SMTP that incorporates TLS. It is sometimes known as "SMTP over TLS."

- **POP (Post Office Protocol)**   This is a protocol used by an end-user e-mail program to retrieve messages from an e-mail server. POP is not particularly secure because user credentials and messages are transported without encryption.

- **IMAP (Internet Message Access Protocol)**   Like POP, this protocol is used by an end-user program to retrieve e-mail messages from an e-mail server.

- **NNTP (Network News Transport Protocol)**   This is the protocol used to transport Usenet news throughout the Internet, and from news servers to end users using news-reading programs. Usenet news has been largely deprecated by web-based applications.

File and Directory Sharing Protocols

- **NFS (Network File System)**   This protocol was developed to make a disk-based resource on another computer appear as a logical volume on a local computer. The NFS protocol transmits the disk requests and replies over the network.

- **RPC (Remote Procedure Call)**   This protocol is used to permit a running process to make a procedure call to a process running on another computer. RPC supports a variety of functions that permit various types of client-server computing.

Session Protocols

- **Telnet**   This is an early protocol that is used to establish a command-line session on a remote computer. Telnet does not encrypt user credentials as they are transmitted over the network.

- **rlogin**   This is an early Unix-based protocol used to establish a command-line session on a remote system. Like Telnet, rlogin does not encrypt authentication or session contents.

- **SSH (Secure Shell)**   This protocol provides a secure channel between two computers whereby all communications between them are encrypted. SSH can also be used as a tunnel to encapsulate and thereby protect other protocols.

- **HTTP (Hypertext Transfer Protocol)**   This protocol is used to transmit web page contents from web servers to users who are using web browsers.

- **HTTPS (Hypertext Transfer Protocol Secure)**   This is similar to HTTP in its use for transporting data between web servers and browsers. HTTPS is not a separate protocol, but instead is the instance where HTTP is encrypted with SSL or TLS.

- **RDP (Remote Desktop Protocol)**   This proprietary protocol from Microsoft is used to establish a graphical console interface to another computer.

Management Protocols

- **SNMP (Simple Network Management Protocol)**   This protocol is used by network devices and systems to transmit management messages indicating a need for administrative attention. SNMP is used to monitor networks and their components; SNMP messages are generated when events warrant attention by network engineers or system engineers. In larger organizations, SNMP messages are collected by a network management system that displays the network topology and devices that require attention.

- **NTP (Network Time Protocol)**   This protocol is used to synchronize the time-of-day clocks on systems, using time-reference standards. The use of NTP is vital because the time clocks in computers often drift (run too fast or too slow), and it is important for all computers' time clocks in an organization to be precisely the same so that complex events can be more easily managed and correlated.

Directory Services Protocols

- **DNS (Domain Name System)**   This is a vital Internet-based service that is used to translate domain names (such as www.isecbooks.com) into IP addresses. A call to a DNS server is a prerequisite for system-to-system communications where one system wants to establish a communications session with another system and where it knows only the domain name for the target system.

- **LDAP (Lightweight Directory Access Protocol)**   This protocol is used as a directory service for people and computing resources. LDAP is frequently used as an enterprise authentication and computing resource service. Microsoft Active Directory is an adaptation of LDAP.

- **X.500**   This protocol is a functional predecessor to LDAP that provides directory services.

TCP/IP Network Devices   Network devices are required to facilitate the transmission of packets among TCP/IP networks. These devices include

- **Router**   This device is used to connect two or more separate TCP/IP networks to each other. A router typically has two or more network interface connectors, each of which is connected to a separate network. A router that is used to connect LANs is typically equipped with Ethernet interfaces, while a router used to connect LANs with WANs will have one or more Ethernet connectors and one or more connectors for WAN protocols such as SONET or MPLS. A router may also have an *access control list* (ACL, which is functionally similar to a firewall) that the router uses to determine whether packets passing through it should be permitted to proceed to their destination.

- **Firewall**   This device is used to control which network packets are permitted to cross network boundaries. Typically, a firewall will block or permit packets to pass based on their source IP address, destination IP address, and protocol. Firewalls are typically used at an organization's network boundary to protect it from unwanted network traffic from the Internet but still permit traffic to the organization's e-mail and web servers, for instance.

- **Application firewall**   This device is used to control packets being sent to an application server, blocking those that contain unwanted or malicious content. An application firewall can help to protect a web server from attacks such as SQL injection or buffer overflow.

- **Intrusion prevention system (IPS)**   This device is used to detect and potentially block network packets that may be malicious.

- **Proxy server**   This device is typically used to control end-user access to web sites on the Internet. A proxy server typically controls access according to policy.

- **Layer 3 switch**   This device routes packets between different VLANs. Functionally, this is the same as a router; a router performs network routing using software running on a microprocessor, while a layer 3 switch performs this routing using a dedicated application-specific integrated circuit (ASIC), giving it much better performance than a router.

- **Layer 4 switch**   This device is used to route packets to destinations based on TCP and UDP port numbers.

- **Layer 4-7 switch**   Also known as a content switch, web switch, or application switch, this device is used to route packets to destinations based on their internal content. Layer 4-7 switches can be used to route incoming network traffic intelligently to various servers based on policy, performance, or availability.

Interestingly, the names of layer 3, layer 4, and layer 4-7 switches are based on their OSI network model layers even though these are TCP network devices.

Other network devices such as hubs, switches, and gateways are discussed in the section "Ethernet," earlier in this chapter.

Software-Defined Networking   *Software-defined networking* (SDN) is a new class of capabilities where network infrastructure is created, configured, and managed in the context of virtualization. In SDN, routers, firewalls, switches, IPSs, and other network devices are no longer physical devices but software programs that run in virtualized environments.

SDN gives organizations greater agility with regard to their network infrastructure: instead of procuring additional network devices as network infrastructure needs grow and change, virtual network devices are instantiated and deployed immediately.

Organizations and groups of organizations are developing SDN standards, such as OpenFlow, to build consistent practices to SDN.

Addresses	Name	Total Number of Networks Available	Addresses per Network
1.0.0.0–126.255.255.255	Class A networks	126	16,777,124
128.0.0.0–191.255.255.255	Class B networks	16,384	65,532
192.0.0.0–223.255.255.255	Class C networks	2,097,152	254

Table 5-10   Internet IP Address Allocation

The Global Internet

The TCP/IP networks owned by businesses, government, military, and educational institutions are interconnected; collectively this is known as the global Internet—or just the Internet. It is in the context of the global Internet that TCP/IP topics such as node addressing, routing, domain naming, and other matters are most relevant.

IP Addressing   The allocation of routable IP addresses is coordinated through a central governing body known as the Internet Assigned Numbers Authority (IANA). This coordination is necessary so that duplicate addresses are not allocated, which would cause confusion and unreachable systems.

The original IP address allocation scheme appears in Table 5-10.

When TCP/IP was established, the entire IP address space (that is, the entire range of possible addresses from 1.1.1.1 through 255.255.255.255) appeared to be far more than would ever be needed. However, it soon became apparent that the original IP address allocation scheme was woefully inadequate. This led to the establishment of ranges for private networks and rules for their use. Private address ranges are listed in Table 5-11.

Availability of a sufficient number of publicly routable IP addresses has been addressed with IPv6. See the sidebar on IPv6 earlier in this chapter.

NOTE   The number of available addresses does not take network IDs and broadcast addresses into account, which will make the number of actual addresses lower. This will vary, based upon how networks are subnetted.

The private addresses listed in Table 5-11 are not "routable." This means that no router on the Internet is permitted to forward a packet with any IP address within any of the private address ranges. These IP addresses are intended for use wholly *within* organizations to facilitate communication among internal systems. When any system with a private address needs to communicate with a system on the Internet, its

Table 5-11
Private Address
Ranges

Address Range	Available Addresses
10.0.0.0–10.255.255.255	16,777,214
172.16.0.0–172.31.255.255	1,048,576
192.168.0.0–192.168.255.255	131,072

communication is required to pass through a gateway that will translate the internal IP address to a public routable IP address. The NAT (Network Address Translation) method is often used for this purpose.

Domain Name System The Internet utilizes the Domain Name System (DNS), a centrally coordinated domain name registration system. Several independent *domain registrars* are licensed to issue new domain names to individuals and corporations in exchange for modest fees. These domain registrars often also provide DNS services on behalf of each domain name's owner.

New and changed domain names are periodically uploaded to the Internet's "root" DNS servers, enabling users to access services by referring to domain names such as www.myblogsite.com.

Network Routing Routers used by Internet service providers (ISPs) receive and forward IP traffic to and from any of the millions of systems that are connected to the Internet. These big routers exchange information on the whereabouts of all publicly reachable networks in large "routing tables" that contain rules about the topology of the Internet and the addresses and locations of networks. Internet routers exchange this information through the use of routing protocols, which are "out-of-band" messages that contain updates to the topology and IP addressing of the Internet. Some of these protocols are

- BGP (Border Gateway Protocol)
- OSPF (Open Shortest Path First)
- IGRP (Interior Gateway Routing Protocol)
- EIGRP (Enhanced Interior Gateway Routing Protocol)
- EGP (Exterior Gateway Protocol, now obsolete)
- IS-IS (Intermediate System to Intermediate System)
- RIP (Routing Information Protocol; this is one of the earliest protocols and no longer used for Internet routing)

Organizations with several internal networks also use one or more of these routing protocols so that their routers can keep track of the changing topology and addressing of its network.

Global Internet Applications Applications are what make the Internet popular. From electronic banking to e-commerce, entertainment, news, television, and movies, applications on the Internet have made it possible for people anywhere to view or receive virtually any kind of information and content.

The World Wide Web The World Wide Web encompasses all of the world's web servers, which are accessible from workstations of many types that use web browser programs. Requests to web servers, and content returned to browsers, are issued using HTTP and HTTPS. Content sent to browsers consists primarily of text written in HTML, as well as rich text, including images and dynamic content such as audio and video.

The World Wide Web rapidly gained in popularity because information and applications could be accessed from anywhere without any special software. Readily available tools simplified the publication of many types of data to the Web.

The most critical service that supports the World Wide Web is DNS. This service translates server domain names into IP addresses. For example, if a user wants to visit www.mheducation.com, the operating system running the user's browser will make a request to a local DNS server for the IP address corresponding to www.mheducation. com. After the DNS server responds with the server's IP address, the user's browser can issue a request to the server (at 52.4.128.203) and then receive content from the server.

Web servers can act as application servers. Authenticated users can receive menus, data entry screens and forms, query results, and reports, all written in HTML, all with only web browser software. Web servers that function as application servers have built-in protocols to communicate to back-end application servers and database management systems.

E-mail　Electronic mail was one of the Internet's first applications. E-mail existed before the Internet, but it was implemented on the Internet as a way to send messages not only *within* organizations but also *between* them. The SMTP, POP, and IMAP protocols were developed and adopted early on, and are still widely used today. SMTP remains the backbone of Internet e-mail transport. Organizations increasingly are using SMTPS to protect the contents of e-mail messages.

Instant Messaging　E-mail, while far more rapid than postal-delivered letters, can still be slow at times. Instant messaging (IM), originally developed on DEC PDP-11 computers in the 1970s and on Unix in the early 1980s, was adapted to the Internet in the early 1990s. Like all other Internet applications, IM is based on the TCP/IP protocol suite and enables people all over the world to communicate in real time via text, voice, and video.

Network Tunneling　*Tunneling* refers to a number of protocols that permit communications between two endpoints to be encapsulated in a logical "tunnel." Often, a tunnel is used to protect communications containing sensitive data that is transported over public networks such as the Internet. Packets in a tunnel can be encrypted, which hides the true endpoint IP addresses as well as the message contents, to prevent any intermediate system from eavesdropping on those communications. Tunnels are frequently called virtual private networks (VPNs), because they provide both security (through encryption and authentication) and abstraction (by hiding the details of the path between systems).

VPNs are frequently used for end-user remote access into an organization's network. When an end user wants to connect to an organization's internal network, the network will establish a session with a VPN server and provide authentication credentials. An encrypted tunnel will then be established that gives the end user the appearance of being connected to the internal network.

Network Management

Network management is the function of ensuring that a data network continues to support business objectives. The activities that take place include monitoring network devices, identifying problems, and applying remedies as needed to restore network operations.

The purpose of network management is the continued reliable operation of an organization's data network. A properly functioning data network, in turn, supports business applications that support critical business processes.

Network Management Tools   Network management requires tools that are used to monitor, troubleshoot, and maintain data networks. This permits an IT organization to ensure the continuous operation of its data network so that it has sufficient capacity and capability to support applications and services vital to the organization's ongoing business operations.

The tools that are used to fulfill this mission include

- **Network management system**   This software application collects network management messages that are sent from network devices and systems. These messages alert the management system that certain conditions exist on the device, some of which may require intervention. Some network management systems also contain the means for network administrators and engineers to diagnose and correct conditions that require attention.

- **Network management report**   Network management systems generally have the ability to generate reports showing key metrics such as network availability, utilization, response time, and downtime. Reports from helpdesk systems or incident management systems also help in communicating the health of an organization's networks.

- **Network management agent**   An agent is a small software module that resides on managed network devices and other systems. Agents monitor operations on the device or system and transmit messages to a centralized network management system when needed.

- **Incident management system**   This is a general-purpose ticketing engine that captures and tracks individual incidents and report on an organization's timely response to them. Often, network management systems and incident management systems can be integrated together so that conditions requiring attention in the network can automatically create a ticket that will be used to track the course of the incident until it is closed.

- **Sniffer**   This software program can be installed on a network-attached system or a separate hard device to capture and analyze network traffic.

- **Security incident and event management (SIEM) system**   A SIEM (pronounced "sim") system collects, correlates, analyzes, reports on, and creates actionable alerts based on the individual error and event messages generated by the systems and devices in an environment.

Organizations employing network management tools often implement a NOC staffed with personnel who monitor and manage network devices and services. Often this function is outsourced to a managed security service provider (MSSP).

Networked Applications

Other than simple end-user tools on a business workstation, business applications are rarely installed and used within the context of an individual computer. Instead, many applications are centrally installed and used by many people who are often in many locations. Data networks facilitate the communications between central servers and business workstations. The applications discussed in the following sections are client-server, web-based, and middleware.

Client-Server   *Client-server applications* are a prior-generation technology used to build high-performance business applications. They consist of one or more central application servers, database servers, and business workstations. The central application servers contain some business logic—primarily the instructions to receive and respond to requests sent from workstations. The remainder of the business logic will reside on each business workstation; primarily this is the logic used to display and process forms and reports for the user.

When a user is using a client-server application, he or she is typically selecting functions to input, view, or change information. When information is input, application logic on the business workstation will request, analyze, and accept the information and then transmit it to the central application server for further processing and storage. When viewing information, a user will typically select a viewing function with, perhaps, criteria specifying which information they want to view. Business logic on the workstation will validate this information and then send a request to the central application server, which in turn will respond with information that is then sent back to the workstation and transformed for easy viewing.

The promise of client-server applications was improved performance by removing all application display logic from the central computer and placing that logic on each individual workstation. This scheme succeeded in principle but failed in practice for two principal reasons:

- **Network performance**   Client-server applications often overburdened the organization's data network, and application performance failed when many people were using it at once. A typical example is a database query issued by a workstation that results in thousands of records being returned to the workstation over the network.

- **Workstation software updates**   Keeping the central application software and the software modules on each workstation in sync proved to be problematic. Often, updates required that all workstations be upgraded at the same time. Invariably, some workstations are down or otherwise unavailable for updates (powered down by end users or taken home if they are laptop computers), potentially resulting in application malfunctions for those users.

Organizations that did implement full-scale client-server applications were often dissatisfied with the results. And at nearly the same time, the World Wide Web was invented and soon proved to be a promising, simpler alternative.

Client-server application design has enjoyed a revival with the advent of smartphone and tablet applications, or *apps*, which are often designed as client-server.

Web-Based Applications   With client-server applications declining in favor, web-based applications were the only way forward. The primary characteristics of web-based applications that make them highly favorable include

- **Centralized business logic**   All business logic resides on one or more centralized servers. There are no longer issues related to pushing software updates to workstations since they run web browsers that rarely require updating.

- **Lightweight and universal display logic**   Display logic, such as forms, lists, and other application controls, is easily written in HTML, a simple markup language that displays well on workstations without any application logic on the workstation.

- **Lightweight network requirements**   Unlike client-server applications that would often send large amounts of data from the centralized server to the workstation, web applications send mainly display data to workstations.

- **Workstations requiring few, if any, updates**   Workstations require only browser software. Updates to applications themselves are entirely server-based.

- **Fewer compatibility issues**   Instead of requiring a narrow choice of workstations, web-based applications can run on nearly every kind of workstation, including Unix, Windows, macOS, Chrome OS, or Linux.

Middleware   *Middleware* is a component used in some client-server or web-based application environments to control the processing of communications or transactions. Middleware manages the interaction between major components in larger application environments.

Some of the common types of middleware include

- **Transaction processing (TP) monitors**   A TP monitor manages transactions between application servers and database servers to ensure the integrity of business transactions among a collection of database servers.

- **RPC gateways**   These systems facilitate communications through the suite of RPC protocols between various components of an application environment.

- **Object request broker (ORB) gateways**   An ORB gateway facilitates the execution of transactions across complex, multiserver application environments that use CORBA (Common Object Request Broker Architecture) or Microsoft COM/DCOM technologies.

- **Message servers**   These systems store and forward transactions between systems and ensure the eventual delivery of transactions to the right systems.

Middleware is typically used in a large, complex application environment, particularly when there are multiple technologies (operating systems, databases, and languages) in use. Middleware can be thought of as glue that helps the application environment operate more smoothly.

Business Resilience

In the context of information systems, *business resilience* is concerned with the resilience of IT systems and business applications that support critical business processes, to ensure the ongoing viability of the organization as well as survival in the event of a major disaster. Given the phenomenon of digital transformation (DX), which represents an increasing dependency of business processes on information technology, ensuring the resilience of IT systems is all the more important. The two primary activities within business resilience are business continuity planning and disaster recovery planning.

Business Continuity Planning

Business continuity planning (BCP) is a business activity that is undertaken to reduce risks related to the onset of disasters and other disruptive events. BCP activities identify the most critical activities and assets in an organization. They identify risks and mitigate those risks through changes or enhancements in technology or business processes so that the impact of disasters is reduced and the time to recovery is lessened. The primary objective of BCP is to improve the chances that the organization will survive a disaster without incurring costly or even fatal damage to its most critical activities.

The activities of BCP development scale for any size organization. BCP has the unfortunate reputation of existing only in the stratospheric, thin air of the largest and wealthiest organizations. This misunderstanding hurts the majority of organizations that are too timid to begin any kind of BCP effort at all because they believe that these activities are too costly and disruptive. The fact is that any size organization, from a one-person home office to a multinational conglomerate, can successfully undertake BCP projects that will bring about immediate benefits as well as take some of the sting out of disruptive events that do occur.

Organizations can benefit from BCP projects, even if a disaster never occurs. The steps in the BCP development process usually bring immediate benefit in the form of process and technology improvements that increase the resilience, integrity, and efficiency of those processes and systems.

 EXAM TIP Business continuity planning is closely related to disaster recovery planning—both are concerned with the recovery of business operations after a disaster.

Disasters

I always tried to turn every disaster into an opportunity.
–John D. Rockefeller

In a business context, disasters are unexpected and unplanned events that result in the disruption of business operations. A disaster could be a regional event spread over a wide geographic area, or it could occur within the confines of a single room. The impact of a disaster will also vary, from a complete interruption of all company operations to a mere slowdown. (The question invariably comes up: when is a disaster a *disaster*? This is somewhat subjective, like asking, "When is a person sick?" Is it when he or she is too ill to report to work, or if he or she just has a sniffle and a scratchy throat? I'll discuss disaster declaration later in this chapter.)

Types of Disasters   BCP professionals broadly classify disasters as natural or human-made, although the origin of a disaster does not figure very much into how we respond to it. Let's examine the types of disasters.

Natural Disasters   Natural disasters are phenomena that occur in the natural world with little or no assistance from mankind. They are a result of the natural processes that occur in, on, and above the earth.

Examples of natural disasters include

- **Earthquakes**   Sudden movements of the earth with the capacity to damage buildings, houses, roads, bridges, and dams; to precipitate landslides and avalanches; and to induce flooding and other secondary events.

- **Volcanoes**   Eruptions of magma, pyroclastic flows, steam, ash, and flying rocks that can cause significant damage over wide geographic regions. Some volcanoes, such as Kilauea in Hawaii, produce a nearly continuous and predictable outpouring of lava in a limited area, whereas others, such as the Mount St. Helens eruption in 1980 in Washington state, caused an ash fall over thousands of square miles that brought many metropolitan areas to a standstill for days and also blocked rivers and damaged roads. Figure 5-23 shows a volcanic eruption as seen from space.

- **Landslides**   Sudden downhill movements of earth, usually down steep slopes, can bury buildings, houses, roads, and public utilities and cause secondary (although still disastrous) effects such as the rerouting of rivers.

Figure 5-23
Mount Etna
volcano in Sicily

- **Avalanches**   Sudden downward flows of snow, rocks, and debris on a mountainside can damage buildings, houses, roads, and utilities, resulting in direct or indirect damage affecting businesses. A *slab* avalanche consists of the movement of a large, stiff layer of compacted snow. A *loose snow* avalanche occurs when the accumulated snowpack exceeds its shear strength. A *power snow* avalanche is the largest type and can travel in excess of 200 mph and exceed 10 million tons of material.

- **Wildfires**   Fires in forests, chaparral, and grasslands are part of the natural order. However, fires can also damage power lines, buildings, equipment, homes, and entire communities, and cause injury and death.

- **Tropical cyclones**   The largest and most violent storms are known in various parts of the world as hurricanes, typhoons, tropical cyclones, tropical storms, and cyclones. Tropical cyclones consist of strong winds that can reach 190 mph, heavy rains, and storm surge that can raise the level of the ocean by as much as 20 feet, all of which can result in widespread coastal flooding and damage to buildings, houses, roads, and utilities and significant loss of life.

- **Tornadoes**   These violent rotating columns of air can cause catastrophic damage to buildings, houses, roads, and utilities when they reach the ground. Most tornadoes can have wind speeds from 40 to 110 mph and travel along the ground for a few miles. Some tornadoes can exceed 300 mph and travel for dozens of miles.

- **Windstorms**   While generally less intense than hurricanes and tornadoes, windstorms can nonetheless cause widespread damage, including damage to buildings, roads, and utilities. Widespread electric power outages are common, as windstorms can uproot trees that can fall into overhead power lines.

- **Lightning**   Atmospheric discharges of electricity occur during thunderstorms, but also during dust storms and volcanic eruptions. Lightning can start fires and also damage buildings and power transmission systems, causing power outages.

- **Ice storms**   Ice storms occur when rain falls through a layer of colder air, causing raindrops to freeze onto whatever surface they strike. They can cause widespread power outages when ice forms on power lines and the resulting weight causes those power lines to collapse. A notable example is the Great Ice Storm of 1998 in eastern Canada, which resulted in millions being without power for as long as two weeks and in the virtual immobilization of the cities of Montreal and Ottawa.

- **Hail**   This form of precipitation consists of ice chunks ranging from 5mm to 150mm in diameter. An example of a damaging hailstorm is the April 1999 storm in Sydney, Australia, where hailstones up to 9.5cm in diameter damaged 40,000 vehicles, 20,000 properties, and 25 airplanes, and caused one direct fatality. The storm caused $1.5 billion in damage.

- **Flooding**   Standing or moving water spills out of its banks and flows into and through buildings and causes significant damage to roads, buildings, and utilities.

Flooding can be a result of locally heavy rains, heavy snowmelt, a dam or levee break, tropical cyclone storm surge, or an avalanche or landslide that displaces lake or river water.

- **Tsunamis**   This series of waves usually results from the sudden vertical displacement of a lake bed or ocean floor, but a tsunami can also be caused by landslides, asteroids, or explosions. A tsunami wave can be barely noticeable in open, deep water, but as it approaches a shoreline, the wave can grow to a height of 50 feet or more. Recent notable examples are the 2004 Indian Ocean tsunami and the 2011 Japan tsunami. Coastline damage from the Japan tsunami is shown in Figure 5-24.

- **Pandemic**   The spread of infectious disease can occur over a wide geographic region, even worldwide. Pandemics have regularly occurred throughout history and are likely to continue occurring, despite advances in sanitation and immunology. A pandemic is the rapid spread of any type of disease, including typhoid, tuberculosis, bubonic plague, or influenza. Pandemics in the 20th century include

Figure 5-24
Damage to structures caused by the 2011 Japan tsunami

Figure 5-25
An auditorium was used as a temporary hospital during the 1918 flu pandemic.

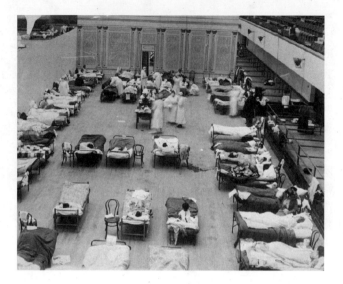

the 1918–1920 Spanish flu, the 1956–1958 Asian flu, the 1968–1969 Hong Kong "swine" flu, and the 2009–2010 swine flu pandemics. Figure 5-25 shows an auditorium that was converted into a hospital during the 1918–1920 pandemic.

- **Extraterrestrial impacts**   This category includes meteorites and other objects that may fall from the sky from way, way up. Sure, these events are extremely rare, and most organizations don't even include these events in their risk analysis, but I've included it here for the sake of rounding out the types of natural events.

Human-Made Disasters   Human-made disasters are events that are directly or indirectly caused by human activity through action or inaction. The results of human-made disasters are similar to natural disasters: localized or widespread damage to businesses that results in potentially lengthy interruptions in operations.

Examples of human-made disasters include

- **Civil disturbances**   These can include protests, demonstrations, riots, strikes, work slowdowns and stoppages, looting, and resulting actions such as curfews, evacuations, or lockdowns.

- **Utility outages**   Failures in electric, natural gas, district heating, water, communications, and other utilities can be caused by equipment failures, sabotage, or natural events such as landslides or flooding.

- **Service outages**   Failures in IT equipment, software programs, and online services can be caused by hardware failures, software bugs, or misconfiguration.

- **Materials shortages**   Interruptions in the supply of food, fuel, supplies, and materials can have a ripple effect on businesses and the services that support them. Readers who are old enough to remember the petroleum shortages of the

Figure 5-26
Citizens wait in long lines to buy fuel during a gas shortage.

mid-1970s know what this is all about; Figure 5-26 shows a line at a gas station during a 1970s-era gasoline shortage. Shortages can result in spikes in the price of commodities, which is almost as damaging as not having any supply at all.

- **Fires** As contrasted to wildfires, human-made fires originate in or involve homes, buildings, equipment, and materials.

- **Hazardous materials spills** Many created or refined substances can be dangerous if they escape their confines. Examples include petroleum substances, gases, pesticides and herbicides, medical substances, and radioactive substances.

- **Transportation accidents** This broad category includes plane crashes, railroad derailments, bridge collapses, and the like.

- **Terrorism and war** Whether they are actions of a nation, nation-state, or group, terrorism and war can have devastating but usually localized effects in cities and regions. Often, terrorism and war precipitate secondary effects such as materials shortages and utility outages.

- **Security events** The actions of a lone hacker or a team of organized cyber-criminals can bring down one system, one network, or many networks, which could result in widespread interruption in services. The hackers' activities can directly result in an outage, or an organization can voluntarily (although reluctantly) shut down an affected service or network to contain the incident.

NOTE It is important to remember that real disasters are usually complex events that involve more than just one type of damaging event. For instance, an earthquake directly damages buildings and equipment, but it can also cause fires and utility outages. A hurricane also brings flooding, utility outages, and sometimes even hazardous materials events and civil disturbances such as looting.

How Disasters Affect Organizations   Disasters have a wide variety of effects on an organization. Many disasters have direct effects, but sometimes it is the secondary effects of a disaster event that are most significant from the perspective of ongoing business operations.

A risk analysis is a part of the BCP process (discussed in the next section) that will identify the ways in which disasters are likely to affect a particular organization. During the risk analysis, the primary, secondary, and downstream effects of likely disaster scenarios need to be identified and considered. Whoever is performing this risk analysis will need to have a broad understanding of the interdependencies of business processes and IT systems, as well as the ways in which a disaster will affect ongoing business operations. Similarly, personnel who are developing contingency and recovery plans also need to be familiar with these effects so that those plans will adequately serve the organization's needs.

Disasters, by our definition, interrupt business operations in some measurable way. An event that has the *appearance* of a disaster may occur, but if it doesn't affect a particular organization, then we would say that no disaster occurred, at least for that particular organization.

It would be shortsighted to say that a disaster affects only *operations*. Rather, it is appropriate to understand the longer term effects that a disaster has on the organization's *image*, *brand*, *reputation*, and ongoing financial viability. The factors affecting image, brand, and reputation have as much to do with how the organization communicates to its customers, suppliers, and shareholders as with how the organization actually handles a disaster in progress.

Some of the ways that a disaster affects an organization's operations include

- **Direct damage**   Events such as earthquakes, floods, and fires directly damage an organization's buildings, equipment, or records. The damage may be severe enough that no salvageable items remain, or it may be less severe, where some equipment and buildings may be salvageable or repairable.

- **Utility interruption**   Even if an organization's buildings and equipment are undamaged, a disaster may affect utilities such as power, natural gas, or water, which can incapacitate some or all business operations. Significant delays in refuse collection can result in unsanitary conditions.

- **Transportation**   A disaster may damage or render transportation systems such as roads, railroads, shipping, or air transport unusable for a period. Damaged transportation systems will interrupt supply lines and personnel.

- **Services and supplier shortage**   Even if a disaster does not have a direct effect on an organization, critical suppliers affected by a disaster can have an undesirable effect on business operations. For instance, a regional baker that cannot produce and ship bread to its corporate customers will soon result in sandwich shops and restaurants without a critical resource.

- **Staff availability**   A community-wide or regional disaster that affects businesses is also likely to affect homes and families. Depending upon the nature of a disaster, employees will place a higher priority on the safety and comfort of family members. Also, workers may not be able or willing to travel to work if transportation systems are affected or if there is a significant materials shortage. Employees may also be unwilling to travel to work if they fear for their personal safety or that of their families.

- **Customer availability**   Various types of disasters may force or dissuade customers from traveling to business locations to conduct business. Many of the factors that keep employees away may also keep customers away.

CAUTION   The kinds of secondary and tertiary effects that a disaster has on a particular organization depend entirely upon its unique set of circumstances that constitute its specific critical needs. A risk analysis should be performed to identify these specific factors.

The Business Continuity Planning Process

The proper way to plan for disaster preparedness is first to know what kinds of disasters are likely and their possible effects on the organization. That is, *plan first, act later*.

The business continuity planning process is a *life cycle process*. In other words, business continuity planning (and disaster recovery planning) is not a one-time event or activity. It's a set of activities that results in the ongoing preparedness for disaster that continually adapts to changing business conditions and that continually improves.

The elements of the BCP process life cycle are

- Develop BCP policy.
- Conduct business impact analysis (BIA).
- Perform criticality analysis.
- Establish recovery targets.
- Develop recovery and continuity strategies and plans.
- Test recovery and continuity plans and procedures.
- Train personnel.
- Maintain strategies, plans, and procedures through periodic reviews and updates.

The BCP life cycle is shown in Figure 5-27. The details of this life cycle are described in detail in this chapter.

BCP Policy   A formal BCP effort must, like any strategic activity, flow from the existence of a formal policy and be included in the overall governance model that is the topic of this chapter. BCP should be an integral part of the IT control framework; it should not lie outside of it. Therefore, BCP policy should include or cite specific controls that ensure that key activities in the BCP life cycle are performed appropriately.

BCP policy should also define the scope of the BCP strategy. This means that the specific business processes (or departments or divisions within an organization) that are included in the BCP effort must be defined. Sometimes the scope will include a geographic boundary. In larger organizations, it is possible to "bite off more than you

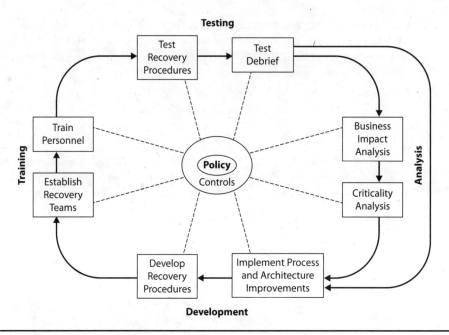

Figure 5-27 The BCP process life cycle

can chew" and define too large a scope for a BCP project, so limiting scope to a smaller, more manageable portion of the organization can be a good approach.

BCP and COBIT Controls The specific COBIT controls that are involved with BCP are contained within *DSS04—Ensure continuous service*. DSS04 has eight specific controls that constitute the entire BCP life cycle:

- Define the business continuity policy, objectives and scope.
- Maintain a continuity strategy.
- Develop and implement a business continuity response.
- Exercise, test and review the BCP.
- Review, maintain and improve the continuity plan.
- Conduct continuity plan training.
- Manage backup arrangements.
- Conduct post-resumption review.

These controls are discussed in this chapter and also in COBIT.

Business Impact Analysis The objective of the *business impact analysis* (BIA) is to identify the impact that different scenarios will have on ongoing business operations. The BIA is one of several steps of critical, detailed analysis that must be carried out before the development of continuity or recovery plans and procedures.

Inventory Key Processes and Systems   The first step in a BIA is the collection of key business processes and IT systems. Within the overall scope of the BCP project, the objective here is to establish a detailed list of all identifiable processes and systems. The usual approach is the development of a questionnaire or intake form that would be circulated to key personnel in end-user departments and also within IT. A sample intake form is shown in Figure 5-28.

Typically, the information that is gathered on intake forms is transferred to a multi-columned spreadsheet, where information on all of the organization's in-scope processes can be viewed together. This will become even more useful in subsequent phases of the BCP project, such as the criticality analysis.

TIP   Use of an intake form is not the only accepted approach when gathering information about critical processes and systems. It's also acceptable to conduct one-on-one interviews or group interviews with key users and IT personnel to identify critical processes and systems. I recommend the use of an intake form (whether paper-based or electronic), even if the interviewer uses it only as a framework for note-taking.

Process or system name	
Interviewee	
Title	
Department	
Contact info	
Date	
Process owner	
Process operator(s)	
Process description	
Customer facing (Y or N)	
IT system(s) used	
Key suppliers	
Communications needed	
Assets needed	
Process dependencies	
Other dependencies	
Documentation location	
Records location	

Figure 5-28   BIA sample intake form for gathering data about key processes

> ## Planning Precedes Action
>
> IT personnel are often eager to get to the fun and meaty parts of a project. Developers are anxious to begin coding before design; system administrators are eager to build systems before they are scoped and designed; and BCP personnel fervently desire to begin designing more robust system architectures and to tinker with replication and backup capabilities before key facts are known. In the case of business continuity and disaster recovery planning, completion of the BIA and other analyses is critical, as the analyses help to define the systems and processes most needed before getting to the fun part.

Statements of Impact   When processes and systems are being inventoried and cataloged, it is also vitally important to obtain one or more *statements of impact* for each process and system. A statement of impact is a qualitative or quantitative description of the impact on the business if the process or system were incapacitated for a time.

For IT systems, you might capture the number of users and the names of departments or functions that are affected by the unavailability of a specific IT system. Include the geography of affected users and functions if that is appropriate. Here are some example statements of impact for IT systems:

- *Three thousand customer support users in France and Italy will be unable to access customer records.*
- *All users in North America will be unable to read or send e-mail.*

Statements of impact for business processes may cite the business functions that would be affected. Here are some examples:

- *Accounts payable and accounts receivable functions will be unable to process.*
- *Legal department will be unable to access contracts and addendums.*

Statements of impact for revenue-generating and revenue-supporting business functions could quantify financial impact per unit of time (be sure to use the same units of time for all functions so that they can be easily compared with one another). Here are some examples:

- *Inability to place orders for appliances will cost at the rate of $12,000 per hour.*
- *Delays in payments will cost $45,000 per day in interest charges.*

As statements of impact are gathered, it may make sense to create several columns in the main worksheet so that like units (names of functions, numbers of users, financial figures) can be sorted and ranked later on.

A complete BIA will have the following information about each process and system:

- Name of the system or process
- Who is responsible for it

- A description of its function
- Dependencies on systems
- Dependencies on suppliers
- Dependencies on key employees
- Quantified statements of impact in terms of revenue, users affected, and/or functions impacted

You're almost home.

Criticality Analysis When all of the BIA information has been collected and charted, the criticality analysis (CA) can be performed.

The *criticality analysis* is a study of each system and process, a consideration of the impact on the organization if it is incapacitated, the likelihood of incapacitation, and the estimated cost of mitigating the risk or impact of incapacitation. In other words, it's a somewhat special type of risk analysis that focuses on key processes and systems.

The criticality analysis needs to include, or reference, a threat analysis. A *threat analysis* is a risk analysis that identifies every threat that has a reasonable probability of occurrence, plus one or more mitigating controls or compensating controls, and new probabilities of occurrence with those mitigating/compensating controls in place. In case you're having a little trouble imagining what this looks like (I'm writing the book and I'm having trouble seeing this!), take a look at Table 5-12, which is a lightweight example of what I'm talking about.

System	Threat	Probability	Mitigating Control	Cost	Mitigated Probability
Application Server	Denial of service	0.1%	High-performance filtering router	$60,000	0.01%
	Malware	1%	Antivirus	$200	0.1%
	Storage failure	2%	RAID-5	$20,000	0.01%
	Administrator error	15%	Configuration management tools	$10,000	1%
	Hardware CPU failure	5%	Server cluster	$15,000	1%
	Application software bug	5%	Source code reviews	$10,000	2%
	Extended power outage	25%	UPS Electric generator	$12,000 $40,000	2% 0.5%
	Flood	2%	Relocate data center	$200,000	0.1%

Table 5-12 Example Threat Analysis Identifies Threats and Controls for Critical Systems and Processes

In the preceding threat analysis, notice the following:

- Multiple threats are listed for a single asset. In the table, I mentioned just eight threats. For all the threats but one, I listed only a single mitigating control. For the extended power outage threat, I listed two mitigating controls.

- Cost of downtime wasn't listed. For systems or processes where you have a cost per unit of time for downtime, you'll need to include it here, along with some calculations to show the payback for each control.

- Some mitigating controls can benefit more than one system. That may not have been obvious in this example, but in the case of a UPS (uninterruptible power supply) and electric generator, many systems can benefit, so the cost for these mitigating controls can be allocated across many systems, thereby lowering the cost for each system. Another example is a high-availability storage area network (SAN) located in two different geographic areas; while initially expensive, many applications can use the SAN for storage, and all will benefit from replication to the counterpart storage system.

- Threat probabilities are arbitrary. In Table 5-12, the probabilities were for a single occurrence in an entire year, so, for example, 5 percent means the threat will be realized once every 20 years.

- The length of outage was not included. You may need to include this also, particularly if you are quantifying downtime per hour or other unit of time.

It is probably becoming obvious that a threat analysis, and the corresponding criticality analysis, can get complicated. The rule here should be this: the complexity of the threat and criticality analyses should be proportional to the value of the assets (or revenue, or both). For example, in a company where application downtime is measured in thousands of dollars per minute, it's probably worth taking a few weeks or even months to work out all of the likely scenarios and a variety of mitigating controls, and to work out which ones are the most cost-effective. On the other hand, for a system or business process where the impact of an outage is far less costly, a good deal less time might be spent on the supporting threat and criticality analysis.

 EXAM TIP   Test-takers should ensure that any question dealing with BIA and CA places the business impact analysis first. Without this analysis, criticality analysis is impossible to evaluate in terms of likelihood or cost-effectiveness in mitigation strategies. The BIA identifies strategic resources and provides a value to their recovery and operation, which is, in turn, consumed in the criticality analysis phase. If presented with a question identifying BCP at a particular stage, make sure that any answers you select facilitate the BIA and then the CA before moving on toward objectives and strategies.

Determine Maximum Tolerable Downtime   The next step for each critical process is the establishment of a metric called *maximum tolerable downtime* (MTD). This is a theoretical time interval, measured from the onset of a disaster, after which the organization's very survival is at risk. Establishing MTD for each critical process is an important step that aids in the establishment of key recovery targets, discussed in the next section.

Establishing Key Recovery Targets   When the cost or impact of downtime has been established and the cost and benefit of mitigating controls has been considered, some key targets can be established for each critical process. These objectives determine how quickly key systems and processes should be made available after the onset of a disaster and the maximum tolerable data loss that results from the disaster. The two key recovery targets are

- **Recovery time objective (RTO)**   This refers to the maximum period that elapses from the onset of a disaster until the resumption of service.
- **Recovery point objective (RPO)**   This refers to the maximum data loss from the onset of a disaster.

Once these target objectives are known, the disaster recovery (DR) team can begin to build system recovery capabilities and procedures that will help the organization economically realize these targets. This is discussed in detail later in this chapter.

Developing Continuity Plans

In the previous section, I discussed the notion of establishing recovery targets and the development of architectures, processes, and procedures. The processes and procedures are related to the normal operation of those new technologies as they will be operated in normal day-to-day operations. When those processes and procedures have been completed, the disaster recovery plans and procedures (actions that will take place during and immediately after a disaster) can be developed.

For example, an organization has established RPO and RTO targets for its critical applications. These targets necessitated the development of server clusters and storage area networks with replication. While implementing those new technologies, the organization developed the operations processes and procedures in support of those new technologies that would be carried out every day during normal business operations. As a separate activity, the organization would then develop the procedures to be performed when a disaster strikes the primary operations center for those applications; those procedures would include all of the steps that must be taken so that the applications can continue operating in an alternate location or in the public cloud.

The procedures for operating critical applications during a disaster are a small part of the entire body of procedures that must be developed. Several other sets of procedures must also be developed, including

- Personnel safety procedures
- Disaster declaration procedures
- Responsibilities
- Contact information

- Recovery procedures
- Continuing operations
- Restoration procedures

All of these are required so that an organization will be adequately prepared in the event a disaster occurs.

Personnel Safety Procedures   When a disaster strikes, measures to ensure the safety of personnel are a top priority and need to be taken immediately. If the disaster has occurred or is about to occur to a building, personnel may need to be evacuated as soon as possible. Arguably, however, in some situations, evacuation is exactly the wrong thing to do; for example, if a hurricane or tornado is bearing down on a facility, the building itself may be the best shelter for personnel, even if it incurs some damage. The point here is that personnel safety procedures need to be carefully developed, and possibly more than one set of procedures will be needed, depending on the event.

TIP   The highest priority in any disaster or emergency situation is the safety of human life.

Personnel safety procedures need to take many factors into account, including

- Ensuring that all personnel are familiar with evacuation and sheltering procedures
- Ensuring that visitors know how to evacuate the premises and the location of sheltering areas
- Posting signs and placards that indicate emergency evacuation routes and gathering areas outside of the building
- Locating emergency lighting to aid in evacuation or sheltering in place
- Providing fire extinguishment equipment (portable fire extinguishers and so on)
- Ensuring that people are able to communicate with public safety and law enforcement authorities, including in situations where communications and electric power have been cut off and when all personnel are outside of the building
- Caring for injured personnel
- Training in CPR and emergency first-aid
- Providing safety personnel who can assist in the evacuation of injured and disabled persons
- Providing the ability to account for visitors and other nonemployees
- Providing emergency shelter in extreme weather conditions
- Providing emergency food and drinking water
- Conducting periodic tests to ensure that evacuation procedures will be adequate in the event of a real emergency

Local emergency management organizations may have additional information available that can assist an organization with its emergency personnel safety procedures.

Disaster Declaration Procedures   Disaster response procedures are initiated when a disaster is declared. However, there needs to be a procedure for the declaration itself so that there will be little doubt as to the conditions that must be present.

Why is a disaster declaration procedure required? Primarily because it's not always clear whether a situation is a real disaster. Sure, a 7.5 earthquake or a major fire is a disaster, but overcooking popcorn in the microwave and setting off a building's fire alarm system might not be. Many "in between" situations may or may not be considered disasters. A disaster declaration procedure must state some basic conditions that will help determine whether a disaster should be declared.

Further, who has the authority to declare a disaster? What if senior management personnel frequently travel and may not be around? Who else can declare a disaster? And, finally, what does it mean to declare a disaster—and what happens next? The following points constitute the primary items that organizations need to consider for their disaster declaration procedure.

Form a Core Team   A core team of personnel needs to be established, all of whom will be familiar with the disaster declaration procedure, as well as the actions that must take place once a disaster has been declared. This core team should consist of middle and upper managers who are familiar with business operations, particularly those that are critical. This core team must be large enough so that a requisite few of them are on hand when a disaster strikes. In organizations that have second shift, third shift, and weekend workers, some of the core team members should be those in supervisory positions during those times. However, some of the core team members can be personnel who work "business hours" and are not on-site all of the time.

Declaration Criteria   The declaration procedure must contain some tangible criteria that a core team member can consult to guide him or her down the "Is this a disaster?" decision path.

The criteria for declaring a disaster should be related to the availability and viability of ongoing critical business operations. Some example criteria include any one or more of the following:

- Forced evacuation of a building containing or supporting critical operations that is likely to last for more than four hours

- Hardware, software, or network failures that result in a critical IT system being incapacitated or unavailable for more than four hours

- A major, prolonged outage by an Internet service provider or cloud service provider

- Any security incident that results in a critical IT system being incapacitated for more than four hours (security incidents could involve malware, break-in, attack, sabotage, and so on)

- Any event causing employee absenteeism or supplier shortages that, in turn, results in one or more critical business processes being incapacitated for more than eight hours

- Any event causing a communications failure that results in critical IT systems being unreachable for more than four hours

The preceding examples are a mostly complete list of criteria for many organizations. The duration periods will vary from organization to organization. For instance, a large, pure-online business such as Salesforce.com would probably declare a disaster if its main web sites were unavailable for more than a few minutes. But in an organization where computers are far less critical, an outage of four hours might *not* be considered a disaster.

Pulling the Trigger   When disaster declaration criteria are met, the disaster should be declared. The procedure for disaster declaration could permit any single core team member to declare the disaster, but it may be better to have two or more core team members agree on whether a disaster should be declared. Whether an organization should use a single-person declaration or a group of two or more is each organization's choice.

All core team members empowered to declare a disaster should have the procedure on hand at all times. In most cases, the criteria should fit on a small, laminated wallet card that each team member can keep close at all times. For organizations that use the consensus method for declaring a disaster, the wallet card should include the names and contact numbers for other core team members so that each will have a way of contacting others.

Next Steps   Declaring a disaster will trigger the start of one or more other response procedures, but not necessarily all of them. For instance, if a disaster is declared because of a serious computer or software malfunction, there is no need to evacuate the building. While this example may be obvious, not all instances will be this clear. Either the disaster declaration procedure itself or each of the subsequent response procedures should contain criteria that will help determine which response procedures should be enacted.

False Alarms   Probably the most common cause of personnel not declaring a disaster is the fear that an actual disaster is not taking place. Core team members empowered with declaring a disaster should not necessarily hesitate. Instead, core team members could convene with additional core team members to reach a firm decision, provided this can be done quickly.

If a disaster has been declared and later it is clear that a disaster has been averted (or did not exist in the first place), the disaster can simply be called off and declared to be over. Response personnel can be contacted and told to cease response activities and return to their normal activities.

 TIP   Depending on the level of effort that takes place in the opening minutes and hours of disaster response, the consequences of declaring a disaster when none exists may or may not be significant. In the spirit of continuous improvement, any organization that has had a few false alarms should seek to improve their disaster declaration criteria or procedures. Well-trained and experienced personnel can usually reduce the frequency of false alarms.

Disaster Responsibilities During a disaster, many important tasks must be performed to evacuate or shelter personnel, assess damage, recover critical processes and systems, and carry out many other functions that are critical to the survival of the enterprise.

About 20 different responsibilities are described here. In a large organization, each responsibility may be staffed with a team of two, three, or many individuals. In small organizations, a few people may incur many responsibilities each, switching from role to role as the situation warrants.

All of these roles should be staffed by people who are available. It is important to remember that many of the "ideal" persons to fill each role may be unavailable during a disaster for several reasons, including the following:

- **Injured, ill, or deceased** Some regional disasters will inflict widespread casualties that will include some proportion of response personnel. Those who are injured, ill (in the case of a pandemic, for instance, or who are recovering from a sickness or surgery when the disaster occurs), or who are killed by the disaster are clearly not going to be showing up to help.

- **Caring for family members** Some types of disasters may cause widespread injury or require mass evacuation. In some of these situations, many personnel will be caring for family members whose immediate needs for safety will take priority over the needs of the workplace.

- **Unavailable transportation** Some types of disasters include localized or widespread damage to transportation infrastructure, which may result in many persons who are willing to be on-site to help with emergency operations being unable to travel to the work site.

- **Out of the area** Some disaster response personnel may be away on business travel or on vacation and be unable to respond. However, some persons being away may actually be opportunities in disguise; unaffected by the physical impact of the disaster, they may be able to help out in other ways, such as communications with suppliers, customers, or other personnel.

- **Communications** Some types of disasters, particularly those that are localized (versus widespread and obvious to an observer), require that disaster response personnel be contacted and asked to help. If a disaster strikes after hours, some personnel may be unreachable.

- **Fear** Some types of disasters (such as pandemic, terrorist attack, flood, and so on) may instill fear for safety on the part of response personnel who will disregard the call to help and stay away from the work site.

NOTE Response personnel in all disciplines and responsibilities will need to be able to piece together whatever functionality they are called on to do, using whatever resources are available—this is part art and part science. Although response and contingency plans may make certain assumptions, personnel may find themselves with fewer resources than they need, requiring them to do the best they can with the resources available.

Figure 5-29   Stress is compounded by the pressure of disaster recovery and the formation of new teams in times of chaos.

Each role will be working with personnel in many other roles, often working with unfamiliar persons. An entire response and recovery operation may be operating almost like a brand-new organization in unfamiliar settings and with an entirely new set of rules. In typical organizations, teams work well when team members are familiar with, and trust, one another. In a response and recovery operation, the stress level is much higher because the stakes—company survival—are higher, and often the teams are composed of persons who have little experience with one another and these new roles. This will cause additional stress that will bring out the best and worst in people, as illustrated in Figure 5-29.

Emergency Response   These are the first responders during a disaster. Their top priorities include evacuation or sheltering of personnel, first aid, triage of injured personnel, and possibly firefighting.

Command and Control (Emergency Management)   During disaster response operations, someone must be in charge. In a disaster, resources may be scarce, and many matters will vie for attention. Someone needs to fill the role of decision maker to keep disaster response activities moving and to handle situations that arise. This role may need to be rotated among various personnel, particularly in smaller organizations, to counteract fatigue.

TIP   Although the first person on the scene may be the person in charge initially, that will definitely change as qualified assigned personnel show up and take charge and as the nature of the disaster and response solidifies. The leadership roles may then be passed among key personnel already designated to be in charge.

Documentation It's vital that one or more persons continually document the important events during disaster response operations. From decisions, to discussions, to status, to roll call, these events must be written down (and later recorded digitally), so that the details of disaster response can be pieced together afterward. This will help the organization better understand how disaster response unfolded, how decisions were made, and who performed which actions, all of which will help the organization be better prepared for future events.

Internal and External Communications In many disaster scenarios, personnel may be stripped of many or all of their normal means of communication, such as desk phone, voicemail, e-mail, smartphone, and instant messaging. Yet never are *communications* as vital as during a disaster, when nothing is going according to plan. Internal communications are needed so that status on various activities can be sent to command and control, and so that priorities and orders can be sent to disaster response personnel.

People outside of the organization also need to know what's going on when a disaster strikes. There's a potentially long list of parties who want or need to know the status of business operations during and after a disaster, including

- Customers
- Suppliers
- Partners
- Shareholders
- Neighbors
- Regulators
- Media
- Law enforcement and public safety authorities

These different audiences need different messages, as well as messages in different forms.

Legal and Compliance Several needs may arise during a disaster that require the attention of inside or outside *legal counsel*. Disasters present unique situations that need legal assistance, such as

- Interpretation of regulations
- Interpretation of contracts with suppliers and customers
- Management of matters of liability to other parties

 TIP Typical legal matters need to be resolved before the onset of a disaster, with this information included in disaster response procedures, since legal staff members may be unavailable during a disaster.

Damage Assessment   Whether a disaster is a physically violent event, such as an earthquake or volcano, or instead involves no physical manifestation, such as a serious security incident, one or more experts are needed who can examine affected assets and accurately assess the damage. Because most organizations own many different types of assets (from buildings, to equipment, to information), qualified experts are needed to assess each asset type involved. It is not necessary to call upon all available experts—only those whose expertise matches the type of event that has occurred need to be consulted.

Some expertise may go well beyond the skills present in an organization, such as a building structural engineer who can assess potential earthquake damage. In such cases, it may be sensible to retain the services of an outside engineer who will respond and provide an assessment on whether a building is safe to occupy after a disaster. In fact, it may make sense to retain more than one, in case one or more of them is affected by a disaster.

Salvage   Disasters destroy assets that the organization uses to make products or perform services. When a disaster occurs, someone (either a qualified employee or an outside expert) needs to examine assets to determine which are salvageable; then a salvage team needs to perform the actual salvage operation at a pace that meets the organization's needs.

In some cases, salvage may be a critical-path activity, where critical processes are paralyzed until salvage and repairs or replacements to critically needed machinery can be performed. In other cases, the salvage operation is performed on inventory of finished goods, raw materials, and other items so that business operations can be resumed. Occasionally, when it is obvious that damaged equipment or materials are a total loss, the salvage effort involves selling the damaged items or materials to another organization.

Assessment of damage to assets may be a high priority when an organization will be filing an insurance claim. Insurance may be a primary source of funding for the organization's recovery effort.

CAUTION   Salvage operations may be a critical-path activity or one that can be carried out well after the disaster. To the greatest extent possible, this should be decided in advance. Otherwise, the command-and-control function will need to decide the priority of salvage operations.

Physical Security   After a disaster, the organization's usual *physical security* controls may be compromised. For instance, fencing, walls, and barricades could be damaged, or video surveillance systems may be disabled or have no electric power. These and other failures could lead to increased risk of loss or damage to assets and personnel until those controls can be restored. Also, security controls in temporary quarters such as hot/warm/cold sites and temporary work centers may be inadequate compared to those in primary locations.

Supplies   During emergency and recovery operations, personnel will require supplies of many kinds, from food and drinking water, writing tablets, and pens, to smartphones, portable generators, and extension cords. This function may also be responsible for ordering replacement assets such as servers and network equipment for a cold site.

Transportation   When workers are operating from a temporary location and/or if regional or local transportation systems have been compromised, many arrangements for all kinds of transportation may be required to support emergency operations. These can include transportation of replacement workers, equipment, or supplies by truck, car, rail, sea, or air. The *transportation* function could also be responsible for arranging for temporary lodging for personnel.

Networks   This technology function is responsible for damage assessment to the organization's voice and data networks, building/configuring networks for emergency operations, or both. This function may require extensive coordination with external telecommunications service providers, who, by the way, may be suffering the effects of a local or regional disaster as well.

Network Services   This function is responsible for network-centric services such as Domain Name System (DNS), Simple Network Management Protocol (SNMP), network routing, and authentication.

Systems   This function is responsible for building, loading, and configuring the servers and systems that support critical services, applications, databases, and other functions. Personnel may have other resources such as virtualization technology to enable additional flexibility.

Database Management Systems   For critical applications that rely upon database management systems, this function is responsible for building databases on recovery systems and for restoring or recovering data from backup media, replication volumes, or e-vaults onto recovery systems. Database personnel will need to work with systems, network, and applications personnel to ensure that databases are operating properly and are available as needed.

Data and Records   This function is responsible for access to and re-creation of electronic and paper business records. This is a business function that supports critical business processes and works with database management personnel and, if necessary, with data-entry personnel to rekey lost data.

Applications   This function is responsible for recovering application functionality on application servers. This may include reloading application software, performing configuration, provisioning roles and user accounts, and connecting the application to databases, network services, and other application integration issues.

Access Management   This function is responsible for creating and managing user accounts for network, system, and application access. Personnel with this responsibility may be especially susceptible to social engineering and be tempted to create user accounts without proper authority or approval.

Information Security and Privacy   Personnel who serve in this capacity are responsible for ensuring that proper security controls are being carried out during recovery and emergency operations. They will be expected to identify risks associated with emergency operations and to require remedies to reduce risks.

Security personnel will also be responsible for enforcing privacy controls so that employee and customer personal data will not be compromised, even as business operations are affected by the disaster.

Off-site Storage   This function is responsible for managing the effort of retrieving backup media from off-site storage facilities and for protecting that media in transit to the scene of recovery operations. If recovery operations take place over an extended period (more than a couple of days), data at the recovery site will need to be backed up and sent to an off-site media storage facility to protect that information should a disaster occur at the hot/warm/cold site (and what bad luck that would be!).

User Hardware   In many organizations, little productive work gets done when employees don't have their workstations, printers, scanners, copiers, and other office equipment. Thus, a *user hardware* function is required to provide, configure, and support the variety of office equipment required by end users working in temporary or alternate locations. This function, like most others, will have to work with many others to ensure that workstations and other equipment are able to communicate with applications and services as needed to support critical processes.

Training   During emergency operations, when response personnel and users are working in new locations (and often on new or different equipment and software), some personnel may need training so that their productivity can be quickly restored. *Training* personnel will need to be familiar with many disaster response and recovery procedures so that they can help people in those roles understand what is expected of them. This function will also need to be able to dispense emergency operations procedures to these personnel.

Restoration   This function comes into play when IT is ready to migrate applications running on hot/warm/cold site systems back to the original (or replacement) processing center.

Contract Information   This function is responsible for understanding and interpreting legal contracts. Most organizations are a party to one or more legal contracts that require them to perform specific activities, provide specific services, and communicate status if service levels have changed. These contracts may or may not have provisions for activities and services during disasters, including communications regarding any changes in service levels.

This function is vital not only during the disaster planning stages but also during actual disaster response. Customers, suppliers, regulators, and other parties need to be informed according to specific contract terms.

Recovery Procedures   Recovery procedures are the instructions that key personnel use to bootstrap services (such as IT systems and other business-enabling technologies) that support the critical business functions identified in the BIA and CA. The recovery procedures should work hand-in-hand with the technologies that may have been added to IT systems to make them more resilient.

An example would be useful here: A fictitious company, Acme Rocket Boots, determines that its order-entry business function is highly critical to the ongoing viability of the business and sets recovery objectives to ensure that order entry would be continued within no more than 48 hours after a disaster. Acme determines that it needs to invest in storage, backup, and replication technologies to make a 48-hour recovery possible. Without these investments, IT systems supporting order-entry would be down for at least ten days until they could be rebuilt from scratch. Acme cannot justify the purchase of systems and software to facilitate an auto-failover of the order-entry application to hot-site DR servers. Instead, the recovery procedure would require that the database be rebuilt from replicated data on cloud-based servers. Other tasks, such as installing recent patches, would also be necessary to make recovery servers ready for production use. All of the tasks required to make the systems ready constitute the body of recovery procedures needed to support the business order-entry function.

This example is, of course, a gross oversimplification. Actual recovery procedures could take potentially dozens of pages of documentation, and procedures would also be necessary for network components, end-user workstations, network services, and other supporting IT services required by the order-entry application. And those are the procedures needed just to get the application running again. More procedures would be needed to keep the applications running properly in the recovery environment.

Continuing Operations Procedures Procedures for continuing operations have more to do with business processes than they do with IT systems. However, the two are related, since the procedures for continuing critical business processes have to fit hand-in-hand with the procedures for operating supporting IT systems that may also (but not necessarily) be operating in a recovery or emergency mode.

Let me clarify that last statement: It is entirely conceivable that a disaster could strike an organization with critical business processes that operate in one city but that are supported by IT systems located in another city. A disaster could strike the city with the critical business function, which means that personnel may have to continue operating that business function in another location, *on the original, fully featured IT application*. It is also possible that a disaster could strike the city with the IT application, forcing it into an emergency/recovery mode in an alternate location, while users of the application are operating in a mostly business-as-usual mode. And, of course, a disaster could strike both locations (or a disaster could strike in one location where both the critical business function *and* its supporting IT applications reside), throwing both the critical business function *and* its supporting IT applications into emergency mode. Any organization's reality could be even more complex than this: just add dependencies on external application service providers, applications with custom interfaces, or critical business functions that operate in multiple cities. If you wondered why disaster recovery and business continuity planning were so complicated, perhaps your appreciation has grown just now.

Restoration Procedures When a disaster has occurred, IT operations need to take up residence temporarily in an alternate processing site while repairs are performed on the original site. Once those repairs are completed, IT operations would need to be transitioned back to the main (or replacement) processing facility. You should expect that the procedures for this transition would also be documented (and *tested*—testing is discussed later in this chapter).

 NOTE Transitioning applications back to the original processing site is not necessarily just a second iteration of the initial move to the cloud/hot/warm/ cold site. Far from it: the recovery site may have been a skeleton (in capacity, functionality, or both) of its original self. The objective is not necessarily to move the functionality at the recovery site back to the original site, but to restore the original functionality to the original site.

Let's continue the Acme Rocket Boots example: The company's order-entry application at the DR site had only basic, not extended, functions. For instance, customers could not look at order history, and they could not place custom orders; they could order only off-the-shelf products. But when the application is moved back to the primary processing facility, the history of orders accumulated on the DR application needs to be merged into the main order history database, *which was not a part of the DR plan*.

Considerations for Continuity and Recovery Plans A considerable amount of detailed planning and logistics must go into continuity and recovery plans if they are to be effective.

Availability of Key Personnel An organization cannot depend upon every member of its regular expert workforce to be available in a disaster. As discussed earlier in this chapter in more detail, personnel may be unavailable for a number of reasons, including

- Injury, illness, or death
- Caring for family members
- Unavailable transportation
- Damaged transportation infrastructure
- Being out of the area
- Lack of communications
- Fear related to the disaster and its effects

 TIP An organization must develop thorough and accurate recovery and continuity documentation as well as cross-training and plan testing. When a disaster strikes, an organization has one chance to survive, and survival depends upon how well the available personnel are able to follow recovery and continuity procedures and to keep critical processes functioning properly.

A successful disaster recovery operation requires available personnel who are located near company operations centers. While the primary response personnel may consist of the individuals and teams responsible for day-to-day corporate operations, others need to be identified. In a disaster, some personnel will be unavailable for many reasons.

Key personnel, as well as their backup persons, need to be identified. Backup personnel can consist of employees who have familiarity with specific technologies, such as operating system, database, and network administration, and who can cover for primary personnel if needed. Sure, it would be desirable for these backup personnel also to be trained in specific recovery operations, but at the very least, if these personnel have access to specific detailed recovery procedures, having them on a call list is probably better than having no available personnel during a disaster.

Besides employees, many other parties need to be notified in the event of a disaster. Outside parties need to be aware of the disaster as well as of basic changes in business conditions.

In a regional disaster such as a hurricane or earthquake, nearby parties will certainly be aware of the disaster and that your organization is involved in it somehow. However, those parties may not be aware of the status of business operations immediately after the disaster: a regional event's effects can range from complete destruction of buildings and equipment to no damage at all and business-as-usual conditions. Unless key parties are notified of the status, they may have no other way to know for sure.

Parties that need to be contacted may include

- **Key suppliers** This may include electric and gas utilities, fuel delivery, and materials delivery. In a disaster, an organization will often need to impart special instructions to one or more suppliers, requesting delivery of extra supplies or temporary cessation of deliveries.

- **Key customers** Many organizations have key customers whose relationships are valued above most others. These customers may depend on a steady delivery of products and services that are critical to their own operations; in a disaster, those customers may have a dire need to know whether such deliveries will be able to continue or not and under what circumstances.

- **Public safety** Police, fire, and other public safety authorities may need to be contacted, not only for emergency operations such as firefighting, but also for any required inspections or other services. It is important that "business office" telephone numbers for these agencies be included on contact lists, as 911 and other emergency lines may be flooded by calls from others.

- **Insurance adjusters** Most organizations rely on insurance companies to protect their assets from damage or loss in a disaster. Because insurance adjustment funds are often a key part of continuing business operations in an emergency, it's important to be able to reach insurers as soon as possible after a disaster has occurred.

- **Regulators** In some industries, organizations are required to notify regulators of certain types of disasters. While regulators obviously may be aware of noteworthy regional disasters, they may not immediately know of an event's specific effects on an organization. Further, some types of disasters are highly localized and may not be newsworthy, even in a local city.

- **Media** Media outlets such as newspapers and television stations may need to be notified as a means of quickly reaching the community or region with information about the effects of a disaster on organizations.

- **Shareholders** Organizations are usually obliged to notify their shareholders of any disastrous event that affects business operations. This may be the case whether the organization is publicly or privately held.

The persons or teams responsible for communicating with these outside parties will need to have all of the individuals and organizations included in a list of parties to contact. This information should all be included in emergency response procedures.

Wallet cards containing emergency contact information should be prepared for core team personnel for the organization as well as for members in each department who would be actively involved in disaster response. Wallet cards are advantageous, because most personnel will have a wallet, notebook, or purse nearby at all times, even when away from home, running errands, traveling, or on vacation. Information on the wallet card should include contact information for fellow team members, a few of the key disaster response personnel, and any conference bridges or emergency call-in numbers that are set up. An example wallet card is shown in Figure 5-30.

Emergency Contacts
Joe Phillips, VP Ops: 213-555-1212 h, 415-555-1212 m
Marie Peterson, CFO: 206-555-1212 h, 425-555-1212 m
Mark Woodward, IT Ops: 360-555-1212 h, 253-555-1212 m
Gary Doan, VP Facilities: 509-555-1212 h, 702-555-1212 m
Jeff Patterson, IT Networks: 760-555-1212 h, 310-555-1212 m
Documentation at briefcase.yahoo.com: Userid = wunderground, password = L0c43Dupt1te
Emergency conference bridge: 1-800-555-1212, host code 443322, PIN 0748
Disaster declaration criteria: 8-hr outage anticipated on critical systems, 2 core members vote, then initiate call tree procedure to notify other response personnel

---

Off-site media storage vendor: 719-555-1212
Telecommunications and network service provider: 312-555-1212
Local emergency response authorities: 714-555-1212
Local health authorities: 702-555-1212
Local law enforcement authorities: 512-555-1212
Local hospitals: 808-555-1212, 913-555-1212
National weather service hotline: 602-555-1212
Regional transportation authority hotline: 312-555-1212
Local building inspectors: 414-555-1212

Figure 5-30 Example laminated wallet card for core team participants with emergency contact information and disaster declaration criteria

Emergency Supplies   The onset of a disaster may cause personnel to be stranded at a work location, possibly for several days. This can be caused by a number of reasons, including inclement weather that makes travel dangerous or a transportation infrastructure that is damaged or blocked with debris.

Emergency supplies should be laid up at a work location and made available to personnel stranded there, regardless of whether they are supporting a recovery effort or not (it's also possible that severe weather or a natural or human-made event could make transportation dangerous or impossible).

A disaster can also prompt employees to report to a work location (at the primary location or at an alternate site) where they may remain for days at a time, even around the clock if necessary. A situation like this may make the need for emergency supplies less critical, but it still may be beneficial to the recovery effort to make supplies available to support recovery personnel.

An organization stocking emergency supplies at a work location should consider including the following items:

- Drinking water
- Food rations
- First-aid supplies
- Blankets
- Flashlights
- Battery or crank-powered radio

Local emergency response authorities may recommend other supplies be kept at a work location as well.

Communications   Communications within organizations, as well as with customers, suppliers, partners, shareholders, regulators, and others, is vital under normal business conditions. During a disaster and subsequent recovery and restoration operations, such communications are more important than ever, while many of the usual means for communications may be impaired.

Disaster response procedures need to include a call tree. This is a method where the first personnel involved in a disaster begin notifying others in the organization, informing them of the developing disaster and enlisting their assistance. Just as the branches of a tree originate at the trunk and are repeatedly subdivided, a call tree is most effective when each person in the tree can make just a few phone calls. Not only will the notification of important personnel proceed more quickly, but each person will not be overburdened with many calls.

Remember that in a disaster a significant portion of personnel may be unavailable or unreachable. Therefore, a call tree should be structured so that there is sufficient flexibility as well as assurance that all critical personnel will be contacted. Figure 5-31 shows an example call tree.

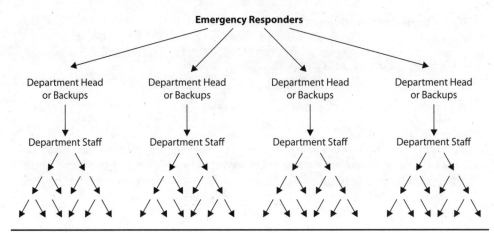

Figure 5-31 Example call tree structure

An organization can also use an automated outcalling system to notify critical personnel of a disaster. Such a system can play a prerecorded message or request that personnel call an information number to hear a prerecorded message. Most outcalling systems keep a log of which personnel have been successfully reached.

An automated calling system should not be located in the same geographic region as the disaster. A regional disaster could damage the system or make it unavailable during a disaster. The system should be Internet accessible so that response personnel can access it to determine which personnel have been notified and to make any needed changes before or during a disaster.

Transportation Some types of disasters may make certain modes of transportation unavailable or unsafe. Widespread natural disasters, such as earthquakes, volcanoes, hurricanes, and floods, can immobilize virtually every form of transportation, including highways, railroads, boats, and airplanes. Other types of disasters may impede one or more types of transportation, which could result in overwhelming demand for the available modes. High volumes of emergency supplies may be needed during and after a disaster, but damaged transportation infrastructure often makes the delivery of those supplies difficult.

Components of a Business Continuity Plan The complete set of business continuity plan documents will include the following:

- **Supporting project documents** These will include the documents created at the beginning of the business continuity project, including the project charter, project plan, statement of scope, and statement of support from executives.

- **Analysis documents**   These include the
  - Business impact analysis (BIA)
  - Threat assessment and risk assessment
  - Criticality analysis
  - Documents defining approved recovery targets such as recovery time objective (RTO) and recovery point objective (RPO)
- **Response documents**   These are all the documents that describe the required action of personnel when a disaster strikes, plus documents containing information required by those same personnel. Examples of these documents include
  - **Business recovery (or resumption) plan**   This describes the activities required to recover and resume critical business processes and activities.
  - **Occupant emergency plan (OEP)**   This describes activities required to care for occupants safely in a business location during a disaster. This will include both evacuation procedures and sheltering procedures, each of which may be required, depending upon the type of disaster that occurs.
  - **Emergency communications plan**   This describes the types of communications imparted to many parties, including emergency response personnel, employees in general, customers, suppliers, regulators, public safety organizations, shareholders, and the public.
  - **Contact lists**   These contain names and contact information for emergency response personnel as well as for critical suppliers, customers, and other parties.
  - **Disaster recovery plan**   This describes the activities required to restore critical IT systems and other critical assets, whether in alternate or primary locations.
  - **Continuity of operations plan (COOP)**   This describes the activities required to continue critical and strategic business functions at an alternate site.
  - **Security incident response plan (SIRP)**   This describes the steps required to deal with a security incident that could reach disastrous proportions.
- **Test and review documents**   This is the entire collection of documents related to tests of all of the different types of business continuity plans, as well as reviews and revisions to documents.

Testing Recovery and Continuity Plans

It's surprising what you can accomplish when no one is concerned about who gets the credit.
–Ronald Reagan

Business continuity and disaster recovery plans may look elegant and even ingenious on paper, but their true business value is unknown until their worth is proven through testing.

The process of testing DR and BC plans uncovers flaws not only in the plans, but also in the systems and processes that they are designed to protect. For example, testing a system recovery procedure may point out the absence of a critically needed hardware component, or a recovery procedure may contain a syntax or grammatical error that misleads the recovery team member and results in recovery delays. Testing is designed to uncover these types of issues.

Recovery and continuity plans need to be tested to prove their viability. Without testing, an organization has no way of really knowing whether its plans are effective. With ineffective plans, an organization has a far smaller chance of surviving a disaster.

Recovery and continuity plans have built-in obsolescence—not by design, but by virtue of the fact that technology and business processes in most organizations are undergoing constant change and improvement. Thus, it is imperative that newly developed or updated plans be tested as soon as possible to ensure their effectiveness.

Types of tests range from lightweight and unobtrusive to intense and disruptive and include the following:

- Document review
- Walkthrough
- Simulation
- Parallel test
- Cutover test

These tests are described in more detail in this section.

 TIP Usually, an organization will perform the less intensive tests first to identify the most obvious flaws and then follow with tests that require more effort.

Each type of test requires advance preparation and recordkeeping. Preparation will consist of several activities, including

- **Participants** The organization needs to identify personnel who will participate in an upcoming test. It is important to identify all relevant skill groups and department stakeholders so that the test will include a full slate of contributors.

- **Schedule** The availability of each participant needs to be confirmed so that the test will include participation from all stakeholders.

- **Facilities** For all but the document review test, proper facilities need to be identified and set up. This might consist of a large conference room or training room. If the test will take place over several hours, one or more meals and/or refreshments may be needed as well.

- **Scripting** The simulation test requires some scripting, usually in the form of one or more documents that describe a developing scenario and related circumstances. Scenario scripting can make parallel and cutover tests more interesting and valuable, but this can be considered optional.

- **Recordkeeping**   For all of the tests except the document review, one or more persons should take good notes that can be collected and organized after the test is completed.

- **Contingency plan**   The cutover test involves the cessation of processing on primary systems and the resumption of processing on recovery systems. This is the highest risk plan, and things can go wrong. A contingency plan to get primary systems running again in case something goes wrong during the test needs to be developed.

These preparation activities are shown in Table 5-13.

The various types of tests are discussed next.

Document Review   A *document review* test is a review of some or all disaster recovery and business continuity plans, procedures, and other documentation. Individuals typically review these documents on their own, at their own pace, but within whatever time constraints or deadlines have been established.

The purpose of a document review test is to review the accuracy and completeness of document content. Reviewers should read each document with a critical eye, point out any errors, and annotate the document with questions or comments that can be sent back to the document's author(s), who can make any necessary changes.

If significant changes are needed in one or more documents, the project team may want to include a second round of document review before moving on to more resource-intensive tests.

The owner or document manager for the organization's business continuity and disaster recovery planning project should document which persons review which documents and perhaps even include the review copies or annotations. This practice will create a more complete record of the activities related to the development and testing of important BCP planning and response documents. It will also help to capture the true cost and effort of the development and testing of BCP capabilities in the organization.

	Document Review	Walkthrough	Simulation	Parallel Test	Cutover Test
Participants	Yes	Yes	Yes	Yes	Yes
Schedule	Yes	Yes	Yes	Yes	Yes
Facilities		Yes	Yes	Yes	Yes
Scripting			Yes	Optional	Optional
Recordkeeping	Yes	Yes	Yes	Yes	Yes
Contingency plan					Yes

Table 5-13   Preparation Activities Required for Each Type of DR/BC Test

Walkthrough   A *walkthrough* is similar to a document review: it's a review of just the BCP documents. However, where a document review is carried out by individuals working on their own, a walkthrough is performed by a group of individuals in a live discussion.

A walkthrough is usually facilitated by a leader who guides the participants page by page through each document. The leader may read sections of the document aloud, describe various scenarios where information in a section might be relevant, and take comments and questions from participants.

A walkthrough is likely to take considerably more time than a document review. One participant's question on some minor point in the document could spark a worthwhile and lively discussion that could last a few minutes to an hour. The group leader or another person will need to take careful notes to record any deficiencies found in any of the documents as well as issues to be handled after the walkthrough. The leader will also need to control the pace of the review so that the group does not get unnecessarily hung up on minor points. Some discussions will need to be cut short or tabled for a later time or for an offline conversation among interested parties.

Even if major revisions are needed in recovery documents, it probably will be infeasible to conduct another walkthrough with updated documents. However, follow-up document reviews are probably warranted to ensure that the documents were updated appropriately, at least in the opinion of the walkthrough participants.

CAUTION   Participants in the walkthrough should carefully consider that the potential audience for recovery procedures may be persons who are not as familiar as they are with systems and processes. They need to remember that the ideal personnel may not be available during a real disaster. Participants also need to realize that the skill level of recovery personnel might be a little below that of the experts who operate systems and processes in normal circumstances. Finally, walkthrough participants need to remember that systems and processes undergo almost continuous change, which could render some parts of the recovery documentation obsolete or incorrect all too soon.

Simulation   A *simulation* is a test of disaster recovery and business continuity procedures where the participants take part in a "mock disaster" to add some realism to the process of thinking their way through procedures in emergency response documents.

A simulation could be an elaborate and choreographed walkthrough test, where a facilitator reads from a script and describes a series of unfolding events in a disaster such as a hurricane or an earthquake. This type of simulation could almost be viewed as "playacting," where the script is the set of emergency response documentation. By stimulating the imagination of simulation participants, it's possible for participants to imagine that a disaster is taking place, which may help them better understand what real disaster conditions could be like. It will help tremendously if the facilitator has experienced one or more disaster scenarios so that he or she can add more realism when describing events.

To make the simulation more credible and valuable, the scenario that is chosen should have a reasonable chance of actually occurring in the local area. Good choices would include an earthquake in San Francisco or Los Angeles, a volcanic eruption in Seattle, or an avalanche in Switzerland. A poor choice would be a hurricane or tsunami in central Asia, because these events would not ever occur there.

A simulation can also go a few steps further. For instance, the simulation can take place at an established emergency operations center, the same place where emergency command and control would operate in a real disaster. Also, the facilitator could change some of the participants' roles to simulate the real absence of certain key personnel to see how remaining personnel might conduct themselves in a real emergency.

 TIP   The facilitator of a simulation is limited only by his or her own imagination when organizing a simulation. One important fact to remember, though, is that a simulation does not actually affect any live or DR systems— it's all as pretend as the make-believe cardboard televisions and computers in furniture stores.

Parallel Test   A *parallel test* is an actual test of disaster recovery and/or business continuity response plans and their supporting IT systems. The purpose of a parallel test is to evaluate the ability of personnel to follow directives in emergency response plans— to set up the actual DR business processing or data processing capability. In a parallel test, personnel set up the IT systems that would be used in an actual disaster and operate those IT systems with real business transactions to determine whether the IT systems correctly perform the processing.

The outcome of a parallel test is threefold:

- It evaluates the accuracy of emergency response procedures.
- It evaluates the ability of personnel to follow the emergency response procedures correctly.
- It evaluates the ability of IT systems and other supporting apparatus to process real business transactions properly.

A parallel test is so named because live production systems continue to operate, while backup IT systems are processing business transactions *in parallel* to see if they process them the same as the live production systems do.

Setting up a valid parallel test is complicated in many cases. In effect, you need to insert a logical "Y cable" into the business process flow so that the information flow will split and flow both to production systems (without interfering with their operation) and to backup systems. Results of transactions need to be compared. Personnel need to be able to determine whether the backup systems would be *able* to output correct data *without actually having them do so*. In many complex environments, you would not want the DR system to actually feed information back into a live environment, because that may cause duplicate events to occur someplace else in the organization (or with customers, suppliers, or other parties). For instance, in a travel reservations system, you would not want a DR system to book actual travel, because that would cost real money and consume available space on an airline or other mode of transportation. But it would be important to know whether the DR system would be *able* to perform those functions. Somewhere along the line, it will be necessary to "unplug" the DR system from the rest of the environment and manually examine results to see if they appear to be correct.

Organizations that do want to see if their backup/DR systems can manage a *real* workload can perform a cutover test, which is discussed next.

Cutover Test   A *cutover test* is the most intrusive type of disaster recovery test. It will also provide the most reliable results in terms of answering the question of whether backup systems have the capacity and correct functionality to shoulder the real workload properly.

The consequences of a failed cutover test, however, might resemble an actual disaster: if any part of the cutover test fails, then real, live business processes will be going without the support of IT applications as though a real outage or disaster were in progress. But even a failure like this would show you that "no, the backup systems won't work in the event a real disaster were to happen later today."

In some respects, a cutover test is easier to perform than a parallel test. A parallel test is a little trickier, since business information is required to flow to the production system and to the backup system, which means that some artificial component has been somehow inserted into the environment. However, with a cutover test, business processing does take place on the backup systems only, which can often be achieved through a simple configuration someplace in the network or the systems layer of the environment.

 TIP   Not all organizations perform cutover tests, because they take a lot of resources to set up and they are risky. Many organizations find that a parallel test is sufficient to determine whether backup systems are accurate, and the risk of an embarrassing incident is almost zero with a parallel test.

Documenting Test Results   Every type and every iteration of DR plan testing needs to be documented. It's not enough to say, "We did the test on September 10, 2019, and it worked." First of all, no test goes perfectly—opportunities for improvement are always identified. But the most important part of testing is to discover *what parts* of the test still need work so that those parts of the plan can be fixed before the next test (or a real disaster).

As with any well-organized project, success is in the details. The road to success is littered with big and little mistakes, and all of the things that are identified in every sort of DR test need to be detailed so that the next iteration of the test will give better results.

Recording and comparing detailed test results from one test to the next will also help the organization to measure progress. By this I mean that the quality of emergency response plans should steadily improve from year to year. Simple mistakes of the past should not be repeated, and the only failures in future tests should be in new and novel parts of the environment that weren't well thought out to begin with. And even these should diminish over time.

Debriefing to Improving Recovery and Continuity Plans   Every test of recovery and response plans should include a debrief or review so that participants can discuss the outcome of the test: what went well, what went wrong, and how things should be done differently next time. All of this information should be collected by someone who will be responsible for making changes to relevant documents. The updated documents should be circulated among the test participants who can confirm whether their discussion and ideas are properly reflected in the document.

Training Personnel

The value and usefulness of a high-quality set of disaster response and continuity plans and procedures will be greatly diminished if those responsible for carrying out the procedures are unfamiliar with them.

A person cannot learn to ride a bicycle by reading even the most detailed how-to instructions on the subject, so it's equally unrealistic to expect personnel to be able to carry out disaster response procedures properly if they are inexperienced in those procedures.

Several forms of training can be made available for the personnel who are expected to be available if a disaster strikes, including

- **Document review**   Personnel can carefully read through procedure documents to become familiar with the nature of the recovery procedures. But, as mentioned earlier, this alone may be insufficient.

- **Participation in walkthroughs**   People who are familiar with specific processes and systems that are the subject of walkthroughs should participate in them. Exposing personnel to the walkthrough process will not only help to improve the walkthrough and recovery procedures, but will also provide a learning experience for participants.

- **Participation in simulations**   Taking part in simulations will similarly benefit the participants by giving them the experience of thinking through a disaster.

- **Participation in parallel and cutover tests**   Other than experiencing an actual disaster and its recovery operations, no experience is quite like participating in parallel and cutover tests. Here, participants will gain actual hands-on experience with critical business processes and IT environments by performing the actual procedures that they would in the event of a disaster. When a disaster strikes, those participants can draw upon their memory of having performed those procedures in the past, instead of just the memory of having read the procedures.

You can see that all of the levels of tests that need to be performed to verify the quality of response plans are also training opportunities for personnel. The development and testing of disaster-related plans and procedures provide a continuous learning experience for all of the personnel involved.

Making Plans Available to Personnel When Needed

When a disaster strikes, often one of the effects is no access to even the most critical IT systems. Given a 40-hour workweek, there is roughly a 25 percent likelihood that critical personnel will be at the business location when a disaster strikes (at least the violent type of disaster that strikes with no warning, such as an earthquake—other types of disasters, such as hurricanes, may afford the organization a little bit of time to anticipate the disaster's impact). The point is that chances are very good that the personnel who are available to respond may be unable to access the procedures and other information that they will need, unless special measures are taken.

 CAUTION Complete BCP documentation often contains details of key systems, operating procedures, recovery strategies, and even vendor and model identification of in-place equipment. This information can be misused if available to unauthorized personnel, so the mechanism selected for ensuring availability must include planning to prevent inadvertent disclosure.

Response and recovery procedures can be made available to personnel during a disaster in several ways:

- **Hard copy** Although many have grown accustomed to the paperless office, disaster recovery and response documentation should be available in hardcopy form. Copies, even multiple copies, should be available for each responder, with a copy at the workplace and another at home, and possibly even a set in the responder's vehicle.

- **Soft copy** Traditionally, softcopy documentation is kept on file servers, but as you might expect, those file servers might be unavailable in a disaster. Soft copies should be available on responders' portable devices (laptops, tablets, and smartphones). An organization can also consider issuing documentation on memory sticks and cards. Depending upon the type of disaster, it can be difficult to know what resources will be available to access documentation, so making it available in more than one form will ensure that at least one copy of it will be available to the personnel who need access to it.

- **Alternate work/processing site** Organizations that utilize a hot/warm/cold site for the recovery of critical operations can maintain hard copies and/or soft copies of recovery documentation there. This makes perfect sense; personnel working at an alternate processing or work site will need to know what to do, and having those procedures on-site will facilitate their work.

- **Online** Soft copies of recovery documentation can be archived on an Internet-based site that includes the ability to store data. Almost any type of online service that includes authentication and the ability to upload documents could be suitable for this purpose.

- **Wallet cards** It's unreasonable to expect to publish recovery documentation on a laminated wallet card, but those cards could be used to store the contact information for core response team members as well as a few other pieces of information, such as conference bridge codes, passwords to online repositories of documentation, and so on. An example wallet card appears earlier in this chapter, in Figure 5-30.

Maintaining Recovery and Continuity Plans

Business processes and technology undergo almost continuous change in most organizations. A business continuity plan that is developed and tested is liable to be outdated within months and obsolete within a year. If much more than a year passes, a DR plan in some organizations may approach uselessness. This section discusses how organizations need to keep their DR plans up-to-date and relevant.

A typical organization needs to establish a schedule whereby the principal DR documents will be reviewed. Depending on the rate of change, this could be as frequently as quarterly or as seldom as every two years.

Further, every change, however insignificant, in business processes and information systems should include a step to review, and possibly update, relevant DR documents. That is, a review of, and possibly changes to, relevant DR documents should be a required step in every business process engineering or information systems change process and a key component of the organization's information systems development life cycle (SDLC). If this is done faithfully, then you would expect that the annual review of DR documents would conclude that few (if any) changes were required, although it is still a good practice to perform a periodic review, just to be sure.

Periodic testing of DR documents and plans, discussed in detail in the preceding section, is another vital activity. Testing validates the accuracy and relevance of DR documents, and any issues or exceptions in the testing process should precipitate updates to appropriate documents.

Sources for Best Practices

It is unnecessary to begin BCP and disaster recovery planning (DRP) by first inventing a practice or methodology. BCP and DRP are advanced professions with several professional associations, professional certifications, international standards, and publications. Any or all of these are, or can lead to, sources of practices, processes, and methodologies:

- **U.S. National Institute of Standards and Technology (NIST)** This branch of the U.S. Department of Commerce is responsible for developing business and technology standards for the federal government. The quality of the standards developed by NIST is exceedingly high, and as a result many private organizations all over the world are adopting them. The NIST web site is at https://www.nist.gov.

- **Business Continuity Institute (BCI)** This membership organization is dedicated to the advancement of business continuity management. BCI has more than 8,000 members in almost 100 countries. BCI holds several events around the world, prints a professional journal, and it has developed a professional certification, the Certificate of the BCI (CBCI). Its web site is at https://www.thebci.org.

- **U.S. National Fire Protection Agency (NFPA)** NFPA has developed a pre-incident planning standard, NFPA 1620, which addresses the protection, construction, and features of buildings and other structures. It also requires the development of pre-incident plans that emergency responders can use to deal with fires and other emergencies. The NFPA web site is at https://www.nfpa.org.

- **U.S. Federal Emergency Management Agency (FEMA)**   FEMA is a part of the Department of Homeland Security (DHS) and is responsible for emergency disaster relief planning information and services. FEMA's most visible activities are its relief operations in the wake of hurricanes and floods in the United States. Its web site is at https://www.fema.gov.

- **Disaster Recovery Institute International (DRI International)**   This professional membership organization provides education and professional certifications for DRP professionals. Its web site is at https://drii.org. Its certifications include

  - Associate Business Continuity Professional (ABCP)
  - Certified Business Continuity Vendor (CBCV)
  - Certified Functional Continuity Professional (CFCP)
  - Certified Business Continuity Professional (CBCP)
  - Master Business Continuity Professional (MBCP)
  - Certified Business Continuity Auditor (CBCA)
  - Certified Business Continuity Lead Auditor (CBCLA)

- **Business Continuity Management Institute (BCM Institute)**   This professional association specializes in education and professional certification. BCM Institute is a co-organizer of the World Continuity Congress, an annual conference that is dedicated to business continuity and disaster recovery planning. Its web site is at https://www.bcm-institute.org. Certifications offered by BCM Institute include

  - Business Continuity Certified Expert (BCCE)
  - Business Continuity Certified Specialist (BCCS)
  - Business Continuity Certified Planner (BCCP)
  - Business Continuity Certified Auditor (BCCA)
  - Business Continuity Certified Lead Auditor (BCCLA)
  - DR Certified Planner (DRCP)
  - Disaster Recovery Certified Expert (DRCE)
  - Disaster Recovery Certified Specialist (DRCS)
  - Crisis Management Certified Planner (CMCP)
  - Crisis Management Certified Specialist (CMCS)
  - Crisis Management Certified Expert (CMCE)
  - Crisis Communication Certified Planner (CCCP)
  - Crisis Communication Certified Specialist (CCCS)
  - Crisis Communication Certified Expert (CCCE)

Disaster Recovery Planning

DRP is undertaken to reduce risks related to the onset of disasters and other events and is closely related to BCP. The groundwork for DRP begins in BCP activities such as the business impact analysis, criticality analysis, establishment of recovery objectives, and testing. The outputs from these activities are the key inputs to DRP:

- The business impact analysis and criticality analysis help to prioritize which business processes (and, therefore, which IT systems) are the most important.
- Key recovery targets specify how quickly specific IT applications are to be recovered. This guides DRP personnel as they develop new IT architectures that make IT systems compliant with those objectives.
- Testing of DRP plans can be performed in coordination with tests of BCP plans to simulate real disasters and disaster response more accurately.

Business continuity planning is discussed in detail in Chapter 2.

Disaster Response Team Roles and Responsibilities

Disaster recovery plans need to specify the teams that are required for disaster response, as well as each team's roles and responsibilities. Table 5-14 describes several teams and their roles.

NOTE   Some of the roles in Table 5-14 may overlap with responsibilities defined in the organization's BCP. DR and BC planners will need to work together to ensure that the organization's overall response to disaster is appropriate and does not overlook vital functions. Also, because of variations in organizations' disaster response plans, some of these teams will not be needed in some organizations.

Recovery Objectives

During the business impact analysis and criticality analysis phases of a BC/DR project, the speed with which each business activity (with its underlying IT systems) needs to be restored after a disaster is determined.

Recovery Time Objective   *Recovery time objective* (RTO) is the period from the onset of an outage until the resumption of service. RTO is usually measured in hours or days. Each process and system in the BIA should have an RTO value.

RTO does not mean that the system (or process) has been recovered to 100 percent of its former capacity. Far from it—in an emergency situation, management may determine that a DR server in another city with, say, 60 percent of the capacity of the original server is adequate. That said, an organization could establish two RTO targets, one for partial capacity and one for full capacity.

NOTE   For a given organization, it's probably best to use one unit of measure for recovery objectives for all systems. That will help to avoid any errors that would occur during a rank-ordering of systems so that, for example, two days does not appear to be a shorter period than four hours.

Team	Responsibilities
Emergency Management	Coordinates activities of all other response teams
First Responders	Usually outside personnel such as police, fire, and rescue who help to extinguish fires, evacuate personnel, and provide emergency medical aid
Communications	Coordinates communication among teams, as well as between teams and outside entities
Damage Assessment	Examines equipment, supplies, furnishing, and assets to determine what can be used immediately in support of critical processes and what will need to be handed off to salvage teams
Salvage	Examines equipment, supplies, furnishings, and other assets to determine what can be salvaged for immediate or long-term reuse
Network Engineering	Establishes and maintains electronic (voice and data) communications in support of critical services during a disaster
Systems Engineering	Establishes and maintains systems as needed to support critical applications and services
Database Engineering	Establishes and maintains database management systems as needed to support critical applications; performs data recovery, using local or remotely stored media as needed
Application Support	Establishes and maintains critical applications in support of critical business processes
Application Development	Makes changes to critical applications as needed during the recovery effort
End-User Computing	Establishes and maintains end-user computing facilities (desktop computers, laptop computers, mobile devices, etc.) as needed in support of critical applications and services
Systems Operations	Performs routine and nonroutine tasks such as backups to keep critical applications running
Transportation	Coordinates transportation of personnel to recovery sites
Relocation	Acquires housing and other resources needed by personnel who are working at remote operations centers
Security	Coordinates physical and logical security activities to ensure the continuous protection of staff, assets, and information
Finance	Facilitates the availability of financial resources as needed to commence and continue emergency response operations

Table 5-14 Disaster Response Teams' Roles and Responsibilities

Further, a system that has been recovered in a disaster situation might not have 100 percent of its functionality. For instance, an application that lets users view transactions that are more than two years old may, in a recovery situation, only contain 30 days' worth of data. Again, such a decision is usually the result of a careful analysis of the cost of recovering different features and functions in an application environment. In a larger, complex environment, some features might be considered critical, while others are less so.

CAUTION   Senior management should be involved in any discussion related to recovery system specifications in terms of capacity, integrity, or functionality.

Recovery Point Objective   A *recovery point objective* (RPO) is the period of time for which recent data will be irretrievably lost in a disaster. Like RTO, RPO is usually measured in hours or days. However, for critical transaction systems, RPO could even be measured in minutes or seconds.

RPO is usually expressed as a worst-case figure; for instance, a transaction processing system RPO will be two hours or less.

The value of a system's RPO is usually a direct result of the frequency of data backup or replication. For example, if an application server is backed up once per day, the RPO is going to be at least 24 hours (or one day, whichever way you like to express it). Maybe it will take three days to rebuild the server, but once data is restored from backup tape, no more than the last 24 hours of transactions are lost. In this case, the RTO is three days and the RPO is one day.

Publishing RTO and RPO Figures   If the storage system for an application takes a snapshot every hour, the RPO could be one hour, unless the storage system itself was damaged in a disaster. If the snapshot is replicated to another storage system four times per day, then the RPO might be better expressed as six to eight hours.

The last example brings up an interesting point. There may not be one "golden" RPO figure for a given system. Instead, the severity of a disrupting event or a disaster will dictate the time to get systems running again (RTO) with a certain amount of data loss (RPO). Here are some examples:

- A server's CPU or memory fails and is replaced and restarted in two hours. No data is lost. The RTO is two hours and the RPO is zero.

- The storage system supporting an application suffers a hardware failure that results in the loss of all data. Data is recovered from a snapshot on another server taken every six hours. The RPO is six hours in this case.

- The database in a transaction application is corrupted and must be recovered. Backups are taken twice per day. The RPO is 12 hours. However, it takes 10 hours to rebuild indexes on the database, so the RTO is closer to 22–24 hours, since the application cannot be returned to service until indexes are available.

 NOTE   When publishing RTO and RPO figures to customers, it's best to publish the worst-case figures: "If our data center burns to the ground, our RTO is X hours and the RPO is Y hours." Saying it that way would be simpler than publishing a chart that shows RPO and RTO figures for various types of disasters.

Pricing RTO and RPO Capabilities   Generally speaking, the shorter the RTO or RPO for a given system, the more expensive it will be to achieve the target. Table 5-15 depicts a range of RTOs along with the technologies needed to achieve them and their relative cost.

RTO/RPO	Technologies Needed	Cost
2 weeks	Backup tapes; purchase a server if the original server has burned or floated away	$
1 week	Backup tapes; replacement server on hand	$$
2 days	Backup tapes; application software installed on replacement server	$$
12 hours	Backup tapes or replication; application server installed and running on replacement server	$$$
1 hour	Server cluster with auto or manual failover; near-real-time replication	$$$$
5 minutes	Load balancing or rapid failover server cluster; real-time replication	$$$$$

Table 5-15   The Lower the RTO, the Higher the Cost to Achieve It

The BCP project team needs to understand the relationship between the *time* required to recover an application and the *cost* required to recover the application within that time. A shorter recovery time is more expensive, and this relationship is not linear. This means that reducing RPO from three days to six hours may mean that the equipment and software investment might double, or it might increase eightfold. There are so many factors involved in the supporting infrastructure for a given application that the BCP project team has to just knuckle down and develop the cost for a few different RTO and RPO figures. Once costs have been analyzed and approved, the actual DR capabilities can be designed and implemented.

The business value of the application itself is the primary driver in determining the amount of investment that senior management is willing to make to reach any arbitrary RTO and RPO figures. This business value may be measured in local currency if the application supports revenue. However, the loss of an application during a disaster may harm the organization's reputation. Again, management will have to make a decision on how much it will be willing to invest in DR capabilities that bring RTO and RPO figures down to acceptable levels. Figure 5-32 illustrates these relationships.

Developing Recovery Strategies

When management has chosen specific RPO and RTO targets for a given system or process, the BCP project team can roll up its sleeves and devise some ways to meet these targets. This section discusses the technologies and logistics associated with various

Figure 5-32
Aim for the sweet spot and balance the costs of downtime and recovery.

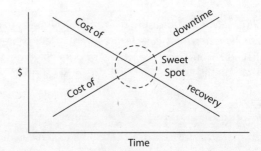

Figure 5-33
Recovery
objective
development
flowchart

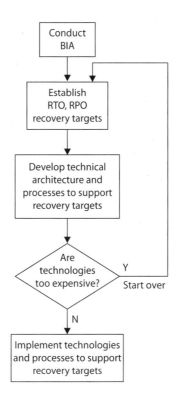

recovery strategies. This will help the project team to decide which types of strategies are best suited for their organization.

Developing recovery strategies to meet specific recovery targets is an iterative process. The project team will develop a strategy to reach specific targets for a specific cost; senior management could well decide that the cost is too high and they are willing to increase RPO and/or RTO targets accordingly. Similarly, the project team could also discover that it is less costly to achieve specific RPO and RTO targets, and management could respond by lowering those targets. This is illustrated in Figure 5-33.

Site Recovery Options   In a worst-case disaster scenario, the site where information systems reside is partially or completely destroyed. In most cases, the organization cannot afford to wait for the damaged or destroyed facility to be restored, as this could take weeks or months. If an organization can take *that* long to recover an application, you'd have to wonder whether it is needed at all. The assumption has got to be that in a disaster scenario, critical applications will be recovered in another location. This other location is called a *recovery site*. There are two dimensions to the process of choosing a recovery site: the first is the speed at which the application will be recovered at the recovery site; the second is the location of the recovery site itself. Both are discussed here.

As you might expect, speed costs. If a system is to be recovered within a few minutes or hours, the costs will be much higher than if the system can be recovered in five days.

	Site Type	Speed to Recovery	Cost
Table 5-16 Relative Costs of Recovery Sites	Hot	0–24 hours	$$$$
	Warm	24 hours–7 days	$$$
	Cold	More than 7 days	$$
	Mobile	2–7 days	$$$–$$$$

Various types of facilities are available for rapid or not-too-rapid recovery. These facilities are called *hot sites*, *warm sites*, and *cold sites*. As the names might suggest, hot sites permit rapid recovery, while cold sites provide a much slower recovery. The costs associated with these are somewhat proportional as well, as illustrated in Table 5-16.

 NOTE The use of a private or public cloud, although not explicitly included in Table 5-16, offers varying degrees of recovery site readiness that can be established in the cloud, which includes both hot and warm sites.

The details about each type of site are discussed in the remainder of this section.

Hot Sites A *hot site* is an alternate processing center where backup systems are already running in some state of near-readiness to assume production workload. The systems at a hot site most likely have application software and database management software already loaded and running, perhaps even at the same patch levels as the systems in the primary processing center.

A hot site is the best choice for systems whose RTO targets range from zero to several hours, perhaps as long as 24 hours.

A hot site may consist of infrastructure in a private or public cloud, or leased rack space (or even a cage for larger installations) at a colocation center. If the organization has its own processing centers, then a hot site for a given system would consist of the required rack space to house the recovery systems. Recovery servers will be installed and running, with the same version and patch level for the operating system, database management system (if used), and application software.

Systems at a hot site require the same level of administration and maintenance as the primary systems. When patches or configuration changes are made to primary systems, they should be made to hot-site systems at the same time or very shortly afterward.

Because systems at a hot site need to be at or very near a state of readiness, a strategy needs to be developed regarding a method for keeping the data on hot standby systems current. This is discussed in detail in the later section "Recovery and Resilience Technologies."

Systems at a hot site should have full network connectivity. A method for quickly directing network traffic toward the recovery servers needs to be worked out in advance so that a switchover can be accomplished. This is also discussed in the "Recovery and Resilience Technologies" section.

When setting up a hot site, the organization will need to send one or more technical staff members to the site to set up systems. But once the systems are operating, much or all of the system- and database-level administration can be performed remotely. However, in a disaster scenario, the organization may need to send the administrative staff to the site for day-to-day management of the systems. This means that workspace for these personnel needs to be identified so that they can perform their duties during the recovery operation.

NOTE   Hot-site planning needs to consider work (desk) space for on-site personnel. Some colocation centers provide limited work areas, but these areas are often shared and often have little privacy for phone discussions. Also, transportation, hotel, and dining accommodations need to be arranged, possibly in advance, if the hot site is in a different city from the primary site.

Warm Sites   A *warm site* is an alternate processing center where recovery systems are present, but at a lower state of readiness than recovery systems at a hot site. For example, while the same version of the operating system may be running on the warm site system, it may be a few patch levels behind primary systems. The same could be said about the versions and patch levels of database management systems (if used) and application software: they may be present, but they're not as up-to-date as they are on the primary systems. Like a hot site, a warm site can be implemented in a private or public cloud, a colocation center, or an organization's own alternate processing center.

A warm site is appropriate for an organization whose RTO figures range from roughly one to seven days. In a disaster scenario, recovery teams would travel to the warm site and work to get the recovery systems to a state of production readiness and to get systems up-to-date with patches and configuration changes to bring the systems into a state of complete readiness.

A warm site is also used when the organization is willing to take the time necessary to recover data from tape or other backup media. Depending upon the size of the database(s), this recovery task can take several hours to a few days.

The primary advantage of a warm site is that its costs are lower than for a hot site, particularly in the effort required to keep the recovery system up-to-date. The site may not require expensive data replication technology, but instead data can be recovered from backup media.

Cold Sites   A *cold site* is an alternate processing center where the degree of readiness for recovery systems is low. At the very least, a cold site is nothing more than an empty rack or allocated space on a computer room floor. It's just an address in someone's data center or colocation site where computers can be set up and used at some future date. A cold site could also exist in the form of an enterprise account established at a public cloud organization, but where no infrastructure has been created and configured.

Often, there is little or no equipment at a cold site. When a disaster or other highly disruptive event occurs in which the outage is expected to exceed seven to fourteen days, the organization will order computers from a manufacturer or perhaps have computers shipped from some other business location, so that they can arrive at the cold site soon after the disaster event has begun. Then personnel would travel to the site and set up

	Cold	Warm	Hot
Computers	Ship to site	On-site	Running
Application Software	To be installed	Installed	Running
Data	To be recovered	To be recovered	Continuously updated
Connectivity	To be established	Ready to go	Already connected
Support Staff	Travel to site	Travel to site	On-site or remotely managed
Cost	Lowest	Moderate	Highest

Table 5-17 Detailed Comparison of Cold, Warm, and Hot Sites

the computers, operating systems, databases, network equipment, and so on, and get applications running within several days.

The advantage of a cold site is its low cost. The main disadvantage is the cost, time, and effort required to bring it to operational readiness in a short period. But for some organizations, a cold site is exactly what is needed.

Table 5-17 shows a comparison of hot, warm, and cold recovery sites and a few characteristics of each.

Mobile Sites   A *mobile site* is a portable recovery center that can be delivered to almost any location in the world. A viable alternative to a fixed location recovery site, a mobile site can be transported by semi-truck and may even have its own generator, communications, and cooling capabilities.

APC and SunGard have mobile sites installed in semi-truck trailers. Oracle has mobile sites that can include a configurable selection of servers and workstations, all housed in shipping containers that can be shipped by truck, rail, ship, or air to any location in the world.

Cloud Sites   Organizations are increasingly using cloud hosting services as their recovery sites. Such sites charge for the utilization of servers and devices in virtual environments. Hence, capital costs for recovery sites is near zero and operational costs come into play as recovery sites are used.

As organizations become accustomed to building recovery sites in the cloud, they are with increasing frequency moving their primary processing sites to the cloud as well.

Reciprocal Sites   A *reciprocal recovery site* is a data center that is operated by another company. Two or more organizations with similar processing needs will draw up a legal contract that obligates one or more of the organizations to house another party's systems temporarily in the event of a disaster.

Often, a reciprocal agreement pledges not only floor space in a data center, but also the use of the reciprocal partner's computer system. This type of arrangement is less common, but it is used by organizations that use mainframe computers and other high-cost systems.

NOTE With the wide use of public cloud and Internet colocation centers, reciprocal sites have fallen out of favor. Still, they may be ideal for organizations with mainframe computers that are otherwise too expensive to deploy to a cold or warm site.

Geographic Site Selection An important factor in the process of recovery site selection is the location of the recovery site. The distance between the main processing site and the recovery site is vital and may figure heavily into the viability and success of a recovery operation.

A recovery site should not be located in the same geographic region as the primary site. A recovery site in the same region may be involved in the same regional disaster as the primary site and may be unavailable for use or be suffering from the same problems present at the primary site.

NOTE "Geographic region" refers to a location that will likely experience the effects of the same regional disaster that affects the primary site. No arbitrarily chosen distance (such as 100 miles) guarantees sufficient separation. In some locales, 50 miles is plenty of distance; in other places, 300 miles is too close—it all depends on the nature of disasters that are likely to occur in these areas. Information on regional disasters should be available from local disaster preparedness authorities or from local disaster recovery experts.

Considerations When Using Third-Party Disaster Recovery Sites Since most organizations cannot afford to implement their own secondary processing site, the only other option is to use a disaster recovery site that is owned by a third party. This could be a colocation center, a disaster services center, or a public cloud provider. An organization considering such a site needs to ensure that its services contract addresses the following:

- **Disaster definition** The definition of disaster needs to be broad enough to meet the organization's requirements.

- **Equipment configuration** IT equipment must be configured as needed to support critical applications during a disaster.

- **Availability of equipment during a disaster** IT equipment needs to be available during a disaster. In the case of disaster service providers, the organization needs to know how the disaster service provider will allocate equipment if many of its customers suffer a disaster simultaneously.

- **Customer priorities** The organization needs to know whether the disaster services provider has any customers (government or military, for example) whose priorities may exceed their own.

- **Data communications** There must be sufficient bandwidth and capacity for the organization plus other customers who may be operating at the disaster provider's center at the same time.

- **Testing**   The organization needs to know what testing it is permitted to perform on the service provider's systems so that the ability to recover from a disaster can be tested in advance.

- **Right to audit**   The organization should have a "right to audit" clause in its contract so that it can verify the presence and effectiveness of all key controls in place at the recovery facility. Note, however, that a right to audit is generally not an option for public cloud providers.

- **Security and environmental controls**   The organization needs to know what security and environmental controls are in place at the disaster recovery facility.

Acquiring Additional Hardware   Many organizations elect to acquire their own server, storage, and network hardware for disaster recovery purposes. How an organization goes about acquiring hardware depends on its high-level recovery strategy:

- **Cold site**   An organization will need to be able to purchase hardware as soon as the disaster occurs.

- **Warm site**   An organization probably will need to purchase hardware in advance of the disaster, but it may be able to purchase hardware when the disaster occurs. The choice will depend on the recovery time objective.

- **Hot site**   An organization will need to purchase its recovery hardware in advance of the disaster.

- **Cloud**   An organization will not need to purchase hardware, as this is provided by the cloud infrastructure provider.

Pros and cons to these strategies are listed in Table 5-18. Warm site strategy is not listed, since an organization could purchase hardware either in advance of the disaster or when it occurs. But because cold, hot, and cloud sites are deterministic, they are included in the table.

Strategy	Advantages	Disadvantages
Hot	Hardware already purchased and ready for use	Capital tied up in equipment that may never be used Higher cost to continue maintaining recovery systems
Cold	Capital spent only if needed Lower costs (until a disaster occurs)	Appropriate equipment may be difficult to find and purchase Difficult to test recovery strategy unless hardware is purchased, leased, or borrowed
Cloud	Zero capital costs Operational costs incurred as cloud-based infrastructure used	Infrastructure owned by a third party

Table 5-18   Hardware Acquisition Pros and Cons for Hot, Cold, and Cloud Recovery Sites

The main reasons for choosing a cloud hosting provider are to eliminate capital costs and to rapidly develop and deploy virtual infrastructure. The cloud hosting provider provides all hardware and charges organizations when the hardware is used.

Dual-Purpose Infrastructure   The primary business reason for not choosing a hot site is the high capital cost required to purchase disaster recovery equipment that may never be used. One way around this obstacle is to put those recovery systems to work every day. For example, recovery systems could be used for development or testing of the same applications that are used in production. This way, systems that are purchased for recovery purposes are being well utilized for other purposes, and they'll be ready in case a disaster occurs.

When a disaster occurs, the organization will be less concerned about development and testing and more concerned about keeping critical production applications running. It will be a small sacrifice to forgo development or testing (or whatever low-criticality functions are using the DR hardware) during a disaster.

Recovery and Resilience Technologies   Once recovery targets have been established, the next major task is to survey and select technologies to enable recovery time and recovery point objectives to be met. Several important factors when considering each technology are

- Does the technology help the information system achieve the RTO and RPO targets?
- Does the cost of the technology meet or exceed budget constraints?
- Can the technology be used to benefit other information systems (thereby lowering the cost for each system)?
- Does the technology fit well into the organization's current IT operations?
- Will operations staff require specialized training on the technology used for recovery?
- Does the technology contribute to the simplicity of the overall IT architecture, or does it complicate it unnecessarily?

These questions are designed to help determine whether a specific technology is a good fit, from a technology perspective as well as from process and operational perspectives.

RAID   Redundant Array of Independent Disks (RAID) is a family of technologies used to improve the reliability, performance, or size of disk-based storage systems. From a disaster recovery or systems resilience perspective, the feature of RAID that is of particular interest is the reliability. RAID is used to create virtual disk volumes over an array (pun intended) of disk storage devices and can be configured so that the failure of any individual disk drive in the array will not affect the availability of data on the disk array.

RAID is usually implemented on a hardware device called a *disk array*, which is a chassis in which several hard disks can be installed and connected to a server. The individual disk drives can usually be "hot swapped" in the chassis while the array is still operating. When the array is configured with RAID, a failure of a single disk drive will have no effect on the disk array's availability to the server to which it is connected. A system operator can be alerted to the disk's failure, and the defective disk drive can be removed and replaced while the array is still fully operational.

There are several options, or *levels*, for RAID configuration:

- **RAID-0** This is known as a *striped volume*, where a disk volume splits data evenly across two or more disks to improve performance.

- **RAID-1** This creates a *mirror*, where data written to one disk in the array is also written to a second disk in the array. RAID-1 makes the volume more reliable through the preservation of data, even when one disk in the array fails.

- **RAID-4** This level of RAID employs data striping at the block level by adding a dedicated parity disk. The parity disk permits the rebuilding of data in the event one of the other disks fails.

- **RAID-5** This is similar to RAID-4 block-level striping, except that the parity data is distributed evenly across all of the disks instead of dedicated on one disk. Like RAID-4, RAID-5 allows for the failure of one disk without losing information.

- **RAID-6** This is an extension of RAID-5, where two parity blocks are used instead of a single parity block. The advantage of RAID-6 is that it can withstand the failure of any two disk drives in the array, instead of a single disk, as is the case with RAID-5.

 NOTE Several nonstandard RAID levels have been developed by various hardware and software companies. Some of these are extensions of RAID standards, while others are entirely different.

Storage systems are hardware devices that are entirely separate from servers—their only purpose is to store a large amount of data and to be highly reliable through the use of redundant components and the use of one or more RAID levels. Storage systems generally come in two forms:

- **Storage area network (SAN)** This stand-alone storage system can be configured to contain several virtual volumes and to connect to several servers through fiber optic cables. The servers' operating systems will often consider this storage to be "local," as though it consisted of one or more hard disks present in the server's own chassis.

- **Network attached storage (NAS)** This stand-alone storage system contains one or more virtual volumes. Servers access these volumes over the network using the NFS or Server Message Block/Common Internet File System (SMB/CIFS) protocols, common on Unix and Windows operating systems, respectively.

NOTE   In public cloud environments, the physical implementation of storage is an abstraction.

Replication   *Replication* is an activity whereby data written to a storage system is also copied over a network to another storage system. The result is the presence of up-to-date data that exists on two or more storage systems, each of which could be located in a different geographic region.

Replication can be handled in several ways and at different levels in the technology stack:

- **Disk storage system**   Data-write operations that take place in a disk storage system (such as a SAN or NAS) can be transmitted over a network to another disk storage system, where the same data will be written to the other system.

- **Operating system**   The operating system can control replication so that updates to a particular file system can be transmitted to another server where those updates will be applied locally on that other server.

- **Database management system**   The database management system (DBMS) can manage replication by sending transactions to a DBMS on another server.

- **Transaction management system**   The transaction management system (TMS) can manage replication by sending transactions to a counterpart TMS located elsewhere.

- **Application**   The application can write its transactions to two different storage systems. This method is not often used.

- **Virtualization**   Virtual machine images can be replicated to recovery sites to speed the recovery of applications.

Replication can take place from one system to another system in *primary-backup* replication. This is the typical setup when data on an application server is sent to a distant storage system for data recovery or disaster recovery purposes.

Replication can also be bidirectional, between two active servers, called *multiprimary* or *multimaster*. This method is more complicated, because simultaneous transactions on different servers could conflict with one another (such as two reservation agents trying to book two passengers in the same seat on an airline flight). Some form of concurrent transaction control would be required, such as a *distributed lock manager*.

In terms of the speed and integrity of replicated information, there are two types of replication:

- **Synchronous replication**   Writing data to a local and to a remote storage system is performed as a single operation, guaranteeing that data on the remote storage system is identical to data on the local storage system. Synchronous replication incurs a performance penalty, as the speed of the entire transaction is slowed to the rate of the remote transaction.

- **Asynchronous replication** Writing data to the remote storage system is not kept in sync with updates on the local storage system. Instead, there may be a time lag, and you have no guarantee that data on the remote system is identical to data on the local storage system. However, performance is improved, because transactions are considered complete when they have been written to the local storage system only. Bursts of local updates to data will take a finite period to replicate to the remote server, subject to the available bandwidth of the network connection between the local and remote storage systems.

 NOTE Replication is often used for applications where the RTO is smaller than the time necessary to recover data from backup media. For example, if a critical application's RTO is established to be two hours, then recovery from backup tape is probably not a viable option, even if backups are performed every two hours. While more expensive than recovery from backup media, replication ensures that up-to-date information is present on a remote storage system that can be brought online in a short period.

Server Clusters A *cluster* is a collection of two or more servers that appears as a single server resource. Clusters are often the technology of choice for applications that require a high degree of availability and a very small RTO, measured in minutes.

When an application is implemented on a cluster, even if one of the servers in the cluster fails, the other server (or servers) in the cluster will continue to run the application, usually with no user awareness that a failure occurred.

There are two typical configurations for clusters, *active-active* and *active-passive*. In active-active mode, all servers in the cluster are running and servicing application requests. This is often used in high-volume applications where many servers are required to service the application workload.

In active-passive mode, one or more servers in the cluster are active and servicing application requests, while one or more servers in the cluster are in "standby" mode; they can service application requests but won't do so unless one of the active servers fails or goes offline for any reason. When an active server goes offline and a standby server takes over, this event is called a *failover*.

A typical server cluster architecture is shown in Figure 5-34.

A server cluster is typically implemented in a single physical location such as a data center. However, a cluster can also be implemented where great distances separate the servers in the cluster. This type of cluster is called a *geographic cluster*, or geo-cluster. Servers in a geo-cluster are connected through a WAN connection. A typical geographic cluster architecture is shown in Figure 5-35.

Network Connectivity and Services An overall application environment that is required to be resilient and have recoverability must have those characteristics present within the network that supports it. A highly resilient application architecture that includes clustering and replication would be of little value if it had only a single network connection that was a single point of failure.

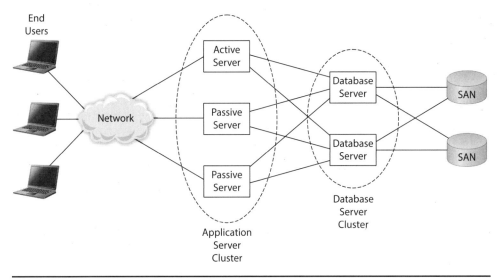

Figure 5-34 Application and database server clusters

An application that requires high availability and resilience may require one or more of the following in the supporting network:

- **Redundant network connections** These may include multiple network adapters on a server, but also a fully redundant network architecture with multiple switches, routers, load balancers, and firewalls. They could also include physically diverse network provider connections, where network service provider feeds enter the building from two different directions.

- **Redundant network services** Certain network services are vital to the continued operation of applications, such as DNS (the function of translating server names like www.mcgraw-hill.com into an IP address), NTP (used to synchronize computer time clocks), SMTP, SNMP, authentication services, and perhaps others. These services are usually operated on servers that may require clustering and/or replication of their own so that the application will be able to continue functioning in the event of a disaster.

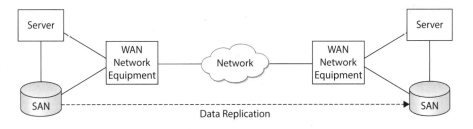

Figure 5-35 Geographic cluster with data replication

Developing Recovery Plans

A DRP effort starts with the initial phases of the BCP project: the business impact analysis (BIA) and criticality analysis (CA) lead to the establishment of recovery objectives that determine how quickly critical business processes need to be back up and running.

With this information, the DR team can determine what additional data processing equipment is needed (if any) and establish a roadmap for acquiring that equipment.

The other major component in the DR project is the development of recovery plans. These are the process and procedure documents that will be vital when a disaster has been declared. These processes and procedures will instruct response personnel how to establish and operate business processes and IT systems after a disaster has occurred. It's not enough to have all of the technology ready if personnel don't know what to do.

Most DR plans are going to have common components:

- **Disaster declaration procedure**   This needs to include criteria for how a disaster is determined and who has the authority to declare a disaster.

- **Roles and responsibilities**   DR plans need to specify what activities need to be performed and specify which persons or teams are best equipped to perform them.

- **Emergency contact lists**   Response personnel need contact information for other personnel so that they may establish and maintain communications as the disaster unfolds and recovery operations begin. These contact lists should include several different ways of contacting personnel, since some disasters have an adverse impact on regional telecommunications infrastructure.

- **System recovery procedures**   These are the detailed steps for getting recovery systems up and running. These procedures will include a lot of detail describing obtaining data, configuring servers and network devices, confirming that the application and business information is healthy, and starting business applications.

- **System operations procedures**   These are detailed steps for operating critical IT systems while they are in recovery mode. These detailed procedures are needed because the systems in recovery mode may need to be operated differently from their production counterparts; further, they may need to be operated by personnel who have not been doing this before.

- **System restoration procedures**   These are the detailed steps to restore IT operations back to the original production systems.

 NOTE   Business continuity and disaster recovery plans work together to get critical business functions operating again after a disaster. Because of this, BC and DR teams need to work closely when developing their respective response procedures to make sure that all activities are covered, but without unnecessary overlap (or gaps).

DR plans need to take into account the likely disaster scenarios that may occur to an organization. Understanding these scenarios can help the DR team take a more pragmatic approach when creating response procedures. The added benefit is that not all disasters result in the entire loss of a computing facility. Most are more limited in their scope, although all of them can result in a complete inability to continue operations. Some of these scenarios are

- Complete loss of network connectivity
- Sustained electric power outage
- Loss of a key system (this could be a server, storage system, or network device)
- Extensive data corruption or data loss

These scenarios are probably more likely to occur than a catastrophe such as a major earthquake or hurricane (depending on where your data center is located).

Data Backup and Recovery

Disasters and other disruptive events can damage information and information systems. It's essential that fresh copies of this information exist elsewhere in a form that enables IT personnel to load this information easily into alternative systems so that processing can resume as quickly as possible.

CAUTION   Testing backups is important; testing recoverability is critical. In other words, performing backups is only valuable to the extent that backed up data can be recovered at a future time.

Backup to Tape and Other Media   In organizations still utilizing their own IT infrastructure, tape backup is just about as ubiquitous as power cords. From a DR perspective, however, the issue probably is not whether the organization *has* tape backup, but whether its current backup capabilities are adequate in the context of disaster recovery. An organization's backup capability may need to be upgraded if

- The current backup system is difficult to manage.
- Whole-system restoration takes too long.
- The system lacks flexibility with regard to DR (for instance, how difficult it would be to recover information onto a different type of system).
- The technology is old or outdated.
- Confidence in the backup technology is low.

Many organizations may consider tape backup as a means for restoring files or databases when errors have occurred, and they may have confidence in their backup system for that purpose. However, the organization may have somewhat less confidence in their backup system and its ability to recover *all* of their critical systems accurately and in a timely manner.

While tape has been the default medium since the 1960s, using hard drives as backup media is growing in popularity: hard disk transfer rates are far higher, and disk is a random-access medium, whereas tape is a sequential-access medium. A *virtual tape library* (VTL) is a type of data storage technology that sets up a disk-based storage system with the appearance of tape storage, permitting existing backup software to continue to back up data to "tape," which is really just more disk storage.

E-vaulting is another viable option for system backup. E-vaulting permits organizations to back up their systems and data to an off-site location, which could be a storage system in another data center or a third-party service provider. This accomplishes two important objectives: reliable backup and off-site storage of backup data.

Backup Schemes   There are three main schemes for backing up data: full, incremental, and differential backups.

- **Full backup**   This is a complete copy of a data set.
- **Incremental backup**   This is a copy of all data that has changed since the last full or incremental backup.
- **Differential backup**   This is a copy of all data that has changed since the last full backup.

The precise nature of the data to be backed up will determine which combination of backup schemes is appropriate for the organization. Some of the considerations for choosing an overall scheme include

- Criticality of the data set
- Size of the data set
- Frequency of change of the data set
- Performance requirements and the impact of backup jobs
- Recovery requirements

An organization that is creating a backup scheme usually starts with the most common scheme, which is a full backup once per week and an incremental or differential backup every day. However, as stated previously, various factors will influence the design of the final backup scheme, such as the following:

- A small data set could be backed up more than once a week, while an especially large data set might be backed up less often.
- A more rapid recovery requirement may induce the organization to perform differential backups instead of incremental backups.
- If a full backup takes a long time to complete, it should probably be performed during times of lower demand or system utilization.

Backup Media Rotation   Organizations will typically want to retain backup media for as long as possible in order to provide a greater range of choices for data recovery. However, the desire to maintain a large library of backup media will be countered by the high cost of media and the space required to store it. And although legal or statutory requirements may dictate that backup media be kept for some minimum period, the organization may be able to find creative ways to comply with such requirements without retaining several generations of such media.

Some example backup media rotation schemes are discussed here.

First In, First Out (FIFO)   In this scheme, there is no specific requirement for retaining any backup media for long periods (such as one year or more). The method in the FIFO rotation scheme specifies that the oldest available backup tape is the next one to be used.

The advantage of this scheme is its simplicity. However, there is a significant disadvantage: any corruption of backed up data needs to be discovered quickly (within the period of media rotation), or else no valid set of data can be recovered. Hence, only low-criticality data without any lengthy retention requirements should be backed up using this scheme.

Grandfather-Father-Son   The most common backup media rotation scheme, grandfather-father-son creates a hierarchical set of backup media that provides for greater retention of backed up data that is still economically feasible.

In the most common form of this scheme, full backups are performed once per week and incremental or differential backups are performed daily.

Daily backup tapes used on Monday are not used again until the following Monday. Backup tapes used on Tuesday, Wednesday, Thursday, Friday, and Saturday are handled in the same way.

Full backup tapes created on Sunday are kept longer. Tapes used on the first Sunday of the month are not used again until the first Sunday of the following month. Similarly, tapes used on the second Sunday are not reused until the second Sunday of the following month, and so on for each week's tapes for Sunday.

For even longer retention, for example, tapes created on the first Sunday of the first month of each calendar quarter can be retained until the first Sunday of the first month of the next quarter. Backup media can be kept for even longer if needed.

Towers of Hanoi   The Towers of Hanoi backup media retention scheme is complex but results in a more efficient scheme for producing a lengthier retention of some backups. Patterned after the Towers of Hanoi puzzle, the scheme is most easily understood visually, as shown in Figure 5-36 in a five-level scheme.

Day of Cycle

	1	2	3	4	5	6	7	8	9	10	11	12	13	14	15	16	17	18	19	20
		∧		∧		∧		∧		∧		A		A		A		A		A
			B				B				B				B				B	
					C								C							
									D									D		
	E																			

Figure 5-36   Towers of Hanoi backup media rotation scheme

Backup Media Storage   Backup media that remains in the same location as backed up systems is adequate for data recovery purposes but completely inadequate for disaster recovery purposes: any event that physically damages information systems (such as fire, smoke, flood, hazardous chemical spill, and so on) is also likely to damage backup media. To provide disaster recovery protection, backup media must be stored off-site in a secure location. Selection of this storage location is as important as the selection of a primary business location: in the event of a disaster, the survival of the organization may depend upon the protection measures in place at the off-site storage location.

EXAM TIP   CISA exam questions relating to off-site backups may include details for safeguarding data during transport and storage, mechanisms for access during restoration procedures, media aging and retention, or other details that may aid you during the exam. Watch for question details involving the type of media, geo-locality (distance, shared disaster spectrum [such as a shared coastline], and so on) of the off-site storage area and the primary site, or access controls during transport and at the storage site, including environmental controls and security safeguards.

The criteria for selection of an off-site media storage facility are similar to the criteria for selection of a hot/warm/cold/cloud recovery site discussed earlier in this chapter. If a media storage location is too close to the primary processing site, it is more likely to be involved in the same regional disaster, which could result in damage to backup media. However, if the media storage location is too far away, it might take too long for a delivery of backup media, which would result in a recovery operation that runs unacceptably long.

Another location consideration is the proximity of the media storage location and the hot/warm/cold recovery site. If a hot site is being used, chances are there is some other near-real-time means (such as replication) for data to get to the hot site. But a warm or cold site may be relying on the arrival of backup media from the off-site media storage facility, so it might make sense for the off-site facility to be near the recovery site. If the public cloud is used as an alternate recovery site, then a different means than tape backup will need to be used to get data to the public cloud, such as e-vaulting or replication.

An important factor when considering off-site media storage is the method of delivery to and from the storage location. Chances are that the backup media is being transported by a courier or a shipping company. It is vital that the backup media arrive safely and intact, and that the opportunities for interception or loss be reduced as much as possible. Not only can a lost backup tape make recovery more difficult, but it can also cause an embarrassing security incident if knowledge of the loss were to become public. From a confidentiality/integrity perspective, encryption of backup tapes is a good idea, although this digresses somewhat from disaster recovery (concerned primarily with availability).

NOTE   The requirements for off-site storage are a little less critical than those for a hot/warm/cold recovery site. All you have to do is be able to get your backup media out of that facility. This can occur even if there is a regional power outage, for instance.

Backup media that must be kept on-site should be stored in locked cabinets or storerooms that are separate from the rooms where backups are performed. This will help to preserve backup media if a relatively small fire (or similar event) breaks out in the room containing computers that are backed up.

Backup Media Records and Destruction To ensure the ability of restoring data from backup media, organizations need to have meticulous records that list all backup volumes in place, where they are located, and which data elements are backed up on them. Without these records, it may prove impossible for an organization to recover data from its backup media library.

Protecting Sensitive Backup Media with Encryption

Information security and data privacy laws are expanding data protection requirements by requiring encryption of backup media in many cases. This is a sensible safeguard, especially for organizations that utilize off-site backup media storage. There is a risk of loss of backup media when it is being transported back and forth from an organization's primary data center and the backup media off-site storage facility.

Laws and regulations may specify maximum periods that specific information may be retained. Organizations need to have good records management that helps them track which business records are on which backup media volumes. When it is time for an organization to stop retaining a specific set of data, those responsible for the backup media library need to identify the backup volumes that can be recycled. If the data on the backup media is sensitive, the backup volume may need to be erased prior to use. Any backup media that is being discarded needs to be destroyed so that no other party can possibly recover data on the volume. Records of this destruction need to be kept.

Testing Disaster Response Plans

Disaster response plans need to be accurate and complete if they are going to result in a successful recovery. It is recommended that recovery and response plans be thoroughly tested.

The types of recovery tests are

- Document review
- Walkthrough
- Simulation
- Parallel test
- Cutover test

These test methods are described in detail earlier in this chapter.

Auditing IT Infrastructure and Operations

Auditing infrastructure and operations requires considerable technical expertise in order for the auditor to fully understand the technology that he or she is examining. If an auditor lacks technical knowledge, interviewed subjects may offer explanations that can evade vital facts that the auditor should be aware of. Auditors need to be familiar with hardware, operating systems, database management systems, networks, IT operations, monitoring, and DRP.

Auditing Information Systems Hardware

Auditing hardware requires attention to several key factors and activities, including

- **Standards** The auditor should examine hardware procurement standards that specify the types of systems the organization uses. These standards should be periodically reviewed and updated. A sample of recent purchases should be examined to determine whether standards are being followed. The scope of this activity should include servers, workstations, network devices, and other hardware used by IT.

- **Maintenance** Maintenance requirements and records should be examined to determine whether any required maintenance is being performed. If service contracts are used, these should be examined to ensure that all critical systems are covered.

- **Capacity** The auditor should examine capacity management and planning processes, procedures, and records. This will help the auditor to understand whether the organization monitors its systems' capacity and does any planning for future expansion.

- **Change management** Change management processes and records should be examined to determine whether hardware changes are being performed in a life cycle process. All changes that are made should be requested and reviewed in advance, approved by management, and recorded.

- **Configuration management** The auditor should examine configuration management records to determine whether the IT organization is tracking the configuration of its systems in a centralized and systematic manner.

 NOTE Audits of these aspects of hardware are applicable to public cloud environments also.

Auditing Operating Systems

Auditing operating systems, whether on-premises or cloud-based, requires attention to many different details, including

- **Standards** The auditor should examine written standards to determine whether they are complete and up-to-date. He or she should then examine a sampling of servers and workstations to ensure that they comply with the organization's written standards.

- **Maintenance and support**   Business records should be examined to see whether the operating systems running on servers or workstations are covered by maintenance or support contracts.

- **Change management**   The auditor should examine operating system change management processes and records to determine whether changes are being performed in a systematic manner. All changes that are made should be requested and reviewed in advance, approved by management, and recorded.

- **Configuration management**   Operating systems are enormously complex; in all but the smallest organizations, configuration management tools should be used to ensure consistency of configuration among systems. The auditor should examine configuration management processes, tools, and recordkeeping.

- **Security management**   The auditor should examine security configurations on a sample of servers and workstations and determine whether they are "hardened" or resemble manufacturer default configurations. This determination should be made in light of the relative risk of various selected systems. An examination should include patch management and administrative access.

Auditing File Systems

File systems containing business information must be examined to ensure that they are properly configured. An examination should include

- **Capacity**   File systems must have adequate capacity to store all of the currently required information, plus room for future growth. The auditor should examine any file storage capacity management tools, processes, and records.

- **Access control**   Files and directories should be accessible only by personnel with a business need. Records of access requests should be examined to see if they correspond to the access permissions observed.

Auditing Database Management Systems

DBMSs are as complex as operating systems. This complexity requires considerable auditor scrutiny in several areas, including

- **Configuration management**   The configuration of DBMSs should be centrally controlled and tracked in larger organizations to ensure consistency among systems. Individual DBMSs and configuration management records should be compared.

- **Change management**   Databases are used to store not only information, but also software in many cases. The auditor should examine DBMS change management processes and records to determine whether changes are being performed in a consistent, systematic manner. All changes that are made should be requested and reviewed in advance, approved by management, tested, implemented, and recorded. Changes to software should be examined in coordination with an audit of the organization's software development life cycle.

- **Capacity management**   The availability and integrity of supported business processes requires sufficient capacity in all underlying databases. The auditor should examine procedures and records related to capacity management to see whether management ensures sufficient capacity for business data.

- **Access management**   Access controls determine which users and systems are able to access and update data. The auditor should examine access control configurations, access requests, and access logs.

Auditing Network Infrastructure

The IS auditor needs to perform a detailed study of the organization's network infrastructure and underlying management processes. An auditor's scrutiny should include

- **Enterprise architecture**   The auditor should examine enterprise architecture documents. There should be overall and detailed schematics and standards.

- **Network architecture**   The auditor should examine network architecture documents. These should include schematics, topology and design, data flow, routing, and addressing.

- **Virtual architecture**   The auditor should examine all aspects of network infrastructure that is implemented in public cloud environments.

- **Security architecture**   Security architecture documents should be examined, including critical and sensitive data flows, network security zones, access control devices and systems, security countermeasures, intrusion detection and prevention systems, firewalls, screening routers, gateways, anti-malware, and security monitoring.

- **Standards**   The auditor should examine standards documents and determine whether they are reasonable and current. Selected devices and equipment should be examined to see whether they conform to these standards.

- **Change management**   All changes to network devices and services should be governed by a change management process. The auditor should review change management procedures and records and examine a sample of devices and systems to ensure that changes are being performed according to the change management policy.

- **Capacity management**   The auditor should determine how the organization measures network capacity, whether capacity management procedures and records exist, and how capacity management affects network operations.

- **Configuration management**   The auditor should determine whether any configuration management standards, procedures, and records exist and are used. He or she should examine the configuration of a sampling of devices to see whether configurations are consistent from device to device.

- **Administrative access management** Access management procedures, records, and configurations should be examined to see whether only authorized persons are able to access and manage network devices and services.

- **Network components** The auditor should examine several components and their configuration to determine how well the organization has constructed its network infrastructure to support business objectives.

- **Log management** The auditor should determine whether administrative activities performed on network devices and services are logged. He or she should examine the configuration of logs to see if they can be altered. The logs themselves should be examined to determine whether any unauthorized activities are taking place.

- **User access management** Often, network-based services provide organization-wide user access controls. The auditor should examine these centralized services to see whether they conform to written security standards. Examination should include user ID convention, password controls, inactivity locking, user account provisioning, user account termination, and password reset procedures.

Auditing Network Operating Controls

The IS auditor needs to examine network operations to determine whether the organization is operating its network effectively. Examinations should include

- **Network operating procedures** The auditor should examine procedures for normal activities for all network devices and services. These activities will include login, startup, shutdown, upgrade, and configuration changes.

- **Restart procedures** Procedures for restarting the entire network (and portions of it for larger organizations) should exist and be tested periodically. A network restart would be needed in the event of a massive power failure, network failure, or significant upgrade.

- **Troubleshooting procedures** The auditor should examine network troubleshooting procedures for all significant network components. Procedures that are specific to the organization's network help network engineers and analysts quickly locate problems and reduce downtime.

- **Security controls** Operational security controls should be examined, including administrator authentication, administrator access control, logging of administrator actions, protection of device configuration data, security configuration reviews, and protection of audit logs.

- **Change management** All changes to network components and services should follow a formal change management life cycle, including request, review, approval by management, testing in a separate environment, implementation, verification, and complete recordkeeping. The auditor should examine change management policy, procedures, and records.

Auditing IT Operations

Auditing IT operations involves examining the processes used to build, maintain, update, and repair computing hardware, operating systems, and network devices. Audits will cover processes, procedures, and records, as well as examinations of information systems.

Auditing Computer Operations

The auditor should examine computer operational processes, including

- **System configuration standards**   The auditor should examine configuration standards that specify the detailed configuration settings for each type of system that is used in the organization.

- **System build procedures**   The auditor should examine the procedures used to install and configure the operating system.

- **System recovery procedures**   The procedures that are used to recover systems from various types of failures should be examined. Usually, this will include reinstalling and configuring the operating system, restoring software and data from backup, and verifying system recovery.

- **System update procedures**   The auditor should examine procedures used for making changes to systems, including configuration changes and component upgrades.

- **Patch management**   The auditor should examine the procedures for receiving security advisories, risk analysis, and decisions regarding when new security patches should be implemented. Procedures should also include testing, implementation, and verification.

- **Daily tasks**   Daily and weekly operating procedures for systems should be examined, which may include data backup, log review, log file cycling, review of performance logs, and system capacity checks.

- **Backup and replication**   The auditor should examine procedures and records for file and database backup, backup verification, replication, recovery testing, backup media control and inventory, and off-site media storage.

- **Media control**   Media control procedures should be examined, which includes backup media retirement procedures, disk media retirement procedures, media custody, and off-site storage.

- **Monitoring**   Computer monitoring is discussed in detail later in this section.

Auditing File Management

The IS auditor should examine file management policies and procedures, including

- **File system standards**   The auditor should examine file system standards that specify file system architecture, directory naming standards, and technical settings that govern disk utilization and performance.

- **Access controls**   The auditor should examine file system access control policy and procedures, the configuration settings that control which users and processes are able to access directories and files, and log files that record access control events such as permission changes and attempted file accesses, including any procedures followed when such events occur.

- **Capacity management**   The settings and controls used to manage the capacity of file systems should be examined. This should include logs that show file system utilization, procedures for adding capacity, and records of capacity-related events.

- **Version control**   In file systems and data repositories that contain documents under version control, the auditor should examine version control configuration settings, file update procedures, and file recovery procedures and records.

Auditing Data Entry

The IS auditor should examine data entry standards and operations, including

- **Data entry procedures**   This may include document control, input procedures, and error recovery procedures.

- **Input verification**   This may include automatic and manual controls used to ensure that data has been entered properly into forms.

- **Batch verification**   This may include automatic and manual controls used to calculate and verify batches of records that are input.

- **Correction procedures**   This may include controls and procedures used to correct individual forms and batches when errors occur.

Auditing Lights-Out Operations

A *lights-out operation* is any production IT environment, such as computers in a data center, that runs without on-site operator intervention. The term "lights out" means that the computers can be in a room with the lights out since no personnel are present to attend to them.

Audit activities of a lights-out operation will fall primarily into the other categories of audits discussed in this chapter, plus a few specific activities, including

- Remote administration procedures
- Remote monitoring procedures

Auditing Problem Management Operations

The auditor should examine the organization's problem management operations, including

- **Problem management policy and processes**   The auditor should examine policy and procedure documents that describe how problem management is supposed to be performed.

- **Problem management records**   A sampling of problems and incidents should be examined to determine whether problems are being properly managed.

- **Problem management timelines**   The time spent on each problem should be examined to see whether resolution falls within the SLA.

- **Problem management reports**   The auditor should examine management reports to ensure that management is aware of all problems.

- **Problem resolution**   The auditor should examine a sample of problems to see which ones required changes in other processes. The other process documents should be examined to determine if they were changed. The auditor also should examine records to see if fixes were verified by another party.

- **Problem recurrence**   The auditor should examine problem records to make sure that the same problems are not coming up over and over again.

Auditing Monitoring Operations

The IS auditor needs to audit system monitoring operations to ensure that it is effective, including

- **Monitoring plan**   The auditor should review any monitoring plan documents that describe the organization's monitoring program, tools, and processes.

- **Response plans**   The auditor should review response plans, as well as records of responses.

- **Problem log**   Monitoring problem logs should be reviewed to see what kinds of problems are being recorded. The auditor should determine whether all devices and systems are represented in problem logs.

- **Preventive maintenance**   The auditor should examine monitoring results, monitoring plan, and preventive maintenance records, and determine whether the level of preventive maintenance is adequate and effective.

- **Management review and action**   Any monitoring reports, meeting minutes, and decision logs should be examined to see whether management is reviewing monitoring reports and whether management actions are being carried out.

Auditing Procurement

The auditor should examine hardware, software, and services procurement processes, procedures, and records to determine whether any of the following activities are being performed:

- **Requirements definition**   All stakeholders (both technical and business, as appropriate) need to develop functional, technical, and security requirements. Each requirement needs to be approved and used to apply scrutiny to candidate products and services. Each candidate supplier's responses need to be scored on their merits regarding their ability to meet requirements. This entire process needs to be transparent and documented. Auditors will need to examine procurement policies, procedures, and records from selected procurement projects.

- **Feasibility studies**   Many requests for service will require an objective feasibility study that will be designed to identify the economic and business benefits that may be derived from the requested service. Auditors need to examine selected feasibility study documents as well as policy and procedure documents for performing feasibility projects.

Auditing Business Continuity Planning

Audits of an organization's business continuity plan are especially difficult, because it is impossible to prove whether the plans will work unless a real disaster is experienced.

The IT auditor has quite a task when it comes to auditing an organization's business continuity. The lion's share of the audit results hinges on the quality of documentation and walkthroughs with key personnel.

As is typical with most audit activities, an audit of an organization's BC program is a top-down analysis of key business objectives and a review of documentation and interviews to determine whether the BC strategy and program details support those key business objectives. This approach is depicted in Figure 5-37.

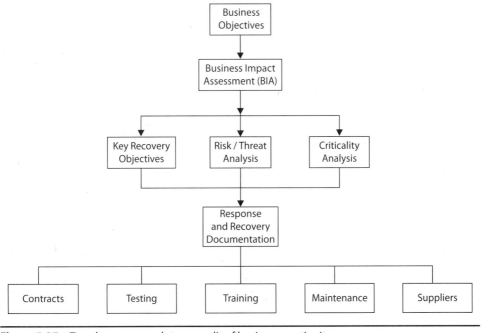

Figure 5-37   Top-down approach to an audit of business continuity

The objectives of an audit of BCP should include the following activities:

- Obtain documentation that describes current business strategies and objectives. Obtain high-level documentation (for example, strategy, charter, objectives) for the BC program, and determine whether the BC program supports business strategies and objectives.

- Obtain the most recent BIA and accompanying threat analysis, risk analysis, and criticality analysis. Determine whether these documents are current and complete, and that they support the BC strategy. Also determine whether the scope of these documents covers those activities considered strategic according to high-level business objectives. Finally, determine whether the methods in these documents represent good practices for these activities.

- Determine whether key personnel are ready to respond during a disaster by reviewing test plans and training plans and results. Find out where emergency procedures are stored and whether key personnel have access to them.

- Verify whether there is a process for the regular review and update of BC documentation. Evaluate the process's effectiveness by reviewing records to see how frequently documents are being reviewed.

These activities are described in more detail in the following sections.

Auditing Business Continuity Documentation

The bulk of an organization's business continuity plan lies in its documentation, so it should be of little surprise that the bulk of the audit effort will lie in the examination of this documentation. The following steps will help the auditor to determine the effectiveness of the organization's BC plans:

- Obtain a copy of business continuity documentation, including response procedures, contact lists, and communication plans.

- Examine samples of distributed copies of BC documentation, and determine whether they are up-to-date. These samples can be obtained during interviews of key response personnel, which are covered in this procedure.

- Determine whether all documents are clear and easy to understand, not just for primary responders, but for alternate personnel who may have specific relevant skills but less familiarity with the organization's critical applications.

- Examine documentation related to the declaration of a disaster and the initiation of disaster response. Determine whether the methods for declaration are likely to be effective in a disaster scenario.

- Obtain emergency contact information, and contact some of the personnel to see whether the contact information is accurate and up-to-date. Also determine whether all response personnel are still employed in the organization and are in the same or similar roles in support of disaster response efforts.

- Contact some or all of the response personnel who are listed in emergency contact lists. Interview them and see how well they understand their disaster response responsibilities and whether they are familiar with disaster response procedures. Ask each interviewee if they have a copy of these procedures. See if their copies are current.

- Determine whether a process exists for the formal review and update of business continuity documentation. Examine records to see how frequently, and how recently, documents have been reviewed and updated.

- Determine whether response personnel receive any formal or informal training on response and recovery procedures. Determine whether personnel are required to receive training and whether any records are kept that show which personnel received training and at what time.

Reviewing Prior Test Results and Action Plans

Effectiveness of business continuity plans relies, to a great degree, on the results and outcomes of tests. An IS auditor needs to examine these tests carefully to determine their effectiveness and to what degree they are used to improve procedures and to train personnel. The following procedure will help the IS auditor determine the effectiveness of business continuity testing:

- Determine whether there is a strategy for testing business continuity procedures. Obtain records for past tests and a plan for future tests. Determine whether prior tests and planned tests are adequate for establishing the effectiveness of response and recovery procedures.

- Examine records for tests that have been performed over the past year or two. Determine the types of tests that were performed. Obtain a list of participants for each test. Compare the participants to lists of key recovery personnel. Examine test work papers to determine the level of participation by key recovery personnel.

- Determine whether there is a formal process for recording test results and for using those results to make improvements in plans and procedures. Examine work papers and records to determine the types of changes that were recommended in prior tests. Examine BC documents to see whether these changes were made as expected.

- Considering the types of tests that were performed, determine the adequacy of testing as an indicator of the effectiveness of the BC program. Did the organization perform only document reviews and walkthroughs, for example, or did the organization also perform parallel or cutover tests?

- If tests have been performed for two years or more, determine whether there's a trend showing continuous improvement in response and recovery procedures.

- If the organization performs parallel tests, determine whether tests are designed in a way that effectively determines the actual readiness of standby systems. Also determine whether parallel tests measure the capacity of standby systems or merely their ability to process correctly but at a lower level of performance.

Interviewing Key Personnel

The knowledge and experience of key personnel are vital to the success of any DR operation. Interviews will help the IT auditor determine whether key personnel are prepared and trained to respond during a disaster. The following procedure will guide the IT auditor in interviews:

- Obtain the name, title, tenure, and full contact information for each person interviewed.
- Ask the interviewee to summarize his or her professional experience and training and current responsibilities in the organization.
- Ask the interviewee whether he or she is familiar with the organization's business continuity and disaster recovery programs.
- Determine whether the interviewee is among the key response personnel expected to respond during a disaster.
- Ask the interviewee if he or she has been issued a copy of any response or recovery procedures. If so, ask to see those procedures; determine whether they are current versions. Ask if the interviewee has additional sets of procedures in any other locations (residence, for example).
- Ask the interviewee if he or she has received any training. Request evidence of this training (certificate, calendar entry, and so on).
- Ask the interviewee if he or she has participated in any tests or evaluations of recovery and response procedures. Ask the interviewee whether the tests were effective, whether management takes the tests seriously, and whether any deficiencies in tests resulted in any improvements to test procedures or other documents.

Reviewing Service Provider Contracts

No organization is an island. Every organization has critical suppliers without which it could not carry out its critical functions. The ability to recover from a disaster also frequently requires the support of one or more service providers or suppliers. The IT auditor should examine contracts for all critical suppliers and consider the following guidelines:

- Does the contract support the organization's requirements for delivery of services and supplies, even in the event of a local or regional disaster?
- Does the service provider have its own disaster recovery capabilities that will ensure its ability to deliver critical services during a disaster?
- Is recourse available should the supplier be unable to provide goods or services during a disaster?

Reviewing Insurance Coverage

The IT auditor should examine the organization's insurance policies related to the loss of property and assets supporting critical business processes. Insurance coverage should cover the actual cost of recovery or a lesser amount if the organization's executive management has accepted a lower amount. The IT auditor should obtain documentation that includes cost estimates for various DR scenarios, including equipment replacement, business interruption, and the cost of performing business functions and operating IT systems in alternate sites. These cost estimates should be compared with the value of insurance policies.

Visiting Media Storage and Alternate Processing Sites

The IT auditor should identify and visit remote sites used for storage of backup media and alternate processing. This will permit the auditor to confirm their existence, verify features and functions of these sites to see if they correspond to details in continuity and recovery plans, and to discover any risks.

Auditing Disaster Recovery Planning

The objectives of an audit of disaster recovery planning should include the following activities:

- Determine the effectiveness of planning and recovery documentation by examining previous test results.

- Evaluate the methods used to store critical information off-site (which may consist of off-site storage, alternate data centers, or e-vaulting).

- Examine environmental and physical security controls in any off-site or alternate sites and determine their effectiveness.

- Note whether off-site or alternate site locations are within the same geographic region—which could mean that both the primary and alternate sites may be involved in common disaster scenarios.

Auditing Disaster Recovery Plans

The following steps will help the auditor determine the effectiveness of the organization's DR plans:

- Obtain a copy of DR documentation, including response procedures, contact lists, and communication plans.

- Examine samples of distributed copies of DR documentation and determine whether they are up-to-date. These samples can be obtained during interviews of key response personnel, which are covered in this procedure.

- Determine whether all documents are clear and easy to understand, not just for primary responders, but for alternate personnel who may have specific relevant skills but less familiarity with the organization's critical applications.

- Obtain contact information for off-site storage providers, hot-site facilities, and critical suppliers. Determine whether these organizations are still providing services to the organization. Call some of the contacts to determine the accuracy of the documented contact information.

- For organizations using third-party recovery sites such as cloud infrastructure providers, obtain contracts that define organization and cloud provider obligations, service levels, and security controls.

- Obtain logical and physical architecture diagrams for key IT applications that support critical business processes. Determine whether BC documentation includes recovery procedures for all components that support those IT applications. See whether documentation includes recovery for end users and administrators for the applications.

- If the organization uses a hot site, examine one or more systems to determine whether they have the proper versions of software, patches, and configurations. Examine procedures and records related to the tasks in support of keeping standby systems current. Determine whether these procedures are effective.

- If the organization has a warm site, examine the procedures used to bring standby systems into operational readiness. Examine warm-site systems to see whether they are in a state where readiness procedures will likely be successful.

- If the organization has a cold site, examine all documentation related to the acquisition of replacement systems and other components. Determine whether the procedures and documentation are likely to result in systems capable of hosting critical IT applications and within the period required to meet key recovery objectives.

- If the organization uses a cloud service provider's service as a recovery site, examine the procedures used to prepare and bring cloud-based systems to operational readiness. Examine procedures and configurations to see whether they are likely to support the organization successfully during a disaster.

- Determine whether any documentation exists regarding the relocation of key personnel to the hot/warm/cold processing site. See whether the documentation specifies which personnel are to be relocated and what accommodations and supporting logistics are provided. Determine the effectiveness of these relocation plans.

- Determine whether backup and off-site (or replication or e-vaulting) storage procedures are being followed. Examine systems to ensure that critical IT applications are being backed up and that proper media are being stored off-site (or that the proper data is being e-vaulted). Determine whether data recovery tests are ever performed and, if so, whether results of those tests are documented and problems are properly dealt with.

- Evaluate procedures for transitioning processing from the alternate processing facility back to the primary processing facility. Determine whether these procedures are complete and effective.

- Determine whether a process exists for the formal review and update of business continuity documentation to ensure continued alignment with DR planning. Examine records to see how frequently, and how recently, documents have been reviewed and updated. Determine whether this is sufficient and effective by interviewing key personnel to understand whether significant changes to applications, systems, networks, or processes are reflected in recovery and response documentation.

- Determine whether response personnel receive any formal or informal training on response and recovery procedures. Determine whether personnel are required to receive training, and whether any records are kept that show which personnel received training and at what time.

- Examine the organization's change control process. Determine whether the process includes any steps or procedures that require personnel to determine whether any change has an impact on DR documentation or procedures.

Reviewing Prior DR Test Results and Action Plans

The effectiveness of DR plans relies on the results and outcomes of tests. The IS auditor needs to examine these plans and activities to determine their effectiveness. The following will help the IS auditor audit DR testing:

- Determine whether there is a strategy for testing DR plans. Obtain records for past tests and a plan for future tests.

- Examine records for tests that have been performed over the past year or two. Determine the types of tests that were performed. Obtain a list of participants for each test. Compare the participants to lists of key recovery personnel. Examine test work papers to determine the level of participation by key recovery personnel.

- Determine whether there is a formal process for recording test results and for using those results to make improvements in plans and procedures. Examine work papers and records to determine the types of changes that were recommended in prior tests. Examine DR documents to see whether these changes were made as expected.

- Considering the types of tests that were performed, determine the adequacy of testing as an indicator of the effectiveness of the DR program. Did the organization perform only document reviews and walkthroughs, for example, or did the organization also perform parallel or cutover tests?

- If tests have been performed for two years or more, determine whether there's a trend showing continuous improvement in response and recovery procedures.

- If the organization performs parallel tests, determine whether tests are designed in a way that effectively determines the actual readiness of standby systems. Also determine whether parallel tests measure the capacity of standby systems or merely their ability to process correctly but at a lower level of performance.

- Determine whether any tests included the retrieval of backup data from off-site storage or e-vaulting facilities.

Evaluating Off-Site Storage

Storage of critical data and other supporting information is a key component in any organization's DR plan. Because some types of disasters can completely destroy a business location, including its vital records, it is imperative that all critical information is backed up and copies moved to an off-site storage facility. The following procedure will help the IS auditor determine the effectiveness of off-site storage:

- Obtain the location of the off-site storage or e-vaulting facility. Determine whether the facility is located in the same geographic region as the organization's primary processing facility.

- If possible, visit the off-site storage facility. Examine its physical security controls as well as its safeguards to prevent damage to stored information in a disaster. Consider the entire spectrum of physical and logical access controls. Examine procedures and records related to the storage and return of backup media and other information that the organization may store there. If it is not possible to visit the off-site storage facility, obtain copies of audits or other attestations of controls effectiveness.

- Take an inventory of backup media and other information stored at the facility. Compare this inventory with a list of critical business processes and supporting IT systems to determine whether all relevant information is, in fact, stored at the off-site storage facility.

- Determine how often the organization performs its own inventory of the off-site facility and whether steps to correct deficiencies are documented and remedied.

- Examine contracts, terms, and conditions for off-site storage providers or e-vaulting facilities, if applicable. Determine whether data can be recovered to the original processing center and to alternate processing centers within a period that will ensure that DR can be completed within RTOs.

- Determine whether the appropriate personnel have current access codes for off-site storage or e-vaulting facilities and whether they have the ability to recover data from those facilities.

- Determine what information, in addition to backup data, exists at the off-site storage facility. Information stored off-site should include architecture diagrams, design documentation, operations procedures, and configuration information for all logical and physical layers of technology and facilities supporting critical IT applications, operations documentation, and application source code.

- Obtain information related to the manner in which backup media and copies of records are transported to and from the off-site storage or e-vaulting facility. Determine the adequacy of controls protecting transported information.

- Obtain records supporting the transport of backup media and records to and from the off-site storage facility. Examine samples of records and determine whether they match other records such as backup logs.

Evaluating Alternate Processing Facilities

The IS auditor needs to examine alternate processing facilities to determine whether they are sufficient to support the organization's BC and DR plans. The following procedure will help the IS auditor to determine whether an alternate processing facility will be effective:

- Obtain addresses and other location information for alternate processing facilities. These will include hot sites, warm sites, cold sites, cloud-based services, and alternate processing centers owned or operated by the organization. Note that exact locations of cloud services are often unavailable for security reasons.

- Determine whether alternate facilities are located within the same geographic region as the primary processing facility and the probability that the alternate facility will be adversely affected by a disaster that strikes the primary facility.

- Perform a threat analysis on the alternate processing site. Determine which threats and hazards pose a significant risk to the organization and its ability to carry out operations effectively during a disaster.

- Determine the types of natural and man-made events likely to take place at the alternate processing facility. Determine whether there are adequate controls to mitigate the effect of these events.

- Examine all environmental controls and determine their adequacy. This should include environmental controls (HVAC), power supply, uninterruptible power supply (UPS), power distribution units (PDUs), and electric generators. Also examine fire detection and suppression systems, including smoke detectors, pull stations, fire extinguishers, sprinklers, and inert gas suppression systems.

- If the alternate processing facility is a separate organization, obtain the legal contract and all exhibits. Examine these documents and determine whether the contract and exhibits support the organization's recovery and testing requirements.

 NOTE Cloud-based service providers often do not permit on-site visits. Instead, they may have one or more external audit reports available through standard audits such as SSAE18, ISAE3402, SOC1, SOC2, ISO, or PCI. Auditors will need to determine whether any such external audit reports may be relied upon, and whether there are any controls that are not covered by such external audits.

Chapter Review

All activities in the IT department should be managed, controlled, and monitored. Activities performed by operations personnel should be a part of a procedure or process that is approved by management. Processes, procedures, and projects should have sufficient recordkeeping to facilitate measurements.

IT operations should be structured in a service management model that is aligned with the IT Infrastructure Library (ITIL) or the COBIT framework of processes. These frameworks ensure that comprehensive coverage of activities is likely to be taking place in most IT organizations.

IS auditors need to have a thorough understanding of information systems hardware and software and how they work to support business objectives. This includes knowing how computer hardware functions; how operating systems are installed, configured, and operated; how end users' workstations are provisioned, managed, and used; and how software applications operate. Because newer technologies are not always implemented properly at first, IS auditors need to understand technologies such as virtualization, virtual desktops, software-defined networking, and mobile devices to ensure that the organization is not incurring unnecessary risk through their use.

Network management tools and systems help management understand a network's utilization, capacity, and problems. Network management should be a part of a larger infrastructure monitoring strategy.

Natural and human-made disasters can damage business facilities, assets, and information systems, thus threatening the viability of the organization by halting its critical processes. Even without direct effects, many secondary or indirect effects from a disaster such as crippled transportation systems, damaged communications systems, and damaged public utilities can seriously harm an organization. The development of business continuity plans helps an organization be better prepared to act when a disaster strikes. A vital part of this preparation is the development of alternative means for continuing the most critical activities, usually in alternate locations that are not damaged by a disaster.

There is an accepted methodology to BC and DR planning, which begins with the development of a BCP policy, a statement of the goals and objectives of a planning effort. This is followed by a BIA, a study of the organization's business processes to determine which are the most critical to the organization's ongoing viability. For each critical process, a statement of impact is developed, which is a brief description of the effect on the organization if the process is incapacitated for any significant period. The statement of impact can be qualitative or quantitative.

A criticality analysis is performed next, where all in-scope business processes are ranked in order of criticality. Ranking can be strictly quantitative, qualitative, or even subjective. The maximum tolerable downtime (MTD) is established for each critical business process. This drives the development of recovery targets.

Next, recovery targets for each critical business process are developed. The key targets are RTO and RPO. These targets specify time to system restoration and maximum data loss, respectively. When these targets have been established, the project team can develop plans that include changes to technical architecture as well as business processes that will help achieve these established recovery objectives.

Continuity plans are then developed. These consist of procedures for personnel safety and disaster declaration, together with definitions of responsibilities, contact information for key personnel, and procedures for recovery, continuity of operations, and restoration of assets.

The effectiveness of business continuity plans can be determined only by testing. There are five types of tests: document review, walkthrough, simulation, parallel test, and cutover test. These five tests represent progressively more complex (and risky) means for testing procedures and IT systems to determine whether they will be able to support critical business processes in a real disaster. The parallel test involves the use of backup IT systems in a way that enables them to process real business transactions while primary systems continue to perform the organization's real work. The cutover test actually transitions business data processing to backup IT systems, where they will process actual business workload for a period.

Response personnel need to be carefully chosen from available staff to ensure that sufficient numbers of personnel will be available in a real disaster. Some personnel may be unable to respond for a variety of reasons that are related to the disaster itself. As a result, some of the personnel who respond in an actual disaster may not be as familiar with the systems and procedures required to recover and maintain them. This makes training and accurate procedures critical for effective disaster recovery.

Recovery and continuity plans need to be periodically updated to reflect changes in information systems, and distributed to or made available to response and recovery personnel.

Auditing an organization's BC capabilities involves the examination of BCP policies, plans, and procedures, as well as contracts and technical architectures. The IT auditor also needs to interview response personnel to gauge their readiness and to visit off-site media storage and alternate processing sites to identify risks present there.

During a DRP project, once acceptable architectures and process changes have been determined, the organization sets out to make investments in these areas to bring its systems and processes closer to the recovery objectives. Procedures for recovering systems and processes are also developed at this time, as well as procedures for other aspects of disaster response, such as emergency communications plans and evacuation plans.

Some of the investment in IT system resilience may involve the establishment of an alternate processing site, where IT systems can be resumed in support of critical business processes. There are several types of alternate sites, including a hot site, where IT systems are in a continual state of near-readiness and can assume production workload within an hour or two; a warm site, where IT systems are present but require several hours to a day of preparation; a cold site, where no systems are present but must be acquired, which may require several days of preparation before those replacement systems are ready to support business processes; and a cloud-based site, in which virtual machines are provided on an on-demand basis, and where the organization will establish a hot, warm, or cold capability therein. Virtual infrastructure in a public cloud can serve as a hot or warm site.

Some of the technologies that may be introduced in IT systems to improve recovery targets include RAID, a technology that improves the reliability of disk storage systems; replication, a technique for copying data in near–real time to an alternate (and usually distant) storage system; e-vaulting, where data is copied to a cloud-based e-vaulting service; and clustering, a technology whereby several servers (including some that can be located in another region) act as one logical server, enabling processing to continue even if one or more servers are incapacitated or unreachable.

Quick Review

- All IT activities should be a part of a documented process, procedure, or project.

- Key systems, applications, and infrastructure should be monitored to ensure that they continue to operate properly in their support of key business processes.

- Software program libraries should be controlled with access and authorization controls, check-out and check-in, version control, and code analysis.

- Media sanitization procedures ensure that data leakage will not result from discarded data storage media.

- Mobile devices such as tablet computers and smartphones are the new endpoints. Lacking mature enterprise management controls and anti-malware tools, and being small enough to easily lose, mobile devices are a popular attack vector. The IS auditor needs to understand how the organization addresses these matters.

- It is as important to understand the internal architecture of computers as it is to understand how computers can be combined to form clusters and multitier application environments.

- Automated monitoring of computing and network infrastructure includes monitoring of internal components such as CPU, power supply, memory, and storage. Monitoring also includes resource utilization such as CPU, memory, disk storage, and network. The external environment, including temperature, humidity, water, and vibration, should also be monitored.

- Software license management ensures that the organization will remain in compliance with its software license agreements and avoid costly and embarrassing legal trouble. Automated tools can help monitor the installation and use of licensed software.

- Although the seven-layer OSI data model has never been implemented in its pure form, it is still important to understand its concepts. Terms from the model are used by IT specialists; for instance, layer 4 switches are a type of network device that routes packets based on their OSI layer 4 characteristics.

- IS auditors need to understand the TCP/IP model and TCP/IP's common protocols well enough to be able to identify risks and control weaknesses.

- A network's logical architecture (star, ring, or bus) often does not match its physical architecture (star, ring, or bus).

- A key place to examine a network is its boundary. Edge devices such as firewalls, routers, wireless access points, and gateways contain configurations that control inbound and outbound traffic. Mistakes here can be costly.

- Most of the older and less secure TCP/IP protocols such as Telnet, FTP, and RCP have been superseded by newer protocols such as SSH, SFTP, and FTPS.

- BCP ensures business recovery following a disaster. Business continuity focuses on maintaining service availability with the least disruption to standard operating parameters during an event, while disaster recovery focuses on post-event recovery and restoration of services.

- BCP encompasses a life cycle beginning with the initial BCP policy, followed by business impact and criticality analysis to evaluate risk and impact factors. Recovery targets facilitate the development of strategies for continuity and recovery, which then must be tested and conveyed to operation personnel through training and exercise. Post-implementation maintenance includes periodic reviews and updates as part of the enterprise continuous-improvement process.

- The business impact analysis (BIA) measures the impact on enterprise operation posed by various identified areas of risk. The output of the BIA is used in the criticality analysis (CA), which measures the impact of each risk against its likelihood and the cost of mitigation. Maximum tolerable downtime (MTD) metrics are established for each critical process.

- The output of the BIA, CA, and MTD activities are used when establishing recovery time objectives (RTOs) and recovery point objectives (RPOs), which can then be measured against relative cost scenarios for each identified risk and mitigation option.

- RTOs and RPOs are fed into the DR process so that staff can develop resilient and recoverable IT architectures supporting critical business processes.

- BC plans must be tested to validate effectiveness through document review, walkthrough, simulation, parallel testing, or cutover testing practices. Regular testing must take place to ensure new objectives and procedures meet the requirements of a living enterprise environment. Participation in these tests provides familiarity and training for engaged operational staff members, raising understanding and awareness of requirements and responsibilities.

- Organizations are increasingly turning to the cloud for their alternate processing sites. IS auditors need to understand how cloud-based infrastructure is procured, protected, and managed.

- Once recovery objectives have been identified, strategies can be developed to meet each objective. Many solutions may include redundant (hot, warm, or cold) alternate sites, redundant service operation or storage in high-availability or distributed-cluster environments, alternative network access strategies, and backup/recovery strategies structured to meet identified recovery time and recovery point requirements.

Questions

1. A web application is displaying information incorrectly and many users have contacted the IT service desk. This matter should be considered a(n)

   A. Incident

   B. Problem

   C. Bug

   D. Outage

2. An IT organization is experiencing many cases of unexpected downtime that are caused by unauthorized changes to application code and operating system configuration. Which process should the IT organization implement to reduce downtime?

   A. Configuration management

   B. Incident management

   C. Change management

   D. Problem management

3. An IT organization manages hundreds of servers, databases, and applications, and is having difficulty tracking changes to the configuration of these systems. What process should be implemented to remedy this?

   A. Configuration management

   B. Change management

   C. Problem management

   D. Incident management

4. A computer's CPU, memory, and peripherals are connected to each other through a

   A. Kernel

   B. FireWire

   C. Pipeline

   D. Bus

5. A database administrator has been asked to configure a database management system so that it records all changes made by users. What should the database administrator implement?

   A. Audit logging

   B. Triggers

   C. Stored procedures

   D. Journaling

6. The layers of the TCP/IP reference model are

   A. Link, Internet, transport, application

   B. Physical, link, Internet, transport, application

   C. Link, transport, Internet, application

   D. Physical, data link, network, transport, session, presentation, application

7. The purpose of the Internet layer in the TCP/IP model is

   A. Encapsulation

   B. Packet delivery on a local network

    C. Packet delivery on a local or remote network

    D. Order of delivery and flow control

8. The purpose of the DHCP protocol is

    A. Control flow on a congested network.

    B. Query a station to discover its IP address.

    C. Assign an IP address to a station.

    D. Assign an Ethernet MAC address to a station.

9. An IS auditor is examining a wireless (Wi-Fi) network and has determined that the network uses WEP encryption. What action should the auditor take?

    A. Recommend that encryption be changed to WPA.

    B. Recommend that encryption be changed to EAP.

    C. Request documentation for the key management process.

    D. Request documentation for the authentication process.

10. 126.0.0.1 is an example of a

    A. MAC address

    B. Loopback address

    C. Class A address

    D. Subnet mask

11. What is the most important consideration when selecting a hot site?

    A. Time zone

    B. Geographic location in relation to the primary site

    C. Proximity to major transportation

    D. Natural hazards

12. An organization has established a recovery point objective of 14 days for its most critical business applications. Which recovery strategy would be the best choice?

    A. Mobile site

    B. Warm site

    C. Hot site

    D. Cold site

13. What technology should an organization use for its application servers to provide continuous service to users?

    A. Dual power supplies

    B. Server clustering

    C. Dual network feeds

    D. Transaction monitoring

14. An organization currently stores its backup media in a cabinet next to the computers being backed up. A consultant told the organization to store backup media at an off-site storage facility. What risk did the consultant most likely have in mind when he made this recommendation?

  A. A disaster that damages computer systems can also damage backup media.

  B. Backup media rotation may result in loss of data backed up several weeks in the past.

  C. Corruption of online data will require rapid data recovery from off-site storage.

  D. Physical controls at the data processing site are insufficient.

15. Which of the following statements about virtual server hardening is true?

  A. The configuration of the host operating system will automatically flow to each guest operating system.

  B. Each guest virtual machine needs to be hardened separately.

  C. Guest operating systems do not need to be hardened because they are protected by the hypervisor.

  D. Virtual servers do not need to be hardened because they do not run directly on computer hardware.

Answers

1. **B.** A problem is defined as a condition that is the result of multiple incidents that exhibit common symptoms. In this example, many users are experiencing the effects of the application error.

2. **C.** Change management is the process of managing change through a life cycle process that consists of request, review, approve, implement, and verify.

3. **A.** Configuration management is the process (often supplemented with automated tools) of tracking configuration changes to systems and system components such as databases and applications.

4. **D.** A bus connects all of the computer's internal components together, including its CPU, main memory, secondary memory, and peripheral devices.

5. **A.** The database administrator should implement audit logging. This will cause the database to record every change that is made to it.

6. **A.** The layers of the TCP/IP model are (from lowest to highest) link, Internet, transport, and application.

7. **C.** The purpose of the Internet layer in the TCP/IP model is the delivery of packets from one station to another, on the same network or on a different network.

8. **C.** The DHCP protocol is used to assign IP addresses to computers on a network.

9. **A.** The WEP protocol has been seriously compromised and should be replaced with WPA or WPA2 encryption.

10. **C.** Class A addresses are in the range 0.0.0.0 to 127.255.255.255. The address 126.0.0.1 falls into this range.

11. **B**. An important selection criterion for a hot site is the geographic location in relation to the primary site. If they are too close together, then a single disaster event may involve both locations.

12. **D.** An organization that has a 14-day recovery time objective (RTO) can use a cold site for its recovery strategy. Fourteen days is enough time for most organizations to acquire hardware and recover applications.

13. **B.** An organization that wants its application servers to be continuously available to its users needs to employ server clustering. This enables at least one server to be always available to service user requests.

14. **A.** The primary reason for employing off-site backup media storage is to mitigate the effects of a disaster that could otherwise destroy computer systems and their backup media.

15. **B.** In a virtualization environment, each guest operating system needs to be hardened; they are no different from operating systems running directly on server (or workstation) hardware.

Information Asset Protection

This chapter covers CISA Domain 5, "Protection of Information Assets," and discusses the following topics:

- Information security management
- Logical access controls
- Network security
- Environmental security
- Physical security
- Privacy

The topics in this chapter represent 27 percent of the CISA examination.

Information assets consist of information and information systems. *Information* includes software, tools, and data. *Information system* is an inclusive term that encompasses servers, workstations, mobile devices, network devices, gateways, appliances, IoT devices, and applications. An information system can be a single device or a collection of systems that work together for some business purpose.

Information Security Management

Information security management is the collection of policies, processes, and procedures that ensures an organization's security program is effective. Security management is composed of a number of distinct and interrelated processes, including policy development and enforcement, risk management, security awareness training, user access management, security incident management, vulnerability management, third-party risk management, encryption, network access management, environmental controls, and physical access controls. Ongoing executive support is key to the success of a security management program.

These and other processes should be periodically audited to confirm their effectiveness. Control failures and exceptions should be documented and action plans developed to improve processes and systems.

Aspects of Information Security Management

The protection of information-related assets is the cornerstone of information security management. Flowing out of IT governance and risk management, information security management is a top-down set of coordinated activities whose key objective is the protection of information systems and other information-related assets.

An organization with sound IT governance and risk management programs will develop strategies, policies, and processes that align with the organization's overall objectives. Through a number of strategic processes, such as business impact assessment (BIA), management will create a clear idea of which information-related assets and functions are the most vital to the organization. Through a risk management program, management will take appropriate measures to protect those assets and functions.

NOTE Rather than being a separate activity, information security management works hand-in-glove with IT governance and risk management, which is the focus of Chapter 2.

Executive Support

Information security management will be effective only with an appropriate level of executive-level support. A level of visible commitment to security management is required, including the ratification of security strategies and policies, support of risk management decisions, delegation of key roles and responsibilities, allocation of resources, prioritization of the use of resources, and leadership by example. Without executive support as a foundation, an organization's information security program cannot hope to succeed and be effective.

Policies and Procedures

An effective information security program depends upon a clear rule of law in the form of an information security policy. A complete information security policy should contain the following elements:

- **Statement of executive support**   The policy document must clearly state that the information security policy has the full and unwavering support of the organization's executives. The policy may include a signature block that shows their support and formal adoption of the policy in writing.

- **Roles and responsibilities**   Information security policy should define security-related roles and responsibilities, including who is responsible for policy development and enforcement. It should also include who is responsible for performing risk assessments and making risk-based decisions. The policy should also describe how the structure of asset ownership works and clearly state how asset owners have some responsibilities in protecting the assets that they control. Finally, the policy should state the responsibilities that all employees have in the protection of information systems and information-related assets.

- **Value of information-related assets**   The information security policy should include the idea that the organization's information system and information are valued assets that deserve protection. Although the tangibility of some assets may be difficult to value monetarily, they are valuable nonetheless and must be protected.

- **Protection of information assets**   Because the organization's information-related assets have value, they must be protected. The policy should describe the ways that information assets are protected through controls to protect their confidentiality, integrity, and availability. There may be dozens and perhaps more than 100 individual topics and statements regarding information asset protection. Some of these statements will describe things that people are required to do, and others will describe things that people are forbidden from doing.

- **Acceptable behavior**   Information security policy must clearly state what is expected of the organization's employees by defining the types of behavior and activities that are required, permitted, discouraged, and forbidden. It also may state the consequences of disobeying the rules for acceptable behavior.

- **Risk management**   The information security policy should describe the manner through which risks are measured and treated. This should include a policy for handling exceptions (circumstances where security policy and organization objectives are at odds with one another).

- **Support of laws and regulations**   Information security policy should clearly state the organization's support of applicable laws and regulations. For instance, policy should include statements of support for intellectual property laws through the use of copyrighted and trademarked works. Also, incident response policies and procedures should include all necessary disclosures of data compromise.

- **Enforcement and consequences**   The policy should state how it is to be enforced and by whom, and a statement of the consequences of willful or negligent violation of security policy should be included. Generally, a policy should state that "violations may result in disciplinary action including termination of employment, as well as civil or criminal legal proceedings."

An organization's security policy should be easily found and understood. The policy can be published on the organization's internal web site or portal. It should be written in a style that makes it easily understood by all personnel.

Security Awareness

Many people do not have particularly good instincts when it comes to the protection of information systems and information-related assets. But people are generally teachable, and they can be trained in the methods used to safeguard the organization's information and systems. A formal security awareness program should include activities that will help employees better understand how information protection measures work and how they should be used. Most employees will agree that organization assets are valuable and should be protected—they just need to know *how* it is done, *why* it is important, and what is expected of them.

The designers of a comprehensive security awareness program need to understand that people have a variety of learning styles, which means that reliance on a single method for disseminating security information is not going to work for everyone. Some of the elements of a security awareness program include

- **Signed acknowledgment of security policy**   To drive home the point of the seriousness of the company's security policy, all employees should be required to sign a statement that says they have read, understood, and will conform to the entire security policy. This should be done at the time of hire, but increasingly, organizations are requiring employees to sign this annually thereafter.

- **Security awareness training upon hire**   Each new employee should receive formal training at the time of hire. This training should serve as an orientation to the organization's security policy and programs of asset protection. This will help the employee understand his or her responsibilities, where to find the policy and additional information, how employees are expected to participate in asset protection, and the consequences for failing to do so.

- **Annual security awareness training**   Many organizations incorporate annual security awareness training for all employees. This gives employees opportunities for "refresher" materials as well as updated information that is based on new technologies, practices, threats, and policies. The state of the art of security threats and safeguards is ever-changing, and security awareness training should be updated accordingly.

- **Intranet**   An internal web site (or other manner through which the organization makes information available to its employees on demand) should include content on security awareness, controls, policies, and other information that employees can access. Like security policy, security awareness information should be easy to understand and use—and employees should be easily able to understand *how* and *why* to use the information there to protect the organization's assets.

- **Periodic messages**   From time to time, it may be necessary to send e-mails to groups of employees (or the entire organization) to make them aware of things that they need to know. Periodic messages also help distribute information to employees who won't bother to visit an internal web site—some rely on the company to "push" information to them that they will read.

- **Posters and flyers**   Sometimes, it may be advantageous to make employees aware of security matters in ways other than web sites and e-mail messages. Posters can be put up where people congregate: kitchens, break rooms, meeting rooms, and auditoriums. An organization should not rely on just one method, such as a web site or e-mail, for communications; posters and flyers are another effective way to get the message to employees.

- **Rewards for desired behavior**   Management should reward its employees for making contributions toward the protection of information assets. For example, employees who notice and report security threats or vulnerabilities, or who find a better way to protect assets, could be rewarded with recognition awards or gift certificates.

 NOTE An effective security awareness program should help to create a culture of participation in the protection of the organization's information assets.

Security Program Monitoring and Auditing

There is a popular mantra in the business world: the only things that can be managed are those that are measured. In an organization's information security program, several key areas need to be monitored and audited. This will help management better understand whether its security policies and controls are effective.

Security analysts and auditors should periodically test the organization's policies and controls (including but not limited to its explicitly stated security controls) to see if they are working properly. Indeed, this is the topic of this entire book and of the CISA certification. Only through monitoring and auditing can an organization really know whether the policies, procedures, and controls that it has established are effective at protecting the organization's information and information systems.

Security monitoring is also discussed in Chapter 2 and is covered in more detail in Chapter 5.

Incident Response

A security incident is an event where the confidentiality, integrity, or availability of information (or an information system) has been or is in danger of being compromised. An organization should have an incident response plan in place that will define how the organization should respond when an incident occurs. Some of the common types of incidents that should be included in a response plan include

- **Information exposure or theft**   Information that is protected by one or more controls may still be exposed to unauthorized persons through a weakness in controls or by deliberate or negligent acts or omissions.

- **Information system theft**   Laptop computers, mobile devices, and other information-processing and storage equipment can be stolen, which may directly or indirectly lead to further compromises. If the stolen device contains retrievable sensitive information or the means to access sensitive information stored elsewhere, then what has started out as a theft of a tangible asset may expand to become a compromise of sensitive information as well.

- **Information system damage**   A human intruder or automated malware may cause temporary or irreversible damage to an information system. This may result in an interruption in the availability of information, as well as loss of information.

- **Information corruption**   A human intruder or automated malware such as a worm or virus may damage information stored on a system. This damage may or may not be readily noticed.

- **Information destruction**   An attack by ransomware or destructware may result in a temporary or permanent loss of information stored on a system.

- **Malware**   Viruses, Trojan horses, worms, and rootkits can penetrate a system and result in consumption of resources or corruption or compromise of information.

Most organizations periodically test their incident response plans to make sure that they will be effective when a real security incident occurs.

Security incident response is described in more detail later in this chapter.

Corrective and Preventive Actions

Any organization that is intent on reducing risk through security-related controls, processes, and activities needs to consider using corrective and preventive actions processes. The purpose of these processes is to track corrective and preventive actions formally so that they will be completed on time and not forgotten.

A corrective and preventive actions process may be as simple as a list of actions tracked on a spreadsheet or as complex as an incident tracking system (sometimes known as a ticketing system or a service desk application). The level of complexity should meet the organization's needs for tracking, reporting, follow-up, and escalation of actions.

Corrective and preventive actions are a part of a culture of continuous improvement. Organizations that adopt a culture of continuous improvement are more likely to have effective controls that protect assets.

Compliance

Organizations need to determine and catalog all applicable laws, regulations, standards, and other legal obligations that are relevant to the protection of information and assets. These may include but are not limited to

- National laws
- State and local laws
- Consumer protection agencies
- Industry standards such as PCI-DSS (Payment Card Industry Data Security Standard), and those published by NERC (North American Electric Reliability Corporation), NIST (National Institute of Standards and Technology), and ISO (International Standards Organization)

Roles and Responsibilities

An effective information security management program requires several key roles and responsibilities, which are held by individuals or groups. These roles and responsibilities should be formally defined in the organization's information security policy. They can also be defined in a charter document that describes the mission, objectives, roles, and responsibilities in the organization's information security program. Either way, this information must be readily available to all employees.

Security-related roles and responsibilities include these core elements:

- **Board of directors**   Responsible for directing executive management to provide adequate resources to the protection of information and assets

- **Audit committee**   A subset of the board of directors, responsible for reviewing internal and external audit reports and requiring executive management to respond to any nonconformities

- **Executive management**   Responsible for ratification and support of information security policy and overall responsibility for asset protection

- **Security steering committee**   A committee of senior-level officials from every department in the organization that is convened for approval of security policies, discussion of risk-related matters, and allocation of resources to carry out asset protection

- **Chief information officer (CIO)**   The senior-level official who is responsible for the deployment and operation of all information systems, and for the management of all information

- **Chief information security officer (CISO) or chief information risk officer (CIRO)**   The senior-level official who is responsible for the operation of the organization's risk management program, and the development and enforcement of security policy and the protection of information assets

- **Chief privacy officer (CPO)**   The senior-level official who is responsible for the proper handling of personally sensitive information belonging to employees and customers to protect their privacy rights

- **Internal audit**   Responsible for auditing the organization's financial management processes and other processes and reporting findings to the audit committee of the board of directors

- **Security auditors**   Responsible for monitoring and testing security controls and delivering written opinions on the effectiveness of those controls

- **Security administrators**   Responsible for operating or monitoring specific security controls such as user access controls, firewalls, or intrusion detection systems

- **Security analyst**   Responsible for implementing and/or enforcing security policy by designing, improving, and/or monitoring security processes and security controls

- **Systems analysts**   Responsible for implementing and/or enforcing security policy by designing application software that includes adequate controls to protect the application as well as the information that it manages and stores

- **Software developers**   Responsible for coding application software that includes controls to prevent application misuse or bypass of controls to protect the integrity and confidentiality of information
- **Managers**   Responsible for the actions of the employees whom they supervise
- **Asset owners**   Responsible for protection and integrity of assets and for approving requests to access the assets they control
- **Employees**   Responsible for supporting security policy by using information systems and handling information assets properly and for reporting incidents and other security matters to management

NOTE   The roles and responsibilities here are considered common practice. There will be minor variations in the roles and responsibilities described here in many organizations.

Business Alignment

An effective security management program needs to be aligned with the organization's mission, strategies, and objectives. Characteristics of a business-aligned security program include but are not limited to

- **Board-level involvement**   The organization's board of directors is involved in the security management program, including asking questions, imposing requirements, or requesting key metrics.
- **Executive involvement**   Business executives are involved in the overall management of security, including any security steering committees.
- **Governance**   Executive control of the security management program includes all relevant aspects of the business.
- **Support of key initiatives**   Information security personnel are involved in the development of new key initiatives.
- **Risk tolerance**   The organization's risk appetite and risk tolerance are in alignment with the organization's mission and objectives.
- **Coordination or integration with enterprise risk management (ERM)** Information security risk management processes align with or are integrated with the organization's ERM program.
- IT and security strategy aligns with business mission, goals, and governance.
- Employees understand the relationships between security and business goals and understand how IT security supports those goals.
- Employees understand their security role in relation to the overall business mission, goals, strategy, and governance.

Asset Inventory and Classification

Information assets fall into two basic categories: information and information systems. *Information* consists of software, tools, and every type of data. *Information system* is an inclusive term that encompasses servers, workstations, mobile devices, network devices, gateways, appliances, and almost every other kind of IT hardware that is used.

Information and information systems both need to be inventoried. This helps management continue to be aware of their existence so that they can be properly managed and protected. The inventory of sensitive data supports an organization's privacy program.

Information and information systems also need to be classified. This will ensure that they will be properly handled according to their criticality, sensitivity, importance, and other criteria. A classification scheme may be developed as a result of a risk assessment, as well as regulations and standards such as Health Insurance Portability and Accountability Act (HIPAA), General Data Protection Regulation (GDPR), and PCI-DSS.

Hardware Asset Inventory

An IT organization that is responsible for the management of information and information systems must have a means for knowing what all of those assets are. More than that, IT needs to acquire and track several characteristics about every hardware asset, including

- **Identification** This includes make, model, serial number, asset tag number, logical name, and any other means for identifying the asset.
- **Value** Initially, this may signify the purchased value, but may also include its depreciated value if an IT asset management program is associated with the organization's financial asset management program.
- **Location** The asset's location needs to be specified so that its existence may be verified in a periodic inventory.
- **Condition** The asset's current capability needs to be noted—for example, whether it is operational or down for upgrades or maintenance.
- **Security classification** Security management programs almost always include a plan for classifying the sensitivity of information and/or information systems. Example classifications include secret, restricted, confidential, and public.
- **Asset group** IT assets may be classified into a hierarchy of asset groups. For example, any of the servers in a data center that support a large application may be assigned to an asset group known as "Application X Servers."
- **Configuration** The configuration of every asset must be managed and known, according to established standards and in compliance with applicable regulations and standards.
- **Owner** This is usually the person or group responsible for the operation of the asset.
- **Custodian** Occasionally, the ownership and operations of assets will be divided into two bodies, where the owner owns them but a custodian operates or maintains them.

Because hardware assets are installed, moved, and eventually retired, it is important to verify the information periodically in the asset inventory by physically verifying the existence of the physical assets. Depending upon the value and sensitivity of systems and data, this inventory "true-up" may be performed as often as monthly or as seldom as once per year. Discrepancies in actual inventory must be investigated to verify that assets have not been moved without authorization or stolen.

Information Assets

Sometimes overlooked because it is intangible, the information that is stored in systems should be treated as an asset. In almost all cases, information such as software and databases has tangible value and should be included in the list of IS assets.

Operating systems and subsystems such as database management systems or applications that reside in virtual machines are considered assets. Like physical assets, these may have tangible value and should be inventoried periodically.

Emerging privacy laws including GDPR and California Consumer Privacy Act (CCPA) are compelling organizations to improve their knowledge and control of information assets, particularly those containing sensitive information about individuals.

Data Classification Overview   In most organizations, various types and sets of information will have varying degrees of sensitivity. These levels of sensitivity will implicitly dictate that information at different levels should be handled accordingly. For instance, the most sensitive information should be encrypted whenever stored or transmitted and should be accessible only to those individuals who have a justified need to use it.

Would it be easier to handle all information the same way that the most sensitive information in the organization is handled? Although it would be easier to remember how to handle and dispose of all information, it might also be an onerous task, particularly if all information is handled at the level warranted for the organization's most sensitive or critical information. Encrypting everything and shredding everything would be a wasteful use of resources. That said, it is incumbent on an organization to build a simple data classification program that is easy to understand and follow. Too many levels of classification would be burdensome and difficult for users to understand and follow.

Data Classification Details   In most organizations, a data classification program can be defined in detail in less than a dozen pages, and the practical portions of it could almost fit on a single page. For many organizations, a simple four-level classification program is a good place to start. The four levels could be labeled as *secret, restricted, confidential*, and *public*. Any information in the organization would be classified into one of these four levels.

Example handling procedures for each of these levels are found in Table 6-1.

The classification and handling guidelines presented in Table 6-1 are meant as an example to illustrate the differences in various forms of data handling for various classification levels. However, the contents of Table 6-1 can serve as a starting point for an actual data classification and handling procedure.

	Secret	Restricted	Confidential	Public
Example Information Types	Passwords, merger and acquisition plans and terms	Credit card numbers, bank account numbers, Social Security numbers, detailed financial records, detailed system configuration, vulnerability scan reports	System documentation, end-user documentation, internal memos, network diagrams	Brochures, press releases
Storage on Server	Must be encrypted, store only on servers labeled sensitive	Must be encrypted	Access controls required	Access controls required for update
Storage on Mobile Device	Must never be stored on mobile device	Must be encrypted	Access controls required	No restrictions
Storage in the Cloud	Must never be stored in the cloud	Must be encrypted	Access controls required	Access controls required for update
E-mail	Must never be e-mailed	Must be encrypted	Authorized recipients only	No restrictions
Web Site	Must never be stored on any web server	Must be encrypted	Access controls required	No restrictions
Fax	Encrypted, manned fax only	Manned fax only, no e-mail–based fax	Manned fax only	No restrictions
Courier and Shipment	Double wrapped, signature and secure storage required	Signature and secure storage required	Signature required	No restrictions
Hardcopy storage	Double locked in authorized locations only	Double locked	Locked	No restrictions
Hardcopy Distribution	Only with owner permission, must be registered	To authorized parties only, only with owner permission	To authorized parties only	No restrictions
Hardcopy Destruction	Cross-cut shred, make a record of destruction	Cross-cut shred	Cross-cut shred or secure waste bin	No restrictions
Softcopy Destruction	Erase with DoD 5220.22-M spec tool	Erase with DoD 5220.22-M spec tool	Delete and empty recycle bin	No restrictions

Table 6-1   Example of Information Handling Guidelines

Access Controls

Access controls are the technology-based methods of controlling access to an information-based resource. Access controls must be actively managed by staff members who are authorized to perform this function and trained to perform it properly.

The workings of access controls are discussed later in this chapter in the section "Logical Access Controls." Access controls also exist in the physical world and are discussed later in this chapter in the section "Physical Security Controls."

Access Control Management

The management of access controls requires that processes and business rules be established that govern how access controls are managed. These processes and rules are used to decide which persons and systems will be permitted to access which data and functions in the organization, as well as the rules governing the request, approval, provisioning, and review of access controls.

Several processes are used to manage access controls:

- **Access control request**   Any new request for access must be formally made via an established request procedure. The request should be approved by the subject's manager as well as by the owner of the resource to which access is being requested.

- **Access control review**   A periodic review of all users' access to systems must be performed to verify that everyone who has access is still entitled to that access and to verify that all access for terminated employees has been removed.

- **Access history review**   A periodic review of users' accesses to systems must be made to determine who has accessed systems. A practical result is the removal of access rights for users who have not accessed systems for a period of time. Users who do not access systems for extended periods of time probably should have those access rights removed.

- **Segregation of duties review**   A periodic review of each user's access rights in all systems must be performed to verify that each employee does not have a combination of access privileges that would constitute a violation of segregation of duties.

- **Employee transfer**   When an employee is transferred from one position to another, the access rights associated with the departed position must be removed and any new access rights for the new position established.

- **Employee termination**   When an employee is no longer employed by the organization, all access rights for that employee must be terminated immediately.

All of these processes must have a robust recordkeeping plan so that all requests, reviews, transfers, and terminations are well documented. These records must themselves be restricted so that only authorized persons may view them. These records also must be protected against tampering.

These activities must include not only an organization's full-time employees, but also temporary workers, contractors, consultants, services providers, and all other parties with access to an organization's systems.

In addition to these processes, there are several audit and monitoring procedures to verify correct operation of these procedures; auditing of access controls is discussed later in this chapter.

Access Control Logs

The preceding section discussed business processes and the records that are associated with them. In addition to those records, the information systems that persons are given permission to access must have automatic records of their own. These systems must record all login and access attempts (successful and failure) made by persons. And like the records associated with business processes, these records must also be protected from alteration. This topic is discussed in more detail later in this chapter in the section "Logical Access Controls."

Privacy

Privacy is the protection of personal information from unauthorized disclosure, use, and distribution. *Personal information* refers to a variety of informational elements about a private citizen, some of which are not well known, including their name in combination with one or more of the following:

- Date and place of birth
- Place of residence
- Fixed and mobile telephone numbers
- Social insurance (such as Social Security) number
- Driver's license number
- Passport number
- Financial account (such as credit card, bank account, retirement account) numbers

 NOTE Some privacy regulations include additional items such as location and IP address as a part of privacy information.

Historically, the concern about privacy stemmed from organizations that collected, aggregated, and then distributed databases containing private citizens' information, which was then used for targeted marketing and other purposes.

More recently, one worry about privacy has concerned the rise in identity theft, which is made possible from the proliferation of private information and the failure to protect that information adequately. Cyber-criminals have had an easy time discovering and stealing this information in order to conduct wide-scale identity theft as well as fraud. Another source of concern about privacy is the improper and unethical use of personal information by corporations and governments.

Organizations that collect any of the previously mentioned items on behalf of customers or other constituents need to develop policies that define what the organization intends to do with this information. Organizations also need to be aware of applicable privacy laws and regulations and ensure they are fully compliant with them. For each item of potentially sensitive information, an organization should be able to specify

- What information it specifically collects
- Why it collects the information
- How it uses the information
- Collection of consent for these and other uses
- How long it retains the information
- How the information can be corrected by its owners
- To what other organizations the information is distributed and why
- Who is responsible for protecting the information
- How an owner can opt out (causing the cessation of storage of that information)

Business processes, procedures, and records should exist for all of these associated uses and actions, which can then be monitored and audited by others as needed.

Third-Party Management

Nearly every organization relies on one or more third-party organizations in the development, support, or operations of its business processes. Often this takes the form of outsourced information systems or related services. Digital transformation has resulted in many organizations outsourcing some IT services that support critical business processes. There are so many specialties and subspecialties in IT that even the largest organizations need to utilize third-party organizations to build, support, or manage their IT environment.

Third Parties and Risk

The use of any third-party organization should not be permitted to result in an increase of overall risk to an organization, at least not without bringing some matching value. When considering outsourcing a service to a third party, a risk assessment should be performed to identify and characterize risks associated with this.

Some of the types of services that third-party service organizations provide include

- Internet connectivity
- Internet hosting and colocation
- Cloud service, whether Software-as-a-Service (SaaS), Infrastructure-as-a-Service (IaaS), or Platform-as-a-Service (PaaS)
- Application services (for e-mail, CRM [customer relationship management], ERP [enterprise resource planning], MRP [materials resource planning], payroll, and expense reporting)

- Managed security services
- IT support
- Software development and testing
- Call centers
- Collection services
- Management and business consulting
- Auditors and security assessments
- Vendors that support hardware and software solutions
- Janitorial and other cleaning
- Shipping and receiving
- Building and equipment maintenance
- Temporary employee services

The primary risk with a third-party service provider is that the service provider will have access to some of the organization's sensitive information or to systems or networks containing or processing such information. Whether the service provider will have access to the organization's applications and data, or whether the organization will be sending data to the service provider, this overall risk needs to be broken down into each component and analyzed.

For each risk identified, remediation needs to be identified, typically so that the risk can be reduced to the same level as though the organization were performing the service on its own.

Types of Third-Party Access

Depending upon the type of service rendered, third-party service providers will have access to the organization's information in a variety of ways, including

- Physical access to hardcopy business records
- Physical access to information systems
- Physical access to storage media such as hard drives, solid-state drives, backup tapes, and optical drives
- Logical access to information systems, sensitive data, or source code

 NOTE A third-party service provider does not necessarily need access to sensitive business records to pose a risk. A service provider that is familiar with the organization's business practices can cause harm to the organization by interfering with business operations or disclosing business practices to outsiders such as customers, competitors, and others. Such interference or disclosure can occur through the action of an internal or external malicious actor or by innocent mistake.

Risks Associated with Third-Party Access

Knowing the type of access that a third-party service provider will have to an organization's information, the types of risks can be identified. Some of these risks include

- Theft of business records
- Exposure of business records to unauthorized parties
- Alteration of business records
- Damage (both deliberate and accidental) to information systems hardware, software, or information
- Failure to perform services in a timely manner
- Failure to perform services accurately
- Failure to perform services professionally

Third-Party Access Countermeasures

As mentioned earlier in this section, the risks associated with a third-party service provider should be no different from associated risks if the organization were performing the service on its own. Even though new risks are introduced when transferring work to a service provider, countermeasures and compensating controls should be introduced that will keep the level of risk acceptably low.

Some of the countermeasures that can be used to mitigate risk include

- Video surveillance with video recording
- Logging all data access and associated accesses to named individuals in the third-party organization
- Access controls that prevent the third party from accessing business records that it does not require in the performance of its services
- Logical access controls that limit the third party's access only to those data fields required to perform their services
- Vulnerability management tools and procedures
- Security awareness training
- Systems to block malware and its actions
- Security monitoring to detect and respond to security events
- Recording of voice or data communications sessions
- Periodic audits of the service provider's activities

Generally, an organization can require that a third-party service organization that has logical access to the organization's systems or stores any of the organization's data protect this data with the same (or higher) level of controls that the organization uses for its own data. This should result in the third-party service organization's *not* being in a situation where the organization's records are more vulnerable to theft, exposure, or compromise. For example, if an organization requires encryption of specific information when processed in your organization's systems, any service provider that processes the same information should also be required to encrypt it or to employ other means that result in the same level and type of protection.

NOTE In any situation where treatment for a specific risk associated with a third-party service provider results in unavoidable residual risk, senior management will need to be made aware of the residual risk and determine whether they are willing to accept that risk.

When an organization is considering use of a third-party service provider, the organization should require the service provider to answer a detailed questionnaire concerning security and other aspects of its operation. The organization should also ask whether the provider has had any external audits of its services; if so, the organization should request to see reports from those audits.

To validate information provided in questionnaires and other materials, an organization should consider requesting key pieces of evidence and perhaps a site visit to the service provider's offices and processing center(s).

Addressing Third-Party Security in Legal Agreements

The services performed by a third-party service provider should be succinctly described in a legal agreement. This will generally include a description of the services that are performed, measures of quantity and quality for services, service levels, remedies or penalties for failures in quality or quantity, rates and payments, and roles and responsibilities for both parties.

Legal agreements with service providers need to include several security provisions, including

- A statement that all of the organization's information and knowledge of its business practices will be kept confidential
- Security- and privacy-related liabilities, roles, and responsibilities
- Security controls required to protect the organization's information
- Acceptable uses for the organization's information
- Persons who will be authorized to access the organization's information
- Background checks, nondisclosure agreements, and acceptable-use agreements for each person who is authorized to access the organization's information
- Required security training for persons authorized to access the organization's information
- Capabilities in place to log and respond to security-related events
- Steps to be taken if a security breach or suspected breach should occur

- Steps to be taken to reduce the likelihood of data loss caused by a natural or manmade disaster
- Identification of who is responsible for security and privacy in the third-party organization
- The right to inspect and audit the third-party organization's premises and operations on short notice
- Proof of compliance with all applicable laws and regulations
- Agreement to adequately destroy all copies of information on request or upon the termination of the agreement

Many additional security-related terms and conditions may be warranted, depending upon the nature of the services provided and the sensitivity and value of the information accessed and used by the service provider. Regulations imposed on the organization regarding the collection, handling, and use of relevant information may result in additional terms and conditions.

Addressing Third-Party Security in Security Policy

Many organizations provide cloud-based commercial applications, which are as easy to set up as filling in a registration form, paying with a credit card, and uploading sensitive data from an employee's workstation. These organizations operate as SaaS, PaaS, IaaS, or other cloud service models.

Often, the persons in an organization have little idea about or regard for the security controls that are used by its service providers. Because of this, organizations can enact a security and business policy that forbids the use of any online service provider (SaaS, PaaS, IaaS, cloud, and so on) unless a risk assessment has first been performed for that service provider. Without such a policy, there is little to stop persons from signing up with various online service providers and potentially putting the organization's sensitive data at risk.

 NOTE An organization should have policies and processes in place to properly assess, measure, and monitor risks related to any third-party service provider.

Third-Party Risk Management Life Cycle

The third-party risk management (TPRM) process is a typical life cycle process. It starts with a decision to consider one or more third parties to perform a service to the organization. Even before selecting a service provider, the organization sends an appropriate questionnaire to each prospective service provider to understand the risk profile of each. Once a third party has been selected, the information gleaned from the questionnaire is used to determine the contents of the legal agreement; for instance, if a third party does not have a security awareness training program, a clause in the legal agreement would stipulate that the third party will implement such a program within a specific period of time. Annually, the organization will send a security questionnaire to each third party to reassess its security posture to ensure that its security programs continue to be acceptably effective.

Each third party represents a different level of risk and criticality to an organization. For this reason, organizations can develop risk levels or "tiers" that each third party is assigned to. For instance, three tiers corresponding to low, medium, and high risk are developed and third parties assigned to one of those tiers. Service providers at the highest tier are assessed with more rigor and at a higher frequency. Service providers at the lowest risk tier may be assessed at onboarding time and seldom thereafter. Each organization needs to determine the standards and procedures for each risk tier and the level and types of assessment performed at each.

Many security leaders build a third-party risk dashboard that depicts changes and trends in the risks associated with the entire portfolio of third parties. This dashboard can show risk "hot spots" and areas requiring more focus and attention. Information in the third-party risk program should be integrated with the organization's risk management life cycle and even with its ERM program if that exists.

Governance should also be a consideration in the TPRM life cycle. Some governance requirements, such as those that come from HIPAA, actually require that third-party service providers be appropriately vetted and must include certain security or privacy measures in their contracts.

Human Resources Security

The hearts of most organizations' business operations are not computers, machinery, or buildings, but people. People design and operate business processes; they design, build, and operate IT systems, and they support processes and systems and help to improve them over time. They interact, directly and indirectly, with vendors, partners, suppliers, and customers. And while people are an organization's greatest asset, they may also be a source of significant risk.

People are entrusted with access to sensitive information and entrusted to design and create information systems to manage sensitive information properly. But an employee in a position of trust can betray that trust and cause a significant amount of damage to the organization's operations and long-term reputation, whether acting out of ignorance, malice, or haste.

Trust is the key: organizations provide access to sensitive information, trusting that their employees will honor that trust and treat information properly. The trust is reciprocal: employees also trust that their employer will treat them with respect, pay them a fair salary, recognize their accomplishments, and give them opportunities to advance.

Organizations need to take several measures to mitigate human resource–related risks. These measures are described in the remainder of this section.

 NOTE In nearly every case in this section, actions that organizations take regarding their employees should also apply to temporary and contract workers and to others who have access to their sensitive information.

Screening and Background Checks

Prior to hiring each employee, an organization should verify the facts that each candidate presents on his or her résumé or curriculum vitae. The confirmation of these and other important facts is commonly known as a background check, and may consist of

- Verification of the candidate's identity
- Confirmation of the candidate's legal right to work in the employer's locale
- Verification of previous employment
- Verification of education
- Verification of professional licenses and certifications
- Investigation into the candidate's criminal history
- Investigation into the candidate's financial history
- Drug test
- Checks for associations with certain persons or groups (such as designated terrorist or hate groups)

Irregularities in any of these areas may be a signal to the employer that further investigation is required if the employer is still intent on hiring the candidate. The organization discovering irregularities in a candidate's background may also rescind a pending offer of employment or decide not to make an offer.

In addition to a background check, an employer will usually check references. This means that the employer will contact one or more professional colleagues to learn more about the candidate. The employer might also make inquiries through its network of professional acquaintances to gather intelligence about the candidate from people who are not references. For example, if a security manager is hiring a security analyst and receives a résumé from an employee at a local organization, the security manager could contact other known colleagues in the organization to determine whether any of them are familiar with the candidate. This can be a source of valuable information, since sometimes a candidate's references may be coached to say certain things or avoid certain topics.

 CAUTION Employers frequently search professional and social networking sites such as LinkedIn, Twitter, Instagram, and Facebook to gather additional intelligence on prospective employees. These and other networking sites often reveal more about a person's character than will be found on a résumé, application for employment, or references.

Another emerging trend in organizations is the practice of repeating background checks throughout an employee's tenure. This can help an employer discover certain facts about recent criminal convictions or significant financial events (such as judgments, collections, or bankruptcy) that may warrant action on the employer's part. Because of the cost associated with a background check, organizations that perform repeat background checks generally limit these checks to those vying for high-risk positions, such as those who handle or manage the use of financial resources.

NOTE   Organizations need to ensure that background screening is performed for temporary workers, contractors, and consultants. Some organizations perform these themselves, while others require that placement agencies or consulting firms screen their own candidates.

Job Descriptions

A job description is an employer's formal statement to an employee that says, "This is what we expect and require of you to perform this job." Employers should have formal job descriptions for each position in the organization. The main reason for this is to document formally the expectations that the organization has for each employee. These expectations should include

- **Position title**   The job title (such as senior security auditor or database administrator)
- **Requirements**   To include necessary education, skills, and work experience
- **Duties and responsibilities**   To include the tasks, projects, and other activities that the employee is expected to perform

The duties and responsibilities section should include a statement that says the employee is required to uphold all of the organization's policies (including security and privacy policies and code of ethics). The job description could list the major policies by name.

Employment Agreements

In locales that permit them, organizations should utilize written employment agreements with each employee. The employment agreement should clearly specify the terms and conditions of employment, including

- **Duties**   The employment agreement should describe the employee's duties in his or her position. This may be similar to what is stated in the employee's job description.
- **Roles and responsibilities**   The employment agreement should define the employee's roles and responsibilities, as well as the responsibilities of the employer. This will be similar to what is in the job description.
- **Confidentiality**   The employee agrees to keep all company secrets confidential, even after termination of employment.
- **Compliance**   The employee must agree to comply with all applicable laws and regulations, as well as with all organization policies. The employment agreement should state the consequences of failing to comply with laws, regulations, and policies.
- **Termination**   The employment agreement should include the conditions and circumstances by which the organization or the employee can sever the agreement.

Some organizations require employees in certain positions to sign noncompete agreements as a way of protecting intellectual property and customer/supplier relationships.

During Employment

Organizations need to enact several safeguards during the span of employment for each employee. These safeguards ensure that each employee's behavior is appropriate and that each employee is able to do only what is required of him or her. These safeguards include

- **Periodic renewal of employment agreements** Documents signed at the time of hire, including nondisclosure, employment, security policy, code of conduct, and other agreements, should be renewed periodically. Organizations that employ this practice do this annually.

- **Repeat background checks** Occasionally, repeating background checks helps to ensure that each employee's background (criminal history in particular) is still acceptable. Some organizations do this only for higher risk positions.

- **Access changes when transferred** Any employee who is transferred from one position to another should have his or her accesses for the former position removed. This helps to prevent the accumulation of privileges over time.

- **Awareness training** Employees should undergo periodic training on important topics, including security awareness training, so that they will continue to be aware of security procedures and requirements.

Policy and Discipline During their service, employees, contractors, temps, and other workers are expected to comply with the organization's security policy and other policies. The organization's security management program needs to include monitoring and internal auditing to ensure that policies are adhered to. When policy violations occur, human resources will need to invoke its disciplinary action process as needed.

Disciplinary action that is related to security policy violations should not be treated differently from any other disciplinary matter. IT security may be asked to provide facts about the matter but should otherwise not be involved. Discipline is usually a matter between an employee's manager and the employee; human resources should be involved only if the matter is serious enough to warrant a letter in the employee's employment file, suspension, demotion, or termination of employment. The organization's legal department will be involved to protect the organization's treatment of the employee to respond when any employee's actions represent a violation of any law or legal agreement.

Equipment Organizations should keep records regarding any equipment, software, licenses, or other assets that are entrusted to the employee, particularly when the asset will be used away from company premises, such as during travel or in the employee's home. Each time an asset is issued to an employee, a simple checkout document should be completed that describes the asset, the employee's name, the date issued, and an agreement that the asset will be returned to the employer on request. The employee should be required to sign this document, and a copy should be placed in his or her employment file.

If the employee transfers to another position or department or leaves the organization altogether, human resources should retrieve all equipment checkout forms and make sure that the employee returns each asset.

Transfers and Terminations

When employees are transferred from one position or department to another, they may be required to return certain assets entrusted to their care if they are no longer needed in the new role. Similarly, after transfer, an employee's access rights should be reviewed and any accesses from the old position that are not required in the new position should be removed. This is covered in more detail in the earlier section "Access Controls."

When an employee's employment is terminated, his or her access to information systems and business premises should be immediately revoked. All equipment, documents, software, and other assets in the employee's care should be returned and accounted for. The access badge and other identifying items should also be returned.

If an employee is being terminated for cause, the organization may elect to do a "look back" in electronic records to determine whether any recent activities represent risk to the organization. For example, a software developer who suspected an imminent termination may have appropriated a large cache of source code to be used in subsequent employment.

Computer Crime

Computers are involved in many criminal acts and enterprises. This section discusses the uses of computers in criminal activities.

Roles of Computers in Crime

Being the flexible, multipurpose tools that they are, computers can be used in several different ways in the commission and support of crimes. And because some computers contain valuable information, they are targets of crimes. There are three main ways in which a computer is involved in a crime: as a target, as an instrument, and as support.

Target of a Crime   A computer or its contents are the target of a crime. Some of the types of crimes are

- **Equipment theft**   The computer itself (or related equipment or media) is stolen.

- **Equipment vandalism**   Computer equipment is damaged or destroyed.

- **Data theft**   Data that is stored on the computer or related media is stolen. This is a more difficult crime to detect, since thieves usually steal a copy of the data, leaving the original data intact and untouched.

- **Data vandalism**   Data that is stored on a computer is deliberately altered, sometimes in ways that go undetected for a time.

- **Trespass**   Someone accesses the computer system or data center without permission or authorization.

Instrument in a Crime   A computer is used as a weapon or tool to commit a crime. Some of the types of crimes that can be perpetrated include

- **Trespass**   Someone makes unauthorized and unlawful entry into a computer or network.
- **Data theft and vandalism**   Intruders access computers or networks and steal or destroy data and programs.
- **Sabotage**   Intruders destroy computer hardware, software, or data.
- **Child pornography**   An individual or group unlawfully stores or distributes child pornography content.
- **Libel and slander**   Someone issues communications that make claims that slander a subject a negative light.
- **Espionage**   An individual or group obtains information considered a military, a political, or an industrial secret.
- **Eavesdropping**   A computer is used to eavesdrop on electronic messaging, such as e-mail, instant messaging, and even voice over IP (VoIP).
- **Phishing and spam**   Computers are used to generate and deliver millions of spam messages every day.

Support of a Crime   Computers can be used to support criminal activities. Some of the ways that this can occur include

- **Storage and transmission of stolen property**   Computers are used to store or transmit stolen information.
- **Recordkeeping**   Computers are used to record criminal activities. For example, a petty thief who breaks into houses tracks the items he steals in a spreadsheet program.
- **Aid and abet**   Computers are used to provide support for other criminals. For instance, a computer is used to send helpful information and funds to an accomplice.
- **Conspiracy**   A computer is used to document the plans for a crime. Criminals use word processing tools to perfect their criminal schemes.

It should be easy to imagine how computers can play multiple roles in crimes: they can be used as weapons as well as storage and recordkeeping systems, for instance.

Categories of Computer Crime

Cyber-crime comes in a lot of flavors, primarily because computers are used as targets for so many purposes. It may be helpful to remember that the information stored in computers has some value—and the nature and value of that information will attract various types of criminal elements. Computer crimes are roughly analogous to crimes in the physical world. People rob banks to get the money; they deface statues in public places to embarrass the government and make a political point; they attack public transportation systems in acts of terrorism; and they steal purses to get quick cash and maybe a photo ID and a few usable credit cards.

The categories of computer crime can be thought of in this way:

- **Military and intelligence**   Attackers are attempting to obtain military or intelligence secrets or disrupt military or intelligence operations. These attacks may occur at any time—during wartime, periods of hostility, or when there are no apparent tensions between governments. Governments as well as nongovernment-sanctioned civilian groups carry out these attacks.

- **Political**   This type of attack may be carried out by one state against another, but more typically, the attacker is a state-sponsored individual or an independent group.

- **Terrorist**   Attackers are attempting to induce fear and panic among a populace by damaging or disrupting critical infrastructure that is controlled or monitored by computers, including utilities, government services, transportation, financial services, health care, education, and other organizations.

- **Financial**   Perpetrators are carrying out activities in an attempt to steal funds, credit card numbers, or bank account numbers, or to perpetrate fraud. Targets include financial institutions and all other organizations that store or process financial data.

- **Business**   This represents a wide variety of purposes, including espionage, extortion, theft, vandalism, denial of service, and any attacks designed to weaken or embarrass a business organization.

- **Grudge**   This is generally motivated by feelings of revenge that an individual or group wants to exact upon an individual, group, or organization.

- **Amusement**   This type of attack is carried out primarily for fun. Nevertheless, these attacks can be lethal and can cause significant damage or embarrassment.

Many attacks are a blend of two or more of the categories discussed here. Understanding these categories can help an organization better understand how to prepare for possible cyber-attacks.

Threats of Cyber-Crime on Organizations

Organizations that use computers to store information of value (whether tangible value or not) or perform high-value activities need to take steps to protect that information and the systems they reside in. The nature of the information does have a bearing on the types of threats that will be most prevalent for a given organization. In general, the threats include those discussed next.

Financial   Organizations that store financial-related information, particularly credit card numbers, bank account numbers, personally identifiable information, and patient health information, are more likely to be the target of crimes whereby criminals will attempt to steal and monetize this information. Organizations may also be the target of one or more types of financial fraud, including

- **Transferring funds**   A web site that is used to send or receive funds will be the target of attackers, who will attempt to trick the application—or its other users—into transferring funds to attackers' accounts.

- **Stealing service**   Intruders attempt to trick a web site into providing free service. For instance, a flaw in a site's payment acceptance program may permit a user to receive service without paying for it.

- **Ransomware**   This highly successful and lucrative technique often pays handsomely for perpetrators who employ malware to encrypt sensitive information and hold it for ransom. Criminals provide a decryption key (sometimes) after the victim organization has paid the ransom.

- **Account hijacking**   This can occur through malware that sniffs user IDs and passwords from existing customers, or phishing schemes that entice customers to click links that take them to imposter sites that appear to be financial institutions.

- **Click fraud**   Many online advertisers pay for clicks on their online ads. Attackers can build malware to generate clicks from victim computers in order to collect payments.

- **Social engineering**   Attackers attempt to trick people into responding to e-mails purporting to be invoices or refund requests, providing users' valuable login credentials to a phony web site.

Encryption or Disclosure of Sensitive Information   If an organization has sensitive information, intruders will attempt to encrypt, steal, or deface it. Sensitive information can be almost anything of value, including bank account and credit card numbers, intellectual property, personally identifiable information, patient health information, and military and government secrets. Perpetrators may try to steal or deface this information, or they may simply discover how to do that and disclose that technique to others.

Blackmail   If hackers or organized crime enterprises successfully break in to an organization's computers or networks, they may be able to encrypt or remove sensitive information and then demand payments to restore that information. *Ransomware* is a common and highly successful method of blackmail.

Sabotage   An attacker may break in to computers or networks to damage their ability to perform their functions. This kind of attack can range from damaging operating systems, application software, or information—whatever it takes to damage or destroy a system. Many strains of malware and attack tools are designed to destroy not only information, but also information systems, permanently. Such wide-scale attacks have crippled large organizations, requiring a ground-up rebuild of a part or all of an organization's IT infrastructure.

Reputation   Intruders may break in to an organization's computers or networks in some obvious way simply for the opportunity to embarrass the organization and damage its reputation.

Legal   Security breaches may invite lawsuits from customers, business partners, and shareholders.

Perpetrators of Cyber-Crime

Many different types of individuals and groups will commit cyber-crimes if they have sufficient motivation. The nature of the organization and the data that it stores on its computers will influence which groups and individuals will be more likely to attack the organization's systems. In no particular order, the perpetrators of cyber-crimes include

- **Cyber-criminal gangs and organized crime**   Lured by big profits, organized crime has moved headlong into the cyber-crime business with worldwide profits that exceed those from drug trafficking, according to the U.S. Treasury Department. Cyber-crime organizations are well organized with investors and capital, research and development budgets, supply chains, employees on payroll, and profit sharing. Owners and employees in cyber-criminal organizations network with one another, develop standards, and attend conferences to further their knowledge and skills.

- **Competing organizations**   Other organizations in the same industry sector may be intent on conducting industrial espionage to obtain trade secrets or to disrupt the operations of a competitor.

- **Military organizations**   Cyber-ops groups within military organizations, such as the PLA Unit 61398 in China, conduct intrusions and attacks to obtain military and commercial secrets as well as to disrupt critical infrastructure and industrial activities.

- **Spies and intelligence agents**   People in intelligence organizations may break into the computers or networks in target governments or industries to collect intelligence information. Often these agents will employ hackers to perform information-gathering activities.

- **Hackers**   Usually lone combatants who have the skills and the tools to break into computer systems and networks can steal or deface information or plant software in an organization's computers for a variety of purposes.

- **Activists**   Organizations with some political or ideological causes may conduct attacks and intrusions to further an agenda.

- **Law enforcement**   Some law enforcement organizations have been known to exceed their authority through illegal surveillance, including trespass into organizations' and private citizens' computers and mobile devices.

- **Terrorists**   State-sponsored, privately sponsored, and just plain rogue groups of individuals perpetrate cyber-crimes against populations to induce fear and intimidation, and eventually to precipitate changes in a nation's foreign policy. There have not been many spectacular terrorism-based cyber-crimes (none that we know of anyway), but it's likely just a matter of time.

- **Script kiddies**   Inexperienced computer hackers obtain hacking tools from others. The term "script kiddies" usually refers to adolescents (kiddies) or simply inexperienced would-be hackers who obtain hacking tools (scripts) to break in o computers for fun or just to pass the time.

- **Social engineers**   These clever individuals will use a variety of means to gain information about an organization's inner workings that they then use to exploit the organization. Social engineers frequently use pretexting (pretending to be someone they aren't) to get employees and private citizens to give up secrets that help them break in to systems.

- **Employees**   People who work in an organization have the means and often the opportunity to steal equipment and information from their employers. Usually all they need is motivation. Employers often deliver motivation on a silver platter as a result of draconian policies and working conditions.

- **Former employees**   People who used to work in organizations know their secrets, vulnerabilities, and inner workings. Terminated and laid-off employees sometimes have sufficient motivation to steal from or embarrass their former employers as a way of getting even for losing their job.

- **Knowledgeable outsiders**   These persons have some knowledge about an organization's internal systems, architecture, or vulnerabilities. These individuals can gain their knowledge through espionage, social engineering, or eavesdropping, or from current or former employees. The point is they know more than most outsiders.

- **Service provider employees**   Personnel employed at service providers are another class of knowledgeable outsiders; through their business relationship with the organization, they possess information about the organization's people, processes, and technology that they can use to harm the organization through illegal means.

Because cyber-crime can be perpetrated by so many different types of people, it is quite a challenge to "think like a cyber-criminal" in order to prepare one's defenses. While such an approach will still be helpful, it requires broad reflection on the part of security analysts and engineers who are responsible for protecting an organization's valuable assets.

Security Incident Management

A *security incident* is defined as any event that represents a violation of an organization's security policy. For instance, if an organization's security policy states that it is not permitted for one person to use another person's computer account, then such a use that results in the disclosure of information would be considered a security incident. There are several types of security incidents:

- **Computer account abuse**   This includes willful account abuse, such as a person sharing user account credentials with others or stealing login credentials from another.

- **Computer or network trespass**   An unauthorized person accesses a computer network. The methods of trespass include installing malware, using stolen credentials, bypassing access credentials, or gaining physical access to the computer or network and connecting to it directly.

- **Interception of information**   An intruder devises a means for eavesdropping on communications. The intruder may be able to intercept e-mail messages, client-server communication, file transfers, login credentials, and network diagnostic information. Eavesdropping methods include installing malware, installing sniffing programs on compromised computers, or connecting directly to computers or networks.

- **Malware**   A worm or virus outbreak may occur in an organization's network. The outbreak may disrupt normal business operations simply through the malware's spread, or the malware may also damage infected systems in other ways, including destroying or altering information. Malware can also be used to eavesdrop on communications and send intercepted sensitive information such as login credentials, credit card numbers, bank account numbers and other sensitive information back to its source. Malware can also be used to perform Bitcoin mining on victim computers, thereby enriching cyber-criminals who use victims' computers at little or no cost.

- **Ransomware**   This specialized malware encrypts sensitive information on local machines as well as on network shares. The ransomware then displays a message that instructs the victim to transfer funds to the perpetrator in exchange for the ability to decrypt and recover the information. Law enforcement agencies generally discourage the payment of ransoms, since about half the time organizations do not recover the information if they do; further, paying a ransom invites subsequent attacks.

- **Destructware**   Similar to ransomware, destructware is designed to destroy information using encryption and other means. Varieties of destructware are designed to destroy computers and equipment. (Stuxnet is a good example of malware designed to destroy nuclear fuel enrichment centrifuges in a hostile country.)

- **Denial-of-service (DoS) attack**   An attacker floods a target computer or network with a volume of traffic that overwhelms the target so that it is unable to carry out its regular functions. For example, an attacker can flood an online banking web site with so much traffic that the bank's depositors are unable to use the site. Sending traffic that causes the target to malfunction or cease functioning is another form of a DoS attack.

- **Distributed denial-of-service (DDoS) attack**   Similar to a DoS attack, a DDoS attack emanates simultaneously from hundreds to thousands of computers. A DDoS attack can be difficult to withstand because of the sheer volume of incoming messages.

- **Equipment theft**   Computer or network equipment is stolen. Information contained in stolen equipment may be easy to extract unless it is encrypted.
- **Disclosure of sensitive information**   Any sensitive information can be disclosed to any unauthorized party.

The examples here should give you an idea of the nature of a security incident. Other types of incidents may be considered security incidents in some organizations.

 NOTE   A vulnerability that is discovered in an organization is not an incident. However, the severity of the vulnerability may prompt a response that is similar to a response for an actual incident. Vulnerabilities should be fixed as soon as possible to prevent future incidents.

Developing Incident Response Plans

The time to repair the roof is when the sun is shining.
–John F. Kennedy

No organization is immune to the effects of a security incident or breach. Thus, it is essential that organizations develop formal incident response plans to prepare for the inevitable. The steps in incident response plan development include

- **Policy**   Formal statements define the need to perform monitoring and prepare for incidents of every kind.
- **Roles and Responsibilities**   These define responsible parties in the organization who monitor and respond to an incident. This goes beyond the actual incident responders and includes legal, corporate communications, and business unit leaders.
- **Incident Procedure Development**   Create high-level procedures to be followed in any incident. Often this is where incident severity levels are defined.
- **Playbook Development**   Create detailed procedures to be followed for specific types of incidents—for example, steps to be followed if a laptop computer is lost or stolen.
- **Training**   Conduct training sessions for incident responders, so that they will be more familiar with those procedures during an actual incident.
- **Incident Response Exercises**   Conduct exercises and simulations to help the organization better understand how to respond during an actual incident.

Phases of Incident Response

An effective response to an incident is organized, documented, and rehearsed. The phases of a formal incident response plan are explained in the following sections.

Planning and Plan Development   This step involves the development of written response procedures that are followed when an incident occurs, as described in detail in the preceding sections.

Detection   Detection occurs when an organization is first aware that a security incident is taking place or has taken place. Because of the variety of events that characterize a security incident, an organization can become aware of an incident in several ways, including

- Application or network malfunction
- Application or network slowdown
- Intrusion detection system alerts
- Logfile alerts
- Alert from a security information and event management system (SIEM)
- Media outlets
- Notification from an employee, business partner, supplier, or customer
- Notification from law enforcement
- Anonymous tips

Initiation   Response to the incident begins at this phase. Typically, this will include notifications that are sent to response team members so that response operations may begin.

Evaluation   In this phase, response team members analyze available data to understand the cause, scope, and impact of the incident. This often includes forensic analysis to determine the precise nature of the incident.

Containment   The organization takes steps to ensure that the incident is not able to continue.

Eradication   Responders take steps to remove the source of the incident. This could involve removing malware, blocking incoming attack messages, or removing an intruder.

Recovery   When the incident has been evaluated and eradicated, often there is a need to recover systems or components to their pre-incident state. This may include restoring data or configurations or replacing damaged or stolen equipment.

Remediation   This activity involves any necessary changes that will reduce or eliminate the possibility of a similar incident occurring in the future. This may take the form of process or technology changes.

Closure   Closure occurs when eradication, recovery, and remediation are completed. Incident response operations are officially closed.

Post-Incident Review   Shortly after the incident closes, incident responders and other personnel meet to discuss the incident: its cause and impact, and the organization's response. The discussion will range from lessons learned to possible improvements in technologies and processes to improve defense and response.

Testing Incident Response

Incident response plans should be not only documented and reviewed—they need to be tested periodically. Incident response testing helps to improve the quality of those plans, which will help the organization to respond more effectively when an incident occurs.

Similar to disaster recovery and business continuity planning, various types of tests should be carried out:

- **Document review** Individual subject matter experts (SMEs) carefully read incident response documentation to understand the procedures and identify any opportunities for improvement.

- **Walkthrough** This is similar to a document review, except that it is performed by a group of SMEs who talk through the response plan. Discussing each step helps to stimulate new ideas, which could lead to improvements in the plan.

- **Simulation** Also known as a tabletop exercise, a facilitator describes a realistic security incident scenario and participants discuss how they will actually respond. A simulation usually takes half a day or longer. It is suggested that the scenario be "scripted" with new information and updates introduced throughout the scenario. A simulation can be limited to the technical aspects of a security incident, or it can involve corporate communications, public relations, legal, and other externally facing parts of the organization that may play a part in a security incident that is known to the public.

- **Parallel or Full-On** Though usually associated with a BCDR test, there is some utility for performing a test in the environment. For instance, a DoS attack on a production environment may render it inoperative or unavailable. In a DoS attack test, "victim" systems can be taken offline, which would trigger automated or manual responses either to remediate the situation on the target system or shift the workload to another system. Such a test would help the organization better understand its ability to respond to such an incident should one actually occur.

These tests should be performed once each year or more often. In the walkthrough and simulation tests, someone should be appointed as note-taker so that any improvements will be recorded and the plan can be updated.

If the incident response plan contains the names and contact information for response personnel, the plan should be reviewed more frequently to ensure that all contact information is up to date.

Incident Prevention

With the appropriate processes and controls in place, many incidents can be prevented from occurring in the first place, and those that occur may have less impact. Incident prevention is primarily accomplished through knowledge of vulnerabilities and actions to remove them. With fewer vulnerabilities, some threats can be reduced or neutralized altogether.

Important elements in the prevention of security incidents include

- **Vulnerability management** This systems management process utilizes tools and techniques to detect vulnerabilities in network devices, servers, and endpoints, along with tools used to install security patches in operating systems, database management systems, applications, and network devices. Many threats are realized through published vulnerabilities. Sometimes intruders are able to fashion tools to exploit vulnerabilities within hours of publication. It is therefore essential that an organization be prepared to mitigate vulnerabilities quickly by deploying security patches or employing other workarounds when it is known that specific vulnerabilities are being exploited in the wild. Vulnerability and patch management are discussed in more detail in the section "Logical Access Controls."

- **Vulnerability and threat monitoring** This involves close monitoring of security advisories published by vendor and vendor-independent services such as US-CERT, Secunia, InfraGard, Full Disclosure, and Bugtraq. These advisories are publications of newly discovered flaws in computer hardware and software, as well as announcements of new threats that are seen in the wild.

- **Situational awareness** This is the result of real-time monitoring of networks, systems, and endpoints, to detect indicators of compromise. The tools used here include software programs and hardware appliances known as intrusion detection systems (IDSs), intrusion prevention systems (IPSs), and security incident and event management (SIEM) systems.

- **Threat hunting** This is the proactive search for intrusions, intruders, and indicators of compromise (IOC).

- **Advanced anti-malware** Antivirus software is no longer considered effective against advanced threats. Thus, organizations need to consider the use of advanced anti-malware solutions at network boundaries and in servers, endpoints, and mobile devices.

- **System hardening** This is the technique of configuring a system so that only its essential services and features are active and all others are deactivated. This helps to reduce the "attack surface" of a system to its essential components only. On a hardened system, only the essential components need to be configured to resist attack; all other components are disabled and removed, resulting in less effort and fewer vulnerabilities. System hardening is discussed in detail in the section "Logical Access Controls."

- **Intrusion detection** IDSs can give early warnings of network- or computer-based attacks. IPSs go one step further by actively blocking activities that resemble attacks.

 NOTE According to contemporary thinking on incident management, it is considered unwise to believe that all incidents can be prevented. Accordingly, organizations need to invest in incident response processes and tools to facilitate rapid and effective response when incidents do occur.

Forensic Investigations

Forensic investigations are required when a security incident has occurred and it is necessary to gather evidence to determine the facts. Because the information gathered in an investigation may later be used in a legal proceeding, a forensic investigator must follow strict procedures when gathering, studying, and retaining information.

Chain of Custody

The key to an effective and successful forensic investigation is the establishment of a sound *chain of custody*. The primary considerations that determine the effectiveness of a forensic investigation are

- **Identification** A description of the evidence that was acquired and the tools and techniques used to acquire it. Evidence may include digital information acquired from computers, network devices, and mobile devices, as well as interviews of involved persons.

- **Preservation** A description of the tools and techniques used to obtain and retain evidence. This will include detailed records that establish the chain of custody, which may be presented and tested in legal proceedings.

- **Analysis** A description of the examination of the evidence gathered, which may include a reconstruction of events that are a subject of the investigation.

- **Presentation** A formal document that describes the entire investigation, evidence gathered, tools used, and findings that express the examiner's opinion of the events that occurred (or did not occur).

The entire chain of custody must be documented in precise detail and include how evidence was protected against tampering through every step of the investigation. Any "holes" in the information acquisition and analysis process will likely fail in legal proceedings, possibly resulting in the organization's failure to convince judicial authorities that the event occurred as described.

Forensic Techniques and Considerations

Computer and network forensics require several specialized techniques that ensure the integrity of the entire forensic investigation and a sound chain of evidence. Some of these techniques are

- **Data acquisition** This is the process of acquiring data for forensic analysis. Subject data may reside on a computer hard drive, in mobile device memory, or in an application's audit log. Several tools are used for forensic data acquisition, including media copiers, which are tools that acquire a copy of a computer's hard drive; USB memory stick; or removable media, such as an external hard drive or a CD/DVD-ROM.

- **Data extraction** If data is being acquired from a running system or from a third party, a forensics analyst must use a secure method to acquire the data and be able to demonstrate the integrity of the process used to acquire the data. This must be done in a way that proves the source of the data and shows that it was not altered during the extraction process.

- **Data protection**   Once data is acquired, the forensic investigator must take every step to ensure its integrity. Computers used for forensic analysis must be physically locked so that no unauthorized persons have access to them. They must not be connected to any network that would allow for the introduction of malware or other agents that could alter acquired data and influence the investigation's outcome.

- **Analysis and transformation**   Often, tools are required to analyze acquired data and search for specific clues. Also, data must frequently be transformed from its native state into a state that is human or tool readable; in many cases, computers store information in a binary format that is not easily read and interpreted by humans. For example, the NTUSER.DAT file used in Windows is a binary representation of the HKEY_LOCAL_USER branch of the system's registry. This file cannot be directly read and requires tools to transform it into human-readable form.

Logical Access Controls

Logical access controls are used to control whether and how subjects (usually persons, but also running programs and computers) are able to access objects (usually systems and/or data). Logical access controls work in a number of different ways:

- **Subject access**   A logical access control uses some means to determine the identity of the subject that is requesting access. Once the subject's identity is known, the access control performs a function to determine whether the subject should be allowed to access the object. If the access is permitted, the subject is allowed to proceed; if the access is denied, the subject is not allowed to proceed. An example of this type of access control is an application that first authenticates a user by requiring a user ID and password before permitting access to the application.

- **Service access**   A logical access control is used to control the types of messages that are allowed to pass through a control point. The logical access control is designed to permit or deny messages of specific types (and may possibly permit or deny based upon origin and destination) to pass. An example of this type of access control is a firewall, screening router, or IPS that makes pass/block decisions based upon the type of traffic, it origin, and its destination.

An analogy of these two types of access is a concert hall with a parking garage. The parking garage (the "service access") permits cars, trucks, and motorcycles to enter but denies oversized vehicles from entering. Upstairs at the concert box office (the "subject access"), persons are admitted if they possess a photo identification that matches a list of prepaid attendees. Certain persons are granted "backstage access" if they possess the required credentials and are not carrying dangerous objects such as firearms.

Access Control Concepts

In discussions about access control, security professionals often use terms that are not used in other IS disciplines:

- **Subject, object** These pronouns refer to access control situations. A *subject* is usually a person, but it could also be a running program, device, or computer. In typical security parlance, a subject is someone (or some*thing*) that wants to access something. An *object* (which could be a computer, application, database, file, record, or other resource) is the thing that the subject wants to access.

- **Fail open, fail closed** This refers to the behaviors of automatic access control systems when they experience a failure. For instance, if power is removed from a keycard building access control system, will all doors be locked or unlocked? The term *fail closed* means that all accesses will be denied if the access control system fails; the term *fail open* means that all accesses will be permitted upon failure. Generally, security professionals like access control systems to fail closed, because it is safer to admit no one than to admit everyone. But there will be exceptions now and then where fail open might be better; for example, building access control systems may need to fail open in some situations to facilitate emergency evacuation of personnel or entrance of emergency services personnel.

- **Least privilege** According to this concept, an individual user should have the lowest privilege possible that will still enable him or her to perform required tasks.

- **Segregation of duties** This concept specifies that single individuals should not have combinations of privileges that would permit them to conduct high-value operations on their own. The classic example is a business accounting department where the functions of creating a payee, requesting a payment, approving a payment, and making a payment should rest with two or more separate individuals. This will prevent any one person from being able to embezzle funds from an organization without notice. In the context of information technology, functions such as requesting user accounts and provisioning user accounts should reside with two different persons so that no single individual could create user accounts on his or her own.

- **Split custody** This is the concept of splitting knowledge of a specific object or task between two persons. One example is splitting the password for a critical encryption key between two parties: one person has the first half and the other has the second half. Similarly, the combination to a bank vault can be split so that two persons have the first half of the combination while two others have the second half.

Access Control Models

Several *access control models* have been developed since the 1970s. These models are simple mechanisms that are used to understand and build access control systems. The early models include Biba, Bell-La Padula, Clark-Wilson, Lattice, Brewer and Nash, Take-Grant, and Non-Interference. The models that are of interest to the IS auditor include

- **Mandatory Access Control (MAC)**   This access model is used to control access to objects (files, directories, databases, systems, networks, and so on) by subjects (persons, programs, and so on). When a subject attempts to access an object, the operating system examines the access properties of the subject and object to determine whether the access should be allowed. The operating system then permits or denies the requested access. Access is administered centrally, and users cannot override it.

- **Discretionary Access Control (DAC)**   In this access model, the owner of an object is able to determine how and by whom the object may be accessed. The discretion of the owner determines which subjects will be permitted access.

 NOTE   The MAC and DAC models offer particular advantages and disadvantages. While DAC offers flexibility by permitting an owner to set access rights, abuse or errors could lead to exposure of sensitive information. MAC's centralized administration and inflexibility are also strengths: users cannot override MAC settings and potentially expose sensitive information to others.

Access Control Threats

Because access controls are often the only means of protection between protected assets and users, access controls are often attacked. Indeed, the majority of attacks against computers and networks containing valuable assets are against access controls in attempts to trick, defeat, or bypass them. Threats represent the intent and ability to do harm to an asset.

Threats against access controls include

- **Malware**   This includes viruses, worms, Trojan horses, rootkits, and spyware. Malware is *malicious code* that is used to perform unauthorized actions on target systems. It is often successful because of known vulnerabilities that can be exploited. In the context of access control, malware presents one of two threats: the ability to record login credentials typed in by a user, and the ability to exploit a vulnerability in an access control system, thereby enabling an attacker to bypass an access control. Vulnerabilities are discussed in more detail in the next section.

- **Eavesdropping**   Attackers will install network- or system-based sniffing tools to listen to network communications to intercept key transmissions such as user IDs and passwords used to access sensitive or valuable information. Usually, attackers will need to use some means such as malware or social engineering to install sniffing tools on a target system. In some instances, however, attackers will have access to the physical network and can directly connect sniffing tools to the network cabling.

- **Logic bombs and back doors**   Computer instructions inserted by programmers or others in the systems development process can result in an application that contains unauthorized code. A *logic bomb* is a set of instructions designed to perform some damaging action when a specific event occurs; a popular example is a *time bomb* that alters or destroys data on a specified date in the future. Some developers install time bombs in code that they manage and periodically advance the date in the time bomb. If the developer is fired from his or her job, the time bomb will activate after termination, and the developer will have gotten revenge on the former employer. A *back door* is a section of code that permits someone to bypass access controls and access data or functions. Back doors are commonly placed in programs during development but removed before development is complete. Sometimes, however, back doors are deliberately planted so that the developer (or someone else) can access data and functions.

- **Scanning attacks**   An attacker performs active or passive scanning in an attempt to discover weak access controls. For example, an attacker can use a *port scanning tool* to discover open and possibly vulnerable ports on target systems. An attacker can search for unprotected modems through *war dialing*. Or an attacker can listen to Wi-Fi network traffic to look for vulnerable wireless access points in *war driving*.

- **Race conditions**   Also known as a time-of-check/time-of-use (TOC/TOU) attack, the attacker is attempting to exploit the small window of time that sometimes exists between the time that a resource is requested and when the resource is available for use.

 NOTE   The potency and frequency of threats on a system are directly proportional to the perceived value of assets that the system contains or protects.

Access Control Vulnerabilities

Vulnerabilities are the weaknesses that may be present in a system that enable a threat to be more easily carried out or to have greater impact.

Vulnerabilities by themselves do not bring about actual harm. Instead, threats and vulnerabilities work together. Most often, a threat exploits a vulnerability, because it is easier to attack a system at its weakest point. Common vulnerabilities include

- **Unpatched systems**   Security patches are designed to remove specific vulnerabilities. A system that is not patched still has vulnerabilities, some of which are easily exploited. Attackers can easily enter and take over systems that lack important security patches.

- **Default system settings** Default settings often include unnecessary services that increase the chances that an attacker can find a way to break into a system. The practice of *system hardening* is used to remove all unnecessary services and to make security configuration changes on a system to make it as secure as possible.

- **Default passwords** Some systems are shipped with default administrative passwords that make it easy for a new customer to configure the system. One problem with this arrangement is that many organizations fail to change these passwords. Hackers have access to extensive lists of default passwords for practically every kind of computer and device that can be connected to a network.

- **Incorrect permissions settings** If the permissions that are set up for files, directories, databases, application servers, or software programs are incorrectly set, this could permit access—and even modification or damage—by persons who should not have access.

- **Vulnerabilities in utilities and applications** System utilities, tools, and applications that are not a part of the base operating system may have exploitable weaknesses that could permit an attacker to compromise a system successfully.

- **Application logic** Software applications—especially those that are accessible via the Internet—that contain inadequate session management, resource management, and input testing controls can potentially permit an intruder to take over a system and steal or damage information.

Familiarity with Technology Is Key to Effective IS Audit

The IS auditor needs to be highly familiar with information technologies to be effective. Without in-depth knowledge of security threats, vulnerabilities, controls, and countermeasures, the IS auditor will not be able to detect as many unsafe practices in a technology environment. Furthermore, without a depth of understanding, IS auditors will not be able to ask probing questions in walkthroughs or be able to interpret evidence correctly.

The IS auditor must understand information technology in general, but he or she must also understand the technology architecture in the specific environment that is being examined. In an environment that has the appearance of being highly secure, a configuration error in a single device can betray that security like a traitor and expose the entire organization to considerable harm. Only an IS auditor with a thorough understanding of information technology would have a chance to detect such a weakness and interpret it correctly.

Access Points and Methods of Entry

Computing and network resources must be accessed in order to support business processes, thereby providing services and value. The majority of information-based resources are accessed via TCP/IP networks; some resources are accessed using other technologies, such as direct hardwired connections (as in the case of some mainframe computers) and non-TCP/IP network technologies. Then there are desktop computers that sometimes themselves contain information and resources.

Modern LAN environments are protected from outside threats with firewalls and other means. Many larger organizations also employ internal firewalls to segment their networks, creating separate zones of trust within the organization. But, generally speaking, LANs are a lot like highway systems within individual countries: once you pass a border checkpoint and show a passport or another credential, you can roam freely inside that country unhindered.

Points of Entry

The main point of entry in many organizations is the internal corporate LAN. A user who can connect to the corporate LAN is able to reach computing resources logically in the organization—subject to the access controls associated with each resource. This makes the notion of protecting corporate accesses by controlling access to the LAN a vital topic.

Increasingly, however, organizations have fewer and fewer internal resources, as a result of the mass migration away from on-premises resources to cloud-based resources. In these organizations, the internal LAN is little more than a means for connecting to a few resources such as printers and scanners, or is primarily a means of accessing the Internet and the organizations' primary business applications that are SaaS-based.

The ease of connectivity to the corporate LAN highlights a number of important security issues. Probably the biggest issue is the ability for nonorganization-owned computers to connect to the network and access network-based resources. By permitting nonorganization-owned systems to connect to the network, the organization is essentially giving up control of the network. Allowing any computer or device connect to the network creates risks, including

- **Exposure to malware**   Any computer that is not actively managed by centralized anti-malware software could be carrying malware that would attempt to propagate itself inside the corporate network. Indeed, worms such as Nimda and Code Red were able to spread in just this way. Laptops that were the personal property of employees would become infected on home networks and then spread the infection inside the corporate LAN in "Typhoid Mary" style. Many instances of malware being imported on vendor-owned computers (for "demo" purposes) are also known.

- **Eavesdropping**   While the IT department can exert some level of control over desktop and server computing by prohibiting (and even preventing) the installation of network-sniffing programs, IT cannot easily control whether nonorganization-owned computers have network-sniffing programs (or malware that does the same thing!).

- **Open access**   A corporate LAN that permits any device to connect will permit a wireless access point to connect to the network. This, in turn, may permit anyone with a Wi-Fi client to connect to the network.

Available technologies can be used to control the systems that are permitted to connect to the corporate LAN. Network access control (NAC) through a network access protocol such as 802.1X is used to control whether a system is permitted to connect to corporate network resources. NAC and 802.1X use an authentication mechanism to determine whether each new device is permitted to connect. If the device lacks the necessary credentials, it cannot connect.

Whether the device is actually able to physically connect is another story. Network switches play a role in NAC and 802.1X; if a device is not permitted onto the network, the workgroup switch will not route any packets from the denied workstation into the LAN. The workstation remains logically disconnected.

 NOTE Many organizations employ cloud-based environments for many or even all of their applications. As a result, corporate LAN environments often have few or no local resources. Accordingly, organizations may need to shift their strategies for the protection of assets.

Remote Access

Remote access is defined as the means of providing remote connectivity to a corporate LAN through a data link. Remote access is provided by many organizations so that employees who are temporarily or permanently off-site can access LAN-based resources from their remote location.

Remote access was initially provided using dial-up modems that included authentication. While remote dial-up is still provided in some instances, most remote access is provided over the Internet itself and typically uses an encrypted tunnel, or *virtual private network* (VPN), to protect transmissions from any eavesdroppers. VPNs are so prevalent in remote access technology that the terms *VPN* and *remote access* have become synonymous. Remote access architectures are depicted in Figure 6-1.

Two security controls are essential for remote access:

- **Authentication**   It is necessary to know who is requesting access to the corporate LAN. Authentication may consist of the same user ID and password that personnel use when on-site, or multifactor authentication may be required.

- **Encryption**   Many on-site network applications do not encrypt sensitive traffic because it is all contained within the physically and logically protected corporate LAN. However, because remote access provides the same function as being on the corporate LAN, and because the applications themselves usually do not provide encryption, the remote access service itself usually provides encryption. Encryption may use SSL (Secure Sockets Layer), IPsec (IP Security), L2TP (Layer 2 Tunneling Protocol), or PPTP (Point-to-Point Tunneling Protocol).

These controls are needed because they are a substitute (or *compensating control*) for the physical access controls that are usually present to control which personnel may enter the building to use the on-site corporate LAN. When personnel are on-site, their identity is confirmed through keycard or other physical access controls. When personnel are off-site using remote access, because the organization cannot "see" the person on the far end of the remote access connection, the authentication used is the next best thing.

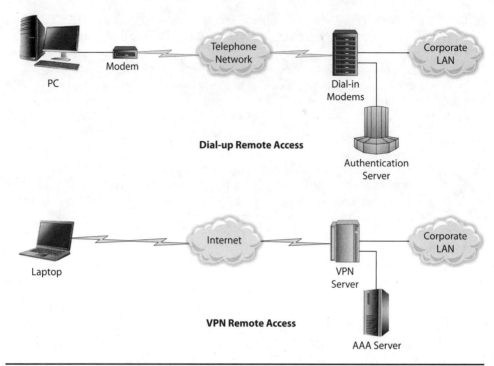

Figure 6-1 Remote access architectures

The migration of corporate resources from internal networks to cloud-based networks is changing the notion of remote access. As a result, organizations are incorporating multifactor authentication for access to the organization's cloud-based resources, regardless of the location of users—whether they are on a corporate LAN, working from home, in the field, or traveling.

The New Remote Access Paradigm

As organizations migrate their business applications to colocation centers and XaaS providers, and after the last internal resource is moved to the cloud, what is the point of remote access? Remote access to *what*?

If we think about this in terms of VPN and the protection afforded through encryption, VPN still makes good business sense, but protecting network traffic from potential eavesdroppers (whether the human or malware variety). For this reason, it's preferred to say "VPN" instead of saying "remote access."

Organizations still need to address several subtopics when considering their VPN architectures in light of cloud migration, such as split tunneling, Internet backhauling, and whether VPN should always automatically activate on workstations away from internal corporate networks.

Identification, Authentication, and Authorization

To control access to computing resources, they are protected by mechanisms that ensure only authorized subjects are permitted to access protected information. Generally, these mechanisms first identify who (or what) wants to access the resource, and then they will determine whether the subject is permitted to access the resource and either grant or deny the access.

Several terms, including *identification*, *authentication*, and *authorization*, are used to describe various activities and are explained here.

Identification

Identification is the act of asserting an identity without providing any proof of it. This is analogous to one person walking up to another and saying, "Hello, my name is _____."
Because it requires no proof, identification is not usually used alone to protect high-value assets or functions.

Identification is often used by web sites to remember someone's profile or preferences. For example, a nationwide bank's web application may use a cookie to store the name of the city in which the customer lives. When the customer returns to the web site, the application will display some photo or news that is related to the customer's location. But when the customer is ready to perform online banking, this simple identification is insufficient to prove the customer's actual identity.

Identification is just the *first* step in the process of gaining entry to a system or application. The next steps are authentication and authorization, which are discussed next.

Authentication

Authentication is similar to identification, where a subject asserts an identity. In identification, no proof of identity is requested or provided, but with authentication, some form of proof of the subject's identity is required. That proof is usually provided in the form of a secret password or some means of higher sophistication and security, such as a token, biometric, smart card, or digital certificate. Each of these is discussed later in this section.

When the user presents his or her user ID plus a second factor, whether a password, token, biometric, or something else, the system will determine whether the login request will be granted or denied. Regardless of the outcome, the system will record the login event in an event log.

Authorization

After a subject has been authenticated, the next step is authorization. This is the process by which the system determines whether the subject should be permitted to access the requested resource in the requested manner. To determine whether the subject is permitted to access the resource, the system will perform some type of a lookup or other confirmation of a business rule. For instance, an access control table associated with the requested resource may have a list of users who are permitted to access it. The system will read through this table to determine whether the user subject's identity appears in the table.

If so (and if the type of requested access matches the type permitted in the table), the system will permit the subject to access the resource. If the user's identity does not appear in the table, he or she will be denied access. Whether the login is successful or not, a record of the access attempt (and its disposition) is recorded in an event log.

The preceding example is simplistic but is often the means used to determine whether a user is authorized to access something. Typically, permissions are centrally stored by the operating system and administered by system administrators, although some environments permit the owners of resources to administer user access. See the section "Access Control Models," earlier in this chapter.

 NOTE The terms *identification, authentication*, and *authorization* are often misused by IT professionals who may not realize the differences between them. Security professionals and IS auditors need to understand the differences.

User IDs and Passwords

User IDs and passwords are the most common means for users to authenticate themselves to a resource—whether it is a network, server, or application.

User IDs   In most environments, a user's user ID will not be a secret; in fact, user IDs may be a derivation of the user's name or an identification number. Some of the common forms of a user's user ID are

- **First initial and last name**   For example, the user ID for John Toman would be jtoman. Some systems may have a limitation on the permitted length of a user ID—for instance, eight characters. If two users' user IDs would be the same (John Brown and James Brown, for example), the IT department could assign jobrown and jabrown, or jbrown and jbrown2.

- **First and middle initials and last name**   This is similar to first initial and last name, but with fewer chances for "collisions" (two persons who would have the same user ID). User James Dean Cunningham would have a user ID jdcunningham.

- **First and last name together**   Systems that permit longer user IDs with special characters such as periods (.) can adopt the common first.last form. User Mark Adams would have the user ID mark.adams.

- **Employee ID number**   Some organizations assign unique identifying numbers to their employees, and these can be used as user IDs if those numbers are not kept secret. One advantage of using an ID number is that the user's name becomes a characteristic of the user ID and not the user ID itself; in many cultures, for example, a woman's name changes when she marries, but in an organization that uses ID numbers, the user ID need not change or reflect a name she no longer uses.

CAUTION Confidential numbers such as social insurance (Social Security in the United States) or driver's license numbers should not be used as user IDs, because these identifying numbers are generally meant to be kept confidential.

Passwords   Whereas a user ID is not necessarily kept confidential, a password *always* is kept confidential. A password, also known as a *pass phrase*, is a secret combination of letters, numbers, and other symbols that is known only to the user who uses it. End users are typically advised the following about passwords:

- **Selecting a password**   Users should select a password that is easy for them to remember but difficult for others to guess. Passwords should not contain common words or the names of their family members or pets, nor should they contain numeric combinations representing birthdays or wedding anniversaries. Many environments require passwords of a minimum length (typically eight characters), and they require that passwords contain some combination of lowercase letters, uppercase letters, numbers, and symbols. Password vaulting tools usually have a means of generating strong, random passwords; this takes the burden from users having to create good passwords on their own, and password vaults also store passwords safely. Many environments also require that passwords be changed periodically, typically every 90 days. They also forbid the use of recently used passwords, which lowers the risk of someone else using a previous password.

- **Sharing passwords**   Users must be told that they should *never* share any password with *any* other person, for *any* reason! User accounts must be used only by the person to whom they are assigned and by no one else in any situation. In many organizations, sharing passwords can result in disciplinary action including termination of employment.

- **Transmitting passwords**   Passwords should never be sent in an e-mail or instant message. An eavesdropper or any person who intercepts the message would then know the password and may be able to use it, compromising the integrity of the user account and possibly of some sensitive business information as well.

- **Writing down passwords**   In environments with many applications, users must remember many passwords. Users will be tempted to write them down or save them in a spreadsheet or text file on their workstation. It would be acceptable for users to write down their passwords, provided they keep the paper with those passwords locked away or on their person always. Password vaulting eliminates the need to write down passwords.

- **Electronic password vaulting**   With so many complex passwords to remember, users could store their passwords in an electronic password vault; a number of good ones are available, including Password Safe, KeePass, and MacPass.

CAUTION Users should be advised *not* to store their passwords in any online password archival service or in a browser.

- **Managing passwords in multiple environments** Users are urged *not* to use the same password for every application. If anyone should discover or learn a user's password in one environment, the person could try that same password in other applications and possibly be able to log in. Difficult as it is, users should use unique passwords for each environment. Password vaults simplify the use of large numbers of passwords by making them readily available to users when they present credentials to a system.

User Account Provisioning When a user is issued a new computer or network user account, he or she needs to know the password to access the resource. Generating and transmitting an initial password to a user can be tricky, because passwords should never be sent in an e-mail message. A sound practice for initial user account provisioning would involve the use of a limited time, one-time password that would be securely provided to the user; upon first use, the system would require that the user change the password to a value that no one else would know.

Several factors influence how passwords are initially determined, including

- **User locations** If a user is located near the administrators who provision user accounts, one of the administrators can personally deliver the new password to the user. If the administrator and the user are not near each other, the administrator can give the password to the user by phone. In no circumstance should the password be sent via e-mail or instant message.

- **System limitations** Some environments do not support initial-use passwords that expire in a short amount of time.

- **Data sensitivity** The value of the data protected by access controls (including user accounts and their initial passwords) should be a factor in determining how user accounts are provisioned. If the data or asset being protected is of high value, more elaborate means (such as those discussed in this section) may be needed. But if the asset value is low, then the rules for initial account provisioning may be more relaxed.

NOTE Ideally, users will be required to change their password as soon as they have their new user account; however, some systems don't even permit this. Security analysts or IS auditors who are examining an environment's user account provisioning procedures should understand the environment's capabilities as well as the risks and value of the assets being protected. Any recommendations should reflect system capabilities and asset value.

Risks with User IDs and Passwords Password-based authentication is among the oldest in use in information systems. While password authentication is still quite prevalent, a number of risks are associated with its use. The risks are all associated with the different ways in which passwords can be discovered and reused by others. Some of these risks are

- **Eavesdropping** Because of system limitations, some user account passwords are transmitted "in the clear" over networks, which permits anyone who is eavesdropping to intercept and reuse the password later on.

- **Key logging** Many types of malware are specifically designed to harvest login credentials that a user types on a keyboard. When credentials are captured in this way, they are sent back to the malware's owner/operator for malicious use.

- **Phishing** If an intruder creates a phishing message and sends it to several users, one or more users may be tricked into entering valid credentials onto a system owned by the intruder, who can then use those captured credentials to access a system.

- **Finding a password written down** If a user neglects to protect the paper that contains written passwords, they may be discovered by a colleague or another person, who could use them or pass them on to another person for malicious use.

- **Finding a stored password** If an intruder (or even a trusted colleague) examines the hard drive of a user's workstation, he or she may discover a file containing stored user IDs and passwords.

- **Exploiting a browser's password store** An intruder may be able to exploit a vulnerability in a browser that will permit him or her to trick the user's browser into providing login credentials. For this reason, it is recommended that browsers *not* be used to remember passwords.

All of these risks follow the same theme: user IDs and passwords are static and, if discovered, can be used by others. For this reason, other, more secure, means for authentication have been developed. The techniques include biometrics, tokens, smart cards, and certificates, all of which are collectively known as *multifactor authentication*.

Multifactor Authentication

Multifactor authentication (MFA) is so-called because it relies not only on "something you know" (namely, a user ID and password), but also upon "something you have" (such as a key card or smart card) and/or "something you are" (such as a fingerprint). Multifactor authentication requires not only a user ID and password, but also requires that the user possess something or use a biometric to form a part of the authentication. Several technologies are used for multifactor authentication, including

- **Tokens** These small electronic devices come in two forms. One form has a small display that shows a string of characters. The characters displayed are typed in during login, and if the characters are correct, the user will be able to log in to the system or network. The advantage of these tokens is that the displayed value will change frequently, making a "replay attack" almost impossible to conduct. The other type of token authentication is the use of a small USB key that contains information associated with the authentication. This information could be a digital certificate or other value.

- **Soft tokens**   These applications run on mobile devices such as smartphones that function like hardware tokens but are implemented as functionally equivalent software programs.

- **SMS tokens**   These values are transmitted to mobile devices such as smartphones. A user who logs in to an application or system first provides a user ID and password. Then a string of characters is transmitted to the user's registered mobile device via carrier text message. The user types those characters into the login screen to complete authentication.

- **Smart cards**   A smart card is a small, credit card–sized device that contains electronic memory and is accessed with a smart card reader. Many laptop computers are equipped with smart card readers for this purpose. A smart card may contain a digital certificate or other identifying information that is difficult or impossible to reproduce.

- **Digital certificates**   This electronic document uses a digital signature to bind a public encryption key with a user's identity. The system containing the digital certificate can be hardened so that the document cannot be exported, cloned, or moved to another computer. Typically, a digital certificate will reside within the workstation's hardware or in a special computer chip, or it may be stored in a USB token.

- **Biometrics**   Any of several technologies that measure a user's physical characteristics. This is discussed in detail in the next section.

Users of multifactor authentication systems need to be trained on their proper use. For example, they need to be told not to store their tokens or smart cards with their computers, and to keep their smartphones or mobile devices locked except when in use.

Biometrics

A number of different biometrics authentication technologies have a common theme: all use some way of measuring a unique physical characteristic of the person who is authenticating. Some of the technologies in use are

- **Fingerprint**   This is one of the most common forms of biometrics, primarily because fingerprint readers are compact and easy to manufacture, fingerprints don't change much over time, and people are generally unafraid to scan their fingers. Many notebook computers have fingerprint scanners built-in, as do some computer mice. A USB fingerprint reader is shown in Figure 6-2.

- **Handprint**   A handprint scanner is designed to measure the geometry of a person's hand. Since the readers are much larger than fingerprint readers, handprint scanners are generally limited to physical access settings where a user is required to enter a PIN and scan his or her hand to gain access to a controlled area. A handprint scanner is shown in Figure 6-3.

Figure 6-2
USB-connected
fingerprint
reader

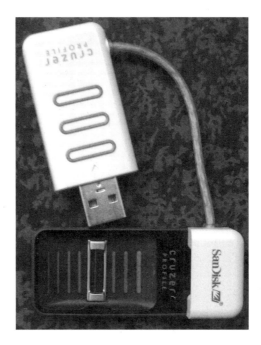

- **Palm vein** Similar to hand scanning, the pattern of veins in a person's palm can be used as a reliable biometric. Palm vein readers resemble a computer mouse; a user places his or her hand a few inches above the reader so that it may read the palm vein patterns.

Figure 6-3
Biometric
hand scanner
(Image courtesy
of Ingersoll
Rand Security
Technologies)

- **Voice recognition** Voice recognition is designed to recognize the specific patterns in the sound of spoken words. One advantage of voice recognition is that it usually does not require additional computer hardware, since most workstations have built-in microphones. Some disadvantages of voice recognition include voice changes during head and chest colds, or changes when a user is angry, sad, or nervous.

- **Iris scan** The human iris (the muscle surrounding the pupil of the eye) is similar to the human fingerprint in that it is unique to each person. A biometric iris scanner takes a high-resolution image of the human iris. This is similar to a retina scan, which is less favored because a subject is required to place his or her eye very close—maybe uncomfortably close—to a retina scanning device.

- **Facial scan** Facial scanning involves fine measurements of the angular dimensions of the human face. This means that computer imaging software will measure the relative distances between key features on a human face. Facial scanning, like voice recognition, can utilize built-in computer hardware (in this case, a camera) and requires only additional software. Some models of laptop computers utilize facial recognition for user authentication.

- **Handwriting** Two primary forms of handwriting recognition are available—both involve the use of a subject signing his or her name. One technology measures the dynamics of the signature as it is written on the signing surface. The other technology measures the acceleration of the pen or stylus while the subject signs his or her name.

Biometric technologies share a number of common operational challenges and traits that are discussed here.

Biometric Registration Each type of biometrics requires some kind of initial registration. Some biometric systems permit a user to self-register on their own workstation, while others require attended or assisted registration. Registration usually involves the biometric system taking several initial measurements so that it can develop an "average" reading for the subject.

Biometric Measurement Variances Biometric measurements are not exact; there will be small differences in the biometric being measured from one authentication to the next. Some of these differences result from the gradual changes that a human body undergoes over time. The biometric system will need to incorporate these newer measurements into a user's baseline so that users will continue to authenticate properly.

Several key measurements in biometric systems are usually adjustable:

- **False reject rate** This is the rate at which valid subjects are rejected. This occurs when the biometric system has too small a margin of error.

- **False accept rate** This is the rate at which invalid subjects are accepted as valid. This occurs when the biometric system has too large a margin of error.

- **Crossover error rate**   This is the point at which the false reject rate (FRR) equals the false accept rate (FAR). This is the ideal point for a well-tuned biometric system.

Biometric Usability Issues   A number of issues will arise in an organization where some employees will be reluctant to use a biometric system:

- **Sanitary**   For biometrics such as door entry systems, many persons will be touching the biometric system in the course of a day. Some employees will cite health-related objections to the use of biometrics on account of spreading germs.

- **Privacy**   Some employees feel that scanning their fingerprints or irises constitutes an invasion of their privacy. What they need to know is that a fingerprint scanner (for instance) does not record the user's actual fingerprint, but instead a computed "hash" of the intersections in the lines in their fingerprint. Few, if any, biometric systems store actual fingerprints.

NOTE   Because biometrics involves the measurement of a subject's physical characteristics, a number of employees are bound to object to its use—sometimes based on valid concerns and sometimes not.

Reduced Sign-On

Reduced sign-on refers to an environment where a centralized directory service such as LDAP (Lightweight Directory Access Protocol), RADIUS (Remote Authentication Dial-in User Service), Diameter, or Microsoft Active Directory is used by several applications for authentication. The term comes from the result of changing each application's authentication from stand-alone to centralized and the resulting reduction in the number of user ID–password pairs that each user is required to remember.

EXAM TIP   The terms "reduced sign-on" and "single sign-on" are often interchanged. Many times, a reduced sign-on environment is labeled as single sign-on. They are not the same, however.

Single Sign-On

Single sign-on refers to an interconnected environment where applications are logically connected to a centralized authentication server that is aware of the logged-in/-out status of each user. At the start of the workday, when a user logs in to an application, he or she will be prompted for login credentials. When the user logs in to another application, the application will consult the central authentication server to determine whether the user is logged in and, if so, the second application will not require the user's credentials. The term refers to the fact that a user needs to sign on only one time, even in a multiple-application environment.

Single sign-on is more complex than reduced sign-on. In a single sign-on environment, each participating application must be able to communicate with a centralized authentication controller and act accordingly by requiring a new user to log in, or not.

Access Control Lists

Access control lists (ACLs) are a common means to administer access controls. ACLs are used by many operating systems and other devices such as routers as a simple means to control access to a resource such as a server or a network.

On many devices and systems, the list of packet-filtering rules (which give a router many of the characteristics of a firewall) is known as an ACL. In the Unix operating system, ACLs can control which users are permitted to access files, directories, and run tools and programs. ACLs in these and other contexts are often simple text files that can be edited with a text editor.

Protecting Stored Information

Information systems store information primarily in the form of databases and flat files. Operating systems and database management systems usually provide minimum protection of databases and files by default; organizations need to determine the correct level of protection that is pursuant to the value and sensitivity of information. The controls that may need to be enacted are discussed in this section.

Access Controls

Access controls are the primary means used to protect stored information from unauthorized accesses and unauthorized users.

Operating system access control settings (often in the form of ACLs) are used to determine which user IDs are permitted to access flat files (as well as the directories containing them). Following the principle of *least privilege*, all flat files containing sensitive information should have access restricted to only those users and processes that must be able to access them. No user or process that doesn't have a need to access specific files should be able to do so.

Access Logging

Operating systems and database management systems should be configured so that all access attempts to files and directories are logged. This practice promotes accountability and provides a trail of evidence in the event that a forensic investigation should be conducted in the future.

Access logs themselves must be highly protected—ideally, they should be stored in a different storage system than the one that stores the data whose access is being logged. Access logs should not be alterable, even by database administrators and system administrators, so that no one will be able to "erase his or her tracks" should someone decide to tamper with sensitive information and then attempt to hide the evidence afterward.

Access logging is effective only if someone actually examines the logs. Because this can be a time-consuming activity, many organizations utilize alert-generating tools such as a SIEM that sends alerts to key personnel when particular audit log entries (such as unauthorized access attempts) appear. These alerts permit personnel to act upon anomalous events when they occur.

Backup and Media Storage

Data stored on information systems can be lost or damaged. Some of the ways in which this can occur include

- **Hardware failure** Many of the components in a storage system—particularly hard disks—are subject to failures, however rare they might be nowadays. These failures can result in data being irretrievable.

- **Administrator error** A system or database administrator can accidentally erase or alter information in a way that is not easily undone.

- **Software bug** An erroneous section of code in application software can inadvertently wipe out data in a database or in flat files. This can occur with an organization's own programs or with programs that are supplied by a software vendor.

- **Malware** Any attack such as ransomware that results in data destruction.

Any of these possibilities should be reason enough for an IT operation to back up all critical data. Backing up data means making copies of it on other media in case the original media (or the system that it is stored on) fails. Then, after the original system is repaired, data can be copied from the backup media and processing can be resumed.

Backup Tools Organizations often use backup tools that help the backup process be as efficient as possible. Some backup tools automatically manage backup media volumes and make data restoration easier than if it had to be done manually.

Protection of Backup Media Because backup media is often transported from place to place, there are opportunities for media to be misplaced or lost in transit. For this reason, data on backup media should be encrypted so that any third party who happens to find a backup media volume will not be able to retrieve any data from it. When backup media is encrypted, a lost tape means only the loss of an inexpensive asset and not a potential compromise of sensitive information.

Off-site Backup Media Storage To protect data from disasters, backup media should be stored at a location away from the original data. For example, if data from a server was backed up onto tape and the backup tapes are stored near the server, both server and backup media could be destroyed in an event such as a fire or flood. If backup media were stored in another location, however, then only the original server would be destroyed, but the system could be recovered using data on backup media at the other location.

Selecting an off-site media storage facility requires the organization to weigh several factors, including distance from the original data (too close means it may be destroyed in a regional disaster; too far away means it may take too long to obtain it when needed), security of the storage facility, security of the transportation of media back and forth between the original location and the off-site storage facility, and recordkeeping available so that it can be easily determined which media volumes are at the off-site facility at any given time. Security of the off-site storage facility should be at least as good as the security in the original location so that the protected information is not more vulnerable at the off-site facility.

E-Vaulting Many organizations are migrating away from tape backup to e-vaulting, where data is copied to a cloud-based e-vaulting service provider. While one disadvantage lies in the potential time it takes to copy a large data set over the Internet, e-vaulting can reduce or eliminate the administrative burden of managing and protecting backup media. With e-vaulting, data can be restored directly over the Internet without having to transport backup media to a location where it is needed.

Restoration Testing The organization should occasionally test backup media and data restoration software to make sure that data is actually being backed up onto the backup media and that it can be retrieved. I personally know of an organization that believed it was backing up its databases every day until it needed to restore one, only to find out that nothing was ever being written to the backup media. Clearly, the organization was not testing its backup system. Restoration tests should be scheduled and their results recorded.

Media Inventory A periodic inventory of all backup media (whether physical in the form of backup tapes, or virtual in the form of e-vaulting volumes), including media at the off-site location, should be performed. This will ensure that all media volumes are being handled properly and that none has been lost or misplaced. The results of each inventory should be recorded and any anomalies corrected.

 NOTE The loss of one or more backup media volumes during an inventory would be considered a security incident, unless the media was known to be encrypted.

Patch Management
Patch management is an IT operational process whereby security and functionality patches are obtained, tested, and installed on information systems. The purpose of patch management is to keep systems running on currently supported vendor software and to ensure that all known security vulnerabilities are closed and software defects fixed.

Patch management is typically managed with tools that are quickly able to assess the "patch level" of many servers and then install patches en masse.

There are different points of view with regard to patches. Should all patches be installed, or just some patches? There are pros and cons to each approach. If all security patches are installed, then indeed all known vulnerabilities will be closed. However, some security patches may be unnecessary because specific components that are patched might not be used. If an organization chooses to install only the most critical patches, a security analyst will need to perform a risk analysis each time a security patch is released so that a formal determination of need can be established. And even if an organization does install

all available security patches, a risk analysis can help to determine how quickly each patch needs to be installed.

The argument against installing patches is that each patch can add a tiny increment of instability to the system. Although the base operating system undergoes exhaustive testing, far less testing is performed on security patches before they are released. This is evidenced by the occasional security patch that breaks some other functionality—this does not happen often, but it does happen sometimes. This is another reason why organizations should first test patches (security and other) on test environments prior to installing them on production systems. Otherwise, there is a small chance that a new patch will cause unexpected problems that could be difficult to isolate.

Patch management is an integral part of the vulnerability management process, discussed next.

Vulnerability Management

The purpose of vulnerability management is to identify and manage vulnerabilities in IT applications and infrastructure. Vulnerabilities can result from errors in configuration, from flaws in the overall architecture, or from newly discovered weaknesses reported by security researchers.

Vulnerability management requires a number of distinct but connected activities.

Subscribing to Security Alerts   Most computer hardware and software manufacturers have a service whereby customers can be made aware of new vulnerabilities, weaknesses, threats, and the remedies for these. Often, the fixes for vulnerabilities, weaknesses, and threats are security patches or bulletins that advise changes in configuration. There are also some high-quality, nonvendor-related sources for security alerts, including Secunia, Bugtraq, InfraGard, Full Disclosure, and US-CERT. Organizations should subscribe both to any available vendor sources as well as one or more of these nonvendor sources to get a full picture of new vulnerabilities as well as guidance on how to mitigate them.

System and Device Hardening   This is concerned with activities to design and implement standards for system and device configuration, to increase security and reduce the risk of compromise. Hardening is discussed in more detail later in this section.

Vulnerability Scanning and Penetration Testing   This involves the use of tools that scan or examine computers, network devices, or application programs with the purpose of finding any vulnerabilities. Organizations that have any computers or applications accessed over the Internet (including simple web sites) should consider performing regular scans to make sure that those computers and applications are free of any high- or medium-risk vulnerabilities. An organization that does not remediate vulnerabilities faces the real threat of the computer or application being attacked and compromised, which could lead to a loss of sensitive information. Many commercial and open-source tools are available to inspect computers and applications for vulnerabilities; the better tools also rank findings by the level of risk and include instructions on how vulnerabilities can be fixed. Organizations also need to remember that scanning a system once and removing all vulnerabilities does not mean that there will never be new vulnerabilities in the future;

this is because security researchers regularly find new vulnerabilities in programs and systems. A system that is secure today will most certainly be less secure tomorrow.

Patch Management This is the process of responding to known vulnerabilities by installing security patches on target systems and devices. This process is described in detail in the preceding section. Patches should be applied proactively, and vulnerability scanning used as a step to confirm that all necessary patches have been installed on all systems.

Corrective Action Process This is the process of recording vulnerabilities into an incident tracking process so that vulnerability remediation can be assigned to a person or team and be formally tracked. Corrective and preventive action processes are discussed early in this chapter.

Threat Management

The purpose of threat management is to acquire intelligence on credible threats that may potentially occur in the organization. When a threat is seen as actionable, the organization will take steps to defend itself against the threat, to prevent the threat outright or—at least—reduce the impact of the threat if it cannot be avoided entirely. The activity of proactively looking for active threats in an environment is known as *threat hunting*. The activity of conducting analysis regarding potential threats is known as *threat modeling*.

Organizations doing threat management will typically obtain information from two types of sources:

- **Internal** Security tools and systems such as IPSs, firewalls, data loss prevention (DLP) systems, malware prevention systems, and web-filtering systems will detect events that may be indicators of compromise (IOCs).

- **External** Organizations may subscribe to one or more threat intelligence feeds that contain information about threats occurring elsewhere.

For threat management to be effective, organizations need to be able to filter threat information so that only relevant and actionable threats are seen. Further, organizations need to know what action is appropriate to take when a credible threat is seen.

System Hardening

System hardening is the process of changing the configuration of a system (which could be a server, subsystem, application, tool, or network device) so that it is more resistant to malfunctions and attacks. The principles behind system hardening consist of the concepts discussed in this section.

Changing Systems from Multifunction to Single-Function An individual server that performs many functions may require the presence of several services, software modules, or applications to be running at once. Consolidation may reduce the number of servers and make an environment simpler, but it also increases risk. A vulnerability on a multifunction server places all services on the server at risk.

In an environment where each server performs a single function, a vulnerability in a function will place only that function at risk. Server virtualization and containerization make it easier to separate functions into separate security zones (known as *guests* in virtualization or *containers* in containerization) while permitting them to continue to run on one physical system.

Removal of Unnecessary Services   Only the services and software features required to support a system's purpose should be installed and running; all other services and features should be disabled and, if possible, removed altogether. Removing unnecessary services reduces the "attack surface" on a system only to those services that are required.

For example, the Sendmail program should be disabled (prevented from running) or removed on Unix systems that do not need to send or receive e-mail. Sendmail is a large, complex program that is the subject of ongoing security research, and new vulnerabilities are discovered from time to time.

Limiting Functionality or Privilege of Necessary Services   After all unnecessary services have been removed from a server, only those that are required for the server's function will remain. The functions that any necessary service is permitted to perform should be reduced to those that are necessary only. Accomplishing this will vary, but limiting functionality should follow the principle whereby any unneeded function should be disabled if the configuration will permit this. For example, if a specific software program should not ever need to drop a table from a database management system, then the user ID that the software program uses to log in to the database management system should not have the privilege to drop a table.

Each necessary service or program should be configured to run at the lowest possible privilege. In the past, it was common for all generic services (and even many applications) to run at root, super-user, or administrator level. Often this is unnecessary, and on systems where the privilege levels can be configured, each service should run at a lower service where possible. The advantage of this is that if a particular service is compromised through a vulnerability, the attacker's ability to compromise the entire system may be limited to the ability afforded by the privilege level assigned to the service.

Changing Default Passwords   One of the easiest ways for an intruder to attack a system is through known default passwords. Often, the manufacturers of systems and software utilize a documented default password that makes it easy for a new user or customer to begin using the system. But all too often, these default credentials are never updated, which results in systems that are vulnerable to attacks that are easy to carry out.

Before being connected to a network, every system should be changed so that all accounts on all devices have nondefault passwords.

Using Nonpredictable Passwords   If an intruder is able to compromise a system, he or she may (if able) attempt to retrieve the system's encrypted user account passwords and crack them to discover the passwords for other user accounts on the system. If the intruder has been able to crack one system's passwords, he or she may attempt to log in to neighboring systems (those in the same organization) using the same user IDs and passwords. If many or all systems use the same passwords, particularly for administrative accounts, the intruder may be able to compromise many or all other systems easily in the environment. Similarly, if the intruder is able to detect a pattern in the use of passwords, many systems may be compromised.

Removing Nonessential User IDs   Exploiting access privileges is one of the easiest techniques available to system hackers for breaking into a target system. Often, a system can be compromised by attacking nonessential user IDs, such as "guest" accounts. Every user account that does not serve a specific, required purpose should be disabled or removed.

Some types of systems require the presence of special accounts, even though they may not be required for interactive login. System engineers should look for a way of preventing interactive logins for these types of accounts without crippling the services that use them. Some operating systems support the notion of a service account that can be used by system and application programs but will not permit interactive login.

NOTE   The use of more advanced authentication technologies, such as two-factor authentication or biometrics, may make it far more difficult for an intruder to attack target systems successfully through user ID and password guessing.

Reducing User Privileges   The privileges required by each end user should be reduced to the minimum privileges necessary for each user to perform his or her tasks. Similar to the principle of reducing privilege levels for system services and applications, user privileges should be reduced so that the user is not permitted to perform any functions beyond what is required. This is similar to the principle of *least privilege* that is discussed earlier in this chapter.

NOTE   Many organizations continue to permit their end users to be local administrators on their workstations. This practice should be discontinued, and local administrator privileges should be granted on an exception basis, documented, and audited.

Reduce or Eliminate Interserver Trust   Some operating systems, such as Unix and Linux, can be configured to trust users on other systems. Some of these trust arrangements (such as *rlogin*) assume the integrity of other systems and are vulnerable to attack. For this reason, interserver trust should be used with care.

Single sign-on (SSO), when configured properly, is considered reliable and need not be eliminated based on the principle of removing interserver trust. However, even modern SSO and other authentication services must be designed and implemented securely to avoid misuse and attack.

System and device hardening have been a topic of discussion and innovation over the past three decades. Consequently, there are many good sources for hardening standards, guidelines, and instructions, including US-CERT, NIST, SANS, and the Center for Internet Security.

Implement Virtual Keyboards In certain high-risk situations on servers and workstations, there may be a particular concern regarding the threat and impact of various types of key loggers. The use of a virtual keyboard can reduce this risk. A *virtual keyboard* is a software program that emulates a keyboard and is operated by clicking on characters on the screen instead of the hardware keyboard.

Securing Virtualization Environments

Many organizations have adopted virtualization technology to make more efficient use of their server hardware. *Virtualization* permits two or more operating systems to run concurrently on a hardware system, each with its own share of resources and each operating as though it were running on its own physical server. Architecturally, virtualization inserts another layer of software between system hardware and the operating system to manage multiple copies of running operating systems. *Containerization* permits two or more tools or applications to run concurrently in respective, isolated *containers* in an operating system.

Like all other types of systems, virtualization and container environments must be hardened to reduce the likelihood and impact of attacks. The principles of hardening virtualization environments are

- Limit and monitor physical access to hardware resources.
- Restrict and periodically review administrative access.
- Remove unnecessary functions and services.
- Maintain current versions of software.
- Enable logging, and review those activity logs.
- For critical systems, monitor for availability and performance.
- Connect mechanisms that generate alerts to a centralized alerting environment.
- Back up all virtual machines and containers, including raw files.
- Use only encrypted remote administration such as Secure Shell (SSH) and multifactor authentication.
- Limit or eliminate file sharing.
- Implement anti-malware software.
- Patch guest OS and VM hypervisors early and often.
- Implement file integrity monitoring, and connect it to the centralized alerting environment.
- Implement time synchronization.
- Disconnect or remove unused devices and peripherals.

If these principles sound familiar, they should. These are similar to the principles used to harden computer operating systems. However, virtualization and container environments are really nothing more than a special kind of operating system, where the applications that run on it are operating systems.

Virtualization technology is discussed in detail in Chapter 5.

Managing User Access

Managing login credentials for end users (as well as for automated processes) requires that user accounts be managed in a highly consistent, organized manner. Because login credentials are often the only barrier between intruders and sensitive or valuable information, the consequences of poor security access management can be devastating to an organization. With the mass migration of business applications to the cloud, access management is considered the new perimeter.

The processes associated with user access are user access provisioning, user access termination, and internal job transfers. Each is discussed here.

User Access Provisioning

User access provisioning is the process whereby user accounts are created for new employees and other personnel. This activity should utilize a formal, documented access request and approval process that specifies who is authorized to request user accounts, who is authorized to approve access requests, and how (and which) activities are recorded.

Requests for administrative or privileged access should require additional approvals. The reason for this is that administrative and privileged accounts have higher risks associated with them (the potential for damage is directly proportional to the level of privilege).

User access provisioning occurs at the time of hire for new employees, but it also occurs when individual (or groups of) employees require additional access to applications or access to new applications. The process of vetting each account should address the following items:

- Is this person still actively employed and in good standing?
- Does this person require this access to perform his or her duties?
- Does the business owner of the system approve access?

A great deal of care is required in this process. The risk of errors can be devastating for an organization: the worst-case scenarios involve unauthorized insiders or outsiders having access to highly sensitive or valuable information. The practical effects of an error in user access management can be as grave as a hacking incident where an attacker is able to access a system to steal or alter sensitive information.

Employee Termination

When a worker's employment or contract ends, all logical and physical access privileges must be removed, and quickly. In many situations, removing access within 24 hours is sufficient, but some situations warrant immediate removal. For example, if an employee is being terminated, the organization should arrange to have the employee's access terminated at once so that the employee does not have *any* opportunity to take emotionally charged revenge against the employer. Also, if the employee has access to high-value information, access should be removed immediately to protect that information from misuse.

User accounts should be locked in a way that prevents any other employees from being able to use the account. For example, if user access administrators change the password to "LOCKED" (or something less blatant than this example), other employees who knew of this method could log in to the terminated employee's account and perpetrate acts that could be blamed on the terminated person (indeed, the terminated employee could also do this). Instead, user accounts should be locked by methods that are sophisticated or effective enough to prevent *anyone* from using them for *any* purpose. Some environments have the ability to lock a user account *administratively*; others must be *effectively* locked by changing the password to prevent anyone from logging in.

The OPM Incident

In 2015, the U.S. Office of Personnel Management (OPM) suffered a major security breach wherein private information (including the details of background checks, as well as more than 5 million sets of fingerprints) on 18–21 million current and former U.S. government employees was stolen. This happened because of the failure or outright absence of controls designed to detect and prevent intrusions and data exfiltration.

The OPM is just the one in a long string of breaches that have occurred in public and private organizations in the past several years (other, more recent, breaches such as Equifax Marriott are comparable in their scale and impact). What is especially egregious about this breach is the breadth and depth of personally identifiable information (PII) that was compromised.

The OPM incident should be a significant lesson for organizations that protect sensitive or valuable information: the process of vetting new access requests cannot be taken lightly, for the consequences of getting it wrong can be devastating.

As with user access provisioning, there must be detailed and accurate recordkeeping associated with terminated users. This includes information on who initiated the termination notification process, as well as the names of user access administrators who terminated each user access account and the date and time when user access was terminated.

Additional safeguards may be warranted, including

- **Notifying personnel/other parties of employee's termination** To prevent the just-terminated employee from being able to conduct social engineering on co-workers and other parties, the organization should notify all relevant parties at once of the termination.

- **Review of terminated employee's actions prior to termination** The employer should presume that a terminated employee may have had some suspicion about being terminated. The employee may have stolen sensitive or valuable information or may have sabotaged systems, devices, or application source code. A thorough review of the terminated employee's activities for days, weeks, or longer prior to the incident may be needed to detect whether any inappropriate activities were performed.

- **Review of terminated employee's actions after termination**   Access logs should be examined to make sure that there are no activities associated with the terminated employee's user accounts after the time of termination. Such activities could be an indication that the terminated employee still had access to information, or that some other employee is attempting to perform unauthorized actions that could be blamed on someone else. This should be done even when the terminated employee's accounts were locked. Anything can happen.

- **Periodic access reviews**   Periodic access reviews should take place in all application and system environments to make sure that all users who have access still need it. These reviews should include a check to ensure that all terminated employee accounts were actually terminated properly and in a timely manner.

 CAUTION   A defense-in-depth method should be used when terminating employee access. For example, in the case of building access, the employer should collect the employee's building access keycard *and* the keycard should be logically disabled so that it can no longer be used.

Employee Transfers

Employees transfer from one position to another in many organizations. These transfers may take place regularly or sparingly, depending on the size and type of organization and the amount of turnover.

Historically speaking, organizations are very practiced with provisioning new employees and transferring employees with new accesses that they require. Organizations are also reasonably effective when handling employee terminations. However, transfers are far more complicated, because, ideally, employees' old access rights *should* be rescinded when their new accesses are provisioned. This often does not take place, however, for a number of reasons. First, employees transferring from one job to another often have lingering responsibilities in their old positions, making immediate revocation disruptive. Unless the user access management department has effective processes and recordkeeping, they are likely to forget to revoke those old accesses later on.

In organizations that do not manage user access changes that are related to employee transfers, a result is a growing number of employees who have a growing list of access privileges. This phenomenon is sometimes known as *accumulation of privileges* (or *privilege creep*).

Password Management

The management of passwords is one of the responsibilities of the user account management function. There are several activities within user account management where passwords are managed or handled in some way. These activities are described next.

New User Account Provisioning   When users are issued new computer or network accounts, a means for transmitting the password to the user needs to be determined. The

password should not be sent via e-mail, since anyone eavesdropping (or reading messages later) would be able to intercept and later reuse those passwords.

Account Lockout   If a user tries several times to log in to an account, the account may be automatically locked. The account may remain locked until one of the following events occurs:

- The user calls a service desk to identify him- or herself and get the password reset.
- A set period of time (usually 15 to 60 minutes) elapses.

Forgotten Passwords   When users forget their passwords, they need to get their password reset somehow so that they can resume using their access account. Several methods are available for resetting passwords, including

- **Self-service with secret question**   Users access a "forgotten password" screen where they are asked a secret question. If they can answer the question successfully, they are taken to a screen where they create a new password.

- **Self-service with password or URL mailed to them**   Users access a "forgotten password" screen, where they cause a new password or one-time URL to be sent to their e-mail. If a password is sent via e-mail, the application should require the user to choose a new password on the first login. If a URL is sent via e-mail, the URL will take the user to a screen where the user is required to choose a new password. This method will not work if the user has forgotten his or her e-mail password.

- **Assisted password reset**   Users call a service desk that uses a reliable means for identifying the user, usually by asking for some information that other employees or persons would not know. When the user has been successfully and properly identified, the service desk provisions a new password and tells it to the user over the phone.

Systems and applications usually contain a number of automatic password controls that are related to the selection and use of passwords. The current practices for automatic password controls include

- **Account lockout**   User accounts become automatically locked after a number of unsuccessful login attempts. This measure is used to prevent automated password attacks against a user account. The lockout threshold is usually from 4 to 10 unsuccessful attempts. If the user successfully logs in or a specific period elapses, the counter is usually reset.

- **Password length**   User accounts are required to contain a minimum number of characters, usually seven or eight, but sometimes longer passwords are used in highly sensitive environments. Many organizations have transitioned from using the word *password* to the term *passphrase* to get users to think of passwords as a group of words instead of a single word. This encourages users to choose longer passwords, which are more difficult for intruders to guess.

- **Password complexity**   Passwords are often required to contain more than one class of character, the classes being lowercase and uppercase letters, numbers, and symbols. Many systems require three or even all four types of characters in passwords.

- **Password expiration**   Systems often require users to change their passwords periodically, as often as every 30 days to as seldom as every year.

- **Password reuse**   Systems can require that users be unable to choose a new password that is the same as the previous password, or even the same as the previous N passwords. This prevents users from switching back to the same familiar passwords.

- **Password rechange**   Systems can require that users wait a minimum period (for instance, seven days) before they can rechange their password. This is designed to prevent users from quickly cycling back to their old familiar password. For example, if a system forbids the use of the last 10 passwords and at least seven days between password changes, it would take a user 70 days to get back to an old familiar password; these settings would discourage such a practice.

NOTE   Password controls should be chosen based upon the settings of other controls, as well as on system limitations, service desk processes, and the value or sensitivity of the information being protected.

Passwords: To Expire, or Not to Expire

We have all become accustomed to (I didn't say *like* or *appreciate*) periodic password expiration, typically every 90 days but as often as 30 days. This has been accepted as a good practice and a defense against situations in which an intruder has obtained a user's login credentials.

In 2019, pundits began a new conversation, suggesting that password expiration no longer reduces risk and may in fact increase risk. More are beginning to listen, although no official standards such as those created by PCI-DSS or NIST have followed suit. I think the conversation will take more time before we in cybersecurity officially change our minds.

The argument against password expiration is this: people who are required to change passwords more frequently will choose weaker passwords and will use a predictable method for creating new passwords (for example, Summer$2019, Fall$2019, Winter$2019, Spring$2020, and so forth). These passwords pass standard complexity requirements but are easily guessable.

Managing Tokens, Certificates, and Biometrics

Multifactor authentication controls that include tokens, certificates, and biometrics require support and management processes that will equip users with the knowledge and devices they require and with support processes to help them in times of trouble. Areas where support processes require additional steps include those described next.

Provisioning   Provisioning user accounts when multifactor authentication is used does require more effort. Whereas user ID-and-password accounts can often be provisioned remotely, multifactor authentication provisioning sometimes requires in-person presence. For instance, users need to be given a hardware token (although one could be shipped to the user), a digital certificate needs to be installed on the user's computer (although this may be possible through a remote network connection), or a user must enroll his or her biometric, which may not be possible if the user is not on-site.

Training   Training in the use of multifactor authentication will teach users how to use it properly. Without adequate or effective training, users will call the service desk more frequently, raising support costs even higher (the cost of implementing multifactor authentication is many times that of ordinary user ID-and-password authentication).

Where hardware tokens (or USB tokens or smart cards) are used, users need to be trained to carry their hardware devices separate from the computers they use. They need to understand that if their computer and hardware authentication device are kept together and stolen, an intruder may have an easier time breaking into the organization's systems.

Authentication Troubles   Multifactor authentication is more complicated, and this can trip up some end users. While digital certificates are relatively hands-off (aside from forgetting the password), tokens and biometrics have their share of support issues. Biometrics that are configured with too low a tolerance for error may lock out legitimate users (and, if configured with too high a tolerance, may admit outsiders), which could require that users re-register or that their systems be examined.

Token and smart card authentication methods use tiny electronic devices that cannot be considered absolutely trouble-free. While these devices are highly reliable, a few things can go wrong that may require their replacement.

The IT service desk will need to develop workaround procedures when users are not able to log in using their multifactor authentication methods. Making a user wait until he or she can be re-registered for biometrics, for instance, will be unacceptable in many instances.

Replacing Devices   As with keycards and other small objects, lost tokens and smart cards will be a semi-regular occurrence in a large organization. Users will lose them, damage them (spilled coffee and so on), or leave them behind in a hotel room or their other suit jacket (the one that's home while they are on location).

The IT service desk will need to develop procedures for emergency authentication while users are awaiting replacement devices. Making users wait for replacements (even when shipped overnight) will be unacceptable in many cases. Instead, information systems may need to be able to fall back to user ID-and-password authentication for emergencies for individual users.

Protecting Mobile Computing

The year 2005 was the first year that laptop computers outsold desktop computers. This development helped IT security professionals recognize that most new end-user computers were not going to be as easy to protect as they once were: there would be more and more laptop computers, containing sensitive data, away from the protection of corporate buildings and firewalls, and less available for automated overnight updates.

Corporations struggled to adjust their PC management and support, as well as policies governing the use of laptop computers. Standard safeguards put in place include endpoint management software capable of communicating with laptops over slower, sporadic communication links; built-in firewalls and antivirus programs; whole-disk encryption; cable locks; policies that require employees to keep their laptops safely locked away or in their custody at all times; and policies that state that laptops are for business use only and for employee use only.

Management capabilities for protecting laptop computers were beginning to mature in the five years since they were outselling desktop computers. Then even more disruptive technological developments occurred: smartphones, mobile devices, and tablet computers.

In just five years after laptop computers outsold their desktop counterparts, smartphones and tablet computers were outselling laptop and desktop computers combined, and this trend continues. Smartphones and mobile devices are far more disruptive than laptop computers were: for the most part, smartphones and mobile devices are being purchased by consumers instead of corporations, and enterprise-class management capabilities for protecting smartphones and tablets are still maturing.

Laptop Controls

Enterprises generally enact a broad suite of policies and controls regarding the use of laptop computers. The most common are

- Whole-disk encryption
- Firewall
- Host-based intrusion prevention system
- Cloud-based web content filtering
- Advanced anti-malware (antivirus software is no longer sufficient)
- Restricted privileges, including limitations on the ability to change configurations and limitations on which applications can be installed
- Removable storage restrictions—usually limiting or prohibiting the use of USB-attached storage and optical media
- Multifactor authentication, such as a smart card or biometric device
- Policies requiring employees to keep laptop computers with them at all times unless they are in a locked room, and often requiring cable locks for settings such as hotel rooms

- Policies permitting only assigned employees to use company-issued laptop computers (no use permitted by other family members or friends)

Smartphone and Mobile Device Controls

The productivity gains that are realized through the use of smartphones, mobile devices, and tablet computers are compelling. However, their use means that sensitive company information now resides in mobile devices that the enterprise does not own and cannot easily control. Enterprises are responding to the onslaught of employee-purchased smartphones and mobile devices that are being used to connect to corporate e-mail and other systems, and they are struggling to control these devices to continue protecting sensitive information. This disruptive phenomenon is known as "bring your own device," or BYOD.

The controls that organizations are implementing for smartphones and mobile devices include

- **Authentication policies**   Many enterprises are requiring employees to enact auto-lock and create longer or complex passwords on their smartphones and mobile devices. This helps to increase the likelihood that an intruder who steals a device will be unable to access it.

- **Encryption**   Where possible, enterprises are enacting controls to cause any locally stored data to be encrypted.

- **Remote wipe**   Enterprises are enacting controls that enable them to wipe any smartphone or mobile device remotely when it is reported lost or stolen. In some instances, an organization will be able to wipe just the corporate data on the devices, but sometimes the only remedy is wiping the entire device. For this reason, employees are often reluctant to report a missing device out of fear that all of their personal content may be destroyed.

- **Download restrictions**   Enterprises are enacting controls to restrict which applications a user may download onto a smartphone or mobile device.

Enterprises are coming to terms with management, control, and policy issues regarding mobile devices. Employees are buying them on their own, often with the expectation that they will be able to access corporate e-mail and other functions. Security and risk managers are cringing because they have just gotten laptops under control, which (relatively speaking) was simpler since the company typically owns them and can more easily control whether they can connect to corporate networks.

But on the positive side, several enterprise management tools, called *mobile device management* (MDM), are available to facilitate more effective control of mobile devices.

NOTE   Security controls for mobile devices are not *additional* controls, but *compensating* controls that reduce data compromise risks because they are usually not protected by other physical and logical protections such as locked doors and firewalls.

Network Security Controls

Enterprise networks—and the network-based services that support systems and applications—require protection and control so that they will be reliable and secure. Networks carry information for virtually all applications and computing services; a compromise of network security could seriously threaten all of the applications, computing services, and information in an organization.

Network Security

Users access sensitive information through networks. While databases and operating systems that contain data will have controls in place to protect information, many controls are required at the network level that protect systems and other network-based resources from various threats. Countermeasures are available to prevent or detect many threats.

Network-Based Threats

Threats are the intent and ability to cause harm. In the context of a network, a threat may have the ability to disrupt network communications or intercept communications in order to acquire sensitive information.

The most prevalent network-based threats include

- **Access by unauthorized persons** Because some network-based resources do not include authentication by their very nature, it is essential to restrict network access at the point of entry. This means that users (and system-based resources) must be authenticated prior to being permitted to communicate on the network. Without that authentication, a user is not permitted to send any messages on the network; nor are they permitted to listen to any network traffic.

- **Spoofing** This is the act of changing the configuration of a device or system in an attempt to masquerade as a different, known, and trusted system. There are several reasons why someone would want to do this; primarily, the reason will be to attract incoming connections in order to steal identities that can later be used illicitly. For example, an intruder may successfully spoof an internal web server and present an authentication page where users will enter their user IDs and passwords. The intruder can save these credentials and use them later to access protected resources in order to steal or alter sensitive or valuable information. Another method is to masquerade as a known, legitimate user or device in order to bypass authentication and access network resources as the other user or device.

- **Eavesdropping** Here, someone installs hardware or software to listen to other network transmissions in an attempt to intercept any available sensitive information. Or, if this is a targeted attack, the intruder will listen for the specifically desired information and then capture it for later use. The intruder could be looking for login credentials, e-mail messages, transferred files, or communications between servers in an application.

- **Malware**   While viruses, worms, Trojan horses, and so on, do not directly attack networks, they do use networks to propagate from one system to another. Especially virulent malware may generate so much traffic that all legitimate network communications may cease. This may be true even if only a small number of infected systems are present and attempting to find new victim hosts to attack and infect.

- **Denial of service (DoS) attacks**   This is when an attacker floods a target with such a large volume of traffic that the target is unable to function normally. Such an attack can cause the target system to malfunction or crash, or the sheer volume of traffic may impair the target's ability to respond to legitimate messages.

- **Access bypass**   An individual can attach an unauthorized access device, such as a Wi-Fi access point or a dial-in modem, to the network, thereby permitting himself (or others) to access the network while bypassing security controls.

- **DNS attack**   This attack is used to alter the results of routine internal domain queries in order to direct new connections to an attacker's system instead of the system that users and systems intend to connect to.

- **Man-in-the-middle (MITM) attack**   This attack is used to take over or disrupt communications that are taking place between two parties. Here, an attacker intercepts communications being sent from one party to another and injects new, altered communications in their place. The attacker must be able to impersonate each party in the communication so that each party believes it is talking directly with the other party.

- **Man-in-the-browser (MITB) attack**   This attack involves the installation of a malicious "browser helper object" (BHO) onto a victim's browser. The malicious BHO alters communication between the browser and the Internet without the victim's knowledge.

There is no single detective or preventive control that is effective against all of these threats. Instead, several controls are needed to protect networks against these and other threats.

Vulnerable Network-Based Services

Many common network-based services are vulnerable to manipulation and can be used to attack other systems. Some of these services are

- **Malicious web sites**   If improperly protected, web sites can be attacked and loaded with malware that will be installed on site visitors' computers. This is typically called a "drive-by attack," because a victim was merely visiting a web site when it installed malware on the victim's computer.

- **E-mail**   The darling of attackers everywhere, e-mail is used to propagate spam, phishing attacks, pharming attacks, and malware.

- **DNS**   When attacked, the service that translates domain names such as www .espn.com into an IP address such as 141.204.13.76 can cause users and systems to connect to imposter systems that attempt to steal login credentials or infect user systems with malware.

- **Instant messaging**   IM networks are used to propagate worms that can be used to install malware on unprotected victims' computers, as well as spam (called "spim" in the context of instant messaging) and phishing (called "smishing" in instant messaging and text messaging).

- **Message boards**   People who search the Internet for solutions to problems often find discussions about their problems on message boards. Because many message boards are operated by volunteers, they often lack security controls and do not block attackers from putting malware on them for victims to install unknowingly on their computers, or links that take users to malicious web sites.

- **Social networking**   Some popular social networking sites allow for "applications" to be downloaded for subscribers' use. Some of these social networking sites do not examine these applications to determine whether they are harmful or malicious in any way.

- **Peer-to-peer networking**   Peer-to-peer networks are a favorite attack vector for malware producers. Because they lack centralized servers with strong anti-malware controls, peer-to-peer networks are a great method for distributing malware.

Network Security Countermeasures

Several controls are needed to ensure the integrity and security of a network as one layer of defense in the protection of valuable or sensitive information.

- **Segmentation**   This technique is used to divide an enterprise network into two or more security zones that are protected with firewalls. A DMZ is a good example of segmentation, but it's wise for organizations to expand their segmentation to reduce lateral propagation of malware.

- **Microsegmentation**   This is a special segmentation technique where individual hosts (whether servers or endpoints) are isolated from one another, either with network firewalls or with firewalls on individual hosts.

- **User authentication controls**   Users can be required to authenticate to the network itself prior to accessing any network-based resources. This may be useful even if servers and other resources on the network have their own separate authentication requirements.

- **Machine authentication controls**   Every node that attaches to the network should itself be authenticated. This can prevent nonorganization-owned assets (such as personally owned computers, unauthorized access points, sniffers, or vendor demo equipment) from being able to access the network. This helps to ensure that only organization-managed devices that have malware controls, including anti-malware software, can attach to the network, thereby reducing the likelihood that malware will be introduced into the environment. The dominant technology for enforcing machine authentication is the IEEE 802.1X standard, which can also perform detailed checks on a node, including patch levels and whether antivirus software is running and up to date.

- **Anti-malware** Many organizations have opted to supplement workstation-based anti-malware software with network-based anti-malware capabilities. Centralized, network-based anti-malware may be used to filter malware and spam from incoming e-mail, or it may act as a silent or active proxy for web traffic, blocking malware that is hosted on web sites. Both measures can greatly improve an organization's ability to prevent malware attacks.

- **Encryption** Sensitive communications can be encrypted to reduce the threat of eavesdropping. Many methods for encryption are available, depending on the network's architecture and the specific traffic that needs to be protected. For instance, tunnels between pairs of servers can be established at the OS level using IPsec or SSH. Tunnels between networks can be established using IPsec between pairs of routers. In both cases, network-based applications and services need not be modified, as they will be completely unaware of the encryption taking place at lower layers in the IP stack.

- **Switched networks** The use of shared-media networks (such as Ethernet through the use of hubs, repeaters, and bridges) invites eavesdroppers who can intercept some or all network transmissions. By changing to switched networks, the only traffic that a node sees are packets sent explicitly to or from the node, as well as some broadcast traffic. This greatly reduces the risk of eavesdropping, since it may not be practical to encrypt all communications.

- **Intrusion detection systems (IDSs)** These systems are used to detect anomalous activities on the network, sending alerts to appropriate personnel when these anomalies occur. Like anti-malware software, IDSs must be updated from time to time to remain effective. Some IDSs can "learn" normal network traffic behavior and generate alarms when nonnormal traffic is detected. IDSs can also alert personnel about traffic to or from known malicious sites. IDSs are available in two forms: network-based IDSs (NIDSs), which usually take the form of network appliances, and host-based IDSs (HIDSs), which consist of software agents installed on each host which are typically monitored and managed with a separate management console.

- **Intrusion prevention systems (IPSs)** These systems, like IDSs, detect anomalies on the network. However, IPSs are also able to block malicious traffic. They can be used to block both internal and external threats, whether they are intruders trying to break in to a system or some malware that has been able to penetrate defenses on an organization-owned device. One drawback with IPSs is that a false positive can result in legitimate traffic being blocked.

- **Web content filtering**   These systems are designed to block users' access to categories of web sites. Web content filtering is often implemented with two purposes in mind: First, it is used to limit employees from visiting sites with little or no business value, thereby preventing some wasted time. Second, some categories of sites are known for hosting malware, so web content filtering helps to reduce malware attacks on an organization's systems. Some web content filtering systems also have the ability to block malicious traffic based on its contents.

- **Data loss prevention (DLP)**   These systems are designed to detect the storage of potentially sensitive information on servers and endpoints and/or transmission of potentially sensitive information into or out of an organization's network. DLP systems may be configured to generate alerts sent to a security incident manager, and some are able to block such transmission altogether. These alerts can be based on general types of sensitive data such as credit card numbers or social insurance numbers, but also on organization-specific data such as internal project names.

- **Application whitelisting**   These systems include agents that are installed on servers and workstations. They examine each executable that is launched; if the executable matches an entry in the tool's whitelist, it is permitted to run. Otherwise, its execution is blocked.

- **Netflow**   These systems are designed to ingest all of a network's metadata— that is, the origination and destination address of every packet, and its protocol. Netflow systems are typically used to troubleshoot network issues (because they can reveal every packet transmitted on the network), but they are handy for security purposes as well, because they can show anomalous network traffic that could be a sign of an intrusion, malware, or data exfiltration.

These and other network security countermeasures should be considered key controls, each of which should have complete process and procedure documentation, managed records, and periodic audits.

IoT Security

Organizations in some industry sectors are seeing a significant increase in the number of nonhuman interaction devices being connected to their networks. These devices include patient monitoring and care equipment in hospitals, IP-connected machinery in manufacturing plants, laboratory equipment in biomedical research organizations, and remote-control and status monitoring equipment in public utility networks. Organizations in other industries are still seeing a moderate increase in IoT devices such as "smart" refrigerators and coffee makers. Many organizations, when they upgrade their video surveillance and door access systems, are moving to IP-connected systems that are connected to internal enterprise networks.

Many IoT devices are manufactured without providing the ability to update their security configurations; this means that IoT devices are vulnerable by design. For instance, a privilege escalation attack on an IoT device could permit an intruder to move laterally to other environments. However, because these devices are often essential for ongoing business processes, other means are needed to protect the organization from vulnerable IoT devices. The primary method is segmentation and even microsegmentation in extreme cases. This serves to isolate IoT devices from the rest of the organization and from other IoT devices. Segmentation control points should be monitored to detect potential attacks.

Securing Client-Server Applications

Though no longer the platform of choice for most new applications, many client-server applications are still in use and require continued, and even improved, protection from evolving threats.

Client-server environments are subject to the same threats and have most or all of the same vulnerabilities as ordinary servers and workstations. The threats and countermeasures that are specific to client-server environments include the following:

- **Access controls** Most client-server applications were developed in an era when the prospect of impersonated client systems seemed remote. However, client-server applications that are designed today would certainly include multifactor authentication between client software and server software (in addition to workstation authentication using 802.1X and end-user authentication to the network). Modern client-server environments may utilize servers in the cloud, possibly operated by service providers, which means that client systems require access to the Internet. Older client-server environments may lack one or more of these authentication components. While altering the existing client-server components themselves may be infeasible, other compensating controls may be viable, including workstation-based integrity management software, anti-malware, firewalls, and workstation hardening.

- **Interception of client-server communications** Eavesdropping and interception of client-server communications can result in a compromise of sensitive or valuable information. Furthermore, a MITM attack can result in intercepted and altered communications, with consequences including compromise of sensitive information and fraud. The most effective countermeasure for traffic interception is encryption between servers and client workstations. These threats are more likely with Internet-based application servers.

- **Attacks on networks** See the earlier section, "Network Security Countermeasures," for details.

- **Change management** When application code changes are considered, the project team making the changes needs to establish comprehensive test and implementation plans to ensure that the change will result in the correct functional changes in the environment. This is further complicated by the fact that code changes will need to be distributed to all of the client workstations in the organization. If some of those workstations are laptop computers, installation of client software updates will be logistically challenging since not all laptops will be available when the IT department intends to update them.

- **Disruption of client software updates**   If clients are unable to receive and install software updates, they may fail to operate properly. In client-server architecture, client software must be in close (if not exact) synchronization with server software, since part of the application's business logic is server-based and part is client-based. An update to the application that requires changes to both the server and all clients may fail for any workstations that cannot install the new updates. The purpose of attacks on the client software distribution mechanism or on client workstations themselves may be the disruption of the entire application in an organization. In addition to system hardening, countermeasures include encryption, reports indicating the success rate of client updates, and tools to troubleshoot client update problems.

- **Stealing data**   Users of client-server applications will be able to steal information if their client workstations include a full operating system and access to external storage devices (this is also a viable threat to web-based applications). In environments where the information being viewed and managed is highly sensitive or valuable, additional countermeasures, such as blocking the use of external storage devices (CD/DVD-ROM and USB-based storage), may be warranted.

Client-Server Applications and Data Protection Laws

Another serious issue in many client-server environments is the need to update these environments to meet new security regulations. New and updated data protection laws and standards such as PCI-DSS, GDPR, and CCPA require protection measures in application environments that were not included in older client-server frameworks. Some of these measures include encryption of transmitted data, encryption of stored data, multifactor authentication, access and transaction logging, and the use of unique user accounts for each individual user. Many client-server environments are simply unable to implement one or more of these controls that are present in newer application environments. This is not to say that countermeasures are impossible; instead, each organization has to weigh the cost of implementing and supporting each required countermeasure to assess the long-term viability of each client-server environment.

Securing Wireless Networks

Innovations in wireless communications have produced a productivity breakthrough for many workers who no longer have to be constrained to a desk in a corporate office. Wireless network technologies have enabled workers to connect to enterprise networks, regardless of their work location. However, some wireless communications technologies have significant vulnerabilities, and most are subject to severe threats.

Early wireless LAN (WLAN, or Wi-Fi) technologies did not encrypt traffic at all. This permitted other users (and outsiders—anyone within range of a WLAN) to use relatively simple tools to intercept, record, and even hijack wireless network sessions, and they did nothing to prevent someone from joining a WLAN and using it for Internet access. At that time, since many internal communications, including login sessions, were not encrypted, sniffing a wireless network from a safe location could yield as much rich information as a sniffer connected directly to the network—minus the risks related to getting a sniffer inside an office building.

Wireless networks are attractive to intruders because they provide an opportunity to penetrate a network easily without the risks associated with breaking into a physical building.

Wireless Network Threats and Vulnerabilities

Early wireless networks had significant vulnerabilities in their design and implementation that drew the attention of intruders. This attention led to research and discovery of more vulnerabilities, which have led to a proliferation of tools designed to exploit them. The threats and vulnerabilities associated with wireless networks are discussed here.

Eavesdropping This is the best-known threat identified with WLANs. Intruders with reasonably simple tools are easily able to listen in on wireless communications, even when communications are encrypted and protected through other means. Because wireless networks use radio frequency (RF) technology, the threat of eavesdropping will never completely disappear.

War Driving and War Chalking In war driving and war chalking, intruders travel in dense urban areas, looking for unprotected Wi-Fi access points. The term *war driving* comes from the practice of searching from within a moving vehicle or on foot.

War chalking is the practice of marking buildings (using chalk) with symbols to indicate the presence of a Wi-Fi access point, including some basic facts about it. The practice was widespread in the early 2000s but is not often used now. Figure 6-4 shows the standard symbols that were used. The practice is thought to be derived from a similar practice during the Great Depression when homeless people would mark buildings that were friendly, unfriendly, and where law enforcement was located.

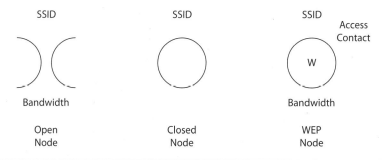

Figure 6-4 Common war chalking symbols indicate the presence of Wi-Fi access points

Weak Encryption The earliest WLANs used no encryption at all—not because it wasn't available, but because it required additional effort to implement. Because wireless access points can be configured to permit "wide open" (no encryption) configuration, many organizations stopped here and never implemented encryption. In addition, many Wi-Fi access points sold for home use did not have encryption enabled by default; most consumers did not bother to implement encryption because they did not know that it was important to do so.

The WEP (Wired Equivalent Privacy) encryption algorithm was developed to protect Wi-Fi networks from eavesdropping. WEP is so-named because its designers intended for WEP to provide confidentiality as effective as a traditional wired LAN. Unfortunately, WEP was soon compromised: intruders with readily available tools can completely compromise a Wi-Fi network protected with WEP within minutes. These tools can derive the WEP encryption key, enabling an intruder to decrypt all encrypted communications easily on a Wi-Fi network protected with WEP.

The WPA (Wi-Fi Protected Access) protocols were adopted as a stronger method for encryption of wireless networks. However, WPA is showing some signs of compromise as well. WPA2 is still considered marginally suitable for most commercial environments. However, organizations processing more sensitive data should consider adding layers of defense such as additional authentication and VPN encryption. In late 2018, WPA3 was announced and represents improvements over weaknesses identified in WPA2.

Spoofing Intruders can use spoofing to impersonate both Wi-Fi access points and Wi-Fi network clients. It is relatively easy for an intruder to establish a rogue access point with the same or a similar name as a legitimate access point. The intruder can use this rogue access point as a gateway to forward legitimate traffic in both directions while watching for and intercepting any sensitive information that may pass by. Or the intruder may use the rogue access point to steal login credentials from users trying to connect to the *real* access point.

Intruders can also spoof legitimate Wi-Fi clients in an attempt to connect to Wi-Fi networks. Some Wi-Fi networks include MAC address ACLs, which means they permit only known computers (identified by their MAC addresses) to connect to the Wi-Fi network. An intruder who eavesdrops on Wi-Fi traffic can easily discern this and change his or her computer's MAC address to that of one of the computers permitted to connect.

Session Hijacking Many Internet web sites (including those used for social networking, blogs, and e-mail) do not force encryption in users' communications. When users' sessions are not encrypted, their session cookies are transmitted unencrypted. On public Wi-Fi hotspots, this makes those users' sessions vulnerable to session hijacking, where an intruder on the same Wi-Fi network can intercept a user's session cookie and then take over the session.

The Firesheep tool made session hijacking a topic of discussion and debate. There are probably many other such tools available for intruders who want to prey on and hijack users' sessions.

Wireless Network Countermeasures

Several protective countermeasures can be taken to reduce risks associated with the use of wireless networks. These countermeasures include

- **Use an obscure SSID**   The SSID (service set identifier) should be changed from the default, but it should not obviously identify the organization that operates it. Doing so would invite intruders and curious persons to try and penetrate a known network. However, in the case of "public hotspots" such as hotels, restaurants, and coffee shops, the SSID often conspicuously and understandably identifies the establishment.

- **Stop broadcast of SSID**   Except for the case of public hotspots, broadcast of the access point's SSID should be disabled. Granted, this is a weak countermeasure because determined intruders who use more advanced tools do not need to see a network's SSID to know it is there: they have tools to sniff packets directly from the airlink, whether the access point is broadcasting its SSID or not. This measure does, however, act as a mild deterrent for those who are less skilled.

- **Reduce transmit power**   The transmit strength of the Wi-Fi RF transmitter should be reduced to the lowest level that will still permit reliable use. This will prevent any distant eavesdropper from easily detecting the network.

- **Use MAC access filtering**   Wi-Fi access points can usually be configured to permit only those computers whose MAC addresses are present in a list of allowed addresses.

- **Use WPA2/3 encryption**   Because WEP and WPA have been compromised, WPA2 or WPA3 encryption should be used.

- **Require VPN**   Organizations that are concerned that WPA protocols may also be compromised can configure their Wi-Fi architecture so that VPN connections must be established for users to connect to the corporate LAN.

- **Change default passwords**   Administrative user IDs and passwords on new Wi-Fi access points should be changed before they are put into use.

- **Patches and upgrades**   Before new Wi-Fi access points are put into general use, network administrators should make sure that they contain the latest firmware or software. This is especially important if any vulnerabilities have been found in older versions.

- **Use a personal Wi-Fi hotspot**   Travelers who often connect to public Wi-Fi hotspots may be prudent to carry and use a personal Wi-Fi hotspot that connects to cellular networks. A personal Wi-Fi hotspot is shown in Figure 6-5.

- **Use VPN software**   Travelers who often connect to public Wi-Fi hotspots should consider the use of VPN software to encapsulate and encrypt their network traffic, so that an intruder eavesdropping on the Wi-Fi network cannot learn the nature of the traveler's communications.

Figure 6-5
Personal Wi-Fi
hotspot

CAUTION   Like system hardening, hardening Wi-Fi access points and supporting infrastructure is not a set-once-and-forget-it affair. Instead, making a system secure and keeping it secure requires vigilance through staying informed on the latest threats and vulnerabilities and taking action as needed.

5G Security

As of the time of writing this book, 5G networks are being introduced in some markets. 5G represents an increase in bandwidth in LTE (Long-Term Evolution) networks from 100Mbit/sec to as high as 500Mbit/sec. The bandwidth increase for 5G is not itself a security concern. Instead, it is the proliferation of a new generation of IoT devices, as well as new capabilities in existing devices, that represents the concern. Mainly, this means the vast increase in the global attack surface of vulnerable devices.

5G makes everything in LTE faster—from individuals and businesses that can be more productive, to a wide range of threats that gives cyber-criminals a faster "getaway car." This includes activities such as over-the-air security scanning, LTE-based DDoS attacks, and data exfiltration via 5G that will all be able to perform far faster than they did via older LTE technologies such as 4G.

Protecting Internet Communications

For decades, the standard practice for commercial organizations that needed to establish data communication connections between locations—or between organizations—was the use of dedicated private communications links leased from telecommunications carriers. Prior to the Internet, using private communications links was the *only* available method for setting up long-distance data communications.

The establishment of the Internet made it possible for organizations to connect to one another simply by connecting to the Internet backbone and letting routers do the rest. Most organizations scoffed at this idea because of the Internet's reputation for unreliable performance, as well as its lack of security. Gradually, however, Internet performance has improved in many parts of the world, and security standards have been developed that make use of the Internet for an inter- and intraorganization communications medium a practical reality.

This section describes the threats, vulnerabilities, and countermeasures needed to protect Internet-based business communications.

Internet Communications Threats and Vulnerabilities

The Internet is not a safe place. Practically all of the threats against organizations' valuable and sensitive information originate from the Internet or use the Internet in their delivery. This is because the Internet is the backbone of nearly all types of data communications, like the one well in the middle of town from which all its citizens draw water—the source of life but also a source of disease when things go wrong.

Internet-related threats and vulnerabilities are discussed in the following sections.

Eavesdropping Any data sent from one place to another over the Internet can be intercepted. While actual interception is infrequent, it is possible, and interception does occur from time to time. Compare this to the use of postcards in the mail. Most of the time, postcards are not read by anyone while in transit; nonetheless, their confidentiality cannot be assured.

Network Analysis Similar to eavesdropping, someone who has access to an organization's data communications can perform network analysis on it. This activity would be the reconnaissance phase of some bigger effort. An eavesdropper with access to an organization's network traffic would, over time, be able to tell quite a lot about the organization's internal network by observing data coming and going. This would be the case even if all the sensitive data in the traffic were encrypted, since the protocol headers (containing useful information such as host names, IP addresses, and so on) typically cannot be encrypted.

Targeted Attack An attacker whose objective is a specific organization's systems will probably use the Internet to transmit the attack to his or her target. An intelligent attacker will relay an attack through a series of compromised systems to conceal his or her actual whereabouts, making it difficult for law enforcement to learn the attacker's real identity and location.

Malware The Internet is the conduit through which virtually all malware travels. Whether it is transmitted in spam, hidden in downloadable software programs, or embedded in web sites, the designers of malware know that the Internet is the way to travel fast and cheap. Botnets use Internet protocols to control their bot armies as well as to spread spam or attack target systems.

Masquerading   An attacker can forge messages that have the appearance of originating elsewhere. TCP/IP itself does not enforce the value in the "From" IP address field in any packet, which makes it easy to send messages to a target system that have the appearance of originating from anywhere.

The SMTP (Simple Mail Transport Protocol, as initially defined in RFC-822) performs no enforcement on the "From" address in any e-mail message, a fact that has contributed to the spam and phishing problem. Many other protocols have similar weaknesses in their design.

Denial of Service   A *denial of service* (DoS) attack is an attack on a target system with the intent of causing it to cease functioning. There are two principal ways to perpetrate a DoS attack: First, it can be carried out by sending an enormous volume of messages to the target system to flood its input buffers and exhaust its available resources. The second method is to send a specially built message that is known to cause a service or application running on the target system to malfunction or stop running altogether. Both types accomplish an attacker's objective of making the target system unavailable for legitimate use.

Another form of a DoS attack is the *distributed denial of service* (DDoS) attack, a flooding attack that originates from a large number of systems simultaneously.

Fraud   Many kinds of fraud are perpetrated on the Internet against systems and people. In a fraud attack, the attacker pretends to be someone or something else (a merchant, bank, or government entity, for instance) and attempts to trick the target into performing an action, such as transferring money or providing private information.

 NOTE   One topic not covered in this section is the variety of reasons and motivations behind attacks on systems. This subject is covered in detail earlier in this chapter.

Masquerading on the Internet

The protocols at the base of the Internet, TCP/IP, were developed a generation ago by designers who assumed that TCP/IP would always be operated on controlled, trusted, and closed networks. The basic design of most of the protocols and services still in use on the Internet today assume that all other parties can be trusted. For this reason, the designers of TCP/IP did not include controls to prevent one system from masquerading as another. It is this design principle that has permitted the proliferation of much spam, phishing, malware, and other malevolence on the Internet.

Internet Communications Security Countermeasures

A wide variety of countermeasures are needed to protect an organization from the assortment of threats. The countermeasures described in this section should begin to look familiar if you are reading through this chapter from beginning to end; the countermeasures used to protect Internet-based threats are not much different from those protecting similar threats in other contexts.

Network- and computer-related security countermeasures discussed elsewhere in this book would often apply when any network, system, or application is opened to the Internet. The Internet represents the worst-case security scenario for any system or application, as it exposes it to the most potent threats that exist.

Firewalls   Firewalls are devices that control the flow of messages between networks. Placed at the boundary between the Internet and an organization's internal network, firewalls enforce security policy by prohibiting all inbound and outbound traffic except for the specific few types of traffic that are permitted to a select few systems. For example, a firewall will

- Permit incoming e-mail to be sent only to the organization's e-mail server.
- Permit incoming HTTPS requests to be sent only to the organization's Internet-facing web server.
- Permit incoming file transfer requests to be sent only to the organization's file transfer gateway.
- Permit outbound e-mail to originate only from the organization's e-mail server.

The last item in this list points out that firewalls control not only what comes *in* to an organization's network, but also what *leaves* an organization's network. Permitting outbound mail to originate only from the e-mail server prevents malware from communicating via command-and-control traffic or exfiltrating stolen information, thereby slowing down the spread and impact of some types of malware.

The two principal types of firewalls are

- **Screening routers**   These simpler firewalls are designed to examine each packet and compare it to an access control list (ACL) to determine whether, based on its source and destination IP addresses and ports, it should be permitted to pass through the firewall.
- **Stateful inspection firewalls**   This type of firewall is designed to record incoming packets and keep track of TCP/IP sessions between external and internal hosts. In TCP, an incoming packet is answered with an outgoing packet; a stateful inspection firewall will examine an outgoing packet and make a go/no-go decision based on whether it believes that the outgoing packet is a part of an active session. Stateful inspection firewalls are more complex and capable of more effectively protecting an organization's network.

Firewalls are available as hardware appliances and as virtual machines for use in virtualization and cloud-based environments.

CAUTION   Firewall rule sets should be periodically reviewed to ensure that every rule is formally approved and justified.

Application Firewalls   Application firewalls are devices that are designed to protect web-based applications from application layer attacks. The types of attacks that application firewalls are designed to recognize and block include

- SQL injection
- Script injection
- Cross-site scripting
- Buffer overflow
- Parameter and session tampering
- Denial of service

Application firewalls were developed because traditional network firewalls examine only the source and destination IP addresses and source and destination port numbers. Network firewalls do not examine the contents of an incoming packet, which could be harmful nonetheless if it is a part of an attack on an application server.

Application firewalls are available as stand-alone appliances (called network-based application firewalls), software applications that can be installed in application servers (known as host-based application firewalls), and virtual machines for use in cloud environments.

An application firewall is not a replacement for a network firewall. Application firewalls are designed to block application layer attacks, but they don't necessarily act as a general-purpose firewall.

Demilitarized Zone Network (DMZ)   An organization with one or more systems that provide services to Internet users may implement a DMZ network architecture. The DMZ is a separate network where Internet-facing systems are attached and isolated with one or more firewalls. The rules in the firewall(s) will permit specific services from the Internet to reach the DMZ servers but will not permit access from the Internet to the internal network.

Typical DMZ architectures are shown in Figure 6-6. Organizations with large numbers of Internet-facing servers may use more complex architectures with layers of DMZ networks.

IDSs and IPSs   An IDS is designed to listen to network traffic and generate alerts if it sees any messages that match a database of attack signatures, as well as messages that match known malicious IP networks and domains. An IPS is a preventive control that listens to network traffic and blocks messages that match a database of attack signatures, and also messages that match known malicious IP networks and domains. IDSs and IPSs are discussed in more detail earlier in this chapter in the section "Network Security."

Honeypots and Honeynets   A *honeypot* is a trap that is designed to detect unauthorized use of information systems. A honeypot will have the appearance of an unprotected and unmonitored system containing valuable information. When an attacker attacks and takes over a honeypot, it provides information that will help the organization learn how to protect its real production computers.

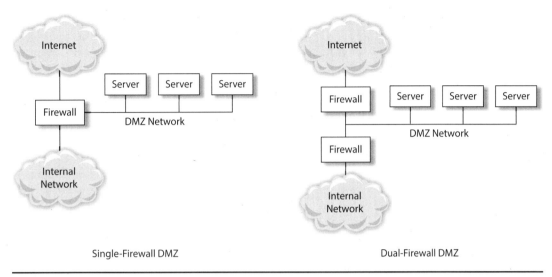

Figure 6-6 Typical DMZ networks

A honeypot helps an organization better understand some important facts:

- Which attackers are sufficiently interested in the organization's information to launch an attack against it
- Which available targets attract attackers
- Which tools and techniques are used by the attacker(s)

A security team in the organization can analyze this information and use it to improve defenses on the systems that actually do contain sensitive or valuable information.

 CAUTION An organization that sets up a honeypot needs to ensure that the honeypot cannot be used as a platform to attack real production systems successfully or to stage an attack on another organization's systems.

A *honeynet* is just what the term implies: a network of computers that are all acting as honeypots to emulate a complex production environment that consists of several computers.

There are two primary types of honeypots and honeynets:

- **High interaction** These are systems that will be partly or entirely unpatched, thereby attracting attackers.
- **Low interaction** These are designed to resemble other production servers in the network. Ordinarily unused, IDSs would trigger alarms if they are accessed, signaling that an intruder may be examining them.

Change Management and Configuration Management   The protection of sensitive and valuable information—particularly information that is exposed to the Internet—depends upon the integrity of the entire environment. The environment's integrity can be assured only to the extent to which it is controlled; this means that all minor and major changes made to the environment must be managed through formal change management and configuration management processes.

These processes are described in detail in Chapter 5.

Vulnerability Management   The security of an organization's environment depends upon the security of all devices that access the Internet and can be accessed from the Internet. Effective vulnerability management processes are essential to ensure that all such devices and systems run current software, are free of exploitable vulnerabilities, and are configured according to hardening standards.

These processes are described in detail in Chapter 5.

Incident Management   Incident management is the two-part process of proactive and responsive activities that help to reduce the likelihood and impact of security incidents. The proactive side of incident management helps to prevent incidents from occurring at all, while the responsive side helps to contain incidents quickly and make changes to reduce the likelihood and impact of future incidents.

Incident management is discussed in detail at the beginning of this chapter in the section "Information Security Management."

Incidents can also result from manmade or natural disasters—this aspect of incident response is addressed through disaster recovery plans and business continuity plans (discussed in Chapter 5).

Threat Management   Threat management is the process of acquiring relevant and actionable threat information. This is done as an attack detection and prevention measure to anticipate and defend against present and future attacks.

Threat management is described in detail earlier in this chapter.

Security Awareness Training   Security awareness training helps people in the organization be more familiar with how their tasks and responsibilities help to protect the organization's assets. Familiarity with security concepts and responsibilities helps each staff member make better decisions that help reduce risk.

This training is discussed in detail at the beginning of this chapter in the section "Information Security Management."

Encryption

Encryption is the act of hiding information in plain sight. It works by scrambling the characters in a message using a method known only to the sender and receiver, making the message useless to any party that intercepts the message.

Encryption plays a crucial role in the protection of sensitive and valuable information. In some situations, it is not practical or feasible to prevent third parties from having logical access to data—for instance, data transmissions over public networks.

This technique can also be used to *authenticate* information that is sent from one party to another. This means that a receiving party can verify that a specific party did, in fact, originate a message and that it is authentic. This enables a receiver to know that a message is genuine and that it has not been forged or altered in transit by any third party.

With encryption, best practices call for system designers to use well-known, robust encryption algorithms. Thus, when a third-party intercepts encrypted data, the third party can know which algorithm is being used but still not be able to read the data. What the third party does not know is the *key* that is used to encrypt and decrypt the data. How this works will be explained further in this section.

NOTE Encryption can be thought of as another layer of access protection. Like user ID and password controls that restrict access to data to everyone but those with login credentials, encryption restricts access to (plaintext) data to everyone but those with encryption keys.

Terms and Concepts Used in Cryptography

Several terms and concepts used in cryptography are not used outside of the field. Security professionals and IS auditors must be familiar with these to be effective in understanding, managing, and auditing IT systems that use cryptography. Terms used in cryptography include

- **Plaintext** An original message, file, or stream of data that can be read by anyone who has access to it
- **Ciphertext** A message, file, or stream of data that has been transformed by an encryption algorithm and rendered unreadable
- **Encryption** The process of transforming plaintext into ciphertext, as depicted in Figure 6-7
- **Hash function** A cryptographic operation on a block of data that returns a fixed-length string of characters, used to verify the integrity of a message
- **Message digest** The output of a cryptographic hash function
- **Digital signature** The result of encrypting the hash of a message with the originator's private encryption key, used to prove the authenticity and integrity of a message, as depicted in Figure 6-8
- **Algorithm** A specific mathematical formula that is used to perform encryption, decryption, message digests, and digital signatures
- **Decryption** The process of transforming ciphertext into plaintext so that a recipient can read it
- **Cryptanalysis** An attack on a cryptosystem where the attacker is attempting to determine the encryption key that is used to encrypt messages
- **Encryption key** A block of characters, used in combination with an encryption algorithm, to encrypt or decrypt a stream or blocks of data; an encryption key is also used to create and verify a digital signature

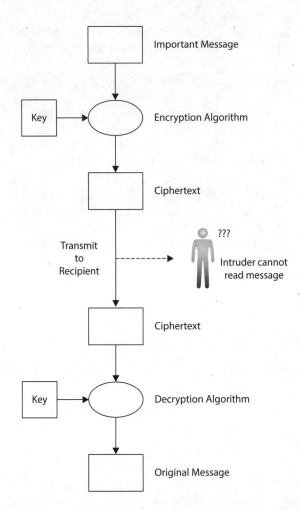

Figure 6-7
Encryption and
decryption utilize
an encryption
algorithm and an
encryption key.

- **Key encrypting key**   An encryption key used to encrypt another encryption key
- **Key length**   The size (measured in bits) of an encryption key; longer encryption keys can take considerably more effort to attack a cryptosystem successfully
- **Block cipher**   An encryption algorithm that operates on blocks of data
- **Stream cipher**   A type of encryption algorithm that operates on a continuous stream of data such as a video or audio feed
- **Initialization vector (IV)**   A random number that is needed by some encryption algorithms to begin the encryption process
- **Symmetric encryption**   A method for encryption and decryption where it is necessary for both parties to possess a common encryption key
- **Asymmetric encryption**, or **public key cryptography**   A method for encryption, decryption, and digital signatures that uses pairs of encryption keys, consisting of a *public key* and a *private key*

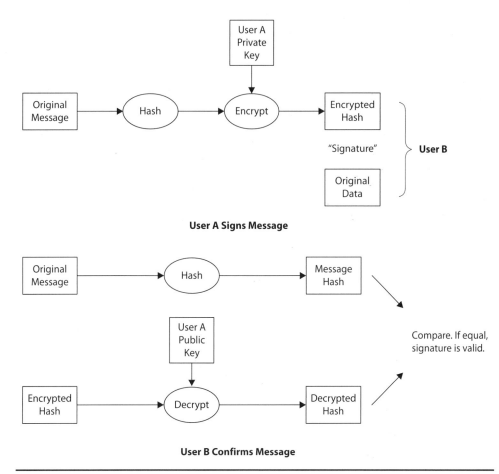

User A Signs Message

User B Confirms Message

Figure 6-8 Digital signature used to verify the integrity of a message

- **Key exchange**   A technique that is used by two parties to establish a symmetric encryption key when there is no secure channel available
- **Nonrepudiation**   The property of digital signatures and encryption that can make it difficult or impossible for a party to later deny having sent a digitally signed message, unless they admit to having lost control of their private encryption key

Private Key Cryptosystems

A private key cryptosystem is based on a symmetric cryptographic algorithm. The primary characteristic of a private key cryptosystem is the necessity for both parties to possess a common encryption key that is used to encrypt and decrypt messages.

The two main challenges with private key cryptography are

- **Key exchange**   An "out-of-band" method for exchanging encryption keys is required before any encrypted messages can be transmitted. This key exchange must occur over a secure channel; if the encryption keys were transmitted over the primary communications channel, anyone who intercepted the encryption key would be able to read any intercepted messages, provided they could determine the encryption algorithm used. For instance, if two parties want to exchange encrypted e-mail, they would need to exchange their encryption key first via telephone or fax, provided they are confident that their telephone and fax transmissions are not being intercepted.

- **Scalability**   Private key cryptosystems require that each sender-receiver pair exchange an encryption key. For a group of 4 parties, 6 encryption keys would need to be exchanged; for a group of 10 parties, 45 keys would need to be exchanged. For a large community of 1,000 parties, many thousands of keys would need to be exchanged.

Some well-known private key algorithms in use include AES (Rijndael), Blowfish, DES, Triple DES, RC4, Serpent, Skipjack, and Twofish.

Secure Key Exchange

Secure key exchange refers to methods used by two parties to establish a symmetric encryption key securely without actually transmitting the key over a channel. Secure key exchange is needed when two parties, previously unknown to each other, need to establish encrypted communications where no out-of-band channel is available.

Two parties can perform a secure key exchange if a third party intercepts their entire conversation. This is because algorithms used for secure key exchange utilize information known by both parties but not transmitted between them.

The most popular algorithm is the Diffie-Hellman Key Exchange Protocol. Another algorithm in limited use is quantum key distribution (QKD).

Public Key Cryptosystems

Public key cryptosystems are based on *asymmetric*, or *public key*, cryptographic algorithms. These algorithms use two-part encryption keys that are handled differently from encryption keys in symmetric key cryptosystems.

Exchanging Initial Encryption Keys

Think about a private key cryptosystem. In an established cryptosystem, two users exchange messages and encrypt/decrypt them using an encryption key. Before they can begin exchanging encrypted messages, one of the users must first get a copy of the key to the other user. They have to do this prior to the establishment of the cryptosystem, so they cannot use the cryptosystem to transmit the key.

Secure key exchange, such as Diffie-Hellman, is used to transmit the key safely from one party to the other party. Once both parties have the key, they can begin sending encrypted messages to each other.

Without secure key exchange, the two parties would have to use some other safe, out-of-band means for getting the encryption key across to the other user.

Key Pair   The encryption keys that are used in public key cryptography are the *public key* and the *private key*. Each user of a public key cryptosystem has these two keys in his or her possession. Together, the public and private keys are known as a *key pair*. The two keys require different handling and are used together but for different purposes, as explained in this section.

When a user generates his or her key pair, the key pair will physically exist as two separate files. The user is free to publish or distribute the public key openly; it could even be posted on a public web site. This is in contrast to the private key, which must be well protected and never published or sent to any other party—like keys in a private key cryptosystem. Most public key cryptosystems will utilize a password mechanism to protect the private key further; without its password, the private key is inaccessible and cannot be used.

Message Security   Public key cryptography is an ideal application for securing messages—e-mail in particular. The reason for this is that users do not need to establish and communicate symmetric encryption keys through a secure channel. With public key cryptography, users who have never contacted each other can immediately send secure messages to one another. Public key cryptography is depicted in Figure 6-9.

Every user is free to publish his or her public encryption key so that it is easily retrievable. There are servers on the Internet where public keys can be published and made available to anyone in the world. Public key cryptography is designed so that open disclosure of a user's public key does not compromise the secrecy of the corresponding private key: a user's private key cannot be derived from the public key.

When User A wants to send an encrypted message to User B, the procedure is as follows:

1. User B publishes his public key to the Internet at a convenient location.

2. User A retrieves User B's public key.

3. User A creates a message and encrypts it with User B's public key and sends the encrypted message to User B.

4. User B decrypts the message with his private key and is able to read the message.

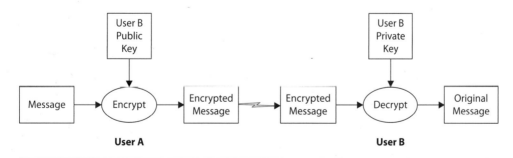

Figure 6-9   Public key cryptography used to transmit a secret message

Note that only User B's encryption key is used in this example. This method is used only to protect the message from eavesdroppers. This method is not used to verify the authenticity of the message.

Public key cryptography can also be used to verify the authenticity and integrity of a message. This is used to verify that a specific party did, in fact, create the message. The procedure is as follows:

1. User A publishes his public key to the Internet at a convenient location.

2. User B retrieves User A's public key and saves it for later use.

3. User A creates a message and digitally signs it with his private key, and then sends the signed message to User B.

4. User B verifies the digital signature using User A's public key. If the message verifies correctly, User B knows that the message originated from User A and has not been altered in transit.

In this example, only the authenticity and integrity of a message are assured. The message is not encrypted, which means that any party that intercepts the message can read it.

Public key cryptography can be used both to encrypt and to digitally sign a message, which will guarantee its confidentiality as well as its authenticity. The procedure is as follows:

1. User A and User B publish their public encryption keys to convenient places.

2. User A retrieves User B's public key, and User B retrieves User A's public key.

3. User A creates a message, then signs it with his private key and encrypts it with User B's public key, and then sends the message to User B.

4. User B decrypts the message with his private key and verifies the digital signature with User A's public key.

Public key cryptography also supports encryption of a message with more than one user's public key. This permits a user to send a single encrypted message to several recipients that is encrypted with each of their public keys. This method does not compromise the secrecy of any user's private key, since a user's private key cannot be derived from the public key.

Elliptic Curve Cryptography

Elliptic curve cryptography (ECC) is attracting interest for use in public key cryptography applications. ECC requires less computational power and bandwidth than other cryptographic algorithms and is thought to be more secure as well. Because of its low power requirements, it is used extensively in mobile devices.

Verifying Public Keys   It is possible for a fraudster to claim the identity of another person and even publish a public key that claims the identity of that person. Four methods are available for verifying a user's public key as genuine:

- **Certificate authority (CA)**   A public key that has been obtained from a trusted, reputable certificate authority can be considered genuine.

- **E-mail address**   Public keys used for e-mail will include the user's e-mail address. If the e-mail address is a part of a corporate or government domain (for example, *adobe.com* or *seattle.gov*), then some level of credence can be attributed to the successful exchange of messages with that e-mail address. However, since e-mail addresses can be spoofed, this should be considered a weak method at best.

- **Directory infrastructure**   A directory services infrastructure such as Microsoft Active Directory, LDAP, or a commercial product can be used to verify a user's public key.

- **Key fingerprint**   Many public key cryptosystems employ a method for verifying a key's identity, known as the key's fingerprint. If a user wants to verify a public key, the user retrieves the public key and calculates the key's fingerprint. The user then contacts the claimed owner of the public key, who runs a function against his or her private key that returns a string of numbers. The user also runs a function against the owner's public key, also returning a string of numbers. If both numbers match, the public key is genuine.

NOTE   When issuing a public key, it is essential that the requestor of the new public key be authenticated, such as by viewing a government-issued ID or by contacting the owner at a publicly listed telephone number.

Hashing and Message Digests

Hashing is the process of applying a cryptographic algorithm on a block of information that results in a compact, fixed-length "digest." The purpose of hashing is to provide a unique "fingerprint" for the message or file—even if the file is very large. A message digest can be used to verify the integrity of a large file, thus assuring that the file has not been altered.

Some of the properties of message digests that make them ideally suited for verifying integrity include

- Any change made to a file—even a single bit or character—will result in a significant change in the hash.

- It is computationally infeasible to make a change to a file without changing its hash.

- It is computationally infeasible to create a message or file that will result in a given hash.

- It is infeasible for any two messages to have the same hash.

One common use of message digests is on software download sites, where the computed hash for a downloadable program is available so that users can verify that the software program has not been altered (provided that the posted hash has not also been compromised).

Digital Signatures

A *digital signature* is a cryptographic operation where a sender "seals" a message or file using his or her identity. The purpose of a digital signature is to authenticate a message and to guarantee its integrity. Digital signatures do not protect the confidentiality of a message, however, as encryption is not one of the operations performed.

Digital signatures work by encrypting hashes of messages; recipients verify the integrity and authenticity of messages by decrypting hashes and comparing them to original messages. In detail, a digital signature works like this:

1. The sender publishes his public key to the Internet at a location that is easily accessible to recipients.

2. The recipient retrieves the sender's public key and saves it for later use.

3. The sender creates a message (or file) and computes a message digest (hash) of the message, and then encrypts the hash with his private key.

4. The sender sends the original file plus the encrypted hash to the recipient.

5. The recipient receives the original file and the encrypted hash. The recipient computes a message digest (hash) of the original file and sets the result aside. She then decrypts the hash with the sender's public key. The recipient compares the hash of the original file and the decrypted hash.

6. If the two hashes are identical, the recipient knows that a) the message in her possession is identical to the message that the sender sent, b) the sender is the originator, and c) the message has not been altered.

The use of digital signatures is depicted earlier in this chapter in Figure 6-6.

Digital Envelopes

One aspect of symmetric (private key) and asymmetric (public key) cryptography that has not been discussed yet is the computing requirements and performance implications of these two types of cryptosystems. In general, public key cryptography requires far more computing power than private key cryptography. The practical implication is that public key encryption of large sets of data can be highly compute-intensive and make its use infeasible in some occasions.

One solution to this is the use of a *digital envelope* that utilizes the convenience of public key cryptography with the lower overhead of private key cryptography. This practice is known as *hybrid cryptography*. The procedure for using digital envelopes works like this:

1. The sender and recipient agree that the sender will transmit a large message to the recipient.

2. The sender selects or creates a symmetric encryption key, known as the *session key*, and encrypts the session key with the recipient's public key.

3. The sender encrypts the message with the session key.

4. The sender sends the encrypted message (encrypted with the session key) and the encrypted session key (encrypted with the recipient's public key) to the recipient.

5. The recipient decrypts the session key with his private key.

6. The recipient decrypts the message with the session key.

The now-deprecated SET (*secure electronic transaction*, a predecessor to SSL/TLS) protocol uses digital envelopes. Digital envelopes require less computing overhead than the Diffie-Hellman key exchange, which is why digital envelopes may be preferred in some circumstances.

Public Key Infrastructure

One of the issues related to public key cryptography is the safe storage of public encryption keys. Although individuals are free to publish public keys online, doing so in a secure and controlled manner requires some central organization and control. A *public key infrastructure* (PKI) is designed to fulfill this and other functions.

A PKI is a centralized function that is used to store and publish public keys and other information. Some of the services provided by a PKI include

- **Digital certificates**   This digital credential consists of a public key and a block of information that identifies the owner of the certificate. The identification portion of a digital certificate will follow a standard, structured format and include such data as the owner's name, organization name, and other identifying information, such as e-mail address. The public key and the identifying information will reside in a document that is itself digitally signed by a trusted party, known as a certificate authority.

- **Certificate authority (CA)**   A CA is a business entity that issues digital certificates and publishes them in the PKI. The CA vouches for the identity of each of the digital certificates in a PKI; the CA undergoes certain safeguards to ensure that each digital certificate is genuine and really does belong to its rightful owner.

- **Registration authority (RA)**   The RA operates within or alongside a CA to accept requests for new digital certificates. The RA vets the request, carefully examines it, and undergoes steps to verify the authenticity of the person making the request. This verification may include viewing government-issued ID cards or passports or taking other steps as needed to ensure that the request is originating from the genuine person. When the RA is satisfied that the requestor is indeed the person making the request, the RA will issue a digital certificate. Part of the certificate issuance will be the delivery of private encryption keys to the requesting party. This may take place in person or over a secured electronic connection.

- **Certificate revocation list (CRL)**   Some circumstances may require that a user's digital certificate be cancelled or revoked. These circumstances include termination of employment (if a person's certificate was issued expressly for employment-related purposes) or loss or compromise of a user's private key. A CRL is an electronic list of digital certificates that have been revoked prior to their expiration date. To be effective, any consumer of digital certificates needs to consult a CRL to be doubly sure that a certificate remains valid.

- **Certification practice statement (CPS)**   This published statement describes the practices used by the CA to issue and manage digital certificates. This helps determine the relative strength and validity of digital certificates that are issued by the CA.

Key Management

The term *key management* refers to the various processes and procedures used by an organization to generate, protect, use, and dispose of encryption keys over its lifetime. Several of the common practices are described in this section.

Key Generation   The start of an encryption key life cycle is its generation. While at first glance it would appear that this process should require little scrutiny, further study shows that this is a critical process that requires safeguards.

The system on which key generation takes place must be highly protected. If keys are generated on a system that has been compromised or is of questionable integrity, it would be difficult to determine whether a bystander could have electronically observed key generation. For instance, if a key logger or other process spying tool were active in the system when keys were generated, the key generation may have been observable and details about keys captured. This would mean that newly minted keys have already been compromised if an outsider knows their identities.

In many situations, it would be reasonable to require that systems used for key generation be highly protected, isolated, and used by as few persons as possible. Regular integrity checks would need to take place to make sure the system continues to be free of any problems.

Furthermore, the key generation process needs to include some randomness (or, as some put it, entropy) so that the key generation process cannot be easily duplicated elsewhere. If key generation were not a random event, it could be possible to duplicate the conditions related to a specific key and then regenerate a key with the very same value. This would instantaneously compromise the integrity and uniqueness of the original key.

Key Protection   Private keys used in public key cryptosystems and keys used in symmetric cryptosystems must be continuously and vigorously protected. At all times they must be accessible *only* to the parties that are authorized to use them. If protection measures for private encryption keys are compromised (or suspected to be), it will be possible for a key compromise to take place, enabling the attacker to view messages encrypted with these keys.

In commercial environments, keys are often protected in a *hardware security module* (HSM), as depicted in Figure 6-10.

Figure 6-10 Hardware security module (Image courtesy of Rstubbs2)

A *key compromise* occurs when a private encryption key has been disclosed to any unauthorized third party. When a key compromise occurs, it will be necessary to re-encrypt all materials encrypted by the compromised key with a new encryption key.

CAUTION   In many applications, an encryption key is protected by a password. The length, complexity, distribution, and expiration of passwords protecting encryption keys must be well designed so that the strength of the cryptosystem (based on its key length and algorithm) is not compromised by a weak password scheme protecting its keys.

Key Encrypting Keys   Applications that utilize encryption must obtain their encryption keys in some way. In many cases, an intruder may be able to examine the application in an attempt to discover an encryption key, so that the intruder may decrypt communications used by the application. A common remedy for this is the use of encryption to protect the encryption key. This additional encryption requires a key of its own, known as a *key encrypting key*. Of course, this key also must reside someplace; often, features of the underlying operating system may be used to protect an encryption key as well as a key encrypting key.

Key Custody   *Key custody* refers to the policies, processes, and procedures regarding the management of keys. This is closely related to key protection but is focused on *who* manages keys and *where* they are kept.

Key Rotation   *Key rotation* is the process of issuing a new encryption key and re-encrypting data protected with the new key. Key rotation may occur when any of the following occurs:

- **Key compromise**   When an encryption key has been compromised, a new key must be generated and used.
- **Key expiration**   In some situations, encryption keys are rotated on a schedule.
- **Rotation of staff**   In some organizations, if any of the persons associated with the creation or management of encryption keys transfers to another position or leaves the organization, keys must be rotated.

Key Disposal *Key disposal* refers to the process of decommissioning encryption keys. This may be done upon receipt of an order to destroy a data set that is encrypted with a specific encryption key—destroying an encryption key can be as effective (and a whole lot easier) than destroying the encrypted data itself.

However, key disposal can present some challenges. If an encryption key is backed up to tape, for instance, disposal of the key will require that backup tapes also be destroyed. Hence, it is crucial to dispose of an encryption key *only* after it is determined that it is no longer needed.

NOTE A novel method for data disposal is the destruction of encryption keys.

Encryption Applications

Several applications utilize encryption algorithms. Many of these are well known and in everyday use.

Secure Sockets Layer/Transport Layer Security (SSL/TLS) SSL and TLS are the encryption protocols used to encrypt web pages requested with the HTTPS (Hypertext Transfer Protocol Secure). Introduced by Netscape Communications for use in its own browser, SSL and its successor, TLS, have become de facto standards for the encryption of web pages.

SSL and TLS provide several cryptographic functions, including public key encryption, private key encryption, and hash functions. These are used for server and client authentication (although in practice, client authentication is seldom used) and session encryption. SSL and TLS support several encryption algorithms, including AES, RC4, IDEA, DES, and Triple DES, and several key lengths, from 40 bits to 256 bits and beyond.

Weaknesses were discovered in all versions of SSL as well as the first version of TLS; therefore, any versions of SSL and TLS 1.0 should not be used.

EXAM TIP Remember that all versions of SSL and the early versions of TLS are now considered deprecated and should no longer be used.

S-HTTP (Secure Hypertext Transfer Protocol) Not to be confused with HTTPS, S-HTTP also provides encryption of web pages between web servers and web browsers. Because Netscape and Microsoft favored HTTPS, S-HTTP never caught on and is not widely supported.

The main difference between HTTPS and S-HTTP is that HTTPS secures the entire channel, regardless of the data that is transmitted through it. S-HTTP protects only individual pieces of data or messages.

Secure/Multipurpose Internet Mail Extensions (S/MIME)   S/MIME is an e-mail security protocol that provides sender and recipient authentication and encryption of message content and attachments. S/MIME is most often used for encryption of e-mail messages.

Secure Shell   SSH is a multipurpose protocol that is used to create a secure channel between two systems. The most popular use of SSH is the replacement of the Telnet and R-series protocols (rsh, rlogin, and so on), but it also supports tunneling of protocols such as X-Windows and File Transfer Protocol (FTP).

Internet Protocol Security   IPsec is a protocol used to create a secure, authenticated channel between two systems. IPsec operates at the Internet layer in the TCP/IP suite; hence, all IP traffic between two systems protected by IPsec is automatically encrypted.

IPsec operates in one of two modes: ESP and AH. If ESP is used, all encapsulated traffic is encrypted. If AH is used, only IPsec's authentication feature is used.

Secure Electronic Transaction (SET)   SET is a now-deprecated protocol designed to protect Internet-based financial transactions. SET never caught on because it required the installation of a separate client program. HTTPS became the standard for encrypting web pages and then became the preferred method for encryption.

SET offered greater protection of credit card transactions through the substitution of tokens for actual credit card numbers. But SET never caught on, and it is no longer used.

Blockchain   A *blockchain* is a distributed ledger used to record cryptographically linked transactions in a peer-to-peer network. Once recorded, transactions in a blockchain cannot be altered or removed. Blockchain is, by design, decentralized. Implementations of blockchain include the Bitcoin cryptocurrency as well as emerging uses in financial services and supply chain management.

Voice over IP

Voice over IP (VoIP) encompasses several technologies that permit telephony that is transported over IP networks. Other terms associated with VoIP include *Internet telephony* and *IP telephony*. These terms all describe services for transporting voice, video, and facsimile over IP networks, including the Internet. Organizations that implement VoIP will incorporate one or more of the following:

- **Trunking**   Replace older technology voice trunks with SIP (Session Initiation Protocol) trunks that have far greater capacity and lower costs. Trunks can connect an organization's private branch exchange (PBX) to telecommunications providers that offer VoIP trunking. Also, an organization can connect its digital PBXs in various locations together via MPLS (Multiprotocol Label Switching) over IP WAN connections.

- **Digital PBX**   Replace older PBX systems with newer PBXs that support VoIP and SIP trunking.

- **VoIP handsets**   Replace digital and analog telephone sets with IP telephone sets that connect to the PBX via TCP/IP over Ethernet or Wi-Fi.

- **VoIP clients**   Replace telephone sets with software programs on workstations that communicate over TCP/IP to the PBX. Often called *softphones*, these programs eliminate the need for separate telephone handsets.

VoIP Threats and Vulnerabilities

The primary threat to VoIP systems is the fact that an organization's telephone network is connected to the TCP/IP network and thus is vulnerable to all the types of attacks that plague workstations and servers. Furthermore, many VoIP components run on devices and systems that use conventional operating systems such as Unix. That means that most VoIP components are vulnerable to the same class of threats that servers and workstations are subject to. These threats include

- **Eavesdropping**   Attackers may attempt to listen in to voice, video, and facsimile transmissions.

- **Spoofing**   Attackers can send packets to VoIP devices, systems, and PBXs that impersonate other devices and systems. Possible reasons include stealing information, altering information, denial of service, toll fraud, and more.

- **Malware**   This includes viruses, worms, Trojan horses, rootkits, and so on.

- **Denial of service**   This attack is designed to disable a target system or network by flooding it either with an enormous volume of traffic or with specially crafted traffic designed to cause the target to malfunction.

- **Toll fraud**   This attack is designed to steal long-distance service by using another organization's telephone network for personal use.

These and other threats are not unique to VoIP but plague all kinds of IP and Internet-connected networks and systems. For a complete discussion on threats and vulnerabilities, see the section "Logical Access Controls," earlier in this chapter.

 CAUTION   An organization that employs VoIP must now take even greater care to protect its networks. For such an organization, an attack on the network will threaten not only computer networks but also voice communications.

Protecting VoIP

Because VoIP systems communicate over TCP/IP, and because many are based on conventional operating systems, VoIP is protected through primarily the same measures that are used to protect other IT systems. The protection measures that are most effective include

- Network segmentation
- System and device hardening

- Strict access controls and access management
- Anti-malware controls
- Security event monitoring
- Firewalls and session border controllers (SBCs)
- Intrusion detection systems

These and other countermeasures are discussed in detail in the section "Logical Access Controls," earlier in this chapter.

Private Branch Exchange

A PBX is a private telephone switch used by an organization to manage its internal telephone calls as well as telephone calls with parties in the public telephone network. Workers in an organization can often call one another with shortened phone numbers, such as four-digit extensions, and call "outside" numbers using a prefix such as "8" or "9."

PBXs are connected to the public-switched telephone network (PSTN) via one or more *trunks*, which are telecommunications circuits designed to carry several simultaneous telephone conversations. Implemented over telephony circuits such as T-1 or E-1, trunks are leased from common-carrier telecommunications carriers.

PBX Threats and Vulnerabilities

A variety of security issues affect PBXs. IT managers and security professionals need to be aware of these threats and vulnerabilities to be able to protect them. Some of these include

- **Default passwords on administrator console**   This can permit anyone with physical access to the PBX to change the configuration of the PBX or extract data from it (including phone records and access controls). Passwords on many PBXs are left at factory default; this is an old practice still in place today.

- **Dial-in modem**   Many PBXs employ an administrative dial-in modem so that the PBX administrator can perform remote administrative duties. Often, dial-in access uses either a default password or no authentication at all.

- **Toll fraud**   One of the most enticing opportunities on a PBX is the ability to commit toll fraud by using it to place long-distance telephone calls. This is done by logging into the PBX (when passwords are weak or nonexistent) and changing its configuration to permit the attacker to place long-distance calls at the PBX owner's expense.

- **Espionage**   PBXs are also the target of attempts to eavesdrop on telephone conversations as well as retrieve phone records.

Many PBXs have IP connections to facilitate remote administrative access. PBXs with IP connectivity are subject to the broader scope of IP-related threats and vulnerabilities that are discussed in detail earlier in this chapter in the section "Logical Access Controls."

PBX Countermeasures

PBXs without IP connectivity are relatively easy to protect. Some of the most effective countermeasures include

- **Administrative access control**   Console and modem access should be configured with the strongest reasonable controls, including strong, complex passwords; multifactor authentication; administrative access logging; and dial-back modems.

- **Physical access control**   Only authorized personnel should have physical access to the PBX. A PBX should be protected with keycard and/or video surveillance so that the organization can positively identify individual personnel who access it.

- **Regular log reviews**   Administrative personnel should regularly review access logs to verify that only authorized personnel are accessing administrative consoles and functions. Furthermore, toll records should be reviewed frequently to ensure that no toll fraud is taking place.

- **Calling restrictions**   Administrative personnel should configure a PBX to block outbound calling to countries that the organization does not call. This will help to combat toll fraud should an intruder gain access to an outbound call trunk.

PBXs with IP connectivity will require additional IP-centric countermeasures that are similar to those required for servers and other network-connected devices.

Malware

Malware is an inclusive term that refers to many types of malicious code, including viruses, worms, Trojan horses, rootkits, and more. Malware is increasingly stealthy and potent, and if the past 20 years is any indication, malware will always be one step ahead of the measures used to try to keep it at bay.

Blocking malware is rarely a matter for discussion, any more than locks on the outside doors. The malware threat is just too real, and the consequences can be devastating.

Malware has many attack vectors, meaning it has many ways to get into an organization, which requires a variety of defenses operating simultaneously. It is no longer sufficient to run only antivirus software on end-user workstations; instead, it is necessary to employ several means of detecting, blocking, and responding to malware.

Malware Threats and Vulnerabilities

Malware is capable of making a wide variety of mischief, as well as serious trouble, for organizations. The earliest viruses were relatively benign, whereas contemporary malware is able to produce a wide range of economic damage.

There are several classes of malware:

- **Viruses**   These fragments of code attach themselves to .exe files (executable programs) in Microsoft operating systems and are activated when the program they are attached to is run.

- **Worms**   These stand-alone programs are capable of human-assisted and automatic propagation.

- **Ransomware**   As a highly successful attack method, ransomware encrypts data on a user's workstation and, optionally, on network shares, and then issues instructions to victims to remit ransom payments to recover their encrypted data.

- **Destructware**   This malware is designed to destroy information irretrievably and, in some cases, render information systems unbootable.

- **Trojan horses**   As the name suggests, these programs are purported to perform one function but actually perform other (or additional) undesired functions. For example, something might be advertised as a game that actually erases files (or does both).

- **Spyware**   This type of software performs one or more surveillance-type actions on a computer, reporting back to the spyware owner. The most insidious form of spyware is the key logger, a software program (and also an implantable hardware device) that records user keystrokes and transmits them back to a central location.

- **Rootkits**   These malware programs are designed to hide from the operating system as well as evade detection by antivirus software. Some rootkits are also able to run "underneath" the operating system so that they are undetectable.

- **Bots**   These are agents implanted by other forms of malware that are programmed to obey remotely issued instructions. Collections of bots are called *bot armies*. These are built to create spam, propagate malware, attack target systems and networks, and host phishing sites.

 CAUTION   Security managers and architects need to understand the different types of malware thoroughly—how they are made, how they propagate, and how they attack systems. But security professionals can't forget the forest for the trees: it is essential to establish a defense-in-depth set of controls to block all types of known and unknown malware and to respond effectively when malware attacks occur.

The types of damage that malware can cause include

- Computer slowdowns and crashes
- Alteration, encryption, or destruction of data
- Eavesdropping on communications
- Theft of sensitive data
- Damage to system hardware
- Attack or damage to other systems

Malware infiltrates an organization through avenues of opportunity. The vulnerabilities that malware is able to exploit include

- **Missing patches**   Many malware programs are designed to exploit known vulnerabilities that remain on many computers that do not have security patches installed.

- **Software flaws**   Malware designers will use various tools to discover and exploit flaws in applications, operating systems, tools, and other programs. Some of these flaws may be known and have patches available, but others may be relatively unknown.

- **Unsecure configuration**   Old, outdated, or incorrectly set configuration settings can leave a computer vulnerable to attack.

- **Faulty architecture**   Flaws in a network's architecture (for example, incorrect placement of a firewall that exposes too many systems) or errors in implementation can leave systems open to attack.

- **Faulty judgment**   Mistakes and decisions that are based on incomplete knowledge can lead to configuration or architecture errors that introduce vulnerabilities.

- **Gullibility**   Often, the target of malware is end users' gullibility and curiosity. They are inclined to click links in phishing messages, open attachments, and visit unknown sites—all of which are nowadays the primary means for injecting malware into their computers.

Malware's most common threat vectors to organizations include

- **Phishing**   Phishing messages impersonate real government and private institutions, pretending to communicate urgent news to customers and others, who need to act quickly. A common ploy is an e-mail message from a bank telling customers that their bank accounts will be locked unless they respond by logging in to an imposter site. People who fall for these schemes inadvertently provide login credentials to thieves, who use them to transfer funds out of their victims' accounts. Many similar schemes exist that attempt to steal money or other valuables from victims.

- **Spam**   Junk e-mail often either contains malware or entices users to connect to web sites that contain malware. Spam also includes e-mail messages that advertise both legitimate goods and services as well as fakes; prescription medication is a good example of the phony merchandise that many people buy in the hopes of saving money or achieving world conquest.

- **Spear phishing**   This is phishing that is specially crafted for a single target organization or audience. Spear phishing is more difficult for end users to discern because the e-mail messages resemble authentic messages originating from within the organization.

- **Whaling**   This is spear phishing that specially targets executives in an organization.

- **Denial of service**   Some malware deliberately causes computers to malfunction. Plus, malware that is designed to spread from computer to computer rapidly over networks will cause high volumes of network traffic that make the networks, as well as computers, unusable.

- **Screen scraping**   Some malware is designed to intercept data displayed on users' computer screens.

- **Key logging**   Some malware is designed to intercept keystrokes and displayed information and relay that data back to a central location. The information of greatest interest is credit card numbers, bank account numbers, and user ID-and-password combinations for high-value sites such as online banking.

Anti-Malware Administrative Controls

Organizations' anti-malware controls need to include several administrative controls to stop the introduction and spread of malware. These controls include policies such as

- **Spam policy**   Security policy and awareness training need to include "don't open strange or unusual e-mail messages, even from people you know" guidance to workers. Even in an environment with effective spam filters, some spam does get through, so this policy helps users think twice before opening them.

- **Only business-related Internet access**   Because some malware spreads through malicious code implanted on web sites (and for other reasons such as lost productivity), organizations may forbid its employees from visiting web sites with no direct business purpose.

- **No removable media**   Malware can be introduced via removable media. In fact, the earliest viruses were spread via floppy disk. Today, many organizations forbid, and even actively block, the use of removable media such as USB drives and memory sticks.

- **No downloading**   Because some malware is implanted in downloadable software, many organizations have enacted policies that forbid the practice of downloading software. Instead, requests are made to the IT service desk if additional software or tools are needed.

- **Restricted privileges**   Earlier versions of popular operating systems by default configured end-user accounts at the same level of privilege as system administrators. The harmful result of this was that malware, introduced by end users, would execute on the computer with administrative privileges and cause significant damage. The new norm is to restrict end-user workstation privileges to the lowest access level, thereby reducing malware potency.

- **No personally owned computers**   In many organizations, it was once okay to access the corporate network remotely using personally owned computers. Because the organization is unable to control the spread of malware on computers it does not own or control, the right place to draw the line is to enact a policy that forbids all but company-owned computers from connecting to any network, local or remote.

- **Restricted smartphone access**   Organizations that don't take the hard line of "no personally owned computers will connect to the network, including smartphones" may take a softer line and permit limited access for smartphones, such as e-mail access only.

Advanced Persistent Threats

The phenomenon known as *advanced persistent threats* (APTs) represents the technique of hard-to-detect and continuous attacks on an organization, through the use of reconnaissance, social engineering attacks, and malware attacks. APTs are particularly difficult to defend against as the attacker is generally focused on attacking a single organization, while personnel in the organization are reacting and trying to always stay one step ahead.

Anti-Malware Management Controls

Several procedural controls are needed to ensure that systems remain free of malware:

- Include anti-malware procedures in employee security awareness training.
- Build servers only from original read-only media.
- Scan all incoming e-mail messages for malware prior to releasing them to users.
- Evaluate all URLs in e-mail messages at the time that users click them to evaluate them for maliciousness.
- Scan all new software (regardless of source) for malware on nonproduction systems prior to use.
- Prohibit any use of personally owned computers for any business purpose, on or off work premises.
- Scan all incoming files for malware prior to releasing them for use.
- Verify all network equipment software releases as genuine and free of malware prior to use.

The Malware Industry

The face of malware is rapidly changing. Once the purview of hacker-hobbyists and script kiddies, malware is now the domain of large organized crime syndicates and cyber-criminal organizations. These are businesses with investors, research and development, profit sharing, and benefits. The only thing that makes them fundamentally different from legitimate businesses is that organized crime is in the business of conducting illegal operations, such as financial fraud.

The U.S. Treasury Department published a report in 2006 that claimed that, on a worldwide scale, organized crime was making more profits from Internet-based fraud than from drug trafficking. And 14 years later, they are just getting better at it.

Malware: Avoiding Repeats of History

For the most part, organizations are serious about stopping malware at the network boundary. This is because they remember malware attacks of the past 20 years that completely incapacitated corporate networks for days at a time. Malware with names like Code Red, Blaster, SQL Slammer, Duqu, Mirai, and Conficker evoke memories of battles to keep corporate networks running.

Those were painful events that resulted in business disruptions that were sometimes severe enough to affect financial results. Pointed questions from senior executives, who often did not understand the rules of the new cyber-wars, distracted IT managers from their primary objective: keep the malware out of the network!

Anti-Malware Technical Controls

Because malware is so potent, and because some kinds of malware are able to spread without any human interaction or assistance, a defense-in-depth strategy for blocking it is needed in most organizations to make sure that malware has few opportunities to enter the network:

- **Advanced anti-malware software**   Antivirus software is no longer sufficient to detect and block malware. Additional software programs and agents installed on endpoint systems are needed to detect and block today's malware.

- **Anti-malware on all servers and workstations**   Every workstation should have current anti-malware software installed, functioning, and up to date. It should be configured to perform real-time malware detection, plus regular scans (daily in high-risk environments, weekly in others). Users should not be able to remove or tamper with anti-malware software, even if they are local administrators for their workstations. However, users should be able to perform scans on demand if they sense that their system may be infected.

- **Anti-malware on e-mail servers**   E-mail servers should have anti-malware programs designed to block malware on incoming and outgoing e-mail. This cannot be ordinary anti-malware software, but should be a type designed to run on an e-mail server and interoperate with the e-mail server programs.

- **Anti-malware on web proxy servers/filters**   Organizations should have active or passive web proxy servers that have anti-malware software on board. This will prevent malware from entering an organization from web sites that users are visiting.

- **Centralized anti-malware console**   Organizations should consider using enterprise versions of anti-malware software that provide central monitoring and configuration consoles. This gives the organization the ability to see the "big picture" instantly with regard to anti-malware controls. For instance, a console will show which workstations' anti-malware programs are having trouble running or getting new updates and where infections are occurring. Centralized consoles can also be used to force selected systems to perform immediate malware signature updates and perform scans if management believes that a malware outbreak is imminent or in progress.

- **Data loss prevention (DLP) systems**   Organizations should consider the use of DLP systems, which detect and can block the unauthorized transfer and exfiltration of sensitive data. While this may be considered a last line of defense against the compromise of sensitive data, DLP systems can nonetheless prevent the loss of valuable and sensitive information.

- **End-user reduced privileges**   Organizations can limit the privilege level that end users have on their workstations. This can help to blunt the impact of malware, since malware generally executes at the same level of privilege as the end user who triggered it. This measure also reduces the ability for end users to tamper with and "improve" their workstations, which can help to reduce support costs.

- **Intrusion prevention systems (IPS)**   Organizations can employ agented or agentless IPSs that will automatically sense activities typical of malware. An IPS has the ability to disconnect an infected system from the network immediately so that it cannot infect other systems or disrupt network traffic. Endpoint-based IPSs can effectively block known command and control traffic, reducing or eliminating the effects of malware.

- **Spam filters**   A lot of malware (not to mention phishing schemes and fraud) enters an organization through e-mail. Centralized spam filters can intercept and block spam before it even reaches the e-mail server. Many spam filters also have antivirus programs on them to scrub viruses from incoming e-mail—even when it comes from legitimate, known persons.

- **Blocking use of removable media**   While external memory devices such as USB sticks and external hard drives are popular, they do represent a number of threats, including malware. Blocking removable media is also one measure that is effective against information leakage.

- **Block outbound network services on servers**   It is rare that a server should need to initiate communications over the Internet, except for specific business connections that may be a part of distributed applications. All other accesses should be blocked. This would effectively block any malware's attempt to communicate information back to its source.

- **Boot servers from protected images**   In virtual environments, it is possible to boot servers from read-only images stored on a centralized storage system. This would prevent malware from being able to install itself on a server permanently, since the next reboot from a clean image would effectively remove it.

- **Block read-only objects**   Except in rare and well-controlled circumstances, software should not be able to write to a hard drive's boot sector or the system's

CMOS (complementary metal oxide semiconductor, the technology used to store a computer's hardware configuration). These and possibly other portions of a system should be protected so that malware cannot alter or destroy them.

CAUTION   Blocking malware is not a one-time effort of procuring and configuring tools. Instead, this should be thought of as the "malware wars" that continue indefinitely and require constant vigilance.

Information Leakage

Information leakage refers to the tendency for sensitive information to leak out of an organization's systems through various means. Blocking opportunities for information leakage is a developing area in IT today.

There are fundamentally two forms of information leakage: accidental and malicious. Accidental leakage occurs when, for instance, an employee selects the wrong recipients in an outgoing e-mail that contains sensitive information and mistakenly sends sensitive information to the wrong external party, resulting in a potential security breach.

Deliberate information leakage occurs when an employee chooses to acquire sensitive data with the intention of taking it out of the organization. There are two primary reasons and motivations for this:

- **Profit**   Some sensitive information such as credit card and bank account numbers are easily sold on the black market.
- **Revenge**   If the employee senses that injustice has occurred—or will occur—in the organization, the employee may plan a form of revenge by taking copies of sensitive information for later use, whether for extortion, exposure, or profit.

Leakage also occurs when malware intercepts login credentials, resulting in a hacker's ability to log in and steal sensitive information. Leakage is multifaceted and extends into other areas, including social engineering, malware, proper HR hiring procedures, and more.

Leakage can also occur when, for example, a user performs a query in an application containing sensitive data and saves the result on a local hard drive, file server, or Internet-based file storage service such as Box or Dropbox. This is generally considered a lack of good judgment in the gray area between accidental and malicious intent.

Because of the numerous means available for users to remove data deliberately from the organization, several measures should be taken to limit those opportunities, including

- **Outbound e-mail filtering**   Outbound e-mail filters that check for information leakage can be used to observe and even block sensitive information that is leaving the organization.
- **Control removable media**   Through centralized automatic policies, organizations can prevent the use of USB media, writing to optical discs, and other actions contributing to information leakage.

- **Blocking Internet access**   Users in the most sensitive functions (those with access to the most sensitive information) should be prevented from accessing any computer or network outside of the organization. This not only reduces the likelihood of malware infecting a sensitive system, but it reduces the opportunity for leakage. Preventing end users from using personal e-mail is a safeguard used by many organizations.

- **Tighter access controls**   Organizations should periodically examine their access controls for the most sensitive information, looking for more ways to reduce the ability for people to access that data, except in situations where they must do so for business purposes. When fewer people have access, there will be fewer opportunities for leakage.

- **Access logging**   The organization should improve access logging so that all accesses (not just updates) to information are logged. This can be an effective detective control, since this would tell the organization who is accessing which data records. If the organization discloses the logging to its workers, this also becomes a deterrent control, not unlike video surveillance.

- **Job rotation**   Staff members should be periodically shifted into other positions so that their opportunities for covertly extracting information are fewer. When organizations shift their employees on short notice and on sporadic schedules, employees are less likely to engage in information-pilfering schemes because they do not want to get caught.

- **Periodic background checks**   Organizations should consider periodic background checks for employees in positions of access to sensitive information. Changes in an employee's current background may provide additional incentives for employees to engage in unauthorized or illegal acts. For instance, an employee whose credit background has gone from good to terrible may be tempted to find ways to supplement his income, such as embezzlement or selling information on the black market. Also, an employee who started employment with a clean criminal record may, over time, turn to the dark side and enter a lifestyle of crime. That two-week vacation last year could actually have been a jail sentence.

- **Implement a DLP system**   Organizations can implement a DLP system that will observe all inbound and outbound network traffic and create alerts when sensitive information is believed to be leaving or entering. Some DLP systems can also block these transmissions, thereby blocking illegitimate attempts to steal information and forcing legitimate activities to use more prudent means such as encryption.

   NOTE   Employers should understand that a patient employee who is determined to remove information from the organization would probably be able to do so despite many controls to detect or prevent it. For systems containing the most sensitive information, security specialists should perform a detailed risk analysis to understand precisely how data leakage can be controlled in their organization.

Environmental Controls

Computers and networks operate in the physical world. Networks consist of devices such as routers, switches, and firewalls, plus cabling within and between buildings. Computer systems and network devices are designed to operate within a narrow band of temperature, humidity, moisture, and cleanliness. When they operate within these bounds, they are likely to provide years of service, but even brief periods outside these bounds can significantly shorten the life of many components.

Organizations that employ computers and networks to support vital business processes need to provide suitable environments for them. Failure to do so can result in higher operating costs and business disruptions resulting from more frequent unscheduled downtime due to environmental conditions. This section discusses the environmental systems and controls required to maintain a suitable environment for computers and networks.

Environmental Threats and Vulnerabilities

Computer systems require special facilities that include reliable electric power, environmental controls, and physical security. By their very nature, the controls that support and protect computer systems are complex and require periodic maintenance to provide reliable service. Redundant controls or systems are often needed for organizations intolerant of downtime.

This section discusses electric power, cooling and humidity controls, fire detection and suppression, and physical security.

Electric Power Vulnerabilities

Computer systems require a steady diet of clean electric power. The quality and delivery of electric power from virtually every public utility falls far short of the needs required by IT systems. Several power-related events threaten the health of computer equipment, including

- **Spike or surge**   A sharp increase in voltage that lasts for only a fraction of a second
- **Inrush**   A sudden increase in current flowing to a device, usually associated with the startup of a large motor, which can cause a voltage drop that lasts several seconds
- **Noise**   The presence of other electromagnetic signals within incoming power
- **Dropout**   A momentary loss of power that lasts from a few milliseconds to a few seconds
- **Brownout**   A sustained drop in voltage that can last from several seconds to several hours
- **Blackout**   A complete loss of electric power for more than a few seconds

All of these phenomena can damage computer and network equipment by damaging internal components that make them fail outright or through latent damage that may shorten the life of an electronic component such as a power supply.

Physical Environment Vulnerabilities

Computer and network equipment is sensitive to changes in environmental conditions. The conditions that warrant discussion here are

- **Temperature**   Computer and network equipment generate potentially large volumes of waste heat that must be continuously siphoned away. Even a brief interruption in environmental systems can cause sharp rises in temperature that can damage equipment. A temperature that is too low can cause condensation on equipment, which can invite corrosion and even cause short circuits when it occurs on electrical components.

- **Humidity**   Computer and network equipment must operate within a narrow band of humidity, usually 40 to 55 percent. When humidity drops below 40 percent, static buildup can occur that can damage sensitive electronics. Excessively high humidity can result in condensation, inviting corrosion and short circuits, causing the failure of computers and network equipment.

- **Dust and dirt**   Computer and network equipment is designed to be used in clean environments that are reasonably free of dust and dirt. Dust and dirt can accelerate wear in mechanical components and clog air filters, causing heat buildup.

- **Smoke and fire**   A fire that is in or near a data center can introduce smoke, which can damage computer and network equipment. Fire extinguishing agents such as water can also damage sensitive equipment. Fire departments often cut electric power to a building when there is a fire, so even equipment that is not threatened by the fire will suffer the effects of a power outage.

- **Sudden unexpected movement**   Earthquakes and landslides can violently shake equipment, pulling it away from its fastenings. Personnel moving equipment may accidentally bump into other devices or snag or damage loose cabling.

Environmental Controls and Countermeasures

Several environmental control systems are required to counteract the threats and vulnerabilities discussed in this section. When designed and operated correctly, these controls will contribute to high reliability and a good service record for IT equipment, which is sensitive to environmental conditions.

Electric Power

Because the quality of commercial utility electric power is usually insufficient for sensitive and critical computing equipment, several additional controls may be needed to improve the quality and/or quantity of available electric power. These controls are described in the following sections and depicted in Figure 6-11.

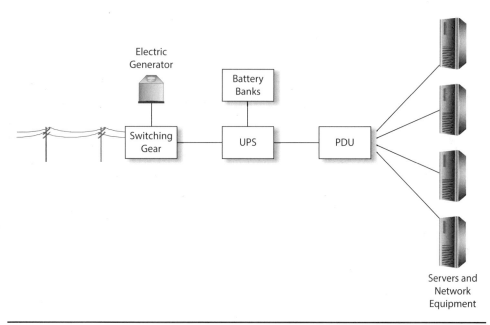

Figure 6-11   Components in a facility power system

Uninterruptible Power Supply (UPS)   This is a system that filters incoming power from spikes and other noise and supplies power for short periods through a bank of batteries. A UPS is sufficient for power outages that last from a few minutes to as long as a few hours (provided there is sufficient battery capacity). A UPS provides a continuous supply of electricity; when there is a brownout or blackout, power delivered to computer systems is unaffected.

Electric Generator   This is a system consisting of an internal combustion engine powered by gasoline, diesel fuel, or natural gas that spins an electric generator. A generator can supply electricity for as long as several days, depending on the size of its fuel supply and whether it can be refueled.

Electric generators require several seconds to a few minutes to start up and provide emergency power. For this reason, electric generators are implemented in conjunction with a UPS system. In the event of a power failure, the UPS provides an uninterrupted flow of power and provides that power via its batteries until the generator has started and is producing electricity. Further, in a sustained power failure, many generators must be shut down for refueling (and indeed for any required maintenance); the UPS once again provides continuous power for this purpose.

Larger facilities employ multiple electric generators for larger workloads and greater overall reliability.

Dual Utility Power Feeds   An organization that is dependent on reliable electric power can consider using two separate electric utility power feeds that would ideally originate from separate utility substations. This safeguard helps to ensure a steady supply of electric power, even in the event of the outage of a utility company distribution line.

Transfer Switch   Facilities that use a UPS, one or more electric generators, and one or more public utility power feeds also employ a system of electrical switching equipment known as a *transfer switch*. A transfer switch automatically routes power among one or more public utility feeds, one or more generators, through one or more UPSs into the facility.

Power Distribution Unit   A *power distribution unit* (PDU) is a device that distributes electric power to a computer room or data center. A PDU may be large and supply dozens of separate power circuits or may be as small as a power strip. Some PDUs also have voltage step-down capabilities, converting higher input voltages into voltage levels used by computer equipment.

Multiple Power Feeds   Some organizations with high reliability requirements may build fully redundant power systems consisting of dual power feeds, dual switchgear, generators, UPSs, and PDUs, delivering fully redundant power to each computer and network device. Organizations that utilize redundant power systems usually refer to their power systems as "A-side" and "B-side" systems. Computer and network equipment that utilizes dual power supplies can take advantage of redundant power systems by connecting one power supply to the A-side and one to the B-side. This permits systems to continue functioning, even in the event of a complete failure of any single component in the facility's power system. All such protected equipment will continue operating without interruption.

Power Planning   It is crucial to understand present and future electric power requirements so that the facility's electric power distribution components discussed here can be appropriately sized. Data centers generally size their power systems by calculating a minimum number of watts delivered to each square foot of data center space or to each cabinet. In the 1990s and early 2000s, data centers were generally configured to provide 40–100 watts per square foot, or as much as 3.125 kW per cabinet. However, with rapid advances in server technology, these figures have become inadequate. Modern data centers that need to get the most out of their IT equipment will plan for 150–200 watts per square foot, or as much as 6.250 kW per cabinet.

Data centers use different methods for calculating power requirements. Power figures often encompass an entire room or cage, which includes hot and cold aisles.

Planning for too high a power density will almost certainly result in excess electrical capacity, which is considered a waste of capital. Correspondingly, however, too small a figure per square foot or per cabinet will result in the data center running out of power before it runs out of space.

Many data centers that experience insufficient electric power are exploring ways of increasing their capacity. One solution is to use ambient air cooling instead of more expensive air conditioning. This is discussed in the next section.

Temperature and Humidity Controls

Because computing and network equipment sheds a large volume of waste heat, highly reliable and adequately sized HVAC (heating, ventilation, and air conditioning) systems are required.

The temperature in rooms containing computer and network equipment should range from 68° to 75°F (20° to 24°C), and humidity should range from 40 to 55 percent. In facilities with a considerable number of computer systems, this will require highly reliable and high-capacity HVAC systems.

It is recommended that facilities utilize an "N + 1" design, which means that there should be at least one additional HVAC system than is required to cool the facility continuously. For example, if a facility requires four HVAC systems for cooling, then at least five HVAC systems should be used. This permits adequate cooling to continue in the event one system fails or is being maintained.

Computer facilities should employ continuous temperature and humidity monitoring that regularly records readings and alerts personnel when readings exceed safe levels. Sensitive equipment should also have internal temperature monitoring capabilities that alert support personnel when readings exceed tolerance. Systems that are sensitive to variations in temperature should have auto-shutdown capabilities in the event that support personnel are unable to respond in time.

Many computer rooms and data centers employ a raised floor system consisting of removable tiles. The space under the tiles acts as an air plenum for air conditioning systems; tiles with holes in them are strategically placed to direct cold air into areas requiring it. Tiled floors are typically 80 to 100 cm (about 30 to 40 in.) above the floor beneath.

Data centers generally employ technology such as refrigeration or chilled water loops for controlling temperature. Many newer data centers employ ambient air cooling, which is less expensive as outside ambient air needs only to be filtered for dust. This approach has been adopted in many data centers trying to increase their power per square foot or power per cabinet figures by using less electric power for air cooling and therefore making more power available for IT equipment.

Fire Prevention, Detection, and Suppression Controls

Virtually every local government authority requires fire detection, prevention, and suppression controls. However, the minimum controls may be considered inadequate for facilities containing expensive computer and network equipment. For example, regulations requiring water-sprinkler suppression systems would certainly extinguish a fire in a data center, but the water would also cause considerable damage to equipment. For this reason, different types of detection and suppression systems are often used to protect valuable equipment from fire and suppression agent damage.

Fire Prevention   Measures that help to prevent fires in the first place contribute to a safer environment. Some measures include

- **Combustibles**   Materials such as packing boxes and manuals should be stored away from computer equipment. Reductions in combustible materials make fires less likely to start or spread.

- **Cleanliness**   Dust can sometimes trigger highly sensitive smoke detectors; this is another reason to practice proper cleanliness measures in data centers.

- **Electrical equipment maintenance**   Maintenance activities such as soldering should not be done near computer equipment. Smoke from soldering can trigger smoke detectors and cause a discharge of fire suppression agents.

Fire Detection   Facilities can be equipped with more than the minimum required capabilities for smoke detection. Highly sensitive smoke and heat detection systems are available that can provide an earlier warning. This gives personnel an added opportunity to identify the cause of the fire and suppress it with limited-impact means such as fire extinguishers or simply cutting power to the offending device. Such measures help to avoid a larger fire that would require more aggressive suppression measures.

Commercial buildings also employ many manually operated fire alarms, often called "pull stations," where someone who sees a fire can pull the lever to set the alarm manually. In most cases, this causes fire alarms to sound but does not trigger fire suppression.

Fire Suppression   Most commercial facilities are required to have automatic or semi-automatic fire suppression systems. While the minimum is usually water-based sprinkler systems and a complement of hand-operated fire extinguishers, often an organization will make an investment in more sophisticated suppression systems that have less of an impact on computing equipment. But in some locations, even where advanced suppression systems are permitted, water-based systems are still required as a backup.

The types of centralized fire suppression systems include

- **Wet pipe**   In this type of system, all sprinkler pipes are filled with water. Each sprinkler head is equipped with a fuse—a heat-sensitive glass bulb—that breaks upon reaching a preset temperature. When this occurs, water is discharged from just that sprinkler head, which is presumably located near a fire. When water begins to flow, an automatic sensor trips a fire alarm. This is the most common type of sprinkler system.

- **Dry pipe**   This type of system is used where ambient temperatures often drop below freezing. In this type of system, pipes are filled with compressed air. When sufficient heat causes one of the sprinkler head fuses to break, a control valve releases water into the piping. A delay of up to one minute occurs as water flows from the control valve to the sprinkler head.

- **Pre-action**   This type of system is used in areas with high-value contents such as data centers. A pre-action system is essentially a dry pipe system until a "preceding" event, such as a smoke detector alarm, occurs; at this time, the system is filled with water and essentially converted in real time to a wet pipe system. Then, if the ambient temperature at any of the sprinkler heads is high enough, those fuses break, releasing water to extinguish the fire. Pre-action systems are more expensive and complicated than wet pipe or dry pipe systems.

- **Deluge**   This type of system has dry pipes and all of the sprinkler heads are open. When the system is operated (for instance, when an alarm is triggered), water flows into the pipes and out of all of the sprinkler heads.

- **Inert gas**   This type of system is often the choice for use in computer centers because of its low impact on computing equipment and high effectiveness in fire suppression. Inert gas systems work by displacing oxygen from the room by bringing down the concentration of oxygen from the usual 21 percent to a lower figure, which slows the advancement of a fire. Through the 1980s, Halon 1301 was the substance of choice for inert gas systems. Declared a greenhouse gas in 1987, Halon 1301 has been replaced by other substances, such as FM-200.

In addition to centralized fire suppression systems, many commercial buildings are required to have hand-operated fire extinguishers. These come in a range of sizes, from 1 to 30 pounds, and have fire retardants of several types:

- **Class A**   Suitable for ordinary solid combustibles such as wood and paper
- **Class B**   Suitable for flammable liquids and gases
- **Class C**   Suitable for energized electrical equipment
- **Class D**   Suitable for combustible metals
- **Class K**   Suitable for cooking oils and fats

NOTE   The types listed here are U.S. standards. Different classifications are used in other countries.

Larger fire extinguishers are used in some facilities that have 50 pounds or more fire retardant. These larger units are mounted on large-wheeled carts that can be pulled to the site of a fire.

NOTE   The laws governing the use of fire detection and suppression systems vary from city to city. When planning a data center facility, it is crucial to understand precisely what is required in any specific location.

Classification of Data Center Reliability

The Telecommunications Industry Association (TIA) released the TIA-942 Telecommunications Infrastructure Standards for Data Centers in 2005 and updated it in 2014 as TIA-942-A. The standard was updated further in 2017 as TIA-942-B. The standard describes various aspects of data center design, including reliability. The standard describes four rating levels of reliability:

- **Rated 1/Tier 1–Basic Site Infrastructure**   Power and cooling distribution are in a single path. There may or may not be a raised floor, UPS, or generator. All maintenance requires downtime.

- **Rated 2/Tier 2–Redundant Capacity Component Site Infrastructure** Power is in a single path; there may be redundant components for cooling. Includes raised floor, UPS, and generator. Most maintenance requires downtime.
- **Rated 3/Tier 3–Concurrently Maintainable Site Infrastructure** Includes multiple power and cooling paths, but with only one path active. Includes sufficient capacity to carry power and cooling load on one path while performing maintenance on the other path. Includes raised floor, UPS, and generator.
- **Rated 4/Tier 4–Fault Tolerant Site Infrastructure** Includes multiple active power and cooling distribution paths. Includes redundant components, including UPS and generator. Includes raised floor.

Cleaning

Facilities containing computing and network equipment need to be kept clean, with dirt, dust, and debris kept to a minimum. While computer rooms do not need to be kept clean to the same extent as "clean rooms" (facilities that manufacture disk drives, computer chips, and orbital satellites), they do need to be regularly cleaned to prevent the buildup of dust, dirt, and other particles that will clog filters and get inside computers and network devices, shortening their life span.

Lighting

Private and commercial data centers are generally designed as "lights out" facilities. However, they do provide lighting to accommodate personnel who occasionally need to work on IT equipment. Such lighting is sometimes automatically controlled (through motion detection) or manually controlled through switches to activate lighting in areas where people are working.

Physical Security Controls

Physical security controls are primarily concerned with the protection of valuable or sensitive facilities (including those with computers and network devices) from unauthorized personnel. Controls are used to detect or prevent the entry of unwanted persons at these facilities. This section describes typical threats and vulnerabilities related to physical security and the controls and countermeasures that can be employed to protect a facility.

Physical Access Threats and Vulnerabilities

The threats and vulnerabilities in the realm of physical security are all associated with unwanted persons at business premises. A site without proper security controls may be subject to one or more threats, including these:

- **Theft** Persons who are able to enter a building may be able to steal equipment, records, or other valuable items.

- **Sabotage**   Persons who may enter a building or work site may be able to damage or destroy valuable equipment or records.

- **Espionage**   Persons may conduct espionage to acquire information about the organization.

- **Covert listening devices**   Commonly known as *bugs*, these listening devices can be placed in a building to overhear conversations and transmit them to a receiver located in a remote location. Sometimes intruders plant bugs; they can also be hidden in articles that are delivered to a building (for example, in flower bouquets or gift baskets).

- **Tailgating**   When attempting to enter a building, an intruder follows an employee into the building without showing his or her security credentials (such as a keycard). This practice is also known as *piggybacking*.

- **Active shooter**   Many organizations are taking this relatively new threat seriously. An armed perpetrator may target a specific workplace and attempt to shoot multiple subjects who may or may not be specifically targeted.

NOTE   While the active shooter threat is not directly related to information security, security leaders and auditors realize that workplace safety is of even higher importance than the protection of business equipment and IT equipment. Further, many of the controls that protect personnel also protect equipment. It is with these two objectives in mind that most workplace physical security plans are developed.

Several vulnerabilities can also increase risks, including

- **Propped doors**   Sometimes a front, rear, or side door that is equipped with security controls will be propped open for various reasons, including hot weather (to permit a cooling breeze to enter and cool the building), frequent traffic moving in or out, or persons going out for a quick smoke who don't want the hassle of having to return to the building through another door.

- **Key-locked doors**   Some facilities still use doors locked with metal keys instead of (or in addition to) keycard entry and have not fully switched over to the exclusive use of keycards. This can result in the organization not knowing who is entering specific buildings or rooms.

- **Poorly managed keycard controls**   The lack of effective management of keycards can result in lost keycards and keycards issued to terminated personnel who are still able to access facilities.

- **Keycards displaying workplace**   Some organizations display their names on keycards. If such a keycard is lost or stolen, it's easy for someone to determine where the keycard can be used, inviting an intrusion. This weakness can be mitigated with PIN pads or biometric controls.

- **Poor visibility**   A facility may have exterior features that permit an unauthorized person to lurk about without being noticed. The person may be able to gain entry if he or she can discover a weakness before being noticed.

- **Inadequate video surveillance**   A facility lacking sufficient video surveillance may have one or more ingress/egress points, paths of approach, or corridors that are unwatched. This could invite intrusions by perpetrators who are able to identify these weaknesses.

- **Poorly protected Knox boxes**   The small metal safes used by fire departments for emergency entry into businesses are, in some cases, not well protected. Attackers may be able to remove them or force them open, giving attackers access to metal keys or key cards (often these are master keys that can open any door) that enable them to enter the building without signs of forced entry.

Physical Access Controls and Countermeasures

Several controls can be used to improve the physical security of a worksite, reducing the threat of intruders and resultant theft or damage. Some of these controls are

- **Keycard systems**   Authorized persons are issued electronically activated ID cards that can be used to activate entry doors that are usually locked. These systems record the date and time that persons entered each door. Some keycard systems are also equipped with a PIN pad that requires the person to enter a numeric PIN before the door unlocks. This helps to prevent someone who finds a keycard from entering a facility. Keycard systems can also utilize biometrics such as palm scan, fingerprint scan, or iris scan. Note that older keycard system technology is vulnerable to keycard cloning, a technique used by an attacker to forge a copy of a keycard; this can occur if a keycard is momentarily located near a keycard cloning device that an attacker could carry and conceal.

- **Cipher locks**   These electronic or mechanical doors are equipped with combination locks. Only persons who know the combination may unlock the door. Some cipher locks can be equipped with different combinations for each person and also record each entry.

- **Fences, walls, and barbed wire**   These barriers are used to prevent unauthorized persons from approaching a building, keeping them at a safe distance away from the structure.

- **Bollards and crash gates**   These barriers prevent the entry of vehicles into protected areas. Some bollards can be retracted or removed when needed. Crash gates are hard barriers that lift into position, preventing the entry (or exit) of unauthorized vehicles, and can be lowered to permit authorized vehicles.

- **Video surveillance**   Video cameras, monitors, and recording systems can record the movement of persons in or near sensitive areas.

- **Visual notices**   This includes signs and placards that warn intruders that premises are monitored and protected.

- **Bug sweeping**   Because most covert listening devices emit radio frequency radiation, it is possible to detect them through the use of a bug sweeper.

- **Security guards**   These personnel control passage at entry points or roam building premises looking for security issues such as unescorted visitors.

- **Guard dogs**   Dogs assist security guards and can be used to apprehend and control trespassers.

 NOTE   A detailed risk analysis, including a study of physical facilities and access controls, should be used to determine which controls are appropriate for a facility for both workplace safety as well as protection of business and IT equipment.

Auditing Asset Protection

Auditing asset protection requires substantial knowledge about IT, threats, vulnerabilities, countermeasures, and common asset protection practices. The IS auditor who lacks this knowledge will likely overlook threats or vulnerabilities that may be obvious to more knowledgeable auditors.

Auditing Security Management

Auditing security management activities requires attention to several key activities, including

- **Policies, processes, procedures, and standards**   The auditor should request and examine information security policies to determine what processes are required. This should be followed by requests to examine process and procedure documentation for key processes that are cited in security policies. The IS auditor should review the entire body of information security policy to determine whether there is adequate coverage on every topic. Rather than examine the organization's security policy in a vacuum, it should be compared to an industry standard, such as current versions of ISO/IEC 27001 or NIST 800-53, to ensure that the organization has not omitted any topic that should be included in its security policy.

- **Records**   For security management processes that usually have associated recordkeeping, the auditor should examine business records to see whether processes are active.

- **Security awareness training**   The auditor should examine training materials, procedures, and records to determine the effectiveness of the organization's security awareness training program. In various walkthroughs on this and other topics, the IS auditor should ask questions related to security awareness training, such as the following: "Have you received security awareness training?" "Does your organization have a security policy?" A still better question is "What security procedures are required for laptop computers?" to determine whether employees can corroborate the effectiveness of the security awareness program.

- **Data ownership and management**   The IS auditor should inquire about the methodology used to determine ownership and management of business data. The key point with data ownership and management is accountability: when someone is responsible for the management of a given data set, that person will ensure that only authorized parties have access to it and will take steps to ensure the continuing integrity of the data. The auditor should determine if there are company-wide policies and procedures on data management, or whether this is a disorganized or undocumented activity.

- **Data custodians**   Often, business owners of information and systems delegate management to the IT department, who will manage access on their behalf. If an organization manages data in this way, the IS auditor should identify whether data custodians effectively carry out the wishes of the data owner or act on their own *as if* they were the owner.

- **Backup and media storage**   The IS auditor should examine policies to see what backup measures are required and how media is to be protected. Next, the IS auditor should examine records of backups and restoration requests and tests to determine the historical viability of backup. The IS auditor should examine inventory records and verify that selected media volumes exist and are in the correct location.

- **Security administrators**   Often, an IT department will handle the day-to-day responsibilities of managing access to, and integrity of, business data. The IS auditor should determine if IT staff are knowledgeable about these duties and qualified to carry them out.

- **New and existing employees**   Data management is implicitly every employee's responsibility. As individuals who are entrusted to access and use company data properly, individual employees are obligated to handle data properly, to keep data confidential, and to be alert for any misuse of data. The IS auditor should determine whether any policies exist on this topic and whether security awareness training covers this subject matter.

Auditing Logical Access Controls

Auditing logical access controls requires attention to several key areas, including

- Network access paths
- User access controls
- User access logs
- Investigative procedures
- Internet points of presence

These topics are discussed in depth in this section.

Auditing Network Access Paths

The IS auditor should conduct an independent review of the IT infrastructure to map out the organization's logical access paths. This will require considerable effort and may require the use of investigative and technical tools as well as specialized experts on IT network architecture. The reason for this is that the IT network may have undocumented access paths that are deliberately hidden from most personnel, or the network may have unexpected access paths resulting from incorrect configuration of even a single device. For instance, the IS auditor or a security specialist may discover a hidden, unauthorized Wi-Fi access point in an office or data center network, or the auditor may discover a network back door in the form of a firewall hole. The presence of deliberate or accidental back doors is a particular problem in larger organizations with highly complex network infrastructures that have many interconnections within the network and with external parties. Any of those connections could be a wide-open back door. Proving the absence of such a path is similar to the analogy of proving that there is no spider in the room where you are now.

The IS auditor should request network architecture and access documentation to compare what was discovered independently against existing documentation. The auditor will need to determine why any discrepancies exist.

Similar investigations should take place for each application to determine all of the documented and undocumented access paths to functions and data. This topic is explored in Chapter 4.

Auditing Access Management

User access controls are often the only barrier between unauthorized parties and sensitive or valuable information. This makes the audit of user access controls particularly significant. Auditing user access controls requires keen attention to several key factors and activities in four areas:

- User access controls, to determine if the controls work as designed
- User access provisioning, to determine if provisioning processes are effective
- Password management, to determine if passwords are effectively managed
- Employee transfers and terminations, to determine if accesses are managed and removed effectively

NOTE   The IS auditor should not become so entrenched in the details of user access controls as to lose sight of the big picture. One of the responsibilities of the IS auditor is to continue to observe user access controls from the "big picture" perspective to determine if the entire set of controls *works together* to manage this important process effectively.

Auditing User Access Controls   Auditing user access controls requires attention to several factors, including

- **Authentication**   The auditor should examine network and system resources to determine whether they require authentication or whether any resources can be accessed without first authenticating.

- **Authentication bypass**   The auditor should examine network and system resources to determine if it is possible to bypass user authentication methods. This may require the use of specialized tools or techniques. This needs to include penetration testing tools and application scanning tools to determine the presence of vulnerabilities that can be exploited to bypass authentication. For highly valued or sensitive data and applications that are Internet-accessible, hackers will certainly try these techniques in attempts to access and steal this information; the organization's security staff should regularly attempt to determine the presence of any such vulnerabilities.

- **Access violations**   The auditor should determine if systems, networks, and authentication mechanisms have the ability to log access violations. These usually exist in the form of system logs showing invalid login attempts, which may indicate intruders who are trying to log in to employee user accounts.

- **User account lockout**   The auditor should determine whether systems and networks have the ability to lock user accounts automatically that are the target of attacks. A typical system configuration will lock a user account after five unsuccessful login attempts within a short period. Such a control helps to thwart automated password-guessing attacks. Without such detective and preventive controls, intruders could write scripts to guess every possible password until a user's correct password is guessed correctly, thereby enabling an intruder to log in to a user account. Systems use different methods for unlocking such locked accounts: some will automatically unlock after a "cooling off period" (usually 30 minutes), or the user is required to contact the IT service desk and, after properly identifying him- or herself, get the account manually unlocked. The IS auditor should obtain policies, procedures, and records for this activity.

- **Intrusion detection and prevention**   The auditor should determine if there are any IDSs or IPSs that would detect authentication-bypass attempts. The auditor should examine these systems to determine whether they have up-to-date configurations and signatures, whether they generate alerts, and whether the recipients of alerts act upon them.

- **Dormant accounts**   The IS auditor should determine whether any automated or manual process exists to identify and close dormant accounts. Dormant accounts are user (or system) accounts that exist but are unused. These accounts represent a risk to the environment, as they represent an additional path between intruders and valuable or sensitive data. A dormant account could also be a back door, deliberately planted for future use. But chances are that most dormant accounts are user accounts that were assigned to persons who ended up not needing to access the environment or terminated employees whose accounts were never removed.

- **Shared accounts**   The IS auditor should determine if there are any shared user accounts; these are user accounts that are routinely (or even infrequently) used by more than one person. The principal risk with shared accounts is the inability to determine accountability for actions performed with the account. Through the 1990s, information systems were routinely designed with shared user accounts, and many systems continue to use shared accounts. To the greatest extent possible, shared user accounts should be identified as audit exceptions and be replaced with individual user accounts.

- **System accounts**   The IS auditor should identify all system-level accounts on networks, systems, and applications. The purpose of each system account should be identified, and it should be determined whether each system account is still required (some may be artifacts of the initial implementation or of an upgrade or a migration). The IS auditor should determine who has the password for each system account, whether accesses by system accounts are logged, and who monitors those logs.

- **Jump servers**   The IS auditor should identify whether jump servers or other logical air gaps exist to protect critical systems and critical data from compromise. The IS auditor should determine who has access to jump servers, whether they can be bypassed, and whether they can be used to exfiltrate data.

Auditing Password Management   The IS auditor needs to examine password configuration settings on information systems to determine how passwords are controlled. Some of the areas requiring examination are

- **Minimum length**   How many characters a password must have and whether there is a maximum length

- **Complexity**   Whether passwords must contain various types of characters (lowercase alphabetic, uppercase alphabetic, numeric, symbols), whether dictionary words are permitted, and whether permutations of the user ID are permitted

- **Expiration**   How frequently passwords must be changed

- **History**   Whether former passwords may be used again

- **Minimum time between changes**   Whether users are permitted to change their passwords frequently (for instance, to cycle back to the familiar password they are used to)

- **Display**   Whether the password is displayed when logging in or when creating a new password

- **Transmission**   Whether the password is encrypted when transmitted over the network or is transmitted in plaintext

- **Storage**   Whether the password is stored encrypted or hashed, or is stored in plaintext; if the password is stored encrypted or in plaintext, the IS auditor needs to determine who has access to it

In addition, auditing password management requires attention to several key technologies and activities:

- **Account lockout**   The IS auditor should determine whether systems automatically lock user accounts after a series of unsuccessful login attempts. The auditor should determine how locked user accounts are unlocked—whether automatically or manually—and whether these events are logged.

- **Access to encrypted passwords**   The IS auditor should determine if end users are able to access encrypted/hashed passwords, which would enable them to use password-cracking tools to discover other users' passwords and administrative passwords.

- **Password vaulting**   The IS auditor should determine if users are encouraged or required to use password vaulting tools for the safe storage of passwords and if administrative passwords are vaulted.

Auditing User Access Provisioning   Auditing the user access provisioning process requires attention to several key activities, including

- **Access request processes**   The IS auditor should identify all user access request processes and determine if these processes are used consistently throughout the organization. The auditor should determine if there is one central user access request process, or if each environment has a separate process. The auditor should identify what data elements are required in a user access request—for instance, if the request specifies *why* and for *how long* the user needs this access. The auditor should examine business records to determine how access requests are documented.

- **Access approvals**   When studying the user access process, the IS auditor needs to determine how requests are approved and by what authority they are approved. The auditor should determine if system or data owners approve access requests, or if any accesses are ever denied (if no access requests are denied, the IS auditor should see if all requests are merely "rubber-stamped" without any real scrutiny). The auditor should examine business records to look for evidence of access approvals.

- **New employee provisioning**   The IS auditor should examine the new employee provisioning process to see how a new employee's user accounts are initially set up. The auditor should determine how a new employee's initial roles are determined: Does a new user have an established "template" of accesses, or do requests simply state, "Make John's access just like Susan's"? The auditor should determine if new employees' managers are aware of the access requests that their employees are given and if they are excessive. Furthermore, the auditor should determine if access to applications requires any initial training of the user of the application, or if the organization just "turns them loose" to figure out how the application is supposed to be used. The auditor also needs to determine how initial user credentials are communicated to the new employee and if the method is secure and reasonable.

- **Segregation of duties (SOD)**   The IS auditor should determine if the organization makes an effort to identify and mitigate segregation of duties issues. This may include whether there are any SOD matrices in existence and if they are actively used to make user access request decisions. Furthermore, the IS auditor should determine if the organization performs SOD reviews to identify persons who have access privileges within or among applications that would constitute SOD violations. The auditor should determine how violations are managed when they are found.

- **Access reviews**   The IS auditor should determine if there are any periodic access reviews and what aspects of user accounts are reviewed; this may include termination reviews, internal transfer reviews, SOD reviews, and dormant account reviews.

Auditing Employee Terminations   Auditing employee terminations requires attention to several key factors, including those listed next.

- **Termination process**   The IS auditor should examine the employee termination process and determine its effectiveness. This examination should include understanding how terminations are performed and how user account management personnel are notified of terminations. The auditor should identify specific security policies to determine how quickly user accounts should be terminated. The auditor should examine HR records to see if all employee terminations correspond to user account management termination records.

- **Timeliness**   The IS auditor should examine employee termination records and the records on individual information systems to determine if user accounts are locked or removed in a timely manner. Typically, user accounts should be locked or removed within one business day, but in environments with particularly valuable or sensitive information, employee terminations should be processed within minutes or hours to ensure that a departing employee cannot access systems immediately afterward (when passions often run high).

- **Access reviews**   The IS auditor should determine if any internal reviews of terminated accounts are performed, which would indicate a pattern of concern for effectiveness in this important activity. If such reviews are performed, the auditor should determine if any missed terminations are identified and if any process improvements are undertaken.

- **Contractor access and terminations**   In many organizations, a contractor's tenure is not managed by HR, so the IS auditor needs to determine how contractor access and termination is managed and if such management is effective. The classic problem with contractors is that it's sometimes difficult to determine precisely when a contractor no longer requires access to a system or network. The reason for this uncertainty lies in the nature of the contracted work: sometimes the contractor performs services sporadically or on request, and sometimes months or even years pass between these events. Furthermore, contractors are often hired and fired by internal managers without any notification to or tracking by HR. In light of these aspects, it can be difficult to determine the effectiveness of contractor-related access management.

Auditing Access Logs

Auditing access logs requires attention to several key points, including

- **Access log contents**   The IS auditor needs to determine what events are recorded in access logs. Events may include every user login and granular information, such as every program run and file accessed, or logs may include only invalid login attempts (or not even that). The IS auditor needs to understand the capabilities of the system being audited and determine if the right events are being logged, or if logging is suppressed on events that should and could be logged.

- **Centralized access logs**   The IS auditor should determine whether the organization's access logs are aggregated or are stored on individual systems.

- **Access log protection**   The IS auditor needs to understand access log protection mechanisms. Primarily, the auditor needs to determine if access logs can be altered, destroyed, or attacked to cause the system to stop logging events. For especially high-value and high-sensitivity environments, the IS auditor needs to determine if logs should be written to digital media that is unalterable, such as optical WORM (write once read many) media.

- **Access log review**   The IS auditor needs to determine if there are policies, processes, or procedures regarding access log review. The auditor should determine if access log reviews take place, who performs them, how issues requiring attention are identified, and what actions are taken when necessary.

- **Access log retention**   The IS auditor should determine how long access logs are retained by the organization and if they are backed up.

- **Access alerts**   The IS auditor should determine whether automated mechanisms are in place that alert appropriate personnel of security alerts related to access logs. This includes but is not limited to alerts related to repeated unsuccessful attempts by a person to log in to a privileged account. The auditor should determine whether written procedures exist for such events, as well as records of their occurrence and response.

Auditing Investigation and Incident Response Procedures

Auditing incident management and investigative procedures requires attention to several key activities, including

- **Investigation policies and procedures**   The IS auditor should determine if there are any policies or procedures regarding security investigations. This would include who is responsible for performing investigations, where information about investigations is stored, and to whom the results of investigations are reported.

- **Computer crime investigations**   The IS auditor should determine if there are policies, processes, procedures, and records regarding computer crime investigations. The auditor should understand how internal investigations are transitioned to law enforcement.

- **Security incident response**   The IS auditor should examine security incident response policies, procedures, and plans to determine whether they are up to date. Interviewing incident responders to gauge their familiarity with incident response procedures can indicate the effectiveness of training and tabletop exercises. The auditor should examine some of the records from actual security incidents to see whether the responses were effective and whether the organization conducted post-incident reviews to identify process improvements.

- **Computer forensics**   The IS auditor should determine whether there are procedures for conducting computer forensics. The auditor should also identify tools and techniques that are available to the organization for the acquisition and custody of forensic data. The auditor should identify whether any employees in the organization have received computer forensics training and are qualified to perform forensic investigations. Because some organizations employ an outside firm for forensics assistance, the auditor should examine any contract in place to see whether this prearranged capability was properly established.

Auditing Internet Points of Presence

The IS auditor who is performing a comprehensive audit of an organization's system and network system needs to perform a "points of presence" audit to discover what technical information is available about the organization's Internet presence. Some of the aspects of this intelligence gathering include those listed next.

- **Search engines**   Google, Yahoo!, DuckDuckGo, Bing, and other search engines should be consulted to see what information about the organization is available. Searches should include the names of company officers and management, key technologists, and any internal-only nomenclature such as the names of projects.

- **Social networking sites**   Social networking sites such as LinkedIn, Facebook, Instagram, Glassdoor, and Twitter should be searched to see what employees, former employees, and others are sharing about the organization. Any authorized or unauthorized "fan pages" should be searched as well.

- **Online sales sites**   Sites such as Craigslist and eBay should be searched to see if anything related to the organization is being sold online.

- **Domain names**   The IS auditor should verify contact information for known domain names as well as related domain names. For instance, for the organization *mycompany.com*, organizations should search for domain names such as *mycompany.net*, *mycompany.info*, and *mycompany.biz* to see if they are registered and what contents are available.

Justification of Online Presence   The IS auditor should examine business records to determine on what basis the organization established online capabilities such as e-mail, Internet-facing web sites, Internet e-commerce, Internet access for employees, and so on. These services add risk to the business and consume resources. The auditor should determine if a viable business case exists to support these services or if they exist as a "benefit" for employees.

Auditing Network Security Controls

Auditing network security controls requires a thorough understanding of network technologies, network security techniques, and the architecture of the organization's network being audited. Any gaps in understanding may lead to insufficient scrutiny of the network, possibly resulting in a failure to identify serious deficiencies.

Performing an Architecture Review

The IS auditor needs to conduct a meticulous review of the organization's network architecture. This will require an examination of architecture diagrams and documents, walkthroughs with key systems and network staff, and inspection of many system and network device configuration files.

 NOTE   The IS auditor needs to conduct an investigation into the available network paths, independent of any examination of documents, to discover any undocumented or unintended paths. This process is explained in more detail earlier in this section.

Auditing architecture requires attention to several key details, including

- **Architecture diagrams**   The IS auditor should obtain and become familiar with high-level and detailed architecture diagrams that show the logical relationships between key network and system features.

- **Architecture documents**   Visual diagrams are usually accompanied by written documents that describe the purpose of various architectural features. The IS auditor should use these documents to supplement diagrams to get a more complete picture of the network architecture.

- **Support of business objectives**   The IS auditor should determine if the network's architecture supports key business objectives.

- **Compliance with security and privacy policy**   The IS auditor should determine if the network's architecture is compliant with the organization's security and privacy policy. This may include the logical segregation of business functions, protection of key assets, and separation of responsibilities between departments.

- **Comparisons of documented versus actual**   The IS auditor should examine several key points in the documented network architecture to see if the network's configuration actually reflects its documented design. The auditor should seek to understand any discrepancies found.

- **Change and review process** The IS auditor should determine if the organization has any processes used to identify, review, and approve any network architecture changes, as well as updates to diagrams and documentation. This is described more fully in the next section.

Auditing Network Access Controls

Auditing network access controls requires attention to several key factors and activities, including those described next.

User Authentication In environments that employ network-centric user authentication (such as Microsoft Active Directory or LDAP), IS auditors need to apply the full range of user access control audit. See the section, "Auditing Access Management," earlier in this chapter for a detailed discussion on this topic.

Firewalls The IS auditor should examine network architecture (described earlier in this section) and understand the role of firewalls in the network. With this understanding, the auditor should carefully examine network security policies, firewall access control lists, and configurations to determine if firewalls support security policy. The auditor should also examine change control records and firewall change records to determine if all firewall changes are approved and applied properly.

Segmentation and Microsegmentation The IS auditor should examine security policy and network architecture to determine the network segmentation and microsegmentation that is required in the organization. This should include an understanding of the business drivers for segmentation, as well as techniques used to determine the effectiveness of segmentation.

Intrusion Detection and Prevention Systems The IS auditor should examine network security policy and IDS/IPS settings and logs to see if they detect intrusions, malware, botnets, and other violations of security policy. IDS/IPS systems should be examined to see whether they perform malware detection and reputation filtering. The auditor should verify whether alerts from IDS/IPS are sent to a SIEM and whether alerts are produced there.

Web Content Filtering The IS auditor should examine network security policy and web content filtering capabilities to see if they prohibit access to high-risk sites. Web-filtering systems should be examined to see whether they perform malware detection and reputation filtering.

Cloud Access Security Broker (CASB) The IS auditor should determine whether CASB systems are in place to monitor and control access to cloud-based resources. The auditor should examine procedures and records to see whether appropriate action takes place when policy violations are detected.

Data Loss Prevention The IS auditor should examine the DLP system to see whether it is properly configured to detect the storage and/or movement of sensitive data and whether there are procedures and records indicating that people do respond to alerts.

Remote Access   The IS auditor should examine remote access policy to determine acceptable remote access scenarios. The auditor should then examine remote access servers and some workstations to determine if remote access infrastructure supports and enforces policy. Some issues to consider when auditing remote access include

- Whether user authentication is any more difficult (such as multifactor) over remote access than on the physical network
- Whether remote access clients allow split tunneling
- Whether remote access permits noncompany-owned computers to access network resources remotely
- Whether workstations missing security patches are permitted to connect via remote access
- Whether workstations with nonfunctioning or out-of-date anti-malware software are permitted to connect
- Whether workstations with noncompliant security configuration settings are permitted to connect
- Whether remote access back doors exist, with tools such as GoToMyPC, for example

Jump Servers   The IS auditor should identify whether jump servers or other logical air gaps exist to protect critical systems and critical data from compromise. The IS auditor should determine whether jump servers can be bypassed and, if so, whether they can be used to exfiltrate data.

Dial-up Modems   The IS auditor should determine if dial-up modems are permitted in the infrastructure. The auditor should use tools to verify independently whether any dial-up modems exist in the infrastructure and, if so, whether they permit access to the network. Access controls should be examined to determine what subjects are permitted to use dial-up modems and when they were last used.

Wi-Fi Access Points   The IS auditor should determine whether Wi-Fi access points are used and, if so, how they are controlled. The auditor should determine whether there are any rogue (unapproved) access points in use and whether the organization routinely scans for them and takes action. The auditor should also determine whether guest access is permitted and, if so, how internal resources (including network bandwidth) are protected against users connecting as a guest.

Auditing Network Change Management

Auditing network change management requires attention to several key factors and activities, including

- **Change control policy**   The IS auditor should examine the organization's change control policy to understand how change is supposed to be controlled and managed.

- **Change logs**   The IS auditor should determine if information systems contain automatic logs that contain all changes to systems and, if so, if these logs are reviewed by IT staff to ensure that only approved changes are being made to systems. The auditor should examine procedures and records to determine what actions are taken when unapproved changes are discovered.

- **Change control procedures**   The IS auditor needs to examine change control procedures and examine records to determine if procedures are effective and are being followed.

- **Emergency changes**   The IS auditor should examine change control policy, procedures, and records to see how emergency changes are handled and how they are approved.

- **Rolled-back changes**   The IS auditor should examine change control records to see what changes needed to be rolled back because of problems. The auditor should determine how these situations were handled.

- **Documentation**   The IS auditor should determine whether change control procedures and records include updates to documentation, including network operations procedures, architecture diagrams, and disaster recovery plans.

- **Linkage to system development life cycle (SDLC)**   The IS auditor should understand how the organization's SDLC is integrated with its change management processes to ensure that only completed and properly approved software changes are proposed for promotion into production.

 NOTE   The IS auditor should examine all of these aspects of change management to understand whether the organization is really in control of its environment.

Auditing Vulnerability Management

Auditing vulnerability management requires attention to several key factors and activities, including

- **System hardening**   The IS auditor should identify any system hardening standards in place. This includes seeing whether standards are periodically reviewed and updated, how standards were implemented, and how compliance to standards is verified.

- **Virtualization**   The IS auditor should examine the organization's virtualization and containerization architecture and standards, and then examine selected virtualization and containerization environments to determine how well these systems are managed and protected.

- **Alert management**   The IS auditor should determine if the organization actively searches for or subscribes to security alert bulletins. The auditor should examine procedures and records to see if any alert bulletins result in responsive actions such as applied security patches or configuration changes.

- **Infrastructure penetration testing**   The IS auditor should determine if the organization performs any penetration testing on its own network and system infrastructure. The auditor should examine procedures and records to determine if the organization's penetration testing program is effective. The auditor should see if vulnerabilities are mitigated and confirmed.

- **Application penetration testing**   The IS auditor should determine if the organization performs any application penetration testing on its software applications to identify vulnerabilities. The auditor should examine procedures and records to determine if the organization's application penetration testing process is effective.

- **Patch management**   The IS auditor should examine procedures and records to determine if the organization performs any patch management activities. These activities may consist of a periodic review of available security and functionality patches, whether any patches are applied to production systems, and whether any SLAs for patching are established and followed. The auditor should determine if patches are tested on nonproduction environment systems to understand their impact.

Complementary Penetration Testing   The IS auditor should consider the use of security scanning or penetration testing during a network security audit. This can help determine whether the organization's own penetration testing of infrastructure and applications is complete and effective.

Auditing Environmental Controls

Auditing environmental controls requires knowledge of building mechanical and electrical systems as well as fire codes. The IS auditor needs to be able to determine if such controls are effective and if they are *cost*-effective. Auditing environmental controls requires attention to these and other factors and activities, including

- **Power conditioning**   The IS auditor should determine if power conditioning equipment, such as UPS, line conditioners, surge protectors, or motor generators, are used to clean electrical anomalies such as noise, surges, sags, and so on. The auditor should examine procedures and records to see how frequently this equipment is inspected and maintained and if this is performed by qualified personnel.

- **Backup power**   The IS auditor should determine if backup power is available via electric generators or UPS and how frequently they are tested. He or she should examine maintenance records to see how frequently these components are maintained and if this is done by qualified personnel.

- **Heating, ventilation, and air conditioning**   The IS auditor should determine if HVAC systems are providing adequate temperature and humidity levels and if they are monitored. Also, the auditor should determine if HVAC systems are properly maintained and if qualified persons do this.

- **Water detection**   The IS auditor should determine if any water detectors are used in rooms where computers are used. If so, the auditor should determine how frequently these are tested and if they are monitored.

- **Fire detection and suppression**   The IS auditor should determine if fire detection equipment is adequate, if staff members understand its function, and if the equipment is tested. The auditor should determine how frequently fire suppression systems are inspected and tested and if the organization has emergency evacuation plans and conducts fire drills. The auditor should examine the inspection tags on fire suppression equipment, including sprinkler valves and fire extinguishers, to see if their inspections are up to date. He or she should check the walls in data centers to ensure that they extend all the way to the real floor and ceiling and not merely down to the raised floor or up to the dropped ceiling.

- **Cleanliness**   The IS auditor should examine data centers for cleanliness. IT equipment air filters and the inside of some IT components should be examined to see if there is an accumulation of dust and dirt.

 NOTE   The IS auditor may need to consult with electrical and mechanical engineers to determine if power conditioning, backup power, HVAC systems, and fire detection and suppression equipment are in good working order and are adequately sized to meet the organization's needs.

Auditing Physical Security Controls

Auditing physical security controls requires knowledge of natural and manmade hazards, physical security controls, and access control systems.

Auditing Siting and Marking

Auditing building siting and marking requires attention to several key factors and features, including

- **Proximity to hazards**   The IS auditor should estimate the building's distance to natural and manmade hazards, such as

  - Dams
  - Rivers, lakes, and canals
  - Natural gas and petroleum pipelines
  - Water mains and pipelines
  - Earthquake faults
  - Areas prone to landslides
  - Volcanoes
  - Severe weather such as hurricanes, cyclones, and tornadoes

- Flood zones
- Military bases
- Airports
- Railroads
- Freeways

The IS auditor should determine if any risk assessment regarding hazards has been performed and if any compensating controls that were recommended have been carried out.

- **Marking**   The IS auditor should inspect the building and surrounding area to see if building(s) containing information-processing equipment identify the organization. Marking may be visible on the building itself but also on signs or parking stickers on vehicles.

Auditing Physical Access Controls

Auditing physical access controls requires attention to several key factors discussed in this section.

Physical Barriers   This category includes fencing, walls, barbed/razor wire, bollards, sally ports, and crash gates. The IS auditor needs to understand how these are used to control access to the facility and determine their effectiveness.

Surveillance   The IS auditor needs to understand how video and human surveillance are used to control and monitor access. He or she needs to understand how (and if) video is recorded and reviewed and if it is effective in preventing or detecting incidents.

Guards and Dogs   The IS auditor needs to understand the use and effectiveness of security guards and guard dogs. Processes, policies, procedures, and records should be examined to understand required activities and how they are carried out.

Keycard Systems   The IS auditor needs to understand how keycard systems are used to control access to the facility. Some points to consider include

- **Controls**   Whether additional controls such as PIN pads or biometrics are utilized for critical locations
- **Work zones**   Whether the facility is divided into security zones and which persons are permitted to access which zones
- **Records**   Whether keycard systems record personnel movement
- **Provisioning**   What processes and procedures are used to issue keycards to employees (see the earlier section, "Auditing Logical Access Controls," for more details)
- **Monitoring**   What processes and records are in place to monitor the keycard system for access violations

- **Access reviews** Whether the organization performs reviews of access logs and user access lists
- **Visitors** How visitors are handled in terms of building access
- **Incidents** What procedures are in place to respond to access incidents

Chapter Review

Information security management is concerned with the identification and protection of valuable and sensitive assets. Security management begins with executive support of the organization's information security program, including the development and enforcement of an organization-wide information security policy. Several processes also support security management, including security monitoring, auditing, security awareness training, incident response procedures, data classification, vulnerability management, service provider management, and corrective and preventive action processes.

Security roles and responsibilities need to be explicitly developed and communicated. Managers and staff need to demonstrate knowledge of their roles and responsibilities through proper decisions and actions.

Access management is a critical activity in a security management program. Access controls are often the only thing standing between valuable or sensitive information and parties who want to access it. Access management consists of several separate but related processes, including user access management, network access management, and access log review.

Computers are used as instruments of crimes, can be used to support criminal activity, and are the target of crimes. Criminal activities are a threat to organizations, whether the activity is espionage, data theft, fraud, or sabotage.

Several techniques are used to protect sensitive and valuable information from disclosure to unauthorized parties. These techniques include user access controls, network access controls, anti-malware, intrusion detection/prevention systems, data loss prevention systems, cloud access security brokers, system and network hardening, and encryption. Many threats exist that require a variety of countermeasures, many of which require continuous vigilance and effort.

Physical and environmental controls are required to safeguard the physical safety and reliability of computing and network equipment. These controls include power system improvements; heating, cooling, and humidity controls; fire control systems; and physical access controls, such as keycard systems, fences, walls, and video surveillance.

Quick Review

- The foundation of an effective information security program is an information security policy that includes executive support and well-defined roles and responsibilities.
- A security awareness program is used to communicate security policy, procedures, and other security-related information to an organization's employees. Security training should be administered upon hire and regularly thereafter.

- An organization must continuously monitor and periodically audit its processes and systems to ensure that security controls effectively protect information systems and assets.

- A data classification program defines levels of sensitivity and handling procedures for each classification level.

- Access controls are used to control access to programs and data. Access control methods include authentication, authorization, access control lists, and encryption, as well as physical access controls. Access controls are usually implemented in several technology layers, including physical, operating system, database, and application. Multifactor authentication is used in higher risk scenarios. Because access controls are subject to a variety of threats, they should be regularly tested to ensure that they remain effective.

- Facility access controls should be designed to meet the organization's requirements for workplace safety and for the protection of sensitive information as well as business and IT equipment.

- Third-party service organizations that store, transmit, or process an organization's information should be required to implement controls that result in a level of risk that is the same as or lower than if the organization managed the information itself. Organizations need to determine periodically whether third parties' controls continue to be effective.

- An organization should implement controls to ensure that its personnel have an appropriate background prior to employment and that their behavior is monitored and controlled during employment.

- Organizations need to implement controls to prevent and processes to respond to computer crimes and security incidents. Response processes should be periodically tested. Some personnel should be trained in forensic investigation techniques or an outside forensic services firm put on retainer.

- Stored information needs to be protected through several controls, including access controls and logging, sound user access management processes, patch management, vulnerability management, web filtering, intrusion detection and prevention systems, cloud access security brokers, anti-malware, system hardening, and backup.

- Organizations need to implement effective network security controls, including firewalls and other access controls, protection of mobile devices, encryption of sensitive communications, protection of wireless networks, and prevention of information leakage, all to control access and prevent or detect security incidents.

- Organizations need to implement effective controls to assure high-integrity environments for their computer systems and networks. These controls include power conditioning and backup power systems, temperature and humidity control, and fire detection and suppression systems.

Questions

1. A fire sprinkler system has water in its pipes, and sprinkler heads emit water only if the ambient temperature reaches 220°F. What type of system is this?

    A. Deluge

    B. Post-action

    C. Wet pipe

    D. Pre-action

2. An organization is building a data center in an area frequented by power outages. The organization cannot tolerate power outages. What power system controls should be selected?

    A. Uninterruptible power supply and electric generator

    B. Uninterruptible power supply and batteries

    C. Electric generator

    D. Electric generator and line conditioning

3. An auditor has discovered several errors in user account management: many terminated employees' computer accounts are still active. What is the best course of action?

    A. Improve the employee termination process.

    B. Shift responsibility for employee terminations to another group.

    C. Audit the process more frequently.

    D. Improve the employee termination process and audit the process more frequently.

4. An auditor has discovered that several administrators in an application share an administrative account. What course of action should the auditor recommend?

    A. Implement activity logging on the administrative account.

    B. Use several named administrative accounts that are not shared.

    C. Implement a host-based intrusion detection system.

    D. Require each administrator to sign nondisclosure and acceptable-use agreements.

5. An organization that has experienced a sudden increase in its long-distance charges has asked an auditor to investigate. What activity is the auditor likely to suspect is responsible for this?

    A. Employees making more long-distance calls

    B. Toll fraud

    C. PBX malfunction

    D. Malware in the PBX

6. An auditor is examining a key management process and has found that the IT department is not following its split-custody procedure. What is the likely result of this failure?

   A. One or more individuals are in possession of the entire password for an encryption key.

   B. One or more individuals are in possession of encrypted files.

   C. Backup tapes are not being stored at an off-site facility.

   D. Two or more employees are sharing an administrative account.

7. A developer is updating an application that saves passwords in plaintext. What is the best method for securely storing passwords?

   A. Encrypted with each user's public key

   B. Encrypted with a public key

   C. Encrypted with a private key

   D. Hashed

8. An organization experiences frequent malware infections on end-user workstations that are received through e-mail, despite the fact that workstations have anti-malware software. What is the best measure for reducing malware?

   A. Anti-malware software on web proxy servers

   B. Firewalls

   C. Anti-malware software on e-mail servers

   D. Intrusion prevention systems

9. An auditor has reviewed the access privileges of some employees and has discovered that employees with longer terms of service have excessive privileges. What can the auditor conclude from this?

   A. Employee privileges are not being removed when they transfer from one position to another.

   B. Long-time employees are able to guess other users' passwords successfully and add to their privileges.

   C. Long-time employees' passwords should be set to expire more frequently.

   D. The organization's termination process is ineffective.

10. An organization wants to reduce the number of user IDs and passwords that its employees need to remember. What is the best available solution to this problem?

    A. Password vaults for storing user IDs and passwords

    B. Token authentication

    C. Single sign-on

    D. Reduced sign-on

11. An IS auditor has discovered that an employee has installed a Wi-Fi access point in his cube. What action should the IS auditor take?

   A. The IS auditor should include this in his audit report.

   B. The IS auditor should immediately report this as a high-risk situation.

   C. The IS auditor should ask the employee to turn off the Wi-Fi access point when it is not being used.

   D. The IS auditor should test the Wi-Fi access point to see whether it properly authenticates users.

12. An auditor is examining an organization's data loss prevention (DLP) system. The DLP system is recording instances of sensitive information that is leaving the organization. There are no records of actions taken. What should the IS auditor recommend?

   A. That management appoint a party responsible for taking action when the DLP system detects that sensitive information is leaving the organization

   B. That management develop procedures for responding to DLP system alerts

   C. That management discontinue use of the DLP system since no one is taking action

   D. That the DLP system be reconfigured to stop issuing alerts

13. An organization's remote access requires a user ID and one-time password token. What weakness does this scheme have?

   A. Someone who finds a one-time password token could log in as the user by guessing the password.

   B. Someone who finds a one-time password token could log in as the user by guessing the user ID.

   C. Someone who knows the user ID could derive the password.

   D. Someone who is able to eavesdrop on the authentication can log in later using a replay attack.

14. An organization has configured its applications to utilize an LDAP server for authentication. The organization has set up

   A. Automatic sign-on

   B. LDAP sign-on

   C. Single sign-on

   D. Reduced sign-on

15. An organization has hundreds of remote locations containing valuable equipment and needs to enact a secure access control system. The locations do not have electricity. What is the best choice for an access control method that can be implemented at these locations?

   A. Keycards

   B. Metal keys

   C. Cipher locks

   D. Video surveillance

Answers

1. **C.** A wet pipe fire sprinkler system is charged with water and will discharge water out of any sprinkler head whose fuse has reached a preset temperature.

2. **A.** The best solution is an electric generator and an uninterruptible power supply (UPS). A UPS responds to a power outage by providing continuous electric power without interruption. An electric generator provides backup power for extended periods.

3. **D.** The best course of action is to improve the employee termination process to reduce the number of exceptions. For a time, the process should be audited more frequently to make sure that the improvement is effective.

4. **B.** Several separate administrative accounts should be used. This will enforce accountability for each administrator's actions.

5. **B.** The auditor is most likely to suspect that intruders have discovered a vulnerability in the organization's PBX and are committing toll fraud.

6. **A.** Someone may be in possession of the entire password for an encryption key. For instance, split custody requires that a password be broken into two or more parts, where each part is in possession of a unique individual. This prevents any one individual from having an entire password.

7. **D.** Passwords should be stored as a hash. This makes it nearly impossible for any person to retrieve a password, which could lead to account compromise.

8. **C.** Implementing anti-malware software on e-mail servers will provide an effective defense-in-depth, which should help to reduce the number of malware attacks on end-user workstations.

9. **A.** User privileges are not being removed from their old position when they transfer to a new position. This results in employees with excessive privileges.

10. **D.** The most direct solution to the problem of too many user credentials is reduced sign-on. This provides a single authentication service (such as LDAP or Active Directory) that many applications can use for centralized user authentication.

11. **B.** Finding an unauthorized access point is a high-risk situation that the IS auditor should report immediately to management.

12. **A.** An organization using a DLP system should be acting on alerts that the DLP system generates in order to curb employee and system behavior.

13. **B.** Someone who finds a one-time password token and then tries to log in to a system and discovers that the site does not request a password could guess the user ID and possibly be able to log in to the system.

14. **D.** Reduced sign-on is the term used to describe an environment where many different systems use a centralized authentication server (such as LDAP).

15. **C.** The best choice for an access control system for many remote locations is cipher locks. They do not require a power supply or remote connectivity, but they can be configured with a different combination for each user, and some retain a memory of which persons used them.

Conducting a Professional Audit

This appendix discusses the following topics:

- Auditing in the real world
- Carrying out the IS audit cycle
- Internal audits versus external audits
- Ethics and independence
- Writing audit reports

The goals and structure of this appendix are slightly different from the rest of this book. Whereas Chapters 1 through 6 convey information to the CISA candidate, in this appendix the focus shifts to the professional world of the information systems (IS) auditor. It addresses the nature of different professional engagements common to IS auditors. I review the stages of, and responsibilities involved in, performing a risk-based IS audit for both internal and external auditors. This appendix also serves to introduce and frame examples of professional situations that may challenge an auditor.

This appendix reviews the process of performing an IS audit, and in doing so, it identifies how sections of the study materials in this book can be applied in the real world. By bringing the subject of conducting an IS audit "up a level," I provide associations between concepts found in the main chapters in this book so you have real-life examples of a number of these concepts. These real-world descriptions should help solidify material you learned from the rest of the book, and should hopefully assist you in recalling information while studying and sitting for the test.

Further, you can use this appendix as a guide (or adapted to create a checklist) when performing or participating in an IS audit. The material here is based on methods used in professional environments that have succeeded in achieving high client satisfaction ratings and delivering quality audits.

Finally, this appendix is designed to benefit both the auditor and the auditee. The more familiar the organization is with the audit process, the better the experience for everyone, and the better the outcome.

To employ an automotive metaphor, the study material in the main chapters of this book may teach you about how a vehicle functions and relates to the road, while this appendix teaches you about driving.

Understanding the Audit Cycle

The IS audit cycle is central to the profession of an IS auditor. The cycle itself could be executed by a single auditor, or the responsibilities could be distributed to individuals making up an audit team. In some professional situations, one or more sections discussed here may be unnecessary. The IS audit cycle described here is not the *only* cycle an IS auditor may perform, as the needs of different situations may require alternative procedures or approaches.

Candidates for the CISA exam will have had some experience with IS auditing, but not all candidates will have had visibility into the whole end-to-end business process. Here, the stages of the cycle are illustrated as they would be considered by someone managing a professional audit.

For IS auditors early in their professional career, this appendix unveils some of the stages that their supervisors may perform. Understanding these phases will help new auditors see the big picture, deliver meaningful work, and hopefully hasten their advancement.

How the IS Audit Cycle Is Discussed

Some components of an IS audit cycle are uniform, regardless of the size of the client and the scope of the audit. Each stage discussed is a valid consideration during the course of performing a moderately complex audit project. This appendix provides a relevant audit skeleton, regardless of whether the auditor serves as an internal auditor within an organization or is brought in from outside the organization being audited. This appendix is relevant for working on a variety of audit services, including PCI, SOC1/SOC2, SOX, OMB Circular A-123 auditing, financial audits, internal audits, report writing, compliance audits, and other services.

Although the focus is on executing an audit involving controls testing, many project stages will apply when performing other projects where an IS auditor's skills are required. It is not meant to be a complete reference when a project's needs go beyond the scope of this appendix. Additional procedures will be required to deliver services supporting other functions, such as enterprise-wide risk assessments, project life cycle evaluations, and disaster recovery planning.

For the sake of "telling the story," terms from outside of the CISA exam terminology are introduced in this appendix.

NOTE I will most often use the term "control testing," which is synonymous with auditing. "Testing" is the IS auditor's vernacular for auditing. It simply means to put a control to the test to see whether it is designed properly and operating effectively. The effectiveness of a control is the opinion that the IS auditor develops after performing a test. The outcome of the test of a control will help the auditor know whether the control is being operated properly and that it contributes to the integrity of the control objective.

"Client" and Other Terms in This Appendix

To ensure that the examples in this appendix are clear to the reader, this section explains how an experienced auditor's vernacular employs the versatile term "client" contextually. In this appendix, the terms "client" and "client organization" refer to the auditee business entity or departments within an audit project's scope.

- **Client**   The organization, department(s), and individual persons being audited
- **Client organization**   The broader legal entity being audited; in some cases, this can be defined as subdepartments within a larger organization

To say "in front of the client" can refer to being with the client outside the building, in a meeting, or sitting with a control owner.

More specific terms are employed for parties encountered within client organizations. These terms will assist in this discussion of the IS auditing process. In this appendix, I use the following definitions to categorize client personnel as having the following roles:

- **Audit sponsor**   The person or committee within the client organization that has determined that the audit needs be performed. When regulations require audits, the lead executive—commonly the CFO (chief financial officer), CIO (chief information officer), CAE (chief audit executive), CRO (chief risk officer), or CCO (chief compliance officer)—over the group being audited is most often the audit sponsor. If, however, an audit is required to fulfill a private legal obligation such as a contract with a customer, the business unit leader who is the auditee may be the audit sponsor.

- **Audit audience**   The party that will review and employ the information contained in a report. In the case of an internal audit, this is most likely the board of directors and/or audit committee of the organization, whereas for PCI or SOC1/SOC2 reporting purposes, this would more likely be the external auditors or customers of client organizations.

- **Primary contact**   The person who serves as the initial point of communication between the audit team and the client organization's control managers and owners. The primary contact has the authority to schedule meetings and address issues, and may be provided regular status reports.

- **Control owners**   The person(s) performing manual control activities or maintaining the successful performance of automated controls.

- **Control managers**   The members of management who oversee control owners. They are ultimately responsible for ensuring the successful execution of control activities, and have a role in remediating issues discovered during testing, particularly when remediation calls for changes to business processes or additional resources.

"Client" as a Term for Internal Auditors

The term "client" usually implies that the auditee and auditor are not under the same roof. In this appendix, "client" means the auditee—whether an audit is external or internal. A department within a larger organization may be the audit "client." (As an example, in an audit focused on reviewing procurement practices, the procurement department is viewed as the "client.")

With internal auditing, though the audit cycle will lack a bidding process, contract negotiation, and engagement letters, an auditor within an organization is still an independent party. Within this appendix, if there are points in the auditing process where there is a recognizable difference between performing work internally as opposed to externally, the difference is noted.

Overview of the IS Audit Cycle

This section describes the IS audit cycle and covers background information that may be pertinent to an auditor's engagement. Included is a discussion on the origination of audits and some of the particularities of different engagement types. Different reasons are addressed regarding why a client organization may initiate a project requiring the assistance of an IS auditor.

The IS audit cycle is a fairly standardized process, in that established steps are agreed upon as providing the basic structure for performing an IS audit. Common milestones have been established. IS audit projects will involve some, if not all, of these milestones. This appendix explores the details of these milestones and activities, but at a high level, they can be viewed as follows:

- Project origination
- Engagement letter or audit charter
- Ethics and independence
- New project launch
- Audit plan development
- Test plan development
- Pre-audit activities
- Testing plan development
- Resource planning
- Control testing activities
- Audit opinions development
- Audit recommendations development
- Supporting documentation management
- Audit results delivery
- Management response to audit findings

- Audit closure
- Audit follow-up

Each of these stages is covered in more detail within this section.

Project Origination

This section addresses the origination of IS audit projects. Project origination is the beginning of the IS audit cycle. The following service areas are included in this discussion, although some of these service areas are not fully covered in this appendix:

- External attestations
- Internal audits
- Incident response and disaster response
- Life cycle reviews
- Governance reviews
- Staffing arrangements

This appendix surveys how the need for audit work in each service area is identified and originates as a project, and it continues with a discussion of how an auditor's help is solicited and the auditor's common roles in supporting certain projects.

 NOTE Central to the risk-based audit approach is the determination of audit objectives, performance of a risk assessment, and determination of audit scope. In some situations, part or all of these stages are performed before an audit project is launched. If persons outside of this process are performing the audit project, audit team members should have a clear understanding of how these stages lead to the audit.

External Attestations

An *attestation* is a statement made by an auditor that certifies or affirms the results of the audit. Often, an attestation takes the form of a letter or report that is signed by an owner or partner in an auditing firm (or by the leader of the audit department in the case of an internal audit).

Many organizations are required to have an audit based on government regulation or contractual obligations. External auditors provide results free from the pressures of a management reporting relationship. Strict ethical, and sometimes legal, guidelines prohibit relationships that can impair independence, whether in fact or in appearance. These independence measures seek to remove obstacles to an auditor's objectivity when confirming the existence of practices and assessing the operation of controls within their organization—think of this as similar to the idea of testing for conflicts related to segregation of duties.

Examples of external attestations include

- Financial audits
- Bank system controls testing
- Lending or equity arrangements
- SOC1/SOC2 and other attest audits
- Certifications such as ISO, PCI-DSS, and PA-DSS

For external attestations services, a bid solicitation process is most commonly followed. The client organization issues a request for proposals (RFP) from external parties. The RFP will identify, at a high level, the scope of the work and some of the technologies involved. Proposals are collected and reviewed by the client organization, often including the audit sponsor and/or primary contact. Proposals are vetted for approach, skills, terms, fees, expenses, and other considerations. The party selected by this process is then brought in to negotiate a contract (discussed further in the section "Engagement Letters and Audit Charters").

As an alternative to an RFP, an organization can issue a request for information (RFI) to solicit information from candidate audit firms to understand their capabilities and approach. This information can help an organization develop an RFP or proceed to an auditor selection.

Management's Need for an Independent Third Party

In addition to externally required attestations, the executive management of an organization can initiate projects for outside auditors. It is not uncommon for management to decide that an independent third party should handle a task. Management may have many reasons for hiring independent third parties to perform audits and reviews, some of which include

- Freedom from institutional bias
- Fresh perspective (a new set of eyes)
- Professional perspective, if a certified or accredited auditor is employed
- Not employing the necessary skills in-house
- Answering inquiries by external parties (that is, performing agreed-upon procedures)
- Support management decision-making (such as "buy versus build" and system selection decisions)
- Gain access to advice from outside professionals with deep industry experience

Projects at the request of management are likely to report to a CFO, CIO, CAE, CRO, or CCO. Such projects may involve testing that supports goals that are not standard audit goals. It is important for auditors to be clear with a client regarding objectives and scope and how to address requests for additional work.

Internal Audits

Internal audit (IA) departments usually report to the organization's audit committee or board of directors (or a similar governing entity). The IA department usually has close ties with and a "dotted line" reporting relationship to finance leadership in order to manage day-to-day activities. This department will launch projects at the request and/ or approval of the governing entity and, to a degree, members of executive management.

Regulation plays a large role in internal audit work. For example, public companies, banks, and government organizations are all subject to a great deal of regulation, much of which requires regular business controls and IS controls testing. Management, as part of their risk management strategy, also requires this testing. External reporting of the results of internal auditing is sometimes necessary.

A common internal audit cycle consists of several categories of projects:

- Risk assessments and audit planning
- Cyclical controls testing (SOX and A-123, for example)
- Review of existing control structures
- Operational and IS audits

The central function of an internal audit department is the entity-wide risk assessment process. Annually, an attempt is made to identify and weigh all risks to an organization. This process results in ranking the organization's "areas of greatest risk" and is provided to the governing entity (commonly the audit committee) to review and determine the scope of the organization's internal audit function. Areas of greater risk warrant more attention by the governing entity. They may choose to have the scope of the IA department's work address these areas.

It is common for the IA department to maintain a multiyear plan (as discussed in Chapter 3), in which it maintains a schedule or rotation of audits. The audit plan is shared with the governing entity, along with the risk assessment document, and the governing entity is asked to review and approve the IA department's plan. The governing entity may seek to include specific reviews in the IA department's audit plan at this point. When an audit plan is approved, the IA department's tasks for the year (and tentative tasks for future years) are determined.

 NOTE The IIA (Institute of Internal Auditors) has excellent guidance for audit planning at https://na.theiia.org.

Even if the risk assessment is carried out by other personnel, IS auditors are often included in a formal risk assessment process. Specific skills are needed to communicate with an organization's IT personnel regarding technology risks. IS auditors will use information from management to identify, evaluate, and rank an organization's main business and technology risks. The outcome of this process may result in IT-related specific audits within the IA department's audit plan. The governing entity may select areas that are financial or operational and that are heavily supported by information systems.

Internal audits may be launched using a project charter, which formalizes the project to audit sponsors, the auditors, and the managers of the department(s) subject to the audit.

 NOTE Some governing entities may not have staff that understands technology risks. IS auditors may find they are educating governing entities on the nature of the risks they face.

Cyclical Controls Testing   A great deal of effort has recently been expended getting organizations to execute a controls testing cycle. Most frequently, these practices are supporting the integrity of controls in financially relevant processes. Public corporations have needed to comply with Sarbanes-Oxley Section 404 requirements, and U.S. government organizations have been subject to OMB Circular A-123, compliance with the Federal Information Security Management Act (FISMA), and other similar requirements. Countries outside of the United States have instituted similar controls testing requirements for publicly traded companies and governmental organizations. Many industries, such as banking, insurance, and health care, are likewise required to perform control testing due to industry-specific regulations.

Financial leadership is required to affirm that controls testing cycles are operating successfully and that controls surrounding financial reporting are operating effectively. This requirement includes control testing by qualified and independent auditors (common regulations require that a portion of the control testing require using an external IS auditor).

Organizations employ software tools to assist with tracking controls testing. These systems track the execution and success of control tests performed as part of a testing cycle and can frequently manage to archive supporting evidence. Organizations may employ IS auditors to implement a system for tracking controls testing.

Many organizations have functioning internal audit departments. Most internal auditors come from a financial background and have limited knowledge of the practice of IS auditing. Organizations that lack an existing internal audit department may outsource their whole internal audit function via the RFP process. IA departments may seek to augment their staff with IS auditors to cover internal shortcomings.

Establishing Controls Testing Cycles   Young or growing organizations may not have established or documented internal controls testing cycles. IS auditors, working in conjunction with individuals focused on manual controls, will participate in the establishment of controls testing. The auditor produces documentation of controls through a series of meetings with management. During the process, auditors will develop process and controls documentation and confirm their accuracy with control owners through the performance of control walkthroughs.

These engagements are likely to occur when companies prepare to go public. Such companies need to comply with Sarbanes-Oxley Section 404 requirements, which involve documenting controls and performing a test of existence, also known as a "test set of 1" or a "walkthrough," for each identified key control.

Private companies will maintain SOX-equivalent documentation to retain the option of seeking public financing, or when lenders or private investors require it. Many organizations will find external resources to assist in the documentation and testing of applicable internal controls.

When auditors are bidding on engagements for establishing controls testing cycles, there are uncertainties regarding the amount of time this process will take. Factors that may add unexpected amounts of time include

- Functions prove more complex or disorganized.

- Documentation provided by management could be out of date.

- Auditors may be needed to produce control procedures where none exist.

- Control weaknesses and failures may be uncovered, requiring unplanned remediation.

- Fraud may be uncovered, resulting in project interruptions and potential turnover of control owners.

If management has documented procedures or experience with controls testing, this process will take less effort on the part of auditors.

 NOTE Budgets and fee arrangements for these engagements should keep in mind how the degree of effort required may not be uncovered until auditors are in the field.

Reviewing Existing Controls   Control structures change as an organization and the regulatory landscape change. Outside the organization, a change in regulations may change the focus of certain processes and controls testing. Guidance covering SOX and A-123 auditing has changed over time. For example, changes over time by the American Institute of Certified Public Accountants (AICPA) and other organizations have allowed a greater degree of reliance upon monitoring controls. Within an organization, business objectives may change, and with them the technologies and procedures. New systems or new lines of business may change which controls are most material. IS auditors are often asked to review and update the individual controls within a controls testing cycle. They will update wording and may advise management on how to bring the controls testing closer in line with external guidance.

Early SOX compliance efforts often led to long lists of control activities that would be considered excessive by today's standards. Older control structures predate more recent directives, causing an excessive operational and testing burden for the organization. Business, process, and technology changes may have left parts of a control structure obsolete or not yet included. Organizations often seek third-party assistance in performing controls rationalization—updating and "streamlining" their list of key control activities to realign their controls with both current regulatory directives and recent risk assessments. IS auditors may be tasked with updating controls documentation as an additional service while performing control tests.

Operational Audits   Operational audits are typically internal audits. These audits involve internal reporting to management and/or an organization's governing committees and can cover any area of the business. These reports are done at the request of a member of executive management or the governing entity and may originate from the discovery of an issue in the business, the annual risk assessment, or the established audit planning cycle. These audits often will be performed over a limited period, have a clearly specified scope, and result in issuing an internal audit report.

Operational audits require an auditor with experience in the function being audited. Many organizations will want to grow out their internal audit function from within their ranks so their auditors have a functional knowledge of the departments they audit. If an organization lacks an internal audit function, they often will seek audit professionals with experience in their industry. Organizations will either hire additional auditors with skills in functions being audited or partake in a staff augmentation arrangement where the auditors with specific skills assist on a specific audit project.

Audits focused on operational elements will employ whatever methods of testing or analysis support the audit's objectives and may not include controls testing. Examples of the objectives for operational and IS audits could include the following:

- Evaluate procedures within a department.
- Perform process reengineering within a complex function.
- Test compliance with policies.
- Prepare for a system implementation.
- Uncover internal inefficiencies.
- Perform data analysis for management decision-making.
- Identify improvement opportunities to existing systems.
- Detect fraud and the risk of fraud.

When an operational area relies heavily on supporting systems, it is common for an IS auditor to own part or all of the cycle of performing operational audits. For certain operational audits, an IS auditor's background with the operation is important. Familiarity with the business of the department and the procedures performed is often required. A project could require an IS auditor with a financial background or experience with certain financial business processes.

 NOTE   Operational audits requested by management are more likely to experience scope expansion during the course of the audit than other audits. The audit sponsor may determine that there is a need for more thorough analysis as preliminary test results are received. Both client and audit management may need to be made aware of resource constraints or competing priorities that may be deferred as a result of including additional work in the audit's scope.

Project Life Cycle Reviews

Project life cycles are a central function of an IT department, and project management practices can come under review as part of risk assessments and other projects. Areas frequently addressed in project life cycle reviews include

- Tasks supporting implementing or upgrading existing software
- System development life cycle (SDLC) methodology
- Asset management
- Change management
- Patch management of critical systems
- Configuration management

IT projects often involve a great investment on the part of an organization. The success of these projects can be critical to an organization's future well-being and may have a bearing on members of management's future with an organization. Management has a strong interest in ensuring that their investment in the project goes well.

An IS auditor can assess life-cycle reviews to cover an IT department from several different perspectives. SDLC reviews can cover segregation of duties of project personnel, quality assurance measures, or a review of issues tracking tools and associated controls. Reviews may be designed to assess whether certain project management best practices are followed, such as maintaining project plans and meeting minutes, performing and documenting appropriate user-level testing, and capturing approvals on customization design documents. These audits may assess compliance with management's policies in addition to looking at common industry practices.

Examples of possible life cycle projects include the following:

- An organization has just implemented new financial accounting software. Financial auditors determine the change to systems is material and seek to gain an understanding of controls in the process of implementation. An IS auditor is called in to review project documentation and speak with key project personnel. The auditor will review scope documents, approvals for customizations, segregation of duties/responsibilities, test plan records, issues tracking, and other key records from the process. The IS auditor reports to the financial audit team whether the process is well controlled, and the audit team incorporates this information into their test plan development.

- Internal audit may perform an IS review that addresses the controls in an organization's SDLC to ensure that proper review, approvals, version retention, and segregation of duties are performed according to controls documentation.

- An organization is experiencing delays on an implementation project. Management is not sure whether this is due to the performance of the project manager or because of an underestimation of the project requirements. An independent reviewer is asked to speak with persons involved in the project and review project documents to provide feedback.

- A government agency is preparing to comply with new legislation and is hoping to clarify the scope of compliance projects. The new legislation will result in increased traffic through their agency. Agency management seeks to learn whether procedures and technology are prepared for the increase of traffic. They don't have the bandwidth to task their staff with the review, so they hire outside reviewers to report on what changes are necessary and what changes may be desired.

- An organization's network security has been successfully compromised by ethical hackers ("ethical hackers," also known as penetration testers, is a term signifying a professional services firm hired to test an organization's security controls). Management has committed to performing remediation activities to prevent future intrusions. IT management is strengthening existing controls and pursuing projects that aim to institute new control measures. IS auditors are brought in at the request of executive management to validate IT management's claims regarding the successful implementation of controls measures.

 NOTE Life cycle reviews may be covered in part by methods discussed in this appendix, but some reviews may require procedures not addressed here.

Implementation Problems Problems from system implementations and data conversions are common, and management may be needed to remediate the issues. Client management may seek the help of IS auditors as additional "bandwidth."

Here is an example: A company is acquiring smaller competitors and migrating their information systems into one consolidated system. Attempts to report using migrated data show problems in the underlying data. Auditors are tasked with learning about the process and controls related to loading data sets onto the system correctly. The auditor will then test report data and attempt to identify the specific problems.

These tasks can be handled by IS auditing techniques. The more the task involves a consulting-style solution, the more the project is likely to stray from the standard IS audit process. When an IS auditor is brought into these situations, the auditor should be very clear about the scope of the work to be performed and ensure they have the appropriate skills to deliver on the task at hand.

IT and IS Governance Reviews

Often, IT and IS governance reviews are required by external regulations. Governance reviews are usually focused on management's risk management and performance measurement responsibilities. Financial auditing procedures require governance evaluations. An auditor's risk analysis could identify information systems as an area material to an organization's control structure, such as within an e-commerce company.

Management's risk analysis could also identify areas of IT governance to review. Management could request that an internal audit department or external reviewers be requested to assess whether an IT department is aligned with a company's strategies or is delivering appropriate value for an organization's investment in IT.

A few examples of IT governance projects include the following:

- Management is facing some long-term budgeting decisions, possibly including eliminating positions. Rather than determining which positions to eliminate, management finds an independent party to provide an impartial perspective on the value each of the groups within the IT department provides. Management wants IS auditors to provide feedback on whether each group within IT is efficiently delivering value to the organization and is appropriately sized.

- A manufacturing company is preparing for growth. The IT department has not changed much since the company was small. Management wants an outside reviewer to recommend ways to "tune-up and tool-up" the IT department ahead of the expansion. Management hopes IS auditors will identify key IT risks facing expansion and work on developing an IT governance structure appropriate for a larger organization.

- Auditors are asked to review management's security policies and offer recommendations for improvement.

Organizations may seek the help of IS auditors to provide recommendations to strengthen their governance function.

Staff Augmentation

When an organization is able to oversee the work of an IS auditor but needs additional resources to get work accomplished, they may opt for outsourced or co-sourced staffing arrangements. It is not uncommon to requisition the help of a skilled IS auditor temporarily to support controls testing or to serve on special teams (such as a CIRT). In this situation, the IS auditor reports directly to management in a client organization. In these situations, the auditor may perform a limited part of the IS auditing cycle.

 NOTE IS audit services will change over time. New audit practices are sure to be introduced with changes in technology, business, regulation, and the economy as other practices become obsolete or dated. Recent history includes the rapid emergence of SOX work as companies implement SOX compliance. There is still considerable work in this subject area, though it has decreased.

Engagement Letters and Audit Charters

Engagement letters define the terms of the audit engagement when external auditors are used. This section lists a few of the general terms and goes into more detail on a few subjects of interest to auditors. General subject areas addressed within the engagement letter include

- Scope of work to be performed
- Distribution of the report

- Rates, time estimates, and fees
- Ownership of workpapers
- Terms for addendums
- Nondisclosure agreements
- Audit charters

Audit organizations and client organizations will both review the contract, and each party may require specific wording. Some contract negotiations can prove lengthy.

When audits are externally required, the party serving as audit sponsor may not be supportive of the audit. In these situations, the audit may not be welcomed by the primary contact or the control managers. Thus, it can be beneficial to give extra attention to the following:

- Audit terms on turnaround time for requests
- Availability of control owners and other key personnel
- The relationship with the primary contact
- Frequency and type of status reporting

 NOTE This is not a legal discussion and makes no claim to be legal advice; instead, it is a general discussion about the contents and nature of standard engagement letters. Additional legal clauses that may be required in an engagement letter are not discussed in this book.

Distribution of the Audit Report

The outcome of an audit is an *audit report*, a written explanation of the audit project, including the project's objectives, the controls tested, and the auditor's opinion of the effectiveness of each control. Most audit reports are solely for use by an organization's management and governing entities. Reports will contain language reflecting the limited distribution and use of the report. The audit organization will reply to inquiries regarding the report only with members of management and no other parties. For example, the cover sheet and the footer on each page of the report can include the following: "This report is restricted to business use by management of XYZ Corporation and is not to be relied upon by any other party for any purpose."

Certain reports, such as an SSAE 18 or SOC1 (formerly SSAE 16) report, *are* for distribution to third parties (but only for audit purposes, and not for other purposes such as marketing). The engagement letter will state clearly the terms under which parties are permitted to receive these reports and will provide a process for getting permission from the audit organization if they seek to provide the report to another party.

As an example of contract terms surrounding a report, SSAE 18 clients are forbidden from distributing a report to parties other than those using the control information in the SSAE 18 report for management's review and to provide to their financial auditors. This stipulation means client organizations are not permitted to share this report with a *potential* client as a sales tool without express written permission from the audit organization. If management does distribute a report beyond the terms of the engagement letter, the audit organization is no longer responsible for the content of that report if relied upon by a nonpermitted third party.

Rates, Time Estimates, and Fees

Part of an engagement letter will address the invoicing for services. Many attestation engagements are fixed-fee engagements, although additional invoices may be agreed upon with time budget overruns or changes in scope. Many nonattestation (in other words, professional services instead of audit) engagements will bill based on hourly rates. Rates could be blended across teams or could identify individual rates for specific resources. The contract could identify the degree of detail the client will receive on their statement.

Expenses are usually addressed in this section. Any conditions on expenses will be spelled out here. Clients may permit only certain kinds of expenses or may ask for invoices with itemizations. Clients often select nearby audit firms that can provide resources without incurring travel or lodging expenses. Larger audits may draw resources from a wide area and may incur sizeable expense bills.

Ownership of Workpapers

For external auditors, ownership of workpapers is different in attestation and internal audit engagements.

When a certified professional is signing off on an audit, he or she retains ownership of workpapers because the auditor may be asked to defend his or her opinion with evidence. In some engagements, auditors may not have a problem providing a copy of part or all of the workpapers to management. Audit documentation of procedures is sometimes shared with management, and the documentation of test results beyond the report may be shared with management to support remediation efforts. In some external audits, ownership of audit workpapers is retained by the auditors, such as a bank requiring compliance testing from service providers.

Internal audit engagements are services done on behalf of management, and management retains ownership of audit documentation. IA departments commonly document their work in a combination of paper and electronic workpapers. Document retention requirements vary by industry and individual organization and should be clearly understood by internal auditors to ensure internal and/or external retention compliance.

The ownership and sharing of workpapers can be addressed in the engagement letter.

Terms for Addendums

Most contracts prepare for the possibility that they can be extended with an addendum or change order. The addendum can increase or remove scope, extend deadlines, and add audit cycles based on the terms of the original engagement letter.

Nondisclosure Agreements

Because auditors gain access to proprietary information during the course of the audit, they are almost always bound by nondisclosure agreements (NDAs). These may be signed by the individual auditors or by auditing firms, and they may be signed at an engagement level covering all team members. It is worth noting that NDAs usually do not cover disclosure to legal or regulatory authorities if fraud or other illegal activities are discovered during an audit. In some cases, an NDA is not signed but similar nondisclosure-type language is included in an engagement letter or contract.

NOTE Some audit firms sign blanket NDAs for their personnel. Audit firms using these often do not permit their auditors to sign individual nondisclosure forms. When auditors arrive at a client locale for the first time and are provided contracts to sign, they may need to address the requirement with audit management. Audit firm lawyers may want to avoid nonapproved language, as well as avoid having their auditors signing individual contracts with a client.

Audit Charters

Audit charters are used for projects internal to an organization. Internal audit projects will often employ an audit charter. They prove useful to ensure management's buy-in within an organization. Audit charters support the project by communicating and formalizing the following:

- Sponsorship by executive management
- The goals of the audit project
- The planned time frame for audit activities
- Obligations of auditor and auditee team members
- Expectations of auditor and auditee team members

Chartered projects will often be started with a kickoff meeting, which will help the team by enabling introductions to be made between team members in different departments. The event also serves to promote teamwork and reinforce the goals, obligations, and expectations of the project.

When an outsourced IS audit resource is brought in to a chartered audit project, it is important that the auditor become familiar with the audit charter, which will enable the auditor to understand what has been communicated to client management and control owners.

NOTE Systems implementation projects involving multiple departments may also employ a similar project charter. IS auditors may be brought into projects working under a project charter as well.

Ethics and Independence

It is important that the auditor maintain independence from the client organization in both fact and appearance. This appendix will provide a few examples; for a comprehensive discussion of the subject, refer to the discussion on ethics, independence, and the ISACA Code of Professional Ethics in Chapter 3.

Independence in Fact

Avoiding issues of independence in "fact" is rather straightforward. An auditor may not audit his or her own work and may not report on testing if the subject of testing is a function owned or managed within the auditor's reporting relationship. The auditor may not design or be part of implementing controls and be called on to test those controls. Examples of this include the following:

- An auditor has had the responsibility of implementing the new AR (accounts receivable) module as part of the ERP (enterprise resource planning) implementation team; the auditor should not be performing control reviews on this system.

- An auditor has been tasked with the daily monitoring of the firewall log. The auditor may not perform testing as to whether the firewall log is regularly monitored.

- An auditor has a reporting relationship with a control manager. The auditor may not test controls managed by that control manager.

In addition, the auditor should avoid testing the work of control owners or control managers when the auditor has family, intimate personal relationships, or external business relationships involved.

Independence in Appearance

Avoiding issues of independence in appearance is where an auditor faces additional challenges. Gifts from the client are one area where judgment can be required. Fortunately, an auditor often can lean upon workplace policies in such situations. Common workplace policies include forbidding gifts over certain values and getting permission to accept certain gifts (such as business dinners or tickets to a sporting event). Regardless of policies, an auditor must exhibit care when accepting gifts. A few examples are discussed here:

- The client organization's CFO offers the team coffee mugs with the company's new logo. Since this item has a limited cost, has marginal value, and is also a promotional tool for the company, there should not be an issue of independence in appearance.

- A control manager at the company offering to pay for a coffee may be a limited and acceptable gift.

- The CFO meets the audit team for dinner and covers the bill. This can be acceptable as a team-building event. The CFO then seeks to fund a night on the town with drinks and entertainment; this may be perceived as crossing the line.

- Small talk with a control owner about her office decorations leads to her offering the auditor a gift from her collection of sports memorabilia. The client could perceive this as impairing independence.

 NOTE This is a subject of broad debate. An auditor should be aware of his or her audit organization's rules and guidelines regarding ethics, independence, and acceptable behavior.

Launching a New Project: Planning an Audit

A new audit project is on the table. The client wants auditors to start work soon, and so the process begins. Often in external audits, clients will limit the information provided until engagement letters and NDAs have been signed. Most external audit organizations severely limit the amount of work auditors are permitted to perform on a project before the client has signed the engagement letter. To ensure that valuable time is not wasted, management waits until both the audit firm and the client have a clear and formal understanding of the scope and purpose of the audit.

 NOTE Planning for an internal audit with internal resources is similar to planning for an external audit but without the need to address cost and payment terms. Otherwise, most of the planning elements are nearly the same.

Understanding the Client's Needs

When a client organization decides that an audit is needed, they will usually describe their needs in writing and use a formal or informal selection process to choose an auditor. This selection process is centered on communication between the audit organization and the client about the client's needs. A client needing a signed attestation still looks for the best audit firm for their needs. A client has more than price to consider when selecting an audit firm. If an audit firm does not have experience in the client's industry or technologies, the auditors may not work effectively with management. If a client is the smallest in an auditor's book of business, the client may be concerned about the level of service they will receive. A firm may be selected because of experience with an area of a client's needs that are peripheral to the audit scope, and management's decision to perform such an audit could relate to these needs. Understanding the reasons behind an audit can be important for successful planning and meeting client expectations.

A client organization may open up with more specific reasons once auditors are selected and NDAs are signed. Having such conversations with the primary contact or the audit sponsor early in the audit can provide valuable information to the audit team.

Examples of a client organization's needs that may factor into an audit include

- Augment documentation of new or changed procedures
- Get an internal audit function operating
- Update an outdated controls infrastructure
- Assist in the education of a new executive
- Support a financing relationship
- Repair relationships damaged by a previous control failure
- Meet contract conditions by providing an audit report by a certain date

Knowing the reason behind management's decision to perform an audit will enable audit personnel to

- Better understand the client's risk environment
- Provide more useful feedback on their controls structure
- More accurately plan for the audit
- Focus extra testing on the most critical control objectives
- Meet client expectations and deadlines
- Provide meaningful reporting based on the results of the audit

IT managers frequently ask their auditor about how they compare with their peers.

Preliminary Discussions   Preliminary discussions between audit management and client management will set the stage for how well the parties will work together. It is important at this phase to anticipate challenges that may be faced during the audit. Common things to address in these initial discussions are

- Clarifying scope by confirming an understanding of client needs and their risk environment
- Acquiring more detailed information on employed technology and a deeper understanding of how it supports the organization's objectives
- Establishing engagement procedures, such as scheduling control owner time and requesting control documentation
- Setting expectations, such as frequency and depth of status reports and review of testing exceptions

Both the client and the audit manager have an important investment in the success of this phase. The client organization is hoping to maximize the benefit of the service, so they may identify areas where they would seek professional advice. The client representative may aim to minimize internal disruptions and ask the auditor to observe certain practices.

Understand the Technologies Employed   The audit manager uses information on employed technologies when developing the audit plan and when assigning resources to test controls.

When involving a third-party audit resource, a client's selection process will limit the amount of information they share publicly about their systems. If there is a bidding process, it may permit formal or informal Q&A, where answers will be provided in response to vendor inquiries to estimate effort. When the audit is launched and NDAs are signed, the client should be willing to share relevant documentation and information freely.

An audit manager also will be gathering information on the nature of testing that will be performed. Some questions an audit manager may consider include

- What kind of security testing is required?
- What kind of process evaluation is required?
- What kind of application testing is required?
- What relevant customizations exist?
- Are any in-house-developed technologies employed?

In these preliminary discussions, the audit manager needs to gather more specific information on the technologies involved and the testing to be performed. The version numbers, implementation dates, and an idea of the transaction volumes are useful information. The audit manager will use such information during audit planning.

Performing a Risk Assessment

A risk assessment process takes into account the inherent risks of a certain operation and considers information from within the organization. Auditors will weigh information from several sources when performing a risk assessment, as illustrated in Figure A-1.

Figure A-1   Different considerations in a risk assessment

It is common to have financial information available for assessing the materiality of certain activities. Here are some examples:

- An organization may have extensive automated transactions in revenue and have very few assets tracked within their asset management system. Therefore, there is less inherent risk surrounding asset tracking, but thorough attention needs to be given to the systems supporting the revenue cycle. There could be a high risk of data redundancy or incomplete capture of information in the event of system failure.

- A debt collection service outsources the software maintenance for their core collections-processing software to a software vendor. Therefore, risks relating to change management controls surrounding their core systems are reduced. However, because it is a high-transaction environment, data backup and restoration controls are elevated in criticality.

A risk assessment is arguably the most important aspect of an audit. Without a risk assessment, high-risk situations may not be addressed sufficiently during an audit. Management may not realize the opportunity to reduce serious risks.

 NOTE In certain situations, it may be necessary for a financial auditor to participate in the risk assessment so that certain business risks that may not be obvious to the IS auditor can be identified. And a financial auditor can help an IS auditor determine which systems controls are most material in a financially based risk assessment.

Audit Methodology

Audit methodologies are designed by audit management and standardize how parts of audits are performed. Methodologies are the procedures used by the audit team to perform an audit. They can be as simple as requiring audit scope to be documented and approved, to employing audit software and detailed procedures that govern the entire audit process.

ISACA considers the following items so central to the audit process that all audits will at least generate documented statements addressing them:

- Audit charter
- Audit scope
- Audit objectives
- Audit testing program

Audit organizations that regularly provide certain services will standardize methodologies for performing their audits. These methodologies can assist an organization in ensuring completeness, maintaining standards, and streamlining the process of management's review of audit work that is done.

Methodologies can include policies, procedures, software tools, templates, checklists, and other means of providing uniformity across the audit process. These methodologies are documented and taught to new members of the organization.

Documented methodologies can serve to govern many stages of the process, such as

- Bidding on RFPs
- Risk assessments
- Scope
- Objectives
- Resource allocations
- Comprehensiveness of testing
- Sample method and size guidelines
- Report templates
- Completion checklists

Methodologies will provide a structure for achieving milestones within the audit process. Here are some examples:

- **Risk assessment** An audit firm's risk assessment approach involves employing a spreadsheet predesigned to compute an aggregate score from several different risk measurements. Form letters may be used to communicate with management and collect their feedback on the client organization's risks. Management's feedback can be populated into the spreadsheet along with auditors' assessments, and the risks are ranked.

- **Budget** A budget tracks time and rates incurred by auditors. A budget will be developed initially in the RFP process and updated in the planning process. Actual time incurred will be compared with the budget so audit management can better understand how to plan for future engagements.

- **Lead sheets** Lead sheets are intake forms used by auditors to capture and organize test information. They provide a uniform method to represent test results and enable audit management to perform a formulaic review of test results.

- **Testing standards** To maintain a rigorous standard of testing to support their reputation, an audit organization institutes testing standards. These standards require different methods of testing to pass a control test. Testing methods are identified as follows: collaborative inquiry, observation, inspection, and reperformance. In addition, each control objective must be supported by one form of substantive testing.

- **Auditing software** Large audit organizations frequently enforce their audit methodology with software that attempts to accommodate as much of the audit process as possible. These programs may accommodate most audit possibilities and enforce that certain procedures be executed by the audit team. They may even manage images of workpapers so that the software captures all audit documentation.

Methodologies used by audit firms may be designed to meet requirements published by regulatory organizations, such as the AICPA or the U.S. Office of Management and Budget.

Developing the Audit Plan

An audit plan is a project plan designed for performing an IS audit. The audit plan, like a project plan, is a tool for tracking tasks and forecasting the time and resource needs of the audit process. It will cite the audit methodology to be used and lay out milestones and sequential dependencies for the different tasks within the audit. The plan is updated with progress milestones and may be adjusted with certain audit changes.

In addition to serving as a high-level audit plan, in the beginning, the audit plan serves to organize the stages of risk assessment, audit objectives, and the initial assessment of client procedures.

The audit plan does not track the detail of audit testing—this is tracked in the audit testing matrix and the lead sheets.

Gathering Information: PBC Lists

A Provided by Client (PBC) list is a common tool used by auditors for managing information requested from the client. It provides a consolidated list that the auditor can use as a record of requests for process documents and records, and provides an effective checklist for tracking receipt of information. It will also help the primary contact manage the fulfillment of auditor information requests. Several PBC lists may be needed during an audit. PBC lists should be dated when they are delivered, and, if possible, they should document an agreed-upon delivery date.

Initial Information Requests   At the beginning of an audit, the auditor will require information about the organization. Common requests include

- Organizational charts
- Company directory
- Controls documentation
- System documentation
- Relevant reports or other information

This information will be used to prepare for and execute the audit. The list may also identify documents that a client has indicated exist, such as an information security policy document.

A Client's Preparedness for an Audit

When an organization is facing its first audit, auditors frequently include an evaluation of the client's preparedness in their plans. A client may need an audit but may not be prepared. In attestation situations, the client organization may not yet be ready for an audit. A few possible examples of this include the following:

- A company hopes to undergo an initial SSAE 18 audit, but the control infrastructure is not yet in place or documented.
- A company has experienced significant growth. New ways have been devised to perform key processes. Procedures are inconsistent, and documentation is incomplete.
- Changes to business products, processes, and supporting technologies have left controls documentation out of date.
- New control procedures have been only partially implemented.
- Logging in key systems hasn't been configured correctly, so there is inadequate capture or retention of audit information.
- There has been turnover of key control owners or control managers.

If a client organization's support for an audit is below par, the first order of business is housekeeping. If the engagement letter does not account for providing services to help the client prepare, it may be necessary to delay the start of the audit. Some challenges may be addressed by expanding the scope of the engagement letter to include the auditors providing assistance (such as with updating procedures) ahead of an audit. This approach is, however, a tricky issue: in an attestation or external audit, this is most frequently not possible or desirable due to independence or regulatory issues—auditors can't audit the structures they help to develop.

Developing Audit Objectives

An audit's objectives clarify the goals of the audit. Audit objectives also ensure the audit complies with applicable standards, laws, regulations, or other legal obligations. Objectives are clarified in a formal document and retained in project workpapers. The objectives provide a basis for measuring the success of testing and are central to an audit report's opinion.

Objectives are developed by considering several different sources:

- The engagement letter or audit charter addresses the nature of the subject of testing and the expectations of reporting, and it provides a central pillar to an audit's objectives, which may focus on external security, operating effectiveness, or the correctness of transactions and processing.
- At this point, auditors will understand the nature of the client organization's business and have discussed the key processes at a high level.
- An overall understanding of the organization's risks from the risk assessment process will be incorporated.
- An understanding of a client's needs for launching the audit will also be considered. This understanding may reveal the goals of management in conducting the audit or clarify the nature of a third party's interests in the outcome of the report.

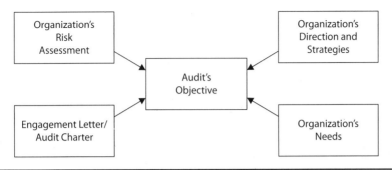

Figure A-2 Audit objectives are developed using information from several sources.

Statements of audit objectives may incorporate additional perspectives. Figure A-2 illustrates how an audit objective is developed through the consideration of many information sources.

For example, an audit engagement letter identifies a client as needing controls documentation and limited financial controls testing. Auditors are aware of new financial systems. The risk assessment shows that financial auditors annually perform test procedures on manual and automated controls within the financial software of an organization. Conversations with management reveal that they hope to update documentation, confirm the success of their system implementation, and provide financial auditors with a report that shows system controls are operating effectively so that they can reduce the scope and cost of the financial audit. The objectives of the audit will be focused on updating procedure and controls documentation for the new system and testing new software controls.

Developing the Scope of an Audit

An audit's scope is documented in a series of statements addressing the processes and/or systems to be reviewed and to what depth. It will address how to enact the audit's objectives. The stages leading to the development of an audit's scope are illustrated in Figure A-3.

A risk assessment has identified the areas with the greatest risk, so an audit scope will be constructed to address areas of greater risk. For example, testing of low-risk areas may focus on a small number of key controls when more robust testing is called for in areas with greater risk.

Similar to casting a net, the scope statement will identify what is included under the net and set the boundaries of what is outside it. A well-defined scope will assist in the development of focused test plans.

Figure A-3 Audit objective and risk assessment help to determine audit scope.

Examples of project scope statements include

- Testing addresses internal and external access to key systems, including procedures to set up accounts within Active Directory, password controls, VPN administration, and reviewing the network configuration and the firewall rule base. Not included in the scope are inquiries into firewall rule-base areas beyond those controlling external access, application access beyond network connectivity, or network penetration tests.

- Controls surrounding files feeding financial information into the financial system are the focus of testing, which includes testing controls and validating report values from systems in the revenue cycle, billing, and AP, which are managed outside of the financial system. Excluded will be any testing of data once it is within the financial system.

If, for some reason, testing issues reveal a need to go beyond the scope of an audit, auditors and the client will need to discuss the expansion of scope. This situation can happen when controls fail and compensating controls need to be tested. When auditors are externally sourced, any augmentation of scope will need to be formalized through a signed addendum to the engagement letter.

 NOTE A client organization may set scope rather than let it be determined by an IS auditor. An example of this is when auditors are brought in to perform an already determined set of tests.

Prior Period Issues   When an audit fails a test, succeeding audits will retest the failed test. When developing scope, audit reports from a prior period must be reviewed so auditors understand which issues require revisiting and additional scrutiny. An exception from a prior period may have been fixed, in which case audit documentation and testing plans may need to adjust to changes. Projects remediating issues to primary controls may be in-process, so only secondary controls are available for testing.

Expanding Scope   In certain audits, such as internal audit reports, management may have some leeway in changing the scope during the reporting period. Understanding procedures or testing exceptions may reveal an area where management needs to dig deeper. It may be more economical to augment the current audit than to perform a procedure as part of a subsequent, currently unscheduled audit. Auditors are most likely available and are currently immersed in the procedures. Management may want to push deeper to get to the root of an issue immediately.

Developing a Test Plan

When an audit's scope has been approved, it's time to develop a test plan. This section covers stages that go into developing the test plan. Audits that are performed on a previously established cycle may base much of their test plan work on plans used in prior audits. However, auditors must avoid any temptation to reuse a prior audit plan. It is very important that an auditor revisit audit objectives and reevaluate the scope of an audit for each audit cycle. Failure to do so can lead to serious audit problems when testing fails to satisfy audit objectives. Avoiding this practice is especially important in situations where new systems have been implemented, changes have occurred in the business, or control issues have been identified in the past.

Understanding the Controls Environment

When an auditor is preparing the test plan, information is drawn from several sources. If the audit is not in its initial year, documentation will be available from previous audits. Auditors who have performed the same audit in prior periods will have historical knowledge. Client management is consulted to update procedure and controls documentation as well as to identify the control owners.

When auditors collect information on the controls environment, they often use PBC lists. Upon review, auditors may find provided information falls short of an auditor's needs, requiring additional information requests. Shortfalls might be due to procedures that are new to the control structure or that have not been previously tested. It is common for auditors to meet with client management during this process.

Understanding the Client's Procedures An auditor must understand a procedure to be tested before he or she can effectively plan and perform testing. Auditors begin by reviewing information provided by the client. Procedure documentation may be provided in several different forms:

- **Financial audit write-ups**   CFOs usually keep copies of the process documentation generated by financial auditors. It is common for a CFO to make these available to audit teams when areas are in scope. These could also include written procedures and systems-level documentation.

- **Internal audit documentation**   If the internal audit department tests controls on a cycle, the department keeps procedure documentation regarding the controls they test. Other auditors can benefit greatly from this documentation when it is within an audit's scope.

- **Management procedure documentation**   Management may have procedure documentation, such as instructional or reference material for employees (for example, desktop procedures). A department's policies may contain procedure documentation. Management may also retain procedure documentation from previous auditors.

- **Instruction manuals**   When management trains many people to perform the same procedures, a training department may provide instruction to employees. Training material may provide instruction on control procedures that are within the scope of the audit.

- **Checklists**   Management may oversee a process with a checklist. If a checklist is provided, it will offer a high-level understanding to auditors (as well as provide evidence of a controlled environment), but follow-up is likely to be required.

- **Walkthroughs** Auditors may determine that they need to perform a walkthrough of a process or transaction to document their understanding of procedures used. The result of these walkthroughs can be a narrative of the process, flowcharts, or a control matrix that documents the control points in place.

Other sources may provide information on procedures as well.

An auditor must understand a procedure in the context of the audit. The impact of a procedure concerning the audit objectives is important when understanding controls within the procedure. This impact will affect the degree or depth of testing that should be employed.

Many auditors bring to the table experience with procedures performed (or technologies employed) at other organizations. An auditor who has experience elsewhere can often more quickly understand a similar procedure (or technology) in a new environment. Such experience can also assist by being available to a junior auditor who is responsible for a subject for the first time.

Understanding the Technology Environment With an understanding of a business procedure, an auditor can then understand how technology is employed to support it. Procedure documentation will often identify existing systems at a high level. To develop an audit program, the audit team needs to "look under the hood." A PBC list may have been sent to the IT department. Conversations with IT personnel may be required to identify what kind of information they keep on their systems. Possible sources of information include

- **Audit documentation** Previous audits of different kinds may have documented certain processes within IT. Because of the speed at which many IT environments change, information from an audit a few years back may no longer be relevant.

- **Network and system diagrams** Information about network and data security can be provided in network diagrams. All network documentation should be dated, and auditors should be sure to inquire about its accuracy and completeness. Diagrams can help auditors quickly identify areas where they will need a greater depth of information.

- **System inventories** An IT department may keep a consolidated list of the systems they support. System inventories are performed to different depths and may not contain exactly the information an auditor seeks, but they are often useful tools for drilling into that information. Auditors can review items on the list and inquire as to their relevance to procedures, or identify where a system's data resides, or whether it is on a standard backup schedule.

- **Management's procedure documentation** Management may have formalized certain procedures as part of developing a controlled environment. This information, when available, is often quite useful.

- **Disaster recovery plans** IT departments may have formalized within disaster recovery plans certain procedures to be performed in the event of an incident.

At times these reflect common procedures performed by management. An auditor may find relevant procedure, technology, and controls information from reviewing a disaster recovery plan.

It is important for an auditor to validate understandings based on documentation received from IT personnel.

In addition to being outdated, it is not uncommon for IT documentation to come up short of auditors' needs. A few examples include the following:

- Documentation may reveal that data entry and processing controls are employed within PeopleSoft, but it might not identify the Linux-hosted Oracle database on the back end, which should be included when testing data security.

- A written description of network security controls might identify the Cisco ASA firewall, but might omit it being used in series with an intrusion prevention system.

These clarifications are important for a test plan to be well designed. It is not uncommon for auditors to sit down with members of IT leadership at this phase to confirm the understanding of key systems and how they are managed.

Changes to IT Environments   Technologies and technological procedures change with some regularity. If the auditors learn of changes, they should be sure to address them with client IT personnel. Conversations with IT should address the landscape of current IT projects and review whether they will have an impact on testing controls.

New system implementations must be considered carefully when designing test procedures. When new systems are employed, there are many questions regarding the success of the deployment. Auditors may seek to review life cycle controls employed during a development process to determine if the system's implementation method introduces control risks. With new systems, there is a risk that documentation was not updated to reflect the use of a new system or that management shared documentation produced ahead of the system going live. "To-be" documentation could contain claims that certain controls exist that were omitted from the production launch.

Further, it is important to know of systems that are due to be implemented before or during a testing period. These can prove problematic to testing plans, as there could be an interruption or a change in control structures with a new system. Here's an example: An SSAE 18 engagement is testing controls over a long period, typically 6 to 12 months. Control objectives are signed off by management ahead of the testing period, and they include performing weekly backups. Four months into the testing period, the IT department upgrades their backup software. In doing so, they change the cycle of backups. This situation introduces some problems:

- **Lack of testing evidence**   The old backup system may have housed records on success and failure of backup jobs. If the system has been retired, records of backup success and failure may no longer be available when auditors request evidence.

- **Outdated control objectives**   Control objectives and control activities may be outdated as documented. The control objective reads that full backups are performed weekly, but the newly implemented practice performs daily incremental backups and full backups only every two weeks. This new practice could fail the stated control objective.

- **Outdated controls and control failures**   The IT department may have encountered problems with the new software performing backups on certain technologies, and may, for a period, fail to perform backups of systems hosted on certain critical servers.

Because of instances such as these, it is important for auditors to be included in communications about potential changes/updates. Without prior knowledge of changes like these, an auditor likely would report failures of control objectives, and client management would argue that failures should not be reported because they have a reasonable controls structure in place. With a full understanding of IT plans, auditors can work with the client to accommodate the changes. Appropriate controls language can be used, and coordination with management can be done to ensure the transition does not interfere with the audit.

Controls and Control Objectives   Controls are selected for testing because they support a control objective. The control objective is achieved when testing shows tested controls are operating effectively. When building a test plan, auditors organize controls they will test by their support of control objectives.

Controls are implemented to mitigate risks within an organization. Multiple controls often work together to mitigate risks within a process or procedure. The control objective statement summarizes the risk-mitigation goals of controls within a procedure. The control objectives will collectively support the audit's objectives.

For use in the test plan, control objectives are listed with their supporting controls. A control objective along with individual controls is depicted in the example in Table A-1.

CO #	Control Objective	Control #	Control Description
1	Full data backups are performed weekly and securely stored off-site.	1.1	Backup system sends e-mail alerts to the backup administrator when jobs are not successful. The backup administrator follows up on issues and records them in the issues tracking system.
		1.2	Backup tapes are numbered and numbers are kept in the tape log. The location of backup tapes is tracked in the tape log.
		1.3	Backup tapes are kept physically secure behind locked doors with limited access. When transferred to storage, they are locked in metal boxes.
		1.4	Tapes are stored securely off-site.

Table A-1   Control Objectives and Their Supporting Controls

Though not all engagements will involve auditors developing lists of control objectives and control activities, many will involve auditors reviewing and providing the client organization feedback on existing controls. Lists such as the example in Table A-1 can provide a great deal of assistance to individuals who are new to an audit or new to auditing in general, as these lists provide a connection between the individual control activities and the true purpose (or objective) for performing and testing those activities; this can be beneficial in helping to understand the "big picture" of why audits are being performed.

Developing Control Objectives and Supporting Controls   When an auditor is tasked with developing the control objectives and the list of controls to test, they must keep the audit's objectives and scope in mind. It is important that control objectives be properly phrased both to reflect the actual control activities performed by management and to support the audit objectives.

When examining existing control objectives and control activities, the auditor should determine whether each control activity supports the control objective. Control activities can exist within procedures that do not support, or poorly support, the control objective. Any such control activities should be removed from the list. A replacement control may need to be identified so that an objective is effectively supported. If an auditor experiences trouble in this area, he or she should consult upward within the organization.

With the list of supporting controls, the auditor should determine whether any of these controls ultimately perform the same function. If two control activities protect against the same problem, the auditor should determine which one should be selected as the key control and remove the other one from the list of controls to be tested. An auditor may want to learn which of these controls can be more efficiently tested before selecting equal controls as key. Management may agree that one of the controls is redundant and elect to cease performing it.

 NOTE   Different methods can be used to arrive at sets of control objectives and control activities. Only one approach is conveyed here.

Key Controls and Compensating Controls   Compensating controls are valuable to identify during this phase of audit planning. When a control failure occurs, the organization relies on a compensating control, which is a secondary measure that is designed to mitigate the same risks addressed by the key control. A good test to determine whether a control is a compensating control is whether a failure of the key control is caught by the compensating control.

An example of a key control is a formal request and approval process for provisioning new user access. A request made by an individual's supervisor with approval by department management is key to ensure an individual's access levels match his or her job responsibilities. If access was provisioned outside of the normal process, a periodic (quarterly/annual) review of all user access may ensure that user access levels overall are appropriate.

In the event of a control failure of a key control, a compensating control can be considered for testing to determine the materiality of the failure of the key control.

Reviewing Control Objectives and Supporting Controls

Over time, an organization will change elements of its controls infrastructure. Control structures may evolve due to changes in the organization's business model, changes in management, or possibly in response to guidance from governing entities, such as how guidance on SOX controls testing now emphasizes a greater focus on governance and monitoring.

When an auditor is tasked with reviewing a control structure, his or her goal is to make three key determinations:

- Do control activities correctly support management's activities?
- Do control activities support the control objectives?
- Do the control objectives effectively mitigate risks?

Auditors usually provide feedback to management on how the client can improve the wording of certain controls. Problems with the control structure could be identified, and management may need to institute additional control measures. Occasionally, auditors will determine that two controls mitigate the same risk and one of them can be relegated to the level of compensating control, be omitted from testing, or even be eliminated from management's control structure altogether.

Helping a Client Understand and Identify Controls

Client management often has the obligation of writing and maintaining their control objectives and control activities. In these situations, auditors often still need to evaluate whether the provided control structure is sound and pertinent to the goals of the audit.

An IS auditor coming in to audit a new organization must keep in mind that not all organizations employ the skills to understand, identify, and document controls. Client organizations may be seeking the assistance of outside auditors to update or even write their controls documentation. If this is the case, auditors should make sure the engagement letter identifies this service.

Certain engagements, such as SSAE 18, agreed-upon procedures (AUPs), and outsourced or co-sourced SOX testing, presume management owns and maintains controls documentation. If a client is seeking these services, the burden is upon client management to have controls identified and documented. These engagements involve testing "management's controls." If management does not have a control structure (which happens), these engagements can run into problems. Consider the following examples:

- A company is undergoing its first SSAE 18 audit. The company is responsible for providing the controls structure for testing, as well as writing "Section 3," which is management's description of controls. This is a small, growing company that doesn't have controls experience in-house. They have agreed with a partner, acquiring company, or a potential client that they will perform an SSAE 18 audit. They figure the auditors they have hired will help them get through a process they have yet to understand.

- A bank has had trouble with an information system conversion. They have data problems, and outside parties have concerns. The bank hires a third-party auditor to perform agreed-upon procedures on converted data, but the auditor is not sure what needs to be tested.

- An internal audit department has relied upon external IS auditors. Since the last testing, a new ERP system has been implemented, but controls documentation has not yet been updated to reflect current controls. Deadlines require testing be completed soon, so they line up auditors to perform the testing, though the controls are not current.

In these situations, the client may presume that the auditors will write the controls that will help them through the process. In the internal audit example, the burden of working with outdated controls may introduce problems meeting the deadline and may introduce problems when attesting to controls over a defined period. Moreover, in the SSAE 18 and agreed-upon procedures examples, there is a line an auditor must not cross. Auditors are not permitted to test controls they have designed. Feedback that does not involve writing controls language can be provided.

Documenting Procedures   Certain projects call for the IS auditor to generate systems and procedure documentation. When an auditor must draft these documents, it may take several meetings with client personnel before documentation goals can be achieved. Providing draft documentation enables an auditor to communicate more effectively with control owners and control managers to confirm an understanding of the subject matter.

The following are examples of documentation formats an auditor may use:

- Written text and lists
- Flowcharts
- Network diagrams
- Spreadsheets
- Data structure and data flow diagrams
- Screenshots
- Text files of command output

The task of creating documentation faces several challenges. When dealing with information systems, an auditor is often attempting to abstract complex concepts in an organized manner to the correct audience. It is common to rely on multiple visual tools to communicate processes and the systems that support them (see Figure A-4).

When developing documentation, the auditor may find it useful to share documentation with control owners and managers. Control owners are often helpful when their area of expertise is being represented in new ways. It is also important for the success of testing that the auditor and control owner agree closely on what is being tested. Draft documentation proves a convenient tool for capturing accurate feedback, as notes and corrections can be written on the draft documentation.

Procedure Flow Diagram

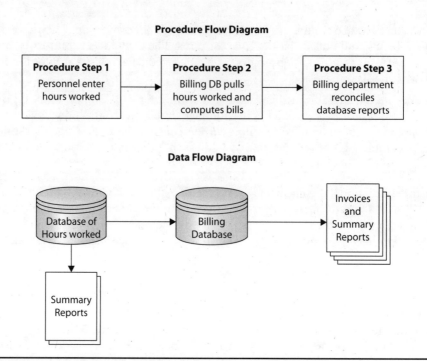

Figure A-4 Different methods of diagramming can support IS auditing.

Documentation frequently reflects a version number, the date of latest update, the name of the person who created the document, and the name of the person who performed the last review and update.

CAUTION Before a document's review is complete, an auditor should take care always to write "DRAFT" on any documentation that is not in final condition. "Final condition" would mean reviewed and accepted (and approved, if possible) by management and ready for inclusion in the audit workpapers. If an auditor has neglected to insert "DRAFT" onto a document before printing, this can simply be written with a pen before presenting it.

Mapping Controls to Documentation For an auditor's purposes, individual control activities are often included in the procedure documentation. These may be cited within the text and repeated at the end of a section of writing, or they could be identified on a process or data flow diagram. This technique of mapping controls to process diagrams is shown in Figure A-5.

One way to confirm that controls documentation is complete is to examine a list of controls and verify that each control is reflected in supporting documentation.

Procedure Flow Diagram

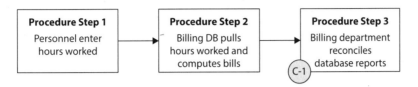

Control #	Control Description
C-1	Billing department reconciles billing summary reports to hours reports and initials …
C-2	…

Data Flow Diagram

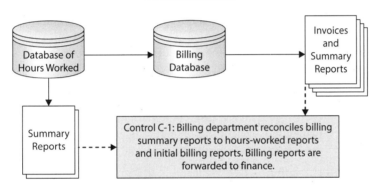

Figure A-5 Diagrammatic process mappings can visually overlay controls and tie them to controls listings.

 NOTE If an IS auditor is developing documentation on behalf of a client, the client may have preferences regarding the technologies employed in documentation. For example, a client may prefer that the documentation utilize certain flowcharting software, as the client may not have knowledge of the software in-house and/or may prefer to avoid purchasing a license to a new application.

Performing a Pre-Audit (or Readiness Assessment)

When audit management is unsure as to whether an audit program will be successful, they will often perform a preliminary review, which may be called a pre-audit or a readiness assessment. This is frequently employed when an organization is facing its initial audit, but it may be performed when employing new auditors or after significant changes to business processes or information systems.

The goals of a readiness assessment are to confirm that the control structure is correctly documented and that control activities are correctly represented. The readiness assessment should serve to avoid the embarrassment and disappointment of failed testing because of misunderstandings. It will determine whether control procedures are implemented as documented, and it hopes to confirm that documentary evidence needed for testing is available. The process involves auditors reviewing controls documentation and conducting meetings with control owners. Auditors may perform some testing to the level of compliance, such as observing controls in walkthroughs, to confirm the existence of key controls.

If the engagement plans to test controls over a defined period, the pre-audit must be performed before the beginning of the test period. Adequate time after a pre-audit gives the client time to correct issues discovered in the pre-audit. It may take time to remediate a control issue.

An example of this would be a company's first SSAE 18 audit, when the client owns the audit program and external auditors are to perform testing on management's stated controls. The auditor will confirm that he or she has learned management's procedures and controls and will determine whether the client is prepared for testing to begin.

This phase is in addition to procedures performed to generate an audit report, and no testing burden or required documentation is generated. Auditors will outline their observations and recommendations to management. Documentation gathered during this phase may contribute to procedure documentation in the audit workpapers but may never be used as documentation in support of testing. It will not serve to reduce any testing to be performed during the testing period because it is collected outside of the testing period.

 NOTE It is important to communicate to management how a pre-audit is different from testing. If the pre-audit has not been thoroughly explained to client personnel, control owners and managers may question why auditors hope to perform a confirmation of certain controls twice.

Presenting Pre-Audit Results

Any deficiencies identified are often presented to management in letter form. Any controls not in place also will be reported to management. The letter can address concerns at a number of different levels. Examples of feedback that may be delivered on a readiness assessment include

- Control language requires updating or is inaccurate.
- Evidence of control activities is not captured.
- Certain transactional records are moved off-site monthly, but testing will require this information to be retained on-site for testing purposes.
- Control practices are not uniform in certain situations.
- Planned system changes will affect the performance or relevance of a control activity during a given period.

Some methodologies involve management agreeing in writing that they understand and will address any deficiencies in controls descriptions or performance before the attestation period begins. If management lacks time for remediation, audit findings are likely. Management may accept an audit despite problems, perhaps citing that they accept the findings in a report and intend to have the issue fixed by the succeeding audit cycle.

Correcting Control Language

Most IS auditors are skilled at writing controls language. When an auditor stumbles upon control wording that is incorrect, he or she should exhibit caution in some situations. Control language is the responsibility of management, and an auditor testing controls is forbidden from writing controls language. Doing so would amount to auditors performing management's function and testing their own work. An auditor can report why a control statement is not accurate and can suggest that management reword the control to reflect the control activity correctly.

Client personnel may be unsure what the audit team is seeking, especially when management currently has limited experience with proper control language. This scenario has the potential to become frustrating for the client. The client is likely looking to expedite the audit progress. Audit management should clearly express to management why this separation of duties is important and can perhaps provide limited advice on what makes effective control language.

Organizing a Testing Plan

After the audit team has reviewed system and procedure documentation and has spoken with control owners about the control environment, they are familiar with the control environment. Once control wording is in its final form, the audit team is ready to assemble the audit's test program, sometimes referred to as the "test plan" or "testing matrix," or abbreviated as the "matrix."

The test program is often in the form of a spreadsheet. Control activities are listed in the document, and auditors design a set of tests for each control. Depending on the control, there could be one to several test actions to perform, which could range from performing inquiries with control owners to complex substantive testing. Certain methodologies may require multiple types of testing to support the passing of each control. The degree of testing required for each control may consider the risk assessment, the audit objectives, and the project's budget.

A test plan outlines the testing down to the individual task level and provides a structure for capturing test results in a central document. The document serves to ensure that the auditors perform testing completely. A test plan is an audit team's internal document. It helps auditors manage the process of testing and serves to track their progress.

 NOTE   If you are working closely with financial auditors, the term "matrix" may refer to a central document in the joint financial-IS audit process.

Contents of a Test Plan

A test plan organizes a set of control objectives and controls within a spreadsheet. The test plan is designed to assist auditors in performing complete testing and tracking their progress, and it will contain many fields that will be populated later during the course of testing. Certain fields will need to be populated before an auditor is ready to start testing, such as the following:

- Control number and name
- Control description
- Control objective supported
- Method of testing
- Date that testing will take place
- Test description
- Control owner
- Auditor resource assigned to test the control

Fields that are prepared by an auditor when developing a test plan include test results in narrative form. This part should provide an answer to a reviewer's question, "Was testing adequately performed?" and may include

- Dates, names, titles, and contact info of people interviewed
- Short responses to inquiries when a full memo is not required
- Short description of the testing process
- Discussion of determinations made during testing
- References to supporting documentation
- Summary of test results
- Testing status
- Test results
- Residual risk
- Recommendations to management

An example test plan, shown in Figure A-6, illustrates how a control may be documented as an entry in a testing plan.

The testing section of the test plan in Figure A-6 is developed to capture test results even though testing has not yet occurred. Auditors could choose to expand this with sections for capturing residual risk and recommendations.

 NOTE   A good rule of thumb is that a test plan should contain enough information about the testing performed that an uninvolved third party could re-create/reperform the test if necessary.

Control objective #	2
Control objective	Accurate import of data files into system
Control #	2.3
Control activity	Reconciliation of validation totals upon file import
Description and control process	Users receive the file from the vendor and record key metrics relating to…
Risk	Data import results in inaccurate, incomplete, or improper transactions
Location performed	IT Department, Seattle, WA
Control validates for:	
Completeness	X
Existence	X
Accuracy	X
Presentation	
Validity	
Rights and obligations	
Cutoff	
Control type	Reconciliation
Control attribute	Preventative
Auto or manual	Manual
Documentary evidence generated	Initials on report
Testing	
Resource assigned to task	Michael, the auditor
Control tests	Manual
1.1	Existence of evidence containing initials
Test 1.1 result	*TBD*
1.2	Sample testing on population of initialed reports
Test 1.2 result	*TBD*
1.3	Corroborative inquiry regarding procedures being followed correctly
Test 1.3 result	*TBD*
1.4	Inquire regarding availability of procedure documentation
Test 1.4 result	*TBD*
Documentary evidence collected	*TBD*

Figure A-6 A testing plan helps to organize the details of an IS audit.

Review of Test Plans

Before testing begins, audit management will approve the test plan. The review will consider the following:

- Do planned test procedures support a valid test of the control?
- Is the degree of testing appropriate to support each control objective and the audit's objective?
- Are all scope areas covered by testing?
- Do planned test procedures appear to fit in the planned time frame?
- Are auditors appropriately skilled to test their assigned controls?

The approved test plan document is placed in the audit's workpapers. Audit management may share this plan (or parts of it) with client personnel, or it may be kept internal to the audit team to protect the integrity of testing. If management knew precisely how each control was going to be tested, control owners could manipulate their controls to pass the audit even if they were not effective controls.

Estimating Effort

Evaluating the time required for testing is important. In the course of designing testing, the time it would take for an auditor to perform the task should be estimated and tracked. Estimates should include the amount of time to schedule meetings, perform interviews, review test materials, document testing results, update the test plan, and file documents. Experience is the best guide for estimating the amount of effort necessary to perform testing.

When reviewing a draft test plan, it can be helpful to review how many hours are estimated for each test, each control objective, and the plan as a whole. Plans should avoid spending too much time on less important controls or control objectives and ensure that testing for the most material control objectives is thorough.

It is important to compare test plan time estimates with the planned time budgets in the audit plan. If the testing plan is much larger than the time allotted, several issues could arise, such as

- Testing is too ambitious, and there may need to be a reduction in test activities, control tests, or even control objectives.
- The scope of testing is appropriate and individual controls tests are appropriately sized; however, testing time estimates were inaccurate. The client may agree to pay for the testing or may want to work with auditors to reduce the scope.

 NOTE Time budgets for testing should build in some buffer time. Some technology tests sometimes don't reveal their magnitude until testing is performed. There could be issues with evidence delivered, unexpected test values, remediation of possible exceptions, and other interruptions.

Resource Planning for the Audit Team

Depending on how many audit professionals are available, resource planning will be more or less complex. For external engagements, the selection and bid solicitation process is the first place where an audit team assesses whether they have the skills available to perform an audit. After more detailed information is gathered from the primary contact, it is time to determine who will perform what work. The most efficient work will be performed by persons who have done testing on that technology (and the supported procedure) in the past. A project will be managed more efficiently with fewer persons involved; however, more hands on deck (with skilled supervision) can accelerate completion—to a point.

An auditor may find it useful to list the technologies in-scope and assign audit resources to the technologies on the list. Such a list helps ensure that auditors have experience in the respective technologies they are assigned to.

If the audit organization has resources with "deep skills" in specific areas, those resources might not need to be included on the team in the field. A skilled auditor can meet with management to gather test materials and then "push down" specific testing tasks to persons with fewer skills. Without bringing them into the field, they can still contribute their skills, perhaps without requiring them to travel or meet with auditors. Here is an example situation:

> Anne is reasonably familiar with Unix and available to the audit team, and Xavier is a Unix expert with limited availability. Anne can own several responsibilities on the audit team, including working with the Unix control owners. When information is gathered for the purposes of testing, Anne can pass the test materials, with detailed testing instructions, to Xavier. Xavier returns test results to Anne, identifying the nature of any exceptions found. Anne is then able to address testing exceptions with the control owner and control manager. Anne has been freed up for other meetings, the testing has been performed by the most capable resource, and the audit has been expedited. Anne also gains valuable Unix testing experience.

 TIP Younger auditors who are mentored can develop the technical skills and expand the experience base of the audit team. Exposure to new processes or technologies is best done when a more senior person is guiding them and able to serve as a backup. By doing so, an organization grows its skills from the inside.

Preparing Staff

Staff members are usually informed of the project when an engagement letter is signed. Details on a project's requirements may be scarce at the time, but management may share with staff a high-level summary of the engagement, the intended roles, and the planned hours per their proposal.

Once resource planning has been completed, it will be clear which personnel will be performing which tasks within an audit. When this occurs, it is important to meet with audit personnel to explain the project and define the roles of auditors during the project. During this meeting, audit management may provide resources or web links for auditors to use when researching the company and update their knowledge on technologies they will review. If audit team members will be tasked with technologies with which they have limited or outdated experience, this is the time to consider providing training.

Once schedules are set for resources visiting the client site, guidelines should be provided to audit staff on the logistics of traveling to their location and, if possible, finding acceptable lodging in the area. This is also a chance for audit personnel to raise questions about the audit. Frequently, dress code, guest Wi-Fi, and other auditee office norms are communicated at this time.

Performing Control Testing

Thorough preparation for testing will reap benefits when the audit team enters the testing phase. It may appear that the effort spent preparing is excessive compared to the task still at hand. Preparation's greatest benefit will be avoiding problems during testing, review, and developing reports. Failure to include a few needed tests may set a team back several days. An error in objectives, scope, or understanding of the test environment can cause even greater problems.

A test plan developed with proper care will provide the audit team with a structure that facilitates effective and efficient testing. Testing is busy enough when it all goes well.

Control testing involves execution of the test plan, consisting of interviews and evidence collection.

Project Planning with the Client

When the readiness assessment is complete and the client has addressed any preparedness issues, the attestation period is approaching. The primary contact will help the audit team plan and schedule testing. Table A-2 is a quick summary of topics to address at this phase.

Gathering Testing Evidence

The process of gathering evidence should be orderly. Several common ways are used to request evidence:

- In person
- E-mail
- PBC (provided by client) lists
- Collaboration sites

It is common when interviewing personnel to make in-person requests while discussing the control being tested. Direct requests may involve an auditor sitting with a control owner observing software controls and gathering screen-shots and other electronic information as evidence. An auditor may confirm the availability of policies, procedures, and disaster recovery plans by asking someone to show where they are located. Direct requests may be made for information to be supplied later. An auditor might follow up a meeting with an e-mail summarizing requested information and what is to be expected.

Subject	Common Considerations
Dates	What schedule works for the client and the auditors? This will center on the availability of key resources and may consider busy periods in the client's cycle, such as financial closing cycles.
Availability of key resources	When will key control owners be away on training or vacation? Are there events or time periods to schedule around? Control managers are often asked to provide availability information on control owners.
Opening meetings	An audit traditionally starts with an opening meeting. In addition to audit management and the primary contact, it may include the audit sponsor, control managers, control owners, and staff auditors. Audit scope, schedules, procedures, permissions, and other subjects are discussed at this time.
Permission to access information	It should be clear to control owners what information they are permitted to provide to auditors and how they may provide it. Clients who manage sensitive information may follow risk-averse practices. For example, the client may forbid the use of flash drives or e-mail to deliver audit evidence. They may require approval prior to sharing certain documents or deliver information on a CD/DVD-ROM of which they later oversee the destruction.
Turn-around time guarantees	The time between when information is requested and when it is provided is sometimes an issue. Turn-around times can cause work bottlenecks for a client and can affect how quickly an auditor completes his or her work.
Learning procedures	How will an auditor get up to speed with the client's procedures? Are meetings with control owners required to confirm documentation is up to date? Is there a need to perform a walkthrough of the controls before testing?
Scheduling testing	Do auditors coordinate with the control owners directly, or does the control manager want to manage their schedules? Also, remember the need for lead time, absences, and vacations.
Auditor workspace and Internet access	Where will auditors set up to do work? During what hours is the workspace accessible? Do auditors require the workspace to be locked? Do auditors require keycards or other means for accessing the client work site? Is Internet access available? Will gaining access require accounts or passwords? Or training on client policies?

Table A-2 Project Planning to Audit Project Planning

PBC lists are a tool that brings order to the process of gathering test information, but they re best employed when an auditor does not need to observe an activity directly. Concise and easy to understand, PBC lists are used by client management to track information they are providing to auditors and by auditors to track what information they have requested and received. PBC lists are ideal for requesting transaction records, data, and process documents.

Depending on the testing being performed, there can be several phases of requests for information supporting testing. The audit team should be orderly regarding requests. If requests are made directly of control owners, the requests should be tracked.

Testing can demand a great deal of time from client personnel, and a client may seek to minimize the impact. When gathering test evidence, the client contact may request that the team limit the frequency of information requests to their staff. Some requests may need to be made through the primary contact or their designee. Clients also may request liberal turnaround times so as not to overburden their personnel.

Sample Testing   Sample testing usually requires multiple rounds of requests. Initial requests are made by auditors for population sizes, from which auditors will select their test populations. Assuming the sample population information is correctly delivered and understandable, auditors then submit a request for test evidence for the selected sample. Unless test results are successful, there could be requests for follow-up information. Unclear sample test results may require further investigation, resulting in requests of additional records or a live discussion with the control owner.

Security and HR Procedure Testing   Testing of information security often covers setup and removal of user account permissions. To determine whether access granting and removal procedures are operating, auditors will involve two key lists:

- Current employee listing
- List of employees terminated within a given period

These lists must be dated and should be provided at the same time. Lists should include (at a minimum) employee name; manager's name, department, or title; employee hire date; and employee termination date. Testing surrounding HR procedures (such as hiring approvals) may require these lists as well. They may be requested early during testing or, in some cases (such as for an SSAE 18), after some time has passed within a test period. These lists may also help auditors determine whether user account permissions are granted appropriately for their role.

NOTE   It may be necessary to explain to a client why an IS audit requires auditors to speak with or make requests of HR personnel.

Requests for Follow-up Information

Often, testing doesn't go precisely as planned. Certain information may be lacking from the provided evidence. This may occur when the course of business requires exceptions to standard procedures. An auditor may not learn of all of these possibilities when meeting with a control owner, but instead the auditor may find out later while examining evidence. Auditors usually need to make follow-up requests or have follow-up discussions to determine whether a notable occurrence during testing is an exception or is acceptable.

Launching the Testing Phase

Because the audit team and client personnel are ready for testing, it is time for auditors to begin. The availability of client personnel may determine the schedule of certain tests.

Planning meetings will set expectations as to when auditors are expected to complete their work. Once schedules are set, logistics should be set for getting auditors into the field (such as securing transportation and lodging).

A testing period often starts with a series of kickoff meetings before interviews are scheduled with individual control owners. These meetings serve to introduce auditors to the control managers and their team of control owners and operators. This forum allows for

- Auditors to meet personnel in person before testing launches
- Auditors to explain the scope of their audit and clarify testing expectations
- Control managers to frame the event for their personnel and to set rules and expectations
- Control owners to raise questions they may have about the process

Control owners may be experiencing some degree of nervousness, especially if they have not spoken with auditors before. Auditors will often find testing interviews work more smoothly when control owners have already met the auditor and have a deeper understanding of the scope and objectives of the audit. Gathering evidence will work more smoothly when control owners have had expectations set by management as to what they can expect during interviews and what they are permitted to provide auditors. In addition, explaining to control owners that results of testing will be reviewed with them before they are reported will often help control owners relax when working with auditors.

Performing Tests of Control Existence

Tests of control existence determine whether a control is in place and operating effectively. They also determine whether the expected control activity occurs. Many controls will pass if a document simply exists or a software configuration setting is confirmed.

Control existence does not imply that a control is operating effectively over time, but whether or not it works when successfully operated. Existence tests are often performed using the following testing methods:

- **Inquiry and corroboration**   Auditor questions control owners about controls.
- **Observation**   Auditor views a control being performed.
- **Inspection**   Auditor reviews material evidencing compliance with stated control.
- **Reperformance**   Auditor performs control activity him/herself.

Many existence tests are performed when accompanying the control owner. Existence testing is a leading method of testing automated controls enforced by software.

Certain controls testing engagements, such as SOX 302 testing and an SSAE 18 Type I, test for a control's existence. An SSAE 18 reports that at one moment in time these controls are in place. SOX 302 requirements also verify that the controls environment is documented and that the controls have been tested once. In contrast, when the burden of controls testing involves confirming operation over a given period, such as SOX 404 or an SSAE 18 Type II report, control tests for existence may be performed multiple times during the test period.

Automated Controls   Automated controls are tested for existence. Many tests involve confirming that software configurations are set to specific values or observing whether systems enforce a rule.

Automated controls are most often observed in person by an auditor, and the auditor documents the occurrence for testing workpapers. Screen-shots or other captured images provide evidence of software configurations. These images can be accompanied with an auditor's descriptive text for use as documentary evidence of the control test.

CAUTION   In certain client situations, a control owner may ask to generate control evidence on their own. If at all possible, documentation of controls settings should be gathered in the presence of the auditor, and preferably the first time an auditor asks to see it. Allowing a control owner to prepare evidence of controls can present certain issues, such as the control owner cutting corners and using images provided to previous auditors.

Governance Controls   Governance controls are often tested for existence—for example, policies, procedure documentation, committee meeting minutes, approvals, and other documents can be tested for existence. The provided documents may be subject to additional review per the test plan. If the evidence does not exist, additional test procedures will not be performed and tests will likely fail.

Testing Existence via Observation   Tests by *observation* are performed by an auditor witnessing whether a control activity is performed. This type of testing can involve the auditor looking over the shoulder of the control owner and requesting the owner perform certain tasks while demonstrating a procedure, or by viewing software settings within applications. Examples of observation testing include

- Confirming that software requires and tracks approvals
- Observing physical and environmental controls for a server room
- Noting the existence of signed policies and a background report in an HR file
- Viewing system-generated alerts reaching a pager
- Reviewing a firewall rule base to confirm settings

Control tests by observation are recorded in writing in testing workpapers, or through retention of screenshots showing configurations. Recording observations should be sure to include the date and time, as well as the full name and title of the control owner. If observations can be supported by documentation beyond an auditor's recorded observations, this is preferable. Not all client or technology situations will provide such evidence.

NOTE   Client organizations may not permit their firewall rule base to be printed or carried off the premises. An auditor may have to observe the rule base and document their review as a test by observation. In cases such as this, it is important to include in workpaper documentation specific details of what was observed so that an uninvolved third party could reperform the observation and come to the same conclusion.

Testing by Inquiry and Corroborative Inquiry   Testing by *inquiry* involves asking questions of control owners. Inquiry is most commonly performed in person, over the phone, or via e-mail. Some standards of testing require *corroborative inquiry*, meaning two persons with knowledge of a control must make agreeing statements. Discussions are documented, often in memos, and placed in the workpapers.

When documenting inquiry in workpapers or reports, the auditor must take care to phrase any statements by management as "representations" made by the client rather than facts. The wording might read, "Per the Unix system administrator, security logs are reviewed on a weekly basis," or "The CIO represented that spending is reviewed monthly."

The audit workpapers will include the record of the conversation and a memo addressing the result of the test.

Testing Existence by Inspection   *Inspection* is performed by reviewing the content of client-provided evidence. Testing may seek to analyze the nature of information discovered within the material being tested, which could be a report, policies, meeting minutes, or another document. Testing by inspection might seek to determine whether

- Forms reflect the proper approvals signatures
- Data backup software schedules and records match documented schedules
- Committee meeting minutes reflect management's discussion of the log file review
- Network and data flow diagrams are dated and current

The audit workpapers should include a memo addressing the results of testing, which identifies the inspected documents and copies of the documents. Any exceptions should be marked in the document and addressed in the memo.

Testing Existence Through Reperformance   Auditors may test security controls and automated controls via *reperformance*. In this type of test, auditors are taking information that is input to a control and performing tasks or calculations on their own to see if they achieve the same results that the control does. Examples of reperformance testing include

- Attempting to set a password that is noncompliant with policies
- Confirming VPN authorization is required and no guest account is enabled
- Checking whether specific employee keycards permit access to a restricted area
- Reproducing report values from business rules and raw data

NOTE Reperformance can be used to perform substantive testing. Recomputing batch totals is a common audit procedure in financial audits.

The audit workpapers should include a description of the reperformance test. Workpapers for a reperformance test may then resemble other forms of testing, such as observation (VPN example) or sample testing (transaction records example).

Control Existence Failures One possible result of testing is that a control being tested is not implemented. The absence of a control activity is often discovered during initial discussions with control owners or during a procedure walkthrough. This absence can occur for several reasons:

- Documentation of controls has not been updated for new procedures. Effective controls may exist, but they are not included in testing programs.
- Changes in personnel resulted in a lack of ownership of the control process.
- Controls were documented as "to be implemented," or implementation was not successful.

When controls are found not to exist, they should be brought quickly to the client's attention. If it is possible (or prudent), validate the absence with a control manager before elevating the issue to the primary contact. A control manager may be able to clear up the confusion and prevent embarrassment, such as identifying a compensating control that could be tested to support audit objectives.

Performing Testing of Control Operating Effectiveness

Tests of control effectiveness confirm that the performance of a control activity has been successful. Audits most often test control effectiveness over a defined period. To test for successful operation, evidence needs to indicate that a control repeatedly occurs correctly or appears to occur without interruption.

There are several methods of testing operating effectiveness, including inspection, reperformance, sample testing, continuous auditing/monitoring, and automated testing methods (not to be confused with testing of automated controls).

Testing Effectiveness by Inspection *Inspection* can be used as a test of effectiveness as well as existence. Inspection can reveal that evidence indicates continued operation of a control activity. To test for control effectiveness, inspection is often used to review system log files or similar reports. Examples of how inspection methods are employed effectively for testing of reports or log files include

- Confirming log entries were captured without interruption
- Reviewing changes to administrator passwords, confirming they are periodically changed in accordance with policy

- Reviewing changes to key settings, confirming that logs were not turned off and that settings were not changed at times during the testing period

Inspection may be employed as a method within sample testing as well. Testing may produce documents that are then tested by inspection.

 NOTE Gathering log file information for testing can be a challenge, as log files can be quite large and reviewing them can take special tools. A client may need to assist an auditor in interpreting the contents of the logs. If filtering is performed on a file before an auditor's inspection, it is best if the auditor observes the filtering operation and documents his or her observations. Some log files are overwritten on a periodic basis, limiting the availability of evidence.

Testing Effectiveness Through Reperformance Effectiveness testing using *reperformance* can involve an auditor reproducing control activities performed by clients. This method can enable auditors to confirm that controls have been operating correctly because they can re-create the control activity themselves. Reperformance can involve recomputing figures or confirming the reported values from source data. Examples of testing by reperformance include

- Comparing a list of active system users against a list of terminated employees to see whether terminated employees' accounts were removed.

- The control owner performs a reconciliation on reports provided by two different systems and initials the documents before processing. To test that the reconciliation was performed correctly, an auditor reviews whether the figures match on a sample of initialed documents.

- A billing application generates reports on hours worked by querying a database of hours worked on each project. An auditor seeks to validate that report totals are accurate. This data is imported into a database, and the auditor runs queries to attempt to reproduce the values generated by the billing application.

If the auditor is using a database or spreadsheet application to manipulate the data, workpapers may include evidence in electronic form. A standard, noneditable format (such as a CD/DVD-ROM) is preferable to rewriteable media. Workpapers should contain a memo discussing the testing methodology and identifying how and where (in the workpapers) the information is stored digitally.

Sample Testing Sample testing is conducted when a control is performed on a regular basis and a record of the control activity exists. An auditor will select a population of control activity records to confirm that the control is being performed correctly. An auditor must review the population of control tests and then request the evidence supporting elements of that population. This technique often involves two rounds of requests from a control owner to gather a sample population and test evidence.

NOTE It is important that an auditor perform procedures to understand that the population provided by the client is complete and accurate. More important, though, is that the auditor document processes or procedures performed by the client to understand how client personnel validates completeness and accuracy of that information.

Auditors may select sample populations by random test sets, or they can judgmentally select a population from the test set. Judgmental selection is often helpful when the materiality or criticality of transactions varies. Auditors might select transactions that relate to a company's largest clients or most critical systems. Judgmental selections may also seek to test a variety of transactions. Auditors might include different kinds of clients or applications hosted on different systems.

When an auditor performs sample testing, the audit workpapers should include

- A written description of the testing process, including a discussion of how sample selection was performed and what sampling criteria were used
- A record of the sampling population
- List of the test set population
- Test results
- At least one example of a successful test and each exception (if all test materials are not retained)

An auditor's workplace may have policies covering workpaper documentation requirements. Testing sometimes includes lengthy printed reports, and some places permit audit management to use their judgment regarding when retaining a sample of the report is sufficient evidence.

Continuous Auditing/Continuous Monitoring   In instances in which the volume of data is very large or the frequency of transactions is high, organizations may choose to utilize tools to perform continuous audits. This type of approach can be done with varying frequency (hourly, daily, weekly, monthly) based on the risk, volume, and type of data, and it incorporates the use of technology to perform an analysis of data/information. This analysis is designed with a level of precision such that anomalies in data are identified and reported upon for further detailed follow-up. Continuous auditing can both provide a greater level of assurance (since high-powered computers can audit 100 percent of a population in much less time than an IT auditor can manually audit a small sample) and make the audit program more efficient (as IT auditors are freed up to perform additional audit tasks, such as a follow-up on continuous audit findings, perform tests where the population or control type does not align with continuous audit techniques, and so on).

In instances related to testing IT general controls, technology may be used continuously to monitor items such as security provisioning. In that case, while there may not be a significant amount of activity over a period of time, tools can be put in place that will send an alert to a responsible party immediately if an unauthorized or inappropriate change in access is made. As mentioned, the use of such a tool can provide a high level of assurance and security, while at the same time enabling an organization to spend less time on periodic access reviews.

Continuous auditing should not be confused with automated testing or testing programs, described next. Although those techniques involve the use of technology, that technology is generally utilized at a particular point in time to assist in the performance of audit procedures.

Automated Testing   Automated testing can quickly provide an auditor with large amounts of critical system information. It often involves the use of testing programs (sometimes off-the-shelf programs) or test scripts. Test scripts may be designed by the audit organization, the software's manufacturer, or a third party. Running scripts should be done only in close cooperation with a control owner, such as a database administrator or operating system administrator, and approved by appropriate client personnel.

Testing programs and scripts may need to be run on a client's system. Many organizations will require that a script or testing program be reviewed before auditors are permitted to run it on their system. A client's review will usually confirm that a script is executing only inquiry commands. Special read-only user accounts may be enabled temporarily for test programs to run. The use of automated testing should be brought up early in conversations with the client, as approval and preparation for their use may take some time.

Testing Programs   Testing programs will often be developed by a software vendor. To assist a client's review of a software program, the client can be provided with the software make and version number, and, if possible, the auditor can provide software documentation.

Examples of automated testing programs include

- Vulnerability scanning tools
- Segregation of duties analysis
- A program that runs on a network to identify all workstations connected to the domain and to confirm that antivirus definitions are current on all workstations
- Network analysis programs that review network components and the protocols enabled on network devices

Testing programs often provide organized reporting of the results of testing. An auditor's test consists of reviewing output reports from the test and recording the observations in a document. In addition to the output report and a record of an auditor's testing, the workpapers should include details on the testing program used, including name, manufacturer, version number, and relevant configuration settings used. The results of this analysis are then recorded in the testing matrix. Finally, a copy of the testing program should be retained.

Test Scripts   Scripts are programs that are run on systems and that usually generate a file showing the commands executed and the results. Scripts are written in scripting languages (such as /bin/sh or SQL) that execute commands sequentially. Scripts can run a query and write query results into an output file. Test procedures will involve reviewing scripts' output files.

When a script is employed, an auditor should observe management running the script and collect the evidence without delay. The audit workpapers should include

- Information on the system being tested, including version, current patches, and relevant configuration settings
- Text of the script itself, plus any information on the publisher, name of the product, and version number
- Output report from running the script
- Results of the auditor's review of the output report

Scripts designed for certain technologies have the issue of expiring as the technology becomes obsolete, so infrastructure is required to keep them current. Unless an auditor is an expert in a given scripting language, he or she should avoid writing or editing scripts. Automated tools are more common with large audit organizations and cutting-edge audit shops.

Discovering Testing Exceptions

Auditors will face problematic test results and will need to determine the nature of any exception. It may not be clear whether an unexpected result equates to a test failure. Despite preparation, an auditor may not immediately understand test results. A clear understanding of the procedure and the role of the control within that procedure is needed so that the auditor can determine whether a nonstandard test result amounts to an exception or simply a test that was run incorrectly. If an auditor reports prematurely on findings, it can lead to challenges with the client relationship and loss of professional integrity for the auditor. Auditors should attempt to confirm an understanding of how the test results amount to an exception.

An auditor should communicate an exception with audit management first. Audit managers will confirm their understanding as to why it appears to be an exception. Then the control manager and primary contact will be informed—perhaps at regular update meetings or more immediately if the finding is highly material.

When an exception is confirmed, it is documented in test matrices and the workpapers. If possible, the description of the exception should accompany the source document, including where it was identified. If the test was discovered in data testing or images of a screen, the evidence should be captured electronically (and perhaps printed), and a written description should be included.

Reporting exceptions in audit reports usually includes reporting to the client the residual risk and making recommendations.

Issues Requiring Follow-up   There can be several reasons why an auditor must return to the control owner for a clear understanding of test results and exceptions. Most often, this will be because a procedure, a control, or the evidence is not completely understood, possibly because control documentation is insufficient or outdated.

When following up with a control owner, the auditor, if e-mail or a short conversation is not possible, should inform the primary contact and control manager that he or she will require more time with control owners. After completing follow-up with control owners, any clarifications the auditor acquires should be documented in the workpapers as support for the results of testing. In addition, procedure and controls documentation could require updating. If follow-up confirms the exception is valid, it must be documented as such.

Confirming an exception with the control owner and control manager should prevent disagreements when an audit report is presented to a client organization.

Here's an example requiring follow-up that involves network security: Upon an initial review of the client's firewall rule base, the firewall appears to permit traffic that includes less secure protocols. The auditor does not yet know if this is an exception. Further inquiry is required for the auditor to learn whether compensating controls address the risk:

- Traffic could additionally be managed by a router, isolating it to specific servers.

- An intrusion prevention system (IPS) may be employed to isolate traffic that introduces security issues into the network.

- Valid business reasons may have led to management accepting the risk of permitting this protocol. Staff may regularly monitor the activity.

Auditors may be told that management is aware of and accepts the risk of these protocols. Auditors would document management's communication in the workpapers, perhaps with an e-mail or a memo recounting the conversation.

Discovering Incidents Requiring Immediate Attention

During the course of testing, an auditor could discover information that requires immediate attention by the audit team, client management, or both. An auditor has a professional duty to be aware of possible indicators of illegal activities, fraud, hacking, or other improper actions. Situations that could require immediate attention include

- Fraudulent evidence provided by client personnel

- Discovery of critical vulnerabilities that compromise the integrity of the environment being audited

- Improper, fraudulent, or unlawful actions on the part of client personnel

- Manipulation of financial figures reported to internal or external parties

- Requests made to auditors that could compromise the integrity of the audit process

An auditor must be sure to understand the nature of the discovery correctly. In many instances, auditors will not have a problem consulting with control owners to confirm their understanding; however, situations such as fraud could require a high degree of confidentiality if a proper investigation is required. If the audit team together is still unclear on how to handle a situation, it is best to consult audit management or certified professionals on how best to proceed.

Discovery of Fraud   If an auditor uncovers evidence of possible fraudulent or criminal activity, it is urgent that he or she address this with audit management. The auditor must begin thoroughly documenting all communications and should write a description of how the discovery was made. The auditor should confidentially consult with fellow auditors to confirm his or her interpretation of the evidence. If the team suspects a possible issue, they must then decide how to proceed.

If there is agreement among auditors that evidence appears to show fraudulent or criminal activity, the audit team will need to notify appropriate client personnel of the incident. The audit team should consider the nature of the incident and carefully consider which members of client management or the governing board are the most appropriate to inform.

In small to middle-sized organizations, the audit team may consider informing the CIO, CFO, legal counsel, internal audit director, or other members of executive management. In larger organizations, a level below executive management may prove more appropriate. In extreme situations, the chair of the audit committee or other governing board may need to be informed first. A meeting should be set up to discuss the evidence and see how the client would like to proceed.

Handling Evidence of Fraud or Criminal Activity   If the auditor possesses documentary evidence of potentially fraudulent activity, he or she will need to isolate the document and establish a *chain of custody* for the potential evidence should criminal investigation proceedings occur. This appendix does not claim to be an authoritative resource on procedures to follow in the event of discovering fraud. If fraud is discovered, a professional investigator should be consulted immediately for guidance. The investigator will advise the audit team on how to act until an investigator is able to take over the chain of custody for evidence and continue the investigation.

An auditor may be required to handle evidence relating to the discovery of fraud or criminal activity. It is preferable to establish the chain of custody of evidence following the instructions of a certified professional. A certified professional may not be able to assume the chain of custody of evidence the day it is identified, so an auditor may be required to perform certain actions. The following points are important to consider when developing a chain of custody of evidence:

- Do not make any marks or additional marks on the evidence or disfigure it in any way (for example, don't punch any holes in it to insert it into a binder).
- Begin an evidence log spreadsheet that will track the location and possession of the evidence. The spreadsheet should be constructed to track the following information:
  - Evidence log number
  - Date and time evidence was received from the source
  - Information on the source of the evidence, including person, source system, report names, and other details
  - Name of person submitting evidence to custody
  - Date and time evidence is entered into the evidence log

- A discussion of the information located within the documentary evidence that may indicate fraud

- The method of storage of the documentary evidence, which should be stored behind locked doors or in locked cabinets when not in the custodian's direct possession

- The name of the person responsible for keeping documentary evidence secure and in his or her possession, and the time and date when the person accepted possession of the evidence; if the security of the evidence is transferred between members of the audit team, the date and time when this transfer of ownership occurs must be recorded

- If the evidence is a piece of paper that has information on only one side, some parties advise that one may write the following on the back of the page: document number, date, and the source of the document, and sign and date it.

- Place the evidence into a tamper-evident envelope.

- Lock the evidence in a locking cabinet or safe.

If anyone on the audit team has experience with fraud investigations, this person should oversee this process, and as soon as possible a certified fraud investigator should be consulted. When a certified fraud investigator arrives, auditors will formally hand over custody of any documentary evidence and the evidence log to the investigator and record the transfer of custody in the evidence log.

 CAUTION When collecting evidence that may later be used in a legal proceeding, strict forensic rules for collecting and protecting evidence must be followed. This situation often requires the services of a trained forensic specialist, who will follow these procedures to protect the evidence and its chain of custody.

Improper Actions by Management Management may behave improperly during the course of the audit, and client personnel may fear for their reputation with client management when auditors are around. Hence, client personnel may behave inappropriately as well. It is important for an auditor to maintain professional composure when client personnel act inappropriately. Less serious issues of inappropriate behavior can be addressed between audit management and the primary contact. More serious issues may require a meeting between control managers and audit sponsors.

Certain improper actions may be severe enough to interfere with the execution of the audit, such as

- Refusing to provide test evidence

- Providing fraudulent or "doctored" evidence

- Requesting audit personnel to act inappropriately

- Threatening audit personnel

Violations at this level will require action by the audit team. Auditors should document and communicate the incident immediately to audit management. Audit management and client management should then meet and address the issue.

Certain improper actions by management could strongly affect the audit execution and the final report. In some situations, refusal to provide evidence or providing fraudulent evidence can be a reason for the audit team to stop performing an audit.

Materiality of Exceptions

The auditor employs judgment to assess the materiality of exceptions. During testing, an auditor will determine whether the exception is serious enough to warrant the immediate attention of management or whether it is a discrepancy of limited consequence. The question of materiality is addressed partly in the testing matrix, when an auditor assesses residual risk for a control that did not pass.

The materiality of controls and control failures is discussed in more detail in Chapter 3.

 CAUTION   Audit management may not always agree with an auditor's assessment of materiality. Hopefully, this situation is resolved quickly and a final determination can be made. A staff auditor may have a client-specific perspective, and management may have more insight into the nature of certain risks.

Assessing Residual Risk   After the nature of a control failure is confirmed, the auditor can assess its residual risk. Certain failures will introduce a relatively limited amount of risk, such as identifying low-access accounts that are not compliant with a password policy. Other failures can be highly material and require immediate attention. Here's an example of a material failure:

Auditors are performing tests of network security controls. When testing a requirement that employees use VPN for external access, auditors learn that RDP (Remote Desktop Protocol) traffic is permitted through the firewall and enabled on workstations. Inquiry reveals that a number of IT personnel work from home and that they access their workstations remotely using RDP. The residual risk is that unencrypted traffic, including authentications, is permitted through the firewall and is potentially visible to third parties. This situation is clearly a material breach of compliance with policies and compromises network security controls.

Examples of how different exceptions from the same test could result in different levels of residual risk are depicted in Table A-3.

In Table A-3, the high-risk example would definitely be brought to the attention of the report's audience; however, it would be up to the auditor whether to bring medium- and low-risk exceptions to the attention of management.

Risk Level	Exception	Residual Risk
Low	No password policy is enforced on a shared account used in a lab for Internet access only.	Inappropriate persons may gain Internet access.
Medium	No password policy is applied to several user accounts with mid-level permissions.	Inappropriate persons may be able to compromise certain tasks within a procedure.
High	No password policy is applied to secure administrator- and executive-level accounts.	Inappropriate persons may gain access to executive-level accounts and perform inappropriate authorizations or access administrative accounts and compromise security administration.

Table A-3   Different Kinds of Exceptions and How Residual Risk Is Evaluated

Categorizing or Ranking Exceptions   In some reports, such as internal audit reports, the severity of exceptions may be weighed. Categorizations of materiality can be selected, such as

- Ranked, most to least important
- Linear, such as low, medium, and high, or on a scale of 1 through 5 or 1 through 10
- Stoplight, with green (controls operating or compliant), yellow (requiring attention), and red (controls not operating or noncompliant)

Several parties can use weighted exceptions:

- Auditors may choose to present only the most material exceptions to the governing entity. These exceptions are again ranked by importance to the governing entity. Exceptions of lesser materiality are addressed with management.
- The IA department can use the ranking when scheduling any retesting of failed controls.
- Management may use the ranking to prioritize their remediation plans.

Weighted results lend effectively to diagrammatic representations of the residual risk. Weighted results help management better understand which residual risks are the most important.

Developing Audit Opinions

Auditors will develop opinions on individual control tests, control objectives, and at times, an audit as a whole. Reviewing test results and developing an opinion can be performed after all testing is complete, any follow-up with the control owner has been performed, and the test evidence is ready to be documented in the workpapers. In the event testing revealed exceptions, the control owner and the auditor would have already agreed to the facts relating to a performed test. An audit opinion is entered into the audit testing matrix.

 NOTE Agreeing on facts ahead of an opinion will reduce disagreements when reporting reveals the exceptions to management.

An auditor will conclude his opinions on all controls supporting a control objective before developing an opinion on a control objective.

Management Representation Letter

When certain licensed professionals are performing an external attestation, it is sometimes the practice to have client management sign a "Management Representation Letter." A Management Representation Letter states that client personnel have provided truthful information throughout the audit process. By signing, management takes responsibility for information provided to auditors. This attestation by the client provides an auditor with a degree of legal protection in the event the report's contents are subject to litigation. When this practice is followed, audit checklists require this letter before the delivery of a signed report to the audit client.

Control Activities

Developing opinions involves weighing the materiality of each exception, its residual risk, and its impact on control or audit objectives. Opinions on control activities will most often take the form of

- Control passes
- Control passes with observations
- Control passes with notable but not material exceptions
- Control fails due to exceptions
- Control fails because the control activity is not performed

Tests that merely "pass" the planned test procedures are easy to handle. Passing controls are entered into the testing matrix and reflect simply that the test passed. There is no burden for the auditor to develop statements of residual risk or recommendations.

Testing observations are generated when a situation is uncovered during the course of testing that relates to the control environment. Inquiry, for example, may reveal control weaknesses outside of the test plan scope. An auditor might also identify possible improvements to the control structure, or note that certain procedures are not always performed consistently.

When an audit test does identify exceptions, but the audit team considers the materiality of the exceptions to not constitute a control failure, the control may pass, but the exceptions may be brought to the attention of management. For example, an Active Directory control states that no shared accounts are permitted on the network. Inquiry confirms that setup of shared accounts is not permitted, but a review of accounts identifies several old shared accounts, though follow-up reveals the access granted to these accounts is appropriately limited and that the accounts were not used by personnel.

Testing a control activity could result in failure before all supporting tests are performed. In these situations, an auditor will need to decide whether to curtail any more testing of that control and conserve effort. An auditor decides whether additional tests of that control will provide any benefit to the client and whether the opinion of the control objective or the audit as a whole is influenced by these control activity test results.

Control Objectives

An auditor opines on control objectives once the opinions of all supporting controls activities have been documented. Auditors will determine how the results of controls testing support the control objective. Opinions on control objectives will state that controls pass with notable observations, or fail. An audit's methodology may provide guidance in determining if a control objective passes or fails. Audit methodologies might provide guidance such as

- Each passed control objective must be supported by at least one substantive test confirming the effectiveness of supporting controls.
- A single control failure shouldn't fail a control objective unless the control is a key control or the auditor documents a clear justification. (Individual audit organizations each have their own tolerance for addressing control failures and any resultant additional testing that can be performed to determine whether a failure is an isolated incident.)
- A failure of two or more control activities should fail a control objective, unless an auditor documents a clear justification of their determination.

If auditors are weighing a control objective, when testing failures exist, auditors must consider how the control objective supports the audit's objectives. In the course of developing an opinion on a control objective, auditors may determine that evidence is inconclusive and that additional testing is needed before a determination can be finalized.

Final determinations on control objectives should be documented in the workpapers and approved by audit management.

Audit Opinions

Certain reports will deliver an opinion on the audit's results. An SSAE 18 Type II report will attest to whether controls appear to be operating effectively. To develop an audit opinion based on control objectives, the opinions on control objectives will be weighed against the audit's objectives. Audit opinions typically pass, pass with qualifying conditions, or fail. A statement supporting this determination should be approved and entered into the workpapers.

Developing Audit Recommendations

At the conclusion of an audit, it is common for an auditor to provide recommendations on improvements to a client's control environment. These recommendations can be delivered formally or informally.

Formal Recommendations

Auditors can provide formal recommendations to the client. This could take the form of internal audit reports or a letter accompanying the audit report. Recommendations included in a report are frequently accompanied by management's responses and possibly remediation plans.

Formal recommendations are carefully worded. Auditors must be careful to advise that management take action to remediate a weakness, avoiding statements that may appear that auditors are making decisions on the part of management. Wording is commonly along the lines of "management should consider" performing a certain action. Auditors may avoid highly specific recommendations, because there are often several options on how a control weakness can be mitigated and clients may argue specific methods rather than agree on a need to fix controls. In other words, auditors may advise a client on *what* to do, but will refrain from describing *how* to do it. However, depending on the audit rules of engagement, and if auditors are free to suggest mitigation approaches, they will often do so. When in doubt, it can't hurt to ask the auditor if they are permitted to advise their client on remediation of findings.

Informal Recommendations

Auditors often discuss informal recommendations with control managers during the course of testing. It is constructive for both the auditor and control managers to discuss improving an organization's controls. Executive management, such as an audit sponsor, may have some pointed questions they would like to ask auditors at the close of an audit. Similar to formal recommendations, auditors should phrase responses with care and maintain impartiality and professionalism in their answer.

Managing Supporting Documentation

In the process of auditing, an auditor will handle a significant volume of audit documents, process documentation, and testing evidence. Having a complete set of documentation is necessary to ensure the integrity of the audit process. In addition, having clear and organized documentation will benefit the execution of the audit. Some of these benefits include the following:

- Auditors will be able to answer detailed questions about test results.
- Audit managers will be able to confirm work is being done to expected standards.
- For auditors in accounting firms, the audit may be subject to a peer review, where other firms review a project's report and its workpapers and scrutinize the audit. An accounting firm may also be audited by the Public Company Accounting Oversight Board (PCAOB), in which case the auditor will be required to show all

of the documentation that has been collected during the audit. Audits of systems according to the Payment Card Industry Data Security Standard (PCI-DSS) and ISO standards have similar oversight structures, including "audits of audits" to ensure that audit procedures are followed and that minimum quality standards are met.

It is important that the format of testing documentation be clear when staff auditors begin testing. Auditors also need to make sure that documentation keeps up with the progress of testing. Memos recording conversations should be inserted promptly into workpapers.

During the course of the audit, it is often convenient to manage testing evidence in binders or electronic folders that are separate from audit documents.

Complete audit documentation will often have most or all of the following sections:

- Table of contents
- Engagement documentation, such as the signed engagement letter
- Contact information for all auditors and auditees
- Memos providing direction on understanding documentation
- Meeting minutes and memos from meetings between auditors and client personnel
- Procedure documentation and background information on key systems
- Testing matrices and lead sheets
- Supporting documentation generated during testing
- Checklists for audit completion
- Testing methods used
- Sample guidance
- Document review

Storing Electronic Documentation

It is increasingly common to retain as much as possible in the form of electronic versions of documentation. Electronic documentation can be stored as files within a file system, such as on a shared network or cloud-based data storage provider, but it is sometimes managed by supporting software.

In some engagements, outside auditors provide a copy of audit workpapers to the client. Sharing electronic versions of documentation can make this easy to do. When delivering electronic documentation, the auditor must confirm the preferred media and schedule of delivery with the client.

Electronic storage can introduce challenges if it is to be archived for a specific period. Storage media preferences evolve and could render documentation difficult to access if it is stored on outdated media. Another consideration is that certain media has a limited shelf life. Data that is to be stored for extended periods (generally, for more than five to ten years) may need to be periodically rearchived onto newer media to ensure that the data can be retrieved if needed.

Storage of data used within audit management software runs the risk of becoming difficult to access in the distant future. Using software can be expensive, and an organization could face the risk of software compatibility issues once the systems that generated the archive files have been upgraded or replaced, or are no longer supported.

Lead Sheets

One common practice for organizing testing documentation is to begin a documentation section for each control with a "lead sheet." Lead sheets often contain similar information to what information was tracked in the testing matrix. Lead sheets provide the reviewer with a tool for following the testing process and understanding the accompanying documentation. Lead sheets can also capture a reviewer's sign-off.

 NOTE Within most spreadsheet software, it is possible to populate information into lead sheets from the testing matrix.

Lead sheets typically end with the result of testing clearly stated, as in Figure A-7. Evaluations of residual risk, auditor opinions, and recommendations will often be tracked in separate tools, but this is not necessary.

Delivering Audit Results

An audit's fieldwork has been completed, and control owners and managers have agreed to the facts of testing. Before delivering audit results, the auditor updates all matrices with test results, residual risks evaluated, and draft versions of audit opinions written. The next task is to compose results into a presentable form.

Typical presentations of audit results can include

- Delivery of a formal report for review by the audit sponsors and other management
- Presentation of the report to the organization's audit committee of the board
- Publication for distribution to and review by third parties (such as SSAE 18, PCI, and ISO audits)
- Memo or letter summarizing audit results and reporting issues to control managers and/or audit management

If IS audit procedures are a subset of a larger audit, IS audit results are communicated to audit management for inclusion in their report.

Discussions with audit sponsors and the primary contact will have clarified what a client expects for their deliverable at the beginning of the audit. The degree of formality will vary depending on client needs and the company culture.

Testing Lead Sheet Company ABC, Inc.	Control ID	2.3
	Tested by	Michael, the auditor
	Date completed	3/29/2010
	Reviewed by	

Control ID	2.3

Control Objective

Accurate import of data files into system

Control Activity

Reconciliation of validation totals upon file import

Tests Performed

Inquiry	X
Inspection	
Observation	
Re-performance	
Sample testing	X

Control Owner

Michael, the auditor

Sample Size

Approximately 440 file imports over the 6-month test period

Test Procedures Performed

1) Inquiry—Corroborate between two different department personnel

2) Sample testing—From a sample of reports, verify that the batch number of the import was recorded on the report and that import totals have been initialed and dated.

Workpaper Reference

2.3a—Memo describing sample selection process
2.3b—Test population
2.3c—Memo describing test results

Test Results

Inquiry
Inquired of file import manager Jane...

Sample Testing
Reviewed 40 out of 440 reviewed import reports and found initials

Conclusion

No exceptions noted

Figure A-7   A testing lead sheet contains comprehensive information on the control and the testing performed.

NOTE In the event of cyclical testing, such as SOX 404 or OMB A-123, the completed tests are often entered into a tracking system. After test completion, depending on the structure of testing and review, a limited amount of additional reporting may be requested. Internal audit management will prepare internal reporting for financial leadership so that they are comfortable signing off on controls supporting financial figures. This process includes a review of exceptions and their remediation projects.

Contributing to Larger Audit Reports

When an IS auditor is working for a team that includes non-IS auditors, typically audit management does not have an IS audit background. In this situation, the IS auditor may have a stronger understanding of the materiality of certain test results and the residual risks than does the audit manager responsible for writing and delivering the report. This situation will require close coordination between the IS and non-IS auditors, which can be a challenge toward the end of an audit when time schedules are tight and several tasks are being pushed to completion. Ensuring that audit results are communicated correctly in final reports and during presentations can be a challenge. If audit reporting over- or under-represents the materiality of information systems risks, it could have consequences to the audit relationship and the reputations of control managers or auditors.

IS auditors should make sure they participate in reviewing the report's representations. The audit manager should be receptive and allow this participation. This situation may be delicate, because the audit team is balancing the success of its relationship with the audit manager with the needs of the audit organization and the client.

Audit Report Contents

Frequently, either the audit organization or the client organization will provide an audit report template. In the case of ISO and PCI-DSS audits, audit report templates from governing organizations are used. At a high level, a report communicates scope, procedures, and conclusions. In audits involving numerous auditors, several parties may contribute content. Coordination between the report writer (frequently the audit manager or senior) and auditors who performed testing is standard during this time. The report writer will confirm with the field auditors that their statements correctly represent audit activities.

An audit report often includes the following:

- Standard language addressing the parties involved, audit scope, and auditing standards invoked during the audit
- Rules regarding the distribution of the report
- If applicable, the audit opinion
- If applicable, statements by client management regarding company history, financial activities, processing activities, and related controls
- Audit objectives
- Controls to be tested and how they support control objectives

- Test results and conclusions from testing, including exceptions, and evaluations of materiality and residual risk
- Auditor recommendations
- Client-provided feedback on exceptions, conclusions, or recommendations

During this process, audit staff and management review how to appropriately present the audit results. Younger auditors tend to experience mentoring, corrections, and rework during this phase.

Audit Management and Staff Disagreements   A staff auditor and an audit manager may draw different conclusions from test results. For an audit opinion to be defensible by audit management, the report and supporting detail must agree. During report writing and review, as audit management becomes familiar with test result details, the practices and judgment of a staff auditor may face criticism. Disagreements can arise surrounding the assessments of the nature of an exception and the residual risks.

When a staff auditor concludes differently about an exception's residual risks than does audit management, a discussion must follow. The following are several scenarios where disagreements may occur:

- A staff auditor may lack a thorough understanding of specific technologies or client procedures, and may draw incorrect conclusions from test results.
- Staff auditors frequently have more familiarity with a procedure than does audit management, so their conclusions may consider as-of-yet-undocumented knowledge of the situation. If an audit staff person does not thoroughly articulate the reasons for their conclusion, they may omit information critical to audit management's review and potentially be overruled. Audit management may require augmenting documentation when they come to understand the reasons behind their judgment.
- A staff auditor may be younger and less experienced with specific technologies than the control owner, and may prove impressionable in the presence of an "expert." A young staff auditor's judgment may be affected by representations of the control owner that an exception is not serious. Staff auditors may require mentoring on the nature of the exception and related risks.

Audit management may need to engage in discussions with the client regarding exceptions. Additional procedures may be required, such as increasing test set size or testing a compensating control. Additional testing may prove frustrating to the client and audit team, as both client and audit team personnel are not expecting additional burdens on their schedules. This situation should be preventable through clear communication during audit procedures and regular oversight by management.

Writing the Report
Once test results are clear, writing the report should be a rather straightforward process. Most audit firms and IA departments have developed reporting templates; in some

cases clients will provide a report template, and sometimes an audit template is provided through a standard such as PCI. When no standard template is provided (or expected), the client may select a report from a similar engagement and benchmark. When developing the shell and structure of a report, the client may identify the parties responsible for providing content for the different sections of the report.

A report can be drafted in sections, even as testing progresses. As soon as a test has been captured fully in the workpapers, the section of a report relating to that test can be drafted for inclusion. It is common for the greatest amount of writing to be done to account for exceptions.

Attention to these few practices will deliver effective audit reports:

- *Write in the clearest way possible.* This can mean breaking up long sentences into single statements using the fewest words. While the auditor may be technically minded and trained, often it is better to compose the report in nontechnical terms so that client management can gain at least a basic understanding of findings.

- *It is often preferable to refer to control owners by their title.* Each person can be listed with his or her title as a participant. A report will be meaningful to more people when individual names are avoided, however, and it will serve as a more effective tool for future management and reviewers.

- *If multiple writers are contributing report sections, employing uniform language throughout the report is essential but can prove challenging.* If dissimilar language is used, more time may be required during review. It is handy to provide writing examples upon which the auditors writing each section can benchmark.

The testing matrix plays an important role when writing the report. Some reports will present results from the full testing matrix, such as SSAE 18, ISO, and PCI-DSS reports. Internal audits may focus reporting on the most material exceptions.

The report is not complete until the workpapers and testing matrix have been reconciled to the report detail. This requires that evidence in the workpapers is organized and supports the content of the report.

 NOTE Auditors may want to sign the audit report digitally, both as a means of ensuring its authenticity and to protect it from tampering. Also, when delivering an audit report via e-mail, auditors may consider encrypting the audit report to protect the contents from eavesdropping by other parties.

Management Response

When the conclusions of the audit report are clear to the audit team, the team sits down with the primary auditee contact, and possibly control managers, and delivers the results of testing. Presentations should share draft language of exceptions wording and audit opinions from testing, which will be included in the final report.

Some report formats seek management's responses to the results of testing. Client management will review the wording and the nature of the audit findings and compose responses. The auditor will include these responses in the final report.

Discussing the Auditor's Wording

Client management may choose to discuss the wording of exceptions or opinions. In some situations, the wording of the audit opinion could trigger confusion for the auditee organization or its customers. So long as a rewording doesn't affect the message or the nature of the opinion, audit management might agree to adjust certain wording.

Here are some examples of wording issues:

- Data backups have been a persistent problem, and the control objective of "daily incremental, weekly full" backups is not being met. Configuration problems existed within the backup software. Because resources were busy on other critical projects, the configuration problems were not addressed. IT management argues the successful weekly full backup is a mitigating factor not mentioned in test results or the opinion, though they agree the control failed as worded.

- Partway through the audit period, an organization replaced a system that had been problematic from a controls issue. Per testing guidance, testing at different points during the period reveals material exceptions. Management impresses the point that the situation is now controlled effectively and argues test wording does not fully reflect the effectiveness of their current and ongoing controls.

Auditors will have to consider these situations carefully. Client management may be seeking to avoid embarrassment for any exceptions, and an auditor must take special care not to give in to pressure or suggestions that result in misrepresenting exceptions or residual risks. If an auditor is unsure whether a change is appropriate, he or she should consult with higher levels of audit management regarding management's requests.

Management's Responses to Auditor Recommendations

Responses from client management about audit recommendations usually involve one of three responses:

- Management performs auditor-suggested remediation.
- Management seeks an alternate solution to their control weakness.
- Management believes no remediation action is necessary and assumes the risk of control failure.

Management may address the audit opinion in their written response to defend their position.

The auditor will then review management's responses and develop his or her own opinion on management's action plans. The auditor may believe that the response is appropriate and agree with management about the plans, but this is not always the case. When management responds by saying no action is necessary, an auditor may be compelled to report this inaction to regulators or governing entities or include in the report that management's responses do not satisfy the auditor's own concerns about the risks involved.

Report Audiences

The audience of an audit report will be defined at the beginning of the audit engagement. The report should be written in language and at a level of depth appropriate to that audience.

Reports to Audit Committees

Reports presented to audit committees are written to communicate at a high level. Audit committees consist of members of the board of directors, who are usually removed from the day-to-day operations of an organization. Their main concern is whether there are problems that they need to be aware of.

Frequently a report will begin with a high-level executive summary. Language in the executive summary must be clear and direct without diving into details. For subjects warranting more thorough attention, additional pages provide supporting detail so that interested members can drill down further into a subject. Auditors will make sure that the issues of greatest concern get the attention of the committee.

Audit committee reports often make a point of

- Clarifying the scope of the audit
- Drawing attention to significant issues
- Communicating management's response to issues

Reports attempting to describe mid-to-low–level operations are generally too detailed for the needs of an audit committee and likely to lose their attention or, in the worst case, confuse members. Be careful not to introduce confusion; this will waste valuable time and may strain the auditor/client relationship.

Audit management will frequently attend the meeting to present results and field any questions the committee may have about the report.

The report typically will be provided to committee members several days in advance of an audit committee meeting. Auditors will need to be aware of the committee's deadlines and procedures for submitting reports on time.

Reports to Client Management

Client management should have a high level of interest in the detailed results of an audit. Reports written for management will contain operational-level information with which they are familiar. The report's audience will include control managers and their directors. It is important that information in the report be accurate to ensure the report is deemed credible. Within the client organization, there may be parties with motives to discredit a report or the audit organization, so an auditor's diligence in presenting undisputable facts will protect his or her reputation.

Reports to management will often contain information on the results of each test performed. Exceptions will be addressed with more detail, and auditors will present their assessment of residual risk and will include recommendations.

In audit situations where management is tasked with providing their own responses addressing exceptions and recommendations, a report's completion can be held up by management delaying in providing their responses. Auditors may need to engage their primary contact and perhaps their audit sponsor to ensure management delivers timely responses.

Frequently, when an audit is being presented to an audit committee, a second, more detailed, report is issued to client management. Providing a more detailed report to management before drafting the report to the audit committee will ensure that all communications with management are complete.

Depending on the organization, a senior executive may ask to sit with auditors and control managers to discuss the detailed report's findings.

Reports to Third Parties   Certain engagements involve presenting testing results to parties outside of the client organization. Here are a few examples of such audits:

- Organizations that provide services to third parties will hire their own auditors to publish an audit report. A service organization thus avoids opening its doors to auditors hired by their customers. The final report is provided to customers and their auditors. An example of this is the transaction-based SSAE 18 reports that are governed by the AICPA.

- When two organizations agree to a partnering relationship or are considering a merger or acquisition, one party may request the results of an audit of the second party.

- Banks and other parties extending credit to an organization may require a set of procedures be performed by auditors as terms of lending.

NOTE   Terms of an audit engagement should clarify what parties are permitted to review the report and under what conditions.

Reviewing the Draft Report

Once the report is in final draft form, it is subject to review by the head of audit management. This person will proofread the report for correct language and will tie the report back to the audit proposal and plan, testing matrix, and supporting workpapers. When a certified professional is signing a report, he or she will go through this process with great care before signing off on the report. Reviews often include reviewers initialing sections as complete during the review, such as initialing lead sheets when review of testing documentation has been completed.

Ideally, a review will go well; certain points of feedback will be delivered to improve the report, testing matrix, and workpapers; and the audit team will have a limited number of points of cleanup—opportunities for feedback and retesting may be required.

In lengthy audit projects, it may also be appropriate for auditors to conduct periodic reviews of audit results throughout the audit, instead of waiting until the end of the audit.

NOTE   Some situations will lead to the testing workpapers not following the same structure as a report. If this occurs, it is important to include a description in the workpapers describing how they can be navigated to support the report.

Signed Reports   Certain reports must be signed by a certified professional. For example, an SSAE 18 audit report must be signed by a certified public accountant (CPA) and a PCI report on compliance (ROC) must be signed by a qualified security assessor (QSA). The certified professional will have taken care to ensure that the audit process has complied with the standards set out by the certifying organization. The audit will have followed guidelines for documentation, review, sample size, internal review, and perhaps other areas. Checklists may be employed that must be completed before an audit may be signed.

Internal audits performed by outside parties may request that the audit report be signed by a certified professional or specialist. Client management can have reasons to seek a certified professional's sign-off on specific testing or internal audit reports. Here's an example: a company has had challenges with its fledgling internal audit department. Another company is seeking to partner with the company but has concerns, and places conditions on the partnership agreement that an outsourced certified internal audit firm provide a signed report.

Delivery of the Report

Audit management will clarify with the client how they would prefer to have the report delivered. Depending on the engagement, a report may be delivered during a closing meeting. Some clients expect a bound hardcopy report, while others will be happy with a printout or electronic file (this information should be agreed upon with the auditee at the commencement of the audit). Reports may be delivered at a formal occasion, such as a closing meeting or an audit committee meeting.

Reports delivered to management often will be provided to specific personnel. Audit management will get a distribution list from the primary contact and provide sufficient copies.

Service providers often need to make their audit reports available to their customers' auditors. Usually this is achieved by mailing hardcopy reports, sending electronic copies via e-mail, or posting audit reports on a web site.

Delivering Electronic Reports   If reports are delivered in electronic form, they should be prepared so that they cannot be altered. Additional controls, such as encrypting the report in transit, that prevent text or figures from being copied out of the report or prevent the report from being printed, may also be appropriate in some circumstances. These controls will help to prevent the original audit report from being misrepresented, abused, or distributed outside of its intended audience.

Additional Engagement Deliverables

A client organization, or the department being tested, could request additional information from an audit process, such as the following:

- Feedback on policies
- Suggestions for improving the control environment
- Test results information in greater detail than in the report
- The feasibility of control mitigation strategies

The client organization may have selected the contracted audit party because of the experience of its team members. Certain audit projects give an auditor a significant understanding of a client organization's environment. After testing, it is not uncommon for clients to ask the auditor how their systems and processes compare to those of their peers.

Auditors can be helpful when asked such questions, but they should be cautious in their responses. There are several potential pitfalls to avoid:

- Auditors should avoid making statements that go beyond their experience with the client and their personal areas of expertise.

- It would be problematic if a manager justifies a decision based on the fact that "the auditor told me we should do it." An audit is usually not a consulting arrangement, and engagement letters often are not written with disclaimers used by business advisors.

- An auditor should exhibit prudence when performing assessments at clients that are business competitors. An auditor should be careful not to reveal details of a competitor's systems. Even without identifying the party, providing certain information could be perceived as unethical and in violation of professional standards. If a client believes an auditor is overly liberal in sharing business information, they may fear that the auditor will treat their sensitive information similarly in dealing with other clients.

An auditor is in no way discouraged from providing advice to management but must do so in accordance with an engagement's requirements and in accordance with ethical and professional standards. Auditors may seek to avoid putting certain comments or advice in writing to protect them from exposure to liability or professional criticisms.

Audit Closing Procedures

The audit process comes to a conclusion when reporting is finalized and workpapers are ready for storage. Methodologies may require certain checklists and that approvals are followed when wrapping up an audit.

Audit Checklists

Audit management may follow checklists for certain milestones during the audit. These may include requirements during the bidding and launching cycle, as well as closing procedures that make sure the audit is complete. Audit closing procedures may include the following:

- The report and workpapers have been reviewed.
- The report has been delivered.
- The signed management representation letter is in the workpapers.
- Workpapers are signed off on and archived.
- Final invoices have been sent.

Audit checklists are typically filed along with the engagement workpapers.

Closing Meetings

At some point after the delivery of reports, audit management and the client will discuss the performance of the audit. If the audit organization plans to continue performing audits for the client in the future, these inquiries help to develop business relationships as well as refine the performance of the audit. It is common to identify points of friction in the audit and seek ways to improve interactions. Clients may prefer to perform testing within certain calendar periods or may want to centralize requests for information. This occasion is a good opportunity to address changes in personnel. A client may choose to have another person serve as the primary contact, or the audit team may announce a change in staffing or management.

When auditors deliver these reports to management, these discussions frequently append the meeting in which reports are delivered. Auditors should be prepared to discuss such points at the end of the audit. It may prove best to address certain issues at a later time. For example, specific details of findings and recommendations for improvement may be best discussed with individual control owners, who may not be participants in the closing meeting.

Final Sign-off with the Client

Audit methodologies may involve formalizing the closing of an audit with a client. Audit organization management may seek closure to know that they can close the book on an audit. Auditors will know all work on a project is complete and no more hours will go against project budgets. Final invoicing can be processed, and the auditor can send a final invoice for audit services to the client.

One way of formalizing the end of an audit is to have management sign a letter accepting its completion. A final document is often signed by the client that states the auditor has provided all services as contracted under the engagement letter. Such letters are placed in the engagement files.

Client Feedback and Evaluations

After an engagement is completed, the audit organization frequently will ask for feedback from client management. Some audit organizations track a complex set of feedback metrics. It is common to use this information for internal performance evaluations and bonuses.

An audit firm may follow up with clients with surveys. These surveys will solicit feedback on different parts of the audit. The client will provide the audit team with different "grades," which the audit firms may consider when seeking to improve service quality in the future. If a client is pleased with the service, this proves an opportunity for the audit firm to ask a client if they may serve as a reference client when the audit firm is bidding on services to a new client.

Some audit firms will bring the audit team together to review the feedback from the client. If audits are performed on a regular schedule, the results of "what went well" and "potential improvements" in a prior audit may be discussed during kickoff meetings to ensure that focus is given to following up on feedback received.

Audit Follow-up

From an auditee's perspective, an audit is a part of an ongoing cycle. After the initial growing pains of the "first time through," an organization usually experiences audits on a regular cycle. Control managers and owners are often familiar with the audit process, though specific testing practices may evolve to fit changes in business, technology, customer needs, and regulation.

A mature audit function will track issues over successive audit periods. The results of testing cycles or prior audit reports will have identified areas of improvement. Management will have agreed to certain remediation measures. The audit cycle provides an auditor with an opportunity to revisit controls that have failed in previous periods.

Follow-up on Management's Action Plans to Remediate Control Failures

Internal audit cycles will suggest improvements to control activities, and management will reply to these recommendations. Sometimes, management implements the auditor's recommendations; sometimes, they reply with alternative approaches to the issue. Often, a project is started by management as remediation and the planned completion date is provided with management's reply. Internal audit departments will track management's remediation plans on the calendar and will follow up with the project owner regarding completion. Testing will be reperformed on failed controls and may be performed on controls newly introduced by a project as well.

Retesting Issues in Succeeding Periods

Controls with audit exceptions will be retested either until improvements are made and the control passes or the control is replaced with a new control activity. A test with repeated control failures will be shared with appropriate executive management and, depending on materiality, may be reported to a governing entity.

External Audit   External audit agreements often approve performing audits over several periods. The audit organization develops in-house knowledge of the client organization's issues. Audit recommendations aim to work with management to improve the controls environment so testing failures in previous periods are avoided. It is standard to retest areas where previous tests have failed.

In the event that tests continue to fail over successive periods, auditors will draw attention to the issues in their reports; audit reports will draw attention to issues that persist. In high-risk areas, audit management may deem the issue material enough to issue a qualified or adverse audit opinion.

When an audit organization is performing its first audit of a client, they will review previous periods' audit reports. These help the auditors evaluate the risk of different areas and include in-scope failed tests and management's remediation plans.

Internal Audit   Internal audit departments frequently track controls to be tested over cycles. Certain controls testing cycles, OMB A-123, for example, will permit less-critical controls testing on a less frequent basis. If a control has passed in previous testing, a risk evaluation may deem the control needs be tested on a two- or three-year cycle only. However, control tests that have experienced exceptions, that have a high level of materiality/risk to an organization, or that include processes that have changed in previous periods probably will need to be retested on a more frequent basis.

Cyclical control testing is only a portion of internal audit work. An internal audit will, at the direction of the board of directors, pursue audits of different functions within an organization. Unlike internal audit testing cycles or external audits, audits of specific functions may be a one-time event. Issues discovered in these reports are tracked within the internal audit department. Internal audit management and the audit committee should allocate time each year to revisit the status of different issues uncovered in these audits.

Management Projects Frequently, management will agree to remediate issues by initiating a project to solve the problem. Information systems projects end up in a priority queue, where they are allocated time based on available resources as well as complexity, relative importance, and other factors. Management is frequently cooperative in understanding the importance of a remediation project, but these are evaluated and prioritized among dozens, if not hundreds, of other IT projects. Auditors may find themselves pressing management on delayed projects relating to ongoing control issues.

Summary

This appendix has provided an in-depth study of the IS audit cycle, with the goal of providing a link between CISA study materials and the discipline of professional IS auditing. This material, which provides real-world associations for the subject materials addressed in this book, will benefit your memory. After all, successfully passing the CISA audit exam requires more than being able to recite facts; it requires you to understand all aspects of IS auditing and many aspects of IT management and security.

An additional goal of this appendix has been to portray the "organic" challenges that auditors face in the field. Examples have illustrated scenarios that experience has shown are reasonable considerations during an audit.

Hopefully, you have a better grasp of the process of IS auditing and an awareness of the challenges encountered in the field. To the experienced auditor, it is frequently the case that as soon as one audit cycle ends, planning for the next period's audit is just around the corner. There are always opportunities to improve a current process, and experience will unveil more perspectives and stories.

Popular Methodologies, Frameworks, and Guidance

This appendix discusses the following topics:

- Common terms and concepts utilized in methodologies, frameworks, and guidance
- Demystifying the various resources available and their value to the CISA

Are you getting ready to develop, document, or audit IT controls? Several methodologies, frameworks, and guides contain detailed information on processes, control objectives, and controls that may assist you in your efforts. This appendix is dedicated to helping you make sense of these available resources and the terminology used within each of them.

The appendix is divided into two main sections. The first section focuses on common terms and concepts, while the second section describes the various methodologies, frameworks, and guides available and provides background information, high points, and a summary of why the resource may be helpful to a CISA-certified professional.

If you are reading this for the first time, it is recommended that you pay close attention to the first section, "Common Terms and Concepts," which provides you with a foundation from which to view the resources. Once you are familiar with the terminology, you can skip to the second section, "Frameworks, Methodologies, and Guidance," and find the resources that most directly apply to you and your organization's objectives. A table is provided at the end of the appendix as guidance for which frameworks may be most relevant to you.

EXAM TIP   You are not going to be tested on details of the various frameworks discussed in the second section of this appendix. The purpose of this appendix is to provide the professional IS auditor with additional tools and techniques that may be required in an organization.

Common Terms and Concepts

This section was created with the intention that it be used for reference when you are working with one of the frameworks discussed in the second section (or another that is not discussed in this book). At some point, you may hear someone refer to one of the

665

frameworks or methodologies described in this appendix or find yourself wondering if a particular framework or methodology may be valuable to you.

When looking for resources, consider the level and type of information you are looking for. Are you looking for information on implementing processes, control objective statements, or detailed guidance on specific controls? Are you developing a set of general IT controls, assessing a process, or writing particular policies and standards? Each of these activities may be covered in complementary resources; however, if you are in a time crunch, it is recommended that you first determine what you are looking for. Using the following common terms and concepts should help you to narrow down the type of information you are on an adventure to find.

Governance

Enterprise governance (or corporate governance) is defined as the responsibilities and practices followed by executive management and the board of directors to ensure that the enterprise's strategic goals and objectives are met, risks are managed, and resources are used responsibly.

ISACA defines governance as follows: *Ensures that stakeholder needs, conditions and options are evaluated to determine balanced, agreed-on enterprise objectives to be achieved; setting direction through prioritization and decision making; and monitoring performance and compliance against agreed-on direction and objectives.*

 NOTE See the ISACA online glossary for other definitions at www.isaca.org/Pages/Glossary.aspx.

Examples of enterprise governance practices would be that of senior management providing direction and oversight, clearly identifying roles and responsibilities, coordinating initiatives, managing resources, identifying and assessing risks, approving budgets, and enforcing compliance. Integrity, ethical behavior, risk management, transparency, and accountability are just a few principles of enterprise governance. Enterprise governance is critical for increasing investor confidence and ensuring compliance and profitability.

IT governance is a vital part of enterprise governance and aims to ensure that IT is meeting strategic goals and managing risks, and that IT investments are generating business value. IT governance is the foundation for all IT strategic and tactical activities. It helps ensure that strategic goals and objectives are set and measured against; activities, resources, and investments are managed and prioritized; and IT risks are identified and managed.

The IT Governance Institute (ITGI; a part of ISACA) has developed an IT governance framework that focuses on strategic alignment of IT with the business strategy, value delivery of IT, IT resource management, IT performance management, and IT risk management. You can find more information on this online in the ITGI publication, *Board Briefing on IT Governance: 2nd Edition.*

Although governance is the focus of the *Certified in the Governance of Enterprise IT* (CGEIT) certification, it is important to understand that IT governance is the foundation of IT management and may affect which processes and controls are prioritized or assessed at any given time.

Goals, Objectives, and Strategies

Often, the terms "goals" and "objectives" are used synonymously in documentation and planning. Both are used to describe a desired end state, or what an organization intends to achieve. Strategies are the means, or actions, by which an organization intends to realize these goals.

One of the most popular terms in the IS world and control and process frameworks is "objective." Keep in mind that an objective is what the enterprise is trying to achieve or the expected result of an activity. It is always set within a context. For example, the COBIT framework describes several IT processes and related objectives. In addition, the framework describes specific control objectives. COBIT is not an objective framework, but aligning IT processes to COBIT may help to achieve objectives.

Business objectives, *process objectives*, and *control objectives* are different from each other. Business objectives are higher level statements that guide the organization. Process objectives describe what the process activities intend to achieve, while control objectives describe what the implemented controls are trying to achieve or risks the controls are attempting to mitigate. It is important to understand that the concept of objectives is widely used, and they need to be kept in proper context. Some examples of different objectives are shown in Table B-1.

Detailed definitions of goals and objectives are provided in the *Business Motivation Model*, which is published by the Business Rules Group. In this publication, *goals* are seen as general statements that are ongoing, longer term, and qualitative, whereas *objectives* are intended to be more specific, shorter term, time-specific, and quantitative. In the same model, *strategies* are said to be the activities that are planned to channel efforts toward goals. The model provides an entire framework for developing mission, vision, goal, objective, strategy, tactic, and directive statements, just to name a few, for an organization.

Type of Objective	Context	Example Objective
Business Objective	Supports Business Goal of Managing IT-Related Business Risks	Implement IT risk quarterly reporting by Q4.
Process Objective	Risk Assessment and Management Process	Ensure all risk mitigation plans are updated by risk owners on a quarterly basis.
Control Objective	Risk Response	Ensure the risk response process identifies risk strategies such as avoidance, reduction, acceptance, or sharing; determines risk responsibilities; and considers risk tolerance levels.

Table B-1 Examples of Objectives

Processes

Simply stated, processes are used to manage and organize a set of activities and to help ensure that organizational goals are being met.

Each process represents a series of steps or activities designed to take one or more inputs and create some sort of output(s) that delivers a service or product to meet specific expectations or desired objectives/goals for a particular group of customers. Usually a process consists of one or more written procedures that describe the actions that people (and/or systems) perform. In summary, processes are put into place to guide how an organization does work in order to produce value for customers.

Example Process

An example of a process would be the assessment and management of IT risks. The process would represent a set of activities and may look like this:

Determine the Context -> Identify Risks -> Assess Risks -> Prioritize -> Respond -> Monitor

- Potential inputs: Internal and external audit reports, business stakeholder interviews, vendor assessments, vulnerability scans
- Potential outputs: Risk registers, risk reports, mitigation tracking reports
- What business goal does this process meet? Manage IT-related business risks

Several frameworks describe the various IT processes, interdependencies, inputs, outputs, and metrics, most notably COBIT and IT Infrastructure Library (ITIL). These frameworks are discussed later in this appendix. For more detailed information on business process design or improvement, you may want to research business process modeling or methodologies and toolkits on the Web, such as RummlerBrache (https://www.rummlerbrache.com/toolkit).

Capability Maturity Models

Initially developed by the Carnegie Mellon Software Engineering Institute as a software evaluation model, *capability maturity models* (CMMs) are used in several frameworks to determine and describe incremental maturity levels of business process and engineering capabilities.

The maturity of a process or system is rated on a scale from 0 to 5, with a level of 0 referring to a nonexistent process and a 5 equating to the greatest maturity in capability. The ideal maturity rating differs for each organization.

CMMs can be used to assist organizations with developing process maturity baselines, benchmarking, prioritizing activities, and defining improvement. They can be useful in conjunction with any process framework adopted. An example of a CMM is that which is used in the COBIT framework to describe the maturity of COBIT-identified processes.

Table B-2 provides an example of a maturity model and the ratings used to measure those processes outlined in COBIT. Figure B-1 represents how this maturity model

Level	Label	Description
0	Nonexistent	Complete lack of any recognizable processes. The enterprise has not even recognized that there is an issue to be addressed.
1	Initial/ad hoc	There is evidence that the enterprise has recognized that the issues exist and need to be addressed. There are, however, no standardized processes; instead, ad hoc approaches tend to be applied on an individual or case-by-case basis. The overall approach to management is disorganized.
2	Repeatable but intuitive	Processes have developed to the stage where similar procedures are followed by different people undertaking the same task. There is no formal training or communication of standard procedures and responsibility is left to the individual. There is a high degree of reliance on the knowledge of individuals and, therefore, errors are likely.
3	Defined process	Procedures have been defined and documented and communicated through training. It is mandated that these processes should be followed; however, it is unlikely that deviations will be detected. The procedures themselves are not sophisticated but are the formalization of existing practices.
4	Managed and measurable	Management monitors and measures compliance with procedures and takes action when processes appear not to be working effectively. Processes are under constant improvement and provide good practice. Automation and tools are used in a limited or fragmented way.
5	Optimized	Processes have been refined to a level of good practice, based on the results of continuous improvement and maturity modeling with other enterprises. IT is used in an integrated way to automate the workflow, providing tools to improve quality and effectiveness, and making the enterprise quick to adapt.

Table B-2   Example Process Maturity Model

Figure B-1
Rating scale for
process maturity

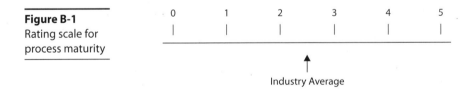

Industry Average

Legend: 0 - No processes at all
1 - Processes are ad hoc and disorganized
2 - Consistent processes
3 - Documented processes
4 - Measured and managed processes
5 - Processes are continuously improved

can be used to show current and future desirable states and for benchmarking against competitors or industry standards.

 NOTE Other capability maturity models exist as well and may be used to evaluate the overall maturity of functions such as an IT audit department, internal audit as a whole, or enterprise risk management.

Controls

Controls are the means by which management establishes and measures processes by which organizational objectives are achieved. Controls may be established to improve effectiveness, efficiency, integrity of operations, and compliance with laws and regulations.

Frameworks may represent collections of controls that work together to achieve an entire range of an organization's objectives. Because many organizations operate similarly, standard frameworks of controls have been established, which can be adopted in whole or in part. Some of these frameworks are discussed later in this appendix.

There are many ways in which the frameworks discuss controls:

- **Internal control** This aggregate system is put into place in an organization to provide management with reasonable assurance that objectives are met. It refers to the many control objectives and related control activities in place to meet business objectives.

- **Control objectives** Control objectives ensure that business objectives are achieved and that undesirable events are prevented or detected and corrected.

- **Control activities/controls** These are the specific policies, procedures, and activities in place to meet the control objectives. Controls may be put into place to help prevent or detect and correct undesired events in the organization.

There are two main types of controls: general controls and application controls. General controls support the functioning of the application controls—both are needed for complete and accurate information processing. General controls apply to all systems and the computing environment, while application controls handle application processing.

Some examples of IT general controls include

- Access controls
- Change management
- Security controls
- Incident management
- System development life cycle (SDLC)
- Source code and versioning controls
- Disaster recovery and business continuity plans

- Monitoring and logging
- Event management

Examples of application controls include

- Authentication
- Authorization
- Completeness checks
- Validation checks
- Input controls
- Output controls
- Identification/access controls

Tips for identifying and documenting controls include the following:

- When looking at processes, define potential risks/points of failure (that is, what could go wrong in a process, or what would happen if this process fails?).
- Identify controls and examine whether they operate at a level of granularity that make them adequate in preventing or detecting errors and irregularities.
- Check to see if the control's strength is commensurate with the level of risk the control is mitigating.
- The cost of implementing a control should not exceed the expected benefit.
- Well-designed internal controls can lead to operating efficiencies and sometimes reduction in costs and risks.
- Effective controls reduce risk, increase the likelihood of value delivery, and improve efficiency because of fewer errors and a consistent management approach.
- Auditors are responsible for the independent evaluation of internal controls and whether they are adequate.

The Deming Cycle

Dr. W. Edwards Deming developed a four-step quality control process known around the world as the Deming Cycle, PDSA (Plan-Do-Study-Act) or PDCA (Plan-Do-Check-Act). The steps in the Deming Cycle are

- **Plan**   Establish objectives to align with desired outcomes and predict results.
- **Do**   Execute the plan in a controlled manner.
- **Study/Check**   Check the results on a regular basis and compare with expectations.
- **Act**   Analyze the results and take corrective actions.

Many of the frameworks described in this appendix are based on this concept, which supports continuous quality monitoring and business process improvement. Each framework defines the set of processes and how they support the different steps. For example, in the project management frameworks, specific processes are necessary for properly planning, executing, and monitoring a project. Although each of the processes is unique, they collectively contribute to continuous quality and improvement.

Projects

Virtually all technology professionals participate in projects. Projects are organized activities intended to bring about a new process or system or a change to a process or system. Projects are generally thought of as unique, one-time, nonrepeated efforts. Examples of projects include

- Design and development of a new software application
- Migration of an application from Windows to Linux
- Development of a new accounts payable process

Most of the time, formal project management techniques will be implemented in conjunction with software or system acquisition and implementation processes.

Here are a few things to keep in mind about projects and project management:

- Projects are a means to organize activities that are not addressed within normal operational limits. Often, projects are used as a means to achieve an organization's strategic objectives.

- Project management consists of a set of processes.

- Projects are similar to operations in that they are performed by people, constrained by resources, planned, executed, and controlled.

- Operations are ongoing, while projects are temporary and unique.

- Project and operational objectives are different. Once project objectives are met, the project is considered complete. Operational objectives are ongoing and are in place to sustain business activities and goals. Once operational objectives are met, new ones are adopted and things keep moving forward.

- Controls exist in projects. Examples include comparing actual with planned budgets and time, analysis of variances, assessment of trends to effect process improvements, evaluation of alternatives, and recommendation of corrective actions.

There are frameworks available to assist you, should you be responsible for planning or managing a project. In addition, the information provided within these frameworks may be helpful if you are responsible for auditing the SDLC or assessing any related project documentation.

Frameworks, Methodologies, and Guidance

Creating appropriate processes and controls can be daunting. This is where frameworks, methodologies, and guidance can become valuable. Many internationally recognized organizations have already conducted the research and documented their conclusions, resulting in the publication of several high-quality frameworks and methodologies.

Before re-creating the wheel, consider utilizing these existing resources as a basis for your process and control discussions, audits, or project planning. Many of the documents available today are quite comprehensive and can save you a great deal of time and heartache. They often outline key processes and controls that can be implemented to meet specific business goals and objectives.

The following sections identify the most renowned and respected resources with regard to managing IT governance, controls, processes, information security, and projects. The background and high points of each resource is described, as well as how each may be useful for a CISA-certified professional.

Keep in mind that the following resources are merely structures of ideas formulated to solve or address complex issues, or outline possible courses of action to represent a preferred and reliable approach to an idea. They are not intended to be the sole source for your efforts.

Business Model for Information Security (BMIS)

Based on research conducted by the Institute for Critical Information Infrastructure Protection at the University of Southern California Marshall School of Business, the Business Model for Information Security (BMIS) was developed in 2009 by ISACA mainly for use by security professionals. Primarily built on a foundation of systems theory, the business model is unique in that it tackles security issues from a systems perspective. The model is not intended to replace security program best practices but should be used to integrate security program components into one complete functioning system.

BMIS Highlights

BMIS is a three-dimensional model, similar to a pyramid, composed of four elements and six dynamic connections, shown in Figure B-2. The model requires balance and can be distorted should one of the elements not be addressed or appropriately managed. Using a business-oriented approach, the model explores the elements and the relationships between them in great detail.

The model's primary objective is to create an "intentional" security culture through instituting awareness campaigns, developing cross-functional teams (such as risk councils and steering committees), and obtaining management support and commitment. In addition, this intentional culture should aim to fulfill enterprise governance needs by ensuring the alignment of information security objectives to business objectives; instituting a risk-based approach to controls; instilling balance among the organization, people, process, and technology; and aligning security strategies across the enterprise.

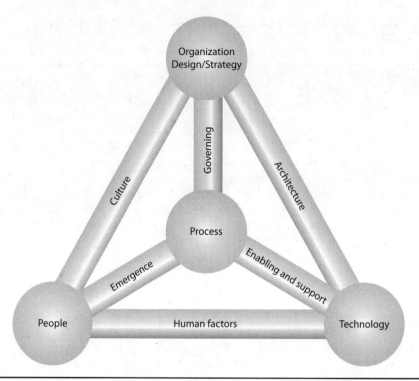

Figure B-2 The Business Model for Information Security

BMIS Value for the CISA

The model is useful for senior executives, information security managers, those responsible for managing business risk, and those responsible for designing, implementing, monitoring, or improving an Information Security Management System (ISMS).

In addition, the model is useful if you are looking for ways to align information security to privacy, risk, physical security, and compliance. It also provides a common language to talk to business management about information security.

COSO Internal Control – Integrated Framework

Originally authored in 1992 by Coopers & Lybrand (now PricewaterhouseCoopers), and updated in 2013, for the Committee of Sponsoring Organizations of the Treadway Commission (COSO), the COSO Internal Control – Integrated Framework is by far one of the most fundamental frameworks available to an IS auditor. It defines internal control and provides guidance for assessing and improving internal control systems. The term "internal control" stems from senior management's need to "control" and be "in control."

Formed in 1985, COSO is a private-sector group in the United States sponsored by the American Institute of Certified Public Accountants (AICPA), American Accounting Association (AAA), Financial Executives International (FEI), The Institute of Internal Auditors (IIA), and The Institute of Management Accountants (IMA).

It is highly recommended that those who are CISA-certified take the time to become familiar with this framework. It is the basis of internal control descriptions and is fundamental to understanding, assessing, and making improvements to an internal control environment successfully.

COSO Highlights

The COSO framework is composed of four volumes, the framework volume being the most widely used, which contains these sections:

- Executive summary
- Framework
- Tools for assessing control effectiveness
- Approaches and examples for internal controls

The framework and appendices focus on one main concept and five interrelated internal control components that compose what many call the COSO "cube" (see Figure B-3).

The COSO cube consists of three dimensions:

- Objectives
- Components
- Business units/areas

Figure B-3
The COSO cube

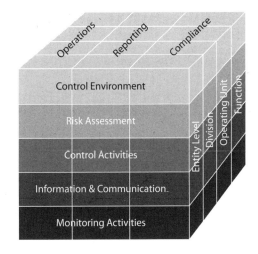

The main concept of the COSO framework is that internal control is a *process, affected by people*, designed to provide *reasonable assurance* that the entity is meeting its *objectives*:

- **Process** A process is not one event, but a series of activities that are integrated in an organization.

- **Affected by people** People across the organization establish objectives and ensure that controls are in place. At the same time, internal controls affect people's actions.

- **Reasonable assurance** Internal control can provide only reasonable, not absolute, assurance that the organization is meeting its objectives, because of limitations such as human judgment and error, potential for controls to be circumvented through collusion, or controls being overridden by management.

- **Objectives** Internal control helps organizations meet the following objectives, all of which are separate but may overlap:

  - Effectiveness and efficiency of operations: performance, profitability goals, safeguarding assets

  - Reliability of financial reporting: prepare reliable financial reports while preventing financial misstatements

  - Compliance with applicable laws and regulations

In addition, the framework describes the following five interrelated components of internal control:

- **Control environment** This is the foundation of how the business operates, where individuals know that they are to conduct activities and carry out control responsibilities. A solid control environment is exhibited by integrity and ethical values, commitment to competence, dedicated board and audit committees, management's philosophy and operating style, the organizational structure, assignment of authority and responsibility, and human resources policies and practices.

- **Risk assessment** The organization should establish mechanisms to identify, assess, and manage the risks to objectives. This component is evident through the establishment of entity-wide and activity-level objectives, risks identified, and how well the organization manages change.

- **Control activities** Control policies and procedures are in place to ensure that the actions and controls needed to ensure objectives are met and that mitigating activities are carried out. Examples of control activities include approvals, authorizations, security of assets, segregation of duties, top-level reviews, information processing, physical controls, and performance indicators. Success in this area occurs when control activities are linked to meeting objectives and are deemed necessary to mitigate risks in meeting the objectives.

- **Information and communication**   Information pertaining to control activities should flow through the organization so that management knows whether its objectives are being met. It should be in a form and time frame that ensures that people can carry out responses. Information and communication can be considered successful when they are flowing up to management and down to employees in sufficient detail and in a timely manner, when established communication channels exist internally and with external parties, and when management is open and receptive to suggestions.

- **Monitoring activities**   The process should be monitored and modified as necessary through ongoing monitoring activities, separate evaluations, or a combination of both. Control deficiencies should be reported upstream, with important issues being communicated to the board or senior management. Management needs information to ensure that the internal control system is effective, to identify whether new risks have developed, and to determine if internal controls are still relevant. Monitoring is considered successful when it is ongoing and built into operations, separate evaluations are conducted, and deficiencies are reported in an open and timely basis.

When is an internal control system effective? When you've assessed and concluded that the five components listed previously are functioning successfully and the organization's objectives are being met:

- The board of directors and management understand operational objectives and whether they are being achieved.

- Financial reporting is prepared reliably.

- Laws and regulations are being complied with.

Making Sense of the COSO Cube

Each organization has three main types of objectives that span across all divisions and groups. To ensure that these objectives are met, the five interrelated internal control components must be in place. There must be a solid control environment, with risk assessments to confirm that adequate control activities are in place to mitigate risk and that risks to objectives are properly managed. In addition, information regarding risk, activities, and deficiencies should be reported through the organization and responded to in a timely manner. Evaluation and monitoring of activities to ensure that objectives are met should occur on a continual basis, with corrective actions taken when necessary.

COSO Value for the CISA

COSO is the basis for the majority of all internal control discussions and process and control frameworks. Whether you are educating others on internal controls, as outlined in the CISA Professional Code of Ethics, or evaluating or testing internal control effectiveness, COSO provides a foundation with which the CISA should be familiar. COSO is a great source for definitions and explanations. Due to the enterprise basis by which COSO has been developed, it is highly recommended that it serve as the foundation, and other frameworks, such as COBIT, ISO/IEC 27001/2, NIST 800-53, and ITIL, build upon this knowledge. Other COSO guidance includes ongoing updates to the Enterprise Risk Management – Integrated Framework and the Internal Control – Integrated Framework, such as *COSO in the Cyber Age*, which provides guidance for utilizing frameworks to evaluate cybersecurity.

COBIT

The COBIT framework was created in 1992 by ISACA and the IT Governance Institute (ITGI). In 1996, the first edition of COBIT was released to the public. Version 5 was released in April 2012 and COBIT 2019, the most current version, was released in 2018. COBIT aligns with and meets COSO internal control requirements.

COBIT was developed to assist companies in maximizing the benefits derived through the strategic use of IT. Broad, yet detailed, the COBIT framework was designed for use by managers, auditors, and IT personnel and contains IT governance guidance. The framework aligns IT goals with general business goals; contains a comprehensive list of IT processes; and links related control objectives, metrics, and roles and responsibilities for carrying out process activities.

COBIT Highlights

The COBIT framework is composed of six elements, covered in multiple documents:

- Executive summary
- Governance and control framework
- Control objectives
- Management guidelines
- Implementation guide
- IT assurance guide

The framework is complex and requires dedicated individuals to implement and compile the elements. The framework is based upon the notion of strong IT governance, stressing alignment to business strategy and goals.

As with many frameworks, COBIT is based on the Deming Cycle, with 37 IT processes falling into the following five domains:

- **Evaluate, Direct, and Monitor (EDM)**   Processes in this domain are focused on the overall governance of IT.
- **Align, Plan, and Organize (APO)**   Processes in this domain are dedicated to ensuring that IT goals are strategically aligned with the business strategy and goals.
- **Build, Acquire, and Implement (BAI)**   Processes for acquiring software, personnel, and external resources are covered in this domain, along with those processes needed to implement them.

- **Deliver, Service, and Support (DSS)**   Operational managers can focus on these processes for delivering and supporting the resources utilized, including people, infrastructure, software, and third-party services.
- **Monitor, Evaluate, and Assess (MEA)**   Processes ensure that the outcome is delivered and measured against initial expectations and that deviations are investigated and result in corrective actions.

Figure B-4 provides an overview of the COBIT framework. Note how the 37 process categories coincide with a cycle similar to that of the Deming Cycle (Plan-Do-Check-Act).

Each process is outlined in the framework and details the associated process objectives, control objectives, roles and responsibilities charts, metrics, and process maturity levels.

COBIT Value for the CISA

The COBIT framework is ideal for those looking for a comprehensive framework to outline how IT goals and processes align with business goals, what processes IT should consider implementing, and related control objectives.

COBIT nicely ties general business goals to IT goals with the use of a balanced scorecard. This enables you to see which IT processes are key in supporting specific IT goals and, ultimately, business goals.

For personnel who are implementing or evaluating a process, the COBIT framework provides an overview of general processes utilized to manage IT. Each process in COBIT includes key activities, control objectives, and metrics that should be in place.

COBIT is one of the most comprehensive and widely used frameworks available, which equates to the development of additional research and documentation being available.

Figure B-4
The COBIT 2019 framework

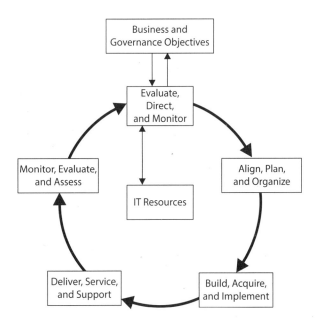

See the ISACA web site for an extensive line of COBIT and COBIT-related documents. Not only will you find COBIT translated into more than eight foreign languages, you also will find documents mapping popular frameworks with COBIT, a "quickstart" guide to implementing COBIT, and guides for utilizing COBIT within various focus areas (such as security, Sarbanes-Oxley, IT assurance, and service management).

GTAG

Global Technology Audit Guides (GTAG) represents a series of documents developed by the IIA to help organizations with their IT control framework and audit practices. The guides are developed to assist with describing the importance of IT controls as part of the internal controls environment, establishing the roles and responsibilities required for ensuring controls are in place and assessed, and addressing the risks inherent in using and managing IT. The first GTAG guide was published in 2005 and it was updated in 2012.

Several groups aid in the development of the guides, including an advanced technology committee and other professional organizations (ACIPA, FEI, ISSA, Sans Institute, and Carnegie Mellon SEI).

The GTAG guides are geared toward chief audit executives and other executives needing a high-level overview of the latest technology issues and how they affect the organization, the associated risks, and necessary IT controls.

GTAG Highlights

Several GTAG guides have been published and are available through the IIA. At the time of writing, these guides are

- Data Analysis Technologies (Previously GTAG 16)
- Developing the IT Audit Plan (Previously GTAG 11)
- Fraud Prevention and Detection in an Automated World (Previously GTAG 13)
- Identity and Access Management (Previously GTAG 9)
- Information Technology Outsourcing, 2nd Edition (Previously GTAG 7)
- Information Technology Risk and Controls, 2nd Edition (Previously GTAG 1)
- Management of IT Auditing, 2nd Edition (Previously GTAG 4)
- Understanding and Auditing Big Data

GTAG Value for the CISA

Although GTAG documents primarily target the chief audit executive, IS auditors can utilize them to learn more about controls and for assistance with describing IT risk and controls in executive terms.

GTAG can be downloaded by IIA members free of charge, or for a reasonable price for nonmembers, from the IIA web site. Hard copies of some guides can also be purchased should you choose to add the publications to your library.

GAIT

The Guide to the Assessment of IT Risk (GAIT) was developed by the IIA to assist with IT general-control risk assessment and scoping for Sarbanes-Oxley Section 404 (SOX 404). The GAIT series provides guidance on assessing risk to the financial statements and key controls that could be implemented within the business and IT sectors, including IT general controls (IT GC) and automated controls.

GAIT Highlights

The methodology provides guidance on identifying risks and related controls needed to protect financially significant applications and related processes and data.

Currently, three practice guides are available:

- *GAIT Methodology* uses a risk-based approach to scope IT GCs
- *GAIT for IT General Controls Deficiency Assessment* (GAIT 2)
- *GAIT for Business and IT Risk* (GAIT-R)

GAIT does not specify key controls, but it does describe the IT GC processes and control objectives that should be addressed.

GAIT is based on four principles, according to the IIA:

- The identification of risks and related controls in IT general control processes (for example, in change management, deployment, access security, and operations) should be a continuation of the top-down and risk-based approach used to identify significant accounts, risks to those accounts, and key controls in the business processes.
- The IT general control process risks that need to be identified are those that affect critical IT functionality in financially significant applications and related data.
- The IT general control process risks that need to be identified exist in processes and at various IT layers: application program code, databases, operating systems, and networks.
- Risks in IT general control processes are mitigated by the achievement of IT control objectives, not individual controls.

GAIT Value for the CISA

If you are asked to scope and identify key IT general controls for SOX 404 compliance or general prevention of financial reporting misstatements, GAIT can help you determine which control objectives and controls are key through the use of a risk assessment. GAIT can be downloaded by IIA members free of charge, or for a reasonable price for nonmembers, from the IIA web site.

ISF Standard of Good Practice for Information Security

Standard of Good Practice for Information Security was first published in 1996 by the Information Security Forum (ISF). The ISF is a nonprofit organization dedicated to the development of information security good practices. Like ISACA, ISF is a paid membership organization with chapters throughout the world. The standard was last updated in October 2018.

ISF Standard of Good Practice for Information Security Highlights

Standard of Good Practice for Information Security contains guidance on security principles, control objectives, and controls in the following areas:

- Enterprise security management
- Critical business applications
- Computer installations
- Networks
- Systems development
- End-user environment

Although the document is divided into these main areas, there are reference tables so that specific control areas that may be present in more than one area can be found easily.

Standard of Good Practice Value for the CISA

Standard of Good Practice for Information Security can provide you with information security control objective statements and describes the controls that should be in place. If you are looking for specific controls, such as access controls or controls around firewalls or e-mails, a reference guide can help point you to the proper section within each area.

ISO/IEC 27001 and 27002

Organizations facing privacy and information security concerns may decide that they need to implement a formal ISMS to ensure that information security is managed, risks are assessed, and appropriate controls are put in place to mitigate risk to information security. Published in 2005 and updated in 2013 by the International Organization for Standardization (ISO) and the International Electrotechnical Commission (IEC), ISO/IEC 27001 is a standard that organizations can use for developing, implementing, controlling, and improving an ISMS. ISO/IEC 27001 provides the general framework for the ISMS, while ISO/IEC 27002 provides a more detailed list of control objectives and recommended controls. The controls presented within the document act as a guide for those who are responsible for initiating, implementing, or maintaining an ISMS.

Organizations may choose to be certified as compliant with ISO/IEC 27001 by an accredited certification body. Similar to other ISO management system certifications, there is a three-stage audit process.

In addition to the ISF *Standard of Good Practice for Information Security* guide, there is complete coverage on the topics found in ISO/IEC 27002, COBIT, CIS 20 Critical

Security Controls, plus a glossary, ISMS auditing guidelines for the management system and controls, implementation guide, and guides on IT network security and application security, to name a few.

ISO/IEC 27001 and 27002 Highlights

The concept of an ISMS centers on the preservation of

- **Confidentiality**   Ensuring that information is accessible only to those authorized to have access
- **Integrity**   Safeguarding the accuracy and completeness of information and processing methods
- **Availability**   Ensuring that authorized users have access to information and associated assets when required

The ISO/IEC standard contains an introductory section and a description of the risk management process framework needed around information security controls. Each organization is expected to perform an information security risk assessment process to determine which regulatory requirements must be satisfied before selecting appropriate controls.

The 14 main domains in ISO/IEC 27001 and 27002 are

- Information security policy
- Organization of information security
- Human resource security
- Asset management
- Access control
- Cryptography
- Physical and environmental security
- Operations security
- Communications security
- System acquisition, development, and maintenance
- Supplier relationships
- Information security incident management
- Information security aspects of business continuity management
- Compliance

Control objectives and controls for each section are listed in the standards and code of practice. ISO/IEC 27001 focuses on the implementation of controls throughout the Deming Cycle, while ISO/IEC 27002 lists the good practice controls an organization can implement.

ISO/IEC 27001 and 27002 Value for the CISA

Those involved with implementing or assessing information security controls or the management of information security risk may find it helpful to look more closely into these standards. ISO/IEC standards documents can be purchased from the International Standards Organization.

NIST SP 800-53 and NIST SP 800-53A

NIST Special Publication 800-53 (NIST SP 800-53), "Security and Privacy Controls for Federal Information Systems and Organizations," provides a comprehensive catalog of security and privacy controls for U.S. federal organizations and information systems to support compliance with the mandatory federal standard FIPS Publication 200 Minimum Security Requirements for Federal Information and Information Systems. Revision 4 of SP 800-53 was published in January 2015, revision 5 is in draft as of this writing.

Of special interest to the IS auditor is the document NIST SP 800-53A, "Assessing Security and Privacy Controls in Federal Information Systems and Organizations." A companion to NIST SP 800-53, this publication guides the IS audit for auditing all the controls in NIST SP 800-53. For each control in NIST SP 800-53, this document describes what the IS auditor should examine, who she should interview, and what to test. Control owners will also derive value as they will know what would be expected of them in an audit; this will lead to better control design and operation.

NIST SP 800-53 Highlights

NIST SP 800-53 revision 4 contains almost 1,000 controls across 18 control families. FIPS Publication 199 requires organizations to categorize information systems as low-impact, moderate-impact, or high-impact, in terms of criticality, based upon the types of information they process. To support this framework, the NIST SP 800-53 has grouped minimum security control requirements security control baselines for low-impact, moderate-impact, and high-impact rated systems to provide a starting point for establishing expected control requirements.

The 18 control families in NIST SP 800-53R4 are

- AC – Access Control
- AU – Audit and Accountability
- AT – Awareness and Training
- CM – Configuration Management
- CP – Contingency Planning
- IA – Identification and Authentication
- IR – Incident Response
- MA – Maintenance
- MP – Media Protection
- PS – Personnel Security

- PE – Physical and Environmental Protection
- PL – Planning
- PM – Program Management
- RA – Risk Assessment
- CA – Security Assessment and Authorization
- SC – System and Communications Protection
- SI – System and Information Integrity
- SA – System and Services Acquisition

Appendix J in the publication contains a catalog of privacy controls. These sections are

- AP – Authority and Purpose
- AR – Accountability, Audit, and Risk Management
- DI – Data Quality and Integrity
- DM – Data Minimization and Retention

Privacy controls in revision 5 of NIST SP 800-53 will be integrated, not separated as they are in revision 4.

NIST SP 800-53 Value for the CISA

Those involved with establishing or auditing U.S. federal information systems and cyber-security programs should be familiar with the NIST SP 800-53 control set. Moreover, IS auditors should also be familiar with NIST SP 800-53A, as this contains detailed guidance on auditing all the controls in NIST SP 800-53.

NIST Cybersecurity Framework

The NIST Cybersecurity Framework (NIST CSF) was published in 2014 as a response to the Presidential Executive Order 13636, Improving Critical Infrastructure Cyber-security. The order directed NIST to work with stakeholders to develop a voluntary framework—based on existing standards, guidelines, and practices—for reducing cyber-risks to critical infrastructure. The CSF is not intended to be another set of standards. Instead, the CSF is a body of work that is built around industry best practices and utilizes direct references to internationally accepted cybersecurity and risk management standards.

The NIST CSF is made up of three main components: the *core, implementation tiers,* and *profiles*. The core is broken down into five functions that each includes categories of cybersecurity outcomes and informative references that provide guidance to standards and practices that illustrate methods to achieve the stated outcomes within each category. The implementation tiers provide context on how well an organization understands its cybersecurity risk and the processes in place to manage that risk. Finally, the profiles assist an organization in defining the outcomes it desires to achieve from the framework categories.

NIST CSF Highlights

The NIST CSF core is broken down into the following five functions:

- **Identify**   Develop an understanding of the business context and resources that support critical operations to enable the organization to identify and prioritize cybersecurity risks that can impact operations.

- **Protect**   Implement appropriate safeguards to minimize the operational impact of a potential cybersecurity event.

- **Detect**   Implement capabilities to detect suspicious and malicious activities.

- **Respond**   Implement capabilities to respond to cybersecurity events properly.

- **Recover**   Maintain plans and activities to enable timely restoration of capabilities or services that might be impaired after a cybersecurity event.

Four tiers are intended to describe an organization's cybersecurity program capabilities in support of organizational goals and objectives. It is important to highlight that the tiers do not represent maturity levels or how well capabilities are executed. The tiers are meant to describe and support decision-making about how to manage cybersecurity risk and prioritization of resources. Here is a summary of the tiers:

- **Partial**   Cybersecurity program may not be formalized and risks are managed in an ad hoc or reactive manner. There is limited awareness of cybersecurity risk across the organization.

- **Risk Informed**   Cybersecurity program activities are approved by management and linked to organizational risk concerns and business objectives. However, cybersecurity considerations in business programs may not be consistent at all levels in the organization.

- **Repeatable**   Cybersecurity program activities are formally approved and supported by policy. Cybersecurity program capabilities are regularly reviewed and updated based on risk management processes and changes in business objectives.

- **Adaptive**   There is a consistent organization-wide approach to managing cybersecurity risk through formal policies, standards, and procedures. Cybersecurity program capabilities are routinely updated based on previous and current cybersecurity events, lessons learned, and predictive indicators. The organization strives to adapt proactively to changing threat landscapes.

NIST CSF Value for the CISA

The CSF can enable the IS auditor to develop and utilize common terminology that is easier for nonsecurity professionals to comprehend. In addition, the informative reference feature makes the NIST CSF a powerful and flexible model to facilitate development and auditing of a cybersecurity program against defined objectives and outcomes.

Payment Card Industry Data Security Standard

If an organization stores, processes, or transmits credit card data, it is subject to the Payment Card Industry Data Security Standard (PCI-DSS). In 2001, Visa launched its Cardholder Information Security Program (CISP), which established a set of security requirements for merchants and merchant service providers. Shortly after, other card brands launched their payment card security programs, such as MasterCard Site Data Protection (SDP) Program, American Express Data Security Operating Procedures (DSOP), and the Discover Information Security & Compliance (DISC) program. This resulted in merchants and service providers that accepted multiple payment card types having to maintain compliance with multiple security programs. The PCI-DSS grew out the need to standardize security requirements across the major card brand security programs. In 2004, the payment card companies came together to establish this comprehensive set of security requirements for merchants and service providers.

The PCI Security Standards Council (PCI SSC) is the independent group that was set up to oversee the standard going forward. An important distinction is that while the PCI SSC manages the technical and operational aspects of the standard, the compliance enforcement actions are the responsibility of the individual card brands. A top-down approach is taken from the card brands where they hold the card-issuing banks (banks that issue consumers a credit card) and acquiring banks (banks that set up merchant accounts and enable merchants to accept credit card payments). The merchant agreement with acquiring banks will include a requirement for the merchant to maintain compliance with the PCI-DSS and requires all service providers that the merchant engages with to uphold those compliance requirements.

PCI-DSS Highlights

PCI-DSS v3.2.1 was released in May 2018. The standard comprises 251 control activities organized within six principles and 12 security requirements.

Build and Maintain a Secure Network and Systems	1. Install and maintain a firewall configuration to protect cardholder data. 2. Do not use vendor-supplied defaults for system passwords and other security parameters.
Protect Cardholder Data	3. Protect stored cardholder data. 4. Encrypt transmission of cardholder data across open, public networks.
Maintain a Vulnerability Management Program	5. Protect all systems against malware and regularly update antivirus software or programs. 6. Develop and maintain secure systems and applications.
Implement Strong Access Control Measures	7. Restrict access to cardholder data by business need to know. 8. Identify and authenticate access to system components. 9. Restrict physical access to cardholder data.
Regularly Monitor and Test Networks	10. Track and monitor all access to network resources and cardholder data. 11. Regularly test security systems and processes.
Maintain an Information Security Policy	12. Maintain a policy that addresses information security for all personnel.

Merchant Levels   Merchants and service providers are classified based on the number of credit card transactions they process. The classification levels dictate how the organization must certify compliance with the PCI-DSS.

Although each card brand maintains its own table of merchant levels, a basic summary of merchant levels is as follows:

- **Level 1**   More than 6 million transactions annually
- **Level 2**   Between 1 and 6 million transactions annually
- **Level 3**   Between 20,000 and 1 million transactions annually
- **Level 4**   Less than 20,000 transactions annually

It is important to note that Visa, MasterCard, and Discover use similar criteria, while American Express and JCB have their own classification criteria. Although American Express and JCB have their own criteria, it is generally accepted that if you are at a level for one provider, you will be considered the same for all.

Level 1 merchants are required to have quarterly external vulnerability scans performed by a PCI approved scanning vendor (ASV) and have an independent validation of compliance conducted by a Qualified Security Assessor (QSA) who tests the implementation of the PCI-DSS control activities and delivers a Report of Compliance (ROC). Level 2–4 merchants, depending on the acquirer's requirements, may simply be required to fill out a much shorter self-evaluation, called a Self-Assessment Questionnaire (SAQ).

Service Provider Levels   A service provider or merchant may use a third-party service provider to store, process, or transmit cardholder data on its behalf, or a service provider may manage components such as routers, firewalls, databases, physical security, and/or servers.

Service providers are classified in a similar manner as merchants. Although each card brand maintains its own table of service provider levels, a basic summary of merchant levels is as follows:

- **Level 1**   More than 300,000 transactions annually
- **Level 2**   Less than 300,000 transactions annually

Like level 1 merchants, Level 1 service providers are required to have quarterly internal and external vulnerability scans performed by a PCI ASV and have an independent validation of compliance conducted by a QSA who tests the implementation of the PCI-DSS control activities and delivers a ROC that the service provider will submit to the respective payment brands.

Similar to merchant levels, it is generally accepted that if you are at a level for one provider, you will be considered the same for all.

PCI-DSS Value for the CISA

The IS auditor may be called upon to assist in preparing an organization for a PCI-DSS compliance assessment. The PCI-DSS is a prescriptive standard by design and includes detailed testing procedures and guidance for each control activity. The PCI SSC publishes a number of supporting documents to enable consistent interpretation of the PCI-DSS.

 NOTE   You can find more information regarding the PCI-DSS and supporting documentation in the document library on the PCI SSC web site, https://www.pcisecuritystandards.org/.

CIS Controls

The Center for Internet Security (CIS) Critical Security Controls (CSC) was first published in 2009 through a partnership with the U.S. National Security Agency, CIS, and SANS Institute as a way to assist the Department of Defense in prioritizing its security initiatives. The working group that was formed utilized the premise that only actual attack information could be used to justify the control activities. Under this premise, the working group focused on gaining consensus to the control activities and the priority of control activities by sharing and analyzing cybersecurity attack experience and data. These exercises resulted in the 20 key control activities. The publication was originally owned by the SANS Institute; ownership of the standard was transferred to CIS in 2015. The framework is now known as the CIS Controls.

Historically, the CIS Controls utilized the order of the controls as the implied order of prioritizing an organization's cybersecurity activities. This approach led to grouping the controls into categories of Basic, Foundational, and Organizational. However, it has been observed that many of the practices found within the CIS Basic grouping of controls can be difficult to implement for organizations with limited resources. This highlighted an opportunity to provide recommended prioritization of specific control activities believed to provide the best risk mitigation based on the real-world attack data reviewed while balancing resource constraints and effective risk mitigation. This resulted in the introduction of implementation groups within version 7.1 of the Controls. These groups are intended to assist organizations in focusing their security resources on specific objectives while leveraging the CIS controls.

The three implementation group categories are

- **Implementation Group 1**   An organization with limited resources and cybersecurity expertise available to implement subcontrols

- **Implementation Group 2**   An organization with moderate resources and cybersecurity expertise available to implement subcontrols

- **Implementation Group 3**   A mature organization with significant resources and cybersecurity expertise available to allocate to subcontrols

Version 7.1 was released in April 2019 and is the latest version as of this writing.

CIS CSC Highlights

The CIS Controls comprise 20 key activities, or critical security controls, that an organization can implement to mitigate cybersecurity attacks. The controls are described in a direct manner that is intended to be understandable by technical and nontechnical individuals:

1. Inventory and Control of Hardware Assets
2. Inventory and Control of Software Assets
3. Continuous Vulnerability Management
4. Controlled Use of Administrative Privileges
5. Secure Configuration for Hardware and Software on Mobile Devices, Laptops, Workstations and Servers
6. Maintenance, Monitoring and Analysis of Audit Logs
7. Email and Web Browser Protections
8. Malware Defenses
9. Limitation and Control of Network Ports, Protocols and Services
10. Data Recovery Capabilities
11. Secure Configuration for Network Devices, such as Firewalls, Routers and Switches
12. Boundary Defense
13. Data Protection
14. Controlled Access Based on the Need to Know
15. Wireless Access Control
16. Account Monitoring and Control
17. Implement a Security Awareness and Training Program
18. Application Software Security
19. Incident Response and Management
20. Penetration Tests and Red Team Exercises

CIS Controls Value for the CISA

The CIS Controls framework strives to provide a balance between providing descriptive, but not overly prescriptive, control activities that enable organizations to build cybersecurity program capabilities in a prioritized manner. The CIS Controls can enable the IS auditor to facilitate discussions utilizing common terminology for descriptions of control activities, which can simplify audit planning and execution.

IT Assurance Framework

In 2006 the ISACA board of directors approved the IT Assurance Framework (ITAF) project to address the need for audit and assurance standards. As the project matured, additional needs, such as taxonomy and guidelines, were identified and addressed. In 2014 ISACA published the third and current edition of *ITAF: A Professional Practices Framework for IT Audit/Assurance.*

The ITAF establishes mandatory standards that address IT audit and assurance professionals' roles and responsibilities, knowledge, skills and diligence, conduct, and reporting requirements. The framework also provides nonmandatory guidance on design, conduct, and reporting on IT audit and assurance engagements and defines common IT assurance terms and concepts.

ITAF Highlights

There are three categories of audit and assurance standards in the document: general, performance, and reporting.

General Standards   These are the guiding principles by which the profession operates. These standards deal with all IT audit and assurance activities conducted, and include

- Audit charter
- Organizational independence
- Professional independence
- Reasonable expectation
- Due professional care
- Proficiency
- Assertions
- Criteria

Performance Standards   These focus on the IT audit or assurance professional's conduct of assurance activities such as the design of audit and assurance activities, evidence, findings, and conclusions. ISACA IS Auditing Standards are the performance standards (current IS Auditing Standards are listed in more detail in Chapter 3). These standards include topics such as

- Engagement planning
- Risk assessment in planning
- Performance and supervision
- Materiality
- Evidence
- Using the work of other experts
- Irregularity and illegal acts

Reporting Standards   These standards cover the report produced by the IT audit or assurance professional and address

- Reporting
- Follow-up activities

The ITAF documentation also outlines guidelines for applying the standards. Guidelines assist the IT audit or assurance professional with understanding enterprise-wide issues and IT management processes as well as processes, procedures, methodologies, and approaches for conducting an IT audit and assurance engagement.

ITAF incorporates ISACA's IS auditing standards and the ISACA Code of Professional Ethics. In addition, all of the ISACA guidance is mapped to the framework. For more detailed information, see the ISACA web site.

ITAF Value for the CISA

The standards within ITAF are mandatory for all CISAs. It is recommended that all CISAs review the standards prior to certification and formulate good habits to ensure that standards are applied to any assurance work conducted. Although not mandatory, these guidelines, tools, and techniques can assist anyone needing to conduct IT audits or assurance activities, and they can even assist those on the receiving end of IT audit or assurance reports.

ITIL

In the 1980s, when the British government determined that the level of IT service quality provided to it was insufficient, it was clear that an IT process framework was needed. The Central Computer and Telecommunications Agency (CCTA) sponsored the development of the Information Technology Infrastructure Library (ITIL, pronounced *EYE-till*), which began guiding organizations on the efficient and financially responsible use of IT resources within public and private entities worldwide.

The current version of ITIL, known as ITIL v4, released in January 2019, consists of a collection of books that contain guidelines for different aspects of good practice around IT service management (ITSM) and aligning IT services to business needs. When all volumes are combined, ITIL presents a comprehensive view of proper provisioning and management of IT services.

ITIL Highlights

ITIL is a high-level, user-focused process framework that defines a common language for ITSM processes. The framework describes the IT service organization that delivers agreed-upon services and maintains the infrastructure on which the services are delivered. One of the critical components of ITIL is that the services and maintenance must be aligned and realigned according to business needs. To do this, the framework closely aligns its five volumes with the Deming Cycle:

- ***ITIL Service Strategy***   This volume focuses on determining potential market opportunities with regard to delivering IT services, with sections dedicated to service portfolio management and financial management.

- *ITIL Service Design*   This volume describes how to design proposed services with adequate processes and resources to support them. Availability management, capacity management, continuity management, and security management are key areas of service design.

- *ITIL Service Transition*   This volume describes the implementation of the design and creation or modification of the IT services. Key areas identified are change management, release management, configuration management, and service knowledge management.

- *ITIL Service Operation*   This volume provides guidance on the activities needed to operate IT services and maintain them according to service-level agreements. It focuses on the key areas of incident management, problem management, event management, and request fulfillment.

- *ITIL Continual Service Improvement*   This volume focuses on how to ensure that the IT services delivered to the business are continually improved through service reporting, service measurement, and service-level management.

ITIL outlines the general IT processes needed to manage IT; the resources, outputs, and inputs utilized; and the controls that must be implemented to ensure business goals are met (such as policies and budgets).

ITIL Value for the CISA

Whether documenting, implementing, or assessing processes, the IS auditor can utilize the ITIL volumes for additional information on specific IT processes, such as change management or incident management. The framework outlines recommended controls to ensure that IT services are delivered as promised.

NOTE   The volumes of ITIL v4 can be purchased online from AXELOS at www .axelos.com.

PMBOK Guide

A Guide to the Project Management Body of Knowledge (PMBOK Guide) is a guide on project management fundamentals and practices. The guide is published by the Project Management Institute (PMI). It began as a whitepaper in 1987 and was published as a guide in 1996. The sixth edition was released in 2017.

Not only is PMBOK a guide to project management, it also is an internationally recognized standard on project management practices. Those with an interest in obtaining certification in this area may want to look into becoming certified as a Project Management Professional (PMP) through the PMI.

PMBOK Highlights

The PMBOK Guide describes the many processes that are often used in managing projects. It consists of five process groups and ten knowledge areas.

Process Groups Forty-seven processes are used by project teams. These processes fall into five groups, which are consistent with the Plan-Do-Check-Act activities of the Deming Cycle:

- **Initiating process group** Defines the project/phase and gathers authorization
- **Planning process group** Defines objectives and courses of actions required to meet objectives and scope
- **Executing process group** Correspond to carrying out the project management plan
- **Monitoring and controlling process group** Regularly monitors progress and identifies variances from the plan; takes corrective actions
- **Closing process group** Concludes that all objectives are met and the service, product, or result is accepted by the customer/sponsor; end of the project

The Project Management Knowledge Areas Ten knowledge areas are needed for an effective project management program and the processes involved, as well as inputs, outputs, tools, and techniques for each. Each process belongs to a process group and is associated with a knowledge area. This section represents the bulk of the guide and details how the 47 processes interrelate. The ten knowledge areas are

- Project Integration Management
- Project Scope Management
- Project Time Management
- Project Cost Management
- Project Quality Management
- Project Human Resource Management
- Project Communications Management
- Project Risk Management
- Project Procurement Management
- Project Stakeholder Management

PMBOK Value for the CISA

As an IS auditor, you may be asked to take a closer look at the process for introducing new applications or systems into your organization. Many times, new applications and systems are delivered via a system/software/solution delivery life cycle and coupled with project management. Solutions are scoped and assessed, projects ensue, and a great deal of activity and documentation occurs throughout the process. Project management methodologies and frameworks can help you make sense of this madness.

In addition, project management skills can be valuable for an IS auditor. Being well versed in project management can help ensure that your IS audit work remains in scope and on budget and that you are planning your time adequately. For example, you will want to ensure that you are giving yourself enough time for audit planning, documentation, and accommodating complex interview schedules.

The PMBOK Guide can be purchased from booksellers worldwide or from the PMI.

PRINCE2

PRojects IN Controlled Environments (PRINCE) is a structured project management standard covering project management fundamentals. The original standard was developed in 1989 by the U.K. Office of Government Commerce (OGC) specifically for IT project management. In 1996, PRINCE2 was released, representing a change in focus from beyond IT to general project management. In 2009, it was relaunched as PRINCE2:2009 Refresh (hereafter referred to as PRINCE2) and updated in 2017. In addition to becoming the de facto standard for project management in the U.K., the standard has been adopted by organizations worldwide, although not as commonly in North America as some of the other frameworks described in this appendix. As with ITIL, an individual may pass an exam to become accredited.

PRINCE2 Highlights

PRINCE2 consists of one main manual: *Managing Successful Projects with PRINCE2.* It is similar to the PMBOK Guide in that it consists of processes and components, but it is different in that it fully describes the methodology and implementation techniques. The main concept behind PRINCE2 is that projects should have an organized and controlled start, middle, and end. Although it is not as comprehensive as PMBOK, PRINCE2 supplements general project management knowledge by specifically describing how to manage projects in a controlled and organized manner.

PRINCE2 is a process-driven framework and integrates well with other processes and practices, such as Agile Scrum. The framework details 45 processes categorized in seven process groups. The process groups lead you through the project life cycle, similar to the Deming Cycle:

1. Starting up a project

2. Directing a project

3. Initiating a project

4. Controlling a stage

5. Managing product delivery

6. Managing stage boundaries

7. Closing a project

Key inputs, outputs, goals, and activities are defined for each process. In addition, a maturity model is available to measure project management capability maturity. Another bonus is that the entire framework can be tailored for each project, as every process has guidance on how to scale it for small or large projects. This results in a flexible, scalable, and fully described framework.

Similar to PMBOK knowledge areas, PRINCE2 details seven "themes" that are deemed critical for project success:

- Business case
- Organization
- Quality
- Plans
- Risk
- Change
- Progress

PRINCE2 Value for the CISA

As an IS auditor, you may be asked to take a closer look at the process for introducing new applications or systems to your organization, including the software/system/solution delivery cycle and associated project management methodology and documentation. In addition, project management skills can be valuable for an IS auditor.

Similar to PMBOK, PRINCE2 will provide you with general guidance on project management processes and controls. PRINCE2 is complementary to PMBOK in that it helps shape and direct the use of PMBOK through the introduction of certain techniques. PMBOK will lay a more comprehensive foundation, whereas PRINCE2 will describe how to start managing projects and put the pieces together.

Risk IT

Published in 2009 by ISACA, Risk IT is the first comprehensive IT-specific risk framework that has been developed. The framework is based upon enterprise risk management frameworks such as COSO ERM and ISO/IEC 31000, making it much easier to integrate the management of IT risks into overall enterprise risk management. Risk IT also complements COBIT. Risk IT provides guidance for managing all aspects of IT-related risks, including project, value delivery, compliance, security, availability, service delivery, and recovery risks.

Risk IT Highlights

Two specifically significant documents have been published by ISACA: *The Risk IT Framework*, containing the principles, process details, management guidelines, and domain maturity models, and *The Risk IT Practitioner Guide*, which provides an overview of the Risk IT process model, describes how Risk IT links to COBIT and Val IT, and describes in detail how to use the model.

To ensure the effective enterprise governance and management of IT risk, *The Risk IT Framework* is based upon the following principles:

- Always align with business objectives.
- Align IT risk management with enterprise risk management.

- Balance the costs and benefits of IT risk management.
- Promote fair and open communication of IT risks.
- Establish the right tone from the top, while defining and enforcing accountability.
- Ensure a continuous process that is a part of daily activities.

There are three main domains in the framework: risk governance, risk evaluation, and risk response. Each of these domains is supported by three processes with various activities. Similar to COBIT, the guidance will provide a list of components, inputs and outputs, RACI charts, goals, and metrics for each process. The framework is depicted in Figure B-5.

In addition to the guiding principles and process model mentioned earlier, the Risk IT Framework contains good practice guidance, domain maturity models, reference materials, and a high-level comparison of risk frameworks.

For more detailed guidance on governing and managing risk, *The Risk IT Practitioner Guide* walks you through the entire process, from defining a risk universe, developing risk appetite and risk tolerance, to setting up risk scenarios, responding to risks, and prioritizing risks.

NOTE You can find more information and download or purchase both documents at the ISACA web site.

Risk IT Practice Value for the CISA

If you are being asked to audit an IT risk program or identify, govern, or manage IT-related risks, *The Risk IT Framework* and *The Risk IT Practitioner's Guide* will be of great value to you. These can also help with assessing risk and comparing it against the organization's risk appetite and risk tolerance, or they can assist with the integration of IT risk management within an existing enterprise risk management program.

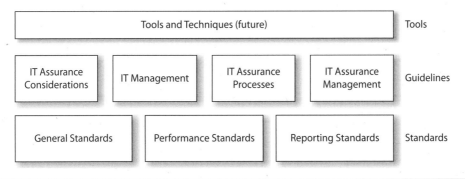

Figure B-5   The Risk IT Framework

Val IT

Developed in 2006 by the ITGI, Val IT is a governance framework focused on the management of the IT-related business investments and portfolios. It is based on and attempts to address the "Four Areas" as described in John Thorp's book *The Information Paradox: Realizing the Business Benefits of Information Technology*:

- Are we doing the right things?
- Are we doing them the right way?
- Are we getting them done well?
- Are we getting the benefits?

Val IT complements COBIT, and in fact the elements covered in VAL IT are included within the scope of COBIT, adding best practices for measuring, monitoring, and maximizing the realization of business value from IT investments. Val IT focuses on the IT investment decision processes and the realization of benefits, whereas COBIT focuses on the execution of IT processes.

Val IT Highlights

There are four Val IT publications: *The Val IT Framework 2.0*; *Getting Started with Value Management*; *The Business Case Guide: Using Val IT 2.0*; and *Value Management Guidance for Assurance Professionals: Using Val IT 2.0*.

The Val IT Framework 2.0 contains information on the framework's seven key principles, three domains, key processes, and related practices.

Val IT is based upon the following seven principles:

- IT-enabled investments will be managed as a portfolio of investments.
- IT-enabled investments will include the full scope of activities required to achieve business value.
- IT-enabled investments will be managed through their full economic life cycle.
- Value delivery practices will recognize that there are different categories of investments that will be evaluated and managed differently.
- Value delivery practices will define and monitor key metrics and respond quickly to any changes or deviations.
- Value delivery practices will engage all stakeholders and assign appropriate accountability for the delivery of capabilities and the realization of business benefits.
- Value delivery practices will be continually monitored, evaluated, and improved.

The principles are applied to three Val IT domains: value governance, portfolio management, and investment management. Each of these domains contains various processes, each enabled by a number of key management practices. Similar to COBIT, for each process identified in Val IT, you can find associated inputs and outputs, RACI charts, goals, and metrics.

Getting Started with Value Management provides various approaches for implementing Val IT. Documentation includes assessment templates, maturity models, and approaches for managing and sustaining change.

The Business Case Guide: Using Val IT 2.0 provides guidance for developing an effective business case. Business cases are developed for IT-enabled investments and consider the following:

- Resources are needed for development
- A technology/IT service that will be supported
- An operational capability that will be enabled
- A business capability that will be created
- Stakeholder value that will be realized

This publication outlines an eight-step process for developing the business case that involves building a fact sheet, analyzing various data and risk, appraising the risk and/or return of the investment, documentation, and review.

Value Management Guidance for Assurance Professionals: Using Val IT 2.0 describes how to use Val IT to support an assurance review of IT investment governance for all three Val IT domains. Included is a set of assurance tests covering the full scope of Val IT as well as guidance for planning and scoping assurance activities.

Val IT Value for the CISA

Val IT publications, especially *Value Management Guidance for Assurance Professionals: Using Val IT 2.0*, can be useful tools should you need to audit or assess how IT investments and the IT portfolio are managed and governed. More information about Val IT can be obtained at the ISACA web site.

Summary of Frameworks

Table B-3 contains a summary of the frameworks discussed in this appendix. The table indicates whether the framework is available for a fee, the primary focus of the framework, and best uses for the framework.

Pointers for Successful Use of Frameworks

- Take time to learn the fundamentals of governance, controls, and processes. Become familiar with COSO, COBIT, and fundamental GTAG documents.
- Not one single framework is the "right" framework.
- There has been a great deal of research on governance, controls, and frameworks. Start here—don't reinvent the wheel.
- Use frameworks for guidance and tailor them to your unique organization.

Title	Summary	Free Online/ Hardcopy Cost	Primary Focus						Best Use
			DemCyc	MatMod	Proc	ContObj	Cont	Gov	
COSO Internal Control – Integrated Framework	Provides general overview of enterprise internal control.	NO/$				X	X	X	To get an overview of what internal control is. Foundational. Can use Illustrative Tools volume to assist with risk, controls, and objectives.
COBIT 2019	Provides detailed framework of IT processes and controls.	YES*/$$	X	X	X	X	X	X	Details on processes, RACI, control objectives, and audit foundation. Links all other frameworks to it; most comprehensive/detailed. Audit and implementation.
GAIT	Assess scope of IT general controls.	YES*/$			X	X			Determine/assess risk and scope IT general controls. Assists with SOX 404 planning.
GTAG	High-level overview of IT audit and controls.	YES*/$			X				Foundational: provides overviews of IT controls in business terminology.
ISF Standard of Good Practice for Information Security	Overview of information security controls/ domains.	NO/$$			X	X			Excellent resource when implementing information security controls.
ISO/IEC 27001	Overview of information security controls/ domains.	NO/$$	X		X	X	X		Overview, details on information systems. Control/activities. Use for audit and implementation of information security controls.
NIST SP 800-53	Detailed controls framework.	YES/0				X	X		Government agencies and their suppliers; orgs that require more cybersecurity rigor.
NIST CSF		YES/0	X	X		X	X		Orgs that need to formalize their cybersecurity efforts.
PCI-DSS	Requirements for all orgs that process cardholder data.	Yes/0				X	X		Compliance for protection of cardholder data; also valuable for protecting other types of sensitive data.

Framework	Description	Free?	DemCyc	MatMod	Proc	ContObj	Cont	Gov	Notes
CIS Critical Controls	Detailed controls framework.	Yes/0					X	X	Excellent controls framework for orgs just starting on cybersecurity controls.
ITAF	Standards and guidance for conducting IT audit and assurance activities.	YES*/$				X			Fundamental framework for every CISA as it contains mandatory standards and several guidelines to assist with conducting IT audit and assurance activities.
ITGI Boardroom Briefing	Overview of IT governance.	YES*/$				X		X	Overview of the five main components of IT governance.
ITIL	Service delivery standards.	NO/$$			X	X			Overview. Use for guidance in improving service delivery processes.
PMBOK Guide	Enterprise project management.	NO/$			X	X			Provides thorough guidance on managing projects: what to do.
PRINCE2	IT project management.	NO/$$			X	X			Guidance on managing projects: how to do it.
RISK IT	IT-related business risk governance and management. Complements COBIT.	YES*/$			X	X		X	Best used for developing or auditing IT risk processes and/or programs.
Val IT	Governance of IT-enabled business investments and the portfolio. Complements COBIT.	YES*/$				X		X	Useful for CISAs needing to audit the IT-enabled business investment or portfolio management processes.

*   Must be an ISACA or IIA member to download the documents free of charge
\$ Denotes materials that can be purchased for less than $100US
\$\$ Denotes materials that can be purchased directly or through membership, more than $100US
Key to Primary Focus Areas:
  DemCyc – Deming Cycle – continuous improvement
  MatMod – maturity model
  Proc – business process
  ContObj – control objectives
  Cont – controls
  Gov – governance

Table B-3   Summary of Frameworks

Notes

- Goals and objectives define what the organization is trying to achieve.
- Governance is what organizations put in place to identify and ensure achievement of goals, objectives, and strategies.
- A process is a set of activities that is put in place to maximize effectiveness and efficiency of operations. Organizations can manage operations through processes.
- Maturity models are often used to measure the maturity of process capabilities.
- The Deming Cycle focuses on continuous improvement through the implementation of a range of processes that address planning, execution, monitoring, and taking corrective actions.
- Control objectives are developed to ensure that business objectives are achieved.
- Control activities support control objectives and can be implemented within processes.
- Projects are temporary, unique, and have specific objectives and controls implemented.

This appendix focused on processes and internal controls, and described the various frameworks, methodologies, and guides available as resources. Now that we have examined the available resources, it's time to put all of this to use. For an overview of conducting professional audits, see Appendix A.

References

- Board Briefing on IT Governance: 2nd Edition; IT Governance Institute. https://www.isaca.org/itgi
- Business Model for Information Security (BMIS); ISACA. https://www.isaca.org/BMIS
- Business Motivation Model; Business Rules Group. https://www.businessrulesgroup.org/bmm.shtml
- Certified in the Governance of Enterprise IT (CGEIT) certification; ISACA. https://www.isaca.org/cgeit
- CIS Controls. https://www.cisecurity.org/controls/
- COBIT; ISACA. https://www.isaca.org/COBIT
- COSO Internal Control – Integrated Framework; Committee of Sponsoring Organizations of the Treadway Commission (COSO). https://www.coso.org/ic.htm

- Enterprise Risk Management – Integrated Framework (2004); COSO. https://www.coso.org/-ERM.htm

- Global Technology Audit Guides (GTAG); Institute of Internal Auditors. https://na.theiia.org

- Guidance for Assurance Professionals Using Val IT 2.0; ISACA. https://www.isaca.org

- Guidance on Monitoring Internal Control Systems; COSO. https://www.coso.org/guidanceonmonitoring.htm

- Guide to the Assessment of IT Risk (GAIT); Institute of Internal Auditors. https://na.theiia.org

- A Guide to the Project Management Body of Knowledge (PMBOK); Project Management Institute (PMI). https://www.pmi.org

- Information Technology Assurance Framework (ITAF): A Professional Practices Framework for IT Assurance; ISACA. https://www.isaca.org/itaf

- Information Technology Infrastructure Library (ITIL) 2011; AXELOS. https://www.axelos.com/best-practice-solutions/itil

- Information technology – Security techniques – Code of practice for information security management (ISO/IEC 27002:2013); ISO. https://www.iso.org

- Information technology – Security techniques – Information security management systems – Requirements (ISO/IEC 27001:2013); ISO. https://www.iso.org

- The ISF Standard of Good Practice for Information Security; Information Security Forum (ISF). https://www.securityforum.org/tool/the-standard-of-good-practice-for-information-security

- Managing Successful Projects with PRINCE2; AXELOS. https://www.axelos.com/best-practice-solutions/prince2

- NIST Cybersecurity Framework. https://www.nist.gov/cyberframework

- NIST SP 800-53R4. https://csrc.nist.gov/

- Payment Card Industry Data Security Standard (PCI-DSS). https://www.pcisecuritystandards.org/

- Risk IT Framework and Risk IT Practitioner Guide; ISACA. https://www.isaca.org/riskit

- The Rummler-Brache Toolkit; RummelerBrache. https://www.rummlerbrache.com/toolkit

- Val IT Framework for Business Technology Management; ISACA. https://www.isaca.org/valit

About the Online Content

This book comes complete with TotalTester Online customizable practice exam software with 300 practice exam questions.

System Requirements

The current and previous major versions of the following desktop browsers are recommended and supported: Chrome, Microsoft Edge, Firefox, and Safari. These browsers update frequently, and sometimes an update may cause compatibility issues with the TotalTester Online or other content hosted on the Training Hub. If you run into a problem using one of these browsers, please try using another until the problem is resolved.

Your Total Seminars Training Hub Account

To get access to the online content you will need to create an account on the Total Seminars Training Hub. Registration is free, and you will be able to track all your online content using your account. You may also opt in if you wish to receive marketing information from McGraw-Hill Education or Total Seminars, but this is not required for you to gain access to the online content.

Privacy Notice

McGraw-Hill Education values your privacy. Please be sure to read the Privacy Notice available during registration to see how the information you have provided will be used. You may view our Corporate Customer Privacy Policy by visiting the McGraw-Hill Education Privacy Center. Visit the **mheducation.com** site and click **Privacy** at the bottom of the page.

Single User License Terms and Conditions

Online access to the digital content included with this book is governed by the McGraw-Hill Education License Agreement outlined next. By using this digital content you agree to the terms of that license.

Access   To register and activate your Total Seminars Training Hub account, simply follow these easy steps.

1. Go to this URL: **hub.totalsem.com/mheclaim**
2. To Register and create a new Training Hub account, enter your e-mail address, name, and password. No further personal information (such as credit card number) is required to create an account.

 NOTE   If you already have a Total Seminars Training Hub account, select **Log in** and enter your e-mail and password. Otherwise, follow the remaining steps.

---

3. Enter your Product Key: `qsvr-df60-7pq6`
4. Click to accept the user license terms.
5. Click **Register and Claim** to create your account. You will be taken to the Training Hub and have access to the content for this book.

Duration of License   Access to your online content through the Total Seminars Training Hub will expire one year from the date the publisher declares the book out of print.

Your purchase of this McGraw-Hill Education product, including its access code, through a retail store is subject to the refund policy of that store.

The Content is a copyrighted work of McGraw-Hill Education, and McGraw-Hill Education reserves all rights in and to the Content. The Work is © 2020 by McGraw-Hill Education, LLC.

Restrictions on Transfer   The user is receiving only a limited right to use the Content for the user's own internal and personal use, dependent on purchase and continued ownership of this book. The user may not reproduce, forward, modify, create derivative works based upon, transmit, distribute, disseminate, sell, publish, or sublicense the Content or in any way commingle the Content with other third-party content without McGraw-Hill Education's consent.

Limited Warranty   The McGraw-Hill Education Content is provided on an "as is" basis. Neither McGraw-Hill Education nor its licensors make any guarantees or warranties of any kind, either express or implied, including, but not limited to, implied warranties of merchantability or fitness for a particular purpose or use as to any McGraw-Hill Education Content or the information therein or any warranties as to the accuracy, completeness, correctness, or results to be obtained from, accessing or using the McGraw-Hill Education Content, or any material referenced in such Content or any information entered into licensee's product by users or other persons and/or any material available on or that can be accessed through the licensee's product (including via any hyperlink or otherwise) or as to non-infringement of third-party rights. Any warranties of any kind, whether express or implied, are disclaimed. Any material or data obtained through use of the McGraw-Hill Education Content is at your own discretion and risk and user understands that it will be solely responsible for any resulting damage to its computer system or loss of data.

Neither McGraw-Hill Education nor its licensors shall be liable to any subscriber or to any user or anyone else for any inaccuracy, delay, interruption in service, error or omission, regardless of cause, or for any damage resulting therefrom.

In no event will McGraw-Hill Education or its licensors be liable for any indirect, special or consequential damages, including but not limited to, lost time, lost money, lost profits or good will, whether in contract, tort, strict liability or otherwise, and whether or not such damages are foreseen or unforeseen with respect to any use of the McGraw-Hill Education Content.

TotalTester Online

TotalTester Online provides you with a simulation of the CISA exam. Exams can be taken in Practice Mode or Exam Mode. Practice Mode provides an assistance window with hints, references to the book, explanations of the correct and incorrect answers, and the option to check your answer as you take the test. Exam Mode provides a simulation of the actual exam. The number of questions, the types of questions, and the time allowed are intended to be an accurate representation of the exam environment. The option to customize your quiz allows you to create custom exams from selected domains or chapters, and you can further customize the number of questions and time allowed.

To take a test, follow the instructions provided in the previous section to register and activate your Total Seminars Training Hub account. When you register you will be taken to the Total Seminars Training Hub. From the Training Hub Home page, select **CISA All-in-One Exam Guide 4th Edition TotalTester** from the Study drop-down menu at the top of the page, or from the list of Your Topics on the Home page. You can then select the option to customize your quiz and begin testing yourself in Practice Mode or Exam Mode. All exams provide an overall grade and a grade broken down by domain.

Technical Support

For questions regarding the TotalTester or operation of the Training Hub, visit **www .totalsem.com** or e-mail **support@totalsem.com**.

For questions regarding book content, visit **www.mheducation.com/customerservice**.

802.1X A standard for network authentication and access control that can mutually authenticate both people and devices connecting to a LAN or a wireless LAN.

802.11 The wireless network standard, commonly known as Wi-Fi, that can transport data up to 108 Mbit/sec up to a distance of 300 meters.

acceptable use A security policy that defines the types of activities that are acceptable and those that are not acceptable to the organization.

access bypass Any attempt by an intruder to bypass access controls in order to gain entry into a system.

access control Any means that detects or prevents unauthorized access and that permits authorized access.

access control list (ACL) An access control method whereby a list of permitted or denied users (or systems, or services, as the case may be) is used to control access to resources.

access control log A record of attempted accesses.

access control policy A statement that defines the policy for the granting, review, and revocation of access to systems and work areas.

access management A formal business process used to control access to networks and information systems.

access point A device that provides communication services using the 802.11 (Wi-Fi) protocol standard.

access review A review of the users, systems, or other subjects that are permitted to access protected objects. The purpose of a review is to ensure that all subjects are authorized to have access.

account lockout An administrative lock that is placed on a user account when a predetermined event occurs, such as when an expiration date is reached or when there have been several unsuccessful attempts to access the user account.

accumulation of privileges A situation in which an employee accumulates system access privileges over a long period of time and after internal transfers or other privilege changes, but old access privileges have not been removed.

Address Resolution Protocol (ARP) A standard network protocol used to obtain the address for another station on a local area network (LAN).

administrative audit   An audit of operational efficiency.

administrative control   Controls in the form of policies, processes, procedures, and standards.

agile development   Software development process whereby a large project team is broken up into smaller teams, and project deliverables are broken up into smaller pieces, each of which can be attained in a few weeks.

algorithm   In cryptography, a specific mathematical formula that is used to perform encryption, decryption, message digests, and digital signatures.

analytics   *See* audit data analytics.

annualized loss expectancy (ALE)   The expected loss of asset value due to threat realization. ALE is defined as single loss expectancy (SLE) × annualized rate of occurrence (ARO).

annualized rate of occurrence (ARO)   An estimate of the number of times that a threat will occur every year.

anti-malware   Software that uses various means to detect and block malware. *See also* antivirus software.

antivirus software   Software that is designed to detect and remove viruses and other forms of malware.

AppleTalk   The suite of protocols developed by Apple Inc. that are used to transmit packets from one station to another over a network.

appliance   A type of computer with preinstalled software that requires little or no maintenance.

application firewall   A device used to control packets being sent to an application server, primarily to block unwanted or malicious content.

application layer (OSI model)   Layer 7 of the OSI network model. *See also* OSI network model.

application layer (TCP/IP model)   Layer 4 of the TCP/IP network model. The purpose of the application layer is the delivery of messages from one process to another on the same network or on different networks. *See also* TCP/IP network model.

application programming language   *See* programming language.

application server   A server that runs application software.

architecture standard   A standard that defines technology architecture at the database, system, or network level.

ARCI   *See* RACI.

arithmetic logic unit (ALU) The part of a central processing unit that performs arithmetic computations. *See* central processing unit (CPU).

asset inventory The process of confirming the existence, location, and condition of assets; also, the results of such a process.

asset management The processes used to manage the inventory, classification, use, and disposal of assets.

asset value (AV) The value of an IT asset, which is usually (but not necessarily) the asset's replacement value.

assets The collection of property that is owned by an organization.

asymmetric encryption A method for encryption, decryption, and digital signatures that uses pairs of encryption keys: a public key and a private key.

asynchronous replication A type of replication whereby writing data to the remote storage system is not kept in sync with updates on the local storage system. Instead, there may be a time lag, and there is no guarantee that data on the remote system is identical to that on the local storage system. *See also* replication.

Asynchronous Transfer Mode (ATM) A LAN and WAN protocol standard for sending messages in the form of cells over networks. On an ATM network, all messages are transmitted in synchronization with a network-based time clock. A station that wants to send a message to another station must wait for the time clock.

atomicity The characteristic of a complex transaction whereby it is either performed completely as a single unit or not performed at all.

attack surface The set of hardware and software components present on a system or in an environment that can potentially be exploited by an attacker.

attribute sampling A sampling technique used to study the characteristics of a population to determine how many samples possess a specific characteristic. *See also* sampling.

audit charter A written document that defines the mission and goals of the audit program as well as roles and responsibilities.

audit data analytics Techniques used to examine audit evidence computationally to assist auditors in determining control effectiveness.

audit hook Components in software applications used to provide additional transaction monitoring and to create alerts when certain events occur.

audit logging A feature in an application, operating system, or database management system whereby events are recorded in a separate log.

audit methodology A set of audit procedures that is used to accomplish a set of audit objectives.

audit objective   The purpose or goals of an audit. Generally, the objective of an audit is to determine whether controls exist and are effective in some specific aspect of business operations in an organization.

audit procedures   The step-by-step instructions and checklists required to perform specific audit activities. Procedures may include a list of people to interview and questions to ask them, evidence to request, audit tools to use, sampling rates, where and how evidence will be archived, and how evidence will be evaluated.

audit program   The plan for conducting audits over a long period.

audit report   The final, written product of an audit. An audit report will include a description of the purpose, scope, and type of audit performed; persons interviewed; evidence collected; rates and methods of sampling; and findings on the existence and effectiveness of each control.

audit scope   The process, procedures, systems, and applications that are the subject of an audit.

authentication   The process of asserting one's identity and providing proof of that identity. Typically, authentication requires a user ID (the assertion) and a password (the proof). However, authentication can also require stronger means of proof, such as a digital certificate, token, smart card, or biometric.

authorization   The process whereby a system determines what rights and privileges a user has.

automated workpapers   Data that has been captured by computer-assisted audit techniques. *See also* computer-assisted audit technique (CAAT).

automatic control   A control that is enacted through some automatic mechanism that requires little or no human intervention.

availability management   The IT function that consists of activities concerned with the availability of IT applications and services. *See also* IT service management (ITSM).

back door   A section of code that permits someone to bypass access controls and access data or functions. Back doors are commonly placed in programs during development but are removed before programming is complete.

background check   The process of verifying an employment candidate's employment history, education records, professional licenses and certifications, criminal background, and financial background.

background verification   *See* background check.

back-out plan   A procedure used to reverse the effect of a change that was not successful.

backup   The process of copying important data to another media device in the event of a hardware failure, error, or software bug, disaster, that causes damage to data.

backup media rotation   Any scheme used to determine how backup media is to be reused.

balanced scorecard (BSC)   A management tool that is used to measure the performance and effectiveness of an organization.

barbed wire   Coiled or straight wire with sharp barbs that may be placed along the top of a fence or wall to prevent or deter passage by unauthorized personnel.

benchmarking   The practice of measuring a process in order to compare its performance and quality with the same process as performed by another firm. The purpose is to discover opportunities for improvement that may result in lower cost, fewer resources, and higher quality.

benefits realization   The result of strategic planning, process development, and systems development, which all contribute toward a launch of business operations to reach a set of business objectives.

biometrics   Any use of a machine-readable characteristic of a user's body that uniquely identifies the user. Biometrics can be used for strong authentication. Types of biometrics include voice recognition, fingerprint, hand scan, palm vein scan, iris scan, retina scan, facial scan, and handwriting. *See also* authentication; multifactor authentication.

blackmail   An attempt to extort money from an individual or organization through a threat of exposure.

blackout   A complete loss of electric power for more than a few seconds.

blade server   A type of computer architecture in which a main chassis equipped with a power supply, cooling, network, and console connectors contains several slots that are fitted with individual computer modules, or blades. Each blade is an independent computer system.

block cipher   An encryption algorithm that operates on blocks of data.

blockchain   A distributed ledger used to record cryptographically linked transactions.

Bluetooth   A short-range airlink standard for data communications between peripherals and low-power consumption devices.

bollard   A barrier that prevents the entry of vehicles into protected areas.

Border Gateway Protocol (BGP)   A TCP/IP routing protocol used to transmit network routing information from one network router to another in order to determine the most efficient path through a large network.

bot   A type of malware in which agents are implanted by other forms of malware and are programmed to obey remotely issued instructions. *See also* botnet.

bot army   *See* bot; botnet.

botnet   A collection of bots that are under the control of an individual. *See also* bot.

bridge   An Ethernet network device used to interconnect two or more Ethernet networks.

broadcast address   The highest numeric IP address in an IP subnet. When a packet is sent to the network's broadcast address, all active stations on the network will receive it.

brownout   A sustained drop in voltage that can last from several seconds to several hours.

budget   A plan for allocating resources over a certain time period.

bug sweeping   The practice of electronically searching for covert listening devices.

bus   A component in a computer that provides the means for the different components of the computer to communicate with one another.

bus topology   A network topology in which each station is connected to a central cable.

business case   An explanation of the expected benefits to the business that will be realized as a result of a program or project.

business continuity planning (BCP)   The activities required to ensure the continuation of critical business processes.

business functional requirements   Formal statements that describe required business functions that a system must support.

business impact analysis (BIA)   A study used to identify the impact that different disaster scenarios will have on ongoing business operations.

business process life cycle (BPLC)   The life cycle process concerned with the development and maintenance of business processes.

business process management (BPM)   Activities concerned with the development, maintenance, and monitoring of business processes.

business process reengineering (BPR)   The set of activities related to the process of making changes to business processes.

business realization   *See* benefits realization.

business recovery plan   The activities required to recover and resume critical business processes and activities. *See also* response document.

call tree   A method for ensuring the timely notification of key personnel when an event such as a disaster occurs.

campus area network (CAN)   The interconnection of LANs for an organization that has buildings in close proximity.

capability maturity model A model used to measure the relative maturity of an organization or of its processes.

Capability Maturity Model Integration (CMMI) A maturity model that represents the aggregation of other maturity models.

capacity management The IT function that consists of activities that confirm that there is sufficient capacity in IT systems and IT processes to meet service needs. Primarily, an IT system or process has sufficient capacity if its performance falls within an acceptable range, as specified in service-level agreements (SLAs). *See also* IT service management (ITSM); service-level agreement (SLA).

Category 3 A twisted-pair cabling standard that is capable of transporting 10MB Ethernet up to 100 meters (328 ft.). *See also* twisted-pair cable.

Category 5/5e A twisted-pair cabling standard that is capable of transporting 10MB, 100MB, and 1000MB (1GB) Ethernet up to 100 meters (328 ft.). *See also* twisted-pair cable.

Category 6 A twisted-pair cabling standard that is capable of transporting 10MB, 100MB, and 1000MB (1GB) Ethernet up to 100 meters (328 ft.). Category 6 has the same transport capability as Category 5, but with better noise resistance. *See also* twisted-pair cable.

Category 7 A twisted-pair cabling standard that is capable of transporting 10GB Ethernet over 100 meters (328 ft.). *See also* twisted-pair cable.

Category 8 A new cable standard, still under development, designed for high-speed networking in data centers. *See also* twisted-pair cable.

cell The protocol data unit (PDU) for the Asynchronous Transfer Mode (ATM) protocol.

Center for Internet Security Controls A security controls framework developed by the Center for Internet Security (CIS).

central processing unit (CPU) The main hardware component of a computer that executes program instructions.

certificate authority (CA) A trusted party that stores digital certificates and public encryption keys.

certificate revocation list (CRL) An electronic list of digital certificates that have been revoked prior to their expiration date.

certification practice statement (CPS) A published statement that describes the practices used by the CA to issue and manage digital certificates.

chain of custody Documentation that shows the acquisition, storage, control, and analysis of evidence. The chain of custody may be needed if the evidence is to be used in a legal proceeding.

change advisory board   The group of stakeholders from IT and business that propose, discuss, and approve changes to IT systems.

change control   *See* change management.

change control board   *See* change advisory board.

change management   The IT function that is used to control changes made to an IT environment. *See also* IT service management (ITSM).

change request   A formal request for a change to be made in an environment. *See also* change management.

change review   A formal review of a requested change. *See also* change request; change management.

channel service unit/data service unit (CSU/DSU)   A device used to connect a telecommunications circuit to a local device such as a router.

cipher lock   An electronic or mechanical door equipped with combination locks. Only persons who know the combination may unlock the door.

ciphertext   A message, file, or stream of data that has been transformed by an encryption algorithm and rendered unreadable.

circuit switched   A WAN technology where a dedicated, end-to-end communications channel is established that lasts for the duration of the connection.

CISC (complex instruction set computer)   A central processing unit design that uses a comprehensive instruction set. *See also* central processing unit (CPU).

class   The characteristics of an object, including its attributes, properties, fields, and the methods it can perform. *See also* object; method.

class library   A repository where classes are stored. *See also* class.

classful network   A TCP/IP network with addressing that fits into one of the network classes: Class A, Class B, or Class C. A classful network will have a predetermined address range and subnet mask.

classless internet domain routing (CIDR)   A method for creating IP subnets that is more efficient than classful networks.

classless network   A TCP/IP network with addressing that does not fit the classful network scheme, but instead uses an arbitrary subnet mask, as determined by the network's physical and logical design.

client-server application   An application design in which the database and some business logic are stored on a central server and additional business logic plus display logic are stored on each user's workstation.

cloud access security broker (CASB)   A system that monitors and, optionally, controls users' access to cloud-based resources.

cloud computing   A technique of providing a dynamically scalable and usually virtualized computing resource as a service.

cluster   A tightly coupled collection of computers that is used to solve a common task. In a cluster, one or more servers actively perform tasks, while zero or more computers may be in a "standby" state, ready to assume active duty should the need arise.

coaxial   A type of network cable that consists of a solid inner conductor surrounded by an insulating jacket, which is surrounded by a metallic shield, which in turn is surrounded by a plastic jacket.

COBIT   A control framework for managing information systems and security. COBIT is published by ISACA.

code division multiple access (CDMA)   An airlink standard for wireless communications between mobile devices and base stations.

code division multiple access 2000 (CDMA2000)   An airlink standard (updated from CDMA) for wireless communications between mobile devices and base stations.

code of ethics   A statement that defines acceptable and unacceptable professional conduct.

codec   A device or program that encodes or decodes a data stream.

cold site   An alternate processing center where the degree of readiness for recovery systems is low. At the very least, a cold site is nothing more than an empty rack or allocated space on a computer room floor.

compensating control   A control that is implemented because another control cannot be implemented or is ineffective.

compliance audit   An audit to determine the level and degree of compliance to a law, regulation, standard, contract provision, or internal control.

compliance testing   A type of testing used to determine whether control procedures have been properly designed and implemented and are operating properly.

component-based development   A system development life cycle process whereby various components of a larger system are developed separately. *See also* system development life cycle (SDLC).

computer trespass   Unlawful entry into a computer or application.

computer-aided software engineering (CASE)   A broad variety of tools that are used to automate various aspects of application software development.

computer-assisted audit technique (CAAT)   Any technique by which computers are used to automate or simplify the audit process.

confidence coefficient   The probability that a sample selected actually represents the entire population. This is usually expressed as a percentage.

configuration item   A configuration setting in an IT asset. *See also* configuration management.

configuration management   The IT function in which the configuration of components in an IT environment is independently recorded. Configuration management is usually supported by the use of automated tools that inventory and control system configurations. *See also* IT service management (ITSM).

configuration management database (CMDB)   A repository for every component in an environment that contains information on every configuration change made on those components.

configuration standard   A standard that defines the detailed configurations that are used in servers, workstations, operating systems, database management systems, applications, network devices, and other systems.

conspiracy   A plan by two or more persons to commit an illegal act.

Constructive Cost Model (COCOMO)   A method for estimating software development projects based on the number of lines of code and the complexity of the software being developed.

contact list   A list of key personnel and various methods used to contact them. *See also* response document.

container   A method of virtualization whereby several isolated operating zones are created in a running server operation, which isolates programs and data to their respective containers.

continuity of operations plan (COOP)   The activities required to continue critical and strategic business functions at an alternate site. *See also* response document.

continuous and intermittent simulation (CIS)   A continuous auditing technique in which flagged transactions are processed in a parallel simulation and the results compared to production processing results.

continuous auditing   An auditing technique in which sampling and testing are automated and occur continuously.

contract   A binding legal agreement between two parties that may be enforceable in a court of law.

control   A policy, process, or procedure that is created to achieve a desired event or to avoid an unwanted event.

control failure   The result of an audit of a control whereby the control is determined to be ineffective.

control objective   A foundational statement that describes desired states or outcomes from business operations.

control risk   The risk that a material error exists that will not be prevented or detected by the organization's control framework.

control self-assessment (CSA)   A methodology used by an organization to review key business objectives, risks, and controls. Control self-assessment is a self-regulation activity.

corrective action   An action that is initiated to correct an undesired condition.

corrective control   A control that is used after an unwanted event has occurred.

corroboration   An audit technique whereby an IS auditor interviews additional personnel to confirm the validity of evidence obtained from others who were interviewed previously.

countermeasure   Any activity or mechanism designed to reduce risk.

crash gate   Hard barriers that lift into position to prevent the entry (or exit) of unauthorized vehicles and that can be lowered to permit authorized vehicles.

critical path methodology (CPM)   A technique used to identify the most critical path in a project to understand which tasks are most likely to affect the project schedule.

criticality analysis (CA)   A study of each system and process, a consideration of the impact on the organization if it is incapacitated, the likelihood of incapacitation, and the estimated cost of mitigating the risk or impact of incapacitation.

cross-over error rate   The point at which the false reject rate equals the false accept rate. This is the ideal point for a well-tuned biometric system. *See also* biometrics; false reject rate (FRR); false accept rate (FAR).

cryptanalysis   An attack on a cryptosystem whereby the attacker is attempting to determine the encryption key used to encrypt messages.

cryptography   The practice of hiding information from unauthorized persons.

cryptosystem   A set of algorithms used to generate an encryption key, to perform encryption, and to perform decryption.

custodian   A person or group delegated to operate or maintain an asset.

customer relationship management (CRM)   An IS application used to track the details of the relationships with each of an organization's customers.

customization   A unique change that is made to a computer program or system.

cutover   The step in the system development life cycle in which an old replaced system is shut down and a new replacement system is started.

cutover test   An actual test of disaster recovery and/or business continuity response plans. Its purpose is to evaluate the ability of personnel to follow directives in emergency response plans—to actually set up the DR business processing or data processing capability. In a cutover test, personnel shut down production systems and operate recovery systems to assume actual business workload. *See also* disaster recovery plan.

Cybersecurity Framework (CSF)   *See* NIST CSF (National Institute for Standards and Technology Cybersecurity Framework).

cyclic redundancy check (CRC)   A hash function used to create a checksum that detects errors in network transmissions. The Ethernet standard uses a CRC to detect errors.

damage assessment   The process of examining assets after a disaster to determine the extent of damage.

data acquisition   The act of obtaining data for later use in a forensic investigation.

data analytics   *See* audit data analytics.

data classification   The process of assigning a sensitivity classification to a data set or information asset.

data classification policy   Policy that defines sensitivity levels and handling procedures for information.

data control language   A procedural language used to control access to a database.

data definition language (DDL)   A procedural language used to describe the structure of data contained in a database.

data dictionary (DD)   A set of data in a database management system that describes the structure of databases stored there.

data file controls   Controls that ensure the security and integrity of data files and their contents.

data flow architecture   The part of network architecture that is closely related to application and data architecture. *See also* data flow diagram.

data flow diagram   A diagram that illustrates the flow of data within and between systems.

data link layer   Layer 2 of the OSI network model. *See also* OSI network model.

data loss prevention (DLP)   Any of several methods of gaining visibility and control into the presence and movement of sensitive data.

data management utility   A type of utility software used to manipulate, list, transform, query, compare, encrypt, decrypt, import, or export data. *See also* utility software.

data manipulation language (DML)   A procedural language used to insert, delete, and modify data in a database.

data restore   The process of copying data from backup media to a target system for the purpose of restoring lost or damaged data.

database   A collection of structured or unstructured information.

database management system (DBMS)   A software program that facilitates the storage and retrieval of potentially large amounts of structured or unstructured information.

database server   A server that contains and facilitates access to one or more databases.

datagram   The protocol data unit (PDU) for the User Datagram Protocol in the TCP/IP suite.

data-oriented system development (DOSD)   A software development life cycle process that starts with a design of data and interfaces to databases and then moves on to program design.

debugging   The activity of searching for the cause of malfunctions in programs or systems.

decryption   The process of transforming ciphertext into plaintext so that a recipient can read it.

default gateway   A station on a network (usually a router) that is used to forward messages to stations on distant networks.

default password   A password associated with a user account or system account that retains its factory default setting.

deluge   A dry pipe fire sprinkler system with all sprinkler heads open. When the system is operated (for instance, when an alarm is triggered), water flows into the pipes and out of the sprinkler heads. *See also* fire sprinkler system.

denial of service (DoS)   An attack on a computer or network with the intention of causing disruption or malfunction of the target.

desktop computer   A computer used by an individual end user and located at the user's workspace.

destructware   Malware that intentionally destroys information or information systems.

detection risk   The risk that an IS auditor will overlook errors or exceptions during an audit.

detective control   A control that is used to detect events.

deterrent control   A control that is designed to deter people from performing unwanted activities.

development   The process where software code is created.

DevOps   An agile software development and operations model.

DevSecOps   An agile and secure software development and operations model.

diameter   An authentication standard that is the successor to RADIUS. *See also* Remote Authentication Dial-in User Service (RADIUS).

Diffie-Hellman   A popular key exchange algorithm. *See also* key exchange.

digital certificate   An electronic document that contains an identity that is signed with the public key of a certificate authority (CA).

digital envelope   A method that uses two layers of encryption. A symmetric key is used to encrypt a message; then a public or private key is used to encrypt the symmetric key.

digital private branch exchange (DPBX)   A private branch exchange (PBX) that supports digital technologies such as Voice over IP (VoIP) and Session Initiation Protocol (SIP). *See also* private branch exchange (PBX); Voice over IP (VoIP); Session Initiation Protocol (SIP).

digital rights management (DRM)   Any technology used to control the distribution and use of electronic content.

digital signature   The result of encrypting the hash of a message with the originator's private encryption key, used to prove the authenticity and integrity of a message.

digital subscriber line (DSL)   A common carrier standard for transporting data from the Internet to homes and businesses.

digital transformation (DX)   The creative use of information technology to support business operations and solve business problems.

directory   A structure in a file system that is used to store files and, optionally, other directories. *See also* file system.

directory system (DS)   *See* data dictionary (DD).

disaster   An unexpected and unplanned event that results in the disruption of business operations.

disaster declaration criteria   The conditions that must be present to declare a disaster, triggering response and recovery operations.

disaster declaration procedure   Instructions to determine whether to declare a disaster and trigger response and recovery operations. *See also* disaster declaration criteria.

disaster recovery and business continuity requirements   Formal statements that describe required recoverability and continuity characteristics that a system must support.

disaster recovery plan   The activities required to restore critical IT systems and other critical assets, whether in alternate or primary locations. *See also* response document.

disaster recovery planning (DRP)   Activities related to the assessment, salvage, repair, and restoration of facilities and assets.

Disaster Recovery-as-a-Service (DRaaS)   A cloud-based set of tools and services that streamline planning and execution of data backup and data replication for disaster recovery purposes.

discovery sampling   A sampling technique by which at least one exception is sought in a population. *See also* sampling.

Discretionary Access Control (DAC)   An access model by which the owner of an object is able to determine how and by whom the object may be accessed. The discretion of the owner determines permitted accesses by subjects.

disk array   A chassis in which several hard disks can be installed and connected to a server. The individual disk drives can be "hot swapped" in the chassis while the array is still operating.

disk management system (DMS)   An information system used to manage disk media, usually for the purpose of performing information backup. *See also* backup.

distributed denial of service (DDoS)   A denial of service (DoS) attack that originates from many computers. *See also* denial of service (DoS).

document review   A review of some or all disaster recovery and business continuity plans, procedures, and other documentation. Individuals typically review these documents on their own and at their own pace, but within whatever time constraints or deadlines that may have been established.

documentation   The inclusive term that describes charters, processes, procedures, standards, requirements, and other written documents.

Domain Name System (DNS)   A TCP/IP application layer protocol used to translate domain names (such as www.isecbooks.com) into IP addresses (such as 216.3.128.12).

dropout   A momentary loss of power that lasts from a few milliseconds to a few seconds.

dry pipe system   A fire sprinkler system used in locales where ambient temperatures often drop below freezing. In this type of system, pipes are filled with compressed air. When sufficient heat causes one of the sprinkler head fuses (heat-sensitive glass bulbs) to break, a control valve releases water into the piping. *See also* fire sprinkler system.

dual power feeds   The use of two physically separate electric power feeds into a facility.

Dynamic Host Configuration Protocol (DHCP)   A TCP/IP application layer protocol used to assign an IP address, subnet mask, default gateway, IP address of DNS servers, and other information to a workstation that has joined the network.

dynamic random access memory (DRAM)   The most common form of semiconductor memory by which data is stored in capacitors that require periodic refreshing.

E-1   A common carrier standard protocol for transporting voice and data. E-1 can support up to 32 separate voice channels of 64 Kbit/sec each and is used primarily in Europe.

E-3   A common carrier standard protocol for transporting voice and data. E-3 can support up to 512 separate voice channels of 64 Kbit/sec each and is used primarily in Europe.

E-vaulting   The process of backing up data to a cloud-based storage provider. E-vaulting is a form of backup, as distinguished from e-journaling.

east–west traffic   Network traffic moving between and among a tier of servers, between servers within a single virtualization environment, or within a data center. *See also* north–south traffic.

eavesdropping   The act of secretly intercepting and recording a voice or data transmission.

electric generator   A system consisting of an internal combustion engine powered by gasoline, diesel fuel, or natural gas that spins an electric generator. A generator can supply electricity for as long as several days, depending upon the size of its fuel supply and whether it can be refueled.

electrically erasable programmable read-only memory (EEPROM)   A form of permanent memory that can be rewritten using a special program on the computer on which it is installed.

electromagnetic interference (EMI)   Any electric field or magnetic field energy that can potentially interfere with a signal being sent via radiofrequency or over a metallic medium.

electronic protected health information (ePHI)   Patient-related healthcare information in electronic form, as defined by the U.S. Healthcare Insurance Portability and Accountability Act (HIPAA).

elliptic curve   A public key cryptography algorithm.

e-mail   A network-based service used to transmit messages between individuals and groups.

embedded audit module (EAM)   A continuous auditing technique that consists of a special software module embedded within a system that is designed to detect processing anomalies.

emergency communications plan   A plan that outlines the communications required during a disaster. *See also* response document.

emergency response The urgent activities that immediately follow a disaster, including evacuation of personnel, first aid, triage of injured personnel, and possibly firefighting.

employee handbook *See* employee policy manual.

employee policy manual A formal statement of the terms of employment, facts about the organization, benefits, compensation, conduct, and policies.

employment agreement A legal contract between an organization and an employee, which may include a description of duties, roles and responsibilities, confidentiality requirements, compliance requirements, and termination information.

encapsulation A practice in which a method can call on another method to help perform its work. *See also* method.

encryption The act of hiding sensitive information in plain sight. Encryption works by scrambling the characters in a message, using a method known only to the sender and receiver, to make the message useless to anyone who intercepts the message.

encryption key A block of characters used in combination with an encryption algorithm to encrypt or decrypt a stream or block of data.

Enhanced Interior Gateway Routing Protocol (EIGRP) A TCP/IP routing protocol used to transmit network routing information from one network router to another to determine the most efficient path through a large network.

enterprise architecture The model used to map business functions into the IT environment and IT systems in increasing levels of detail, with activities that ensure important business needs are met by IT systems.

erasable programmable read-only memory (EPROM) A form of permanent memory that can be erased by shining ultraviolet (UV) light through a quartz window on the top of the chip.

error handling Functions that are performed when errors in processing are encountered.

espionage The act of spying on an organization.

Ethernet A standard protocol for assembling a stream of data into frames for transport over a physical medium from one station to another on a local area network. On an Ethernet network, any station is free to transmit a packet at any time, provided that another station is not already doing so.

evacuation procedure Instructions to evacuate a work facility safely in the event of a fire, earthquake, or other disaster.

evidence Information gathered by the auditor that provides proof that a control exists and is being operated.

expected error rate   An estimate that expresses the percent of errors or exceptions that may exist in an entire population.

exposure factor (EF)   The financial loss that results from the realization of a threat, expressed as a percentage of the asset's total value.

extreme programming (XP)   An iterative software development methodology that consists of short development cycles intended to improve quality and respond to changing requirements.

false accept rate (FAR)   The rate at which invalid subjects are accepted as valid. This occurs when the biometric system has too large a margin of error. *See also* biometrics.

false reject rate (FRR)   The rate at which valid subjects are rejected as invalid. This occurs when the biometric system has too small a margin of error. *See also* biometrics.

feasibility study   An activity that seeks to determine the expected benefits of a program or project.

fence   A structure that prevents or deters passage by unauthorized personnel.

Fiber Distributed Data Interface (FDDI)   A local area network technology that consists of a "dual ring" with redundant network cabling and counter-rotating logical tokens.

fiber optics   A cabling standard that uses optical fiber instead of metal conductors.

Fibre Channel   A standard protocol for assembling a stream of data into frames for transport over a physical medium from one station to another on a local area network. Fibre Channel is most often found in storage area networks. *See also* storage area network (SAN).

field   A unit of storage in a relational database management system that consists of a single data item within a row. *See also* relational database management system (RDBMS); table; row.

file   A sequence of zero or more characters that is stored as a whole in a file system. A file may be a document, spreadsheet, image, sound file, computer program, or data that is used by a program. *See also* file system.

file activity monitoring (FAM)   Software that detects accesses to sensitive files, usually operating system files.

File Allocation Table (FAT)   A file system used by the MS-DOS operating system as well as by early versions of the Microsoft Windows operating system.

file integrity monitoring (FIM)   Software that detects tampering with sensitive files, usually operating system files.

file server   A server that is used to store files in a central location, usually to make them available to many users.

file system   A logical structure that facilitates the storage of data on a digital storage medium such as a hard drive, CD/DVD-ROM, or flash memory device.

File Transfer Protocol (FTP)   An early and still widely used TCP/IP application layer protocol used for the batch transfer of files or entire directories from one system to another.

File Transfer Protocol Secure (FTPS)   A TCP/IP application layer protocol that is an extension of FTP, in which authentication and transport are encrypted using SSL or TLS. *See also* File Transfer Protocol (FTP); Secure Sockets Layer (SSL); Transport Layer Security (TLS).

financial audit   An audit of an accounting system, accounting department processes, and accounting procedures to determine whether business controls are sufficient to ensure the integrity of financial statements.

financial management   Management for IT services that consists of several activities, including budgeting, capital investment, expense management, project accounting, and project ROI. *See also* IT service management (ITSM); return on investment (ROI).

fire extinguisher   A hand-operated fire suppression device used for fighting small fires.

fire sprinkler system   A fire suppression system that extinguishes a fire by spraying water on it.

firewall   A device that controls the flow of network messages between networks. Placed at the boundary between the Internet and an organization's internal network, firewalls enforce security policy by prohibiting all inbound traffic except for the specific few types of traffic that are permitted to a select few systems.

firmware   A computer's special-purpose storage that is usually used to store the instructions required to start the computer system. Firmware is usually implemented in ROM, PROM, EPROM, EEPROM, or flash.

first in, first out (FIFO)   A backup media rotation scheme in which the oldest backup volumes are used next. *See also* backup media rotation.

flash   A form of permanent memory that can be rewritten by the computer that it is installed on. Flash memory is used by several types of devices, including SD (Secure Digital) cards, Compact Flash, Memory Stick, and USB drives.

foreign key   A field in a table in a relational database management system that references a unique primary key in another table. *See also* relational database management system (RDBMS); table; row; field.

forensic audit   An audit that is performed in support of an anticipated or active legal proceeding.

forensics   The application of procedures and tools during an investigation of a computer or network-related event.

fourth-generation language (4GL) A variety of tools that are used in the development of applications, or that are parts of the applications themselves.

frame The protocol data unit (PDU) at the transport layer of TCP/IP (namely, for Ethernet), and layer 2 of the OSI model.

Frame Relay A common carrier standard for transporting packets from one network to another. Frame Relay is being replaced by MPLS. *See also* Multiprotocol Label Switching (MPLS).

fraud The intentional deception made for personal gain or for damage to another party.

function point analysis (FPA) A method for estimating software development projects based on the number of user inputs, outputs, queries, files, and external interfaces.

functional requirements Statements that describe required characteristics that software must have to support business needs.

functional testing The portion of software testing in which functional requirements are verified.

gate process Any business process that consists of one or more review/approval gates, which must be completed before the process may continue.

gateway A device that acts as a protocol converter or that performs some other type of transformation of messages.

general computing controls (GCC) Controls that are general in nature and implemented across most or all information systems and applications.

General Packet Radio Service (GPRS) An airlink standard for wireless communications between mobile devices and base stations.

generalized audit software (GAS) Audit software that is designed to read data directly from database platforms and flat files.

governance Management's control over policy and processes.

grandfather-father-son A hierarchical backup media rotation scheme that provides for longer retention of some backups. *See also* backup media rotation.

grid computing A large number of loosely coupled computers that are used to solve a common task.

guard dogs Dogs that assist security guards and that can be used to apprehend and control trespassers.

guest A virtual machine running under a hypervisor.

hacker Someone who interferes with or accesses another's computer without authorization.

hardening The technique of configuring a system so that only its essential services and features are active and all others are deactivated. This helps to reduce the attack surface of a system to its essential components only.

hardware monitoring Tools and processes used continuously to observe the health, performance, and capacity of one or more computers.

hardware security module (HSM) A device used to store and protect encryption keys.

hash function A cryptographic operation on a block of data that returns a fixed-length string of characters, used to verify the integrity of a message.

Health Insurance Portability and Accountability Act (HIPAA) A U.S. regulation requiring healthcare delivery organizations, health insurance companies, and other healthcare industry organizations to secure and maintain privacy for electronic protected health information (ePHI).

heating, ventilation, and air conditioning (HVAC) A system that controls temperature and humidity in a facility.

Hierarchical File System (HFS) A file system used on computers running the Mac OS X operating system. *See also* file system.

honeynet A network of computers acting as a honeypot. *See also* honeypot.

honeypot A trap that is designed to detect unauthorized use of information systems.

host-based intrusion detection system (HIDS) An intrusion detection system that is installed on a system and watches for anomalies that could be signs of intrusion. *See also* intrusion detection system (IDS).

hot site An alternate processing center where backup systems are already running and in some state of near-readiness to assume production workload. The systems at a hot site most likely have application software and database management software already loaded and running, perhaps even at the same patch levels as the systems in the primary processing center.

hub An Ethernet network device that is used to connect devices to the network. A hub can be thought of as a multiport repeater.

humidity The amount of water moisture in the air.

hybrid cryptography A cryptosystem that employs two or more iterations or types of cryptography.

Hypertext Transfer Protocol (HTTP) A TCP/IP application layer protocol used to transmit web page contents from web servers to users who are using web browsers.

Hypertext Transfer Protocol Secure (HTTPS) A TCP/IP application layer protocol that is similar to HTTP in its use for transporting data between web servers and browsers. HTTPS is not a separate protocol, but instead is the instance where HTTP is encrypted with SSL or TLS. *See also* Hypertext Transfer Protocol (HTTP); Secure Sockets Layer (SSL); Transport Layer Security (TLS).

hypervisor   Virtualization software that facilitates the operation of one or more virtual machines.

identification   The process of asserting one's identity without providing proof of that identity. *See also* authentication.

identity management   The activity of managing the identity of each employee, contractor, temporary worker, and, optionally, customer, in a single environment or multiple environments.

impact   The actual or expected result from some action such as a threat or disaster.

impact analysis   The analysis of a threat and the impact it would have if it were realized.

implementation   A step in the software development life cycle where new or updated software is placed into the production environment and started.

incident   Any event that is not part of the standard operation of a service and that causes, or may cause, interruption to or a reduction in the quality of that service.

incident management   The IT function that analyzes service outages, service slowdowns, security incidents, and software bugs, and seeks to resolve them to restore normal service. *See also* IT service management (ITSM).

incident prevention   Proactive steps taken to reduce the probability and/or impact of security incidents.

independence   The characteristic of an auditor and his or her relationship to a party being audited. An auditor should be independent of the auditee; this permits the auditor to be objective.

index   An entity in a relational database management system that facilitates rapid searching for specific rows in a table based on a field other than the primary key. *See also* relational database management system (RDBMS); table; row; field; primary key.

indicator of compromise (IoC)   An observation on a network or in an operating system that indicates evidence of a network or computer intrusion.

inert gas system   A fire suppression system that floods a room with an inert gas, displacing oxygen from the room and extinguishing the fire.

information classification   *See* data classification.

information leakage   The tendency for sensitive information to leak out of an organization's databases through various means, most of which are perpetrated by the organization's personnel.

information security management   The aggregation of policies, processes, procedures, and activities implemented to ensure that an organization's security policy is effective.

Information Security Management System (ISMS)   The collection of activities for managing information security, as defined by ISO/IEC 27001.

information security policy   A statement that defines how an organization will classify and protect its important assets.

Infrared Data Association (IrDA)   The organization that has developed technical standards for point-to-point data communications using infrared light. IrDA has largely been replaced with Bluetooth and USB.

infrastructure   The collection of networks, network services, devices, facilities, and system software that facilitates access to, communications with, and protection of business applications.

Infrastructure-as-a-Service (IaaS)   A cloud computing model in which a service provider makes computers and other infrastructure components available to subscribers. *See also* cloud computing.

inherent risk   The risk that material weaknesses are present in existing business processes and no compensating controls are able to detect or prevent them.

inheritance   The property of a class whereby the class's attributes are passed to its children. *See also* class.

initialization vector (IV)   A random number that is needed by some encryption algorithms to begin the encryption process.

input authorization   Controls that ensure that all data input into an information system is authorized by management.

input controls   Administrative and technical controls that determine what data is permitted to be input into an information system. These controls exist to ensure the integrity of information in a system.

input validation   Controls that ensure the type and values of information that are input into a system are appropriate and reasonable.

input/output (I/O) device   Any device that can be connected to a computer that enables the computer to send data to the device as well as receive data from the device.

inquiry and observation   An audit technique whereby an IS auditor asks questions of interviewees and makes observations about personnel behavior and the way they perform work tasks.

inrush   A sudden increase in current flowing to a device, usually associated with the startup of a large motor. This can cause a voltage drop that lasts several seconds.

insourcing   A form of sourcing whereby an employer will use its own employees to perform a function.

instant messaging (IM)   Any of several TCP/IP application layer protocols and tools used to send short text messages over a network.

integrated audit   An audit that combines an operational audit and a financial audit. *See also* operational audit; financial audit.

Integrated Services Digital Network (ISDN)   A common carrier telephone network used to carry voice and data over landlines. ISDN can be thought of as a digital version of the PSTN. *See also* public-switched telephone network (PSTN).

integrated test facility (ITF)   A type of automated test in which an auditor creates fictitious transactions to trace their integrity through the system.

intellectual property   A class of assets owned by an organization, including the organization's designs, architectures, software source code, processes, and procedures.

Interior Gateway Routing Protocol (IGRP)   A TCP/IP routing protocol used to transmit network routing information from one network router to another to determine the most efficient path through a large network.

Intermediate System to Intermediate System (IS-IS)   A TCP/IP routing protocol used to transmit network routing information from one network router to another to determine the most efficient path through a large network.

Internet   The interconnection of the world's TCP/IP networks.

Internet Control Message Protocol (ICMP)   A communications diagnostics protocol that is a part of the TCP/IP suite of protocols.

Internet Group Management Protocol (IGMP)   A TCP/IP Internet layer protocol used to manage group membership in multicast networks.

Internet Key Exchange (IKE)   A protocol used to establish security associations (logical connections) between hosts using the IPsec protocol.

Internet layer (TCP/IP model)   Layer 2 of the TCP/IP network model. The purpose of the Internet layer is the delivery of messages (called packets) from one station to another on the same network or on different networks. *See also* TCP/IP network model.

Internet Message Access Protocol (IMAP)   A TCP/IP application layer protocol used by an end-user program to retrieve e-mail messages from an e-mail server.

Internet Protocol (IP)   The network layer protocol used in the TCP/IP suite of protocols. IP is concerned with the delivery of packets from one station to another, whether the stations are on the same network or on different networks.

Internet Protocol Security (IPsec)   A suite of protocols used to secure IP-based communications by using authentication and encryption.

interprocess communications (IPC) Any of several protocols used for communications between running processes on one system or between systems.

intrusion detection system (IDS) A hardware or software system that detects anomalies that may be signs of an intrusion.

intrusion prevention system (IPS) A hardware or software system that detects and blocks anomalies that may be signs of an intrusion.

IP address An address assigned to a station on a TCP/IP network.

irregularity An event that represents an action that is contrary to accepted practices or policy.

IS audit An audit of an information systems department's operations and systems.

IS operations The day-to-day control of the information systems, applications, and infrastructure that support organizational objectives and processes.

ISACA audit guidelines Published documents that help the IS auditor apply ISACA audit standards.

ISACA audit procedures Published documents that provide sample procedures for performing various audit activities and for auditing various types of technologies and systems.

ISACA audit standards The minimum standards of performance related to security, audits, and the actions that result from audits. The standards are published by ISACA and updated periodically. ISACA audit standards are considered mandatory.

ISAE 3402 (International Standard on Assurance Engagement) audit An external audit of a service provider. An ISAE 3402 audit is performed according to rules established by the International Auditing and Assurance Standards Board (IAASB).

ISO/IEC 15504 An ISO/IEC standard for evaluating the maturity of a software development process.

ISO/IEC 20000 An ISO/IEC standard for IT service management (ITSM).

ISO/IEC 27001 An ISO/IEC standard for IT security management.

ISO/IEC 27002 An ISO/IEC standard for IT security controls.

ISO/IEC 38500 An ISO/IEC standard for corporate governance of information technology.

ISO/IEC 9000 An ISO/IEC standard for a quality management system.

ISO/IEC 9126 An ISO/IEC standard for evaluating the quality of software.

ISO/IEC 9660 An ISO/IEC standard file system used on CD-ROM and DVD-ROM media.

IT Assurance Framework (ITAF) An end-to-end framework developed to guide organizations in developing and managing IT assurance and IT audit.

IT balanced scorecard (IT-BSC) A balanced scorecard used to measure IT organization performance and results. *See also* balanced scorecard (BSC).

IT governance Management's control over IT policy and processes.

IT Infrastructure Library (ITIL) *See* IT service management (ITSM).

IT service management (ITSM) The set of activities that ensures the delivery of IT services is efficient and effective, through active management and the continuous improvement of processes.

IT steering committee A body of senior managers or executives that discusses high-level and long-term issues in the organization.

iterative development process A software development process that consists of one or more repeating loops of planning, requirements, design, coding, and testing until development and implementation are considered complete.

job description A written description of a job in an organization. A job description usually contains a job title, experience requirements, and knowledge requirements.

job rotation The practice of moving personnel from position to position, sometimes with little or no notice, as a means for deterring personnel from engaging in prohibited or illegal practices.

JSON-RPC A protocol used in application environments to facilitate a client request made to a server.

judgmental sampling A sampling technique in which items are chosen based upon the auditor's judgment, usually based on risk or materiality. *See also* sampling.

Kanban A lean software development methodology that uses a visual Kanban board to track and plan the assignment and completion of tasks in a project.

key *See* encryption key.

key compromise Any unauthorized disclosure or damage to an encryption key. *See also* key management.

key custody The policies, processes, and procedures regarding the management of keys. *See also* key management.

key disposal The process of decommissioning encryption keys. *See also* key management.

key encrypting key An encryption key that is used to encrypt another encryption key.

key exchange A technique that is used by two parties to establish a symmetric encryption key when no secure channel is available.

key fingerprint   A short sequence of characters used to authenticate a public key.

key generation   The initial generation of an encryption key. *See also* key management.

key length   The size (measured in bits) of an encryption key. Longer encryption keys mean that it takes greater effort to attack a cryptosystem successfully.

key logger   A hardware device or a type of malware that records a user's keystrokes and, optionally, mouse movements and clicks and sends them to the key logger's owner.

key management   The various processes and procedures used by an organization to generate, protect, use, and dispose of encryption keys over their lifetime.

key performance indicator (KPI)   Measure of business processes' performance and quality, used to reveal trends related to efficiency and effectiveness of key processes in the organization.

key protection   All means used to protect encryption keys from unauthorized disclosure and harm. *See also* key management.

key rotation   The process of issuing a new encryption key and re-encrypting data protected with the new key. *See also* key management.

keycard system   A physical access control system by which personnel are able to enter a workspace by waving a keycard near a reader or inserting it into a reader, activating a door lock to unlock the door briefly.

known error   An incident that has been seen before, and its root cause is known.

laptop computer   A portable computer used by an individual user.

last in, first out (LIFO)   A backup media rotation scheme whereby the newest backup volumes are used next. *See also* backup media rotation.

Layer 2 Tunneling Protocol (L2TP)   A TCP/IP tunneling protocol.

layer 3 switch   A device that routes packets between different TCP/IP networks.

layer 4 switch   A device used to route packets to destinations based on TCP and UDP port numbers.

layer 4-7 switch   A device that routes packets to destinations based on their internal content.

lean   A project management approach that emphasizes focus on value and efficiency. Lean is derived from lean manufacturing techniques developed at Toyota in Japan in the 1990s.

least privilege   The concept by which an individual user should have the lowest privilege possible that will still enable him or her to perform necessary tasks.

Lightweight Directory Access Protocol (LDAP)   A TCP/IP application layer protocol used as a directory service for people and computing resources.

link layer   Layer 1 of the TCP/IP network model. The purpose of the link layer is the delivery of messages (usually called frames) from one station to another on a local network. *See also* TCP/IP network model.

local area network (LAN)   A network that connects computers and devices together in a small building or a residence.

logic bomb   A set of instructions designed to perform some damaging action when a specific event occurs; a popular example is a time bomb that alters or destroys data on a specified date in the future.

logical network architecture   The part of network architecture concerned with the depiction of network communications at a local, campus, regional, and global level.

loopback address   The IP address 127.0.0.1 (or any other address in the entire 127 address block). A packet sent to a loopback address is sent to the station at which it originated.

LTE (Long Term Evolution)   A wireless telecommunications standard for use by mobile devices, considered an upgrade of older GSM and CDMA2000 standards.

machine authentication controls   Access controls used to authenticate a device to determine whether it will be permitted to access resources.

main storage   A computer's short-term storage of information, usually implemented with electronic components such as random access memory (RAM).

mainframe   A large central computer capable of performing complex tasks for several users simultaneously.

malware   The broad class of programs designed to inflict harm on computers, networks, or information. Types of malware include viruses, worms, Trojan horses, spyware, and rootkits.

managed security service provider (MSSP)   An organization that provides security monitoring and/or management services for customers.

mandatory access control (MAC)   An access model used to control access to objects (files, directories, databases, systems, networks, and so on) by subjects (persons, programs, and so on). When a subject attempts to access an object, the operating system examines the access properties of the subject and object to determine whether the access should be allowed. The operating system then permits or denies the requested access.

mandatory vacation   A policy established by some organizations that requires each employee to take a vacation every year.

man-in-the-browser (MITB) attack   An attack on an end user's browser whereby a malicious browser helper object (BHO) interferes with the browser's operation.

man-in-the-middle (MITM) attack An attack used to take over communications occurring between two parties. Here, an attacker intercepts communications being sent from one party to another and injects new, altered communications in their place. The attacker must be able to impersonate each party in the communication so that each party believes it is talking directly with the other party.

man-made disaster A disaster that is directly or indirectly caused by human activity, through action or inaction. *See also* disaster.

manual control A control that requires a human to operate it.

marking The act of affixing a classification label to a document.

mash-up A web-based application that contains components that originate from other web applications.

materiality In financial audits, a dollar-amount threshold that alters the results on an organization's financial statements. In IS audits, materiality is the threshold at which serious errors, omissions, irregularities, or illegal acts could occur.

maximum tolerable downtime (MTD) A theoretical time period, measured from the onset of a disaster, after which the organization's ongoing viability would be at risk.

maximum transmission unit (MTU) The size of the largest protocol data unit (PDU) that can be transmitted on a network.

Media Access Control (MAC) A framing protocol used by Ethernet, DSL, MPLS, and ISDN.

Media Access Control (MAC) address Node addressing used on an Ethernet network in which the address is expressed as a six-byte hexadecimal value. A typical address is displayed in a notation separated by colons or dashes, such as F0:E3:67:AB:98:02.

media control A set of processes for controlling the security of storage media.

media destruction *See* media sanitization.

media sanitization The process of ensuring the destruction of data on digital media.

message digest The result of a cryptographic hash function.

message server A system in a distributed processing environment that stores and forwards transactions between systems.

message switched A WAN communications technology in which each message is switched to its destination when a communications path is available.

method The actions that an object can perform. *See also* object.

methodology standard A standard that specifies the practices used by the IT organization.

metropolitan area network (MAN)　An interconnection of LANs that spans a city or regional area.

microsegmentation　A segmentation technique in which individual hosts are isolated with network access controls, typically with network or host firewalls.

middleware　A component in an application environment that is used to control or monitor transactions.

midrange computer　A large central computer capable of performing complex tasks for users.

migration　The process of transferring data from one system to a replacement system.

mitigating control　*See* compensating control.

mobile device　A portable computer in the form of a smartphone, tablet computer, or wearable device.

mobile device management (MDM)　A class of enterprise tools used to manage mobile devices such as smartphones and tablet computers.

mobile site　A portable recovery center that can be delivered to almost any location in the world.

modem (modulator-demodulator)　A device used to connect a local computer or network to a telecommunications network.

monitoring　The continuous or regular evaluation of a system or control to determine its operation or effectiveness.

multifactor authentication　Any means used to authenticate a user that is stronger than the use of a user ID and password. Examples of multifactor authentication include digital certificate, token, smart card, and biometrics.

multiplexor　A device used to connect several separate signals and combine them into a single data stream.

Multiprotocol Label Switching (MPLS)　A packet-switched network technology that utilizes a variable-length packet. In an MPLS network, each packet has one or more labels affixed to it that contain information that helps MPLS routers make packet-forwarding decisions without examining the contents of the packet itself (for an IP address, for instance).

multistation access unit (MAU)　A Token Ring network device used to connect stations to the network.

N + 1　The practice of employing one more than the minimum required number of systems so that in the event of a planned or unplanned outage of one of the systems, the other systems will continue functioning and provide service. This term usually applies to

HVAC, UPS, and electric generators. *See also* heating, ventilation, and air conditioning (HVAC); uninterruptible power supply (UPS); electric generator.

natural disaster A disaster that occurs in the natural world with little or no assistance from mankind. *See also* disaster.

near-field communications (NFC) A standard for extremely short-distance radiofrequency data communications.

nearshore outsourcing Outsourced personnel are located in a nearby country.

netbook computer A miniature laptop computer, usually with more limited storage and peripheral connectivity than a laptop computer.

netflow A network diagnostic tool that collects all network metadata, which can be used for network diagnostic or security purposes.

network access control (NAC) An approach for network authentication and access control for devices designed to attach to a LAN or wireless LAN.

network address translation (NAT) A method of translating IP addresses at network boundaries, most notably to convert private internal network addresses to publicly-routable network addresses.

network analysis A reconnaissance operation on an organization's network.

network architecture The overall design of an organization's network.

network attached storage (NAS) A stand-alone storage system that contains one or more virtual volumes. Servers access these volumes over the network using the Network File System (NFS) or Server Message Block/Common Internet File System (SMB/CIFS) protocols, common on Unix and Windows operating systems, respectively.

network authentication A network-based service that is used to authenticate persons to network-based resources.

Network Basic Input/Output System (NetBIOS) A network protocol that permits applications to communicate with one another using the legacy NetBIOS API.

Network File System (NFS) A TCP/IP application layer protocol used to make a disk-based resource on another computer appear as a logical volume on a local computer.

network interface card (NIC) A device that is directly connected to a computer's bus and contains one or more connectors to which a network cable may be connected.

network layer Layer 3 of the OSI network model. *See also* OSI network model.

network management A class of software program that is used to monitor and manage devices connected to a network. Also refers to the business processes used for the same purpose.

Network News Transfer Protocol (NNTP)   A TCP/IP application layer protocol used to transport Usenet news throughout the Internet and from news servers to end users using news reading programs. Usenet news has been largely deprecated by web-based applications.

network operations center (NOC)   An IT function whereby personnel centrally monitor operations within an organization's network, and often also its systems and applications.

network segmentation   The design process that results in the creation of network security zones, which are defined and controlled by firewalls or other stateful ACLs that limit access between zones.

Network Time Protocol (NTP)   A TCP/IP application layer protocol used to synchronize the time-of-day clocks on systems with time reference standards.

network-based intrusion detection system (NIDS)   An intrusion detection system that attaches to a network and listens for network-based anomalies. *See also* intrusion detection system (IDS).

NIST CSF (National Institute for Standards and Technology Cybersecurity Framework)   A framework consisting of standards, guidelines, and best practices to manage cybersecurity-related risk, developed by the U.S. National Institute for Standards and Technology.

noise   The presence of other electromagnetic signals within incoming power.

nonrepudiation   The property of digital signatures and encryption that can make it difficult or impossible for a party to deny having sent a digitally signed message—unless they admit to having lost control of their private encryption key.

north–south traffic   Network traffic that crosses virtual server boundaries, server tier boundaries, or data center boundaries. *See also* east–west traffic.

NoSQL   An inclusive term referring to several nonrelational database management system designs.

notebook computer   *See* laptop computer.

NT File System (NTFS)   The file system used by Windows operating system to store and retrieve files on a hard disk.

object   1) The instantiation of a class. If a class is thought of as a design, an object can be thought of as a running example of the class. *See also* class. 2) A resource, such as a computer, application, database, file, or record. *See also* subject.

object breakdown structure (OBS)   A representation of the components of a project in graphical or tabular form.

object database   *See* object database management system (ODBMS).

object database management system (ODBMS) A type of database management system in which information is represented as objects that are used in object-oriented programming languages.

object request broker (ORB) gateway A system that facilitates the processing of transactions across a distributed environment that uses the CORBA (Common Object Request Broker Architecture) or Microsoft COM/DCOM standards.

objectivity The characteristic of a person that relates to his or her ability to develop an opinion that is not influenced by external pressures.

object-oriented (OO) system development Development of information systems using object-oriented languages and tools.

occupant emergency plan (OEP) Activities required to care for occupants in a business location safely during a disaster. *See also* response document.

off-shoring A form of sourcing whereby an employer will source a function with employees or contractors located in another country or continent.

off-site media storage The practice of storing media such as backup tapes at an off-site facility located away from the primary computing facility.

online inquiry An auditing technique whereby an auditor can log on to an application to retrieve detailed information on specific transactions.

onshore outsourcing Outsourced personnel are located in the same country.

Open Shortest Path First (OSPF) A TCP/IP routing protocol used to transmit network routing information from one network router to another to determine the most efficient path through a large network.

operating system A large, general-purpose program used to control computer hardware and facilitate the use of software applications.

operational audit An audit of IS controls, security controls, or business controls to determine control existence and effectiveness.

optical carrier (OC) level Classifications of data throughput over wide area fiber telecommunications networks.

organization chart A diagram that depicts the manager-subordinate relationships within an organization or within a part of an organization.

OSI network model The seven-layer network model that incorporates encapsulation of messages. The OSI model has been extensively studied but has never been entirely implemented. *See also* TCP/IP network model.

output controls Controls that ensure the accuracy and validity of final calculations and transformations.

outsourcing A form of sourcing in which an employer uses contract employees to perform a function. The contract employees may be located on-site or off-site.

owner A person or group responsible for the operation of an asset.

packet The protocol data unit (PDU) at the IP layer of TCP/IP and layer 3 of the OSI model.

packet switched A WAN technology in which communications between endpoints take place over a stream of packets that are routed through switches until they reach their destination.

parallel test An actual test of disaster recovery (DR) and/or business continuity response plans. The purpose of a parallel test is to evaluate the ability of personnel to follow directives in emergency response plans—to set up the DR business processing or data processing capability. In a parallel test, personnel operate recovery systems in parallel with production systems to compare the results between the two to determine the actual capabilities of recovery systems.

password An identifier that is created by a system manager or a user; a secret combination of letters, numbers, and other symbols used to log into an account, system, or network.

password complexity The characteristics required of user account passwords. For example, a password may not contain dictionary words and must contain uppercase letters, lowercase letters, numbers, and symbols.

password length The minimum and maximum number of characters permitted for a user password associated with a computer, network, application, or system account.

password reset The process of changing a user account password and unlocking the user account so that the user's use of the account may resume.

password reuse The act of reusing a prior password for a user account. Some information systems can prevent the use of prior passwords in case any were compromised with or without the user's knowledge.

password vaulting The process of storing a password in a secure location for later use.

patch management The process of identifying, analyzing, and applying patches (including security patches) to systems.

Payment Card Industry Data Security Standard (PCI-DSS) A security standard intended to protect credit card numbers in storage, while being processed, and while being transmitted. The standard was developed by the PCI Standards Council, which is a consortium of credit card companies, including Visa, MasterCard, American Express, Discover, and JCB.

performance evaluation A process whereby an employer evaluates the performance of each employee for the purpose of promotion, salary increase, bonus, or retention.

personal area network (PAN)   A network that is generally used by a single individual and is usually limited to about 3 meters in size.

phishing   A social engineering attack on unsuspecting individuals in which e-mail messages that resemble official communications entice victims to visit imposter web sites that contain malware or request credentials to sensitive or valuable assets.

physical control   Controls that employ physical means.

physical layer   Layer 1 of the OSI network model. *See also* OSI network model.

physical network architecture   The part of network architecture concerned with the physical locations of network equipment and network media.

piggybacking   *See* tailgating.

plain old telephone service (POTS)   Another name for the public-switched telephone network (PSTN). *See also* public-switched telephone network (PSTN).

plaintext   An original message, file, or stream of data that can be read by anyone who has access to it.

Platform-as-a-Service (PaaS)   A cloud computing delivery model whereby the service provider supplies the platform on which an organization can build and run software.

Point-to-Point Protocol (PPP)   A network protocol used to transport TCP/IP packets over point-to-point serial connections (usually RS-232 and dial-up connections).

policy   A statement that specifies a course, principle, or method of action that has been adopted or proposed in an organization. A policy usually defines who is responsible for monitoring and enforcing the policy.

polymorphism   A feature of a programming language that enables an object to behave in different ways, depending upon the data passed to it. *See also* object.

population   A complete set of subjects, entities, transactions, or events that are the subject of an audit.

Post Office Protocol (POP)   A TCP/IP application layer protocol used to retrieve e-mail messages from an e-mail server.

power distribution unit (PDU)   A device that distributes electric power to a computer room or data center.

pre-action system   A fire sprinkler system used in areas with high-value contents, such as data centers. A pre-action system is essentially a dry pipe system until a "preceding" event such as a smoke detector alarm occurs; at this time, the system is filled with water and becomes a wet pipe system. Then, if the ambient temperature at any of the sprinkler heads is high enough, fuses (heat-sensitive glass bulbs) break, releasing water to extinguish the fire. *See also* fire sprinkler system; dry pipe system; wet pipe system.

pre-audit   An examination of business processes, controls, and records in anticipation of an upcoming audit.

precision   A measure of how closely a sample represents the entire population.

presentation layer   Layer 6 of the OSI network model. *See also* OSI network model.

preventive action   An action that is initiated to prevent an undesired event or condition.

preventive control   A control that is used to prevent unwanted events from happening.

primary key   One of the fields in a table in a relational database management system that contains values that are unique for each record (row). *See also* relational database management system (RDBMS); table; row; field.

print server   A server used to coordinate printing to shared printers.

privacy   The protection of personal information from unauthorized disclosure, use, and distribution.

privacy policy   A policy statement that defines how an organization will protect, manage, and handle private information.

privacy requirements   Formal statements that describe required privacy safeguards that a system must support.

private address   An IP address that falls into one of the following ranges: 10.0.0.0–10.255.255.255, 172.16.0.0–172.31.255.255, or 192.168.0.0–192.168.255.255. Packets with a private address destination cannot be transported over the global Internet.

privilege creep   *See* accumulation of privileges.

probability analysis   The analysis of a threat and the probability of its realization.

problem   An incident—often multiple incidents—that exhibits common symptoms and whose root cause is not known.

problem management   The IT function that analyzes chronic incidents and seeks to resolve them, and also enacts proactive measures in an effort to avoid problems. *See also* IT service management (ITSM).

procedure   A written sequence of instructions used to complete a task.

process   1) A collection of one or more procedures used to perform a business function. *See also* procedure. 2) A logical container in an operating system in which a program executes.

process isolation   A basic feature of an operating system that prevents one process from accessing the resources used by another process.

processing controls   Controls that ensure the correct processing of information.

program An organization of many large, complex activities; it can be thought of as a set of projects that work to fulfill one or more key business objectives or goals.

program charter A formal definition of the objectives of a program, its main timelines, sources of funding, the names of its principal leaders and managers, and the business executive(s) who are sponsoring the program.

program management The management of a group of projects that exists to fulfill a business goal or objective.

programmable read-only memory (PROM) A form of permanent memory that cannot be modified.

programming language A vocabulary and set of rules used to construct a human-readable computer program.

project A coordinated and managed sequence of tasks that results in the realization of an objective or goal.

project change management The process of controlling a project plan and budget through formal reviews of changes.

Project Evaluation and Review Technique (PERT) A visual representation of a project plan that shows project tasks, timelines, and dependencies.

project management The activities that are used to control, measure, and manage the activities in a project.

Project Management Body of Knowledge (PMBOK) A project management guide that defines the essentials of project management.

project plan The chart of tasks in a project, which also includes start and completion dates, resources required, and dependencies and relationships between tasks.

project planning The activities related to the development and management of a project.

project schedule The chart of tasks in a project with their expected start and completion dates.

PRojects IN Controlled Environments 2 (PRINCE2) A project management framework.

proof of concept A method for demonstrating the ability to build or implement complex systems through the use of simpler models.

protocol analyzer A device that is connected to a network to view network communications at a detailed level.

protocol data unit (PDU) A discrete term that is used to signify a message that is created at various layers of encapsulated protocols such as TCP/IP.

protocol standard   A standard that specifies the protocols used by the IT organization.

prototyping   An alternative software development process whereby rapidly developed application prototypes are developed with user input and continuous involvement.

provided by client (PBC)   A list of evidence requested of an auditee at the onset of an audit.

proxy server   A device or system used to control end-user access to Internet web sites.

public key cryptography   *See* asymmetric encryption.

public key infrastructure (PKI)   A centralized function that is used to store and publish public keys and other information.

public-switched telephone network (PSTN)   The common carrier-switched telephone network used to carry voice telephone calls over landlines.

qualitative risk analysis   A risk analysis methodology by which risks are classified on a nonquantified scale, such as "High, Medium, Low," or on a simple numeric scale, such as 1 through 5.

quality assurance testing (QAT)   The portion of software testing in which system specifications and technologies are formally tested.

quality management   Methods and processes by which business processes are controlled, monitored, and managed to bring about continuous improvement.

quality of service (QoS)   Any of several schemes in networks that ensure the quality of interactive, jitter-sensitive protocols such as telephony and streaming video.

quantitative risk analysis   A risk analysis methodology whereby risks are estimated in the form of actual cost amounts.

race condition   A type of attack in which an attacker is attempting to exploit a small window of time that may exist between the time that a resource is requested and when it is available for use.

RACI   Responsible, Accountable, Consulted, and Informed. The responsibility model used to describe and track individual responsibilities in a business process or a project.

Radio Resource Control (RRC)   A part of the Universal Mobile Telecommunications System (UMTS) Wideband Code Division Multiple Access (WCDMA) wireless telecommunications protocol that is used to facilitate the allocation of connections between mobile devices and base stations.

random access memory (RAM)   A type of semiconductor memory usually used for a computer's main storage.

ransomware   Malware that performs some malicious action, requiring payment from the victim to reverse the action. Such actions include data erasure, data encryption, and system damage.

rapid application development (RAD)   A software development life cycle process characterized by small development teams, prototypes, design sessions with end users, and development tools that integrate data design, data flow, user interface, and prototyping.

razor wire   Coiled wire with razorlike barbs that may be placed along the top of a fence or wall to prevent or deter passage by unauthorized personnel.

read-only memory (ROM)   An early form of permanent memory that cannot be modified.

reciprocal site   A data center that is operated by another company. Two or more organizations with similar processing needs will draw up a legal contract that obligates one or more of the organizations to house another party's systems temporarily at a reciprocal site in the event of a disaster.

records   Documents describing business events such as meeting minutes, contracts, financial transactions, decisions, purchase orders, logs, and reports.

recovery control   A control that is used after an unwanted event to restore a system or process to its pre-event state.

recovery point objective (RPO)   The time during which recent data will be irretrievably lost in a disaster. RPO is usually measured in hours or days.

recovery procedure   Instructions that key personnel use to bootstrap services that support critical business functions identified in the business impact assessment (BIA).

recovery strategy   A high-level plan for the resumption of business operations after a disaster.

recovery time objective (RTO)   The period of time from the onset of an outage until the resumption of service. RTO is usually measured in hours or days.

reduced sign-on   The use of a centralized directory service (such as LDAP or Microsoft Active Directory) for authentication into systems and applications. Users will need to log in to each system and application, using only one set of login credentials.

Redundant Array of Independent Disks (RAID)   A family of technologies that combines multiple physical disk drive components into one or more logical units to improve the reliability, performance, or capacity of disk-based storage systems.

referential integrity   The characteristic of relational database management systems that requires the database management system maintain the parent-child relationships between records in different tables and prohibits activities such as deleting parent records and transforming child records into orphans. *See also* relational database management system (RDBMS).

registration authority (RA)   An entity that works within or alongside a certificate authority (CA) to accept requests for new digital certificates.

regulatory requirements   Formal statements, derived from laws and regulations, that describe the required characteristics a system must support.

relational database management system (RDBMS)   A database management system that permits the design of a database consisting of one or more tables that can contain fields that refer to rows in other tables. This is currently the most popular type of database management system.

release management   The IT function that controls the release of software programs, applications, and environments. *See also* IT service management (ITSM).

release process   The IT process whereby changes to software programs, applications, and environments are requested, reviewed, approved, and implemented.

remote access   A service that permits a user to establish a network connection from a remote location so that the user can access network resources remotely.

Remote Authentication Dial-in User Service (RADIUS)   A network authentication protocol.

remote copy (rcp)   A TCP/IP application layer protocol that is an early file transfer protocol used to copy files or directories from system to system.

Remote Desktop Protocol (RDP)   A proprietary protocol from Microsoft that is used to establish a graphic interface connection with another computer.

remote destruct   The act of commanding a device, such as a laptop computer or mobile device, to destroy stored data. Remote destruct is sometimes used when a device is lost or stolen to prevent anyone from being able to read data stored on the device.

remote login (rlogin)   A TCP/IP application layer protocol used to establish a command-line session on a remote system. Like Telnet, rlogin does not encrypt authentication or session contents and has been largely replaced by Secure Shell (SSH). *See also* Telnet; Secure Shell (SSH).

Remote Procedure Call (RPC)   A network protocol that permits an application to execute a subroutine or procedure on another computer.

repeater   An Ethernet network device that receives and retransmits signals on the network.

reperformance   An audit technique whereby an IS auditor repeats actual tasks performed by auditees to confirm they were performed properly.

replication   An activity in which data that is written to a storage system is also copied over a network to another storage system and written. The result is the presence of up-to-date data that exists on two or more storage systems, each of which could be located in a different geographic region.

request for change (RFC)   *See* change request.

request for information (RFI)   A formal process whereby an organization solicits detailed product or service information from one or more vendors.

request for proposals (RFP)   A formal process whereby an organization solicits solution proposals from one or more vendors. The process usually includes formal requirements and desired terms and conditions. It is used to evaluate vendor proposals to make a selection.

requirements   Formal statements that describe required (and desired) characteristics of a system that is to be changed, developed, or acquired.

residual risk   The risk that remains after being reduced through other risk treatment options.

response document   A document that outlines required action of personnel after a disaster strikes. Includes business recovery plan, occupant emergency plan, emergency communication plan, contact lists, disaster recovery plan, continuity of operations plan (COOP), and security incident response plan (SIRP).

responsibility   A stated expectation of activities and performance.

return on investment (ROI)   The ratio of money gained or lost as compared to an original investment.

Reverse Address Resolution Protocol (RARP)   A TCP/IP link layer protocol that is used by a station that needs to know the IP address that has been assigned to it. RARP has been largely superseded by DHCP. *See also* Dynamic Host Configuration Protocol (DHCP).

reverse engineering   The process of analyzing a system to see how it functions, usually as a means for developing a similar system. Reverse engineering is usually not permitted when it is applied to commercial software programs.

right to audit   A clause in a contract that grants one party the right to conduct an audit of the other party's operations.

ring topology   A network topology in which connections are made from one station to the next, in a complete loop.

RISC (reduced instruction set computer)   A central processing unit design that uses a smaller instruction set, which leads to simpler microprocessor design. *See also* central processing unit (CPU).

risk   Generally, the fact that undesired events can happen that may damage property or disrupt operations; specifically, an event scenario that can result in property damage or disruption.

risk acceptance   The risk treatment option in which management chooses to accept the risk as-is.

risk analysis   The process of identifying and studying risks in an organization.

risk appetite   The level of risk that an organization is willing to accept while in pursuit of its mission, strategy, and objectives, and before action is needed to treat or manage the risk.

risk assessment   A process in which risks, in the form of threats and vulnerabilities, are identified for each asset.

risk avoidance   The risk treatment option involving a cessation of the activity that introduces identified risk.

Risk IT Framework   A risk management model that approaches risk from the enterprise perspective.

risk management   The management activities used to identify, analyze, and treat risks.

risk mitigation   The risk treatment option involving implementation of a solution that will reduce an identified risk.

risk tolerance   The amount of variation from the risk appetite that an organization is willing to accept in a particular situation. *See* risk appetite.

risk transfer   The risk treatment option involving the act of transferring risk to another party, such as an insurance company.

risk treatment   The decision to manage an identified risk. The available choices are mitigate the risk, avoid the risk, transfer the risk, or accept the risk.

role   A set of privileges in an application. Also a formally defined set of work tasks assigned to an individual.

rollback   A step in the system development life cycle in which system changes need to be reversed, returning the system to its previous state.

rootkit   A type of malware that is designed to evade detection.

router   A device that is used to interconnect two or more networks.

Routing Information Protocol (RIP)   A TCP/IP routing protocol that is used to transmit network routing information from one network router to another to determine the most efficient path through a network. RIP is one of the earliest routing protocols and is not used for Internet routing.

row   A unit of storage in a relational database management system that consists of a single record in a table. *See also* relational database management system (RDBMS); table.

RPC gateway   A system that facilitates communication through the RPC suite of protocols between components in an application environment.

RS-232   A standard protocol for sending serial data between computers.

RS-449 A standard protocol for sending serial data between network devices.

sabotage Deliberate damage of an organization's asset.

salvage The process of recovering components or assets that still have value after a disaster.

sample A portion of a population of records that is selected for auditing.

sample mean The sum of all samples divided by the number of samples.

sample standard deviation A computation of the variance of sample values from the sample mean. This is a measurement of the "spread" of values in the sample.

sampling A technique used to select a portion of a population when it is not feasible to test an entire population.

sampling risk The probability that a sample selected does not represent the entire population. This is usually expressed as a percentage, as the numeric inverse of the confidence coefficient. *See also* confidence coefficient.

SAS 70 (Statement of Accounting Standards No. 70) An external audit of a service provider. An SAS 70 audit is performed according to rules established by the American Institute of Certified Public Accountants (AICPA). Deprecated by SSAE 16 and by SSAE18. *See also* SSAE 18.

scanning attack An attack on a computer or network with the intention of discovering potentially vulnerable computers or programs.

screened shielded twisted pair (S/STP) A type of twisted-pair cable in which a thick metal shield protects each pair of conductors and an outer shield protects all of the conductors together. *See also* twisted-pair cable.

screened unshielded twisted pair (S/UTP) A type of twisted-pair cable in which a thick metal shield surrounds and protects the cables. *See also* twisted-pair cable.

screening router A network device that filters network traffic based on source and destination IP addresses and ports. *See also* firewall.

script kiddie An inexperienced computer hacker who uses tools developed by others to access computers and networks illegally.

Scrum An iterative and incremental methodology used for rapid and agile software development.

Scrumban An iterative and incremental methodology used for software development. Scrumban is derived from the terms "Scrum" and "Kanban" (Japanese). *See also* Kanban; Scrum.

secondary storage A computer's long-term storage of information, usually implemented with hard disk drives or static random access memory (SRAM).

Secure Copy (SCP)   A TCP/IP application layer protocol used as a file transfer protocol that is similar to remote copy (rcp) but is protected using Secure Shell (SSH). *See also* remote copy (rcp); Secure Shell (SSH).

secure electronic transaction (SET)   A protocol used to protect credit card transactions that uses a digital envelope. SET has been deprecated by Secure Sockets Layer (SSL) and Transport Layer Security (TLS). *See also* digital envelope; Secure Sockets Layer (SSL); Transport Layer Security (TLS).

Secure File Transfer Protocol (SFTP)   A TCP/IP application layer protocol that is an extension of the File Transfer Protocol, in which authentication and file transfer are encrypted using SSH. Sometimes referred to as SSH File Transfer Protocol. *See also* File Transfer Protocol (FTP); Secure Shell (SSH).

Secure Hypertext Transfer Protocol (SHTTP)   A protocol used to encrypt web pages between web servers and web browsers. Often confused with Hypertext Transfer Protocol Secure (HTTPS).

Secure Multipurpose Internet Mail Extensions (S/MIME)   An e-mail security protocol that provides sender and recipient authentication and encryption of message content and attachments.

Secure Shell (SSH)   A TCP/IP application layer protocol that provides a secure channel between two computers whereby all communications between them are encrypted. SSH can also be used as a tunnel to encapsulate and thereby protect other protocols.

Secure Sockets Layer (SSL)   An encryption protocol used to encrypt web pages requested with the HTTPS URL. Deprecated by Transport Layer Security (TLS). *See also* Transport Layer Security (TLS); Hypertext Transfer Protocol Secure (HTTPS).

security awareness   A formal program used to educate employees, users, customers, or constituents on required, acceptable, and unacceptable security-related behaviors.

security governance   Management's control over an organization's security program.

security guards   Personnel who control passage at entry points or roam building premises looking for security issues such as unescorted visitors.

security incident   An event in which the confidentiality, integrity, or availability of information (or an information system) has been compromised.

security incident response   The formal, planned response that is enacted when a security incident has occurred. *See also* security incident.

security operations center (SOC)   An IT function wherein personnel centrally monitor and manage security functions and devices and watch for security anomalies and incidents.

security policy   *See* information security policy.

security requirements Formal statements that describe the required security characteristics that a system must support.

segment The term used to identify the protocol data unit (PDU) in the TCP of the TCP/IP suite of protocols.

segmentation The practice of dividing a network into two or more security zones, with network access controls restricting and monitoring traffic between those zones.

segregation of duties The concept that ensures single individuals do not possess excess privileges that could result in unauthorized activities such as fraud or the manipulation or exposure of sensitive data.

separation of duties *See* segregation of duties.

Serial Line Interface Protocol (SLIP) A network protocol used to transport TCP/IP packets over point-to-point serial connections (usually RS-232).

server A centralized computer used to perform a specific task.

service continuity management The IT function that consists of activities concerned with the organization's ability to continue providing services, primarily in the event that a natural or man-made disaster has occurred. *See also* IT service management (ITSM); business continuity planning (BCP); disaster recovery planning (DRP).

service desk The IT function that handles incidents and service requests on behalf of customers by acting as a single point of contact. *See also* IT service management (ITSM).

service provider audit An audit of a third-party organization that provides services to other organizations.

service set identifier (SSID) A friendly name that identifies a particular 802.11 wireless network.

service-level agreement (SLA) An agreement that specifies service levels in terms of the quantity and quality of work, timeliness, and remedies for shortfalls in quality or quantity.

service-level management The IT function that confirms whether IT is providing adequate service to its customers. This is accomplished through continuous monitoring and periodic review of IT service delivery. *See also* IT service management (ITSM).

session border controller A device deployed in a VoIP network to control VoIP security, connectivity, quality of service, and metering.

session hijacking An attack on a user's browser session whereby the attacker intercepts the user's session cookie from an unencrypted wired or wireless network and then uses the cookie to take over the victim's browser session.

Session Initiation Protocol (SIP)   The network protocol used to set up and tear down Voice over IP (VoIP) and other communications connections. *See also* Voice over IP (VoIP).

session layer   Layer 5 of the OSI network model. *See also* OSI network model.

shielded twisted pair (STP)   A type of twisted-pair cable in which a thin metal shield protects each pair of conductors. *See also* twisted-pair cable.

Simple Mail Transfer Protocol (SMTP)   A TCP/IP application layer protocol that is used to transport e-mail messages.

Simple Network Management Protocol (SNMP)   A TCP/IP application layer protocol used by network devices and systems to transmit management messages indicating a need for administrative attention.

Simple Object Access Protocol (SOAP)   A protocol used to facilitate the exchange of structured information between systems.

simulation   A test of disaster recovery, business continuity, or security incident response procedures in which the participants take part in a "mock disaster" or incident to add some realism to the process of thinking their way through the emergency response process.

single loss expectancy (SLE)   The financial loss when a threat is realized one time. SLE is defined as AV × EF. *See also* asset value (AV); exposure factor (EF).

single sign-on (SSO)   An interconnected environment in which applications are logically connected to a centralized authentication server that is aware of the logged-in/logged-out status of each user. A user can log in once to the environment; each application and system is aware of a user's log-in status and will not require the user to log in to each one separately.

site classification policy   Policy that defines sensitivity levels, security controls, and security procedures for information processing sites and work centers.

Six Sigma   A quantitative, statistical technique used to identify and remediate defects in business processes.

smart card   A small, credit card–sized device that contains electronic memory and is accessed with a smart card reader and used in two-factor authentication.

smartphone   A mobile phone equipped with an operating system and software applications.

smishing   Phishing in the context of instant messaging. *See also* phishing.

snapshot   A continuous auditing technique that involves the use of special audit modules embedded in online applications that sample specific transactions. The module copies key database records that can be examined later on.

sniffer   A program that can be installed on a network-attached system to capture network traffic being transmitted to or from the system.

social engineering   The act of using deception to trick an individual into revealing secrets.

softphone   A software program with the functionality of a VoIP telephone.

software licensing   The process of maintaining accurate records regarding the permitted use of software programs.

software maintenance   An activity in the software development life cycle whereby modifications are made to the software code.

Software Process Improvement and Capability dEtermination (SPICE)   A maturity model based on the SEI CMM maturity model. SPICE has been made an international standard: ISO/IEC 15504.

software program library   The repository that contains program source code and that usually includes tools to manage the maintenance of source code.

Software-as-a-Service (SaaS)   A software delivery model whereby an organization obtains a software application for use by its employees and the software application is hosted by the software provider, as opposed to the customer organization.

software-defined networking (SDN)   A class of capabilities in which network infrastructure devices such as routers, switches, and firewalls are created, configured, and managed as virtual devices in virtualization environments.

source code management   The techniques and tools used to manage application source code.

source lines of code (SLOC)   A sizing technique for software development projects that represents the size of the planned program, expressed as the number of lines of code.

sourcing   The choices that organizations make when selecting the personnel who will perform functions and where those functions will be performed.

spam   Unsolicited and unwanted e-mail.

spam filter   A central program or device that examines incoming e-mail and removes all messages identified as spam.

spear phishing   Phishing that is specially crafted for a specific target organization or group. *See also* phishing.

spike   A sharp increase in voltage that lasts for only a fraction of a second.

spim   Spam in the context of instant messaging. *See also* spam.

spiral model   A software development life cycle process in which the activities of requirements definition and software design go through several cycles until the project is complete. *See also* system development life cycle (SDLC).

split custody   The concept of splitting knowledge of a specific object or task between two persons.

spoofing   The act of changing the configuration of a device or system in an attempt to masquerade as a different, known, and trusted system or user.

sprint   A portion of a project in which an individual or a team will accomplish a set of objectives within a specified timeframe.

spyware   A type of malware software that performs one or more surveillance-type actions on a computer, reporting back to the spyware owner.

SSAE 16 (Statements on Standards for Attestation Engagements No. 16)   An external audit of a service provider. SSAE 16 has been superseded by SSAE 18.

SSAE 18 (Statements on Standards for Attestation Engagements No. 18)   An external audit of a service provider. An SSAE 18 audit is performed according to rules established by the American Institute of Certified Public Accountants (AICPA).

standard   A statement that defines the technologies, protocols, suppliers, and methods used by an IT organization.

standard IT balanced scorecard   A management tool that is used to measure the performance and effectiveness of an IT organization.

star topology   A network topology in which a separate connection is made from a central device to each station.

stateful inspection firewall   A network device that filters network traffic based on source and destination IP addresses and ports and keeps track of individual TCP/IP sessions to make filtering decisions, permitting established connections. *See also* firewall.

statement of impact   A description of the impact a disaster will have on a business or business process.

static random access memory (SRAM)   A form of semiconductor memory that does not require refreshing.

statistical sampling   A sampling technique in which items are chosen at random; each item has a statistically equal probability of being chosen. *See also* sampling.

stop-or-go sampling   A sampling technique used to permit sampling to stop at the earliest possible time. This technique is used when the auditor believes that there is low risk or a low rate of exceptions in the population. *See also* sampling.

storage area network (SAN)   A stand-alone storage system that can be configured to contain several virtual volumes and is connected to many servers through fiber optic cables.

strategic planning   Activities used to develop and refine long-term plans and objectives.

stratified sampling A sampling technique whereby a population is divided into classes or strata, based upon the value of one of the attributes. Samples are then selected from each class. *See also* sampling.

stream cipher A type of encryption algorithm that operates on a continuous stream of data, such as a video or audio feed.

strong authentication *See* multifactor authentication.

structured data Data that resides in database management systems and in other forms, as part of information systems and business applications. *See also* unstructured data.

subject A person or a system. *See also* object.

subnet mask A numeric value that determines which portion of an IP address is used to identify the network and which portion is used to identify a station on the network. *See also* IP address.

substantive testing A type of testing used to determine the accuracy and integrity of transactions that flow through processes and systems.

supercomputer The largest type of computer that is capable of performing large, complex calculations such as weather forecasting and earthquake simulations.

surge *See* spike.

switch A device used to connect computers and other devices to a network. Unlike a hub, which sends all network packets to all stations on the network, a switch sends packets only to intended destination stations on the network.

symmetric encryption A method for encryption and decryption that requires both parties to possess a common encryption key.

Synchronous Optical Networking (SONET) A class of common carrier telecommunications network technologies used to transport voice and data over fiber optic networks at very high speeds.

synchronous replication A type of replication in which writing data to a local and to a remote storage system is performed as a single operation, guaranteeing that data on the remote storage system is identical to data on the local storage system. *See also* replication.

system classification policy Policy that specifies levels of security for systems storing classified information.

system development life cycle (SDLC) The life cycle process used to develop or acquire and maintain information systems. Also known as software development life cycle.

system hardening *See* hardening.

system testing The portion of software testing in which an entire system is tested.

Systems control audit review file and embedded audit modules (SCARF/EAM) The development and embedding of specialized audit software directly into production applications.

T-1 A common carrier standard protocol for transporting voice and data. T-1 can support up to 24 separate voice channels of 64 Kbit/sec each and is used primarily in North America.

T-3 A common carrier standard protocol for transporting voice and data. T-3 can support up to 672 separate voice channels of 64 Kbit/sec each and is used primarily in North America.

T-Carrier A class of multiplexed carrier network technologies developed to transport voice and data communications over long distances using copper cabling.

table A unit of storage in a relational database management system that can be thought of as a list of records. *See also* relational database management system (RDBMS).

tablet A mobile device with a touchscreen interface. *See also* mobile device.

tabletop An exercise, usually of security incident response plans, that consists of a scripted simulation of an actual incident or event.

tailgating A technique used by an intruder to attempt to enter an access-controlled building, typically executed by following closely behind an employee entering the building and "piggybacking" on the employee's security credentials.

tape management system (TMS) An information system used to manage tape media, usually for the purpose of performing information backup. *See also* backup.

TCP/IP network model The four-layer network model that incorporates encapsulation of messages. The TCP/IP suite of protocols is built on the TCP/IP network model.

technical control A control that is implemented in IT systems and applications.

technical requirements Formal statements that describe the required technical characteristics that a system must support.

technology standard A standard that specifies the software and hardware technologies used by the IT organization.

Telnet A TCP/IP application layer protocol that is used to establish a command-line session on a remote computer. Telnet does not encrypt user credentials as they are transmitted over the network and has been largely replaced by SSH. *See also* Secure Shell (SSH).

terminal emulation A software program that runs on a workstation that emulates an older style computer terminal.

termination The process of discontinuing employment of an employee or a contractor.

terrorist A person or group who perpetrates violence for political or other reasons.

test plan The list of tests that are to be carried out during a unit test or system test. *See also* unit testing; system testing.

test server Any type of server that is used to test features; a test server does not perform production tasks.

thick client A workstation that contains a fully functional operating system and application programs.

thin client A workstation that contains a minimal operating system and little or no data storage.

threat An event that, if realized, would bring harm to an asset.

threat hunting The proactive search for intrusions, intruders, and indicators of compromise.

threat management Activities undertaken by an organization to learn of relevant security threats, so that the organization can take appropriate action to counter the threats.

threat modeling The activity of looking for potential threats in a business process, an information system, or a software application.

Thunderbolt A hardware interface standard combining PCI Express and DisplayPort (DP) technologies.

time bomb *See* logic bomb.

Time Division Multiple Access (TDMA) An airlink standard for wireless communications between mobile devices and base stations.

time of check/time of use (TOC/TOU) *See* race condition.

time synchronization A network-based service used to synchronize the time clocks on computers connected to a network.

timebox management A project management technique in which a large project is broken down into smaller components and time periods.

token A small electronic device used in two-factor authentication. A token may display a number that the user types in to a login field, or it may be plugged into a workstation to complete authentication. *See also* two-factor authentication.

Token Ring A standard protocol for assembling a stream of data into frames for transport over a physical medium from one station to another on a local area network. On a Token Ring network, a three-byte token is passed from station to station over the network. A station may not transmit a packet to another station until it has first received the token.

tolerable error rate   The highest number of errors that can exist without a result being materially misstated.

Tolkien Ring   A wireless network used for communications among beings wearing magic rings created by Sauron. Used in Middle-earth.

toll fraud   An attack on a private branch exchange (PBX) that results in stolen long-distance telephone service.

Towers of Hanoi   A complex backup media rotation scheme that provides for more lengthy retention of some backup media. Based on the Towers of Hanoi puzzle. *See also* backup media rotation.

training   1) The process of educating personnel. 2) To impart information or provide an environment where personnel can practice a new skill.

transaction processing (TP) monitor   A system that manages transactions between application servers and database servers in a distributed processing environment.

transfer   The process of changing an employee's job title, department, and/or responsibilities.

transfer switch   A system of electrical switches that automatically routes electric power from one or more public utility feeds, one or more generators, through one or more UPSs, to a data center facility.

Transmission Control Protocol (TCP)   The connection-oriented protocol used in the TCP/IP suite of protocols to establish a connection and transport messages from one station to another over a network during a communication session.

transport layer (OSI model)   Layer 4 of the OSI network model. *See also* OSI network model.

transport layer (TCP/IP model)   Layer 3 of the TCP/IP network model. The purpose of the transport layer is the controlled and ordered delivery of messages (called packets) from one application on a station to another on the same network or on different networks. *See also* TCP/IP network model.

Transport Layer Security (TLS)   An encryption protocol used to encrypt web pages requested with the HTTPS URL. Replacement for Secure Sockets Layer (SSL). *See also* Secure Sockets Layer (SSL); Hypertext Transfer Protocol Secure (HTTPS).

Trojan horse   A type of malware program that purports to perform one function but actually performs other (or additional) undesired functions.

trunk   A telecommunications network technique in which several communications can share a set of lines or frequencies.

tunneling   The practice of encapsulating messages within another protocol.

twinax   A type of coaxial cable that uses two inner conductors.

twisted-pair cable　A type of network cabling that consists of a thick cable containing four pairs of insulated copper conductors, all surrounded by a protective jacket.

two-factor authentication　*See* multifactor authentication.

uninterruptible power supply (UPS)　A system that filters the incoming power of spikes and other noise and supplies power for short periods through a bank of batteries.

unit testing　The portion of software testing in which individual modules are tested.

Universal Disk Format (UDF)　An optical media file system considered a replacement for ISO/IEC 9660. *See also* ISO/IEC 9660; file system.

Universal Mobile Telecommunications System (UMTS)　An airlink standard for wireless communications between mobile devices and base stations.

Universal Serial Bus (USB)　An external bus technology used to connect computers to peripherals such as mice, keyboards, storage devices, printers, scanners, cameras, and network adaptors. However, the USB specification contains full networking capabilities, facilitated through the use of a USB hub.

Unix file system (UFS)　A file system used by many Unix operating systems. *See also* file system.

unshielded twisted pair (UTP)　A type of twisted-pair cable with no shielding—just four pairs of twisted conductors and the outer protective jacket. *See also* twisted-pair cable.

unstructured data　Data that resides on end-user workstations and network file shares, usually as a result of the creation of reports and extracts *See also* structured data.

user　A business or customer who uses an information system.

user acceptance testing (UAT)　The portion of software testing in which end users test software programs for correct functional operation and usability.

User Datagram Protocol (UDP)　The connectionless protocol used in the TCP/IP suite of protocols used to transport messages from one station to another over a network.

user ID　An identifier created by a system manager and issued to a user for the purpose of identification or authentication.

utility software　The broad class of programs that support the development or use of networks, systems, and applications. Utility software is most often used by IT specialists whose responsibilities include some aspect of system development, support, or operations.

V.35　A standard protocol for sending serial data between computers.

variable sampling　A sampling technique used to study the characteristics of a population to determine the numeric total of a specific attribute from the entire population. *See also* sampling.

vendor standard   A standard that specifies which suppliers and vendors are used for various types of products and services.

version control   The techniques and tools used to manage different versions of source code files.

video surveillance   The use of video cameras, monitors, and recording systems to record the movement of persons in or near sensitive areas.

virtual circuit   A logical communications channel between two endpoints on a packet-switched network.

virtual desktop infrastructure (VDI)   A technology by which user workstations use operating systems that are stored and run on central servers.

virtual keyboard   An interactive software program that emulates the use of a physical keyboard. Virtual keyboards are used when key logging is a credible threat.

virtual local area network (VLAN)   A logical network that may share a physical medium with one or more other virtual networks.

virtual machine   A software implementation of a computer, usually an operating system or other program running within a hypervisor. *See also* hypervisor.

virtual private network (VPN)   Any network encapsulation protocol that utilizes authentication and encryption; used primarily for protecting remote access traffic and for protecting traffic between two networks. *See also* tunneling; encapsulation.

virtual server   An active instantiation of a server operating system, running on a system that is designed to house two or more such virtual servers. Each virtual server is logically partitioned from every other server so that each runs as though it were on its own physically separate machine.

virtual tape library (VTL)   A disk-based storage system that emulates a tape-based storage system.

virus   A type of malware in which fragments of code attach themselves to executable programs and are activated when the program they are attached to is run.

visual notice   A sign or symbol used to inform personnel of security controls and/or to warn unauthorized persons.

Voice over IP (VoIP)   Several technologies that permit telephony transported over IP networks.

VoIP client   A computer program designed to communicate using VoIP. *See also* Voice over IP (VoIP).

VoIP handset   A digital telephone designed to communicate using VoIP. *See also* Voice over IP (VoIP).

vulnerability   A weakness that may be present in a system that makes the probability of one or more threats more likely.

vulnerability management   A formal business process used to identify and mitigate vulnerabilities in an IT environment.

walkthrough   A review of some or all disaster recovery and business continuity plans, procedures, and other documentation. A walkthrough is performed by an entire group of individuals in a live discussion.

wall   A structure that prevents or deters passage by unauthorized personnel.

WAN switch   A general term encompassing several types of wide area network switching devices, including ATM switches, Frame Relay switches, MPLS switches, and ISDN switches.

war chalking   The practice of marking buildings (using chalk) with symbols to indicate the presence of a Wi-Fi access point, including some basic facts about it, to inform hackers of potential targets. *See also* war driving; Wi-Fi.

war dialing   An attack designed to discover unprotected remote access modems by dialing phone numbers sequentially and recording those with modems.

war driving   An attack on a wireless network in which attackers intercept and record information about Wi-Fi access points.

warm site   An alternate processing center where recovery systems are present, but at a lower state of readiness than recovery systems at a hot site. For example, although the same version of the operating system may be running on the warm site system, it may be a few patch levels behind primary systems.

waterfall model   A software development life cycle process whereby activities are sequential and are executed one time in a software project. *See also* system development life cycle (SDLC).

web content filter   A central program or device that monitors and, optionally, filters web communications. A web content filter is often used to control the sites (or categories of sites) that users are permitted to access from the workplace. Some web content filters can also protect an organization from malware.

web server   A server that runs specialized software that makes static and dynamic HTML pages available to users.

web services   A means for system-to-system communications using HTTP.

Web Services Description Language (WSDL)   An XML-based language used to describe web services. *See also* web services.

web-based application   An application design in which the database and all business logic are stored on central servers and user workstations use only web browsers to access the application.

web-based application development   A software development effort in which the application's user interface is based on the HTTP (Hypertext Transport Protocol) and HTML (Hypertext Markup Language) standards.

wet pipe system   A fire sprinkler system in which all sprinkler pipes are filled with water. Each sprinkler head is equipped with a fuse—a heat-sensitive glass bulb—that breaks upon reaching a preset temperature. When this occurs, water is discharged from just that sprinkler head, which is presumably located near a fire. *See also* fire sprinkler system.

whaling   Spear phishing that targets executives and other high-value and high-privilege individuals in an organization. *See also* phishing; spear phishing.

wide area network (WAN)   1) A network that ranges in size from regional to international. 2) A single point-to-point connection between two distant locations (a WAN connection).

Wi-Fi   The common name for a wireless LAN protocol. *See also* 802.11.

Wi-Fi Protected Access (WPA)   An encryption standard for 802.11 wireless networks. The final version of WPA is WPA-2. *See also* 802.11.

WiMAX   A wireless telecommunications standard with data rates ranging from 30 Mbit/sec to 1 GBit/sec.

Wired Equivalent Privacy (WEP)   An encryption standard for 802.11 wireless networks. WEP has been compromised and should be replaced with WPA-2. *See also* 802.11; Wi-Fi Protected Access (WPA).

Wireless USB (WUSB)   A short-range, high-bandwidth standard wireless communications protocol used to connect computer peripherals.

work breakdown structure (WBS)   A logical representation of the high-level and detailed tasks that must be performed to complete a project.

worm   A type of malware containing stand-alone programs capable of human-assisted and automatic propagation.

Zachman framework   An enterprise architecture framework used to describe an IT architecture in increasing levels of detail.

zero trust   An architecture model in which a portion of an environment is considered to be untrusted.

INDEX

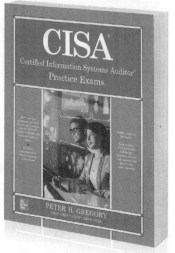

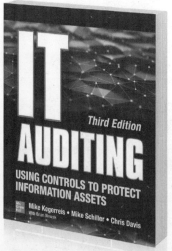